Decolonizing Linguistics

Decolonizing Linguistics

Edited by
Anne H. Charity Hudley
Christine Mallinson
Mary Bucholtz

OXFORD
UNIVERSITY PRESS

Oxford University Press is a department of the University of Oxford. It furthers
the University's objective of excellence in research, scholarship, and education
by publishing worldwide. Oxford is a registered trade mark of Oxford University
Press in the UK and certain other countries.

Published in the United States of America by Oxford University Press
198 Madison Avenue, New York, NY 10016, United States of America.

© Anne H. Charity Hudley, Christine Mallinson, and Mary Bucholtz 2024

Some rights reserved. No part of this publication may be reproduced, stored in
a retrieval system, or transmitted, in any form or by any means, for commercial purposes,
without the prior permission in writing of Oxford University Press, or as expressly
permitted by law, by licence or under terms agreed with the appropriate
reprographics rights organization.

This is an open access publication, available online and distributed under the terms of a
Creative Commons Attribution – Non Commercial – No Derivatives 4.0
International licence (CC BY-NC-ND 4.0), a copy of which is available at
http://creativecommons.org/licenses/by-nc-nd/4.0/.

You must not circulate this work in any other form
and you must impose this same condition on any acquirer.

Library of Congress Cataloging-in-Publication Data
Names: Charity Hudley, Anne H., editor. | Mallinson, Christine, editor. |
Bucholtz, Mary, 1966– editor.
Title: Decolonizing Linguistics / Anne Charity Hudley, Christine Mallinson,
Mary Bucholtz.
Description: New York, NY : Oxford University Press, 2024. | Includes
bibliographical references and index.
Identifiers: LCCN 2023049338 (print) | LCCN 2023049339 (ebook) |
ISBN 9780197755259 (hardback) | ISBN 9780197755266 (paperback) |
ISBN 9780197755280 (epub)
Subjects: LCSH: Linguistics—Study and teaching—Social aspects. | Social
justice. | Educational equalization. | LCGFT: Essays.
Classification: LCC P53.8 .I48 2024 (print) | LCC P53.8 (ebook) |
DDC 410.8—dc23/eng/20231220
LC record available at https://lccn.loc.gov/2023049338
LC ebook record available at https://lccn.loc.gov/2023049339

DOI: 10.1093/oso/9780197755259.001.0001

Paperback printed by Marquis Book Printing, Canada
Hardback printed by Bridgeport National Bindery, Inc., United States of America

How you language is beautiful. Don't let anyone tell you your language is wrong. Your languaging is the story of your life.
—Jon Henner

We dedicate this volume to the memory of our friend and colleague, Jon Henner.

Jon, it was a joy and pleasure to work with and learn from you. In one of our email exchanges during the final editing of this volume, you wrote, "What do we do if not argue for inclusion?"

Thank you for teaching us how to crip linguistics brilliantly, inclusively, and authentically. Your memory is a blessing, and your life and work are an inspiration to us all.

Contents

Preface   *xi*

Introduction: Decolonizing Linguistics   **1**
Anne H. Charity Hudley, Ignacio L. Montoya,
Christine Mallinson, and Mary Bucholtz

PART 1: DECOLONIZING LINGUISTICS AND THE ACADEMY

1. **Manifestations of Colonialism in Linguistics and Opportunities for Decolonization Through Refusal**   **25**
   Ignacio L. Montoya

2. **Racialization, Language Science, and Nineteenth-Century Anthropometrics**   **47**
   Margaret Thomas

3. **The Colonial Geography of Linguistics: A View from the Caribbean**   **63**
   Ben Braithwaite and Kristian Ali

4. **We Like the Idea of You But Not the Reality of You: The Whole Scholar as Disruptor of Default Colonial Practices in Linguistics**   **81**
   Nicté Fuller Medina

5. **Apolitical Linguistics Doesn't Exist, and It Shouldn't: Developing a Black Feminist Praxis Toward Political Transparency**   **101**
   Aris Moreno Clemons

6. **Unpacking Experiences of Racism in European Applied Linguistics**   **121**
   Kamran Khan

7. **Centering Race and Multilingualism in French Linguistics**   **139**
   Maya Angela Smith

8. **Decolonizing (Psycho)linguistics Means Dropping the Language Gap Rhetoric**   **157**
   Megan Figueroa

viii   Contents

PART 2: DECOLONIZING METHODS OF TEACHING AND RESEARCH

9. **From Gatekeeping to Inclusion in the Introductory Linguistics Curriculum: Decolonizing Our Teaching, Our Psyches, Our Institutions, and Our Field**   175
   Lynnette Arnold

10. **Decolonizing Historical Linguistics in the Classroom and Beyond**   195
    Claire Bowern and Rikker Dockum

11. **Towards a Decolonial Syntax: Research, Teaching, Publishing**   219
    Hannah Gibson, Kyle Jerro, Savithry Namboodiripad, and Kristina Riedel

12. **Decolonising Methodologies Through Collaboration: Reflections on Partnerships and Funding Flows from Working Between the South and the North**   245
    Rajendra Chetty, Hannah Gibson, and Colin Reilly

13. **Open Methods: Decolonizing (or Not) Research Methods in Linguistics**   263
    Dan Villarreal and Lauren Collister

14. **Revitalizing Attitudes Toward Creole Languages**   293
    Ariana Bancu, Joy P. G. Peltier, Felicia Bisnath, Danielle Burgess, Sophia Eakins, Wilkinson Daniel Wong Gonzales, Moira Saltzman, Yourdanis Sedarous, Alicia Stevers, and Marlyse Baptista

PART 3: DECOLONIZING RESEARCH BY CENTERING COMMUNITY AND ACTIVISM

15. **Solidarity and Collectivity in Decolonizing Linguistics: A Black Diasporic Perspective**   323
    Anne H. Charity Hudley, Christine Mallinson, Kahdeidra Monét Martin, Aris Moreno Clemons, L. J. Randolph Jr., Mary Bucholtz, Kendra Calhoun, Shenika Hankerson, Joy P. G. Peltier, Jamie A. Thomas, Deana Lacy McQuitty, and Kara Seidel

16. **Growing a Bigger Linguistics Through a Zapotec Agenda: The Ticha Project**   363
    May Helena Plumb, Alejandra Dubcovsky, Moisés García Guzmán, Brook Danielle Lillehaugen, and Felipe H. Lopez

Contents ix

17. Decolonizing Creolistics Through Popular Culture: The Case of Dancehall 381
Rashana Vikara Lydner

18. Prioritizing Community Partners' Goals in Projects to Support Indigenous Language Revitalization 393
Katherine J. Riestenberg, Ally Freemond, Brook Danielle Lillehaugen, and Jonathan N. Washington

19. Promoting Decolonized Classrooms Through an Introductory Linguistics Course for Future Teachers in Alaska 409
Ève Ryan, Matt Ford, and Giovanna Wilde

20. An Interdisciplinary Approach to Language Activism from Community Colleges: Linguistics Meets Communication Studies 423
Carlos de Cuba, Poppy Slocum, and Laura Spinu

Conclusion: Decolonizing Linguistics 445
Anne H. Charity Hudley, Ignacio L. Montoya, Christine Mallinson, and Mary Bucholtz

Preface

Anne H. Charity Hudley (she/her)
Stanford University

Christine Mallinson (she/her)
University of Maryland, Baltimore County

Mary Bucholtz (she/her, they/them)
University of California, Santa Barbara

This volume and its companion, *Inclusion in Linguistics,* were invited by Meredith Keffer, senior acquisitions editor at Oxford University Press. We couldn't have had a more knowledgeable or supportive editor than Meredith, to whom we are deeply grateful. As a scholar in folklore and mythology as well as anthropology herself, Meredith was well aware of the intellectual and practical need for decolonization and inclusion in linguistics in alignment with similar efforts in other disciplines that have been traditionally dominated by Western and Global North white cis male discourse, including anthropology, education, and sociology. Grounded in her efforts to continue to diversify the linguistics catalog at OUP, Meredith reached out to Anne to begin the conversation about proposing these volumes in order to advance efforts to decolonize linguistics and create a more inclusive discipline and profession.

We refer to linguistics as a discipline here intentionally—as opposed to the broader, more inclusive and interdisciplinary vision of linguistics that we advocate throughout both volumes—as a nod to the scholarly communities and power dynamics in the particular scholarly tradition of the study of language that has shaped our careers as researchers and educators. We recognize both the challenges and the benefits of our professional and personal experiences, which have informed our editorial lens and the work that we have done throughout our careers. In line with the contributions throughout each of these volumes, we also discuss in this preface who we are and how our positionalities and subjectivities have shaped our lives and careers.

xii Preface

Anne: I grew up in Varina, Virginia, a rural area zoned for agriculture just east of Richmond, Virginia. I was born there to two Black physicians who were part of two large economically privileged Black families in the Upper South. My local affiliations and my dedication to my community are the driving forces behind my most fundamental interests as an academic. In the Black educational narrative, I represent the prep-school-to-professor experience. I attended St. Catherine's School in Richmond for 13 years, where I had an early interest in studying linguistics and in being a college professor and administrator. I was granted early admission to Harvard and found myself surrounded by supportive faculty and students. My senior/master's thesis explored the idiolect of the African American blues singer Ms. Bessie Smith over time—that is, how her individual language and singing style changed over the years. Through this work, I learned about Southern Black and African American language and culture from a linguistics standpoint, and it was an important start to the work I do today.

After Harvard, I attended graduate school at the University of Pennsylvania, where I began studying in earnest how discrimination based on language and culture leads to educational inequalities. I also became very interested both in the transition from high school to college and in undergraduate research through my work with the Center for Africana Studies Summer Institute for Pre-Freshmen and the Penn McNair Scholars Program. At that time, I thought that my interests in linguistics and in supporting underrepresented students and scholars were somewhat unrelated—but as I began to see how they overlap in crucial ways, it shaped my career path, leading me to where I am today.

For 12 years, I worked in my home community at the College of William & Mary in Williamsburg, Virginia, where I was the first William & Mary Professor of Community Studies and where I co-created the William & Mary Scholars Undergraduate Research Experience (WMSURE) program to support WM Scholars—students who are awarded merit tuition based on their academic excellence. Their experiences are the backbone of all of my work. They are my family, my community, and my home.

For four years after that, I was the North Hall Endowed Chair in the Linguistics of African America at the University of California, Santa Barbara (UCSB), where I was also the Director of Undergraduate Research for the Office of Undergraduate Education for three years. These positions brought together my passions for linguistics and for supporting underrepresented students in their research endeavors. I am also dedicated to the craft of teaching and was a faculty fellow in the Center for Innovative Teaching, Research, and Learning at UCSB, where I worked with other faculty to improve their teaching, particularly with regard to empowering Black students as well as other students who have been underrepresented at Historically White Institutions. In addition, I was a faculty in residence, which means that when I wasn't teaching or doing research, students could often find me hosting parties and barbecues, where we talked about life and what it means to be a college student.

I am now Associate Dean of Educational Affairs and the Bonnie Katz Tenenbaum Professor of Education in the Stanford University Graduate School of Education. In my current role, I oversee degree programs and work with students and faculty to ensure a rich educational experience. I am also affiliated with Stanford's Center for Comparative Studies in Race and Ethnicity, the Program in African and African American Studies, and the Department of Linguistics. I consider myself a humanistic social scientist who describes and documents the linguistic, literary, and cultural experiences of Black learners across their lives. I use a community-based participatory research methodology in all of my work and co-construct information and findings with students, community members, and large teams of researchers. I have a particular focus on sharing those findings with in-service educators who most immediately need them. I have a longstanding relationship with the American Federation of Teachers that I am particularly proud of, as it keeps my work centered on the interests and experiences of large numbers of in-service educators.

My desire to see greater and immediate inclusion of Black students in the academy and in research has led me to design innovative undergraduate and graduate curricula and advising programs as we create liberatory and reparative models for what universities can be both now and in the future. We got this. I'm proud to be at Stanford as we work to establish African and African American Studies as a university department. I am also fortunate to be a faculty member at the same university my nieces attend as undergraduate students. We experience college as a family, and their perspective is invaluable as I do this work. It is, ultimately, for them.

Christine: I am an interdisciplinary scholar of language, culture, and society and have devoted my career to studying linguistic and cultural diversity and inclusion in ways that are shaped by my formative life experiences. I grew up in a small town in North Carolina, in the Southern region of the US where both pride and stigma surrounding Southern language run deep. My parents were first-generation college students, having moved from New York and Pennsylvania to North Carolina to attend college; they both ended up pursuing master's degrees and careers in helping professions related to counseling and social work.

xiv Preface

My maternal grandparents, who lived nearby and were the only grandparents I knew, were immigrants from Germany, without a high school education. From them I got my earliest understanding of how complicated language can be. Some of my earliest childhood memories are of my grandmother singing songs in German and reading me books and telling nursery rhymes, and we shared that identity and culture together through language. But I also saw how linguistic insecurity, bias, and discrimination can often surround those who are perceived as speaking differently within a community. As I attended school, I became aware that white Southern English and the local Southern variety of African American English, two important varieties of English used by my peers and teachers, also were subjected to this same complicated mix of social value and stigma. I became intrigued by the social dimension of linguistic differences—the ways that language reflects culture and identity, but also social boundaries and social divisions—which set me on a path of figuring out how to think about and study these dimensions in all their interrelated complexities.

In college and graduate school, my studies were interdisciplinary, centered on sociology, anthropology, gender studies, and linguistics. I completed my master's degree in English linguistics and my PhD in sociology and anthropology at North Carolina State University, working with Walt Wolfram to study how language is used in white and Black communities in the Appalachian region of North Carolina in ways that applied my linguistic, anthropological, and sociological training. In the years I spent studying while working with community members, I added richer scholarly as well as personal understandings of the social dimensions of language use that informed how I understood my own lived experiences with language and the social dynamics that I had seen in the world. I arrived at several key principles that have undergirded and shaped my work ever since: language and society are inseparable, language is a cultural artifact that belongs to those people and communities who use it, and addressing power dynamics and inequalities surrounding language is central to social justice, equity, and inclusion.

After graduate school, I moved to the University of Maryland, Baltimore County (UMBC)—a Minority Serving Institution and a campus known for its innovative teaching, inclusive culture, and dedication to supporting the success of students from historically underserved groups. My interdisciplinary background was a perfect fit for my faculty position in the Language, Literacy, and Culture Program, where I work with faculty and graduate students from numerous fields and disciplines that converge around the study of language and society. When I was on the job market and interviewing for other positions at prominent institutions across the country, I was told by several linguistics departments that my work was not "linguistic enough," and by several sociology departments that my work was not "sociological enough." I rejected those false binaries and the boundary-setting culture of academia, both then and now. Since that time, linguistics has become more open to interdisciplinarity and inclusivity in terms of how we conceptualize language and approach the study of language use—although much more progress needs to be made.

At UMBC, most of the courses I teach focus on language as central to education, equality, social change, and social justice. I am deeply committed to being a mentor and an advocate for graduate students from groups that have been systemically underrepresented in higher education, which includes students of color, women, first-generation students, and members of the LGBTQ+ community. As a white woman, I see my role and responsibility as a professor and mentor as a central part of my dedication to promoting social justice and decolonizing academia through dismantling traditional power structures and established hierarchies and expanding pathways for inclusion. In addition to my faculty positions as professor in the Language, Literacy, and Culture Program and affiliate professor in the Department of Gender, Women's & Sexuality Studies, I hold an appointment as the 2023–2024 Lipitz Distinguished Professor of the Arts, Humanities, and Social Sciences at UMBC. In my administrative roles, I am also the director of the Center for Social Science Scholarship, UMBC's comprehensive social science research center, and Special Assistant for Research and Creative Achievement in UMBC's Office of the Vice President for Research, where I work across our campus to grow social science research, connect it to practice and policy, and foster cross-disciplinary collaborations. The social sciences are critical to tackling pressing social issues, challenging bias and discrimination, addressing social inequalities, and promoting social action.

Across my research leadership, teaching, and mentorship roles, my true academic joys are bringing together great minds and helping faculty, graduate students, and undergraduate students realize their scholarly goals and ambitions. And above all, I do the work that I do for my family—especially for my two children, who already recognize the beauty of language in all its diversity and who, I hope, will always also intentionally work for greater equity and inclusion.

Mary: I became a linguistics professor because I love languages and teaching, but I stayed in linguistics to fight against injustice. My personal and professional commitment to social justice is informed in part from my own first-hand experiences of educational inequity based on my gender and social class. Growing up poor in a very small town in northern Indiana, I was

xvi Preface

discouraged from going to college by my guidance counselor, who advised secretarial school as a more appropriate aspiration. In college, my (male) professors disparaged my interest in education and in youth language and steered me toward fields and topics they considered more respectable. In graduate school at the University of California, Berkeley, I quickly changed my research specialization from historical linguistics to sociolinguistics after other women students warned me of rampant sexual harassment by male faculty and students in that field (as well as others). This decision, however, did not protect me from being stalked by a faculty member, among many other harassing incidents. Nor did my interest in social issues meet with faculty approval. Several linguistics professors mocked and dismissed my interest in gender in particular, and my piles of assigned linguistics articles languished unread while I devoured books on gender, sexuality, race, and social justice, reading these texts not "for fun" but as a form of self-care in Audre Lorde's (1988) sense, as a lifeline in a hostile environment. In my first semester of graduate school I spoke with the chair of the Department of Ethnic Studies about transferring to that program, but I changed my mind after my conversation with another linguistics professor that semester. I had gone to his office hours in some distress and expressed dissatisfaction with the program's decontextualized, asocial approach to language. His response was to discourage me from continuing in linguistics and to blame his wife and child for frustrations in his own career. At that point, I decided to stay in the department, and the field, simply to prove that I refused to be driven out.

Fortunately, I found supportive colleagues among my fellow graduate students, one of whom, Kira Hall, became my closest collaborator. And I found an advisor, Robin Tolmach Lakoff, who at that time was not only one of the few women among the linguistics faculty but also the only Berkeley linguist writing about issues of power and injustice. (For further discussion of the need for linguistics to become a more just and inclusive discipline, see Bucholtz & miles-hercules, 2021; for a discussion of Lakoff's contributions to linguistics and social justice, see Bucholtz, 2004.)

Given the reception of my ideas in graduate school, I have not been surprised to face opposition from the linguistics establishment throughout my career—and I have had a far easier time than my friends and colleagues from more minoritized positionalities. As a graduate student and a junior faculty member writing critically both about race and about cherished assumptions in linguistics, I was often the target of harsh comments and sometimes even angry attacks from senior white male faculty. But I also received supportive comments, especially from faculty of color as well as junior scholars and graduate students, which made it easier to keep doing the work I needed to do. I am deeply indebted to the many linguists and linguistic anthropologists of color who went far out of their way to offer me material support early in my career in the form of recommendation letters, feedback on my work, and professional guidance, among them John Baugh, John Rickford, Marcyliena Morgan, and Ana Celia Zentella. I pledged to pay their generosity forward to the next generation of linguists, and especially linguists of color, an obligation I continue to fulfill to this day.

Linguistics has changed a great deal since I entered the field, and it is encouraging to see the ranks of linguists slowly diversifying, with an accompanying transformation of the discipline's research questions, methods, and professional practices. But this change is far too slow, and now that I am a senior scholar I believe that the greatest impact I can make on linguistics is not through traditional research—after all, the most exciting ideas have always come from those who bring new perspectives to the field rather than those who are firmly established. Instead, I aim to make an impact by using the structural and institutional power I hold as a senior white, cis, relatively able-bodied scholar to make linguistics a welcoming place for students and scholars whose lived experiences and resulting ideas remain marginalized and devalued within the discipline. Although my three-year stint as department chair enabled me to do some of this work, I was frustrated to discover that academic administration is designed to reproduce rather than to undo structural injustice. More important and more rewarding have been my efforts behind the scenes and in collaboration with others—as represented by these two volumes, among many other activities. The lesson I have learned in my career as an academic linguist striving to make our field more inclusive, more equitable, and more humane is that in the never-ending struggle for social justice, the greatest force for change is social connection and collective action, in forms large and small.

Creating *Inclusion in Linguistics* and *Decolonizing Linguistics*

These volumes are directly informed by previous formative collaborations involving the three editors. First was a proceedings paper that we published in 2019 and that led to the first-ever Statement on Race for the Linguistic Society of America, which was adopted by the association. We then drew on this statement to write a subsequent theoretical article, "Toward Racial

xviii Preface

Justice in Linguistics" (Charity Hudley, Mallinson, & Bucholtz, 2020a), which appeared in the discipline's flagship journal, *Language*, along with a set of responses on racial equity in the field, to which we in turn responded (Charity Hudley, Mallinson, & Bucholtz, 2020b). Brian Joseph, former president of the Linguistic Society of America, referred to this work in his presidential address, published later in *Language* (Joseph, 2020). These efforts and others have pushed the discipline to be more fully inclusive and decolonial and have inspired scholars, departments, universities, and professional organizations to put forward their own initiatives: to host webinars on racial equity for faculty and students, to form workshops and workgroups for white allies, to design new courses on racial justice, and to craft and implement departmental action plans on racial justice.

In our response to the published commentaries that accompanied our *Language* article, we included our call for contributions to these two volumes, and we also spread the word widely online through virtual talks, emails, and social media. In addition, we directly invited scholars from across subfields, regions, and institutions whom we knew had an interest and expertise in these topics. We intentionally invited both well-established senior researchers and emerging scholars to ensure that we were all in conversation with each other. At the same time, we acknowledge that there are persistent challenges in being globally inclusive, given the structural biases of professional networks, and we continue to strive to undo those barriers and hope that future work will continue to do the same.

Interest in the volumes was widespread. We accepted 40 contributions across both volumes, all of which went through an intentionally inclusive process of development, workshopping, and revision, which we adopted in deliberate contrast to the traditional paradigm of scholarly writing, editing, revision, and anonymous critique. That traditional approach is often isolated and isolating, as well as susceptible to processes of injustice, exclusion, and colonization. Through these volumes, we aim to challenge that paradigm and change that process. All contributors met in large and small groups during multiple author sessions, sharing project ideas and feedback, and went through multiple rounds of peer and editors' review. Both *Decolonizing Linguistics* and *Inclusion in Linguistics* were developed simultaneously in order to ensure coverage of and dialogue around core themes across the volumes. To broaden the perspectives we were able to represent, we also invited two linguists whose professional and lived experiences were different from our own, Ignacio Montoya and Jon Henner, to coauthor the introduction and conclusion of each volume, respectively. (See the introductions to both volumes for more detail about the process of creating these books.)

We are deeply indebted to our editorial and production team, including Julia Steer, Lacey Harvey, Stuart Allison, Anne Sanow and Sarah Yamashita. We also sincerely thank our external reviewers, as well as all of the volume contributors for their insights, support, and participation throughout the process of putting together these volumes. We are incredibly grateful to UMBC Language, Literacy & Culture doctoral student Kara Seidel, whose spectacular project management skills allowed the compilation of these volumes to proceed smoothly from start to finish and who was an integral member of our editorial team.

We are immensely grateful for the support of the National Science Foundation's Build and Broaden Program, Awards #SMA-2126414 and 2126405, "Linguistic Production, Perception, and Identity in the Career Mobility of Black Faculty in Linguistics and the Language Sciences," which supported both of these volumes, particularly Chapters 5, 14, and 15 in *Decolonizing Linguistics* and Chapters 11 and 12 in *Inclusion in Linguistics*. We thank our Build and Broaden research scholars network, who continue to advance critical work in pursuit of Black linguistic liberation.

We also thank the Bonnie Katz Tenenbaum endowed professorship at Stanford University in support of Anne Charity Hudley's research, and we gratefully acknowledge Stanford University's support of Anne Charity Hudley's Black Academic Lab, https://badlab.stanford.edu/. We also express our appreciation for UMBC's support of Christine Mallinson's research, including the 2023–2024 Lipitz Distinguished Professorship in the Arts, Humanities, and Social Sciences and the College of Arts, Humanities, and Social Sciences Student Research Assistance award for Faculty Research and Creative Achievement. We thank UCSB for ongoing support of Mary Bucholtz's research. We further thank the following institutions for supporting open access for these volumes: Stanford University, Swarthmore College, UCSB, UMBC, University of Michigan, University of Pennsylvania, University of Pittsburgh, and University of South Carolina.

The volumes, and the models of decolonized and inclusive research, teaching, advocacy, and action that they present, inform and are informed by each other. We strongly encourage readers to engage with them as a pair. We also encourage using the volumes both as guides for scholarly work and for pedagogical purposes, including as course readers, and we invite readers to consult the supplementary website associated with these volumes for further materials and resources in teaching contexts. We look forward to the ongoing conversations and the decolonizing and inclusive models of linguistics that will result from scholarly engagement with the chapters in these volumes for years to come.

xx Preface

About the Companion Website

www.oup.com/us/decolonizinglinguistics

Oxford has created a website to accompany *Decolonizing Linguistics*. Material that cannot be made available in a book, namely author photos, bios, and additional resources for readers are provided here. The reader is encouraged to consult this resource in conjunction with the chapters.

References

Bucholtz, Mary. (2004). Changing places: *Language and Woman's Place* in context. In Mary Bucholtz (Ed.), *Language and woman's place: Text and commentaries*, original text by Robin Tolmach Lakoff (pp. 121–128). Revised and expanded edition. Oxford University Press.

Bucholtz, Mary, & miles-hercules, deandre. (2021). The displacement of race in language and gender studies. *Gender and Language, 15*(3), 414–422. https://doi.org/10.1558/genl.20882

Charity Hudley, Anne H., Mallinson, Christine, & Bucholtz, Mary. (2020a). Toward racial justice in linguistics: Interdisciplinary insights into theorizing race in the discipline and diversifying the profession. *Language, 96*(4), e200–e235. https://doi.org/10.1353/lan.2020.0074

Charity Hudley, Anne H., Mallinson, Christine, & Bucholtz, Mary. (2020b). From theory to action: Working collectively toward a more antiracist linguistics (Response to commentators). *Language, 96*(4), e307–e319. http://doi.org/10.1353/lan.2020.0081

Joseph, Brian D. (2020). What is time (and why should linguists care about it)? *Language, 96*(4), 908–937. https://doi.org/10.1353/lan.2020.0066

Lorde, Audre. (1988). *A burst of light*. Firebrand Books.

Abstract: This introduction to *Decolonizing Linguistics* begins by explaining the motivation for the volume and its grounding in decolonizing initiatives within linguistics, the academy, and society more broadly. We discuss the volume's understanding of decolonization as centering Black, Native, and Indigenous perspectives and explain the distinction between decolonization and inclusion, as well as why a specifically decolonizing perspective is necessary. Next, we describe the process of developing and creating the volume as an example of decolonizing and inclusive scholarly practice. We provide an overview of the chapters, contextualizing the volume's major themes—decolonizing the discipline and the academy, decolonizing methods of research and teaching, and decolonizing linguistics by centering communities and activism—in relation to six key principles of decolonization work. Finally, we highlight the importance of engaging in decolonizing efforts holistically, collectively, and systemically as crucial to the ongoing project of advancing justice for Black, Native, and Indigenous scholars, students, and communities within linguistics.

Key Words: Black Diaspora, decolonization, epistemologies, Indigeneity, liberation, Native people

Introduction

Decolonizing Linguistics

Anne H. Charity Hudley (she/her)
Stanford University

Ignacio L. Montoya (he/his)
University of Nevada, Reno

Christine Mallinson (she/her)
University of Maryland, Baltimore County

Mary Bucholtz (she/her, they/them)
University of California, Santa Barbara

Introduction

Decolonizing Linguistics is informed by Faye V. Harrison's groundbreaking book *Decolonizing Anthropology*, now in its third edition (Harrison, 2011), as well as the larger ongoing movement of Black and Native scholars in anthropology and related areas to decolonize their disciplines and the academy. Our sense of responsibility calls for us to do similar work in linguistics, in solidarity with these scholars and others who seek to decolonize the discipline.

In this introduction, we first examine the ongoing impact of the history of colonization in academia in general (e.g., Lee & Ahtone, 2020; Wilder, 2013) and in linguistics in particular (Bolton & Hutton, 2000; Errington, 2008), with a focus on the US context, with which we are most familiar. We then describe our own decolonizing practices in the creation of this volume. Next, we outline our working model of decolonization—informed by what we have learned from the work of the scholars who have led the way in decolonizing academia—and offer our own version of what it means to decolonize linguistics. Finally, we discuss the range of issues that the volume's contributors address in approaching decolonization from their disciplinary and subdisciplinary perspectives and grounded in their lived experiences.

Charity Hudley, Montoya, Mallinson, Bucholtz, *Introduction* In: *Decolonizing Linguistics*. Edited by:
Anne H. Charity Hudley, Christine Mallinson, and Mary Bucholtz, Oxford University Press.
© Anne H. Charity Hudley, Christine Mallinson, and Mary Bucholtz 2024. DOI: 10.1093/oso/9780197755259.003.0001

2 Decolonizing Linguistics

Colonialism in the Academy and in Linguistics

The modern university was founded by and for colonialism and continues to advance colonial interests (Cupples & Grosfoguel, 2018). In the United States, many of the oldest colleges and universities were established as "Indian Schools" and funded with the financial fruits of the labor of enslaved Black people. As historian Craig Steven Wilder explains, "The academy never stood apart from American slavery—in fact, it stood beside church and state as the third pillar of a civilization built on bondage" (2013, p. 12). This strategy of leveraging colonialism to establish higher education institutions continued with the creation of so-called land-grant universities via the 1862 Morrill Act, through which tribal lands were seized and redistributed to educate white people's children, forming what have been aptly renamed "land-grab universities" (Lee & Ahtone, 2020). Our own departments and programs directly benefited from these practices. Complicity with colonial oppression persists if we do not remember and recount this shameful legacy to those who currently work and learn at our home institutions—and it persists if we do not find ways to make direct reparations for these historical and ongoing harms to Black and Native people.

Colonial oppression is also at the heart of linguistics, and the colonial roots and history of the discipline have been interrogated for several decades. Like many fields, like the university system, and like academia itself, linguistics still operates according to logics of domination and extraction (Wilder, 2013; Leonard, 2017; Motha, 2014; Pennycook, 2007; Davis, 2017; among many others). Calls to decolonize linguistics are now being put forward, much as they have been and continue to be in neighboring disciplines with similar histories, such as education (see, e.g., Smith, 2021; Paris & Winn, 2016; Makoni et al., 2022) and anthropology (McGranahan, Roland, & Williams 2016; Gupta, 2021) (see also Charity Hudley, Mallinson, & Bucholtz, 2020). Decolonizing efforts, with crucial leadership by linguists of color, have come from several directions. Not surprisingly, in the North American context most of this work has been undertaken by scholars working outside of the hegemonic core of "theoretical" linguistics, including linguistic anthropologists Jenny Davis and Krystal Smalls (2021), Barbra Meek (2011), and Bernard Perley (2012); applied linguists Suresh Canagarajah (2022) and Ryuko Kubota (2020); Sinfree Makoni, Cristine Severo, Ashraf Abdelhay, and Anna Kaiper-Marquez (2022), and Bassey Antia and Makoni (2023); and Suhantie Motha (2020) (see also Charity Hudley et al., this volume); Native and Indigenous linguists working on language reclamation and revitalization, such as K. A. B. Chew (2019), Emiliana Cruz Cruz (2020), Hilaria Cruz (2020), Wesley Leonard

(2017, 2021; 2024), Adrienne Tsikewa (2021), and scholars who appear in this volume; and Black linguists in African American and Creole studies, including Michel DeGraff (2005), Hubert Devonish (1986), Marcyliena Morgan (1994), and Arthur Spears and Leanne Hinton (2010), and scholars who appear in this volume. (It is important to note that a number of these scholars work across these disciplinary and subdisciplinary divisions as well, which is another decolonizing move.)

Linguistics in general has been slow to take up this charge to decolonize the discipline, however, especially in subfields other than language documentation and revitalization/reclamation, linguistic anthropology, and sociolinguistics; for example, scholars in the areas of syntax, phonology, psycholinguistics, and computational linguistics often view their work as largely detached from social issues, due to notions of objectivity and commitments to abstract formal theory that are pervasive in such traditions (Charity Hudley et al., 2020). *Decolonizing Linguistics* firmly rejects such assumptions by interrogating how colonial thinking and white-supremacist ideals undergird linguistics and academia and by offering models and pathways for comprehensively decolonizing the discipline in both theory and praxis (see summaries of chapters presented thematically below as well as those in the companion volume *Inclusion in Linguistics* (Charity Hudley, Mallinson & Bucholtz 2024). These cross-cutting conversations move forward the broader disciplinary conversation about decolonizing linguistics by providing models for direct action.

One way that we decolonize linguistics is to have an open and real discussion about how research on Indigenous and Black people's languages has been conducted and how longstanding colonizing approaches need to change—with respect to both the ways research is traditionally conducted in and "on" communities and how it is often represented and circulated in academic scholarship. Important frameworks to be taken into account in this process include Indigenous models of land ownership from the perspective of Indigenous studies, anthropology, and literature, as developed by ethnic studies scholars such as Eve Tuck and K. Wayne Yang (2012), as well as Black Diasporic models of reparations that are informed by Indigenous models of decolonization, as developed by historians such as Tiya Miles (2015) and Malinda Maynor Lowery (2010). These models are among other relevant work by myriad scholars from Black studies, sociology, education, and history. Although decolonization necessarily looks different for Black Diasporic and Indigenous—including Black Indigenous—communities, it is informed by the same goal of dismantling the structures of colonialism and undoing its enduring effects.

4 Decolonizing Linguistics

Decolonization is therefore distinct from but related to concepts that often circulate more widely in academic institutional diversity discourse (Calhoun, 2021), such as inclusion, equity, and social justice. Unlike these other concepts, decolonization is grounded in a recognition of the specific forms of oppression that Indigenous and Black Diasporic people have experienced historically and that also continue today, both via intergenerational trauma and through neocolonizing processes. That is, colonizing processes are not only rooted in the past; they persist into the present day—a crucial point that is captured in the distinction between colonialism and coloniality (Quijano, 2007). To decolonize the study of language therefore requires that we expose and challenge the ways that institutions of higher education, as well as our own discipline, are investing in new forms of colonization—such as technological advances that have brought about dispossession and disenfranchisement (Hao, 2022).

Processes of decolonization equally acknowledge the specific forms of agency, resilience, and knowledge that Indigenous and Black Diasporic people have sustained and nurtured against these oppressive forces. Taking a decolonizing perspective within linguistics can therefore advance the institutional goals of inclusion, equity, and social justice; however, when decolonization is not centered, a fully inclusive, equitable, and just linguistics cannot be achieved. We must collectively resist colonizing norms and practices of higher education and linguistics so that the burden of taking up this work is not placed on individuals whose communities have been and continue to be the most negatively affected by colonizing processes.

Fundamentally, to decolonize is to expand our world through global collaboration, partnership, and action. For those of us from colonized communities, to decolonize is to collectively return the benefits of our work to the communities that have sustained us and to lead and accompany them from within. For those of us from colonizing communities, to decolonize is to honor the epistemological authority of our colleagues and partners who have experienced first-hand the harms of colonialism and its aftermath; to prioritize their goals for their communities; and to transform our research, teaching, and community partnerships accordingly.

Decolonizing *Decolonizing Linguistics*

It was critically important to the co-editors that *Decolonizing Linguistics* and the companion volume *Inclusion in Linguistics* reflect decolonization as a multifaceted concept, practice, and process. Here, we describe how Anne,

Christine, and Mary created a decolonizing process for developing and editing this volume, as well as how Ignacio became part of this collaboration.

In reviewing and selecting contributions to this volume, the co-editors prioritized the inclusion of authors with a wide range of distinctive lived experiences that inform their theorizing about and practice of decolonization in their scholarship, teaching, and community partnerships. After all the contributors were selected, we worked to actively decolonize both volumes through a collaborative and supportive writing and editorial process. We intentionally used an inclusive process of development, workshopping, and revision of chapters, which we adopted in deliberate contrast to the traditional paradigm of scholarly writing, editing, revision, and anonymous critique that is often isolated and isolating, as well as susceptible to processes of injustice and exclusion. The co-editors regularly held Zoom meetings during which the authors met in large and small groups across both volumes to discuss and develop their work. The editors also often met with authors one-on-one, in order to develop their individual chapters and to think through how their work fit within their overall scholarly trajectory and in relation to the other contributions to this volume and to *Inclusion in Linguistics*. Multiple rounds of peer and editorial review helped ensure that chapter authors were in conversation with each other. In addition, the co-editors worked with the publisher to ensure that the publication process was inclusive—for instance, retaining authors' preferred spelling and other stylistic preferences and including provided pronouns for each author—and that it was carried out in ways that aligned with the decolonizing principles that undergird the volumes and the work that appears in it. (For additional details on our process, see also the preface to both volumes and the introduction to *Inclusion in Linguistics*.)

The co-editors invited Ignacio to coauthor the introduction and conclusion for this volume in order to broaden perspectives on decolonizing linguistics. At the first stage of the co-authorship process, Anne and Ignacio met regularly to discuss their views on the most pressing issues regarding decolonization and incorporated these ideas with others generated by the editorial team in order to develop the introduction and conclusion. Anne and Ignacio aimed to create a human-facing narrative surrounding decolonization that would be in conversation with the authors in the volume. As part of this process, they worked to highlight the relationship between inclusion and decolonization but were particularly careful to show how these concepts are not the same. Christine and Mary also wove in their own ideas and insights, and the final texts represent a collaboration of all four of us, informed by feedback from the contributors.

Decolonizing Linguistics is divided into three parts. Part 1 of the volume focuses on decolonizing linguistics and the academy, addressing the ways that traditional academic research and scholarly practices are extractive and have served to colonize linguistic communities and marginalize scholars and language users from these communities. Part 2 focuses on decolonizing methods, with examples at the synergistic intersections of teaching and research that readers can adapt to their own practices. Part 3 focuses on decolonizing research by centering community and activism, with chapters that illustrate models of linguistic research and engagement that center on humanizing both researchers and language users in order to strengthen communities.

In the sections that follow, we present six key tenets that comprise our model of decolonization. Rather than addressing each chapter in this volume linearly within each section, we weave a discussion of the chapters into our discussion of these six tenets. In this way, the chapters in this volume illustrate how the concepts and practices of decolonization can be an active, central part of linguistic research, teaching, community partnerships, public engagement, and institutional and professional service.

To Decolonize Is to Humanize

Our first tenet is that *to decolonize is to humanize*. All too often, conducting research dehumanizes individual participants for an audience that rarely includes the research participants or their communities (Tuck & Yang, 2014). As scholars, we assert that we must decide upon and dedicate ourselves to the humanization of research that benefits the participants. One illustration of the persistent colonial logics of linguistics is the problematic concept of "fieldwork." What a colonizing linguistics exoticizes as "the field" is quite simply someone's home, their community, the places and people that they love. We decolonize linguistics by understanding our work as linguists as situated not in "the field" but in communities, and as linguists we avow that we work in communities, not in fields. This shift in language and mindset disrupts the pervasive white colonizing gaze in linguistic research by reframing whom our work is with and whom it is for and by inspiring further action and re-praxis.

We also assert that humanizing entails offering our own experiences with colonization and decolonization. As a model, and as the lead authors of this introduction, Anne and Ignacio engage with this tenet by offering here their own statements of positionality and intentionality regarding decolonization. (In the preface of each volume, each of the co-editors also provides more detail on their positionality, subjectivity, and intentionality for doing this work.)

Anne: In the Southern African American tradition, my work is not just for me but is work across generations. My family is from Varina and Charles City County, Virginia, which were both original parishes in the colony of Virginia. Before that act of colonization, these locales were home to Indigenous communities, which led to a tri-racial model of colonization and segregation. I grew up among that tri-racial divide between Black, White, and Native, witnessing separate schools, churches, and community sites for what were all members of my own family and neighborhoods.

My local affiliations and dedication to my community are the driving forces behind my most fundamental interests as a linguist. For the first twelve years of my career, I was a faculty member at the College of William and Mary—a university that is adjacent to colonial Williamsburg, a living monument to colonialism. My grandmother, Sarah Adkins Charity, who was also from Varina and lived her adult life in Charles City, thought that the College of William & Mary should educate more African American students—especially the ones who lived nearby. She never wanted me to forget that many members of the Adkins family were Native and were my cousins. Above all, she wanted me to remember family, community, and history. She knew that my life would be Black and that the history of the relationship between Black and Native people in Virginia was complicated and often tenuous. Indeed, there is still an unresolved tension between the Black and Indigenous Adkinses in my own family that I am trying to make sense of. While I personally identify as Black, I am aware that the lack of high schools for Native people in my home area of Virginia forced people, including my great-grandfather, to make tough life choices. To decolonize is to reverse that erasure. My grandmother didn't live to see that dream come to fruition, but I have.

My goal is to be successful as a scholar and as a faculty member in a way that is universal yet respects the focus of my grandmother's local vision. Such work honors the integrity and dreams of those who, like my grandmother, were never afforded the opportunity to become scholars and researchers at public colleges or universities in Virginia. In my career, I have supported the Native salutatorian of Charles City High School and the Black salutatorian of Varina High School. It is a scene my grandmother would have loved—a community and a family. My grandmother wanted something better for all of us, something more complicated but also more nuanced. Decolonization of our intellectual space allows for that complexity and nuance.

Ignacio: My engagement with decolonization did not emerge from learning about decolonial theory but rather through interactions with Indigenous people. My perspectives are grounded in my experiences with the Indigenous communities of the United States—in particular the Western United

8   Decolonizing Linguistics

States: the Great Basin and the Southwest. These experiences began with work on Diné that was initially focused on grammatical structure, consistent with my training in conventional linguistic theories and methodologies. As I engaged with the language, though, I began to engage with communities, such as through the Navajo Language Academy, from whom I learned about Diné language and culture through my summers on the Navajo Nation.

After completing my dissertation, I moved to Reno, Nevada to begin a position as assistant professor at the University of Nevada, Reno (UNR). Knowing that I wanted my linguistic work to be connected to the people whose languages I work with, I decided to focus on the Indigenous languages of the area where I would be living and working. As with Diné, I learned about the language by connecting to the Numu community, through, for instance, the various activities of the Language and Culture Program and by taking community classes in Numu (Northern Paiute) through the Reno-Sparks Indian Colony. This type of engagement gave me a deep and meaningful appreciation for the people of the land where I now live and work.

As I met people in these locations who were interested in language reclamation and revitalization, I made myself available as someone who can potentially support them in these efforts. I also realized that, though many Indigenous communities are eager for support from linguists in their language reclamation and revitalization projects, not all of the work we do with communities actually benefits those communities. In fact, the "theoretical" linguistic work that is often most valued in the field is often irrelevant and sometimes even harmful to communities. My first engagement with decolonization was through the idea that some of our work is harmful to communities and therefore unethical. It may be born out of relationships with communities but then results in products that are not at all useful to them. I didn't have the term "decolonization" in mind (since it's not a standard part of training in linguistics, and I hadn't been encouraged to explore beyond the discipline), but I did have the sense that doing work in this way was wrong. I found myself unwilling to engage in the kind of linguistic work that I began to see as extractive—work that drew from the intellectual traditions of communities to create products that benefit only academia.

As a result, my research has moved further and further in the direction of exclusively community-engaged work, and it has become more and more informed by principles of decolonization. It is telling that I came to notions of decolonization not through my own training in linguistics, but rather through engagement with other scholars in UNR's English Department, my home department, and other departments, especially the Department of Gender, Race, and Identity. My current perspective on linguistic research is that, whether we intend it or not, the work we do reproduces and/or disrupts a status quo that is rooted in colonialism. As a matter of ethics and intellectual integrity, I am committed to interrogating the impact my own work has—on the field of linguistics, on the communities with whom I work, and at my university—as I strive to enact principles of decolonization through my scholarship.

Beyond our models as co-authors here and elsewhere in these volumes, many other contributors humanize their work through personalization and discussion of how their lived experiences with language, culture, and community inform how they do (and don't do) linguistics. By incorporating their lived experiences, the authors critique extractive models of research, offer new models for reciprocally working with communities, and make transparent how their own positionalities shape their scholarship. Indeed, if to decolonize is to humanize, then to decolonize is also to connect us through our shared humanity.

To Decolonize Is to Respect and Respond to the Local and the Particular

Colonization takes multiple forms and is experienced differently in different contexts; thus, a decolonizing perspective is one that recognizes the specificity of colonial processes in local contexts. Colonizing scholarship and teaching often favors generalization and the erasure of distinctive practices, identities, and experiences; a key step toward decolonizing our work as linguists is therefore to attend to the varied and culturally situated ways that individuals, groups, and communities use language. Many of the authors in this volume center the local and the particular by detailing projects that are context-specific and integrated with local needs, priorities, and traditions in ways that align with decolonial perspectives. Informed by their experiences in these contexts, they also offer concrete, action-oriented recommendations that contribute meaningfully to a global conversation about decolonizing linguistics.

For example, in Chapter 15, "Solidarity and Collectivity in Decolonizing Linguistics: A Black Disaporic Perspective," Anne H. Charity Hudley, Christine Mallinson, Kahdeidra Monét Martin, Aris Moreno Clemons, L. J. Randolph Jr., Mary Bucholtz, Kendra Calhoun, Shenika Hankerson, Joy P. G. Peltier, Jamie A. Thomas, Deana Lacy McQuitty, and Kara Seidel offer a model grounded in solidarity and collectivity for decolonizing linguistics, writ large, from a Black Diasporic perspective. Drawing upon personal and professional insights collected from the individual authors, from interviews with additional Black Diasporic scholars and white allies who are navigating

10   Decolonizing Linguistics

their careers in the US, and from recent autobiographical scholarship by three prominent Black Diasporic linguists, the scholars discuss how decolonization is happening in specific domains across research, teaching, practice, and advocacy and offer a set of recommendations for further advancing decolonization in linguistics across various subfields.

In Chapter 20, "An Interdisciplinary Approach to Language Activism from Community Colleges: Linguistics Meets Communication Studies," Carlos de Cuba, Poppy Slocum, and Laura Spinu ground their work in their own experiences as linguists working in communication studies programs at community colleges. Informed by their perspectives and training as linguists working in communication studies, they critique the standard language ideology prevalent in that field, a fundamentally colonial ideology that reinforces deficit approaches in research presentations, textbooks, professional development, and teaching. Through their activism the authors strive to decolonize linguistics by decolonizing a key adjacent discipline.

Respecting the local is a decolonial practice because it recognizes that the work we do as linguists is always situated in a particular context, even for those who may imagine themselves to be "objective" or those who aspire to make theoretical generalizations across situations (see Clemons, this volume). Becoming aware of situated context also requires honoring the histories and present conditions of the people we are working with. This point is addressed in Chapter 3, "The Colonial Geography of Linguistics: A View from the Caribbean" by Ben Braithwaite and Kristian Ali, who theorize the role of geography in the perpetuation of global colonial patterns, pointing to the liberatory linguistic traditions from the Caribbean as a means both of elevating Global South knowledge, which remains marginalized in linguistics, and of offering alternative approaches for linguists in the Global North. The authors show that geography directly informs research through the questions we ask, the methodologies we employ, and the scholars we cite.

Offering a related perspective, in Chapter 17, "Decolonizing Creolistics Through Popular Culture: The Case of Dancehall," Rashana Vikara Lydner examines the decolonizing potential of researching multilingualism in Guyane (French Guiana), employing the musical genre of dancehall as a lens for exploring the workings of race, gender, and power in Caribbean Creole identities in ways that are also situated in Guyanese culture and history. Her analysis is locally situated while also connecting to a wide range of areas of linguistic study, including language and identity, language and gender, language contact, and language change.

Centering the individuals with and for whom we are working is another critical component of respecting the particular in a decolonial approach. In

Chapter 19, "Promoting Decolonized Classrooms Through an Introductory Linguistics Course for Future Teachers in Alaska," Ève Ryan, Matt Ford, and Giovanna Wilde exemplify this commitment. They describe the process of decolonizing a linguistics course for future teachers of Indigenous students, and in doing so they center the voice of Giovanna Wilde, an Indigenous student in the class. Wilde expresses a key motivation for respecting and responding to the local as critical to decolonization—namely, that Indigenous experiences cannot be assumed to be readily mapped onto Western experiences. The chapter demonstrates that centering the experiences of marginalized groups yields perspectives, knowledge, and ways of thinking that are ignored in colonizing approaches.

As a decolonial scholarly practice, a focus on the local and the particular challenges notions of objectivity and generalizability. By centering the perspectives of marginalized groups yield new insights and by acknowledging the trauma of colonization and working to heal it, opportunities are created to repair and strengthen relationships with groups whose marginalization academics have contributed to. We are also reminded once again as linguists to critically reflect on how our own locations—personal, cultural, geographic, and otherwise—influence and have influenced our scholarship and our positionalities as scholars.

To Decolonize Is to Critically Reflect on the Past and Present

Resisting colonization requires us to remember the colonial history of our own institutions and, as discussed above, to directly reject the colonizing principles on which those institutions of higher education were founded. It also requires us to critically reflect on the past and present of our discipline. The histories and development of the languages and language varieties that linguists study are also histories of people, of power, and of oppression. Yet for the most part, linguists and linguistics too often treat language as disembodied and apolitical.

This noncritical approach to linguistics is evident in accounts of how linguistics scholarship has unfolded that are detached from the ideologies of the scholars who shaped the field. In Chapter 2, "Racialization, Language Science, and Nineteenth-Century Anthropometrics," Margaret Thomas reveals one such example by critically examining the discipline's reception of Paul Broca. Thomas demonstrates that Broca's work on language was subject to colonial ideologies of the time, including those that we can now recognize as racist.

As she argues, it is important to examine and reflect on how the ideologies of scholars such as Broca have shaped their scholarship and hence linguistics, so that we can be aware of how racism and colonialism, among other forms of bias and inequality, have distorted scholarship and may continue to do so (see also Dockum & Green, 2024).

As a decolonizing practice that counteracts claims of scholarly objectivity, the authors in both volumes explicitly acknowledge that who we are affects our scholarship. In each chapter, the authors make their positionalities clear and discuss how they impact their scholarship, from research questions to methods and analyses to engagement with communities, from classrooms to the internet. Some contributors write from their perspective as white scholars who recognize the privilege afforded to them as a result of coloniality and structural racism in society and in academia, and they leverage their privilege to call out and work to dismantle those forces. In Chapter 10, "Decolonizing Historical Linguistics in the Classroom and Beyond," Claire Bowern and Rikker Dockum recognize that their lived experiences and their linguistic training left them without significant knowledge about decolonization. Harnessing their agency to address their knowledge gap, they used their expertise as researchers and educators to inform themselves about how to teach historical linguistics, a subfield with a deep colonial legacy, in decolonizing ways and to develop and test strategies in dialogue with their students and colleagues. Other authors similarly reflect on and discuss their whiteness as a decolonizing scholarly practice.

In Chapter 9, "From Gatekeeping to Inclusion in the Introductory Linguistics Curriculum: Decolonizing Our Teaching, Our Psyches, Our Institutions, and Our Field," Lynnette Arnold recounts how her efforts to incorporate language and race into her introductory course had been effective in a largely white section of the class but not in a section that enrolled mostly students of color. Arnold reflects on this experience and offers suggestions for reshaping introductory courses to incorporate a focus on race and language in ways that center the experiences of students of color and draw them more fully into learning about linguistics through a decolonial lens.

Theorization about language is also often detached from the everyday language practices of real people; given the colonialist roots of linguistics, this means that purportedly objective accounts of language are not objective at all but rather are erasures of the intellectual, cultural, and linguistic traditions and lifeways of the people and communities whose language patterns linguists most often study. Some of the authors in the volume write from perspectives that have traditionally been marginalized and minoritized in academia and in linguistics, courageously sharing experiences that are rarely encountered in scholarly writing and are often actively suppressed. In Chapter 6, "Unpacking Experiences of Racism in European Applied Linguistics," Kamran Khan explores the European context of academic colonialities through his positionality as a British-Pakistani Muslim scholar. Khan discusses how the historical legacy of colonialism and racism continues to pervade applied linguistics in Europe, as illustrated in part by the types of aggressions he himself has experienced. The chapter concludes with a series of questions to decolonize linguistics and unsettle the hegemonic whiteness of the discipline.

In Chapter 7, "Centering Race and Multilingualism in French Linguistics," Maya Angela Smith, writing from the perspective of French linguistics, describes her multiple forms of marginalization as a linguist in a literature-dominated field; as a scholar of the topic of race and language, which is neglected in French studies; as an adult language learner of French; and as a Black woman in an overwhelmingly white field. Smith discusses how drawing upon her own background as a minoritized scholar allowed her to more fully connect with her research participants in her work on language and race in the Senegalese diaspora. She highlights the importance of researcher reflexivity about our positionalities not only in our written work but also in our interactions with our research participants, in ways that make the research more meaningful and valuable for everyone.

Confronting the colonizing processes of whiteness from the standpoint of lived experience is also central to Chapter 8, "Decolonizing (Psycho)linguistics Means Dropping the Language Gap Rhetoric," in which Megan Figueroa challenges the widespread and false claim within psycholinguistics and related fields that children from racially and economically minoritized backgrounds experience a "language gap." She does so not only by making use of academic forms of evidence but also by drawing upon her own experiences growing up as someone whose language was racialized through constructs such as the language gap she writes about.

An awareness of how our positionalities shape our thinking is beneficial not only when it allows us to see and understand colonial issues in new ways but also when it reveals what we didn't see or were unable to do. Throughout the volume, contributors' reflective approach to their research, teaching, and community collaborations allows them space to acknowledge the limitations of their work, while paving the way for future scholars to use their example to move the field further toward decolonization. As demonstrated throughout this section, scholarship that is grounded in critical reflection of both the past and present requires that the work of decolonization be tangible, personal, specific, and productive.

To Decolonize Is to Return and Recenter

In certain scholarly and activist frameworks, decolonization means the actual return of land, intellectual property, and allocations (e.g., Deloria, 1969/1988; Landback, 2022; Tuck & Yang, 2012). To decolonize is thus to actively and directly return stolen land, intellectual property, cultural artifacts, and ancestral remains, as well as to provide monetary and other material allocations and reparations. These models are premised on a direct return model as a primary motivation for decolonizing scholarship. This focus is key for us to grapple with in linguistics, as it highlights where theory and action intersect in the processes of decolonization and reparations. In a decolonizing model, what should reparations in linguistics look like? Throughout this volume, contributors engage with this question through work that centers on returning and recentering, in individual and collective models.

In addition to the literal returning of linguistic materials to the groups from which they were taken (addressed, for example, by Nicté Fuller Medina as discussed below), returning and recentering involves returning control to marginalized language users and their communities, which can be done both by increasing the participation of community members in linguistic research and by ensuring that this participation is meaningful. Several authors take this approach by rethinking how nonacademic perspectives are shared and received within linguistic research. In Chapter 14, "Revitalizing Attitudes Toward Creole Languages," Ariana Bancu, Joy P. G. Peltier, Felicia Bisnath, Danielle Burgess, Sophia Eakins, Wilkinson Daniel Wong Gonzales, Moira Saltzman, Yourdanis Sedarous, Alicia Stevers, and Marlyse Baptista examine Creole language users' attitudes toward their languages. They assert that Creole language users have a central role in how Creole languages are described and presented to others, an approach that is all too rare in traditional research on Creole and other languages whose histories are entangled with colonialism. Reframing language users as language experts and conceptualizing their goal as "revitalizing" language attitudes to support Creole communities, the authors provide a model for community-centered linguistic research.

As this example indicates, returning and recentering also entail that linguistic work is driven by community needs, which cannot be taken for granted, even in collaborative models. Given the deep entrenchment of power structures in academia and in linguistics, it is not enough to simply have members of marginalized groups listed as collaborators in a superficial or tacked-on fashion; we must ensure that the needs of these individuals and their communities drive the project and that they and their priorities are centered in the work. In Chapter 5, "Apolitical Linguistics Doesn't Exist, and It Shouldn't: Developing A Black Feminist Praxis toward Political Transparency," Aris Moreno Clemons argues that a community-centered linguistics is crucial to a justice-centered linguistics, and she rejects traditional research models that perpetuate white supremacy and coloniality. Clemons calls for "political transparency" in linguistic research, including the clear articulation of our frameworks of analysis and the goals for our research, as a necessary step toward challenging prevailing power structures. This form of decolonization involves an awareness and deliberate contraction of our privileges as academics.

In Chapter 16, "Growing a Bigger Linguistics Through a Zapotec Agenda: The Ticha Project," May Helena Plumb, Alejandra Dubcovsky, Moisés García Guzmán, Brook Danielle Lillehaugen, and Felipe H. Lopez describe how principles related to returning and recentering drive their collaborative model of work with Zapotec communities. Their goal is not merely to advance academic scholarship but more importantly, guided by Zapotec activists, to produce knowledge that will serve the needs of Zapotec people, both individually and collectively. This model works toward scholarship that is reciprocal, in which both Indigenous and non-Indigenous experts develop and pursue shared and overlapping goals to the benefit of Indigenous community.

A similar commitment informs Chapter 18, "Prioritizing Community Partners' Goals in Projects to Support Indigenous Language Revitalization," in which Katherine J. Riestenberg, Ally Freemond, Brook Danielle Lillehaugen, and Jonathan N. Washington explore the preconditions and consequences of centering community goals over academic goals in linguistic scholarship. Drawing on the insights of community members and students who engaged in two community-centered language revitalization projects, the authors detail the conditions that are necessary in order to alter the balance of power in linguistic research. As these authors assert, returning and recentering entail a ceding of structural privilege and a sharing of institutional resources.

Recentering can be hard for some scholars to accept because it requires a shifting of priorities, which may feel like a loss (of control, of power, of framing) to the privileged. In Chapter 4, "We Like the Idea of You But Not the Reality of You: The Whole Scholar as Disruptor of Default Colonial Practices in Linguistics," Nicté Fuller Medina tackles this issue by discussing extractivist models of linguistic research on the Global South, including the positioning of "native speakers" as data brokers, which she illustrates with her own experiences. She offers as an alternative project to repatriate and restitute original sound recordings and develop through collaborative creation a language archive for community use. Aiming to disrupt colonizing research practices, Fuller Medina deprioritizes access to the archive by researchers

16   Decolonizing Linguistics

from the Global North. Decolonizing linguistic research through recentering may thus limit or even deny structurally privileged scholars access that is taken for granted in colonial models.

To Decolonize Is to Critically Examine and to Transform Our Approaches

The decentering approach described above challenges colonialist linguistic research, which centers European and North American white cis male frameworks and paradigms and establishes them as the assumed default. In colonial frameworks, a great deal of energy is expended in challenging research from different traditions as not sufficiently abstract, technical, or methodologically rigorous. Who is served by a scholarly framework that is centered on obscure categorizations and frets over questions of narrow technicality? When those with greater resources claim that they "advance the discipline" through modes of study that fail to take into account knowledge and input from the individuals or communities from whom language data has been colonially extracted, the result is to create esoteric linguistic analyses—indeed, to create an entire discipline of study—that language users cannot recognize themselves in and have little access to or domain over.

Decolonization therefore requires that scholars interrogate hegemonic epistemologies and methodologies and elevate new approaches—those that have been suppressed and devalued in colonialist academic practice. Returning to Chapter 7, "Centering Race and Multilingualism in French Linguistics," Maya Angela Smith notes that linguists are not the only experts on language; everyday language users are also experts who have key insights into what language is and how it is used. Linguists should look to this wisdom, which requires us to critically examine our own scholarly assumptions and the traditions that have been established by our predecessors in the discipline.

Many chapters in this volume bring to the light unspoken assumptions of linguistic research that have been accepted as default. The authors critique these assumptions, revealing the flawed foundations underlying them, and they offer alternative frameworks across a variety of linguistic subfields and across areas of engagement and application. In Chapter 11, "Towards a Decolonial Syntax: Research, Teaching, Publishing," Hannah Gibson, Kyle Jerro, Savithry Namboodiripad, and Kristina Riedel offer such an interrogation with regard to the field of syntax. In their chapter, they argue that syntax emerged from a colonial perspective that relies on ideologies that reproduce inequities of race, gender, and other dimensions of social difference. The idea that syntax is built on a colonial legacy is not generally acknowledged, which is often also the case in other subfields of linguistics that claim to be "theoretical"; Gibson and colleagues unpack examples of such a legacy in teaching, research and citation practices and call for the development of a decolonial syntax.

Change within linguistics also requires recognizing and dismantling the power structures that permeate academia. In Chapter 13, "Open Methods: Decolonizing (or Not) Research Methods in Linguistics," Dan Villarreal and Lauren Collister explore the potential of Open Methods as a way of leveling unequal access to research resources, while also acknowledging the potential pitfalls if this approach is adopted uncritically. They present a cautionary tale of Open Access in academic publishing, demonstrating how its use has often led to further privileging those who are already structurally and institutionally privileged. As Villarreal and Collister suggest, without transformation, new frameworks that are uncritically built on old models run the risk of reproducing colonial structures. Instead, in a decolonial approach, transparency, intentionality, and critical reflexivity are essential.

To be truly decolonial, change must also take place at all levels of the research process. In Chapter 12, "Decolonising Methodologies Through Collaboration: Reflections on Partnerships and Funding Flows from Working Between the South and the North," Rajendra Chetty, Hannah Gibson, and Colin Reilly reflect on the role of power dynamics involving academic institutions and funding agencies in collaborative partnerships between the Global North and the Global South. Drawing on their experiences in forging such partnerships in the UK and South Africa, they argue that moving toward decolonizing collaborative research involves a commitment from Global North scholars to a fundamental rethinking—and recentering—of the role of Global South scholars and scholarship. The authors detail the transformative practices necessary at multiple levels—that of the individual researcher, the academic institution, and the funding agency—in order for decolonial partnerships to be possible across geographic divides.

Finally, change is also needed to decolonize the incentive structure and the traditional conceptualizations of value and worth that undergird academia. As Katherine J. Riestenberg, Ally Freemond, Brook Danielle Lillehaugen, and Jonathan N. Washington call for in Chapter 18, "Prioritizing Community Partners' Goals in Projects to Support Indigenous Language Revitalization," it is necessary for those who hold positions of institutional power to be agents of change and advocacy for work that is currently marginalized, especially work that is collaborative and community-driven. Decolonizing linguistics needs to take place on committees, in review processes, and in any academic context where behind-the-scenes gatekeeping and resource decisions are made.

18 Decolonizing Linguistics

To Decolonize Is to Embrace Refusal

Decolonization is typically discussed in terms of actions that can be taken. Indeed, throughout this volume, authors share many actions that we can engage in to resist colonialist practices and reshape our work in linguistics and in academia. Even with our best efforts, however, obstacles to progress still abound. When that happens, as Ignacio L. Montoya argues in Chapter 1, "Manifestations of Colonialism in Linguistics and Opportunities for Decolonization Through Refusal," we have three options: we can acquiesce, we can resist, or we can refuse. Refusal, a concept drawn from anthropology and Indigenous studies (cf. Simpson, 2014), refers to the rejection of conventional structures. Decolonization is not about more diversity rhetoric or more practices of inclusion that maintain the scholarly status quo; it is about changing the institutional structures that have been created by colonization and that perpetuate colonial practices. Through refusal, we can directly challenge those structures by deliberately choosing not to engage in practices that reproduce power imbalances.

Sometimes active refusal is necessary. For example, when scholars face the prospect of engaging in work that may reinforce colonialist structures and replicate oppressive structures and processes, however well-intentioned it may be, we may actively push back. As Montoya states, refusal includes saying no to extractive research practices, saying no to violently imposing theoretical frameworks on such data, saying no to exclusionary forms of dissemination that deny community members access to knowledge created using their language. Refusal also means interrogating disciplinary norms and boundaries. Our field has longstanding and deep biases that favor approaches that disconnect languages from their users, with a perspective that puts formal, abstract linguistics at the core of the field and relegates the so-called applied, context-based fields to the periphery. We instead envision a decolonial approach to linguistics that challenges those assumptions and that refuses to be pushed to the margins.

Conclusion

Decolonization can transform linguistics into a discipline that is more expansive, more relevant, and more just. As the authors of the chapters throughout this volume make clear, however, decolonization should not be envisioned as a one-size-fits-all solution; rather, it requires an honest assessment and transformation of the approaches—holistically defined—that we use in our linguistic and professional work. Comprehensive change historically has required sacrifice. We now ask: How can we as scholars engage this work collectively so that it does not overburden the individual scholar but rather presses for systemic change? Whether through direct or indirect action, the authors in this volume offer a wide range of specific suggestions for change that spans from the local to the systemic. We return to these recommendations in the conclusion to this volume, where we also put forward additional suggestions for further steps toward decolonization.

References

Antia, Bassey E., & Makoni, Sinfree (Eds.). (2023). *Southernizing sociolinguistics: Colonialism, racism, and patriarchy in language in the Global South*. Routledge.

Bolton, Kingsley, & Hutton, Christopher (Eds.). (2000). Orientalism and linguistics. Special issue of *Interventions*, *2*(1), 1–5. https://doi.org/10.1080/136980100360751

Calhoun, Kendra N. (2021). *Competing discourses of diversity and inclusion: Institutional rhetoric and graduate student narratives at two Minority Serving Institutions* [Doctoral dissertation, University of California, Santa Barbara].

Canagarajah, Suresh. (2022). Language diversity in academic writing: Toward decolonizing scholarly publishing. *Journal of Multicultural Discourses*, *17*(2), 107–128. https://doi.org/10.1080/17447143.2022.2063873

Charity Hudley, Anne H., Mallinson, Christine, & Bucholtz, Mary. (2020). Toward racial justice in linguistics: Interdisciplinary insights into theorizing race in the discipline and diversifying the profession. *Language*, *96*(4), e200–e235. https://doi.org/10.1353/lan.2020.0074

Charity Hudley, Anne H., Mallinson, Christine, and Bucholtz, Mary (Eds.). (2024). Inclusion in linguistics. Oxford University Press.

Chew, K. A. B. (2019). Weaving words: Conceptualizing language reclamation through culturally-significant metaphor. *Canadian Journal of Native Education*, *41*(1), 168–185. https://doi.org/10.14288/cjne.v41i1.196608

Cruz, Hilaria. (2020). Between insiders and outsiders: When an Indigenous researcher conducts studies in her own community (E. A. Wood, trans.). *Language Documentation & Conservation Special Publication No. 23*, 43–62.

Cruz Cruz, Emiliana (Ed.). (2020). *Theoretical reflections around the role of fieldwork in linguistics and linguistic anthropology: Contributions of Indigenous researchers from southern Mexico*. (Megan J. Crowhurst, Nora C. England, Patience L. Epps, Sofia G. Pierson, May Helena Plumb, James B. Tandy, Paige Erin Wheeler, Elizabeth A. Wood, & Anthony C. Woodbury, Trans.). *Language Documentation & Conservation*, *23*. https://scholarspace.manoa.hawaii.edu/server/api/core/bitstreams/fd5f3303-300e-40fe-aaf8-949284e7e56a/content

Cupples, Julie, & Grosfoguel, Ramón (Eds.). (2018). *Unsettling Eurocentrism in the westernized university*. Routledge.

Davis, Jenny L. (2017). Resisting rhetorics of language endangerment: Reclamation through Indigenous language survivance. *Language and Description, 14*, 37–58.

Davis, Jenny L., & Smalls, Krystal A. (2021). Dis/possession afoot: American (anthropological) traditions of anti-Blackness and coloniality. *Journal of Linguistic Anthropology*, *31*(2), 275–282. https://doi.org/10.1111/jola.12327

20 Decolonizing Linguistics

DeGraff, Michel. (2005). Linguists' most dangerous myth: The fallacy of Creole Exceptionalism. *Language in Society, 34*(4), 533–591. https://doi.org/10.1017/S0047404505050207

Deloria, Vine Jr. (1988). *Custer died for your sins: An Indian manifesto.* University of Oklahoma Press.

Devonish, Hubert. (1986). *Language and liberation: Creole language politics in the Caribbean.* Karia Press.

Dockum, Rikker, & Green, Caitlin M. (2024). Toward a big tent linguistics: Inclusion and the myth of the lone genius. In Anne H. Charity Hudley, Christine Mallinson, & Mary Bucholtz (Eds.). *Inclusion in linguistics.* Oxford University Press.

Errington, Joseph. (2008). *Linguistics in a colonial world: A story of language, meaning, and power.* Blackwell.

Gupta, Akhil. (2021, Nov. 20) *Decolonizing U.S. anthropology* [2021 Presidential Address]. American Anthropological Association Annual Meeting, Baltimore, MD, United States.

Hao, Karen. (2022, April 19). Artificial intelligence is creating a new colonial world order. *MIT Technology Review.* https://www.technologyreview.com/2022/04/19/1049592/artificial-intelligence-colonialism/

Harrison, Faye V. (2011). *Decolonizing anthropology: Moving further toward an anthropology for liberation.* American Anthropological Association.

Kubota, Ryuko. (2020). Confronting epistemological racism, decolonizing scholarly knowledge: Race and gender in applied linguistics. *Applied Linguistics, 41*(5), 712–732. https://doi.org/10.1093/applin/amz033

Landback. (2022). Manifesto. https://landback.org/manifesto/

Lee, Robert, & Ahtone, Tristan. (2020, March 30). Land-grab universities. *High Country News.* https://www.hcn.org/issues/52.4/indigenous-affairs-education-land-grab-universities

Leonard, Wesley Y. (2017). Producing language reclamation by decolonising "language." *Language Documentation and Description, 14,* 15–36.

Leonard, Wesley Y. (2021). Toward an anti-racist linguistic anthropology: An Indigenous response to white supremacy. *Journal of Linguistic Anthropology, 31*(2), 218–237. https://doi.org/10.1111/jola.12319.

Leonard, Wesley Y. (2023). Refusing "endangered languages" narratives. *Daedalus, 152*(3): 69–83. https://www.amacad.org/daedalus/language-social-justice-united-states

Lowery, Malinda Maynor. (2010). *Lumbee Indians in the Jim Crow South: Race, identity, and the making of a nation.* University of North Carolina Press.

Makoni, Sinfree, Severo, Cristine G., Abdelhay, Ashraf, & Kaiper-Marquez, Anna (Eds.). (2022). *The languaging of higher education in the Global South: De-colonizing the language of scholarship and pedagogy.* Routledge.

McGranahan, Carole, Roland, Kaifa, & Williams, Bianca C. (2016). *Decolonizing anthropology: A conversation with Faye V. Harrison.* 2 parts. Savage Minds. https://savageminds.org/2016/05/02/decolonizing-anthropology-a-conversation-with-faye-v-harrison-part-i/

Meek, Barbra A. (2011). Failing American Indian languages. *American Indian Culture and Research Journal, 35*(2), 43–60. https://doi.org/10.17953/aicr.35.2.m272376nl73v332t

Miles, Tiya. (2015). *Ties that bind: The story of an Afro-Cherokee family in slavery and freedom.* University of California Press.

Morgan, Marcyliena (Ed.). (1994). *Language and the social construction of identity in creole situations.* Center for Afro-American Studies, UCLA.

Motha, Suhantie. (2014). *Race, empire, and English language teaching: Creating responsible and ethical anti-racist practice.* Teachers College Press.

Motha, Suhantie. (2020). Is an antiracist and decolonizing applied linguistics possible? *Annual Review of Applied Linguistics, 40,* 128–133. https://doi.org/10.1017/S0267190520000100

Paris, Django, & Winn, Maisha T. (Eds.) (2016). *Humanizing research: Decolonizing qualitative inquiry with youth and communities.* SAGE Publishing.

Pennycook, Alastair. (2007). Language, localization, and the real: Hip-hop and the global spread of authenticity. *Journal of Language, Identity, and Education, 6*(2), 101–115. http://dx.doi.org/10.1080/15348450701341246

Perley, Bernard C. (2012). Zombie linguistics: Experts, endangered languages and the curse of undead voices. *Anthropological Forum, 22*(2), 133–149. https://doi.org/10.1080/00664 677.2012.694170

Quijano, Aníbal. (2007). Coloniality and modernity/rationality. *Cultural Studies, 21*(2–3), 168–178. https://doi.org/10.1080/09502380601164353

Simpson, Audra. (2014). *Mohawk interruptus: Political life across the borders of settler states.* Duke University Press.

Smith, Linda Tuhiwai. (2021). *Decolonizing methodologies: Research and Indigenous peoples.* Third edition. Bloomsbury Press.

Spears, Arthur K., & Hinton, Leanne. (2010). Language, inequality, and endangerment: African Americans and Native Americans. *Transforming Anthropology, 18*(1), 3–14. https://doi.org/10.1111/j.1548-7466.2010.01065.x

Tsikewa, Adrienne. (2021). Reimagining the current praxis of field linguistics training: Decolonial considerations. *Language, 97*(4), e293–e319. https://doi.org/10.1353/lan.2021.0080

Tuck, Eve, & Yang, K. Wayne. (2012). Decolonization is not a metaphor. *Decolonization: Indigeneity, Education and Society, 1*(1), 1–40. https://doi.org/10.25058/20112742.n38.04

Tuck, Eve, & Yang, K. Wayne. (2014). Unbecoming claims: Pedagogies of refusal in qualitative research. *Qualitative Inquiry, 20*(6), 811–818. https://doi.org/10.1177/1077800414530265

Wilder, Craig Steven. (2013). *Ebony and ivory: Race, slavery, and the troubled history of America's universities.* Bloomsbury.

PART 1

DECOLONIZING LINGUISTICS AND THE ACADEMY

Ignacio Montoya was born in New Mexico and raised in a very small town on the border of the United States and Mexico. At the age of 13, he moved with his mother, two younger brothers, and grandmother to the Phoenix area, where his family continues to live. Ignacio attended Harvard College, earning a bachelor's degree in psychology. Between college and his doctoral program he was an elementary and middle school teacher for several years, working in a wide variety of classrooms in Los Angeles and New York City. He earned a master's degree in education at Teachers College, Columbia University and a PhD in linguistics from the Graduate Center, City University of New York. Ignacio is currently assistant professor at the University of Nevada, Reno. His current research program focuses on the intersection of linguistic theory, language revitalization/reclamation, and decolonization.

Abstract: This chapter focuses on how colonialism manifests in the field of Linguistics and how academic linguists can contribute to decolonization. By identifying the ways in which the processes and products of academic linguistic work are based on a colonial legacy and continue to be extractive of the knowledge and cultural resources of Indigenous peoples, academic linguists working with Indigenous languages can identify ways to refuse the privileges afforded them by their association with settler-colonial institutions in order to allow for Indigenous control of linguistic and cultural resources. In doing so, new possibilities are created that make the field more ethical and inclusive and that broaden how we think about linguistic scholarship.

Key Words: decolonization, refusal, community-engaged scholarship, liberatory linguistics, language reclamation

1
Manifestations of Colonialism in Linguistics and Opportunities for Decolonization Through Refusal

Ignacio L. Montoya (he/him)
University of Nevada, Reno

Introduction

This chapter applies the notion of decolonization to linguistic work with Indigenous communities. My understanding of the term *decolonization* in this chapter is based primarily though not exclusively on its use in Indigenous Studies, drawing from scholars such as Eve Tuck and Wayne K. Yang (2012), who argue that decolonization entails a return of resources to Indigenous communities. I discuss different contexts of colonization which lead to different, though related, notions of decolonization. I apply that construct to the field of Linguistics specifically, and more generally to academia—both of which have been and continue to be instruments of colonization, as discussed in the third part of this chapter. My primary target audience is academic linguists who work with Indigenous communities, though many of the observations and arguments presented are relevant for academics working with other communities and/or engaging with antiracist, abolitionist, and liberation work more generally. The ideas presented in this chapter are informed by my own experiences as a non-Indigenous academic linguist working with Indigenous communities (for a discussion of my positionality, see Introduction, this volume), as well as by scholarship in Linguistics and other fields, such as Anthropology and Indigenous Studies. (Following Wesley Leonard (2017), I use capital letters to designate a formally recognized field of study in the academy and lower-case letters for what is studied in that field.)

If our aim is to contribute to the decolonizing of Linguistics, it is necessary first to interrogate the ways in which we as academic linguists collectively and individually reproduce and reinforce colonial structures, including through the products we create, such as our publications. Then, we can develop

---

Ignacio L. Montoya, *Manifestations of Colonialism in Linguistics and Opportunities for Decolonization Through Refusal*
In: *Decolonizing Linguistics*. Edited by: Anne H. Charity Hudley, Christine Mallinson, and Mary Bucholtz, Oxford University Press.
© Anne H. Charity Hudley, Christine Mallinson, and Mary Bucholtz 2024. DOI: 10.1093/oso/9780197755259.003.0002

theories and practices for actively countering colonial structures and expectations. To do so, I argue, requires *refusal*, a notion drawn from Anthropology and Indigenous Studies, especially Audra Simpson (2014). As I discuss later in this chapter, refusal involves the rejection of conventional modes of recognition, such as our academic reward structures. Refusal, as this term is used theoretically, is not simply saying no; it is a generative process that engages with alternative methodologies, epistemologies, and value systems. By refusing to partake in the creation of extractive products in Linguistics, we create new possibilities of decolonial work in the field, possibilities that elevate Indigenous knowledge systems, broaden our insights about language, and make Linguistics more inclusive.

Background on Decolonization

Decolonization can be defined as the undoing of the impact of colonization; it is "a process designed to shed and recover from the ill effects of colonization" (Miller, 2008, p. 15). Given that colonization has manifested differently across various historical, political, cultural, and geographic situations, scholars and activists operating in distinct contexts might have different, though related, expectations of what decolonization entails. To understand the nuances of a particular use of this construct, it is important to be attuned to historical and contemporary details of the context to which the construct is being applied. I begin with an overview of colonization in general, followed by a discussion of the connection of colonization to the academy generally and then linguistics specifically.

One broad distinction that informs different understandings of decolonization is the distinction between what I am referring to as *exploitation colonization* and *settler-colonialism*. Though both types of colonization involve outsiders moving to a new territory and extracting resources for their own benefit, the goals of the colonizers in each of these situations are distinct and they result in significantly different conceptualizations and treatments of the existing inhabitants of that territory. Exploitation colonization—also known as franchise or dependent colonialism—focuses on the acquisition of resources from the occupied land, whereas settler-colonialism involves acquiring the land itself (Wolfe, 1999). In the former, the Indigenous populations are perceived either as sources of labor for extracting the resources of that territory, or the people themselves are perceived as resources for profit (e.g., for forced labor outside of the territory). The British Empire enacted both types of colonization. South Asia and Africa represent sites of British extractive colonial activity involving the extraction of material resources, such as gold, cotton, spices, silk, and gems, as well as forced labor of the Indigenous populations. Management of the Indigenous populations in extractive colonial contexts also involves an assault on the culture, political systems, and psychological well-being of colonized groups and individuals (Ngũgĩ, 1986). Notably, though, because the Indigenous population is critical for the extraction of resources, their elimination is decidedly not a goal of exploitation colonization. In the case of settler-colonialism, on the other hand, because Indigenous people are a threat to the legitimacy of the colonial occupation of their land, a crucial goal of settler-colonialism is the elimination of Indigenous people and culture altogether (Wolfe, 2006). This involves both a literal elimination of Indigenous bodies through strategies such as genocide and displacement as well as an elimination of Indigenous lifeways through different forms of assimilation (e.g., residential schools that aim to "kill the Indian . . . [to] save the man" (Pratt, 1973/1892; Adams, 1995)). Examples of settler-colonialism are evident in North America and Australia, dominated by the movement of Europeans to the occupied territories abroad with the concomitant attempted elimination of the Indigenous people of those lands.

These differences in the experiences of different colonial subjects also account for the current experiences of Indigenous peoples in those places. In the case of exploitation colonization, for instance, in places where the imperial power has retreated, typically as a result of revolutionary actions, it is reasonable to speak about a postcolonial context in formerly occupied lands that are currently under formal self-rule of the previously dominated people. Indeed, the field of Postcolonial Studies explores those contexts to understand the lingering effects of colonization in formerly colonized territories. In these cases, decolonization focuses on managing these postimperial effects, by, for instance, choosing to embrace the traditional language of an area in place of the colonial language (Ngũgĩ, 1986). In settler-colonial states, however, since the territory continues to be governed by a settler-colonial authority, there is no postcolonial context. In settler-colonial states, therefore, decolonization carries a different resonance since the current political, cultural, and economic structures continue to actively oppress Indigenous people. Therefore, it is not surprising that for some activists and scholars in Indigenous Studies, decolonization involves the reversal of the structures of power, as well as the return of land to Indigenous peoples (Tuck & Yang, 2012). The distinction between extraction colonization and settler-colonialism is simply one dimension along which we can view colonization, decolonization, and related ideas. Given that these concepts can be understood in a multiplicity of distinct ways, it is important for us to be mindful about the historical and contemporary particularities of the situation we are exploring and to be explicit about how we are using these constructs.

Though it is important to be mindful of how colonization and decolonization are conceptualized in different contexts, we can also observe many similarities across distinct contexts, similarities which we can explore in order to further our understanding of colonial structures more generally. Across different manifestations of colonization, regardless of whether the goal is to exploit or eliminate the Indigenous population, the colonial power aims to delegitimize the Indigenous cultures, traditions, and ways of life. The framing of European cultures, religions, and worldviews as superior offers justification for the exploitation or elimination of Indigenous people. As Wa Thiongoʻo Ngũgĩ (1986) writes, colonialism brings with it "the destruction or the deliberate undervaluing of a people's culture, their art, dances, religions, history, geography, education, orature and literature" (p. 16). Coupled with the devaluation of Indigenous knowledge systems is the elevation of the knowledge systems of the colonizers, a process rooted in notions of white supremacy and Western cultural hegemony.

As an institution charged with the production of knowledge, the academy is a crucial promoter of the idea of Western methodologies and epistemologies as superior (Smith, 2012). The subordinate position of non-Western knowledge systems is evident in the fact that basic assumptions about the nature of knowledge from Western traditions are taken for granted as the default (e.g., Bonilla-Silva & Zuberi, 2008, in Sociology; Czyakowska-Higgins, 2009, in Linguistics). In contrast, when other knowledge systems are considered in the academy, they are treated as objects to be explored and evaluated. Though some scholars do recognize that Indigenous knowledge systems have been undervalued and therefore have begun to engage with them more meaningfully, we still rarely consider the ways in which Western worldviews are overvalued by the academy.

Critical to decolonization, therefore, is the recognition and valuing of Indigenous knowledge that is actively or passively suppressed under colonization. In the context of knowledge systems, decolonization involves the elevation of Indigenous knowledge, especially in institutions connected to the production and dissemination of knowledge, such as museums, schools, and universities. A first step toward the incorporation of Indigenous knowledge is recognizing that the existing theories and methodologies of these colonial institutions are themselves based on a particular way of understanding the world. Educators and scholars operating under conventional academic frameworks often are not aware that their own assumptions reflect a particular ideology that is grounded in colonialism, instead assuming that their perspective is objective or neutral (see discussion in Clemons, this volume). Yet as Linda Tuhiwai Smith (2012) points out, "it is surely difficult to discuss *research methodology* and *indigenous peoples* together, in the same breath, without having an analysis of imperialism, without understanding the complex ways in which the pursuit of knowledge is deeply embedded in multiple layers of imperial and colonial practices" (p. 2). Recognition of the ways in which conventional institutions of knowledge are rooted in the colonial enterprise is a critical step toward meaningfully allowing Indigenous and other suppressed voices to be heard. Decolonization of knowledge institutions is not achieved simply through the inclusion of Indigenous experiences if those experiences continue to be understood through conventional academic frames. Rather, as Smith and others argue, the very frameworks and methodologies of the academy need to be interrogated and informed by Indigenous knowledge.

With regard to the present chapter, my understanding of the construct of decolonization draws primarily from its use in Indigenous Studies, particularly in the context of the United States and Canada. I adopt the essence of Eve Tuck and Wayne K. Yang's (2012) notion of decolonization. They offer a key insight that I argue is critical for engaging in the decolonization of Linguistics and the academy more broadly: decolonization necessitates challenging colonial structures by redistributing the power, privilege, and resources that come from participation in and association with a colonial context. As discussed further below, the field of Linguistics is rooted in an extractive model based in exploitation colonization in which the flow of resources is unidirectional, from colonized to the colonizer. A decolonial framework, therefore, disrupts this unidirectional flow and reestablishes Indigenous control of Indigenous knowledge and resources. Critically, as discussed later in this chapter, it also requires that those of us who have been granted power and privilege by a colonial institution cede some of those powers and privileges to Indigenous people.

Given that I am working with Indigenous communities in the United States, I see first-hand the importance of being intentional about the use of the term *decolonization*. The notion of decolonization can be a meaningful and powerful construct. It is, therefore, important that we make explicit the principles behind our use of that term, both because an essential component of decolonization is recognition of the local context and because it helps mitigate against a performative use of the term, which is often used in a rather generic way, more or less equivalent to "anti-racist," "equitable," "just," "inclusive." For instance, calls for "decolonizing the syllabus" have recently become more popular among university-level instructors. Among the practices recommended for achieving this goal are the inclusion of a diversity of authors, a wider range of pedagogical techniques, and a greater variety of assessment tools. Such practices are certainly of value and support antiracist work, and, to the extent that antiracist work overlaps with decolonization, these practices may also support decolonization. However, it is not clear to what extent they are based on a solid understanding of the effects of colonization and/or on an intentional drive to directly incorporate Indigenous epistemologies and methodologies, apart from perhaps the inclusion of Indigenous authors in the syllabus. As Eve Tuck and Wayne K. Yang (2012) point out, antiracism is not equivalent to decolonization, and there may in fact be instances when the two are incommensurable. Though there is certainly overlap between work in antiracism and work in decolonization, these constructs arise from different contexts and speak to the different particularities of those contexts. In the United States, for example, though Indigenous people of course experience racism along with other people of color, this experience interacts with their unique position as members of sovereign nations, with a history and political relationship to the government distinct from those of other people of color (Leonard, 2020). To use the term *decolonization* without articulating the basis of one's use of the term (e.g., whether in the sense of Tuck and Yang involving the return of land, resources, and privileges or in the sense articulated by other authors in this volume) runs the risk of excluding Indigenous experiences by ignoring the unique features of the oppression of Indigenous people in the United States. This type of erasure of Indigenous experiences undermines the goals of both antiracism and decolonization, and it in fact replicates colonial structures that seek to eliminate Indigeneity. As discussed in this section, there are a variety of legitimate ways of understanding and expressing decolonization. In order to ensure that this construct indeed serves to disrupt and undo the effects of colonization, we must be mindful that our use of the term is rooted in an awareness of the varied and complex structures that drive colonialism of various types and that devalue and erase the experiences of colonized people.

Colonization and Decolonization in Linguistics

The history of linguistic work in the Americas is inextricably linked to a colonial legacy. The European empires that colonized the Americas required a mastery of the languages spoken by Indigenous populations, a task that necessitated recording, analyzing, and synthesizing linguistic data. The grammars created through this process then served to advance the imperial agenda, which included religious conversion, incorporation into the economies of the empire, and assimilation into European cultural paradigms (Errington, 2008). Linguistic work in that era was intentionally extractive and exploitative, even if, given the belief in the superiority of European knowledge systems, it was framed as a means of benefiting Indigenous populations.

Notably, the overall model of linguistic work in the colonial era continues to be essentially the same model we employ today when we conduct research on the languages and language varieties of Indigenous and other marginalized communities: as did linguists of the colonial era, linguists today go into marginalized communities, access their knowledge, record it for their own use, analyze and synthesize it, and present it in a format that serves the linguist and the agenda of the colonial institution (e.g., the academy). Moreover, linguists typically do this work in a way that dissociates languages from the lived experiences and relationships of the people who use them, an example of linguistic extraction (Davis, 2017). Both then and now, the languages of Indigenous people are viewed as objects that can be appropriated and used by others without regard to Indigenous claims and wishes (Gaby & Woods, 2020). The overall agenda of linguistic work may have changed: this agenda formerly involved the assimilation of Indigenous populations and exploitation of their labor and currently involves making purported "contributions to human knowledge" (Hill, 2002, p. 121), as well as advancing linguists' professional objectives. However, the overall methodology remains the same: we go into communities; record Indigenous people's stories, linguistic tokens, verb paradigms, and so on; and then leave to analyze and synthesize the data, ultimately presenting our conclusions in formats that serve our professional goals.

Though our goals as academic linguists may be different than those of colonial linguists in that they serve the expectations of the academy rather than the expectations of the empire, we should acknowledge that the work is still driven primarily by our goals rather than by the goals of the communities with whom we work (Gerdts, 2017). Indeed, the initial contacts that academic linguists often make with communities are motivated by a desire to advance professionally, through production of a dissertation, articles, or conference presentations that we can use to procure a degree, a job, promotions, tenure, grants, or general prestige. In addition, our work also benefits others who are associated in some way with the academy. For instance, the university system benefits from what we produce, as our grant proposals generate money for the institution and our publications bring prestige. Other academy-adjacent institutions, such as academic presses and grant funding agencies, also rely on our research for their existence. Importantly, of course, the Indigenous communities who serve as sources for our work are not built into this system as beneficiaries (Grenoble, 2009). Though some linguists do end up making direct contributions to the communities on which they rely, (a) these contributions are not an inherent component of the conventional academic work, (b) projects that support communities are typically seen as secondary and associated with less prestige (more on that below), and (c) such projects are undertaken by individuals who have built personal relationships with members of the community and not by institutions such as universities and academic presses who also profit from Indigenous cultural and linguistic resources.

Community-Based Research and Language Reclamation

The idea that conventional research in our field has exploited Indigenous communities has begun to be addressed by some linguists (e.g., Gerdts, 2017; Gaby & Woods, 2020). In the last few decades, scholars have published work that recognizes that Indigenous communities have needs, interests, and goals that diverge from those of non-Indigenous academics (Collins, 1992; Tsikewa, 2021) and that argues that ethical engagement with Indigenous people entails attending to community priorities (Rice, 2006). Such work has come both from Indigenous scholars themselves (e.g., Leonard, 2018) and from non-Indigenous scholars who have built long-term relationships with specific Indigenous communities (e.g., Fitzgerald, 2018). Indeed, many individual linguists who develop strong connections with Indigenous communities contribute substantively to community language revitalization goals (e.g., Montoya et al., 2020). These contributions are based on the desire to ensure that one's work is respectful, relevant, reciprocal, and responsible (Kirkness & Barnhardt, 1991). It is important to note that this impetus typically results from relationships developed during the research process rather than from any incentives by the academy, whose reward structures in fact disincentivize relationship-building (Montoya, 2020). Notably, relationality as the basis of research is a characteristic of Indigenous research methodologies. As Shawn Wilson (2008) explains, Indigenous methodologies stem from the researcher's relations to others and to the environment, and the researcher is ultimately accountable to those in the community. Thus, building on and fostering relationships is at the root of Indigenously attuned scholarship. In order to ensure that Indigenous concerns are taken into consideration on a more systematic basis, we need models that explicitly incorporate Indigenous methodologies, epistemologies, and goals.

In order to impact the structures of the academy, we should incorporate decolonial approaches into our theories, which at a minimum involves a consideration of the goals of the Indigenous communities with whom we work (see also Chetty et al., this volume; Riestenberg et al., this volume). This process involves clarifying what we mean by community-based research. As Ewa Czyakowska-Higgins (2009) notes, a variety of models purport to be community-based, ranging from those that seek to be more ethical while nevertheless remaining linguist-focused to those based on advocacy for and empowerment of Indigenous communities. This type of theorizing allows for the elucidation of what is essential for linguistic research to be considered community-based, that is "research that is *on* a language, and that is conducted *for, with,* and *by* the language-speaking community within which the research takes place and which it affects" (p. 24; original emphasis). Such frameworks present decolonization in the currency valued by the academy (e.g., peer-reviewed journal articles) and form the basis of further discussions that build on these frameworks (e.g., Leonard & Haynes, 2010). Because theory on linguistic research in relation to communities touches on principles of decolonization, it offers tools for evaluating what type of work might qualify as decolonially oriented.

Another theoretical construct that engages with decolonization and language work is language reclamation, which is defined as distinct from language revitalization. Wesley Leonard (2012) describes language reclamation as "a larger effort by a community to claim its right to speak a language and to set associated goals in response to community needs and perspectives" (p. 539). Whereas the conventional focus of language revitalization is on intergenerational transmission of grammatical fluency, this is rarely the only or sometimes even the primary goal of the community. Moreover, under a decolonial framework, it is up to the community to decide what intergenerational transmission of the language looks like based on that community's needs and resources (De Korne & Leonard, 2017). Working from a foundation of language reclamation entails basing language documentation, description, and revitalization on Indigenous priorities, needs, and interests.

These more community-based frameworks have helped bring principles of decolonization to Linguistics by offering more just and equitable models for how linguists can engage with Indigenous communities. They do not, however, necessarily change the extractive nature of Linguistic work overall (see also Fuller Medina, this volume). Because community-based work is typically viewed as secondary to the actual work of Linguistics, the colonial structures of the field remain essentially intact because the reward systems remain intact

34 Decolonizing Linguistics

(Alperin et al., 2019). The kinds of activities that most directly support community goals (e.g., developing pedagogical materials and cultural resources, training community members to teach language classes, or consulting on grant-writing for language reclamation projects) are considered supplemental to so-called real linguistic work, which is conventionally measured by the number of peer-reviewed articles one publishes in prestigious journals (Montoya, 2020). Though community-based work is praised and touted as valuable service to the community—after all, it helps bolster the public image of Linguistics and of linguists' academic institutions—it is typically relegated to the status of a side project. Indeed, the more a university relies on prestige for its branding, the less community-based work at that university tends to be rewarded, which helps account for why work that directly serves communities tends to be more likely to be conducted in non–research-intensive, public institutions, especially tribal colleges. Overall, linguists interested in engaging in community-based work are often counseled either to wait until they have procured tenure or to first ensure that a conventional academic publication can come from that work. Such practices, of course, disincentivize community-based work and make invisible the kind of relationship-building that is essential for true collaborative engagement with communities.

It is therefore not enough to build more community-based models for linguists. Though such models do indeed make the process of conventional academic research in Linguistics more inclusive of Indigenous priorities (see also Villarreal & Collister, this volume), the fact that meaningful community-based work is relegated to the status of a side project or an after-thought means that the extractive products of the field remain unchanged and therefore the colonial reward systems remain intact. If our aim is decolonization of the field, we will not make substantive progress without targeting the colonial products through which we measure the worth of our scholarship: research journal articles, books published by academic presses, research grants, and presentations at academic conferences. The audience for these products is other academic linguists (with some exceptions, noted below), and these products as currently configured are essentially inaccessible to anyone outside of the field. In many instances, published work in Linguistics is difficult to obtain or even locate without an academic affiliation. Moreover, most of this work is written in a highly technical manner that is unintelligible to the untrained—even, in some cases, to linguists not trained in particular theoretical frameworks or methodologies. If we focus on making only the process of linguistic research more equitable, we nevertheless allow for the continued creation of extractive products. Because such products remain the gold standard by which scholarship is judged, we continue to replicate the colonial practices of the field. If we are incentivized to produce extractive products, we will continue to engage in extractive work.

If we truly want to engage with decolonization in Linguistics, we need to acknowledge the deep ways in which our scholarly products are extractive and how our valuing of them only further entrenches colonialism. Despite our efforts at making the process of engaging with communities more decolonial, we will not make significant progress toward decolonization without changing the products. We need to reject the conventional modes of recognition; we need to engage in refusal.

Refusal as a Framework for Decolonization

Refusal is a theoretical construct from fields such as Anthropology and Indigenous Studies (e.g., McGranahan, 2016). As articulated by Audra Simpson (2014), refusal refers to the rejection of conventional modes of recognition. Simpson illustrates the power that acts of refusal have to reframe narratives, value systems, and political structures. One example she offers is the act of refusal of the Iroquois Nationals Lacrosse Team, which served as a means of assertion of the Haudenosaunee (Iroquois) community's identity as a people with their own independent political systems rooted in their own history and culture. The team received significant media attention in 2010 when they withdrew from the World Lacrosse League Championship in England because the United Kingdom did not view their Haudenosaunee passport as sufficiently secure to grant entry into the country. Though members of the lacrosse team could have entered using Canadian or American passports, to which they were entitled, they instead literally and metaphorically "refus[ed] to play the game" (Simpson, 2014, p. 25). In so doing, they exerted themselves as Haudenosaunee, as first and foremost citizens of the Iroquois Confederacy: "they refuse to be Canadian or American. They refuse the 'gifts' of American and Canadian citizenship; they insist upon the integrity of Haudenosaunee governance" (p. 7). In the process, the lacrosse team reinforced for themselves, other members of the community, and the outside world the political sovereignty of the Haudenosaunee, and they highlighted the historical and contemporary presence of the Haudenosaunee on their traditional land. This act, as Simpson points out, comes from a "productive place of refusal" (p. 12). It is not simply saying no, but rather a generative act that rejects one set of modes of recognition and opens up possibilities for others. As this example shows, refusal is a strategy for dealing with oppressive structures.

Refusal is only one of the possible responses to structures of oppression: we can give in to them (e.g., assimilate), we can resist them (i.e., fight against them), or we can reject them (i.e., refuse). Refusal can be enacted in the political arena, as the Haudenosaunee example illustrates, and it can also be enacted in academia: "Refusal, and stances of refusal in research, are attempts to place limits on conquest and colonization of knowledge by marking what is off limits, what is not up for grabs or discussion, what is sacred, what can't be known" (Tuck & Yang, 2014, p. 225). Simpson (2014) herself enacts refusal as a scholar by "refus[ing] to practice the type of ethnography that claims to tell the whole story and have all the answers" (p. 34). Instead of uncritically adopting conventional anthropological methods of analysis, she focuses on a variety of narratives without claiming to be comprehensive. She aims to give voice to the people whose stories she writes about in ways that incorporate Indigenous epistemologies and experiences and that challenge conventional methods of Anthropology, which are overly narrow and do not typically include a wide variety of voices. Thus, Simpson demonstrates the potential for working within a particular discipline and engaging with its conventional methods but in a way that incorporates Indigenous epistemologies and methodologies and, in the process, also broadens the discipline.

Refusal can be enacted by Indigenous communities through setting boundaries on who has access to their traditional knowledge, and it can be enacted by non-Indigenous scholars through choosing not to engage in extractive research practices and not to create products designed to benefit the academy exclusively. If we aim to advance meaningful decolonization efforts in Linguistics, we need to refuse to participate in the creation of extractive products (see also Fuller Medina, this volume). This entails not going into communities with the sole purpose of gathering linguistic data for us to analyze, not taking a standard theory and applying it to data that was collected in this extractive way (either by us or someone else), and not creating conventional products that are based on extraction. In so doing, we can make space for envisioning and enacting new possibilities for what work in Linguistics can be. Though the most effective acts of refusal are those that fully reject extractive products, even incremental steps in that direction support decolonization, which is especially important for the most vulnerable scholars to keep in mind. What follows is a discussion of three principles that can guide us in our efforts: (1) acknowledging of colonial structures in Linguistics, (2) building on existing decolonial work, and (3) replacing colonial structures with decolonial frameworks and expectations.

Acknowledging Colonial Structures in Linguistics

Because the colonial legacy of Linguistics is generally invisible and yet permeates most of our theories and methods, simply recognizing that our conventional products are extractive can be powerful. Doing so validates the experiences of Indigenous people who have an understandable mistrust of academic research, and it allows us to understand precisely which research practices reinforce colonial approaches. For instance, publications drawing on Indigenous languages are not necessarily colonial in and of themselves. Knowing that the colonial legacy of the field sets up a unidirectional flow of linguistic and cultural resources to the benefit of the academy allows us to make more ethical choices about what we publish. Decolonization is a process, and contributing to it necessitates continued honest reflection on what effects our choices have. We need to ask ourselves: In what ways does my work take from rather than give to an Indigenous community? Who benefits from my work and who doesn't? Who has access to what I produce and who doesn't? Because the academy is inherently a colonial institution and because colonialism is systemic, all of us who approach language work from positions within the academy are set up to be complicit in ways big and small in the maintenance of colonial structures. Our good intentions and strong personal relationships with members of the communities with whom we work are not sufficient to undo structures that are founded in colonialism and designed to replicate colonial systems.

It is also important to acknowledge that it is a risky endeavor for those of us in academic positions to engage in meaningful decolonization work by refusing to participate in the creation of extractive scholarly products. These products perpetuate the status quo in part by molding new scholars into the existing system, so those who refuse to participate in creating them run the risk of being excluded from the system. Therefore, it takes courage to embrace alternative theoretical frameworks and methodologies and to create unconventional, decolonizing products, particularly the more precarious one's position in the academy. These risks are very present for me as a pretenure junior scholar, and they are even more present for scholars who are on the job market. For instance, one risk I have encountered is that, because my work with language reclamation in the local Numu (Northern Paiute) community is at the intersection of community engagement, decolonization, and linguistics (cf. Montoya et al., 2020), it does not straightforwardly fit the conventional expectations of what research looks like. Though my work connects to all three components of my role as an academic—research, teaching, and service—it was initially considered primarily service, the least valued of the

38 Decolonizing Linguistics

three components. Having my work recognized as scholarship has necessitated additional justification on my part and on the part of allies senior to me, justification not expected of my peers whose work fits more readily into existing paradigms. Though the result of my efforts and those of my allies to highlight the intellectual worth of community-engaged scholarship remains uncertain, as I have yet to go through the tenure application process, I have developed some strategies for making my work legible to others, as discussed further in the remainder of this chapter, and I have actively engaged in meaningful self-reflection regarding my values and goals and those of the communities with whom I work.

Through my experiences, I have learned that adopting a stance of refusal requires intellectual integrity, a solid ethical foundation, and a strong sense of one's own values and goals. We should be strategic about the choices we make (e.g., considering what acts of refusal will be the most productive), committed to our ultimate goals (e.g., ethical work with communities), and clear-headed about the risks and alternative options (e.g., opportunities outside of academia). Those who are most vulnerable might opt to take incremental steps toward the refusal of extractive products. Though producing a conventional, extractive product while engaging in community-based work does not directly target colonial structures, doing so may be a necessary first step for a vulnerable scholar to gain more job security in the field. For instance, a doctoral student whose advisor expects the student's dissertation to exhibit mastery of conventional frameworks can negotiate to include a chapter that critiques those methodologies or that offers alternative frameworks. Doing so allows the graduate student to meet the advisor's expectations while also cultivating a critical stance toward colonial epistemologies and methodologies. In this way, the student can mitigate some of the extraction involved in the production of the dissertation and start to set up future work that is fundamentally decolonial. It is also important to clarify one's personal and professional goals and to be aware of the different means for achieving them. Though being a faculty member certainly can provide time, resources, and prestige to support a community's language reclamation efforts, participation in such projects does not necessitate being an academic. A clear sense of one's ultimate aspiration offers a useful heuristic for how much compromise might be important in the short term in order to achieve long-term goals.

Moreover, scholars in vulnerable positions should recognize that allies and fellow decolonial scholars can be found both in the field and in our institutions. As evidenced by the existence of this volume, scholarship on decolonization is on the rise, and the value of decolonial work is receiving more recognition in the field. Connecting with like-minded individuals and tapping into broader intellectual movements associated with decolonization helps us deepen our intellectual work, generate ideas for community-based projects, build solidarity, and connect to broader networks of support.

Building on Existing Decolonial Work

As discussed earlier in this chapter, Linguistics already offers some frameworks for and models of meaningful community-based work that are consistent with decolonization. Therefore, another principle to follow when refusing extractive products is to build on existing decolonial work. Authors cited in this chapter provide examples of collaborative work that is grounded in the needs and interests of Indigenous communities. In addition, certain publication and presentation venues in Linguistics have moved toward more inclusive practices that make room for nonacademic Indigenous voices and for community-engaged work that does not necessarily fit the mold of what is conventionally considered core theories and methods in Linguistics. For instance, the Symposium on American Indian Languages (SAIL), many of whose organizers are Indigenous, actively invites the participation of non-academic Indigenous community members and is open to scholarship from a variety of theoretical frameworks. Also, some academic journals, such as *Language Documentation & Conservation*, have been open to publications on community-engaged scholarship, and some very conventional journals are now more open to the value of community-engaged scholarship (e.g., the new section of *Language* focused on language revitalization and documentation; cf. Fitzgerald, 2021). Venues such as these make space for scholars in Linguistics who refuse to engage in the creation of extractive products. Therefore, these venues serve both as resources for linguists looking for models of community-based projects and as sites for publishing their work. In addition, linguists adopting a decolonial stance can also turn to resources outside of Linguistics and even outside of the academy (e.g., the Imagining America consortium of "scholars, artists, designers, humanists, and organizers to imagine, study, and enact a more just and liberatory 'America' and world" (Imagining America, 2022). We can also look at more grassroots sources of information, such as podcasts, YouTube, and other online community forums. Identifying and connecting to broader projects and organizations that draw upon principles of decolonization and related intellectual and justice-oriented constructs is a key strategy for linguists working toward decolonization of the field.

The existence of spaces such as the above is connected to another strategy for protecting oneself while engaging in work that challenges the status quo: making decolonial work legible to those working under conventional colonial structures. As I argue elsewhere (Montoya, 2020), many of the principles that purportedly underlie academia are not inherently incompatible with ethical community-based work. For instance, dissemination of information and accountability are at the heart of peer review, and they are also important to decolonial work, since they contribute to relationship-building and to material benefits for communities. Indeed, peer review can be restructured so it includes more voices—such as members of the communities whose languages we study—while maintaining its grounding in expert evaluation of scholarship. Framing our community-engaged projects using the language of the academy can be an effective means of helping those in power understand the value of our work, especially if it appears in an unconventional format. In this endeavor, we can leverage rhetoric that is consistent with decolonization and that has become part of the repertoire of the academy generally and Linguistics specifically. For instance, many universities have begun incorporating language about the value of community-engaged research in their bylaws and policies (e.g., Pelco & Howard, 2016). In the case of my institution, these statements of support for community-engaged research are related to the university's recent Community-Engaged designation by the Carnegie Foundation for the Advancement of Teaching and the American Council on Education (Carnegie Elective Classifications, 2022). The establishment of this designation speaks to a broader movement among academic institutions toward greater recognition of the importance of the impact that institutions can have on communities. (For additional resources that make the case for community-engaged scholarship, see Hurd, 2022.) In the field of Linguistics, the Linguistic Society of America statement entitled "Evaluation of Language Documentation for Hiring, Tenure, and Promotion" (Linguistic Society of America, 2018) recognizes the intellectual value of alternative forms of publication and can therefore be used to justify the development of pedagogical materials that directly benefit language reclamation. For those of us working in institutions that are beginning to embrace the rhetoric of community engagement, the fact that decolonial work is inherently based on incorporating Indigenous priorities can serve as a justification for the value of our work that is consistent with the stated values of the institution.

Replacing Colonial Structures with Decolonial Frameworks and Expectations

In addition to building on previous work that is intentional about not being extractive, we should also focus on replacing extractive approaches and models with new ones. Indeed, this is critical for decolonial work since the overall aim is to undo the colonial legacy. In fact, if we are adopting a stance of productive refusal, one goal is to imagine and enact new visions and possibilities.

As the work on community-based research discussed above demonstrates, a decolonial stance can lead to methodological frameworks that better serve Indigenous interests. Enacting disciplinary practices that recognize and validate the knowledge, experiences, and goals of communities also presents us with new possibilities for modifying the structures of academia. Given that Western academic institutions are predicated on a belief that Western epistemologies and methodologies are superior, the academic structures we work with reinforce that belief in fundamental ways, some of them subtle. For instance, the notion of peer review, which is a pillar of the academy, is predicated in conceptualizations of "peer" and "expert" that exclude the expertise of the native users of the Indigenous languages we work with. Restructuring peer review such that community members are included in the process is one possibility for making our academic structures more inclusive. Another way we can emphasize the expertise of community members is to include them as coauthors, rather than simply thanking them for their contributions in a footnote (see a number of the chapters in this volume for example). Just as publications based in laboratory work often include multiple authors as an acknowledgment of the different types of contributions that go into a publication, publications based in community engagement can do the same, given that they too involve a diversity of contributions. By actively countering academic practices that privilege academic linguists' interests and priorities, we can begin to reverse the conventional unidirectional flow of resources so that Indigenous communities can better benefit from their engagement with linguists.

The colonial legacy of Linguistics has given us extractive methodologies, and this legacy has also shaped our theories, which have been formed under intellectual ideologies that treat Western epistemologies as superior (Charity Hudley et al., 2020). Indigenous linguists' theorizing in Linguistics builds on a foundation of Indigenous cultural knowledge. Kari Chew (2019), for instance, explores competing values and ideologies in language reclamation through the lens of Chickasaw finger-weaving, and Melvatha Chee (2019) describes Navajo verb structure using Navajo cultural constructs, giving us a sense of what novel theorizing in Linguistics might look like. Indeed, decolonial language work with Indigenous communities necessitates "engagement with community definitions of 'language' and with community beliefs and analyses about how it functions" (Leonard, 2018, p. 59). As discussed earlier in this chapter, Western epistemologies serve as the unquestioned foundations of the academy and permeate all academic theorizing

42 Decolonizing Linguistics

about language. Indeed, current formal linguistic theories are firmly rooted in Western thinking, following a trajectory from Ancient Greek philosophy to modern Euro American intellectual traditions. By being more open to Indigenous people's conceptualizations of their languages, non-Indigenous linguists can enrich our understanding of language more generally, which can lead to linguistic theories that are more comprehensive and expansive. Given that dominant linguistic theories are completely disconnected from Indigenous understandings of language, we can hardly begin to imagine what insights about language we can gain from centering Indigenous epistemologies until we decenter Western ways of knowing. Challenging Western intellectual hegemony and elevating Indigenous epistemologies can broaden our understanding of Indigenous languages specifically but also of language more generally. A first step toward opening up those possibilities is refusing to create scholarly products that treat Indigenous knowledge as a commodity to be exploited for the benefit of academics.

Conclusion

Linguistics has a deep colonial legacy that continues to be enacted in contemporary work with Indigenous and other marginalized communities. The products that the discipline values most—technical publications peer-reviewed by other academic linguists—are inaccessible to those outside of the field and, when they involve Indigenous languages, are based in fundamentally extractive work that mines Indigenous knowledge to serve the interests of the academy. Such products are the basis of our reward systems in academia and therefore serve to replicate colonial structures by disincentivizing community-based work, strengthening hierarchical conceptualizations of knowledge that place Western intellectual traditions at the top, and promoting scholars whose work maintains the status quo (see also Dockum & Green, 2024).

Decolonization offers a framework for interrupting the replication of colonial structures. In order to use this construct meaningfully, it is important to be intentional about our adoption of the term and to articulate the context through which we are understanding it, lest it be appropriated in such a way that causes harm to the very communities it is intended to support. In Linguistics, we have made some progress toward research practices with Indigenous and other marginalized communities that are more genuinely collaborative and inclusive of community interests. These practices contribute to the decolonization of the process of linguistic work. However, unless we target extractive products as well, we limit how far along we can move toward decolonization since the gold standard of the field continues to be products built on the extraction of community knowledge.

Refusal, the rejection of conventional modes of recognition, can be a generative means of decolonization. Given the fundamentally colonial nature of the conventional products of the field, refusal must entail being intentional about what we do with the knowledge we gather from Indigenous communities and what products we create with that knowledge. This can indeed be a risky endeavor, particularly for those in the academy who are in more precarious positions. A first step we can all take toward decolonization is to acknowledge the colonial structures of Linguistics and to consider the impact they have on our work and on the communities with whom we work. We can also recognize that we are not alone in this endeavor and that other scholars have engaged and are engaging with theories and methodologies that advance decolonization in our field. Ultimately, if non-Indigenous linguists are willing to give up some of our structural power, we all stand to gain from challenging the colonial frameworks and expectations that permeate the intellectual tradition of Linguistics. Indeed, adopting a productive stance of refusal toward the creation and promotion of extractive products opens possibilities for new methodologies and theoretical approaches and for a broader and more inclusive Linguistics.

References

Adams, David Wallace. (1995). *Education for extinction: American Indians and the boarding school experience, 1875–1926.* University Press of Kansas.

Alperin, Juan P., Muñoz Nieves, Carol, Schimanski, Lesley A., Fischman, Gustavo E., Niles, Meredith T., & McKiernan, Erin C. (2019). How significant are the public dimensions of faculty work in review, promotion and tenure documents? *eLife* 2019; 8:e42254 doi: 10.7554/eLife.42254

Bonilla-Silva, Eduardo, & Zuberi, Tukufu. (2008). Toward a definition of white logic and white methods. In Eduardo Bonilla-Silva & Tukufu Zuberi (Eds.) *White logic, white methods: Racism and methodology* (pp. 3–30). Rowman and Littlefield Publishers.

Carnegie Elective Classifications. (2022). https://carnegieelectiveclassifications.org

Charity Hudley, Anne H., Mallinson, Christine, & Bucholtz, Mary. (2020). Toward racial justice in linguistics: Interdisciplinary insights into theorizing race in the discipline and diversifying the profession. *Language 96*(4), e200–e235.

Chee, Melvatha R. (2019). "Explaining child verb acquisition through shared cultural knowledge." Paper presented at the Symposium on American Indian Languages, Tucson, AZ, April 12, 2019.

Chew, Kari A. B. (2019). Weaving words: Conceptualizing language reclamation through a culturally-significant metaphor. *Canadian Journal of Native Education*, 41(1).

Collins, James. (1992). Our ideologies and theirs. *Pragmatics*, 2(3), 405–415.

44 Decolonizing Linguistics

Czaykowska-Higgins, Ewa. (2009). Research models, community engagement, and linguistic fieldwork: Reflections on working with Canadian Indigenous communities. *Language Documentation and Conservation, 3*(1), 15–50.

De Korne, Haley, & Leonard, Wesley Y. (2017). Reclaiming languages: Contesting and decolonising "language endangerment" from the ground up. In Wesley Y. Leonard & Haley De Korne (Eds.), *Language Documentation and Description, vol. 14* (pp. 5–14). EL Publishing.

Davis, Jenny L. (2017). Resisting rhetorics of language endangerment: Reclamation through Indigenous language survivance. *Language Documentation and Description, 14*: 37–58.

Dockum, Rikker, & Green, Caitlin M. (2024). Toward a big tent linguistics: Inclusion and the myth of the lone genius. In Anne H. Charity Hudley, Christine Mallinson, & Mary Bucholtz (Eds.), *Inclusion in linguistics*. Oxford University Press.

Errington, Joseph. (2008). *Linguistics in a colonial world: A story of language, meaning, and power*. Blackwell Publishing Ltd.

Fitzgerald, Colleen M. (2018). Reflections on language community training. In Bradley McDonnell, Andrea L. Berez-Kroeker, & Gary Holton (Eds.), *Reflections on Language Documentation: 20 Years after Himmelmann 1998* (pp. 86–99). University of Hawai'I Press.

Fitzgerald, Colleen M. (2021). A framework for language revitalization and documentation. *Language, 97*(1), e1–e11.

Gaby, Alice, & Woods, Lesley. (2020). Toward linguistic justice for Indigenous people: A response to Charity Hudley, Mallinson, and Bucholtz. *Language 96*(4), e268–e280.

Gerdts, Donna B. (2017). Indigenous linguists: Bringing research into language revitalization. *International Journal of American Linguistics 83*(4), 607–617.

Grenoble, Lenore A. (2009). Linguistic cages and the limits of linguists. In Jon Reyner & Louise Lockard (Eds.), *Indigenous language revitalization: Encouragement, guidance, and lessons learned* (pp. 61–69). Northern Arizona University Press.

Hill, Jane H. (2002). Expert rhetorics in advocacy for endangered languages: Who is listening, and what do they hear? *Journal of Linguistic Anthropology, 12*(2), 119–133.

Hurt, C. A. (2022). Tenure and promotion for engaged scholarship: A repository. *Campus Compact.* https://compact.org/resources/tenure-and-promotion-for-engaged-scholarship-a-repository?f%255B0%255D%3Dresource_tag=698

Imagining America. (2022). https://imaginingamerica.org

Kirkness, Verna J., & Barnhardt, Ray. (1991). First Nations and higher education: The four R's—Respect, relevance, reciprocity, responsibility. *Journal of American Indian Education*, 1–15.

Leonard, Weseley Y. (2012). Framing language reclamation programmes for everybody's empowerment. *Gender and Language, 6*(2), 339–367.

Leonard, Wesley Y. (2017). Producing language reclamation by decolonising "language." *Language Documentation and Description, 14*: 15–36.

Leonard, Wesley Y. (2018). Reflections on (de)colonialism in language documentation. In Bradley McDonnell, Andrea L. Berez-Kroeker & Gary Holton (Eds.), *Reflections on language documentation: 20 Years after Himmelmann 1998* (pp. 55–65). University of Hawai'I Press.

Leonard, Wesley Y. (2020). Toward linguistic justice for Indigenous people: A response to Charity Hudley, Mallinson, and Bucholtz. *Language 96*(4), e281–e291.

Leonard, Wesley Y., & Haynes, Erin. (2010). Making "collaboration" collaborative: An examination of perspectives that frame linguistic field research. *Language Documentation and Conservation 4*: 268–293.

Linguistic Society of America. (2018). Evaluation of language documentation for hiring, tenure, and promotion. https://www.linguisticsociety.org/resource/statement-evaluation-language-documentation-hiring-tenure-and-promotion

McGranahan, Carole. (2016). Theorizing refusal: An introduction. *Cultural Anthropology, 31*(3), 319–325.

Miller, Susan A. (2008). Native America writes back: The origin of the Indigenous paradigm in historiography. *Wicazo Sa Review, 23*(2), 9–28.

Montoya, Ignacio L. (2020). Enabling excellence and racial justice in universities by addressing structural obstacles to work by and with people from racially minoritized communities: A response to Charity Hudley, Mallinson, and Bucholtz. *Language, 96*(4), e236–e246.

Montoya, Ignacio L., Harry, Debra, & Burns, Jennie. (2020). A collaborative development of workshops for teachers of Great Basin languages using principles of decolonization and language reclamation. *Language Documentation & Conservation, 14*, 462–487.

Ngũgĩ Wa Thiong'o. (1986). *Decolonising the mind: The politics of language in African literature.* James Currey Ltd.

Pelco, Lynn E., & Howard, Catherine. (2016). Incorporating community engagement language into promotion and tenure policies: One university's journey. *Metropolitan Universities 27*(2), 7–18. doi: 10.18060/21129

Pratt, Richard Henry. (1892/1973). *Official Report of the Nineteenth Annual Conference of Charities and Correction (1892)*, 46–59. Reprinted in Richard H. Pratt, "The Advantages of Mingling Indians with Whites," *Americanizing the American Indians: Writings by the "Friends of the Indian" 1880–1900*, 260–271. Harvard University Press.

Rice, Keren. (2006). Ethical issues in linguistic fieldwork: An overview. *Journal of Academic Ethics, 4*, 123–155.

Simpson, Audra. (2014). *Mohawk interruptus: Political life Across the borders of settler states,* Duke University Press.

Smith, Linda Tuhiwai. (2012). *Decolonizing methodologies: Research and Indigenous peoples.* 2nd edition. Zed Books Ltd.

Tsikewa, Adrienne. (2021). Reimagining the current praxis of field linguistics training: Decolonial considerations. *Language, 97*(4), e293–e319.

Tuck, Eve, & Yang, Wayne K. (2012). Decolonizing is not a metaphor. *Decolonization: Indigeneity, Education & Society, 1*(1), 1–40.

Tuck, Eve, & Yang, Wayne K. (2014). R-words: refusing research. In Django Paris & Maisha T. Winn (Eds.), *Humanizing research: Decolonizing qualitative inquiry with youth and communities* (pp. 223–247). SAGE Publishing.

Wilson, Shawn. (2008). *Research is ceremony: Indigenous research methods.* Fernwood Publishing.

Wolfe, Patrick. (1999). *Settler colonialism and the transformation of anthropology: The politics and poetics of an ethnographic event.* Cassell.

Wolfe, Patrick. (2006). Settler colonialism and the elimination of the native. *Journal of Genocide Research, 8*(4), 387–409.

Margaret Thomas teaches broadly across several subfields of linguistics at Boston College, including courses in psycholinguistics, sociolinguistics, theoretical linguistics, field methods, the structure of Japanese, and the history of linguistics. Her research is similarly heterogeneous, with recent books entitled *Formalism and Functionalism in Linguistics* (2020) and *Fifty Key Thinkers in Language and Linguistics* (2011). She is currently working on a monograph about scientific racism and the 1924 foundation of the Linguistic Society of America.

Abstract: French surgeon and physical anthropologist Paul Broca (1824–1880) is remembered in linguistics for his insight into localization of language in the human brain, in that he demonstrated an association between damage to the left frontal lobe and a specific variety of aphasia. Less acknowledged is that Broca's work overall—including his studies of aphasia, and his lesser-known publications on human olfaction and on ethnic hybridity in the French population—was shaped by ideological assumptions about the superiority of humans over animals, men over women, and a commitment to a racial hierarchy that presupposed the supremacy of whites. Those assumptions went unquestioned by Broca and his contemporaries, but should be reincorporated into his modern reputation. The chapter closes with a meditation on the difficult but urgent necessity, on moral as on scientific grounds, of identifying and confronting our research assumptions which, like Broca, are taken for granted.

Key Words: Paul Broca, nineteenth-century anthropometrics, racism in anthropology, racism in linguistics, history of linguistics

2

Racialization, Language Science, and Nineteenth-Century Anthropometrics

Margaret Thomas (she/her)
Boston College

Introduction

In May 2019, the executive committee of the Linguistic Society of America approved a "Statement on Race," which puts on record the society's opposition to racialization in the study of language, and in the discipline of linguistics itself.[1] As examples of racialization, the statement cites such phenomena as "English only" initiatives; the imposition on research participants of mono-racial self-identification categories; the treatment of white upper-middle-class language as normative; and the devaluation of varieties of speech associated with stigmatized groups as inherently deficient. The LSA's statement aims to "encourage linguists to critically reflect on the changing nature of academic, social, cultural, and linguistic understandings of race," reminding readers that "all linguistic research has the potential to reproduce or challenge racial notions" ("Preamble"). The statement goes on to decry a lack of racial diversity within the discipline in the United States.

In a commentary on the composition of the statement, the three co-editors of the present volume—Anne H. Charity Hudley, Christine Mallinson, and Mary Bucholtz—argued that the modern discipline "urgently needs an interdisciplinarily-informed theoretical engagement with race and racism" (Charity Hudley et al., 2020, e200). The editors make a case for the common failure of linguists to take seriously how integral race is to the study of language, and for linguists' failure to confront insidious racialization in their own work. They also document the failure of modern American linguistics to effectively welcome and incorporate the insights of racially minoritized language scholars. In their words, "acknowledging and addressing rather than denying our discipline's role in the reproduction of racism is central to ensuring equity and inclusion in the theory, practice, and teaching of linguistics" (Charity Hudley et al., 2020, e223).

Margaret Thomas, *Racialization, Language Science, and Nineteenth-Century Anthropometrics* In: *Decolonizing Linguistics.*
Edited by: Anne H. Charity Hudley, Christine Mallinson, and Mary Bucholtz, Oxford University Press.
© Anne H. Charity Hudley, Christine Mallinson, and Mary Bucholtz 2024. DOI: 10.1093/oso/9780197755259.003.0003

Charity Hudley et al. acknowledge the value of probing into the history of the field as a tool for understanding the present, a stance developed in Charity Hudley (2017). But they do not look back beyond a shoutout to Haitian scholar Anténor Firmin (1850–1911), whose largely ignored refutation of nineteenth-century "scientific racism" (Firmin, 1885/2000) predated by more than 25 years Franz Boas's (1858–1942) campaign against racism in anthropology and public life (Boas, 1911; 1940). Adding a historical dimension to discussion of race and racialization in linguistics is important, I believe, for at least two reasons. A first reason is that greater time depth sometimes paradoxically opens up greater clarity about the ways in which racism is embedded in present day cultural practices and conventions, including those of the study of language. A second reason is that historical context helps reduce the temptation to view racism as simply the damage done by individuals, which might be removed by playing what Adam Hodges (2016) calls the "hunting for 'racists' language game," that is, by naming and exposing specific individuals responsible for racist acts. To do so distracts us from the harder work of confronting racism as a complex, intractable, structural, and institutional affliction within which individuals choose to do what they do—or, within which individuals have varying extents of agency over what they do.

This essay brings forward a case study of blatant racist ideology in linguistics, as one facet in the backdrop behind current work in the discipline. It may seem to "hunt for 'racists'" in that I focus on the record of a particular scholar, Paul Broca, whose work now appears very problematic. But my hope is that working through the historical record may demonstrate not so much where one person went wrong, as what it means to belong to an intellectual community where racialization is taken for granted in ways that now seem painfully obvious. Historians of eighteenth- through early twentieth-century racism like Barkan (1992) and Gossett (1963/1997) narrate how saturated a culture can become with the notion that groups of people belong, by "nature," to a hierarchy across which privileges and rights are differentially distributed. A culture can, in fact, become so saturated with this notion that scholars bend the collection and interpretation of scientific data to serve their racialized preconceptions. When language scholarship that echoes racist ideas falls short of meeting scientific standards, it needs to be criticized both for its content and for its epistemological faults. I conclude with a brief personal reflection on the challenge of recognizing and unmasking one's own tacit presuppositions. Sometimes failure to meet that challenge merely limits or destabilizes one's work. In cases like that of Broca, his failure to do so distorted the scientific basis of his work and—much worse—contributed to damaging, excluding, and disparaging fellow humans. That this challenge is difficult to meet in no way exculpates racism in the study of language. Rather, recognizing it as a challenge, and fortifying ourselves to meet that challenge, may help us redress the structural and personal failures that Charity Hudley and her co-authors (2020) articulate.

Language and Nineteenth-Century Anthropometrics

My case study concerns the nineteenth-century French surgeon and physical anthropologist Pierre Paul Broca (1824–1880). Most contemporary students of linguistics encounter Broca as a far-seeing scholar who put modern evidence-based neurolinguistics into motion. Although the last 40 years have not been kind to Broca's reputation, even today no one disputes that he was a brilliant, highly trained empiricist and freethinker remembered as one of the founders of French physical anthropology. It was Broca's lifework to understand human physical variation, especially the anatomy of the brain and the light that craniometry—the measurement of brain size and shape—might bring to mental function.

In 1861 Broca performed an autopsy on a man named Louis Victor Leborgne, who for 20 years had suffered only being able to utter a single monosyllable, "tan." The third frontal convolution of Leborgne's left brain showed clear damage; on observing this fact, Broca confirmed—in some versions of the story, discovered—humans' left-hemispheric dominance for language.[2] A few months later he examined through autopsy the brain of an older man, Lazare Lelong, who had lost virtually all speech. Broca's analysis of Lelong's brain strengthened his confidence that a critical area for productive language is asymmetrically located in the left hemisphere (Broca, 1861; 1865), in the region now identified as "Broca's area." With this conclusion, he publicly broke with the dogma that human brain function is necessarily bilaterally symmetrical. In the usual narrative, Broca's meticulous powers of observation, diagnostic perspicuity, and commitment to empirical analysis made him the first to attribute a specific constellation of language deficits to damage at a specific location in the left brain. Although twenty-first-century neuroscience has access to imaging technology and a corpus of accumulated data that goes far beyond what was available in the 1800s, Broca's core insight remains largely intact (Grodzinsky & Santi, 2008). This is the conventional representation of Broca's contribution to scientific study of language.

We are familiar with the debunking of the reputations of heroic historical figures, so it is not surprising to learn that this representation has its faults.

50 Decolonizing Linguistics

Most consequentially, it gives a false picture of the goals Broca pursued in his research on brain/language connections, as in his anthropometric research overall. But the totality of the case against Broca's reputation goes beyond a routine takedown of a pioneering, prescient figure. It calls attention to the necessity for scholars in general to engage in disciplined interrogation of why and how they pursue a particular object of study, and what goals their studies ultimately serve. Public awareness of the damage racism does has intensified in the United States in the second decade of the twenty-first century; with this, American linguists need to diligently probe into the personally and culturally imposed preconceptions that deform our research. We need to do this even though the effort may be doomed, for several reasons. One reason is that it may be difficult to distinguish bias from the valuable creative resource called intuition. Another reason is that it may not be entirely possible to assess one's own professional commitments as if from outside the context within which those commitments developed and are valued, because, as Charity Hudley et al. put it, "researchers' own identities and subjectivities inform the topics they choose to study, the research questions they ask, and the methodologies they use" (2020, e219). Nevertheless, we must try to accomplish this difficult task. The 40 or so years that followed the centenary of Broca's death have brought to light multiple object lessons in what can go wrong—and even what can accidentally go right—when scientists' preconceptions unwittingly contaminate their evaluation and interpretation of evidence. Just as it is essential to remember Broca for the informed leap of imagination that led him to identify left-lateralization of language in the brain, it is essential to reintegrate into his modern reputation an awareness of the racist context within which Broca worked, and which his work embraced and reinforced.

Since the 1980s, three separate initiatives have undermined scholarly regard for Broca as a scientist. Among these three, the first involves Broca's claims about brain size and shape; the second, his analysis of the ethnic population of France; and the third, his work on the human olfactory system. Not all of these threats to his reputation are directly relevant to language issues, but they all bear on Broca's legacy. They have a consistent logical structure: in each case, modern scholars have asserted that Broca harbored sociopolitical commitments and prejudices that contaminated his scientific work.[3]

Broca's Craniometry Revisited

In a survey of textbooks introducing psycholinguistics to English-speaking university students, I found that they uncritically present four features of Broca's legacy: that he participated in ongoing debate about variation in form and size of the human brain; that he had outstanding powers of observation, and carefully measured and recorded many facts about the topography of the brain and the volume of the human skull; that he brought those empirical data to bear on debate about language and the brain; and that he was a pioneer in the identification, through autopsy, of a specific anatomical basis for language faculties.[4]

A counternarrative starts in 1981 with the publication of Harvard paleontologist Stephen Jay Gould's book *The Mismeasure of Man*. Gould's thesis is that since at least the mid-nineteenth century, European and American social science has erred in treating human intelligence as an attribute that is "unitary, rankable, innate, and effectively unchangeable" (1981/1996, pp. 27–28). On that dubious basis, Gould goes on to show how—in a textbook example of what Charity Hudley et al. (2020) identify as racialization—scientists assigned different intrinsic levels of intelligence to different ethnic and racial groups. With aching predictability, white Europeans come out on top in this scenario. Driven toward that foregone conclusion in what looks like a classic instance of confirmation bias (Chambers, 2017), scientists searched for a physical basis to the purported intellectual superiority of white Europeans. Paul Broca's craniological research is one of Gould's parade cases. Unlike the data of other historical figures, such as the University of Pennsylvania physician and craniologist Samuel George Morton (1799–1851), whose claims about intelligence Gould debunks, Gould finds the accuracy and consistency of Broca's physiological measurements to be without serious flaws. But where Broca went wrong was in his assumption that brain size correlates with intelligence. Worse, in Gould's words, Broca then "used facts as illustrations, not as constraining documents. [He] began with conclusions, peered through the facts, and came back in a circle to [the] same conclusions" (Gould, 1981/1996, p. 117). Broca applied this method repeatedly in his exploration of variation in brain size. For example, he presupposed that greater brain size indicates greater intellectual capacity, and that males are more intelligent than females. On observing that the average adult male brain is larger than the average adult female brain, he then used that observation to support his assumption of male intellectual superiority (Broca, 1861/1960).

Broca also studied the brain volume of people of different races and social classes. Whenever his specimens showed that Europeans—most particularly white, educated European men of high social and professional standing—did not have the largest brains in a given sample, Broca would selectively open the analysis to mitigating factors. For example, he attributed the unexpectedly low volume of the brain of one highly educated male European in his sample to the effects of advanced age, since age diminishes cerebral volume. Conversely, he speculated that the brain of a convicted criminal found to be unexpectedly large might have been due to swelling induced by execution by hanging (Gould, 1981/1996, p. 126). Members of higher social classes were necessarily more intelligent, in Broca's logic, and would therefore necessarily have larger brains; he accounted for deviations from that principle by noting that, for instance, laboratory techniques of preservation varied, plausibly affecting the accuracy of measurement. Among these mitigating factors is one that is most salient to us, namely, Broca's contention that even if the overall brain volume of an individual high-status white European male specimen was unimpressive, the front part of the brain would be relatively larger, or at least relatively more intricately developed (Gould 1981/1996, pp. 129–130).

Gould hardly adverts to localization of language in the front part of the brain, which is the finding that made Broca famous among linguists. But in the 1800s as now, language had crown-jewel status among cognitive faculties. Therefore, Broca's discovery of a language center in the front of the brain—the area he asserted to be largest (or at least most developed) in the brains of his favored groups—was thoroughly amenable to his preconceptions about race, ethnicity, gender, class, and brain anatomy. Twenty-first-century neurolinguistics has complicated the details of Broca's claims about localization, while conceding that he was right about the special status of the left frontal lobe. But it is unsettling to recognize that Broca made essentially the right call within an extended analysis that presupposed what appears to us now as a grotesque tableau of unwarranted, unacknowledged, self-serving, sociopolitical biases. What Broca took for granted, we now repudiate on two grounds: first, on scientific grounds, because (at least in Gould's telling) Broca had not proven, but only had assumed from the start, that intelligence can be reduced to a fixed trait linked to craniometric measurement and further that certain groups are obviously more intellectually endowed than others; and, second, on sociocultural grounds, because we reject not only the specific rankings that Broca arrived at, but the whole conception of ranking people's intelligence on the basis of their membership in an apocryphal racial or cultural group. It is worth noting that the minutes of mid- to late nineteenth-century scholarly meetings at which Broca presented his results record no protest from his colleagues on any of these bases.[5]

Revisiting Broca's Polygenism

The disquiet that Gould interjected into the reception of Broca's research on craniometry has spread to other topics Broca studied. It surfaces in publications by Claude Blanckaert, a contemporary historian of anthropology at the Centre National de la Recherche Scientifique in Paris, about how French writers and scholars have represented racialized groups. Without mentioning Gould, Blanckaert (2003) magnifies the matter Gould raised, depicting Broca as having led a life dedicated to race classification in his support for polygenism, that is, the hypothesis that different human races comprise independent lines of descent from different ancestral species. Broca's deep-rooted skepticism of religious authority made polygenism attractive to him, since polygenism disrupted the nineteenth-century Biblical understanding of human history. Moreover, many polygenists claimed that, if modern humans descended from several distinct but related species of primates, then cross-species hybridity among humans would lead to degeneration over time. As support, polygenists cited the sexual sterility of mules, produced as they are by breeding a horse with a donkey. On those grounds (and in the absence of evidence from the study of human beings) polygenists predicted that humans born of parents categorized as belonging to different races would be incapable of producing healthy, fertile offspring.

Given Broca's commitment to polygenism, his craniometric research rendered the "mule problem" a crisis for him. Broca analyzed physical-anthropological data culled in the late 1800s from the records of military recruits in diverse parts of France (Broca, 1867; 1870; 1873). He concluded that the population of France was in general a hybrid of what he considered to be two races: the short, dark, wide-skulled Celts and the tall, blonde, long-skulled "Kymris," who predominate between the Seine and the Rhine rivers. According to Broca's polygenist assumptions, the hybridity of the Celts and Kymris in the French population would predict cultural and physical degeneration of the overall group. Broca, however, saw little evidence of degeneration. To reconcile polygenism with that lack of evidence, he disputed the tenet that hybridity necessarily led to corruption, countering the "mule problem" by citing the fact that cross-breeding a rabbit with a hare yields a healthy, fertile animal known as a leporide (1860, pp. 574–577). He therefore split hybridity into four subcategories, which would admit both the sterility of mules and the fecundity of leporides (1860, pp. 533–536). On one extreme, the "sterile hybridity" of mules obtained where there was maximal disaffinity between the two parents. In between, Broca posited two types of partially fertile hybridity. On the other extreme, minimal disaffinity between the two parents led to "eugensic hybridity" (that is, nondisruptive hybridity, where the two parties are deemed to be highly similar) and a wholesome reproductive outlook, as in the case of the leporide and as attested among Celts and Kymris in France.[6]

In this way, Broca found a means to harmonize his polygenism with his conviction that, in his words, "we [French] can sleep easily [because] the fatherland is not in danger" (1867, p. 55). According to Blanckaert, Broca "us[ed] natural history to verify and plant the seeds of a republican political history" (2003, p. 63), by arguing that the nature of the French population—"mixed," but nondisruptively so—formed a creative, complementary basis for the success of the French Revolution. But Broca's writings on the hybridity of the French people remind one of Gould's complaint about what he calls "[Broca's] method," namely that Broca problematically "shift[ed] [his] criteria to work through good data toward desired conclusions" (1981/1996, p. 134). Here the conclusion—the assertion that all was well with the French gene pool, despite its evident mixed ethnic stock—seems to have been Broca's tacit goal from the start. He managed to reach that goal while retaining his fidelity to polygenism. In doing so, Broca again fails as a model of how to do science.

Polygenism fell out of currency in the latter decades of the 1800s. But in the rhetoric of eugenics and scientific racism, popular and academic classification of humans by race into stratified classes has continued through the twentieth into the twenty-first century (Barkan, 1992; Hutton, 1999; Okrent, 2019). As one example, in the early 1920s, at the midpoint between Broca's day and the present, the American paleontologist and eugenicist Henry Fairfield Osborn (1857–1935) was deep into his career as president of New York's American Museum of Natural History. Among other accomplishments, Osborn expanded the institution's popular outreach. As a scientist whose views were influential in the culture at large, he spread his conviction in the global superiority of "Nordic" people both through his scholarly writings and through the design of exhibits in the museum. Notwithstanding the demise of Broca-style polygenism, Osborn and his colleagues such as the leading American conservationist and eugenicist Madison Grant (1864–1937) modernized and propagated racist ideas. In the United States, those ideas fortified Jim Crow initiatives; in Europe they supported Adolf Hilter's delusions, both with catastrophic effects (Grant, 1916; Osborn, 1921; Spiro, 2009, p. 357).

Revisiting Broca's Research on Human Olfactory Capacity

A third threat to Broca's scientific legacy was brought forward in a paper published in the spring of 2017 by psychologist John McGann of Rutgers University. McGann tested humans versus other mammals for olfactory discrimination and found that, comparatively speaking, human beings have a good sense of smell. This finding contradicts a popular folk belief that humans have a poor sense of smell relative to other animals (see Majid, 2020). McGann

(2017, p. 1) labels the derogation of human olfactory perception a nineteenth-century "myth," which he attributes specifically to Paul Broca. Among Broca's many anthropometric studies, he accurately observed that the olfactory bulb takes up a proportionally much smaller area of human brain than it does of the mouse brain; he then concluded that humans have a comparatively weak sense of smell (Broca, 1879). McGann speculates that it was important to Broca to locate a material basis for the uniqueness of humans among other animals because, in accord with his commitments as a freethinker, Broca rejected the notion that the presence of an immaterial, immortal soul was the cornerstone of human distinctiveness (2017, p. 1). However, McGann points out that the absolute size of the olfactory bulb in humans is still far larger than that in mice, because of the much larger overall volume of the human brain versus the mouse brain (2017, pp. 2–3). Broca apparently failed to consider the issue of absolute size, and moreover failed to carry out any empirical investigation of human versus nonhuman sensitivity to smells. The proportionally small size of the human olfactory bulb was to Broca enough to settle the issue: a poverty of olfactory ability—not the presence of an immortal soul—distinguished humans as a higher species. To quote Gould again, Broca had "peered through the facts" to reach his desired conclusions, and with that, closed the case.

McGann goes on to write that Broca made sense of his exposition of the poverty of human sense of smell by claiming that atrophy of the olfactory bulb near the bottom of the brain made room for greater development of the frontal lobe of the human brain, where "intellectual life is centralized," and which became "enlarged at the expense of the others" (McGann 2017, p. 6, citing Broca, 1879). In Broca (1877b, p. 655), a publication that McGann does not cite, Broca asserts that differential atrophy of the olfactory bulb can be discerned in the morphology of brains of "men of the white race" compared to the brains of the "inferior races." Broca presumes that in white men the olfactory bulb is especially reduced because of compensatory hyper-development of intellectual abilities. Whether it is materialized as a bigger brain or as a worse sense of smell, the superiority of whites is both his beginning and his endpoint.

Dismantling Raciolinguistic Ideologies

Neither Broca the polygenist's rescue of France's racial hybridity nor Broca the anatomist's specious derogation of the human sense of smell bears specifically on language issues, and neither holds up to modern scientific scrutiny. In contrast, Broca's identification of the key role of the front brain in language is

56 Decolonizing Linguistics

consistent with modern neurolinguistics. But all three of these research results rest on—and build up—unacknowledged, unexamined presuppositions that are obnoxious to the twenty-first century. All three cases also fail as models of lawful application of scientific reasoning. Blanckaert (1997, p. 40) grapples with this feature of Broca's legacy in writing that "Il y aurait donc deux Broca, face diurne et face nocturne" ("There are therefore two sides to Broca, day and night").

However, I'm not convinced that splitting Broca's reputation in two—one part sunny, one part dismal—puts the matter to rest. That Broca's work had a dismal side was not apparent to him or to his contemporaries. It only looks dismal to us, now. Our own dismal places are likewise hidden to us, and may remain that way until somehow, someday, the lights go up on them. When that happens, what will our intellectual descendants see then, that we do not see now? One can only hope that they will be shocked and dismayed by, for example, the extent to which early twenty-first-century linguistics continues to, in the words of Charity Hudley et al., either "simply 'count' race, mechanically classify[ing] participants racially, or assume that race is irrelevant" (2020, e219). Against that, Charity Hudley et al. urge us to "dismantle raciolinguistic ideologies in linguistic research" (2020, e212). As a first step, we need to pay attention to the history of unnoticed, deep-seated biases and presuppositions that deform the analysis of language and make the discipline of linguistics inhospitable to racially minoritized language scholars. (See Ignacio L. Montoya's chapter in this volume for an extrapolation, expressed in the rhetoric of "refusal.")

I will conclude with an autobiographical anecdote. My first few years of professional work in linguistics were devoted to a topic that was all the rage in the late 1980s, generative grammar's Binding Principles, specifically Principle A, which governs structural relations between anaphors and their antecedents. I got to the early dissertation stage just as Rita Manzini and Kenneth Wexler published an article in *Linguistic Inquiry* (1987) that offered a way to parameterize the Binding Principles, rendering the attested cross-linguistic variation in anaphora tractable under Chomsky's "principles and parameters" syntactic model. I spent far too long collecting far too much data on the second-language acquisition of anaphora, and was pleased to find little evidence that contravened Wexler and Manzini's proposals (Thomas, 1991; 1993). However, I realize now that, from the start, I was expecting and covertly hoping to find that result so that my work could reinforce (if only in a very low-profile manner) the general consensus that all human languages, including those produced by adult learners, can be treated on a par with each other and are amenable to theoretical analysis.

When I look back on my first publications based on the dissertation, several thoughts come to mind. First, I am struck by how limited this topic is: even at the time, I could have seen (but didn't) that the theoretical basis of my work was eroding quickly amidst the high turnover of generative theory. Second, I am relieved to find in my methods and analysis no evidence of gross scientific impropriety, only a certain crudeness of conception and execution. Nor, as far as I can see now, did that work contribute to racialization in the terms that Charity Hudley et al. (2020) depict it. Nevertheless, I recognize that the presupposition of parity across languages learned in childhood and languages learned (at least in part) by formal study, was present in my research even before that research started. In that sense, like Broca, I "peered through the facts" to arrive at my conclusions. The issues my work addressed are not as politically and socially charged as the issues that Broca trafficked in. Still, it stands out to me now that no advisor I worked with, nor any journal reviewer who assessed the products of my research, called attention to—much less challenged—my presuppositions. I conceived the project; I gathered the data; I analyzed the results; I wrote it all up; but I never consciously opened my imagination to the possibility that all languages might not be equally theoretically tractable. In fact, I still believe they are all equally theoretically tractable; I communicate that conviction to my students all the time, and that stance seems unremarkable in the pages of contemporary journals in linguistics and in the corridors and meeting rooms of conferences that linguists attend.

To be clear, this reflection on my own early work is intended to neither support nor to detract from any notion of the theoretical (in)tractability of all languages. I include it only as an illustration of how easy it is to uncritically pick up and run with an idea that seems plausible and is taken for granted by the community in which one works. My experience is salient to Broca's legacy in that it highlights that although people in another century may hold beliefs (polygenism, ranking of people by race, correlation of brain size with intelligence) that are quite alien from modern beliefs (the theoretical tractability of all languages); nevertheless, those people's intellectual frailties may be quite familiar to us.

As a graduate student and new PhD, like Broca, I unreflectively brought a received understanding to bear on my collected data and was gratified by the apparent harmony of the data with that understanding. Broca likewise seemed never to have reflected on his own assumptions about race, ethnicity, sex, or species. There is no evidence that his colleagues did so either, in the pages of the *Bullétins de la Société d'Anthropologie,* or in the corridors and meeting rooms of Paris Society for Anthropology where Broca presented his research. Had Broca had any students, he too would probably have tacitly

58 Decolonizing Linguistics

communicated to them the full weight of his presuppositions. He was sure he was right and was pleased that his research proved consistent with his convictions—which seems remarkable only to us, only now.

Notes

1. A version of this essay appeared on the blog "History and Philosophy of the Language Sciences" on June 8, 2020, https://hiphilangsci.net/2020/06/08/racialization-language-science/.
2. Samuel Greenblatt (1984) reviews the historical complexities of Broca's role in the emergence of multiple new ways of thinking about the mind, the structure of the brain, and the role of clinical versus experimental study of the basis of language.
3. There is a fourth—better known—threat that I do not address here. This comprised a polite struggle, already underway during Broca's lifetime, regarding whether he was actually the first person to locate a dedicated language center in the left front brain. See Broca (1877a), and modern analysis in Joynt and Benton (1964), Cubelli and Montagna (1994), Roe and Finger (1996), Finger and Roe (1996; 1999), and Buckingham (2006). I set aside the dispute over historical priority, as it has a different complexion from other threats to Broca's reputation.
4. Textbooks surveyed include Berko-Gleason and Ratner (1998), Carroll (2008), Harley (2008), Fernández and Smith Cairns (2011), Traxler (2012), and Sedivy (2014).
5. I would add that Gould's (1981/1996) thesis and his own scientific objectivity met with resistance after the publication of *The Mismeasure of Man*. A review that challenges Gould's analysis, Lewis et al. (2011), was followed by a *Nature* editorial, "Mismeasure for mismeasure" (2011) and by Mitchell and Michael (2019).
6. Claire Bowern (personal communication) points out that a eugenic-engineering stance infused late nineteenth- to early twentieth-century Australian national policy. A. O. Neville, in his role as "Chief Protector of Aborigines," separated lighter-skinned Aboriginal children from their families in an explicit effort to dilute their racial distinctiveness from white immigrants. See also Bernasconi and Dotson (2005).

References

Barkan, Elazar. 1992. *The retreat from scientific racism: Changing concepts of race in Britain and the United States between the World Wars*. Cambridge University Press.

Berko Gleason, Jean, & Bernstein Ratner, Nan. 1998. *Psycholinguistics*, 2nd ed. Harcourt Brace.

Bernasconi, Robert, & Dotson, Kristie (Eds.). 2005. *Race, hybridity, and miscegenation*. Thoemmes Continuum.

Blanckaert, Claude. 1997. "Paul Broca: des chiffre et des crânes." *L'Histoire*, *214*(October), 40.

Blanckaert, Claude. 2003. "Of monstrous métis? Hybridity, fear of miscegenation, and patriotism from Buffon to Paul Broca." In Sue Peabody & Tyler Stovall (Eds.), *The color of liberty: Histories of race in France* (pp. 42–70). Duke University Press.

Boas, Franz. 1911. *Mind of primitive man*. Macmillan.

Boas, Franz. 1940. *Race, language and culture*. Macmillan.

Broca, Paul. 1860. "Mémoire sur l'hybridité en général, sur la distinction de espèces animales et sur les métis obtenus par le croisement du lièvre et du lapin." In *Recherches sur l'hybridité animale en général et sur l'hybridité humaine en particulier* (pp. 433–593). J. Claye.

Broca, Paul. 1861. "Sur le volume et la forme du cerveau suivant les individus et suivant les races." *Bullétins de la Société d'Anthropologie de Paris, 2*, 139–204.

Broca, Paul. 1865. "Sur le siège de la faculté du langage articulé." *Bullétins de la Société d'Anthropologie de Paris, 6*, 377–393.

Broca, Paul. 1867. *Sur la prétendue dégénerescence de la population française.* E Martinet.

Broca, Paul. 1870. "Nouvelles recherches sur l'anthropologie de la France en général, et la Basse Bretagne en particulier." *Journal of Anthropology, 1*(1), 89–94.

Broca, Paul. 1873. "Sur la question celtique. Crânes des Bas-Bretons et des Auvergnats." *Bulletins de la Société d'Anthropologie de Paris, 1*(8), 313–328.

Broca, Paul. 1877a. "Recherches sur la circulation cérébrale." *Bullétins de l'Académie Impériale de Médecine 6*, 508–539.

Broca, Paul. 1877b. "Sur la circonvolution limbique et la scissure limbique." *Bulletins et Mémoires de la Société d'Anthropologie de Paris, Series II 12*, 646–657.

Broca, Paul. 1879. "Recherches sur les centres olfactifs." *Bulletin de l'Académie de Médecine 2*.

Buckingham, Hugh W. 2006. "The Marc Dax (1770–1837)/Paul Broca (1824–1880) controversy over priority in science: Left hemisphere specificity for seat of articulate language and for lesions that cause aphemia." *Clinical Linguistics and Phonetics, 20*(7–8), 613–619.

Carroll, David W. 2008. *Psychology of language*, 5th ed. Thomson Wadsworth.

Chambers, Chris. 2017. *The seven deadly sins of psychology: A manifesto for reforming the culture of scientific practice.* Princeton University Press.

Charity Hudley, Anne H. 2017. Language and racialization. In Ofelia García, Nelson Flores, & Massimiliano Spotti (Eds.), *The Oxford handbook of language and society* (pp. 381–402). Oxford University Press.

Charity Hudley, Anne H., Mallinson, Christine, & Bucholtz, Mary. 2020. Toward racial justice in linguistics: Interdisciplinary insights into theorizing race in the discipline and diversifying the profession. *Language, 96*(December 4), e200–e35. https://doi.org/10.1353/lan.2020.0074

Cubelli, Roberto, & C. G. Montagna. 1994. *A reappraisal of the controversy of Dax and Broca. Journal of the history of the neurosciences, 3(4)*, 215–226.

Fernández, Eva M., & Cairns, Helen Smith. 2011. *Fundamentals of psycholinguistics.* Wiley-Blackwell.

Firmin, Anténor. 1885/2000. *The equality of the human races (Positivist anthropology)*, translated by Asselin Charles with an introduction by Carolyn Fluehr-Lobban. Garland Press.

Finger, Stanley, & Roe, Daniel. 1996. Gustave Dax and the early history of cerebral dominance. *Archives of Neurology, 53*, 806–813.

Finger, Stanley, & Roe, Daniel. 1999. Does Gustave Dax deserve to be forgotten? The temporal lobe theory and other contributions of an overlooked figure in the history of language and cerebral Dominance. *Brain and Language, 69*, 16–30.

Gossett, Thomas. 1963/1997. *Race: The history of an idea in America*, new ed. Oxford University Press.

Gould, Stephen Jay. 1981/1996. *The mismeasure of man.* Norton.

Grant, Maison. 1916. *The passing of the great race: Or, the racial basis of European history.* Scribner's.

Greenblatt, Samuel H. 1984. The multiple roles of Broca's discovery in the development of the modern neurosciences. *Brain and Cognition, 3*(3), 249–258.

Grodzinsky, Yosef, & Santi, Andrea. 2008. The battle for Broca's region. *Trends in cognitive sciences, 12*, 474–480.

Harley, Trevor A. 2008. *The psychology of language: From data to theory*, 3rd ed. Psychology Press.

60 Decolonizing Linguistics

Hodges, Adam. 2016. Accusatory and exculpatory moves in the hunting for "racists" language game. *Language and Communication, 47*, 1–14.

Hutton, Christopher M. 1999. *Linguistics and the Third Reich: Mother-tongue fascism, race, and the science of language.* Routledge.

Joynt, Robert J., & Benton, Arthur L. 1964. The memoir of Marc Dax on aphasia. *Neurology, 14*(9), 851–854.

Lewis, Jason E., DeGusta, David, Meyer, Marc R., Mong, Janet M., Man, Alan E., & Holloway, Ralph L. 2011. The mismeasure of science: Stephen Jay Gould versus Samuel George Morton on skulls and bias. *PLoS Biology, 9*(6), e1001071.

Linguistic Society of America. 2019. Statement on race. https://www.linguisticsociety.org/content/lsa-statement-race

Majid, Asifa. 2020. Human olfaction at the intersection of language, culture, and biology. *Trends in Cognitive Science, 25*(2), 111–123.

Manzini, M. Rita, & Wexler, Kenneth. 1987. Parameters, binding theory, and learnability. *Linguistic Inquiry, 18*, 413–444.

McGann, John P. 2017. Poor human olfaction is a 19th-century myth. *Science, 356*(no. 6338, eaam7263), 1–6.

Mismeasure for Mismeasure. 2011. Editorial, *Nature, 474*(June 22), 419. doi:10. 1038/474419a

Mitchell, Paul Wolff, & Michael, John S. 2019. Bias, brains, and skulls: Tracing the legacy of scientific racism in the nineteenth-century works of Samuel George Morton and Friedrich Tiedemann. In Jamie A. Thomas & Christina Jackson (Eds.), *Embodied difference: Divergent bodies in public discourse* (pp. 77–98). Lexington Books.

Okrent, Daniel. 2019. *The guarded gate: Bigotry, eugenics, and the law that kept two generations of Jews, Italians, and other European immigrants out of America.* Scribner.

Osborn, Henry Fairfield. 1921. "Preface" to the 1916 1st ed., and to the 1917 2nd ed. In Madison Grant (Ed.), *The passing of the great race: Or, the racial basis of European history* (pp. vii–xiii). Scribner's.

Roe, Daniel, & Finger, Stanley. 1996. Gustave Dax and his fight for recognition: An overlooked chapter in the early history of cerebral dominance. *Journal of the History of the Neurosciences, 5*(3), 228–240.

Sedivy, Julie. 2014. *Language in mind: An introduction to psycholinguistics.* Sinauer Associates, Inc.

Spiro, Jonathan Peter. 2009. *Defending the master race: Conservation, eugenics, and the legacy of Madison Grant.* University of Vermont Press.

Thomas, Margaret. 1991. Universal grammar and the interpretation of reflexives in a second language. *Language, 67*, 211–239.

Thomas, Margaret. 1993. *Knowledge of reflexives in a second language.* John Benjamins Press.

Traxler, Matthew J. 2012. *Introduction to psycholinguistics: Understanding language science.* Wiley-Blackwell.

Ben Braithwaite is lecturer in linguistics and is the coordinator of a Diploma in Caribbean Sign Language Interpreting at the University of the West Indies, St Augustine. He has been involved in multidisciplinary, community-based work and activism with deaf signing communities in various parts of the Caribbean for over 15 years. He is broadly interested in signed languages of the Caribbean, language rights, language documentation, maintenance and advocacy, Caribbean methodologies and research goals, and the empowerment of Caribbean deaf researchers. His recent work has appeared in *Language and Communication,* the *Journal of Sociolinguistics*, and *Language*.

Kristian Ali is Chancellor's Fellow and PhD student at the University of California, Santa Barbara. She is a mixed Indo-Trinidadian, born and raised ·in an interracial family in Trinidad and Tobago, where she completed her undergraduate degree in Linguistics at the University of the West Indies, St Augustine Campus, and wrote an MPhil thesis on the history and structure of Bay Islands Sign Language. She has published on Caribbean signed languages and Caribbean research methodologies, and worked on documenting signed languages in Trinidad and Tobago, Guyana, and the Bay Islands of Honduras.

Abstract: The colonial structure of the field of linguistics is rooted in its history and is also deeply entrenched in its geography. Wealth, power, and prestige are hoarded in elite institutions of the Global North, in ways that shape who can be a professional linguist, and whose concerns are considered important to the field. Drawing on their experiences of being linguists in the Caribbean, the authors discuss some of the ways in which this colonial geography structures and upholds unequal access to opportunities and reproduces a parochial outlook which tends to overlook rich traditions of linguistic study from outside the current centres of institutional power. The chapter provides a brief sketch of one such tradition from the Caribbean and argues that the rootedness in place and explicit commitment to linguistic liberation provides a powerful model for linguists elsewhere committed to advancing liberatory linguistics.

Key Words: language and liberation, liberatory linguistics, Caribbean linguistics, Caribbean, colonial linguistics, decolonial linguistics, Global South linguistics

3

The Colonial Geography of Linguistics

A View from the Caribbean

Ben Braithwaite (he, him)
The University of the West Indies, St. Augustine

Kristian Ali (she, her)
University of California, Santa Barbara

Introduction

"Decolonization," wrote Franz Fanon, "is a historical process" (Fanon, 1963, p. 36). In the ongoing efforts to recognize and challenge the coloniality of contemporary linguistics, there has been an important emphasis on the ways in which the field's history has shaped its structures, methods, and categorizations. Ignoring that history and viewing linguistic theories as naturalized and decontextualized obscures colonial ideological underpinnings. Therefore, in their call to action, Anne Charity Hudley, Christine Mallinson, and Mary Bucholtz (2020a) encourage linguists to critically examine the history of the field, to "fully acknowledge the ongoing legacy of the field's history of racism and colonialism" (e212). Michel DeGraff's (2020) work on what he calls "the racist origins of contemporary beliefs about Creole languages" (e294) provides a particularly clear and rigorous example of how this can be done. In this chapter, we explore the ways in which the geography of linguistics, rooted in colonial histories, ongoing systems of exploitation and extraction, and deeply entrenched inequalities, continues to shape and organize the field of linguistics globally. While it is well understood that languages are molded by the geographies, demographics, social networks, and migrations of linguistic communities, the idea that linguistic theories are subject to much the same kinds of forces has largely been overlooked. Alongside the naturalization of the historical forces that have shaped academia, Donna Haraway (1988) describes "the God trick," in which knowledge has been (mis) represented as a "view from above, from nowhere" (p. 5). In fact, all knowledge is located, situated, and embodied. This is especially important in a field like

Ben Braithwaite, Kristian Ali, *The Colonial Geography of Linguistics* In: *Decolonizing Linguistics*. Edited by: Anne H. Charity Hudley, Christine Mallinson, and Mary Bucholtz, Oxford University Press.
© Anne H. Charity Hudley, Christine Mallinson, and Mary Bucholtz 2024. DOI: 10.1093/oso/9780197755259.003.0004

64 Decolonizing Linguistics

linguistics in which subject of inquiry itself is the located, situated, embodied linguistic knowledge and behaviour of communities around the world.

We believe that attempts to decolonize the academic field of linguistics must grapple with the colonial geography of the field: the ways in which power and opportunity are concentrated in certain parts of the world, the ways that data is extracted from other parts of the world, and the ways that such factors shape the lives of linguists from different parts of the world, and the field as a whole. Notions of core and periphery within the field of linguistics are surely tied to geographical cores and peripheries. This chapter can barely scratch the surface of a topic as huge as this. No doubt the geographies of academia affect people in different parts of the world differently, and we hope that more linguists from different places will share their own reflections in the future. Moreover, the migrations of academia may be experienced very differently by different people. In this chapter we tend to focus on the some of the negative aspects of such migrations, on the dislocation and isolation that we know can be the result of having to move far from home and community to pursue the hope of being a professional linguist. We also recognise that these migrations can be enriching, nourishing, and transformative. Guyanese linguist John Rickford writes of the awakening of a Black consciousness when he came to the US, initially as a student, expecting to move back to teach at a high school in Guyana when he was finished. It was here that he saw himself, for the first time, as Black, and found a new understanding of and love for his own language: "Learning to love Black Talk (my native Creolese and African American Vernacular English, or 'AAVE') was of a piece with learning to love my black self, the African strands of my ancestry, my me" (Rickford, 2022, p. 13). Indeed, we recognise that the geography of the place from which we write, the Caribbean, must be understood in terms of migration and diaspora. As Pat Noxolo puts it, "the Caribbean not only *has* a diaspora . . . the Caribbean *is* a diaspora" (Noxolo, 2016, p. 833).

Both the central importance and the complexity of diaspora in the Caribbean can be briefly exemplified in the work of a small sample of Trinbagonian linguists. Peggy Mohan carried out research on Trinidad Bhojpuri (Mohan, 1978; Mohan & Zador, 1986), the language which emerged from the communities of Indian indentured labourers who came to Trinidad in the post-Emancipation period. She went on to teach linguistics at Jawaharla Nehru University in India. Maureen Warner-Lewis has published extensively on Yoruba language and culture in Trinidad (Warner Lewis, 1991; 1999), and was for a short time a visiting lecturer at the University of Ife, Nigeria, spending the majority of her career the University of the West Indies in Jamaica. Mervyn Alleyne situated his work on the study of Caribbean Creole languages (though he argued against this particular classification) within a wider framework of what he called Afro-American (Alleyne, 1980). Jo-Anne Ferreira has described the cultural and linguistic legacy of Portuguese immigrants to the Caribbean (Ferreira, 1999; 2006). In the work of these linguists and many others, we see what Fanon (1963, p. 170) called "passionate research," which engages with the distortions and destructions of colonisation and seeks to rediscover and reconnect across times and places.

Notions of diaspora critically complicate simplistic conceptions of geography, identity, and language. As Stuart Hall put it, "The diasporic is the moment of the double inscription, of creolization and multiple belongings" (Hall, 2017, p. 144). We also recognise the internal complexity of the Caribbean. Many Caribbean linguists working in the Caribbean may nonetheless be away from home. Sandra Evans has written about the alienation and isolation of being a St Lucian linguist living and working in Trinidad and Tobago (Esnard et al., 2017).

Our focus the coloniality of geography in academia is by no means original. In their introduction to the book *Anthropological Locations: Boundaries and Grounds of a Field Science*, Akhil Gupta and James Ferguson (1997) deconstruct the influences of geography in anthropology. They describe how funding in the US is distributed according to the locations of fieldsites, in ways which are heavily influenced by contemporary geopolitics and the geographic areas in which states promote research. Thus, according to the geopolitics of the time, research in some geographical areas is strongly funded while other research is not. Additionally, the authors give a pointed description of anthropology as having a center and a periphery, with the center being the Euro American and French canon, and all other traditions of anthropology peripheral to these. This division between the center and periphery has crucial consequences for researchers' professional careers. Anthropologists in the periphery must engage with the work of the center or else they will be seen as parochial and backwards, whereas the center never needs to professionally engage with the methods, traditions, and imperatives of the periphery. Another crucial point the authors make is that for many graduate students, the choice of a fieldsite is monumental. While in reality this choice may be made for a multitude of practical reasons, fieldwork grant applications must be written as if the choice was based purely on scientific reasons, and in order to appear "objective." The point is clear: field-based disciplines like anthropology and linguistics are critically shaped and defined by geography in multiple ways. In the second section of this chapter we discuss some specific ways in which the field of linguistics is shaped by colonial geography, with a focus on the Global South. We define *the Global South* as a collective of geographic

66 Decolonizing Linguistics

spaces which have endured the repercussions of colonialism and imperialism and *the Global North* as those territories which have settled in, colonized, and plundered them.

As Boaventura de Sousa Santos argues, there is no social justice without cognitive justice (de Sousa Santos, 2015); that is, different forms of knowledge should be treated equally. This involves unraveling ourselves from Global North colonization and ownership of knowledge in academia. One way in which this can be approached is for scholars to read and cite more widely from traditions outside of the Global North. In the third part of this chapter, we provide a brief sketch of some features that we consider to be characteristic of a Caribbean linguistics tradition, which we argue provides a valuable guide to those interested in achieving cognitive justice in linguistics.

We both have spent the majority of our careers as linguists in the Caribbean. Kristian was born and raised in Trinidad and Tobago, where she completed her first two academic degrees at the University of the West Indies, St Augustine Campus, before moving to the University of California, Santa Barbara to pursue her PhD. A colleague and former student of Ben, she does research in Caribbean communities. Ben was born and grew up in a middle-class white family in England. He completed his PhD at the University of Newcastle and moved to Trinidad and Tobago in 2007 to take up a lecturer position at the University of the West Indies, St Augustine Campus. He has worked there ever since. Our perspectives on the issues we discuss in this chapter are shaped by our interest in collaborative community-based research, and crucially by our different relationships with the places and communities of the Caribbean in which we have lived and worked. We conclude the chapter with some personal reflections on how our engagement with linguistics has been shaped by colonial geography.

The Colonial Geography of Linguistics

The colonial geography of academia is most obviously manifested in the hoarding of wealth, power, and prestige in North America and Europe. This is where the most influential, best-paid professional linguists are, working at institutions whose wealth was often built directly on colonial settlement and exploitation. Tristan Ahtone and Robert Lee's work on "Land-Grab Universities" and Craig Steven Wilder's (2013) exploration of the foundations of US academic institutions in slavery and racism are important examples of work in the North American context that make this ongoing institutional coloniality explicit. It is in these places where publishing and funding decisions are made, and disciplinary gatekeeping is exercised (see also Chetty et al., this volume). It is through these mechanisms that "institutional whiteness [is] a structuring force in academia" (Charity Hudley et al., 2020a, e201) is sustained on a global scale. In this section, we provide a few examples of how we think these processes work in linguistics. We highlight some issues which have material consequences for researchers in and from the Global South, and which linguists with institutional power in the Global North could take practical steps to address, specifically: (1) the editorial boards of linguistics journals; (2) the English language requirements for entry to graduate schools in North America and Europe; and (3) the ways in which linguistic fieldwork is typically carried out in the Global South.

Márton Demeter (2020) identifies the composition of the editorial boards of prominent academic journals as one way in which disciplinary power is geographically structured and exercised. Table 3.1 provides information on the locations of the institutional affiliations of members of the editorial boards of several prominent journals in linguistics. Unsurprisingly, academics based in the US, Europe, and the UK dominate the boards of all of these journals, with large parts of the world barely represented, or not represented at all. The *Journal of Sociolinguistics* has by far the most geographically diverse editorial board, demonstrating that there is nothing inevitable about the distributions found in other journals. The lack of diversity is perhaps particularly problematic in those journals which purport to publish—and thereby help to define the boundaries of—"general linguistics" (e.g., *Glossa*, *Journal of Linguistics*, *Language*). Even journals dedicated to languages predominantly spoken outside the Global North generally have editorial boards dominated by researchers based in Europe and the US. For example, the *Journal of Pidgin and Creole Languages*, in which a significant proportion of articles concern languages spoken in the Caribbean, has only one Caribbean-based researcher among its editors and editorial board. Donald Winford, a Trinidadian who works at Ohio State University, is also listed as an honorary editor. Of the 21 members of the Editorial Advisory Committee, one more is based in the Caribbean, Nick Faraclas at the University of Puerto Rico.

The rate of submissions of papers by authors from different parts of the world seems to mirror the constitutions of the editorial boards. For example, between 2016 and 2020, over 77% of submissions to *Glossa* came from a first author located in Europe or North America, "with Asia comprising the bulk of the remaining papers" (Ubiquity, 2021). Moreover, as Demeter (2020, p. 162) argues, having an editorial board member of a journal at an institution increases the likelihood that colleagues at the same institution will have an article published in that journal.

68 Decolonizing Linguistics

Table 3.1 Nationality of institutional affiliations of editorial boards of linguistics journals

Journal name	Locations of the institutional affiliations of editorial boards
Glossa	17: Europe 11: USA 3: UK 1: Australia, Singapore, Mexico, UK / South Africa, Korea, Israel, Canada, Japan, Taiwan, Hong Kong
Theoretical Linguistics	5: Europe 3: USA
Journal of Linguistics	16: UK 14: Europe 4: USA 1: Hong Kong, Taiwan, China, Canada, Israel
Applied Linguistics	12: USA 7: UK 4: Europe 2: Brazil, Australia, Hong Kong 1: Colombia, Canada, Singapore
Language	16: USA 3: Europe 2: UK 1: Australia, Canada
Linguistic Typology	6: Europe 4: USA 1: Canada, UK, Israel, Fiji
Language in Society	13: USA 8: UK 6: Europe 3: Canada 2: Australia, Singapore, Brazil, Hong Kong, Japan, Israel 1: Bangladesh, South Africa, Philippines
Journal of Sociolinguistics	9: Europe 8: USA 4: UK 3: Brazil 2: South Africa, Australia 1: Perú, Uruguay, Colombia, Mexico, Sri Lanka, India, Qatar, Mozambique, Ethiopia, Morocco, Russia, Azerbaijan, New Zealand, Hong Kong, China, Singapore, Japan, Korea
Journal of Creole and Pidgin Languages	9: USA 6: Europe 2: Australia 1: UK, Singapore, Brazil, Jamaica, South Africa, Hong Kong, USA/South Africa

We acknowledge a point made to us by Anne Charity Hudley that by focusing on the locations of institutional affiliations, without closely examining the nationalities and identities of the individuals who make up these editorial boards, we may be overlooking additional complexities. We nonetheless think that it is important to draw attention to the ways in which power is overwhelmingly located in the *institutions* of the Global North, and hope that future research might look more closely into the ways in which individual identities and transnational diasporic networks might provide a more nuanced picture.

The Colonial Geography of Linguistics 69

We do not wish to imply that scholars in the Global South have no agency in relation to publishing their work. As we discuss below, Caribbean linguists have often aimed their publications at audiences in the Caribbean rather than at academics in the Global North, and, as Rickford (1986) discusses, the choice to publish locally is often quite deliberate. Nonetheless, publications that consider their scope to be global would benefit greatly from addressing some of the current barriers which tend to keep their content parochially Northern in outlook and coverage.

Many researchers have pointed out that the dominance of the English language in academic publishing erects and maintains barriers to professional advancement, particularly for already marginalized scholars from outside the geographical centres of power (Canagarajah, 2002). The ways in which graduate linguistics departments apply English language requirements and the geographical bases of exemptions often reveal biases quite starkly. For example, in 2022, Cornell University specified that all applicants who are not US citizens must prove their English language proficiency via IELTS or TOEFL test scores. Exemptions were granted on the basis of citizenship to applicants from the United Kingdom, Ireland, Australia, New Zealand, or Canada (except Quebec). The situation is not much different in Europe. Leiden University provides exemptions to "applicants who completed their secondary or higher education in the US, the UK, Ireland, New Zealand, Australia, Canada (except French-taught programmes in Canada), Singapore, South-Africa or Malta" (University of Leiden, 2022).

These kinds of policies have direct consequences for Caribbean students like Kristian, who completed her education from primary to tertiary level in English, only to be asked to prove her English language proficiency just to apply to certain schools. These institutional barriers sanction racialized students in the Caribbean whose Englishes are not regarded equally with the Englishes of white students from the Global North. The cost of taking the IELTS Academic exam in Trinidad and Tobago is currently around USD$325, more than enough to make this requirement alone prohibitive for many would-be applicants. We encourage linguists to check the English language requirements at their own institutions and to consider whether they should be adjusted.

Additionally, the way in which linguistics is represented in textbooks shapes the experiences and expectations of students, and can shape the field in profound ways. Elizabeth Peterson (2020, e249) discusses a survey of textbooks and teaching materials used by linguists around the world, which found that textbooks written by North American scholars, and those from the UK and Ireland, were especially widely used and therefore influential. The colonial

70 Decolonizing Linguistics

geography of academic conferences is also evident (see also Hou & Ali, 2024). Attendance and presentations at conferences matter because they are the nuclei of academic networking. For many linguists conferencing often leads to jobs, PhD positions, collaborations, and more, as well as developing academic (including linguistic) skills (Demeter, 2020). However, the cost and difficulty of travel to linguistics conferences which are usually held in the Global North, including the geopolitics of visas, are prohibitive, as is the cost of registration for conferences and membership of scholarly societies. Some societies offer discounts, but these are often based on flawed metrics such as national GDP, which fails to take into consideration the massive levels of inequality within countries. As a result, such discounts may be ineffective, particularly in countries like Trinidad and Tobago where oil and gas revenues mean that GDP is relatively high, but starkly unequal economic distribution means that this is not a useful measure of the economic circumstances of most citizens. Inevitably, it is those from the most disadvantaged backgrounds for whom such barriers are most prohibitive. We offer no simple solutions to societies wishing address their membership pricing structures, but encourage them to think carefully about the ways in which their organisations mediate academic power. We also urge them to do all they can to reduce the extent to which access is dependent on economic and other forms of privilege, particularly for those outside the Global North, who may already be barely represented in organisational leadership.

These structures also mean that professional linguists often live very far from the communities they study, not to mention the places they grew up in and their families and friends. This dislocation, a general problem in the professional academia of the Global North, has particular consequences in linguistics, and as with the history of the field, this geography is usually naturalized and taken for granted. Ben's recent review of guides to linguistic fieldwork, for example, shows that these texts are almost always addressed (at least implicitly) to students living in the Global North, who may be interested in conducting research in the Global South, but never the reverse (Braithwaite, 2020, p. 191). Because the majority of jobs for linguists are located in the Global North, it has been normalized for researchers who work on languages used in the Global South to live very far from the communities whose languages they study, whether or not they are themselves members of those communities. This situation greatly affects the financial, temporal, and environmental costs of research. It restricts the time researchers can usually spend in language communities, and inevitably limits meaningful community engagement. Researchers and advocates from Global South linguistic communities who wish to pursue careers as linguists may find themselves removed from those communities, damaging their relationships, and exacerbating the problems which they are attempting to fix. As we discussed earlier, we recognise that academic migration may also be productive and empowering, and may be enriched by diasporic connections. We believe that it is important to document the experiences both of those academic migrants who went on to sparkling successes, as well as those for whom the experience may have been more traumatic, or for whom migration was not an option. It tends to be those who fall into the latter categories whose experiences are least represented.

This state of affairs is bad for the field of linguistics, bad for linguistic justice, and bad for individual linguists. Increasingly the literature on field research describes the unhappiness and alienation, even "catastrophic identity fragmentation" (Wengle, 1988, p. x) that new field researchers experience (Macaulay, 2004). We argue that such experiences are, to a large degree, a product of the colonial geography of linguistics. The absurdity of the situation is particularly acute for researchers from outside the Global North pursuing a career in linguistics, who must often move thousands of miles from home in order to attend graduate school or get a job in which they can continue to work with the communities from which they are thereby dislocated (see also De Jesus, 2024). Brain drain is not a by-product of the system but a design feature, driven by national and regional funding bodies and serving foreign policy agendas, which explicitly aim to induce researchers from the South to move to the North by "attracting talent from abroad" (European Research Council website).

A View from the Caribbean

Charity Hudley et al. (2020b) challenge us with the question: "Why is your linguistics so small?" (e312). The narrowly prescribed conceptions of linguistics they are challenging can be connected to a wider pattern within the intellectual traditions of elite academic institutions in the Global North. Trinidadian philosopher Lloyd Best (2001), speaking about the experiences that he and others from the Caribbean had when they went abroad to England to study in the immediate postindependence period, observed:

> [V. S.] Naipaul says that the most provincial Universities that you could imagine are Oxford and Cambridge, where I was educated. He says they teach the economics of England and they teach it as the economics of the world! They appropriate the whole world within their concept. They have no concept that the rest of the world is somewhere else. And we go to these Universities and we're brilliant up there and

72 Decolonizing Linguistics

we congratulate ourselves about how little we know about ourselves. [laughter] (Best, 2001)

Outside of US-European linguistics, there are rich traditions of linguistic study that are deeply rooted in Global South places and communities, broad in their scope and explicitly liberatory in their ambitions (see also Bancu, Peltier, et al., this volume). In this section we briefly describe some features of one such tradition from the Caribbean, which can be traced to the work of Trinidadian linguist John Jacob Thomas, whose grammatical description of the French Creole of Trinidad was published in 1869. Thomas, born just a few years after emancipation, was motivated by observing the injustices that French Creole speakers experienced, for example in the English-based justice system. We see several features of Thomas's work as characteristic of the tradition of Caribbean linguistic research that has followed it. Thomas's work was explicitly liberatory. Apart from his grammar, Thomas was best known for his book *Froudacity* (1889), in which he provided a demolition of James Anthony Froude's *The English in the West Indies*, which had argued that Indo- and Afro-Caribbean people were not capable of governing themselves. Thomas is particularly derisive of Froude's methodological approach to trying to understand Black Trinidadians, which consisted of observations from a distance while driving around the country. Although Thomas had not himself grown up as a French Creole speaker, he makes it clear that the methodology for his grammar was grounded in direct observation and participation. Thomas's grammar was intended to be of immediate practical value as a resource to support interpreting and translation.

Several features of Thomas's work—an explicitly liberatory and anti-colonial purpose; a broad scope in which political, historical, and racial issues are central; the production of work intended to be of immediate practical use to Caribbean communities; a failure to conform to disciplinary boundaries established elsewhere; and a methodological emphasis on direct observation and long-term community participation—are characteristic of much of the Caribbean intellectual tradition, in linguistics and beyond, that followed.

In the Caribbean tradition, liberation has continued to be explicitly at the heart of the practice of linguistics. In *Language and Liberation*, Hubert Devonish states that his interest is in freeing the countries of the Caribbean from imperialism, a process that requires an examination of "the role which Creole languages, the ordinary everyday language of millions of people across the region, can and should play in the process of national liberation" (Devonish, 1986, p. 6). Similarly, in the introduction to his *Dictionary of Caribbean English Usage*, Richard Allsopp (2003) writes that the *Dictionary* "should be an inward and spiritual operator of regional integration even more powerful as a signal of unity than a national flag would be" (p. xxxi).

Moreover, issues of race are treated by many Caribbean linguists not as peripheral matters, but integrally connected to linguistic concerns. Mervyn Alleyne, for example, has written extensively on the subject in his 2002 book *The Construction and Representation of Race and Ethnicity in the Caribbean and the World*. And like Thomas, Caribbean linguists have often written widely, with little concern for the kinds of disciplinary gatekeeping which has sometimes tried to narrow the scope of what is considered "real linguistics." For instance, Hubert Devonish and Byron Jones (2017) trace the competition between English and Jamaican language in Jamaican musical traditions over the decades since independence, culminating in an analysis of the role of Jamaican language, via music, in the military confrontation in West Kingston/ Tivoli Gardens in May 2010.

Thomas's concern with the effects of linguistic discrimination in legal settings has continued through Guyanese linguist John Rickford's vital and well-known work on linguistic discrimination in the trial of George Zimmerman for the murder of Trayvon Martin (Rickford & King, 2016), the equally critical work by Sandra Evans on the treatment of French Creole speakers in the justice system of St Lucia (Evans, 2016; 2021; Robertson & Evans, 2020), and Celia Brown-Blake's (2008; 2017) work on linguistic discrimination and the need for justice reform in Jamaica through language policy change. Additionally, Kadian Walters (2017) has examined the linguistic discrimination faced by Jamaican Creole speakers in public service encounters, and there is an extensive literature on linguistic discrimination within the systems of formal education in the Caribbean (for example, among many others, Craig, 1985, Mohammed, 2021). The idea that linguistics can and should be empowering is embedded in teaching practices, as discussed by Kouwenberg et al. (2011).

Integrated in their academic work, Caribbean linguists have often focused on the production of accessible products which directly benefit Caribbean societies (Walicek, 2011, p. 122; see also Bancu, Peltier, et al., this volume). Denis Solomon addresses his grammar of Trinidadian English Creole to "the educated lay person, and above all the teacher of language arts" (Solomon, 1993, p. 1). John Bennett, a Guyanese Lokono linguist, produced an Arawak-English dictionary (Bennett, 1994) and teaching guide (Bennett, 1995) because he was concerned that younger members of his community were no longer speaking the language.

Caribbean linguists have employed the tools of linguistic analysis with social needs in mind, such as in Samantha Jackson's (2019) study of language acquisition by Trinidadian children, which provides the basis for local norms of language development to replace the foreign norms that underpin imported assessment instruments. Telford Rose et al. (2020) similarly discuss comparative phonological analysis as a tool for speech-language pathologists in Guyana. Theoretical engagement is robust, but theoretical concerns without immediate social consequences have been explicitly treated as secondary, as illustrated by Alleyne (1994, p. 7) and Carrington (1992, p. 93), who emphasize the connections which bind researchers in the Caribbean to places and communities, and the social responsibilities which flow from this. Such concerns have been embedded in institutions created by Caribbean linguists, such as the Jamaican Language Unit at the University of the West Indies, Mona Campus, which advocates for protection against discrimination on the basis of language (Jamaican Language Unit, n.d.). Among the Unit's most recent activities has been *Braadkyaas Jamiekan*, which broadcasts radio content in the Jamaican language, including news and public health information (Braadkyaas Jamiekan, n.d.). Meanwhile, the Guyanese Language Unit, based at the University of Guyana, has worked with Indigenous communities across the country to produce translations of public health information into various regional languages (Department of Language & Cultural Studies, n.d.).

Personal Reflections

We end the chapter by sharing some personal reflections on how our engagement with linguistics has been shaped by colonial geography. In pursuing work in linguistics, both of us have moved between academic institutions in the Global North and the University of the West Indies in the Caribbean, though in different directions, and for different reasons.

In 2022, Kristian moved to California to take up a position in a PhD programme there. Her move thousands of miles away from home was based on issues of funding and networking (see also De Jesus, 2024; Mantenuto et al., 2024). It is not uncommon in Trinidad for students like Kristian to be told "If you want to succeed in academia, you must go away," meaning relocate to the Global North. And yet such a move can be antithetical to the mission of carrying out liberatory linguistics in Caribbean communities. Brain drain is not wholly attributable to the imbalance of material resources in the Global South but also to the marginalization and devalorisation of our theoretical traditions. But it is extremely difficult to separate these issues when brain drain is so deeply entrenched in Caribbean societies, inevitably worsening the marginalization of our theoretical traditions. The training Kristian received at the University of the West Indies was steeped in the Caribbean tradition of liberatory linguistics. The issues of Caribbean people and languages were forefronted, and Creole linguistics, language documentation, and issues of language and social justice were always salient. Critical review of methodology was highly encouraged. Students like Kristian in these departments may exit their bachelor's degree with a desire to do work that many linguists in the Global North may deem as "not linguistics." Being part of the first generation in her family to go to university felt natural to Kristian as most of the other students in her cohort who benefited from free tertiary education were also first-generation students (cf. Mantenuto et al., 2024). It felt natural to many of us to want to practice liberatory linguistics, already being close to the issues of social justice and language in daily life. Kristian ended up in the extremely fortunate position of having a fully funded position in a linguistics department that highly encourages her way of thinking about linguistics. For other students in the region, the option of graduate studies in linguistics is less likely. To take one example, many young highly educated professionals are trained in Guyana yet very few remain, leading to one of the worst levels of brain drain in the world in the Caribbean country which produced John Rickford (himself part of the brain drain process).

Ben moved in 2007 from the UK, where he had completed his PhD, to Trinidad and Tobago. During the course of his PhD, he had worked on a project at the University of Newcastle investigating theoretical issues concerning the morphological, syntactic, and phonological structure of the Nuu-chah-nulth language, indigenous to Vancouver Island, Canada. The project involved the analysis of an electronic corpus of Nuu-chah-nulth data, with very limited scope for and no training in field and community-based research. Dislocated geographically from the community whose language he was analyzing, he was also completely disconnected from the interests, needs, and concerns of that community, pursuing a research agenda which was of interest only to a fairly small subset of other academic linguists. As he gradually realized the deep problems with this model of research, he understood how naive he had been in applying to the studentship which supported his PhD, associated with this project on a language with which he had no connection. He also came to understand some of the structural forces which underpinned the situation. The project was funded by a UK national funding body. Because of this and the way that tuition fees in the UK are tied to student nationality, only an applicant with UK citizenship would be eligible for the studentship. In effect, the way in which the research was funded determined that only applicants with no connection to the community whose language was to be studied would be eligible for support (for further discussion of how funding in the Global

North shapes research in the Global South, see Chetty et al., this volume). Moving to the Caribbean in the hope of finding a way to apply his technical knowledge of linguistics in more meaningful and engaged ways, he gradually learned a different way of being a linguist. Ben recognizes the many kinds of privilege which enabled him to migrate to the Caribbean, and to take up one of the very small number of professional positions as a linguist in the Caribbean, and the fact that doing so has meant that there is one less opportunity for Caribbean-born linguists who would love to work in the region from which they are from.

Conclusion

We believe that the Caribbean linguistic tradition, and other Global South traditions like it, can provide powerful situated models for those in the Global North who wish to pursue what Charity Hudley has called liberatory linguistics (e.g., Charity Hudley et al., 2022). We recognise that the structures that underpin the colonial geographies of linguistics are deep, and are tied to powerful forces and interests, but we also believe that linguists have the power to make significant changes to address issues such as the ones we have identified, including the composition of editorial boards, English language policies, and fieldwork practices. We encourage linguists in the Global North to read, cite, and collaborate with scholars from and in the Global South, and to draw on the rich traditions of thought and action such as the Caribbean tradition we have sketched here, to broaden their own horizons and those of the field. We believe that the ways that languages are theorized in linguistics is profoundly shaped by the demographics, migrations, and geographies of the field, all of which continue to be shaped in colonial ways. We wonder how different the general understanding of Creole languages would be if the work of Caribbean Creolists had been as widely read and cited as work within the Language Bioprogram Hypothesis model (Bickerton, 1984), conducted predominantly by linguists outside the Caribbean (cf. Bancu, Peltier, et al., this volume). How different could the field of linguistics be if research funding was less contingent on where researchers lived, if it was usual for researchers who worked on languages in the Global South to live close to those communities, and if the conferences and journals through which our field articulates what it sees as its core concerns did more to challenge the hegemony of institutions located in the Global North?

Acknowledgements

We thank Marlyse Baptista, Ariana Biancu, Mary Bucholtz, Anne Charity Hudley, Ryan Durgasingh, Samantha Jackson, Christine Mallinson, Joy Peltier, and Nicha Selvon-Ramkissoon for their invaluable feedback and support on this chapter.

References

Alleyne, Mervyn C. (1980). *Comparative Afro-American: An historical-comparative study of English-based Afro-American dialects of the New World*. Karoma.

Alleyne, Mervyn C. (1994). Problems of standardization of Creole languages. Marcyliena Morgan (Ed.) *Language and the social construction of identity in Creole situations* (pp.7–18). *Language inequality* (pp. 273–284). Center for Afro-American Studies, University of California.

Alleyne, Mervyn C. (2002). *The construction and representation of race and ethnicity in the Caribbean and the World*. University of West Indies Press.

Allsopp, Richard, & Allsopp, Jeannette (Eds.). (2003). *Dictionary of Caribbean English usage*. University of West Indies Press.

Best, Lloyd. (2001). *Race, class and ethnicity: A Caribbean interpretation*. The Third Annual Jagan Lecture presented at York University on March 3, 2001, 1–25.

Bennett, John P. (1994). *An Arawak-English Dictionary with an English word list*. Georgetown: Walter Roth Museum of Anthropology, Archaeology and Anthropology.

Bennett, John P. (1995). *Twenty-eight lessons in Loko (Arawak): A teaching guide*. Georgetown: Walter Roth Museum.

Bickerton, Derek. (1984). The language bioprogram hypothesis. *Behavioral and Brain Sciences*, 7(2), 173–188.

Brown-Blake, Celia. (2008). The right to linguistic non-discrimination and Creole language situations: The case of Jamaica. *Journal of Pidgin and Creole Languages*, 23(1), 32–73.

Brown-Blake, Celia. (2017). Supporting justice reform in Jamaica through language policy change. *Caribbean Studies*, 45(1–2),183–215.

Braithwaite, Ben. (2020). Ideologies of linguistic research on small sign languages in the Global South: A Caribbean perspective. *Language & Communication*, 74, 182–194.

Canagarajah, A. Suresh. (2002). *A geopolitics of academic writing*. University of Pittsburgh Press.

Carrington, Lawrence D. (1992). Images of Creole space. *Journal of Pidgin Creole Languages*, 7, 93–99.

Charity Hudley, Anne, Mallinson, Christine, & Bucholtz, Mary. (2020a). Toward racial justice in linguistics: Interdisciplinary insights into theorizing race in the discipline and diversifying the profession. *Language*, 96(4), e200–e235.

Charity Hudley, Anne, Mallinson, Christine, & Bucholtz, Mary. (2020b). From theory to action: Working collectively toward a more antiracist linguistics (Response to commentators). *Language*, 96(4), e307–e319.

Charity Hudley, Anne. H., Mallinson, Christine, & Bucholtz, Mary. (2022). *Talking college: Making space for Black language practices in higher education*. Teachers College Press.

Craig, Dennis, R. (1985). The sociology of language learning and teaching in a creole situation. In Ness Wolfson & Joan Manes (Eds.), *Language inequality* (pp. 273–284). Mouton.

DeGraff, Michel. (2020). Toward racial justice in linguistics: The case of Creole studies (Response to Charity Hudley et al.). *Language, 96*(4), e292–e306.

De Jesus, Julien. (2024). We need to be telling our own stories: Creating a home for Filipinx Americans in linguistics. In Anne H. Charity Hudley, Christine Mallinson, & Mary Bucholtz (Eds.), *Inclusion in linguistics*. Oxford University Press.

Demeter, Márton. (2020). *Academic knowledge production and the global south: Questioning inequality and under-representation*. London: Palgrave Macmillan.

De Sousa Santos, Boaventura. (2015). *Epistemologies of the South: Justice against epistemicide*. Routledge.

Devonish, Hubert. (1986). *Language and liberation: Creole language politics in the Caribbean*. Karia Press.

Devonish, Hubert, & Jones, Byron. (2017). Jamaica: A state of language, music and crisis of nation. *Volume!. La revue des musiques populaires, 13*(2). https://journals.openedition.org/volume/5321

Esnard, Talia, Descartes, Christine, Evans, Sandra, and Joseph, Kyneata. (2017). Framing our professional identity: Experiences of emerging Caribbean academics. *Social and Economic Studies, 66*(3/4), 123–150.

Evans, R. Sandra. (2016). *An examination of the language use patterns and practices of the legal system in St. Lucia* [Doctoral dissertation, University of the West Indies, St Augustine Campus].

Evans, R. Sandra. (2021). "Ou ni right-la pou remain silans": The case for a standard Kwéyòl translation of the pre-trial right to silence. *Journal of Pidgin and Creole Languages, 36*(1), 175–200.

European Research Council. Website. https://erc.europa.eu/about-erc/mission.

Fanon, Franz. (1963). *The wretched of the earth*. Grove Press.

Ferreira, Jo-Anne S. (1999). *The Portuguese language in Trinidad and Tobago: A study of language shift and language death* [Doctoral dissertation, University of the West Indies, St Augustine Campus].

Ferreira, Jo-Anne S. (2006). Madeiran Portuguese Migration to Guyana, St. Vincent, Antigua and Trinidad: A Comparative Overview. *Portuguese Studies Review, 14*(2), 63–85.

Gupta, Akhil, & Ferguson, James (Eds.). (1997). *Anthropological locations: Boundaries and grounds of a field science*. University of California Press.

Hall, Stuart. (2017). *Familiar stranger: A life between two islands*. Duke University Press.

Haraway, Donna. (1988). Situated knowledges: The science question in feminism and the privilege of partial perspective. *Feminist Studies, 14*(3), 575–599.

Hou, Lynn, & Ali, Kristian. (2024). Critically examining inclusion and parity for deaf Global South researchers of color in the field of sign language linguistics. In Anne H. Charity Hudley, Christine Mallinson, & Mary Bucholtz (Eds.), *Inclusion in linguistics*. Oxford University Press.

Jackson, Samantha. (2019). *Wee talk Trini: Acquisition of phonology in Trinidadian preschoolers* [Unpublished doctoral dissertation, University of the West Indies, St Augustine Campus].

Kouwenberg, Silvia, Anderson-Brown, Winne, Barrett, Terri-Ann, Dean, Shyrel-Ann, De Lisser, Tamirand, Douglas, Havenol, Forbes, Marsha, France, Autense, Gordon, Lorna, Jones, Byron, McLean, Novelette, & Scott, Jodianne. (2011). Linguistics in the Caribbean: Empowerment through creole language awareness. *Journal of Pidgin and Creole languages, 26*(2), 387–403.

Macaulay, Monica. (2004). Training linguistics students for the realities of fieldwork. *Anthropological Linguistics, 46*, 194–209.

Mantenuto, Iara, Levy, Tamaya, Reyes, Stephanie, & Zhang, Zhongyin. (2024). Increasing access and equity for first-generation scholars in linguistics. In Anne H. Charity Hudley, Christine Mallinson, & Mary Bucholtz (Eds.), *Inclusion in linguistics*. Oxford University Press.

Mohammed, Noor-ud-din. (2021). Deaf students' linguistic access in online education: The case of Trinidad. *Deafness & Education International, 23*(3), 217–233.

Mohan, Peggy Ramesar. (1978). *Trinidad Bhojpuri: A morphological study* [Doctoral Dissertation, University of Michigan].

Mohan, Peggy, and Zador, Paul. (1986). Discontinuity in a life cycle: The death of Trinidad Bhojpuri. *Language, 62*(2), 291–319.

Noxolo, Pat. (2016). Locating Caribbean studies in unending conversation. *Environment and Planning D: Society and Space, 34*(5), 830–835.

Peterson, Elizabeth. (2020). The US is not enough: Why the real world of linguistics needs your voice (Response to Charity Hudley et al.). *Language, 96*(4), e247-e253.

Rickford, John. (1986). Review of L. Carrington in collaboration with D. Craig and R. Todd-Dandaré, eds. Studies in Caribbean Language. *Journal of Caribbean Education*, 13 (1/2) 125–132.

Rickford, John R., & King, Sharese. (2016). Language and linguistics on trial: Hearing Rachel Jeantel (and other vernacular speakers) in the courtroom and beyond. *Language, 92*(4), 948–988.

Rickford, John R. (2021). *Speaking My Soul: Race, Life and Language*. Routledge.

Robertson, Ian E., & Evans, R. Sandra. (2020). Systemic linguistic discrimination and disenfranchisement in the Creolophone Caribbean: The case of the St. Lucian legal system. In Renée Blake & Isabelle Buchstaller (Eds.), *The Routledge Companion to the Work of John R. Rickford* (pp. 46–51. Routledge.

Solomon, Denis. (1993). *The speech of Trinidad: A reference grammar*. University of the West Indies, School of Continuing Studies.

Thomas, John Jacob. (1869). *The theory and practice of Creole grammar*. Port-of-Spain: Chronicle Publishing Office.

Thomas, John Jacob. (1889). *Froudacity: West Indian fables by James Anthony Froude*. TF Unwin.

Telford Rose, Sulare L., Payne, Kay T., De Lisser, Tamirand N., Harris, Ovetta L., & Elie, Martine. (2020). A comparative phonological analysis of Guyanese Creole and Standard American English: A guide for speech-language pathologists. *Perspectives of the ASHA Special Interest Groups, 5*(6), 1813–1819.

Ubiquity. (2021). *Glossa: Five Years of Publishing*. Website. https://blog.ubiquitypress.com/glossa-five-years-of-publishing-fb42b472a1d5.

Walicek, Don E. 2011. Linguistics for the Caribbean region: An interview with Mervyn Alleyne. *Sargasso II: Language rights and language policy in the Caribbean. (pp.111-122). University of Puerto Rico Press*.

Walters, Kadian. N. (2017). *"I got what I wanted but how did they make me feel?": the anatomy of linguistic discrimination in a diglossic situation* [Doctoral dissertation, University of the West Indies, Mona Campus].

Warner-Lewis, Maureen. (1991). *Guinea's other suns: The African dynamic in Trinidad culture*. The Majority Press.

Warner-Lewis, Maureen. (1999). *Trinidad Yoruba: From mother tongue to memory*. University of West Indies Press.

Wengle, John L. 1988. *Ethnographers in the field: The psychology of research*. University of Alabama Press.

Wilder, Craig Steven. 2013. *Ebony and ivy: Race, slavery, and the troubled history of America's universities*. Bloomsbury Publishing.

Nicté Fuller Medina is a quantitative linguist and interdisciplinary scholar who studies the mechanisms underlying multilingual speech to both inform linguistic science and challenge narratives of deficiency with respect to racialized language varieties. She leads two ongoing projects: the Language Contact in Belize project, which examines Spanish-Kriol-English contact, and Language, Culture and History: Belize in a Digital Age, which focuses on developing a decolonial framework for the digital preservation and repatriation of legacy linguistic data and other sound recordings. Her most recent publications appear in *archipelagos: a Caribbean journal of digital praxis*, the volume *When Creole and Spanish Collide: Language and Cultural Contact in the Caribbean*, and the *Canadian Journal of Linguistics*. She is an insider/outsider researcher, a Belizeanist, Central Americanist, and Caribbeanist.

Abstract: As a field that emerged in the context of coloniality, extractivism is built into linguistics. Language is seen as extractible from people and context and thus routinely removed from marginalized communities for the enrichment of smaller, more powerful groups. This chapter highlights two methodological issues which fallout from the extractivist nature of linguistics research: the idealization of the vernacular and the positioning of native speakers as data brokers, both of which lead to narrow science and have negative material consequences for communities and minoritized scholars. As a way of disrupting these colonial ideations and practices, the author proposes shifts in thinking, making alternative paths possible, followed by direct actions. By way of illustration, the author discusses her own reframing of linguistic research and the direct actions she takes working with research assistants as whole scholars and in the repatriation and restitution of legacy data to communities.

Key Words: decolonial linguistics, Belize, multilingualism, Creoles, participatory archives

4

We Like the Idea of You But Not the Reality of You

The Whole Scholar as Disruptor of Default Colonial Practices in Linguistics

Nicté Fuller Medina (she, ella, shee/ih)
Swarthmore College

Introduction

I argue in this chapter that broader extractivist models of research that persist as part of the colonial project directly undermine scholars who are Black, Indigenous, people of color (BIPOC), and/or from the Global South; minoritized language user communities; and the field of linguistics in ways that work against the very goals we hope to achieve in the study of language. These models impede our ability to cultivate transformative collaborative relationships with local communities and to situate linguistics in service to greater visibility and justice for language users. In order to illustrate these points, I draw from my research on multilingual speech in Belize, located on the Caribbean coast of Central America, (Fuller Medina, 2005; 2015; 2020a; 2020b; 2020c; 2021).

The Global South typically, though not unproblematically, refers to geographic regions that have experienced colonization. I use the term to also encompass conditions of inequality experienced in relation to the Global North, thus, "Global South refers to the people, places, and ideas that have been left out of the grand narrative of modernity" (Pennycook & Makoni, 2020, p. 1). Furthermore, even within those regions these conditions of inequality produced by colonialism continue to prevail between the nation-state and Indigenous Peoples as well as other minoritized communities (see also Chetty et al., this volume). *Extractivism* refers to the removal of natural resources and raw materials, such as oil or minerals, from the Global South for the benefit of the Global North, a process that impoverishes local communities (Gudynas, 2018). Drawing parallels to extractivism in

Nicté Fuller Medina, *We Like the Idea of You But Not the Reality of You* In: *Decolonizing Linguistics*. Edited by: Anne H. Charity Hudley, Christine Mallinson, and Mary Bucholtz, Oxford University Press.
© Anne H. Charity Hudley, Christine Mallinson, and Mary Bucholtz 2024. DOI: 10.1093/oso/9780197755259.003.0005

82 Decolonizing Linguistics

linguistics research, I first note methodological issues related to the vernacular (the "natural resource" in linguistics) and the positioning of the native speaker as a data broker (a component of the extraction process). From my positionality as a Creole-Mestizx scholar from the Global South living with disability, I then describe how I reframe my approach to (socio)linguistics research as counter stance to coloniality: the economic, political, and social structures that persist after the political system of colonialism has ended (Quijano, 2000). This reframing has led me to reject the notion of data broker both for myself and for community members, instead envisioning ways of working with community members as full-fledged collaborators; that is, as whole people, which naturally leads to a concomitant reframing of sociolinguistic corpus building as a process which considers community needs. Finally, I detail how I disrupt default colonial practices via the process of creating community-centered corpora of legacy data and new ways of working with research assistants. Throughout, I aim to make explicit the extractivist nature of research as well as some of the material consequences for communities and minoritized scholars.

As a transnational scholar, I occupy multiple spaces at the same time and I am socially located differently in each of these spaces. In addition, I am speaking to multiple audiences at once, though primarily to scholars, broadly defined, in the Global North. As a consequence, my positionality as described here is a challenge to summarize and therefore incomplete. Finally, terminologies used in this chapter may not have the same meanings in all the spaces I occupy. I describe myself as an insider/outsider researcher (cf. Nero, 2015; Tuhiwai Smith, 1999), and in addition to being a linguist trained in variationist sociolinguistics, I work in language and cultural preservation. I am a Belizeanist, Caribbeanist, Central Americanist, and Latin Americanist. Thus, I aim to center and advocate for these epistemologies. The rich linguistic ecology of these regions has much to offer language science, but on its own terms. At the same time, language science has much to offer these regions if applied within a language justice community-centered framework (see for example DeGraff, 2020 on work in Haiti). In the US and Canada, I am Black Latinx (or Afro-Latinx), where Black means "of African descent." In addition, I consider myself to be BIPOC and use that term not only to describe myself but to recognize some of the shared experiences I may have with other Black, Indigenous, and people of color. In Belize, describing myself as Creole-Mestiza may be more legible. Also implicated here are multiple aspects of my positionality related to class, gender and gender-identity expression, sexual orientation, and disability; their interpretations in Belize, in the diaspora, and in primarily white Anglophone spaces; as well as the relationship of these aspects to research. Finally, I am also plurilingual (see Galante, 2020): I speak two varieties of English, Belize Kriol (an English-lexified Creole) and Spanish. When speaking with other plurilingual speakers I make use of all these languages in the same utterance which I describe by the umbrella term language mixing. My research focus is on these empirical linguistic practices in Belize, specifically among those who also language mix as shown in the example (1) below. For convenience, in the examples that follow, non-Spanish items are bolded and ellipses represent portions left out of the quote. Alphanumeric codes refer to speaker number, region, and age group; NFM stands for my name; and BSEK stands for the Belizean Spanish, English, and Kriol corpus (Fuller Medina, 2016).

1. **kriol,** yo lo hablo como lo hablan acá en **Orange Walk** . . . mi **kriol** mío es diferente, es diferente a cómo lo hablan en Belice . . . ellos son más **raw Kriol,** la mía es más como **mixed into Spanish** también . . .

(58NY/BSEK)

Kriol, I speak it the way they speak it here in Orange Walk . . . my Kriol is different, it is different from how they speak it in Belize . . . they are more raw Kriol, mine is more like mixed into Spanish too . . .

It is important to note, however, that not all Belizean Spanish speakers engage in this robust language mixing. Many participants who I interviewed between 2013 and 2014 use highly monolingual Spanish in everyday interactions (see Le Page & Tabouret-Keller, 1985, and Fuller Medina, 2021 for more extensive descriptions of multilingualism across Belize).

My approach to linguistics research aligns with decoloniality in its attempt to deconstruct positivism and "its hegemony on contemporary science, as well as the enhancement of epistemologies or ways of knowing specific to the Global South" (Piron et al., 2019, p. 318). As noted above, I include here as well communities in the Global North that have been impoverished via the colonial project. From this reframing of research, direct actions emerge to disrupt and interrupt the flow of resources and knowledge production from margin to center which are rooted in the colonial systems from which linguistics emerged (Leonard 2017; 2020). This approach has entailed leveraging my experiences of marginalization to enact epistemic fugitivity (cf. Harney & Moten, 2013; Patel, 2016) by developing my own models for working with students from local and broader communities and re-imagining corpus creation from the perspective of decoloniality. The design and development of the first corpus, the Older Recordings of Belizean varieties of Spanish, is part

84 Decolonizing Linguistics

of a larger project, Language, Culture and History: Belize in a Digital Age, which aims to procure, preserve, and make sound recordings, such as sociolinguistic interviews, widely available to diaspora and source communities as well as a broad range scholars, including but not limited to linguists (Fuller Medina, 2022).

Extractivism in Linguistics Research

The process of extractivism is intimately tied to the exploitation of the labor of Black and Brown bodies which has historical roots in colonial systems of enslavement and other systems such as indentureship. In addition, the unidirectional flow of resources from South to North is also observed within both the Global North and the Global South between more privileged and minoritized groups. In linguistics research, the privileged group is a small set of scholars, who are primarily white (LSA, 2020) and often far removed from communities they research which leads to the field being characterized in large part by "unequal partnerships" between language communities and scholars of language (Rickford, 1997). The natural resource in linguistics is language data and the subfield of variationist sociolinguistics (Labov, 1972) specifically focuses on language used in everyday communication known as the vernacular or naturalistic speech. In early approaches, or what has been conceptualized by some scholars as the "first wave" of sociolinguistics, the vernacular is considered the "classic natural object of scientific inquiry, untouched by the reflexivity of human agency" (Eckert, 2012, p. 88) as a result of being produced with least attention paid to language use (Labov,1982). Agency in this wave was not considered, since variation was analyzed in terms of correlations between language use (below the level of consciousness) and macrosocial categories; in other words, patterned in relation to existing social structures (Eckert, 2012). Based on this first wave understanding of the vernacular, it is assumed that if the interviewer and the interviewee share the same vernacular or language variety, then it will be possible to mitigate any shifts away from naturalistic language use that can be triggered by the interview setting itself and/or varieties perceived as standardized or distinct from the language user's variety. Thus emerges the privileging of the idealized "native speaker" reflecting both idealized language use and a historical focus on spoken language (see also Winford, 2003). This invention of the ideal language user is conflated with community insider status and constitutes an important criterion for both collecting and validating data as authentic. Where lead researchers are in a position of power (e.g., via funding, supervisory role) but do not share the interviewees' variety, the privileging of the community insider can extend beyond data collection to the data preparation stages; that is, labor involved in processing the resource. In fact, many large-scale sociolinguistic corpora have been created in this way such that BIPOC students or community members are highly represented at the data collection stage as both data producers and collectors, but less so at decision-making stages (e.g., stewardship and data-curation) and in knowledge production (e.g., publications).[1] These conditions ultimately result in BIPOC scholars constituting a very small percentage of the professoriate in general and in specifically in linguistics, as has been documented both in the US (Leonard, 2020) and Canada (CAUT, 2018). These data hold true even when the languages themselves constitute an entire area of study in the field, as is the case for Native American languages (Leonard, 2020) and African American Language (Rickford, 1997). A similar profile can be observed in the production of knowledge where African American scholars are under-represented in peer-reviewed publications on African American Language (Lanehart & Malik, 2020), as is the case for Creoleophone scholars on so-called Creole languages (cf. Kouwenberg, 2011, on scholars from the University of the West Indies). Likewise, scholars from the Global South are sorely underrepresented in scholarship for a host of reasons (e.g., lack of research resources, Anglocentrism) even where that scholarship is about their contexts and may have direct relevance for their communities. In sum, by viewing insider researchers as data brokers, extractivist research models align with colonial logics marginalizing scholars like myself, who themselves are BIPOC and/or from the racialized communities we work in (see also De Jesus, 2024). This idealization also leaves unanalyzed the ways in which white privilege and/or privilege of the Global North works to facilitate outsiders' entry to marginalized communities.

Experiential Data and Methodological Issues

The practices described above characterized my experience in linguistics as someone who grew up in the Global South—specifically Belize, which straddles both the Caribbean and Central America—and as an insider/outsider scholar who trained at primarily white institutions including a linguistics doctoral program that aligned with first-wave approaches to multilingual settings. As a PhD candidate, I was the only Black-Latinx student in my program and one of only a few students living with nonvisible physical disability. These experiences, particularly as I prepared for and carried out my fieldwork in Belize, made evident to me the ways in which linguistics research, particularly first-wave approaches, coincide with colonial extractivist practices. The first is what Shondel Nero (2015) calls the authenticity trap (or trope) where the insider/

86 Decolonizing Linguistics

outsider researcher is subjected to the pressure "of being expected to maintain a cultural connection to the community that appears genuine, indexed through a host of dispositions including language, while keeping enough distance to examine cultural biases" (p. 364) or otherwise complete research in the community. Recall that the connection between community membership and language is tied to the notion of authentic data, yet this trope is built on a colonial view of community as a monolith. Even where a community is viewed as linguistically and ethnoracially homogeneous, it comprises subgroups based on age, gender identities, class, and so forth. This complexity increases when the researcher must collect data from multiple communities, as I did, in order to be accountable to those communities and language varieties. Thus, a binary view of community membership contributes to cementing racially minoritized scholars as data brokers, whether they are located in the Global North or are transnational scholars from the Global South like myself. By failing to problematize the position of the researcher we fail to adequately situate data and fail to benefit from the methodological advances such an analysis could produce.

During my PhD program, the "authenticity trap" manifested for me as a positive highlighting of my insider status with a simultaneous dismissal of my other capabilities by supervisory faculty in my home department illustrating how the idea of BIPOC and/or insider scholars is often well-received but not the reality of them as whole scholars. In one case, one such faculty member was unsupportive of me moving forward with my fieldwork, saying "you don't even know what you are doing." This, despite the fact that I had carried out fieldwork in multiple localities in Belize for my MA research and had been awarded multiple entrance scholarships based on proposals extending that work. In another instance, another faculty member indicated that I should remove from my dissertation discussions problematizing researcher positionality. On another occasion, they questioned my ability to be a future scholar on the tenure track in direct response to my request for disability-related accommodations (to which I was legally entitled). Posing such a question exemplified the ableist juxtaposition of disability and deficiency (Ben Moshe & Magaña, 2014) and its intersection with the racialized view of the utility and centrality of the Black or Brown body for the extraction, processing, and production of goods. Thus, the idea of the insider is positively received but not necessarily the reality of the whole scholar.

These interactions may appear as simply unkind or inappropriate, but these comments and evaluations came from faculty in roles designated to evaluate me both formally as well as informally. I therefore share these examples as data which reflect the systematic dismissal of racially minoritized scholars' knowledge. One need only consult the two-volume work *Presumed Incompetent*

The Whole Scholar as Disruptor   87

(Flores Neiman et al., 2020; Gutierrez y Muhs et al., 2012) and the Twitter hashtag #BlackInTheIvory for context. Also reflected in those interactions is a reluctance to see us as "thinking and knowledge producing subjects" (see Chetty et al., this volume) or, in other words, as whole scholars since to do so unsettles their idea of us. These types of comments along with the material consequences are only possible because they align with the view of racialized and disabled scholars as one-dimensional and because racist colonial structures are in place that allow such behaviors to go unchecked or even unnoticed by departmental and university leaders.

A second methodological issue is the characterization of the vernacular as one single true vernacular that is, in Penelope Eckert's words quoted above, "untouched by the reflexivity of human agency" (Eckert, 2012), a view which persists despite multiple critiques (Becker, 2013; Milroy & Gordon, 2003; Rickford in Mengesha, 2019; Rickford & McNair Fox, 1994; Weldon, 2022). Language is embedded in a hierarchically structured linguistic landscape in which plurilingual language users enact agency in negotiating multiple languages, contexts, and linguistic ideologies at any given moment as illustrated in the examples below. These examples, from my corpus of spoken language (Belizean Spanish, English and Kriol corpus), demonstrate both speaker agency, in asserting or querying language choice, as well as the navigation of language in relation to context. In example (2), the interviewee's agency is evident in the choice to do the interview in English, even though we communicated in Spanish, Kriol, and mixed discourse several times over a two-day period preceding the interview. Here the interviewee has likely taken into account the interview context, the interviewer (insider/outsider), and the stigma associated with Kriol and Belizean varieties of Spanish (Fuller Medina, 2021). In example (3), the speaker verbalizes this navigation, interrupting me in the interview to verify what language variety or discourse mode they should be using.

2. NFM [in Spanish]: ¿Creció aquí en-? (Did you grow up here -?)
    50N [in English]: In English better, I can express myself in English better. (50NO/BSEK)
3. NFM [in Spanish]: ¿Hay como una cooperativa de los artesanos...?
    63N [interrupts, asks in English]: so how do you want me to speak? In English, Spanish, or...?

Translation:
    NFM [in Spanish]: Is there like a co-op for the artisans...?
    63N [interrupts, asks in English]: so how do you want me to speak? In English, Spanish, or...?   (Fuller Medina, 2021, p. 16)

As someone who grew up speaking Spanish, English, and Kriol, I have navigated the interplay of these languages in the Belizean linguistic landscape for most of my life and, because I had previously conducted interviews in Belize, I knew this could present a methodological issue. Yet nothing in my first wave sociolinguistics training contemplated this reality. In multilingual contexts where languages are hierarchically structured, constrained by hegemonic ideologies, awareness of language and context is often close to the surface. In other words, for multilingual speakers of minoritized varieties who are constantly navigating contexts, multiple languages and linguistic ideologies, it is likely that they naturally pay a lot of attention to speech since not doing so can have material consequences for them. Thus, the attention to speech model (Labov, 1972) needs to be further problematized in such settings as reducing the focus on how one speaks is more complex in these cases. Examples (2) and (3), as well as example (1), repeated here as (4), show a reality of language use in stark contrast to the above idea of the vernacular and the native speaker as broker of language data or speech samples. Note the rich sociolinguistic knowledge that the speaker presents in example (4). She notes variability in Belize Kriol: Orange Walk Kriol versus the Belize City Kriol ("raw" Kriol, or what linguists call "deep Creole"). She further specifies that in her idiolect, Kriol is mixed with Spanish.

4. **kriol,** yo lo hablo como lo hablan acá en **Orange Walk** . . . mi **kriol** mío es diferente, es diferente a como lo hablan en Belice. . . . ellos son más **raw Kriol,** la mía es más como **mixed into Spanish** también. . . .   (58NY/BSEK)
Kriol, I speak it the way they speak it here in Orange Walk . . . my Kriol is different, it is different from how they speak it in Belize . . . they are more raw Kriol, mine is more like mixed into Spanish too.

This speaker demonstrates keen awareness of the linguistic ecology of Belize, insights which an insider researcher could bring to the table if they were valued as a whole scholar. If an insider researcher is only valued at the data collection stage but not at the level of research design, data analysis and knowledge production, then valuable insights are potentially lost.

Disrupting and Interrupting Extractivism

Beyond identifying inequities and methodological issues discussed above, a shift in thinking or "cognitive decolonization" is required in order to disrupt and interrupt extractivism (Mboa Nkoudou, 2020). For Western scholarship, this process involves an "epistemological rupture to better understand all the potential, nuances, and limits" that Western scholars cannot or choose not to see (Mboa Nkoudou, 2020, p. 35). Such a rupture is required in order to shift away from the over focus on disciplinary norms and the overrepresentation of Western perspectives orienting instead toward creating socially relevant knowledge for minoritized communities (Charity Hudley et al., 2020). This shift then makes available direct actions that previously may not have been contemplated if one were strictly adhering to disciplinary norms. By reconceptualizing linguistics research for myself to more closely align with decolonial approaches, for example, I could be intentional in the actions I chose to take and the ones I refused to take (see Montoya, this volume). I took my experiences in my doctoral program as a playbook for what not to do, particularly regarding both how I work with research assistants and how I work with data. It is pervasive in linguistics to consider data as a collection of disembodied objects to be owned and centrally archived away from the communities which they document, a practice I could not and would not participate in. In addition, it has rarely been evident to me how communities benefit from sociolinguistics research. Local communities in the Global South, in addition to generally not benefitting from research outputs, are less likely to receive the economic and experiential benefits of the research process (see also Chetty et al., this volume). The same can be said of racially minoritized students in the Global North, likely because fewer opportunities are presented to them (Charity Hudley et al., 2017). Consequently, I have developed practices for seeking out and working with research assistants as collaborators rather than bodies to labor in processing a resource. I also made a decision not to have data from my fieldwork archived in an institutional repository. In addition, when the opportunity arose to receive and add legacy data to my research corpora, I developed a vision to instead repatriate and restitute this data to Belize under my umbrella project: Language, Culture and History: Belize in a Digital Age, thereby retroactively disrupting the colonial flow of resources (Fuller Medina, 2022). In so doing, I also aim to build capacity among people for whom the data has relevance rather than using data to enrich a select few who are far removed from source communities.

Thus, through a community-collaborative process, I am working to digitally preserve legacy data (sound recordings in analog format) and repatriate and restitute it to Belize and diaspora Belizeans. Digitized recordings will be available online as well as locally in Belize. The first dataset is a collection of interviews carried out by US-ian Timothy W. Hagerty in 1978–1979 for

90 Decolonizing Linguistics

his PhD dissertation at UCLA (Hagerty, 1979), now compiled in the Older Recordings of Belizean varieties of Spanish and for which I currently hold copyright (Fuller Medina, 2018; 2022). To date, this project has involved three main activities: digitizing analog formats; creating time logs, metadata, and time-aligned transcripts in ELAN (Eudico Linguistic Annotator, Sloetjes & Wittenburg, 2008); and developing frameworks for community consultation which had previously been indefinitely postponed in light of the ongoing COVID-19 pandemic (Fuller Medina, 2020b; 2022). This project departs from traditional sociolinguistic approaches of centralizing data in locations far from communities or privatizing it by keeping it solely in a personal research collection. At minimum, such a departure disrupts the flow of data along colonial pathways from South to North (see Robin Gray, 2018 on repatriation as decolonization). That scholars in the Global North will have access once the collection is online is secondary in these efforts. In this way, this project also differs from emerging Open Methods and Open Access projects in linguistics and the social sciences where scholars are the intended end-users and community access for those with necessary technology is simply a fortunate coincidence (see Villarreal & Collister, this volume). Consequently, the corpus is described as community centered where community is conceptualized as multifaceted: interviewee communities in Belize; local students and scholars; local memory institutions (e.g., libraries, archives, museums); the broader Belizean community; Central American region; the Caribbean and the diaspora.

With respect to capacity building, I have worked with several cohorts of research assistants across multiple institutions, multiple countries (Canada, Belize, and the US), and varying levels of resources. Over the course of this work, it became clear to me which research tasks do not require formal linguistics training, which skills can be taught and which ones cannot, such as the language and cultural expertise that come with lived experience. In fact, it became very clear that formal training in linguistics and/or proficiency in Spanish are not sufficient criteria for working with the minoritized language varieties I research since tasks such as transcription are a political process (Bucholtz, 2000; Fuller Medina et al., 2021). Examples (5) and (6) illustrate this point. An advanced PhD student and native speaker of a prestige variety of Spanish was hired to assist in transcription, but as the examples show, data was mistranscribed. Kriol forms in the original transcription are in bold in line *a* of the transcription of the interview while the mistranscription is underlined in line *b*. Translations appear in the third line of each example. In (5) the Kriol word *bway* ("boy") is transcribed as Spanish *va y* ("go and"). Because *va* could be either the second-person formal or the third-person singular form and it is sentence-initial, this mistranscription not only erases the Kriol form but it renders an utterance that lacks coherence.

5. a. **Bway,** y le digo a Susana . . .
   b. <u>Va</u> y le digo a Susana . . .
      Boy, and I tell Susana . . .

In (6), the Kriol future tense marker *ahn* is transcribed as English future *will* in a contraction with *we* in the first instance, while in the second instance it is transcribed as the present tense of *to be*, once again imposing erasure and incoherence when the transcriber failed to recognize that the speaker was perfectly coherent making full use of their linguistic resources in systematic ways.

6. a. me dice, . . . we **ahn** sell everything we got but we **ahn** make sure this thing happen.
   b. me dice: . . . <u>we´ll</u> sell everything we got but we <u>are</u> make sure this thing happen.
      He says to me . . . we will sell everything we have, but we will make sure this thing happens.

Such transcriptions not only render inaccurate data but constitute epistemic violence. They further fail to be accountable to the data and speaker despite the transcriber's expertise in the language and in linguistics. These distortions reaffirmed for me my decision to prioritize the language and cultural expertise of community members, some of whom had no formal linguistics training via coursework. I also developed screening protocols as part of hiring procedures, which now include a sample transcription. Nonetheless, I aim to highlight the contributive value from speakers of minoritized varieties rather than reinforcing hegemonic ideologies. Therefore, the very features that are socially marked in Belizean and other Central American varieties of Spanish are recognized and sought out, as are the critical perspectives of those who have experienced linguistic discrimination first-hand. In other words, the cultural and linguistic knowledge along with a critical approach are deemed necessary for accountable research.

I started to develop these frameworks for working more equitably with transcribers/research assistants when I was still a doctoral student. By the time I was writing the dissertation, for example, I found myself recruiting, training, and supervising four student transcribers. My then institution's center for students with disabilities agreed, only after much advocacy on my part, to provide funding for transcription but did not provide assistance with recruitment, hiring, and supervision. This is a case where, despite the burden, I leveraged the lack of oversight in order to be intentional about facilitating research experience and the paid opportunity for a community member. I was able to hire a Belizean student who was a speaker of Northern Belizean Spanish.

Building on this first experience supervising research assistants, I aim to ensure that research assistantships are not merely transactional. Consequently, I provide training that includes workshops, discussions of readings, and opportunities to attend conference presentations (sometimes including my own so they could see the impact of their work), as well as to co-present our collaborative work (Fuller Medina et al., 2018; 2021). I make work practices as transparent as possible to make clear potential benefits (skills development, training, compensation), expectations (specific tasks, the contribution of their expertise), how their work fits into the larger research project, and how their work would be credited in publications and presentations. Additionally, I emphasize the opportunity to go beyond incidental exposure to research, a line on the CV, part-time income, and/or completing service learning. The goal was and is to provide the opportunity for BIPOC students and community members primarily from Belize, Central America, or the Caribbean to experience themselves as successful, to see themselves reflected in research, and to experience themselves as an integral part of the process.

By re-envisioning the required qualifications for research assistants in linguistics, a natural outcome was that the research opportunities became more available to a diversity of candidates and not just those in linguistics, where minoritized scholars are underrepresented. In addition, by intentionally recruiting widely and specifically in groups where the necessary language expertise could be found, these research opportunities were presented in spaces where minoritized students would see them. Finally, centering communities and cross-disciplinary research for me means making research outputs broadly available where possible and participating in conversations with the scholarly community in Belize (Fuller Medina, 2015), in the region (Fuller Medina, 2020c), and in cross-disciplinary spaces (Fuller Medina, 2020b; 2022) while still producing publications in more traditional venues in linguistics (Fuller Medina, 2020a; 2021).

Direct Action

There is no one set of instructions for countering extractivist practices, but the chapters in this volume and references therein provide much guidance (see also Antia et al., 2023). While the field is in need of swift, multifaceted, and large-scale change, the issues I have outlined in this chapter demonstrate that we need not—and cannot—wait for large grants, tenure-track positions, or tenure to act. To wait for conditions to be ideal before acting would be a form of what Kristie Dotson (2012) describes as "pessimism about epistemic fairness as it assumes an all-or-nothing stance . . . [which] is an over- simplification of the many options available" (p. 25). Small movements like the ones I made (even during times when I had no funding) can be impactful. In fact, the precursor to action, the process of cognitive decolonization, can begin immediately. In what follows, I offer some recommendations.

For those who are students and early career scholars who are BIPOC and/ or from the Global South, first, choose your battles. Second, the standard advice of finding mentorship and allies outside your department and university applies regardless of your situation. This strategy is just good professional sense, but it is particularly important if your supervisory relationships break down, you have difficulty getting letters of recommendation, or find that supervisory faculty are impeding your progress. Mentorship can come in many forms, ranging from one-time advice from senior scholars at a conference to a long-term trust relationship. Social media groups such as the Scholars of Color in Language Studies groups (SCiLS) and other academic-oriented Facebook groups specifically for Black, Indigenous and/or POC scholars can be helpful. Third, given the frequency with which racially minoritized scholars are presumed incompetent (Flores Neiman et al., 2020; Gutierrez y Muhs et al., 2012), it is important to remember that you know more than others may be willing to recognize and that you know what you are doing even when you may not feel that you do. One reviewer of this chapter asked that I make clear what frameworks I used to develop the work and practices I describe here, but the truth is that while I was a student it was rarely clear how to proceed and I had to create the paths I walked on. You may have to do the same.

If you are an outsider researcher from the Global North, the first question to ask is: Do you need to do research in the Global South? In academia, where the "cult of uniqueness" prevails, scholars are often under pressure to demonstrate the uniqueness or exceptionalness of the area of investigation in question (Aceto, 2020, p. 200). Within the prevailing colonial framework, the Global South is constructed as "exotic," "untouched," understudied, and so on. In the case of Belize, it is not uncommon to see research described in exotic terms or for outsider researchers to frame how they came to work in Belize as a "falling in love" while on vacation, retreat, or adventure trip akin to tropes found in literature and travel writing (Metro, 2018; cf. also De Jesus, 2024). Such perspectives, unfortunately, reinforce colonial extractivist notions of the Global South as an untapped source of raw material lying dormant waiting

94 Decolonizing Linguistics

to be mined for the benefit of the researcher rather than local communities and scholars. In Rosalie Metro's (2018) words, it is "an imperialist fantasy," one that needs to be critically examined regardless of whether you are a white scholar, a racially minoritized scholar from the Global North, or a scholar in/ from the Global South benefitting from internal colonialism.

If you are already doing research in the Global South or if you are moving forward with a plan to do so, there are basic ethical and often legal requirements to be aware of. It may be a challenge to determine if you need permission to conduct research, but you must do your due diligence to ensure you are in legal and ethical compliance. In Belize, for example, a permit is required to conduct research as per the National Institute of Culture and History Act (NICH Act Revised Edition, 2011). Legal deposit is also required according to Sections 20 (2) and (3) of the Belize National Library Service and Information System Act, with serious consequences for noncompliance ("Legal Publication," 2014). You can search "legal deposit" for the specific context where you are conducting research (e.g., Jasion, 2019) or seek assistance from your institution's librarians. It is also worth familiarizing yourself with the copyright process and ethical issues related to linguistic data (Collister, 2022; Fuller Medina, 2022; Holton et al., 2022). All of these issues should factor into a research data management plan.

Ethical responsibilities, however, go far beyond basic legal requirements. If consulting with local scholars, community leaders, and memory or cultural heritage workers, recognize that they will not have the same resources, allocated research time, or income that is more often found in the Global North. Budget for honoraria if you can and think of how you will approach offering compensation in local contexts. If there is leeway in hiring research assistants, then be intentional about highlighting whether skills can be learned on the job and be detailed about the degree of language proficiency required, keeping in mind that languaging matters for the many language users who have been told that their variety is deficient. If doing community-based or community-engaged research, be transparent and clearly define what is meant by these terms. For me, the former entails community-generated research questions that benefit the community, while the latter entails reciprocity ideally as determined collaboratively or by the community. In addition, epistemologies from the South, and especially from the specific community you are working with, should be centered and their perspectives uplifted. Accomplishing this goal includes being in conversation in equitable and substantive ways and can include assisting scholars who are not allocated research time or resources with publishing their work both locally and internationally, with yourself as mentor/facilitator, second or third author. It is not uncommon for white scholars from the Global North to co-author with local knowledge bearers about local knowledge but list themselves as first authors, then framing the work as inclusive community engagement when it is evident that the work relies almost entirely on the local contributor. Finally, if you are part of a transnational collaboration or plan to be, recognize that transnational work can entail substantive invisible labor because default colonial systems do not encompass minoritized realities. As noted by Chetty et al. (this volume), systems in the Global North are not set up to efficiently work with partners in the Global South. Part of your work may well entail mitigating the disproportionate impact this can have on partners in the South.

Another ethical imperative is to make linguistic data accessible to the community from which it originates. Do you have legacy data from the Caribbean or Central America in your personal research collection? Are you a senior scholar who can collaborate on funding proposals for repatriation and restitution efforts? Reach out to insider/outsider scholars like myself who are committed to repatriating and restituting data within decolonial frameworks (Fuller Medina, 2022).

The goals of language science must prioritize communities regarding the curation of their own stories and oral histories and give genuine consideration of their rights (Collister, 2022; Fuller Medina, 2022; Holton et al., 2022). For this reason, my final recommendation, regardless of your positionality, but especially if you are from the Global North, is to refuse to engage with people from the Global South from a place of coloniality and instead engage with us as equals, as whole people, as whole scholars.

Note

1. This issue deserves further attention but is beyond the scope of this piece. In some cases, for example, interviews were originally carried out by BIPOC students for their own work but then data were later archived at their institution becoming part of a lab or project while other corpora were created by scholars who I would describe as insider/outsiders. Nonetheless, the fact remains that BIPOC scholars are woefully underrepresented in linguistics.

References

Aceto, Michael. (2020). English in the Caribbean and the Central American Rim. In D. Schreier, M. Hundt, & E. W. Schneider (Eds.), *The Cambridge handbook of World Englishes* (pp. 185–209). Cambridge University Press.

96 Decolonizing Linguistics

Antia, Bassey E., & Makoni, Sinfree (Eds.). (2023). Southernizing sociolinguistics: Colonialism, racism, and
patriarchy in language in the Global South. Routledge.

Becker, Kara. (2013). The sociolinguistic interview. In C. Mallinson, B. Childs, & G. Van Herk (Eds.), *Data collection in sociolinguistics* (pp. 107–133). Routledge.

Ben-Moshe, Liat, & Magaña, Sandy. (2014). An introduction to race, gender, and disability: Intersectionality, disability studies, and families of color. *Women, Gender, and Families of Color, 2* (2), 105–114.

Bucholtz, Mary. (2000). The politics of transcription. *Journal of Pragmatics, 32*(10), 1439–1465.

Canadian Association of University Teachers (CAUT). (2018). Underrepresented & underpaid diversity & equity among Canada's post-secondary education teachers. https://www.caut.ca/sites/default/files/caut_equity_report_2018–04final.pdf

Charity Hudley, Anne, Mallinson, Christine, & Bucholtz, Mary. (2020). Toward racial justice in linguistics: Interdisciplinary insights into theorizing race in the discipline and diversifying the profession. *Language, 96*(4), e200–e235.

Charity Hudley, Anne, Dickter, Cheryl L., & Franz, Hannah A. (2017). *The indispensable guide to undergraduate research: Success in and beyond college.* Teachers College Press.

Collister, Lauren. (2022). Copyright and sharing linguistic data. In Andrea L. Berez-Kroeker, Bradley McDonnel, Eve Koller, & Lauren Collister (Eds.), *The open handbook of linguistic data management.* (pp. 117–128). MIT Press.

DeGraff, Michel. (2020). The politics of education in post-colonies: Kreyòl in Haiti as a case study of language as technology for power and liberation. *Journal of Postcolonial Linguistics, 3,* 89–125.

De Jesus, Julien. (2024). We need to be telling our own stories: Creating a home for Filipinx Americans in linguistics. In Anne H. Charity Hudley, Christine Mallinson, & Mary Bucholtz (Eds.), *Inclusion in linguistics.* Oxford University Press.

Dotson, Kristie. (2012). A cautionary tale: On limiting epistemic oppression. *Frontiers: A Journal of Women Studies, 33*(1), 24–47.

Eckert, Penelope. (2012). Three waves of variation study: The emergence of meaning in the study of sociolinguistic variation. *Annual Review of Anthropology, 41,* 87–100.

Flores Neimann, Yolanda, Gutierrez y Muhs, Gabriella, & Gonzalez, Carmen. (2020). *Presumed incompetent II: Race, class, power, and resistance of women in academia.* University of Utah Press.

Fuller Medina, Nicté (2005). Spanish-English contact in Belize: the case of 'HACER+ V'. *Proceedings of the Canadian linguistic association.* (pp 1-9) https://cla-acl.ca/pdfs/actes-2005/FullerMedina.pdf

Fuller Medina, Nicté. (2015). Let's talk about Spanish: A sociolinguistic study of Spanish in Belize. In Nigel Encalada, Rolando Cocom, Phylicia Pelayo, & Giovanni Pinelo (Eds.), *Research reports in Belizean history and anthropology, Volume 3: Proceedings of the XII Annual Belize Archaeology and Anthropology Symposium* (pp. 166–176). BRC Printing.

Fuller Medina, Nicté. (2016). *Language mixing in Northern and Western Belize: A comparative variationist approach* [Doctoral Dissertation, Université d'Ottawa/University of Ottawa].

Fuller Medina, Nicté. (2018). Sociolinguistic data as cultural patrimony: challenges, solutions and lessons learned in the preservation of legacy data. Caribbean Studies Forum, University of Belize, March 4–11.

Fuller Medina, Nicté. (2020a). How bilingual verbs are built: Evidence from Belizean varieties of contact Spanish. *Canadian Journal of Linguistics/Revue Canadienne de Linguistique, 65*(1), 122–132.

Fuller Medina, Nicté. (2020b). Repatriating sociolinguistic data to Belize: Can a decolonial model still work in times of COVID 19? *CLIR COVID (Re) Collections* (blog), June 22, 2020.

https://www.clir.org/2020/06/repatriating-sociolinguistic-data-to-belize-can-a-decolonial-model-still-work-in-times-of-covid-19/.

Fuller Medina, Nicté. (2020c). Belizean varieties of Spanish: Language contact and plurilingual practices. *Anuario de Estudios Centroamericanos: Dossier on Belize, 46*(1) (December), 1–29.

Fuller Medina, Nicté. (2021). "Lo que hacen mix es el Kriol y el English": How Spanish speakers reconcile linguistic encounters with English and Kriol in Belize. In Glenda A. Leung & Miki Loschky (Eds.), *When Creole and Spanish collide: Language and cultural contact in the Caribbean* (pp. 126–154). Brill.

Fuller Medina, Nicté. (2022). Data is patrimony: On developing a decolonial model for access and repatriation of sociolinguistic data. *Archipelagos: A Journal of Caribbean Digital Praxis.* https://archipelagosjournal.org/issue06/fuller-data.html

Fuller Medina, Nicté, Moreira, Erson, & Moreira, Kennion. (2018). Building research Capacity through service learning: notes from the language, culture and history project. Poster presented at the 1st National Research Conference, University of Belize, Belmopan, Belize, March 21–22.

Fuller Medina, Nicté, Hernández Castro, Daniela, Padron, Griselly, & González Paz, Alexander. (2021). Towards an ethics of care in representing minoritized voices through transcription. Presented at the *UCLA Library Research Forum,* UCLA, Los Angeles, CA, March 23.

Galante, Angelica. (2020). Plurilingual and pluricultural competence (PPC) scale: the inseparability of language and culture. *International Journal of Multilingualism* (ahead of print) 1–22. https://doi.org/10.1080/14790718.2020.1753747

Gray, Robin R. (2018). Repatriation and decolonization: Thoughts on ownership, access, and control. In F. Gunderson, R. C. Lancefield, & B. Woods (Eds.). *The Oxford handbook of musical repatriation* (pp. 723–738). Oxford University Press.

Gudynas, Eduardo. (2018). Extractivisms: Tendencies and consequences. In Ronaldo Munck & Raúl Delgado Wise (Eds.), *Reframing Latin American development* (pp. 61–76). Routledge.

Gutierrez y Muhs, Gabriella, Niemann, Yolanda Flores, Gonzalez, Carmen G., & Harris, Angela P. (Eds.) (2012). *Presumed incompetent: The intersections of race and class for women in academia.* Utah State University Press.

Hagerty, Timothy W. (1979). *A phonological analysis of the Spanish of Belize* [Doctoral Dissertation, University of California, Los Angeles].

Harney, Stefano, & Moten, Fred. (2013). *The undercommons: Fugitive planning and Black study.* Research Collection Lee Kong Chian School of Business. https://ink.library.smu.edu.sg/lkcsb_research/5025

Holton, Gary, Leonard, Wesley Y., & Pulsifer, Peter L. (2022). Indigenous peoples, ethics, and linguistic data. In Andrea L. Berez-Kroeker, Bradley McDonnel, Eve Koller, & Lauren Collister (Eds.), *The open handbook of linguistic data management.* (pp. 49–60). MIT Press.

Jasion, Jan T. (2019). *The international guide to legal deposit.* Routledge.

Kouwenberg, Sylvia. (2011). Linguistics in the Caribbean: Between theory and practice. *Journal of Pidgin and Creole Languages, 26*(1), 219–233.

Labov, William. (1972). *Sociolinguistic patterns.* University of Pennsylvania Press.

Lanehart, Sonja, & Malik, Ayesha. (2020). Diversity and inclusion in language variationist and sociolinguistics research journals. [Conference presentation] Annual Meeting of the American Dialect Society, New Orleans.

Legal Publication Deposit. (2014, May 16). The gray area. *Amandala.* http://amandala.com.bz/news/legal-publication-deposit-gray-area/

Leonard, Wesley Y. (2017). Producing language reclamation by decolonising "language." *Language Documentation and Description 14*, 15–36.

Leonard, Wesley. Y. (2020). Insights from Native American Studies for theorizing race and racism in linguistics (response to Charity Hudley, Mallinson, and Bucholtz). *Language, 96*(4), e281–291.

98 Decolonizing Linguistics

Le Page, Robert. B., & Tabouret-Keller, Andrée. (1985). *Acts of identity: Creole-based approaches to language and ethnicity.* Reprinted (2006). (2. éd. augmentée). Éd. Modulaires Européennes.

Linguistic Society of America (LSA). (2020) The State of Linguistics in Higher Education Annual Report 2020. https://www.linguisticsociety.org/sites/default/files/Annual%20Report%202020%20Jan2021%20-%20final_0.pdf

Mboa Ndoukou, Thomas H. (2020). Epistemic alienation in African scholarly communications: open access as a pharmakon. In M. P. Eve & J. Gray (Eds.), *Reassembling scholarly communications: Histories, infrastructures, and global politics of open access* (pp. 25–41. MIT Press. https://doi.org/10.7551/mitpress/11885.003.0006

Mengesha, Zion. (2019). Interview with John R. Rickford. *Journal of English Linguistics, 47*(4), 335–356.

Metro, Rosalie. (2018). White travel writers, please stop saying you fell in love with a country full of Brown people. Blog. *Los Angeles Review of Books.* https://blog.lareviewofbooks.org/essays/white-travel-writers-please-stop-saying-fell-love-country-full-brown-people/

Milroy, Lesley, & Gordon, Matthew (2003). *Sociolinguistics: Method and interpretation.* Blackwell.

National Institute of Culture and History (NICH) Act Chapter 331 Revised Edition 2011. https://www.belizejudiciary.org/download/LAWS-of-Belize-rev2011/Laws-of-Belize-Update-2011/VOLUME%2015B_2/Cap%20331%20National%20Institute%20of%20Culture%20and%20History%20Act.pdf

Nero, Shondel. (2015). Language, identity, and insider/outsider positionality in Caribbean Creole English research. *Applied Linguistics Review, 6*(3), 341–368.

Patel, Leigh. (2016). Pedagogies of resistance and survivance: Learning as marronage. *Equity & Excellence in Education, 49*(4), 397–401.

Pennycook, Alastair, & Makoni, Sinfree. (2020). *Innovations and challenges in applied linguistics from the Global South.* Routledge.

Piron, Florence, Mboa Nkoudou, Thomas, Madiba, Marie Sophie, Alladatin, Judicaël ,Achaffert, Rhissa Hamissou, & Pierre, Anderson. (2019). Toward African and Haitian universities in service to sustainable local development: The contribution of fair open science. In L. Chan, A. Okune, R. Hillyer, D. Albornoz, & A. Posada (Eds.), *Contextualizing openness: Situating open science,* (pp. 311–331). University of Ottawa Press.

Quijano, Anibal. (2000). Coloniality of power, Eurocentrism, and Latin America. *Nepantla: Views from South, 1*(3), 533–580.

Rickford, John. R. (1997). Unequal partnership: Sociolinguistics and the African American speech community. *Language in Society 26*(2), 161–197.

Rickford, John R., & McNair-Knox, Faye. (1994). Addressee-and topic-influenced style shift: A quantitative sociolinguistic study. In Douglas Biber & Edward Finegan (Eds.), *Sociolinguistic perspectives on register* (pp. 235–276). Oxford University Press.

Sloetjes, Han, & Wittenburg, Peter. (2008). Annotation by category—ELAN and ISO DCR. *In Proceedings of the 6th International Conference on Language Resources and Evaluation (LREC), May, 2008.* European Language Resources Association.

Smith, Linda Tuhiwai. (1999). *Decolonizing methodologies: Research and Indigenous peoples.* Zed Books and University of Tago Press.

Weldon, Tracey. L. (2022). Visibly invisible: The study of middle class African American English. *Language and Linguistics Compass, 16*(11), e12477. https://doi.org/10.1111/lnc3.12477

Winford, Donald (2003). Ideologies of language and socially realistic linguistics. In Sinfree Makoni, Geneva Smitherman, Arnetha Ball and Arthur Spears (Eds.), Black linguistics: Language, society and politics in Africa and the Americas (pp. 21–39). Routledge.

Aris Moreno Clemons is assistant professor of Hispanic Linguistics in the World Languages and Cultures department at the University of Tennessee Knoxville. Having completed her doctoral degree in the Spanish and Portuguese Department and the Mexican American and Latina/o Studies Department at the University of Texas at Austin, her work spans the fields of linguistics, education, anthropology, and Black and Latinx studies in order to interrogate the intersections of language, race, and identity. Originally from (all over) the Bay Area in California, she has been steeped in the traditions of anti-racist pedagogies and has dedicated herself to developing and sustaining these practices in her own research and teaching. As such, her research agenda is rooted in social change through an examination of the ways that what appears to be common knowledge is often constructed and ideologically maintained by various social institutions. Overarchingly, Aris questions the linguistic mechanisms—repetitions, stance taking, tropicalizations, and so on—responsible for the (re)construction and maintenance of racializing and marginalizing ideologies.

Abstract: This chapter discusses the implications of privileging value-based political research agendas in linguistics and affirms the impossibility of neutral and objective scientific linguistic research. Instead, the author argues that linguists must cultivate a practice of transparency, noting not only their positionalities but also in their political motivations, relationships with the language communities they investigate, and ensuring access to investigative work beyond the academy. In this way decisions about research questions, frames, and interpretations become clearer. Using the traditions of research on African American language (AAL) as a case study, the author argues that linguistic researchers must become transparent about the political goals of their research in order to progress the field in ways that disrupt colonial frames of power. Specifically, the ways in which political transparency has been enacted as Black feminist praxis is reviewed, and several provocations are provided toward a transparency-based approach in linguistics that resists formerly constructed categorizations of linguistics as either theoretical or social. Finally, the chapter discusses the benefits of this practice through an example of a value-based research project, which applied African American English (AAE) research traditions to an exploration of Dominican language practices. Through this application, the author argues for a Hemispheric Black Community of Practice approach to the study of Caribbean Spanish, ultimately destabilizing the generative and variationist approaches that have dominated the study of Caribbean Spanish in linguistic traditions.

Este capítulo analiza las implicaciones de privilegiar las agendas de investigación basadas en valores políticas en el campo lingüístico y afirma la imposibilidad de una investigación lingüística científica neutral y objetiva. En cambio, la autora argumenta que los lingüistas deben cultivar una práctica de transparencia, teniendo en cuenta no solo sus posiciones (ver Lin 2015; Clemons y Lawrence 2020 para referencia a estas llamadas) sino también sus motivaciones políticas, relaciones con las comunidades lingüísticas que investigan y garantizar acceso al trabajo más allá de la academia. De esta manera, las decisiones sobre las preguntas de investigación, los marcos teóricos y las interpretaciones se vuelven más claras. Utilizando las tradiciones de investigación sobre la lengua afroamericana (AAL) como estudio de caso, la autora aurgumenta que los investigadores lingüísticos deben practicar una ética de transparencia sobre los objetivos políticos de sus investigaciones. Así podemos progresar en el campo de manera que rompa los marcos coloniales de poder.

Key Words: liberatory linguistics, political transparency, Black language, community of practice, Black feminist praxis

5

Apolitical Linguistics Doesn't Exist, and It Shouldn't

Developing a Black Feminist Praxis Toward Political Transparency

Aris Moreno Clemons (she/her)
University of Tennessee Knoxville

Introduction

> Rule 4: Forget about the spelling, let the syntax carry you
>
> —**Jordan (1988, p. 175)**

Recent work has established scientific objectivity as a myth, both broadly (Bourke, 2014; Parsons, 2008), and in language research specifically (Lin, 2015; McCarty, 2018). Nevertheless, linguistics departments, journals, and associations are still largely impacted by an ideology of scientific objectivism and structuralism (Charity Hudley et. al., 2023). The overreliance on that which is deemed empirical is largely upheld by political motivations of those who occupy positions of power within the academic organizations that guide us (Charity Hudley et al., 2020). A continued reliance on positivist modes of research insists on defining the objective, which ultimately upholds colonial formations of power (Flores & Rosa, 2015; Kubota, 2012; Reagan, 2004) and suggests that scientific linguistics can exist in some sort of value-neutral state. Within these colonial frames of power, the production and proliferation of linguistic scholarship is intimately tied to economic modes of production. In other words, linguistic scholarship has been bound to the ways that academic endeavors produce capital for the ruling classes (e.g., federal grants that provide revenue for institutions, the recruitment of graduate labor pools that drive undergraduate education and the dollars it pours in, the production of knowledge that fuel several publishing industries, and more) (see Hutton, 2020 for review). Historically, the economics of linguistics has resulted in

---

Aris Moreno Clemons, *Apolitical Linguistics Doesn't Exist, and It Shouldn't* In: *Decolonizing Linguistics*. Edited by:
Anne H. Charity Hudley, Christine Mallinson, and Mary Bucholtz, Oxford University Press.
© Anne H. Charity Hudley, Christine Mallinson, and Mary Bucholtz 2024. DOI: 10.1093/oso/9780197755259.003.0006

the privileging of certain voices over others, often with the most divisive characters gaining cult figure status (see Dockum & Green, 2024, for a review of the dangers of Great Man narratives in linguistics). I contend that we must investigate how definitions of linguistics require us to answer the questions of whether linguistics exists solely as an academic endeavor or whether it can be used to push society toward a more equitable and socially just future. To wit, what responsibility do we as linguists have to our communities, to the communities that we investigate, and to society at large? Following the examples laid out for justice-oriented research in fields such as education and sociology (Charity Hudley et. Al, 2020), I suggest that linguistics can be central in informing liberatory praxis (hooks, 1991; Wilson et al., 2019). I am particularly interested in defining how liberatory, that is, decolonial, linguistic praxis as a key intervention in linguistic research can be organized by using a Black feminist praxis of political transparency.

Despite assertions of linguistics as an empirical rather than value-based enterprise (Joseph and Taylor, 2014; Newmeyer, 1986), no research is devoid of political and social motivation (i.e., no work is value-neutral) (Boveda & Bhattacharya, 2019; Hassanpour 2000). As such, I suggest that scholars can and must develop research practices of political transparency. Political transparency insists that all investigators be explicit in defining the motivations and orientations toward their research questions, methodological approaches, theoretical frames, and ultimately the interpretations at which they arrive. Linguists can and must conduct research aimed toward more equitable and just understandings of language communities and society at large. This claim underscores the historical ways in which scientific objectivism has been used to uphold systems of white supremacy, such as the "science" of eugenics, as critiqued by scholars such as Steven Selden (2000) and Marius Turda and Paul J. Weindling (2007); IQ tests where race is an intervening factor, as critiqued by Noam Chomsky (1972) and Subira Kifano & Ernie A. Smith (2005); and recently the ever-growing attention to medical scales that negatively impact health outcomes of women of color (Vyas et al., 2021). The damage caused by the inability of science to grapple with the fact that it can never be free from ideology, and thus with its inability to be objective, makes clear the need for a concerted focus on social justice and anti-racism in any scientific endeavor. Moreover, drawing primarily on Black feminist theory (Hill Collins, 2000), a praxis of political transparency in social science research provides space for individuals and communities to determine their own humanity with dignity (Alagraa, 2018; McKittrick, 2006; 2015). A central element in this required self-determination is the ability to define, describe, and perform one's own language practices. Therefore, linguists need to critically engage speech communities, especially those of minoritized or marginalized language varieties, as political practice. Ana Celia Zentella encapsulates the inextricable link between language studies and politics when she notes, "there can be no language without politics" (Zentella, 2018, p. 191). Drawing from this assertion, I define politics as the set of ideas that come together to formulate strategies for the formation of a particular ideology, policy, or social structure. Therefore, a model of political transparency in linguistics demands that researchers contend with their own social ideologies as they map onto investigations of language practices. Additionally, political transparency calls on researchers to be explicit in naming the social motivations for conducting one's research, to embrace the subjective nature of language-based research, and to ensure the work is accessible to the community under investigations along with the communities who would most benefit from thorough analyses of said language practices.

In establishing an approach of political transparency as linguistic justice, I evoke Boveda and Bhattacharya's (2019) call for an "orientation of love that centers the agencies of those who have been forgotten, silenced, erased and/or minimized" (p. 8). In their call for "love" as an onto-epistemological shift in approaches toward de/coloniality in urban education, the authors center their mothers' exigent love to provide a model for navigating the complexity and contradiction within social research. In doing so, they are able to provide a love-based model for urban education research that both centers the humanity of the research subjectivities while demanding accountability to the communities that will be most impacted by the production of the work. In this vein, and noting the complexity and contradictory nature of language studies as social science, I propose this chapter as an intervention in the theorization of political transparency as Black feminist praxis. The aim of this chapter is to highlight the ways that political transparency impacts the production of linguistic scholarship. Specifically, I review the ways in which political transparency has been enacted as Black feminist praxis and provide several provocations toward a transparency-based approach. The following examples focus primarily on Black women who have built a model of sociopolitical transparency in their research praxis. The scholars position themselves as crucial to the investigation and the analysis, blurring the lines between researcher and research community, while also locating the speaking community under investigation as the intended audience. Their work represents a shift in creating knowledge primarily for the benefit of the academe, as well as a shift in presenting knowledge for knowledge-sake. In centering their work alongside my own, I note key moves toward political transparency as part and parcel of a Black feminist praxis.

104   Decolonizing Linguistics

As suggested by the title of this volume, language scholars and social scientists in general are more frequently challenging the colonial frames of power upon which many academic fields were built in Western societies; in short, to decolonize the field. These calls are not new, but rather represent the traditions of academic activism generated primarily by scholars from marginalized groups around the globe (Mufwene, 2020). Additionally, recent scholarship on language and race maintains that much of our global societies function on a system of white supremacy (Smalls et al., 2021), which can be evidenced by the many rules and regulations that govern these societies and that create racial hierarchies (Clemons, 2021). In attending to this call to decolonize the field, Mufwene (2020) offers a definition, stating that "decolonial linguistics simply entails reducing the Western bias and hegemony in how languages of the Global South and the (socio)linguistic behaviors of their speakers and writers are analyzed" (p. 288). In order to reduce this "Western bias and hegemony," I argue that one must be explicit in their decolonial motivations. Herein, and drawing on arguments that competing definitions of linguistic terms and the ideologies behind them also shape the field (cf. Bancu, Peltier, et al., this volume), I offer the current commentary and provocations toward political transparency in linguistics. In doing so, I suggest that political transparency can shape the field in ways that extend beyond interpretations of linguistic data to the epistemology of linguistics. More specifically, I ask how being transparent about the relationships you have with the linguistic communities that shape your investigations can impact research questions, adoption of theoretical frames, and methodological incursions into subsequent data interpretation. Further, I ask how stating your subject, research, and political positionality disambiguate the conceptual frameworks from which you present your analyses. Lastly, I argue that we must seriously consider who our analyses are for. What audiences are meant to benefit from our work? Who is considered data and who is considered consumer?

These questions have recently been deeply engaged in Black sociolinguistics, with scholars such as Geneva Smitherman (2022) and John Rickford (2022) providing detailed insight into their lives and relationships with language. The linguistic autobiography, described in an open-source course developed by creolist scholar Michel DeGraff (MIT Open Learning, 2021–2023), and taken up in projects such as *Understanding English Language Variation in US Classrooms* (Charity Hudley & Mallinson, 2011), *Talking College: Making Space for Black Language Practices* (Charity Hudley et al., 2022), and the National Science Foundation Build and Broaden Grant that helped support work published in these volumes (see Preface, both volumes; Charity Hudley et al., this volume), provide a template for the ways that we should engage our own linguistic histories and ideologies when approaching linguistic scholarship. What is clear from these projects is that scholarship on and about language is deeply personal, whether the project is about your own language or a differing community, though the relationship described will differ in the former versus the latter case.

Black Language Studies as a Model for Political Transparency

For many scholars, the option to produce "neutral" or apolitical work simply does not exist. In an oft-cited quote, Toni Morrison wisely explains:

> The function, the very serious function of racism is distraction. It keeps you from doing your work. It keeps you explaining, over and over again, your reason for being. Somebody says you have no language, and you spend twenty years proving that you do. Somebody says your head isn't shaped properly so you have scientists working on the fact that it is. Somebody says you have no art, so you dredge that up. Somebody says you have no kingdoms, so you dredge that up. None of this is necessary. There will always be one more thing. (Morrison, 1975)

Since the 1970s, in the midst (or aftermath) of Black liberation and power movements, Black linguists worked to define and exemplify the structural validity of Black English as a dialectal variety of English (Baugh, 1979; Hoover, 1990; King, 2020; Mufwene et al., 2021; Rickford 1999; Spears, 1992). Of importance is the way that many of the earliest scholars of linguistic variation (e.g., Labov and Wolfram) have made field-defining impacts through their exploration of Black language often in relation to educational outcomes (King, 2020). Nonetheless, the work of Black linguists, who often suffer critiques of subjectivity and lack of methodological rigor (see Charity Hudley et al, this volume), have been vocal in expressing their work as a response to the erasure of Black language practices as valid forms of communication in educational spaces as well as the stigmatization of these forms in popular ideology (see Rosa, 2016 for a definition of ideologies of languagelessness). The explicit contestation of marginalizing ideologies surrounding Black language is evidence of a praxis of political transparency in these studies. Additionally, Black linguists used historical, syntactic, phonological, and lexical approaches toward the description of several varieties of Black English(es) across the United States (Bailey et al., 2013; Lanehart, 2015). And while these literatures have significantly impacted the ways that linguists understand language,

106 Decolonizing Linguistics

stigmatizing ideologies surrounding Black language use by Black language users persist. Due to the constant derogation of Black language users, Black scholars have consistently reminded us that Black culture, histories, and bodies cannot be separated from their language practices (Anya, 2016; Jordan, 1973; Smitherman, 1973a). It is not an understatement to say that Black linguists have been at the forefront of proposing and adapting disciplinary and interdisciplinary research models and pedagogies that require political transparency. Community-based and participatory research methods (CBPR) as applied to linguistic research is one example. Described as a research practice of ensuring the target research community is part of every aspect of the research process, CBPR suggests the co-construction of methodology and research practices alongside community members, the stating of researcher subject positionality and relationship to the community and ensuring that research participants are actively engaged in the entirety of your project (for examples relevant to linguistics, see Charity Hudley & Mallinson, 2017; Charity Hudley et al., , 2022; Czaykowska-Higgins, 2009; Leonard & Haynes, 2010).

Additionally, much of Black linguistics is characterized by the desire for self-discovery, spurred by the impulse to contest deficiency frames, which situate our natural language practices as deviant and substandard parts of an educated and appropriate whole. Several scholarly productions on Black language have evidenced a liberatory praxis toward defining, analyzing, and evidencing Black language across the globe. This is particularly true in educational contexts, where as early as 1933, education scholar Carter G. Woodson (1933/2006) noted that "the 'educated Negroes' have the attitude of contempt toward their own people because in their own as well as in their mixed schools Negroes are taught to admire the Hebrew, the Greek, the Latin and the Teuton and to despise the African" (p. 5). What Woodson is underscoring in this quote is that Black language users are often socialized into the belief that their own language practices are unworthy, and thus being "educated" means a divorcing of self from home language practices. April Baker Bell, a Black language and education scholar, provides a powerful description of how and where these socializations occur for Black children in US educational spaces in the contemporary moment. Specifically, she understands these experiences as part and parcel of Anti-Black linguistic racism, which she defines as:

> the linguistic violence, persecution, dehumanization, and marginalization that Black Language (BL) speakers endure when using their language in schools and in everyday life. It includes teachers' silencing, correcting, and policing students when they communicate in BL. It is the belief that there is something inherently

wrong with BL; therefore, it should be eradicated. It is denying Black students the right to use their native language as a linguistic resource during their language and literacy learning. It is requiring that Black students reject their language and culture to acquire White Mainstream English (WME), and it is also insisting that Black students code-switch to avoid discrimination. (Baker-Bell 2020, p. 9)

This popular understanding of Black language as obscure, obscene, unstructured, and unworthy of academic instruction has not only been the lived and understood experience of Black language users (Charity Hudley et al., 2022), but has also resulted in a tradition of Black language scholarship that calls upon positionality and political transparency as a source of analytic rigor. In 1998 Arthur K Spears provided an example of this practice in his essay on Black language use and ideologies:

I have tried to be objective, but it goes without saying that it is possible that some biases based on my own position and personal history in society have inadvertently influenced my discussions. I should also point out that well over a hundred people, students and others, the great majority of whom are African Americans who are culturally African American, have read and discussed with me various versions of this paper, and that it currently incorporates information they have given me. (Spears, 1998, p. 1)

In this example, Spears notes his consultation with "African Americans who are culturally African American," underlining the importance of not only their ascribed identities but also their cultural identity.[1] Spears, in noting his attempt at objectivity, both recognizes the desires of his field while affirming its impossibility.

Black Feminist Praxis of Political Transparency: Ensuring Accessibility to Audiences Beyond the Academy

Much in the way that current media representations of Black English are formulated as "youth speak" or "internet language" (Bucholtz, 2002; Reyes, 2005; Smalls, 2018), the study of Black language in abstraction from its communities becomes an exercise in appropriation for fame, notoriety, and success in academe. I use this example because it has been made patently clear that the structure of Black English cannot be divorced from Black experience of surviving constant threats of "annihilation" (Jordan, 1988); and thus, there can be no study of Black language without attendance to Black sociohistoric locations within their respective societies, just as there can be no study of Black people without the study of their language. Poet and literary scholar June Jordan tells us that "syntax, the structure of an idea, leads you to the worldview of a speaker and reveals her values. The syntax of a sentence equals the structure of your consciousness" (p. 175). In the essay, Jordan expertly weaves the communal construction of a Black English Grammar with the story of a Black boy, who, in suffering an incomprehensible loss, represents Black personhood in all of its complexities. In doing so, Jordan finds the human in the language, exemplifying the ways in which Black English is person-centered. A person-centered emphasis often runs counter to the ways that we conduct linguistic research, at least since the Chompskian traditions of Universal Grammar that deny the need for empirical data (Charity Hudley et al., 2023). Therefore, if scientific, generative, positivist linguistics requires us to abstract language from the community of users, but the language privileges and is only logical through its connection with the person, the subject, "anybody alive" (Jordan, 1988, p. 175) in that idea, then an abstracted language study cannot be valid. Subjectivity, which is generally seen as the antithesis of objectivity required for scientific research, thus becomes a necessary aspect of language study, particularly for marginalized communities. This subjectivity is central to Black feminist praxis, which calls us to draw the most marginalized to the center; in doing so provides the basis for liberatory frameworks for all (hooks, 1984).

Literacy scholar Jacqueline Jones Royster exemplifies this in her article "When the First Voice You Hear is Not Your Own." She states, "this essay emerged from my desire to examine closely moments of personal challenge that seem to have import for cross boundary discourse" (Royster, 1996, p. 29). She then notes that "subjectivity as a defining value pays attention dynamically to context, ways of knowing, language abilities, and experiences, and by doing so it has a consequent potential to deepen, broaden, and enrich our interpretive views in dynamic ways as well" (p. 29). Anti-Black linguistic racism has required Black language scholars to develop and deepen their subject positionalities in defense of their work. This apparent contradiction to scientific objectivism has allowed these scholars to move beyond colonial frames of power, which have deemed both their research and their language unacceptable.

Beyond moments where Black women have called on their own experiences to justify their work, there are instances when Black language itself is used within these investigations. In addition to June Jordan and other Black language scholars, one scholar who is particularly apt in this endeavor is Geneva Smitherman, who consistently incorporates Black English into her scholarship, effectively demonstrating the ways that "the syntax of a sentence equals the structure of your consciousness" (Jordan, 1988). In her article "White English in Blackface, or Who Do I Be?" Smitherman (1973b, p. 32) uses Black English throughout, providing an obvious counter to the notion that academic or educated English is standard white English.

> Ain nothin in a long time lit up the English teaching profession like the current hassle over Black English. One finds beaucoup sociolinguistics research studies and language projects for the "disadvantaged" on the scene in nearly every sizable black community in the country. And educators from K-Grad School bees debating whether: (1) blacks should learn and use only standard white English (hereafter referred to as WE); (2) blacks should command both dialects, i.e., be bidialectal (hereafter BD); (3) blacks should be allowed (??????) to use standard Black English (hereafter BE or BI).

In the quote above, we see Smitherman's expert use of Black English alongside the debates as structured by previous academic arguments provided in her enumeration of questions about what could be described as standard white English. In breaking the conventions of "standard English," not only in her use of Black English but also in writing conventions —six parenthetical question marks to indicate her stance toward the third assertion—Smitherman evidences the ridiculousness of convention, that is, white standard English, to make clear her arguments. In laying out these questions Smitherman may have captured it best when she goes on to say, "the appropriate choice having everything to do with American political reality, which is usually ignored, and nothing to do with the educational process, which is usually claimed" (Smitherman, 1973b, p. 828). The choice she is referring to is not only regarding selecting one of the above options in the debate regarding Black students and language education, but also in her own choice and the choice of all language researchers to take up their home language practices in the production of academic scholarship. In her recent memoir Smitherman makes clear the politics in these choices, naming her motivations (and role in) working through what she called the language wars, where she served on juries, fought for educational rights for African Americans, and maintained a commitment to Black liberation spurred on by the 1960s Black power movements (Smitherman, 2022).

Responding directly to Saussure's (1916) call for language study to be of some concern or another to everybody, we must ensure that we are producing scholarship that in whatever ways possible is accessible to as many people as possible, but most importantly to the people who would benefit from a shift in logics about their own language practices toward liberation. Much like stating your position in relation to your population is a matter of ethics, your citation practices provide insight into what and whose knowledges are valued. I note here the work of many scholars to bring recognition to a population of scholars working within their own communities with little to no recognition in the form of scholarly citations. To counter these patterns, movements such as #CiteBlackWomen were initiated to point out the value of knowledge produced by members of historically marginalized populations.

(a) What is my relationship with language related fields such as education, speech language sciences, rhetoric and communications, and other disciplines? Who am I citing and why?
(b) Why is interdisciplinarity selectively de-intellectualized and thus devalued and how can I break from this pattern?
(c) How can I ensure that I have published across a wide range of formats to disseminate my research?

As an example of a political praxis of accessibility, I go back to June Jordan's (1988) essay. In it, she describes the ways that her students of Black English (all native speakers) struggle with the decision to send a letter to a local newspaper about the killing of their classmate's brother by the police. The students were set on sending the letter but could not decide whether it should be sent in white American English or in Black American English. "But if we sought to express ourselves by abandoning our language wouldn't that mean our suicide on top of Reggie's murder" (Jordan 1988, p. 178)? In the end, the students decided that maintaining their dialect was not only possible, but necessary. They applied what they had learned in their class to a situation that would have deep intellectual and personal impact. I wish to note that many members of the communities that garner attention from linguistic scholars have already formed strong ideologies about their own language, its value and position within particular societies, and its usefulness for advancement in that society. Many are intimately connected to understandings of linguistic discrimination (Thomas, 2024) and thus are able to situate and set powerful research agendas toward linguistic justice. This example shows that accessibility goes beyond the ability to widely disseminate one's research, but also involves the language, genre, style, and format of the text. In this case, the decision to use a particular variety of language is a political act, telling us who the audience is and how important they are to the work itself.

Moving from these paradigms allows scholars to push beyond ideologies of deficiency, oppression, or subjugation and into the most beautifully human parts of language production within a community of language users. In addition to these practices, we need to think about how we are defining linguistics for the next generation of linguists. In other words, are we educating a generation of linguists who are prepared to make the world a more equitable place for all? In the following section, I provide an example of how a model of political transparency has impacted the development and interpretation of language data in one of my own projects. By analyzing the formation of this project alongside practices of self and community identification, we can more fully understand my interpretations of the data collected.

Political Transparency as Linguistic Praxis: Dominican Spanish as Black Language Practice

Political transparency has guided the way that I approach my own linguistic investigations. In a recent study on Dominican language practices, my aim was to introduce a methodological incursion for investigating constructions of *Dominicanidad* and more importantly for investigating the reconstruction, and possible expansion, of Blackness and Latinidad as they are currently conceived in the United States. Before I describe the study, I follow Black feminist practices of naming my subject positionality and my relationship with the populations under investigation. As a child I was sent to an African Montessori school where instruction happened in English, French, and Swahili, and I was raised around a Black Diaspora consisting of African Americans, West Indians, and recent African Migrants. These coalitions around which I was formed grounded me in both a passion for language diversity and for Black liberatory struggles. At 19, I decided to continue my undergraduate studies in Spain after having become conversational in Spanish during a three-month study abroad trip a few years prior. While there, I was frequently re-ethnicized as a Dominican since it was very clear to many that I was neither sub-Saharan African nor American in what had been imagined as a United Statesian. When people saw me, they saw a Black Latina. I was mostly ethnicized as a Dominican but sometimes I got an *oye cubana* thrown at me. In any case, as I began interacting more and more with Dominicans, I began to notice the cultural similarities between Dominican cultural practices and those of my West Indian family. Growing up in a diasporic enclave where heritage from any of the West Indian islands made you automatic family, I begin to question the separation between what amounted to Anglo, Dutch, and French Caribbean from the Spanish Caribbean. What language and racial ideologies allow for this separation? These questions have driven much of my research,

112 Decolonizing Linguistics

and, of course, now that I am armed with historical knowledge, my goal is to demystify the separation.

To contend with the shift in ideological constructions of Blackness in the United States, I first focused on recognizing both the commonalities and differences between race constructions across the Americas. While the US was formed under a racial dichotomy of Black and white, the Dominican Republic relied on ideologies of *mestizaje* or *mulatez*, which allow for tripartite conceptualization of race as Black, white, and mixed. Drawing on my own experiences of ethno-racial ambiguity and attending to the formation of Blackness across the Americas, the question became, what racial scripts are people taking up as they engage in digital literacy practices? In other words, who gets to be Black in the United States? Moving toward this question, I investigated public stances toward Blackness as an identity category for Dominican (Americans), a group with a representative population of individuals who would be marked and identified as Black in the United States, regardless of how they themselves might identify. I wish to note here that the question itself stemmed from my own interactions with Dominicans and African Americans who often found themselves on opposite ends of arguments about what it meant to exist within the ethnoracial category of Black. As such, my motivations for the study were rooted in a desire to complicate and disambiguate the often-oppositional arguments for boundaries of difference between African Americans and Dominicans that were presented in these disagreements (Clemons, 2020). I argued that through an investigation of Dominican digital literacy practices alongside African American linguistic and cultural productions, we could come to appreciate the basis for the formulation of "new Blackness," one that expands our notions of diaspora, race, and Black language in the Americas.

Approaching my study on Dominican language as Black language practice required me to draw on a variety of theoretical frames from fields which contend with linguistic and racial formation: anthropology, sociolinguistics, and ethnic studies. I was able to employ these theories based on the driving motivation for Black scholars, including myself, to read beyond their own fields in an effort to find their own humanity in theory—again recalling Black feminist praxis of self-determination. The result of extensive reading was the creation of a fairly complex theoretical framework based on an understanding of what has been defined in sociolinguistic research as a "community of practice." Penny Eckert and Sally McConnell-Ginet describe a community of practice as

> an aggregate of people who come together around mutual engagement in an endeavor. Ways of doing things, ways of talking, beliefs, values, power relations—in

> short, practices—emerge in the course of this mutual endeavor. As a social con-
> struct, a Community of Practice is different from the traditional community, prima-
> rily because it is defined simultaneously by its membership and by the practice in
> which that membership engages. (Eckert & McConnell-Ginet, 1992, p. 464)

I then asserted that to understand a Black American Community of Practice beyond the boundaries of nation-state and through an investigation of language, we must engage three theoretical frames: raciolinguistic ideologies, stance-taking, and Black self-determination.

In her work on the system of Black vocabulary, Geneva Smitherman notes a difference between African Americans and other Afro-Diasporic beings in that in general the latter are not minorities in their own countries (Smitherman, 1991). These comments, however, drew on understandings of Anglo-speaking Black Diasporic beings, such as Jamaicans, Bajans, and Ghanains. I argued that by looking at practices of Black subjects across national as well as linguistic bounds, we find parallel lexical processes that evidence a shared experience of Blackness. This experience marks both Dominicans and African Americans as part of a singular community of practice, bounded by Black language processes. Drawing on research in African American English, I used the study to draw parallels between African American and Dominican Language practices through what I called Black Language Processes. Specifically, for the purposes of this study, I focused on Black lexical processes, that is, the ways that Black language users create meaning in their use and mobilization of vocabulary. Data was drawn from Dominican youth's digital practices across three social media platforms (Twitter, Instagram, and Facebook) and included three types of artifacts: memes, tweets, and Instagram posts. From this corpus, I was able to perform an analysis of Dominican Spanish as a Black language practice by finding parallels with five African American English lexicalization processes: (1) semantic inversions; (2) phonological evolutions; (3) innovative abbreviations (acronyms); (4) double-voicing; (5) Black naming practices. Each of these processes was evidenced in several digital artifacts collected over a seven-month period. Though the scope of this chapter does not allow for the exposition of the practices explored, the above examples suggested consistency in Black lexical practices that affirmed the positing of "new Blackness" (Clemons, 2020).

Most importantly, I used this study to interrogate the ways that Dominican youth viewed their own linguistic practices on and offline. I drew from previous literature conducted by Black Dominican scholar Almeida Jacqueline Toribio (2000a; 2000b; 2003), considering the linguistic structures of Dominican Spanish within sociohistoric and political contexts of the Dominican dialect

114　Decolonizing Linguistics

while underscoring the consequences of racial discrimination on the production of Dominican Spanish by white versus Black Dominicans. In using this work, I consulted frequently with former high school students who I had developed relationships with as a teacher, mentor, and community member. As we went through the memes students would laugh, often explaining meanings that helped me further make connections between Dominican and African American cultural practices. I invited these students to attend my talks about Dominican language as Black language practice in both English and Spanish and often shared video recordings with them. We were also able to have several conversations about the validity of the linguistic forms that were displayed in the internet artifacts, debating the existence of proper language (i.e., standard language ideologies) in Spanish as well as English. By the end of our time together, several students noted that they did speak in English in nearly the same way as their African American counterparts, but that because they had Spanish to distinguish themselves, they didn't realize that they could be part of the same language community.

Calling attention to practices that are widespread in Dominican Spanish in relation to the practices mirrored in African American English is an example of linguistic justice. Namely, the research itself is an action that redresses linguistic racism since Dominican Spanish and African American English often suffer from stigmatizations in the wider US and Latin American schemas, resulting in erasure from larger academic curricula (cf. Arnold, this volume). With that, I offer some redirections to questions that are frequent when speaking about Blackness in Dominican (and often all over America) contexts. Firstly, how can I claim that Dominican Spanish is a Black language practice, even if people of all races (and social stratifications) use it in their daily lives? The answer becomes simple: if we remove the ideology that culture, with a big C, is created and maintained by the hegemonic, which is grounded in white supremacist understandings of hemispheric American society, then we can position these practices in relation to the Afro-historical contexts that shape every facet of hemispheric American life. Moreover, in the first majority Black republic in the Americas, it is not in the least surprising that Black language practices are the dominant (if not hegemonic) language practices. Ultimately, my aim was to provide foundations for the development of new language to contend with the linguistic complexities of racial logics. That is, instead of focusing on how we survive colonial systems of power, I seek to understand how we transform those systems by refusing to engage within the frames that have been laid out for us.

Conclusion

In positing Blackness as a central fact, as a mode of being, I followed the tradition of many Black feminists drawing the margins of the margins into the center (Hill Collins, 2000; hooks, 1984). I ask: What systems are built to eradicate Black language practices? And what systems are built to edify them? In what ways are anti-Black ideologies institutionalized in these efforts? And how do we continue to push against these systems across a range of activities, institutions, and cross-ethnic solidarities? Further, I look to communities to understand the ways that activism, linguistic and otherwise, can disrupt the racial hierarchies that have dominated social institutions across the Americas since colonial times. I question the ways in which language allows for the commodification of Blackness, while continuing to relegate Black language users to the margins. Finally, with a push toward justice, I evidenced one way that linguistic research can be primary in our understanding of race and ethnicity, expanding the scope of what has traditionally constituted linguistic research, while at the same time pushing up against the notion that we can deconstruct racial logics within a singular disciplinary field.

The current chapter makes the case that scientific objectivity itself, and the idealization of it, is an ideology that privileges certain politics. Ignoring the social background and context of a language community, and the researchers who study them, is a political act. It is clear that there is no investigation of language or society that is free from ideology. As such, a reconstitution of linguistic research that requires investigators to posit their political motivations, subject positionalities, and sociohistoric understandings of language communities is past due (cf. Fuller Medina, this volume). Liberatory linguistics is not new. Scholars such as Ignacio Montoya (this volume), Jon Henner (2024), and Julie Hochgesang (in Fisher et al., 2021) have dedicated themselves to liberatory frames in their work on Indigenous languages, Crip linguistics, and Deaf linguistics, respectively. In the end, we must be creative and transparent in our endeavors to combat anti-Black racism as a social structure that impacts every facet of life, including but not limited to those that impact our understanding of language. Stated plainly, I ask what we can learn from reading Black women who were explicit in who they were, why they were doing their work, and who they were doing their work for. Black feminist political transparency removes the mental gymnastics that must be done to assert social science as value-neutral, providing space to take in the arguments, analyses, and interpretations more honestly so that those who have been stripped of

116 Decolonizing Linguistics

knowledges, access to, and pride in their own linguistic varieties. I'll end with a quote from Black feminist creative writer Octavia Butler that elucidates the need for iterative political transparency in research practices. She says, "all that you touch, you change. All that you change changes you. The only lasting truth is change" (Butler, 1993, p. 3). It is my belief that as researchers we can collectively shape and change the world in change.

Note

1. I note here that racial ascription relies on the full range of signifiers including physical appearance, national origin, language and culture practices, etc. Additionally, I note that these ascriptions and mutable and contextual.

References

Alagraa, Bedour. (2018). Homo narrans and the science of the word: Toward a Caribbean radical imagination. *Critical Ethnic Studies*, *4*(2), 164–181.

Anya, Uju. (2016). *Racialized identities in second language learning: Speaking Blackness in Brazil*. Routledge.

Bailey, Guy, Baugh, John, Mufwene, Salikoko S., & Rickford John R. (Eds.). (2013). *African-American English: Structure, history and use*. Routledge.

Baker-Bell, April. (2020). Dismantling anti-Black linguistic racism in English language arts classrooms: Toward an anti-racist Black language pedagogy. *Theory into Practice*, *59*(1), 8–21.

Baugh Jr., John G. (1979). *Linguistic style-shifting in Black English*. University of Pennsylvania.

Bourke, Brian. (2014). Positionality: Reflecting on the research process. *Qualitative Report*, *19*(33), 1-9.

Boveda, Mildred, & Bhattacharya, Kakali. (2019). Love as de/colonial onto-epistemology: A post-oppositional approach to contextualized research ethics. *The Urban Review*, *51*(1), 5–25.

Bucholtz, Mary. (2002). Youth and cultural practice. *Annual Review of Anthropology*, *31*(1), 525–552.

Butler, Octavia. (1993). *Parable of the sower*. Grand Central.

Charity Hudley, Anne H., & Mallinson, Christine (2017) "It's worth our time": A model of culturally and linguistically supportive professional development for K-12 STEM educators. *Cultural Studies of Science Education*, 12, 637-660.

Charity Hudley, Anne H., Clemons, Aris M., & Villarreal, Dan. (2023). Language across the disciplines. *Annual Review of Linguistics 9*, 253–272.

Charity Hudley, Anne H., & Flores, Nelson. (2022). Social justice in applied linguistics: Not a conclusion, but a way forward. *Annual Review of Applied Linguistics*, *42*, 144–154.

Charity Hudley, Anne H., Mallinson, Christine, & Bucholtz, Mary. (2020). Toward racial justice in linguistics: Interdisciplinary insights into theorizing race in the discipline and diversifying the profession. *Language*, *96*(4), e200–e235.

Charity Hudley, Anne H., Mallinson, Christine, & Bucholtz, Mary. (2022). *Talking college: Making space for Black language practices in higher education*. Teachers College Press.

Charity Hudley, Anne H. & Mallinson, Christine. (2011). Understanding English language variation in U.S. schools. Teachers College Press.

Chomsky, Noam. (1972). IQ tests: Building blocks for the new class system. *Ramparts*, *11*(2), 24–30.

Clemons, Aris M. (2020). New Blacks: language, DNA, and the construction of the African American/Dominican boundary of difference. *Genealogy*, *5*(1), 1.

Clemons, Aris M. (2021). *Spanish people be like: Dominican ethno-raciolinguistic stancetaking and the construction of Black Latinidades in the United States* [Doctoral dissertation, University of Texas at Austin].

Czaykowska-Higgins, Ewa. (2009). Research models, community engagement, and linguistic fieldwork: Reflections on working within Canadian Indigenous communities. *Language Documentation & Conservation*, *3*(1), 182–215

De Saussure, Ferdinand. (1916). *Course in General Linguistics*. Columbia University Press.

Dockum, Rikker, & Green, Caitlin M. (2024). Toward a big tent linguistics: Inclusion and the myth of the lone genius. In Anne H. Charity Hudley, Christine Mallinson, & Mary Bucholtz (Eds.), *Inclusion in linguistics*. Oxford University Press.

Eckert, Penelope, & McConnell-Ginet, Sally. (1992). Think practically and look locally: Language and gender as community-based practice. *Annual Review of Anthropology*, *21*(1), 461–488.

Flores, Nelson, & Rosa, Jonathan. (2015). Undoing appropriateness: Raciolinguistic ideologies and language diversity in education. *Harvard Educational Review*, *85*(2), 149–171.

Fisher, Jami N., Hochgesang, Julie A., Tamminga, Meredith, & Miller, Robyn. (2021). Uncovering the lived experiences of elderly Deaf Philadelphians. In R. Pfau, A. Göksel & J. Hosemann (Eds.), *Our lives—our stories: Life experiences of elderly Deaf people* (pp. 277–232). DeGruyter Mouton.

Hassanpour, Amir. (2000). The politics of a-political linguistics: Linguists and linguicide. In Robert Phillipson (Ed.). *Rights to language: Equity, power, and education* (pp. 33–40). Routledge.

Henner, Jon. (2024). How to train your abled linguist: A crip linguistics perspective on pragmatic research. In Anne H. Charity Hudley, Christine Mallinson, & Mary Bucholtz (Eds.), *Inclusion in linguistics*. Oxford University Press.

Hill Collins, Patricia. (2000). *Black feminist thought: Knowledge, consciousness, and the politics of empowerment*, 2nd edition. Routledge.

hooks, bell. (1984). *Feminist theory: From margin to center*. South End Press.

hooks, bell. (1991). Theory as liberatory practice. *Yale Journal of Law & Feminism*, *4*(1): 59–75.

Hoover, Mary R. (1990). A vindicationist perspective on the role of Ebonics (Black language) and other aspects of ethnic studies in the university. *American Behavioral Scientist*, *34*(2), 251–262.

Hutton, Christopher. (2020). Linguistics and the state: How funding and politics shape a field. *International Journal of the Sociology of Language*, *263*, 31–36.

Jordan, June. (1973). Black English; the Politics of Translation. *School Library Journal*.

Jordan, June. (1988). Nobody mean more to me than you and the future life of Willie Jordan. *Harvard Educational Review*, *58*(3), 363–375.

Joseph, John E., & Taylor, Talbot J. (Eds.). (2014). *Ideologies of language (RLE linguistics A: General linguistics)*. Routledge.

Kifano, Subira, & Smith, Ernie A. (2005). Ebonics and education in the context of culture: Meeting the language and cultural needs of English learning African American students. In David J. Ramirez et al. (Ed). *Ebonics: The Urban Educational Debate* (pp. 62–95). Multilingual Matters.

King, Sharese. (2020). From African American Vernacular English to African American Language: Rethinking the study of race and language in African Americans' speech. *Annual Review of Linguistics*, 6, 285–300.

Kubota, Ryuko. (2012). Critical approaches to intercultural discourse and communication. In Paulston et al. (Eds.). *The handbook of intercultural discourse and communication* (pp. 90–109). Wiley.

Lanehart, Sanja. (Ed.). (2015). *The Oxford handbook of African American language*. Oxford University Press.

Leonard, Wesley Y., & Haynes, Erin. (2010). Making "collaboration" collaborative: An examination of perspectives that frame linguistic field research. *Language Documentation & Conservation*, 4, 269–293.

Lin, Angel M. (2015). Researcher positionality. *Research methods in language policy and planning: A practical guide*, 21–32.

Lipski, John M. (1993). *On the non-Creole basis for Afro-Caribbean Spanish*. https://digitalrepository.unm.edu/laii_research/18

Lipski, John M. (2018). Languages in contact: Pidginization and creolization, Spanish in the Caribbean. In Mendéz (Ed.). *Biculturalism and Spanish in contact* (pp. 95–118). Routledge.

McCarty, Teresa L. (2018). Comparing "new speakerhood": Context, positionality, and power in the new sociolinguistic order. *Journal of Multilingual and Multicultural Development*, 39(5), 470–474.

McKittrick, Katherine. (2006). *Demonic grounds: Black women and the cartographies of struggle*. University of Minnesota Press.

McKittrick, Katherine. (Ed.). (2015). *Sylvia Wynter: On being human as praxis*. Duke University Press.

MIT Open Learning (2021–2023). Creole languages and Caribbean identities. https://ocw.mit.edu/courses/24-908-creole-languages-and-caribbean-identities-spring-2017/pages/assignments/

Morrison, Toni. (1975). Black Studies Center public dialogue. Portland State Public Lecture. May 30, 1975. Portland State Library Special Collections.

Mufwene, Salikoko S. (2020). Decolonial linguistics as paradigm shift: A commentary. In Deumert (Ed.). *Colonial and decolonial linguistics* (pp. 289–300). Oxford University Press.

Mufwene, Salikoko S., Rickford, John R., Bailey, Guy, & Baugh, John. (Eds.). (2021). *African-American English: Structure, history, and use*. Routledge.

Neymeyer, Frederick. (1986). *The politics of linguistics*. University of Chicago Press.

Parsons, Eileen R. Carlton. (2008). Positionality of African Americans and a theoretical accommodation of it: Rethinking science education research. *Science Education*, 92(6), 1127–1144.

Reagan, Timothy. (2004). Objectification, positivism and language studies: A reconsideration. *Critical Inquiry In Language Studies: An International Journal*, 1(1), 41–60.

Reyes, Angela. (2005). Appropriation of African American slang by Asian American youth. *Journal of Sociolinguistics*, 9(4), 509–532.

Rickford, John R. (1999). The Ebonics controversy in my backyard: A sociolinguist's experiences and reflections. *Journal of Sociolinguistics*, 3(2), 267–266.

Rickford, John R. (2022). *Speaking my soul: Race, life, and language*. Taylor & Francis.

Rosa, Jonathan. (2016). Standardization, racialization, languagelessness: Raciolinguistic ideologies across communicative contexts. *Journal of Linguistic Anthropology*, 26(2), 162–183.

Royster, Jacqueline Jones. (1996). When the first voice you hear is not your own. *College Composition and Communication*, 47(1), 29–40.

Selden, Steven. (2000). Eugenics and the social construction of merit, race and disability. *Journal of Curriculum Studies*, 32(2), 235–252.

Smalls, Krystal A. (2018). Languages of liberation: Digital discourses of emphatic blackness. In Avineri et al. (Eds.). *Language and Social Justice in Practice* (pp. 52–60). Routledge.

Smalls, Krystal A. (2020). Race, SIGNS, and the body: Towards a theory of racial semiotics. In Alim et al. (Eds.). *The Oxford handbook of language and race* (p. 233-260). Oxford University Press.

Smalls, Krystal A., Spears, Arthur K., & Rosa, Jonathan. (2021). Introduction: Language and white supremacy. *Journal of Linguistic Anthropology*, *31*(2), 152–156.

Smitherman, Geneva. (1973a). "God don't never change": Black English from a Black perspective. *College English*, *34*(6), 828–833.

Smitherman, Geneva. (1973b). White English in blackface or, Who do I be?. *The Black Scholar*, *4*(8–9), 32–39.

Smitherman, Geneva. (1991). "What Is Africa to me?": Language, ideology, and *African American. American Speech*, *66*(2), 115–132.

Smitherman, Geneva. (2022). *My soul look back in wonder: Memories from a life of study, struggle, and doin battle in the Language Wars*. Routledge.

Spears, Arthur K. (1992). Reassessing the status of Black English. *Language in Society*, *21*(4), 675–682.

Spears, Arthur K. (1998). African-American language use: Ideology and so-called obscenity. In Mufwene et al. (Eds.). *African-American English: Structure, history, and use* (pp. 226–250). Routledge.

Thomas, Jamie A. (2024). Community college linguistics for educational justice: Content and assessment strategies that support antiracist and inclusive teaching. In Anne H. Charity Hudley, Christine Mallinson, & Mary Bucholtz (Eds.), *Inclusion in linguistics*. Oxford University Press.

Toribio, Almeida J. (2000a). Nosotros somos dominicanos: Language and self-definition among Dominicans. In Roca (Ed.). *Research on Spanish in the United States: Linguistic issues and challenges* (pp. 252–270). Cascadilla Press.

Toribio, Almeida J. (2000b). Language variation and the linguistic enactment of identity among Dominicans. *Linguistics*, *38*(5), 1133–1159.

Toribio, Almeida J. (2003). The social significance of Spanish language loyalty among Black and White Dominicans in New York. *Bilingual Review / La Revista Bilingüe*, *27*(1), 3–11.

Turda, Marius, & Weindling, Paul J. (2007). *Eugenics, race and nation in central and southeast Europe, 1900–1940: A historiography*. CEU Press.

Vyas, Darshali. A., Eisenstein, Leo G., & Jones, David S. (2021). Hidden in plain sight—Reconsidering the use of race correction in clinical algorithms. *Obstetrical & Gynecological Survey*, *76*(1), 5–7.

Wilson, Camille M., Hanna, Margaret O. Hanna, & Li, Michelle. (2019). Imagining and enacting liberatory pedagogical praxis in a politically divisive era. *Equity & excellence in education*, *52*(2–3), 346–363.

Woodson, Carter G. (2006). *The mis-education of the Negro*. Book Tree.

Zentella, Ana Celia. (2018) LatinUs and linguistics: Complaints, conflicts, and contradictions - The anthro-political linguistics solution. In N. L. Shin & D. Erker (Eds.), *Questioning theoretical primitives in linguistic inquiry: Papers in honor of Ricardo Otheguy* (pp. 189–207). John Benjamins.

Kamran Khan is director of the Mosaic research group into multilingualism at the University of Birmingham. At the time of writing this chapter he was a recipient of the prestigious Marie Sklodowska-Curie Fellowship financed by Horizon 2020 with the European Commission at Copenhagen University. He researches the proliferation of security practices in adult language education through countering violent extremism involving the Prevent program in the UK and the ghetto policy in Denmark. He was a teacher of ESOL (English for Speakers of Other Language) adult language education before entering academia. He gained his PhD after winning the Universitas 21 College of Social Sciences scholarship at the University of Birmingham and University of Melbourne. He was the winner of the Edward Cadbury Award for best PhD in education. He was also the Economic Social Research Council research associate at the University of Leicester for a British citizenship project and co-led a British Academy project on Sociolinguistics and Security at King's College London. He is the author of *Becoming a Citizen: Linguistic Trials and Negotiations.*

Abstract: This chapter focuses on three experiences as a racially minoritized academic in European applied linguistics. These three experiences centre on being unknowingly targeted as a subject of a study, dealing with professional gatekeeping from a white researcher who researched the author's community and experiences of recruitment. Theoretically, the author analyses these instances using Koritha Mitchell's know your place aggression to examine how whiteness is present and perpetuated in the European context. The author situates aggressions towards him within broader colonial and racial histories in Europe which perpetuate white supremacy while subordinating racially minoritised people and communities. Using this analysis, he then provides a test with a series of questions to reanalyse scholarship on racially minoritised communities and to reorient future work. This provides a practical activity to create a more socially just field.

Key Words: race, language, European racism, academic trajectory, whiteness, disciplinary whiteness

6

Unpacking Experiences of Racism in European Applied Linguistics

Kamran Khan (he/him)
University of Birmingham (United Kingdom)

Introduction

I have never been able to look up to someone like me in European applied linguistics. I have never seen someone like me become a professor or even lead a project. It has become normalised for some white academics to believe that people like me do not have a place as professional equals, much less in senior positions. They cannot believe what they cannot see and neither can I. Jason Arday, one of the very few Black professors in the United Kingdom and a specialist in higher education, stated, "If someone asked me what the blueprint is to become an academic, I'd have to say that if you are Black or Asian it is 'how much can you suffer?', whereas if you are white there is actually a blueprint about getting into academia because if you are a person of colour the goalposts move all the time" (BBC, 2021a). Given that we do not have "blueprints," how do those of us who do not cohere to these "racial somatic norms of academia" (Purwar, 2004, p. 52) negotiate this daunting path? Academics like me are "decolonising from the imperial centre" (Bhambra et al., 2018, p. 3)—both operating within the beating heart of racism in Europe and subject to it. Within this small space with an asymmetric racial power dynamic, always outnumbered and often casually demeaned, we must find ways to exist and succeed.

Despite the volume of applied linguistics research about racially minoritised communities in Europe, there is little recognition of the need to address the pipeline for producing and retaining racially minoritised applied linguists in Europe. Of course, even within these pipelines, not all racial groups are affected equally. Several reports have documented the disgraceful statistics around the recruitment and retention of Black academics (BBC, 2021b). Furthermore, groups may have their own internal dynamics

Kamran Khan, *Unpacking Experiences of Racism in European Applied Linguistics* In: *Decolonizing Linguistics*. Edited by: Anne H. Charity Hudley, Christine Mallinson, and Mary Bucholtz, Oxford University Press.
© Anne H. Charity Hudley, Christine Mallinson, and Mary Bucholtz 2024. DOI: 10.1093/oso/9780197755259.003.0007

and hierarchies around class and caste, for example (see Punnoose & Haneefa, 2024). Including a few minoritized academics reinforces hierarchies against others and thus proves that mere inclusion cannot be the sole goal.

Charity Hudley et al. (2020) and Bhattacharya et al. (2020) recent publications outline the challenges both general and applied linguistics face in relation to knowledge production, equality, and inclusion in North America, but much of their discussion is relevant too in Europe. The question is: If European applied linguists—particularly those in established, powerful positions—are committed to anti-racism, why haven't they used their resources and power to make similar statements with concrete steps on dismantling white supremacy in Europe? The silence among many of those whose careers are based on social inequalities and social justice connected to racially minoritised communities is perhaps indicative of a willingness to extract from our communities for professional gain but it excludes those from these communities who seek collective advancement. Therefore, the spoils of academic labour are concentrated among a few. Perhaps this dynamic is indicative of how racism operates in European linguistics as a reformulation of colonial extraction, exclusion, and concentration. More concretely, there are no statistics about the racial background of linguists in many European contexts. This is not indicative of a lack of racism but denotes an unwillingness to engage with systemic forms of exclusion and a complicity in the reproduction of racism. In fact, there appear few if any initiatives to investigate this issue. As an illustrative example, I shared the 2020 article written by Anne H. Charity Hudley, Christine Mallinson, and Mary Bucholtz with the Iberian-based applied linguistics representative organisation, EdiSo (Asociación de Estudios sobre Discurso y Sociedad), and asked that anyone interested in addressing the issues raised to contact me in order to collaborate. Despite the presence of "critical" researchers in EdiSo, including those specialising in social inequalities and those with leadership positions in the organisation, I received zero response. Goldberg (2006) notes the need to account for the specificities of European racism, especially given its substantive role in racial and colonial projects. This task requires extensive theorisation specifically in applied linguistics.

With such a dire starting point, there is little in the way of providing evidence for the systemic exclusion of racially minoritised academics in Europe even though we *know* it exists. It is visible in the composition of departments and programs, roles within journals, grant evaluations, and those held as disciplinary leaders. It is visible in how these compositions are created, maintained, and perpetuated, as academics in those positions reproduce the field in the image they see fit. In short, these spaces are rarely occupied by racially minoritised linguists. In a similar vein to Ryuko Kubota (2020), I provide three examples from my own experiences as a British-Pakistani Muslim applied linguist who has worked in England and Spain, and I use these experiences as a heuristic to demonstrate how racism pervades the field.

It is worth mentioning where my career is now at the time of writing this chapter to contextualise those past experiences. I am the recipient of a Marie Sklodowska-Curie Fellowship in Sociology, funded by Horizon 2020 with the European Commission. I applied for the fellowship, which is the most prestigious and competitive in Europe, because I wanted to overcome the exclusion I had faced due to my race and religion. I also wanted to pit my wits against other scholars from a wide field, thereby taking disciplinary racial biases out of the equation with a more standard assessment rather than vague notions of "fit." I applied in sociology because there appeared to be an openness to including scholarship on this topic around racism and colonialism. Consequently, I did not meet the same level of resistance and racialised disciplinary gatekeeping that I did in European applied linguistics. I competed against over 11,000 people for around 1,000 places across all fields across Europe. Having received the fellowship placed me in the curious position of being recognised by the European Commission to be within the top 10 to 15% of scholars across all fields at European level at this point in my career trajectory, despite the fact that I had never had a permanent position and therefore have no permanent scholarly place in my own field of applied linguistics. The structure of this chapter proceeds as follows. First, I will outline the theoretical orientation of my work situating Koritha Mitchell's idea of "know your place" aggression within histories of racial formation, and then conceptualising whiteness within European applied linguistics. Second, I will apply these orientations to three personal experiences. This is significant, as Julien De Jesus (2024) notes in the treatment of Filipinx Americans, a similarly excluded profile of linguists, "we need to be telling our own stories." Then, I will propose some ways to (re)read scholarship from Europe about racially minoritised communities and to push organisations, academics, and departments from complicity in racism towards more inclusive practices.

Know Your Place Aggression

"Know your place" aggression is characterised by the commitment to maintain social and racial orders. Koritha Mitchell explains this term as follows: "any progress by those who are not white, straight or male is answered by . . . violence . . . that essentially says 'know your place!'" (253). This violence serves to

124 Decolonizing Linguistics

reaffirm a racial hierarchy that subordinates racialised minorities based on a "colonial order" (Ahmed, 2021).

Fatima El Tayib (2011) and David Theo Goldberg (2006) have pointed to the white and Christian historical foundations of Europe leading to the persecution of those not deemed to be reproducing these foundational qualities. The nature of contemporary European racism is especially problematic (Hesse, 2004; Goldberg, 2006; El Tayib, 2011; De Genova, 2016) due to the myth that racism is extraneous to Europe rather than as a central organising principle (Lentin, 2008). Barnor Hesse explains: "Racism is accounted for in terms of residuum and exceptionalism rather than continuity and conventionality. This is partly due to the failure to understand the western political culture of colonialism, both its historical continuities and contemporary specificities" (2004, p. 142). But it is more than a "failure to understand," as Hesse points out; a willingness to engage in reproducing colonial relations would seem more apt. Thus, invoking "know your place" aggression means drawing upon colonially produced racial hierarchies within an interaction or event and imposing them on minoritised others.

European whiteness requires further theorisation to understand its unique complexities. Nicholas De Genova (2016, p. 90) reminds us that Europe must be situated within "postcolonial whiteness." He points out that "this certainly does not mean that all Europeans are equally white, or white in the same ways. Like the racial formation of whiteness itself, the homogenizing character of a racial formation of Europenness (or European whiteness) is precisely devoted to obfuscating and suturing what are otherwise profound and consequential differences and inequalities." Further, "silence" around colonial legacies and racism in Europe (El Tayib, 2011; Lentin, 2008) leads to a false sense of "innocence" (Wekker, 2016) that is often challenged by the discrepancy between European self-image and the realities of racism (Lentin, 2018).

Not all countries in Europe deal with racism in explicit ways, as some adopt "colourblindness" or "racelessness" (El Tayib, 2011; Goldberg, 2006), which situates whiteness as an unspoken default (Beaman, 2019). El Tayib refers to this process as "invisible racialisation" which involves "a regime of continentwide recognised visual markers that construct nonwhiteness as non-Europeaness. . . . [and] a discourse of colourblindness that claims not to 'see' racialised difference" (El Tayib, 2011, p. xxiv). This process effectively means that race in Europe "has been rendered invisible, untouchable, as unnoticeably polluting as the toxic air we breathe" (Goldberg 2006, p. 339). Since race cannot be mentioned, it cannot be blamed because it does not exist—if only for those who benefit from it (Lentin, 2020). To confront and make visible racial power (Lentin, 2020) is to lose innocence (Wekker, 2016) rather than addressing key issues around racial justice, and thus the defence of innocence becomes the focal point white innocence is often defended through moral arguments in defence of white innocence, which obfuscate the historical and material dimensions of how racism is reproduced and thereby enacts "know your place" aggression which impacts on racially minoritised scholars.

Whiteness in European Applied Linguistics

European applied linguistics manifests whiteness in two main ways: (1) knowledge production and (2) inclusion and representation. These two factors are essentially interdependent (Kubota, 2020), but I will disentangle them here for clarity. The first manifestation is the preponderance for "methodological whiteness," or a way of structuring the world and producing knowledge that fails to recognise or ignores the fact that race is often rooted in colonial legacies (Bhambra, 2017; 2019). This perspective is especially marked in Europe and therefore in European applied linguistics. Methodological whiteness aligns with Kubota's discussion (2019) of "epistemological racism," which addresses how applied linguistics reproduces racial and gendered inequalities through systemic bias in knowledge production and consumption. It could be argued that European applied linguistics perpetuates many of the characteristics of methodological whiteness (Bhambra, 2019) by avoiding interrogating the pervasive effects of colonialism in society and in the field (Rosa & Flores, 2021). Perhaps more telling is the fact that there is a plethora of fashionable academic concepts related to studying diversity (Pavlenko, 2018), and indeed many academics themselves who engage with "studying" racially minoritised communities in seemingly emancipatory ways without dealing with the enduring colonial legacies of race and the construction of whiteness which are central to the past, present, and future of Europe (Rosa & Flores, 2021). These racial hierarchies are reproduced (Kubota, 2020) in the name of addressing racial and other inequalities.

An unwillingness or perhaps inability to engage with racism and whiteness is one thing, but it is often coupled with what Lentin (2020) refers to as "discursive racist violence" or "not racism." Lentin (2018, p. 11) explains: "The demand to not be reminded of racism is what drives 'not racism.' 'Not racism' goes beyond denial . . . by claiming ownership over the definition of racism." This strategy effectively seizes the discursive terrain upon which racism can be discussed, in itself producing racism. Thus, it would seem that the very project of challenging racism in fact leads to more racism (UCU, 2016). Such backlash has a disciplining effect by intimidating scholars from developing

126 Decolonizing Linguistics

anti-racist scholarship and by making them aware that there will be a likely onslaught, should they try. "Not racism" denies material realities of scholars of colour and epistemological perspectives while also reifying the position of methodologically white scholars as disciplinary gatekeepers inasmuch as racism is racism when they decide it is. It also reinforces the concept that minoritised scholars should know their place.

These factors lead to what we "inherit" as a discipline and who its heirs are. Sara Ahmed (2007, pp. 153–154) states, "Colonialism makes the world white . . . If whiteness is inherited, then it is also reproduced." Thus, whiteness is what we enter when we enter academia and the capability to reproduce it is belongs to the heirs groomed to align to its ideals. Perhaps this is why certain academics and certain types of scholarship are able to achieve professional success through the impression of "empty empiricisms" (Alexander, 2017). Through this more vacuous approach academics can use methodologically white research to appear transgressive and edgy due to a proximity to racially minoritised communities with vague notions of challenging power. This happens despite the fact that they do little to challenge racism and colonial legacies (Rosa & Flores, 2021) when it is as necessary to do so as it has ever been.

European applied linguistics is overwhelmingly and structurally white in terms of representation in departments and associations. This whiteness is often manifested in the subjects covered—and not covered. Scholarship centres around the sensibilities and anxieties of methodologically white academics rather than the gravity of problems facing racially minoritised populations in contemporary society. In this respect, "comfort"[1] becomes a guiding principle in which "whiteness is the embodiment of disciplinary normality" (Liu 2021, p. 9). Ahmed explains, "whiteness may function as a form of public service by *allowing bodies to extend into spaces that have already taken their shape*" (2007, p. 158—original emphasis). That is to say, the spaces are opened up to welcome white scholars in a way that allows them to enter seamlessly in contrast to the resistances experienced by many racially minoritised scholars. This point demonstrates the taken for granted assumptions around who belongs in applied linguistics, why they belong, and the forms of knowledge production which enforces belonging. In other words, comfort and inheritance are connected, since the spaces that we enter are dependent on the colonial histories that have shaped and continue to shape them.

It is worth pointing out that if comfort us central to academic belonging then so too is discomfort. Any notions of comfort for some result in discomfort for others. Avoiding colonial legacies is comfortable. Whiteness is comfortable. Racism is comfortable. Working in spaces where there are predominantly white academics is comfortable. How this comfort affects racially minoritised academics is rarely a matter of importance. Driving out racially minoritised academics, particularly those who study race, leaves no space for substantive examinations of European racism to grow—which is comfortable for some. Richardson (2018, pp. 237–238) explains:

> Interpersonal and institutional racism within academia ensures that scholars of colour don't survive within racism, and don't have the social power to set research agendas or directly challenge their more privileged peers. As with generalised colonial violence, the agenda-setting power of racism in academia is contingent on understanding that eliminating people from institutions also eliminates the intellectual agendas and knowledges embodied within those same people. People of colour in academia must contend with white peers who were socialised into similar racial logics and ideologies to those that led to the colonial violence mentioned above. This socialisation encourages behaviour that makes scholars of colour, particularly women of colour, feel unwelcomed, unappreciated and marginalised.

The academic canon, which combines methodologically white scholarship as hegemonic on one side, with silence around racism and hostility to anti-racism on the other side, also pushes out those who challenge whiteness and white supremacy. Whiteness and white supremacy cannot coexist harmoniously with equality; they can only ever dominate and subordinate (Morrison, 2018). Racism within universities is predicated on a "politics of exclusion" which "works to situate the body of colour firmly on the outside: this is one of the characteristics of institutional racism" (Sian, 2019, pp. 23–24). Due to investments in whiteness (Lipsitz, 1995; Ahmed, 2021), racially minoritised academics and especially those who engage in anti-racism and decolonising work become threats rather than potential collaborators or colleagues (Liu, 2021). For people like me, it is inevitable we see links between our embodiment as an existential threat to academia and other spheres of life where this is the case, such as migrants at borders, illegal detention, and global wars. The academic context is usually far less immediately lethal, but the foundations upon which racialized violence is predicated are the same. For this reason, oppressed groups may find solidarities in dismantling together the structures that create these inequalities (Teltumbde & Yengde, 2018). The shared experience of racism creates a global basis for allyship among scholars of colour across geographical territories to create new possibilities and communities which seek to move beyond extractive forms of scholarship (see also Chetty et al., this volume).

Personal Experiences with Racism in European Applied Linguistics

While the previous sections have been somewhat theoretical, I will now turn to more personal experiences to better situate how racism permeates the everyday lives of scholars of colour. There are a number of examples I could have used for this section on personal experiences with racism in European applied linguistics, many of which are in fact far more violent and repulsive than what I present here. Perhaps I will one day be in a position to share these more extreme examples; however, each disclosure is a risk. I have chosen the following examples for their "unremarkability" (Ahmed, 2021).

> Example 1: I was the only racially minoritised academic and the only Muslim academic in my department. When I moved to a new European country, Academic A asked to observe a class of mine within weeks of me starting this new position. Although this request was strange, I agreed. Unknown to me and without my consent, Academic A and their PhD student thereafter began collecting data about me through interviews with my students under the pretence that it was for a funded project. I was not part of any such project and the projects in the department had nothing to do with me. I only realised I was being "studied" when I recognised myself in a conference abstract. I complained to the head of department, who was also their project leader, and requested to read the data about me.. I was unsupported by the head of department, who actively supported Academic A. When pressed, Academic A and their PhD student later claimed they had deleted the data they collected about me. Academic A was seeking the equivalent of tenure and so was protected in order for their position to remain unimpeded. I was told in no uncertain terms to "let it go" by the head of department. I was in the position of lacking the most basic protection and pressured to accept the mistreatment.

To understand this experience, I highlight Sian's concept of invisibility/hypervisibility (Sian, 2019). Racially minoritised scholars are hypervisible in that our presence challenges whiteness and in doing so our embodiment is a threat. To put it directly, we have an immediate target on our backs. At the same time, we are also invisible. Sian (2019, p. 47) explains, "invisibility produced by whiteness is performed through the dismissing, devaluing, lessening and rejection of the racialized body. Fundamentally, it is a way of undermining their very existence through the failure to acknowledge their being." At no point was my recourse to the data or even my right to work in a dignified manner ever considered. Academic A and their PhD student at no point apologised. I had to know my place and once I complained, the head of department decided that those who were secretly studying me needed to be protected rather than me.

Given that the historical base of Europe is white and Christian, the one person in the department that embodied otherness from this base—me—was also the same person who was researched against his will. There is also the element of surveillance in this example which many Muslims must confront and which immediately positions us as an automatic threat. In this example, my performance in class was being research and evaluated without me ever knowing. I was also surveilled in other ways on that campus, including being followed into the toilet cubicles by security. Those experiences form a wider pattern of mistreatment in the same space.

This example additionally illustrates a shared investment in whiteness. Ahmed (2021, p. 113) notes "Complaints challenge other people's investments in persons." The above example involves three generations of white academics—a PhD student and pretenure academic positioned as the heirs to the head of department. From the perspective of the institutional investment in whiteness, they cannot be impeded from taking up their rightful place. Ethics exist to protect the integrity of research and those being researched yet it does not protect racially minoritised individuals who are the targets of research. Thus, the investment in whiteness is so significant that it can override universally agreed ethical principles and professional standards to the detriment of racially minoritised academics.

> Example 2: I am part of a community that Academic B has researched. After a period of part-time adjunct teaching and academic precarity, I won a postdoctoral fellowship based on my scholarly merit. As part of my fellowship application, I provided two academic references as is standard, and both of them were professors I knew well and who could comment on my work. Unknown to me, Academic B gave an unsolicited and unflattering reference for me, despite us having rarely interacted. For example, we almost never worked on the same campus. This intervention endangered my opportunity for full-time work in a moment of immense professional precarity. In more human terms, I was also a new father to baby twins, earning around 80 euros a week. The full-time hours and salary were extremely needed. Thankfully, Academic B's poor reference was disregarded, and I was able to begin my postdoc. My family could have suffered greatly with consequences for where we could afford to live and access to education for our children.

The relationship between white academics who research racially minoritised communities and academics from those communities is often overlooked (but see Braithwaite and Ali, this volume). A lack of racial literacy (Lentin, 2020) often equates proximity to a community with a lack of racism—yet white academics can and sometimes do reproduce colonial relations in which extraction from a community is for their own benefit. Sian (2019) uses the term "academic frenemy," which she describes as "somebody who exploits our [people of color's] experiences for their own personal gain . . . [they] will often work to undermine racially marked academics, as they are not committed to structural change; they actively perpetuate discourses of whiteness to maintain their power" (pp. 163–164). Access to communities like mine by white academics is an orientalism that is often lauded by other academics whose own investment in methodological whiteness means they have little regard to, awareness of, or motivation to address the potential damage that can be caused. Instead, there is more emphasis on an uncritical, sensationalised exoticism of entering "marginalised" areas with little rigour about the deeper significance and potential for extractive relations. In some cases, there may be a recognition that communities of colour and white academia are completely different worlds but more kudos is given to a white academic entering a community like mine than for me to enter white academia. Charity Hudley et al. (2022) addresses this issue by noting that any published research that is conducted by a nonmember of that community should explicitly confront how the inclusion of members from that community in the research process has been handled, and how efforts have been made to increase participation of community members at the researcher's university in the same department and the research area.

In the above example, Academic B perceived that they had a level of gatekeeping power to decide who can enter an academic space, which they exercised first by intervening in my fellowship process and also by having the confidence to be heard in a white academic space in different institutions. Academic B felt that they had the right to comment on my suitability for this position merely because they had studied a community that I am a part of. I did not know it but I was a threat to Academic B (Liu, 2022). For me to move from a precarious, part-time position to an improved position was perceived as exceeding where I should rightfully be. Again, I must know my place. Yet to do so meant endangering my financial security and therefore my possibilities of remaining in academia. Writing about bullying in academia, Susanne Täuber and Morteza Mahmoudi note, "members of underrepresented groups report that they are targets of bullying with the intent to sabotage their careers. Some anecdotes suggest that bullies spring into action when their targets become too successful for their liking—and thus viable competition" (2022, p. 475). Täuber and Mahmoudi also explain that such harmful interventions

Unpacking Experiences of Racism   **131**

are often tools employed by mediocre academics seeking to maintain their prestige in the face of a threat to the hierarchies that their own career progression has benefitted from. In other words, such actions weaponise racial and social power to maintain established hierarchies by utilising know your place aggression.

Since whiteness is rarely questioned, it is comfortable for these types of practices to appear normal and for academic references to appear credible. Ahmed notes, "What people say about you, even if you don't know who is saying what, *you can feel what is being said* in how people react to you, speak to you, address you' (2021, p. 127, original emphasis). Academic B holds positions in academic journals and organisations and is generally viewed as benevolent due to their proximity to my community. Their word carries weight in spaces where word of mouth and personal references are important. The result of this experience was that the little academic space I can operate within was made even smaller, as I subsequently avoided interacting with Academic B, knowing the threat that they pose.

> Example 3: I applied for a job as part of a fellowship in Catalonia and was accepted for an interview in an English department. The all-white panel of interviewers were unaware of the correct interview evaluation format and provided highly irregular scoring patterns for my case, compared to other interviewees in other disciplines who were interviewed at that time for the same fellowship. One member of the panel overemphasised my Pakistani heritage, despite the fact that I am British and have only ever visited Pakistan for a few weeks. Furthermore, both of my names were routinely spelt incorrectly in public documents by different people. The gatekeepers were so dismissive of my candidacy that I was not afforded the basic dignity of proper acknowledgement of my own name. I complained about the process both to the government and to the university, not due to the result but due to the systemic biases, in order to provide suggestions for improving their practices to avoid such othering in the future.

Recruitment is a key part of selecting inheritors of whiteness and maintaining comfort. Sara Ahmed (2007) notes, "Recruitment functions as a technology for the reproduction of whiteness' which is the 'ego ideal of the institution" (pp. 157–158). Recruitment demonstrates how departments and institutions envision their ideal future; that is to say, they recruit aligning to the future that they desire. In the above example, perhaps what occurred was not a failure of policy but the desired outcome, since an all-white panel rejected my application and recruited a white academic to join the historically all-white department. The presence of racially minoritised academic may have been a "disturbance" (Ahmed, 2021) to white comfort and threat to the inheritance of whiteness.

In this example, I was the only racially minoritised academic who was interviewed and the only interviewee who was listed with an incorrect name. These documents, which contained the incorrect name, were then made public. That the fellowship committee either did not know or did not care how my name was spelt gave me an impression of how I was viewed. This is not insignificant. Mary Bucholtz (2016) underlines how names are the site of contestations of power. References to my Pakistani heritage were also completely unnecessary and othered me in a way that used heritage as "floating signifer" for race (Hall, 1997). Thus, I was viewed through allusions to race over nationality. This was marked given that it seemed to devalue my British identity while indirectly highlighting how I was neither white nor Christian. This experience reveals how racism operates in universities as a "politics of exclusion" (Sian, 2019). In some countries the local government and university organise and administer interviews, as employees are viewed as public servants. In some countries, universities (this one included) do not include race within equality and diversity policies. Thus, university policy reproduces state level "racelessness" (El Tayib, 2011). Moreover, in Catalonia and Spain, no data is collected as to racial representation at most levels, which extends to university spaces (Khan & Balsà, 2021).

I complained about my experience and the treatment I received. In her ground-breaking work *Complaint!*, Sara Ahmed (2021) points out that complaints are necessary because they highlight inadequacies of policies and the need for new ones. I first wrote to the representatives of Catalan government, who oversee the coordination of the fellowship, who in turn told me they could not do anything and passed me on to the university. The university finally corrected my names on public documents but ignored the rest of my concerns. No one was interested in creating equitable recruitment practices that did not reproduce racism. To change the system is to risk not reproducing the racial hierarchy (Ahmed, 2021). One would believe that universities would want to establish practices that increase the chances of widening the pool to identify the best applicant. Yet as Koritha Mitchell (2021) explains, "Institutions are not overwhelmingly white because white people are the best the world has to offer, but because every positive trait is attached to individuals simply because they are straight and/or white and/or male." Again, whiteness is institutionalized and whiteness is comfortable. The comfort of finding heirs that align with the white-supremacist legacy of the institution means that whiteness, not equality, almost always wins in academia.

Next Steps

Addressing racism in Europe is no mean feat, as it would require a departure from many years of practices and history (Hesse, 2004). In my life, I have taken inspiration from contexts where changes have made some difference. In this section, I try to tie together many of the issues raised in this chapter with a view to questions that can be asked that challenge the roots of white comfort and white inheritance. I was inspired to write these questions by a series of tests which are used to scrutinise representation in films, such as the Bechdel Test for gender inclusion, the Ava Duverney Test for Black representation, and the Riz Hussain Test for representations of Muslims. Such tests can be effective because they force viewers to reassess previous work and put forth more equitable models going forward for future generations (see, e.g., The Riz Test, 2018). In a similar way, I hope that my questions for reflection and guidance can act as a starting point—that others can develop and refine these questions as they apply them to (re)reading scholarship emanating from Europe about racially minoritised communities.

The Linguistics Test for Decolonial Scholarship

Charity Hudley and Flores (2022) outline several issues around ensuring a socially just field. These range from the exclusion created by racial gatekeeping, addressing the disciplinary career pipeline, and challenging traditional hierarchical models that actively devalue the work of racially minoritised scholars in favour in reproducing canonical whiteness. Below, I have sought to use my own experiences in engaging with Charity Hudley and Flores's call to benefit other scholars in a practical manner to contribute to a more socially just field.

1. **Is the work methodologically white?** Does the work avoid acknowledging race and colonial legacies in shaping knowledge and the world? Rosa and Flores (2021) note the superficial nature of addressing social justice issues which appeal to marginal changes rather than interrogating colonial histories. Going forward, research on migrants, for example, must consider the role of colonialism in creating both the inequalities leading to mobility and the conditions and racial dynamics upon arrival (for example, see De Genova, 2016).
2. **Does the scholar use an equitable number of racially minoritised academics as cited sources (especially from the Global South)? Does this include racially minoritised women?** This question focuses on

citational politics. We must challenge academic norms to create more inclusive reference lists and to expand the epistemological perspectives which move the periphery into the centre (Piller, 2022).

3. **Does the scholar, especially if they are not a community member, explain their motivations for researching a racialised community/individuals and how whiteness is considered?** The point here is to both make visible "invisibilised racial power" (Lentin, 2020) by naming whiteness and to encourage collaboration (Bucholtz, 2021). The rationale behind working with racialised communities should not be assumed or taken for granted. Racially minoritised academics often feel the need to make visible their intentions for researching their communities. When white academics are not required to do the same their position and positionality are reified as somehow being the universal, objective norm.

4. **Does the scholar reflect on their previous work and/or experiences involving other racialised communities or individuals? Do they explain how their racial positionality is shaped?** Linked to the previous question, this question aims to encourage race reflection as an ongoing process rather than a single statement. Doing so pushes scholars to differentiate between research that is aimed at personal advancement from research that is grounded in collaboration and that aims to destabilise colonial relations (Ahmed, 2021).

5. **Does the scholar collaborate with multiple permanently employed racially minoritised academics who occupy spaces at various parts of the career trajectory?** This question aims to encourage change where applied linguists can: in our immediate vicinity. The point here is to foster a collaborative spirit in working with (rather than on) racialized communities. If white, senior scholars are unwilling to share their professional environments, or to advocate for racially minoritised scholars to join them as part of their permanent ranks, they do not deserve to study us.

People like me learn early in life that we must enter white spaces and simply hope they become multiracial to progress. Most white academics never have to leave a comfortable, inherited white space, especially in Europe. In fact, if a space becomes multiracial, it becomes "uncomfortable" and threatening for some white academics in Europe. Perhaps when we see white academic spaces we should not think of inclusion without also thinking about how hostile they can be for some—as well as how comfortable they are for others. White academic spaces can be so inhospitable that racially minoritised academics cannot progress. More accounts are needed (see, e.g., De Jesus, 2024) from other racialised groups, particularly Black linguists in Europe and those at the intersection of oppressive structures. There is also a responsibility on white linguists to act upon these accounts to extricate themselves from racist structures and to engage with a socially just discipline. The key going forward is to find ways of collaborating to create a better field to address rather than reproduce racism in every space that we inhabit. Either way, it is imperative that we hold scholars, institutions, departments, and organisations accountable.

Note

1. I acknowledge and thank Nelson Flores for inspiring me to consider "comfort" through his usage of the word and concept.

References

Ahmed, Sara. (2007). A phenomenology of whiteness. *Feminist Theory*, 8(2), 149-168 https://doi.org/10.1177/1464700107078139

Ahmed, Sara. (2021). *Complaint!* Duke University Press.

Alexander, Claire. (2017). Breaking black: the death of ethnic and racial studies in Britain. *Ethnic and Racial Studies*, 41(6), 1034–1054.

BBC. (2021a). Universities to combat race bias in research. *BBC News*. https://www.bbc.com/news/science-environment-59307390

BBC. (2021b). Only 1% of university professors are Black. *BBC News*. https://www.bbc.com/news/education-55723120#:~:text=Only%20155%20out%20of%20more,than%203%2C000%20in%20that%20time.

Bhambra, Gurminder K., Gebriel, Dalia., & Nişancıoğlu. Kerem. (2018). Introduction: Decolonising the university. In K. Gurminder, Dalia Gebriel Bhambra, & Kerem Nişancıoğlu (Eds.), *Decolonising the university* (pp. 1–18). Pluto Books.

Bhambra, Gurminder, K. (2017). Brexit, Trump, and "methodological whiteness": on the misrecognition of race and class. *British Journal of Sociology*, 68(1), S214–S232.

Bhambra, Gurminder, K. (2019). Methodological whiteness. Global Social Theory. https://globalsocialtheory.org/concepts/methodological-whiteness/#:~:text=In%20effect%2C%20'methodological%20whiteness',situation%20of%20non%2Dwhite%20others.

Bhattacharya, Usree., Jiang, Lei, & Canagarajah, Suresh. (2020). Race, representation, and diversity in the American Association for Applied Linguistics. *Applied Linguistics*, 41(6), 999–1004. Doi: https://doi.org/10.1093/applin/amz003

Bucholtz, Mary. (2016). On being called out of one's name: Indexical bleaching as a technique of deracialization. In H. Samy Alim, John R. Rickford, & Arnetha F. Ball (Eds.), *Raciolinguistics. How language shapes our ideas about race* (pp. 273–289). Oxford University Press.

Bucholtz, Mary. (2021). Community-centred collaboration in applied linguistics. *Applied Linguistics*, 42(6), 1153–1161.

De Genova, Nicholas. (2016). The European question: Migration, race and postcoloniality. *Social Text*, 34(3), 75–102.

136 Decolonizing Linguistics

De Jesus, Julien. (2024). We need to be telling our own stories: Creating a home for Filipinx Americans in linguistics. In Anne H. Charity Hudley, Christine Mallinson, & Mary Bucholtz (Eds.), *Inclusion in linguistics*. Oxford University Press.

El- Tayeb, Fatima. (2011). *European others: Queering ethnicity in postnational Europe*. University of Minnesota Press.

Goldberg. David Theo. (2006). Racial Europeanization. *Ethnic and Racial Studies*, *29*(2), 331364.

Hall, Stuart. (1997). Race, the floating signifier: What more is there to say about "race"? In S. Hall, *Selected writings on race and difference* (pp. 359–373). Durham University Press.

Hesse, Barnor. (2004). Discourse on institutional racism, the genealogy of a concept. In I. Law, D. Phillips, & L. Turney (Eds.), *Institutional racism in higher education* (pp. 49–58). Trentham Books.

Charity Hudley, Anne H., and Nelson Flores. (2022) Social justice in applied linguistics: Not a conclusion, but a way forward *Annual Review of Applied Linguistics* 42: 144-154.

Charity Hudley, Anne H., Mallinson, Christine, & Bucholtz, Mary. (2022). *Talking college: Making space for Black language practices in higher education*. Teachers College Press.

Charity Hudley, Anne H., Mallinson, Christine, & Bucholtz, Mary. (2020). Toward racial justice in linguistics: Interdisciplinary insights into theorizing race in the discipline and diversifying the profession. *Language*, *96*(4), e200–e235.

Kamran Khan, & LíDIA Gallego-Balsà. (2021) Racialized Trajectories to Catalan Higher Education: Language, Anti-Racism and the 'Politics of Listening'. *Applied Linguistics*, 42(6), 1083–1096. https://doi.org/10.1093/applin/amab055

Kubota, Ryuko. (2020). Confronting epistemological racism, decolonizing scholarly knowledge: Race and gender in applied linguistics. *Applied Linguistics*, *41*(5), 712–732.

Lentin, Alana. (2008). Europe and its silence on race. *European Journal of Social Theory*, 11, 487–504.

Lentin, Alana. (2018). Beyond denial: Not racism as racist violence. *Journal of Media & Cultural Studies 32*(4). https://doi.org/10.1080/10304312.2018.1480309

Lentin, Alana. (2020). *Why race still matters* Polity Press.

Lipsitz, George. (1995). The possessive investment in whiteness: Racialized social democracy and the "white" problem in American studies. *American Quarterly*, *47*(3), 369–387.

Liu, Helena. (2022). How we learn whiteness: Disciplining and resisting management knowledge. *Management Learning*, 53(5), 776-796

Mitchell, Koritha. (2018). Identifying white mediocrity and know-your-place aggression: A form of self-care. *African American Review 51*(4), 253–262. Doi:10.1353/afa.2018.0045.

Mitchell, Koritha. (2021). Hannah-Jones tenure case shows white people overvalued in academia. Reuters. https://news.trust.org/item/20210713160623-y1bxz/

Morrison, Toni. (2018). Making America white again. *The New Yorker*. https://www.newyorker.com/magazine/2016/11/21/making-america-white-again?mbid=social_twitter

Pavlenko, Aneta. (2018). Superdiversity and why it isn't: Reflections on terminological innovation and academic branding. In E. Schmenk, S. Breidbach, & L. Küster (Eds.), *Sloganisation in education discourse* (pp. 142–168). Multilingual Matters.

Piller, Ingrid, Jie Zhang, and Jia Li. (2022) Peripheral multilingual scholars confronting epistemic exclusion in global academic knowledge production: A positive case study. *Multilingua* 41(6), 639-662.

Punnoose, Reenu, & Haneefa, Muhammed. (2024). Towards greater inclusion in practice among practitioners: The case for an experience-based linguistics in India. In Anne H. Charity Hudley, Christine Mallinson, & Mary Bucholtz (Eds.), *Inclusion in linguistics*. Oxford University Press.

Purwar, Nirmal. (2004). Fish in or out of water: a theoretical framework for race and space of academia. In I. Law, D. Phillips, & L. Turney (Eds.), *Institutional racism in higher education* (pp. 49–58). Trentham Books.

Richardson, William Jamal. (2018). Understanding Eurocentrism as a structural problem of undone science. In G. K. Bhambra, D. Gebriel, & K. Niçancioglu (Eds.), *Decolonising the University* (pp. 231–248). Pluto Press.

Rosa, Jonathan, & Flores, Nelson. (2021). Decolonization, language, and race in applied linguistics and social justice. *Applied Linguistics*, *42*(6), 1162–1167.

Sian, Katy P. (2019). *Navigating institutional racism in British universities*. Palgrave.

Täuber, Susanne., & Mahmoudi, Morteza. (2022). How bullying becomes a career tool. *Nature Human Behaviour*, *6*(4), 475–475.

Teltumbde, Anand, & Yengde, Suraj. (2018). Reclaiming the radical in Ambdekar. In Teltumbde, Anand, & Yengde, Suraj (Eds.). *The radical in Ambdekar* (pp. xi–1) . Penguin Random House India.

The Riz Test. (2018). https://www.riztest.com/

Wekker, Gloria. (2016). *White innocence*. Duke University Press.

University and College Union. (2016). *Witness*. https://www.youtube.com/watch?v=SGOM EXQe63Eandt=427s

Maya Angela Smith is associate professor of French and Associate Dean for Equity, Justice, and Inclusion at the University of Washington, having earned her doctorate in Romance Languages and Linguistics from the University of California, Berkeley. Her scholarship broadly focuses on the intersection of racial and linguistic identity formations among marginalized groups in the African diaspora, particularly in the postcolonial Francophone world. In addition to *Senegal Abroad*, which won the MLA's Aldo and Jeanne Scaglione Francophone Book Award, Smith has published on French heritage language learning in *Critical Multilingualism Studies*, on language and race in Martinique in *Francosphères*, and on multilingual hip-hop in the edited volume *Africa Everyday*. Her most recent publications look at improving DEI in both French and Italian curricula with a recently published chapter in *Diversity and Decolonization in French Studies*, an article in the *ADFL Bulletin*, and an article in *Diversity and Decolonization in Italian Studies*.

Abstract: This chapter reflects on the author's journey to explore language and Blackness in the traditionally anti-Black disciplines of linguistics and French studies. Her research interests and intellectual trajectory emerged from her personal experiences with language acquisition and racialization, the challenges she has encountered from a lack of resources on how to analyze racial identity formation in linguistics, and the strategies she has devised to confront these challenges. Through her research centering on qualitative interviews of members of the Francophone African diaspora, the author has learned how participants' reflections on real-world language acquisition can counter the ongoing impacts of colonial linguistic hegemony and can help dismantle white supremacy, which relies on language ideologies to commodify, erase, and invalidate the linguistic experiences of members of the global majority. This chapter thus argues for expanding knowledge production, engaging in reflexivity, centering the voices that are least heard, and championing multilingual practices as methods for decolonizing linguistics and language study.

Ce chapitre est une réflexion sur le parcours de l'auteure pour explorer la langue et la négritude dans les disciplines traditionnellement anti-noires de la linguistique et des études françaises. Ses intérêts de recherche et sa trajectoire intellectuelle ont émergé de ses expériences personnelles avec l'acquisition du langage et la racialisation, les défis qu'elle a rencontrés en raison d'un manque de ressources sur la façon d'analyser la formation de l'identité raciale en linguistique, et les stratégies qu'elle a conçues pour faire face à ces défis. À travers ses recherches, qui se concentrent sur des entretiens qualitatifs avec des membres de la diaspora africaine francophone, l'auteure a appris comment les réflexions des participants sur l'acquisition des langues dans le monde réel peuvent lutter contre les impacts continus de l'hégémonie linguistique coloniale et peuvent aider à démanteler la suprématie blanche, qui repose sur les idéologies linguistiques pour marchandiser, effacer et invalider les expériences linguistiques des membres de la majorité mondiale. Ce chapitre plaide donc pour élargir la production de connaissances, s'engager dans la réflexivité, centrer les voix les moins entendues et défendre les pratiques multilingues comme méthodes de décolonisation de la linguistique et de l'étude des langues.

Key Words: racialization, French and Francophone studies, language ideologies, multilingualism, translanguaging, reflexivity

7

Centering Race and Multilingualism in French Linguistics

Maya Angela Smith (she/her/elle)
University of Washington

Introduction

As a linguist housed in a French and Italian studies department and as someone who conducts qualitative research in a humanities-based field, I have spent my career making my research legible to multiple disciplines and audiences. Even though interdisciplinarity has been touted as an ideal to achieve, gatekeepers in academic societies, publishing, and other scholarly environments have often pushed back against interdisciplinary research (Frodeman et al., 2017; Hicks et al., 2010). For instance, in 2014, a literary studies colleague, a linguistics colleague, and I submitted a proposal to the Modern Language Association's (MLA) annual conference entitled "Legitimate Voices in Contested Spaces" under the rubric of linguistics, arguing for new categories in understanding the relationship between linguistics and literature. Our panel was rejected, and while we were given no feedback as to why, we suspect it was in part from the MLA's resistance to dismantling the artificial boundaries between these fields. Then in 2022, I was on an MLA conference roundtable titled "Increasing the Representation of Linguistics in the MLA" where several linguists detailed our difficulties in feeling accepted at the MLA, which supports my hunch about my earlier rejected proposal but also indicates a possible positive change in that our experiences are finally being heard in officially sanctioned spaces such as the annual conference.

I risk further alienation both in American academia and in French studies because my research centers the relationship between racial and linguistic identity formation. In a country such as the United States where demonizing Critical Race Theory has become a rallying cry for the right wing and in a world where discussions about race are silenced in numerous contexts, investigating racialization is a fraught enterprise. As Shu-mei Shih (2008) argues in her special issue on comparative racializations published in the MLA's journal

---

Maya Angela Smith, *Centering Race and Multilingualism in French Linguistics* In: *Decolonizing Linguistics*.
Edited by: Anne H. Charity Hudley, Christine Mallinson, and Mary Bucholtz, Oxford University Press.
© Anne H. Charity Hudley, Christine Mallinson, and Mary Bucholtz 2024. DOI: 10.1093/oso/9780197755259.003.0008

140 Decolonizing Linguistics

PMLA, French departments are especially averse to conceptualizing and exploring race:

> Broadly speaking, cultural and political discourses undergirded by European republican ideology, especially in France, have posited the political and analytic lens of race as differentialist, divisive, and even illiberal, when in fact discrimination is rampant under the unacknowledged but highly operative sign of race. . . . French-derived critical theory has continued, in the United States academy, to relegate race to the margins, and theories of race developed in ethnic studies and other disciplines continue not to be recognized as theory. (p. 1348)

The fact that French departments are overwhelmingly white further inhibits real engagement with race. According to the American Council of Education, 80% of full-time faculty in Academia are white (2019). Unfortunately, neither the MLA nor the American Association of Teachers of French keep statistics on the racial and cultural backgrounds of instructors. However, according to Zippia.com, a website that gives job seekers information to evaluate employment opportunities, 76% of French teachers in the US (at all levels) are white, 10% are Latinx, 7.7% are Black, 3.3% are Asian, 0.5% are American Indian or Alaskan Native, and 1.7% are of unknown racial/ethnic origin (Zippia, n.d.). In my own department, I am the sole current tenure-line faculty member and only the second ever hired who is from the global majority—a term for Black, Brown, Asian, and Indigenous peoples who make up around 80% of the world's population but who are minoritized and marginalized by a global white minority (Campbell-Stephens, 2021). This lack of racial diversity in French departments is particularly egregious considering the immense racial diversity of the French-speaking world and the fact that France sees the future of the French language as tied to Francophone Africa (French Ministry of Foreign and European Affairs, 2022).

However, people like me, who are minoritized not just because of our embodied racial identities but also the type of research we conduct, are making headway in the field. The Movement for Black Lives and on-campus student activism have forced gatekeepers to begin to respond to entreaties for racial justice and meaningful inclusion. In the past few years, I have seen a shift in the MLA. Six years after my interdisciplinary panel was rejected, my book *Senegal Abroad: Linguistic Borders, Racial Formations, and Diasporic Imaginaries* won the MLA's French and Francophone Studies book prize. Furthermore, my article "Creating a More Diverse, Equitable, and Inclusive French Foreign Language Classroom" was published in the *ADFL Bulletin*, a subsidiary of the MLA. In that article, I call for critical language awareness

(Fairclough, 1992, p. 7) in teaching French, and I contend that by bringing real-world linguistic examples to second language pedagogy such as those in *Senegal Abroad*, educators "can interrogate the monolingual, native-speaker norm that champions a seemingly correct version of French and can instead center students' experiences as multilingual speakers and creative explorers of language" (Smith, 2022a, p. 12). These recent nods to linguistic and racial inquiry in modern language studies prove that change is possible, albeit slow, and that those who fight to decolonize our classrooms must continue marching forward (see also Burkette & Warhol, 2021; Clemons, this volume; Chung & dela Cruz, 2024). This chapter reflects on my journey to explore language and Blackness from the perspectives of linguistics and French studies, the challenges I have encountered along the way, and the strategies I have devised to confront these challenges. Often, we researchers are so siloed in our disciplines that we miss creative and novel methods happening more broadly. I am excited to share my experiences and be in conversation with the people in this volume who come from various backgrounds and intellectual traditions as we all work toward our collective goal of decolonizing the study of language(s).

My Positionality and My Journey: Exploring Language and Blackness

My research interests and intellectual trajectory emerged from my own experiences with language acquisition and racialization (Smith, 2021a). As a public elementary school student in Houston, Texas in the late 1980s, I attended mandatory speech classes to correct my pronunciation of the letter S, and auditory discrimination issues since childhood have affected my ability to acquire spoken languages and build confidence in speaking them. Learning differences were not the only considerations that contributed to my classroom anxiety. Attending a prestigious, wealthy, predominantly white private high school as an out-of-place Black scholarship student in the 1990s exacerbated my discomfort. I was hyperaware of my status as the lone Black student in most of my classes. Dealing with the phenomenon of stereotype threat, I worried that any academic or linguistic mistakes would be attributed to my race (Anya 2017; Alim & Smitherman, 2012; Aronson et al., 2002; Holliday & Squires, 2021; Solórzano et al., 2000).

This alienation persisted throughout higher education. I navigated marginalization and minoritization as a college student at New York University in the early 2000s where, as part of my Romance languages major, I spent spring of sophomore year in Madrid, fall of junior year in Paris, and spring of junior year in Dakar. In Paris, I shared many of the insecurities of my fellow American classmates concerning making linguistic errors in a country such as France that places tremendous value on the standard language (Coppel, 2007; Drewelow & Theobald, 2007). At the same time, my white classmates and I diverged in how we were received by the local population. I was the only one followed by sales associates in stores or stopped for document checks by police on the street. It was obvious to me that these encounters were due to racial profiling, and yet when I brought this up to French friends, they repeated the prevailing myth that France was a colorblind society (Beaman, 2017; Keaton et al., 2012; Lozès, 2012; Ndiaye, 2008). I had naively thought that going to France would help me escape the racism and marginalization to which I was so accustomed in the United States, only to encounter a French version of anti-Blackness. As such, these experiences influenced my investment in French and a French-speaking identity (Norton, 2000).

Meanwhile, my sojourn in Dakar the following semester shattered many of the narratives I had about language, Blackness, and the intersection of the two. It was my first time living in a majority-Black country, and it was refreshing not to have the constant reminder of my racial difference. Furthermore, while French courses in the US and societal discourse in France had positioned standard metropolitan French as the norm against which all other varieties were measured, continuing French-language studies in Senegal forced me to interrogate the notion of "correct" French, its relationship to colonial discourse, and the widely held belief that "good" French was synonymous with whiteness (Fanon, 1967). Equally important, the pressure to learn French "perfectly" abated because Dakar was a multilingual space where I heard Wolof, French, Sereer, Pulaar, and other languages on a regular basis. Encountering exuberant multilingualism and linguistic variation helped me reframe what being a competent and legitimate user of a language meant, because I no longer measured myself solely against the monolingual native-speaker model espoused in most second language classrooms (Anya, 2017; Benaglia & Smith, 2022; Kramsch, 1997; 2009; Kubota, 2009).

Due to these experiences with language and race, I decided to attend graduate school so I could systematically research these phenomena. However, when I chose an interdisciplinary degree in Romance languages and linguistics through UC Berkeley's French department in the mid-2000s, I encountered a lack of resources on how to analyze race in linguistics. My advisor was very supportive, but these concerns were not an active part of his research agenda at the time. Few of my courses, whether in French studies, Spanish studies, Italian studies, linguistics, or education, discussed race.

I was fortunate to come across Susan Talburt and Melissa Stewart's (1999) article on the experiences of an African American woman studying abroad in Spain, which validated my own experiences abroad. Other scholars (Ellis, 2008; Gardner & Lambert, 1972; Goldstein, 1987; Gunaratnam, 2003; Harris & Rampton, 2003; Ibrahim, 1999) further helped me theorize race and/or ethnicity in Second Language Acquisition, but most of the time I felt I was wading in uncharted waters. It is worth noting that often those who study race have never experienced minoritized racialization themselves. I wondered if my schooling had adequately prepared me to ask what I saw as pressing and valuable questions out in the field. In the end, I decided that the need for a rigorous investigation of language and race outweighed my anxieties about embarking on research without a full toolkit. Through trial and error, I cobbled together various research methods that I continue to refine and improve.

This background informs my current ethnographic, sociolinguistic approach to research on the Senegalese diaspora in Paris, Rome, and New York City.[1] As documented in *Senegal Abroad*, while the convergence of language, race, and identity influences the lived experiences of anyone who has been racially othered, this convergence has traditionally been overlooked in linguistics. My work stands alongside notable exceptions to this omission that have proven the value of racially conscious linguistic inquiry (e.g., Alim et al., 2016; Bonfiglio, 2002; Charity Hudley et al., 2020; Hill, 1998; Ibrahim, 1999; Flores & Rosa, 2015; Kubota, 2009; Lippi-Green 1997; Makoni et al., 2003; Motha, 2014; Norton, 2000; Rampton, 1995; Rosa & Flores, 2017). Through interviews with over 80 people of Senegalese descent in Paris, Rome, and New York, I learned how they understood language, race, and belonging. Not only did they migrate from the Senegalese context, where race was not a major concern, to the European and North American contexts, where they experienced racialization daily, but their linguistic experiences also heavily influenced this racialization. Now that I have published on language acquisition and Blackness, I feel compelled to impart what I have learned to others who may be struggling with racial inquiry in linguistics.

Challenges in and Strategies for Studying Language and Race

Looking back on the difficulties I have encountered in the 15 years since I started my scholarly work, in some ways little has changed. Robert Squizzero and colleagues' (2021) white paper on race and ethnicity in linguistics reviewed 61 linguistics methods textbooks and found that "only two make explicit mention of conceptualizing race or ethnicity as part of study design" (p. 6). These two texts are Lesley Milroy and Matthew Gordon (2003) and Monica Heller, Sari Pietikänen, and Joan Pujolar (2018). Students are seldom trained in racial methodology. Furthermore, not until 2019 did the Linguistics Society of America publish a formal statement on race (LSA, 2019). This prolonged silence was troubling because, as Anne Charity Hudley (2016) points out, "Disciplines related to linguistics, including psychology, sociology, and anthropology, have formally outlined the historical and social motivations for current racial categories and the ways in which linguistic thought has contributed to racialization" (p. 383).

I have also had to confront the dominant discourses on race in my research sites, which often minimizes the experiences of racialized individuals, and the reticence of my participants to talk about race, ethnicity, and other forms of difference, which are seen as taboo topics (Ben-Ghiat & Fuller, 2005; Keaton et al., 2012; Lozès, 2012; Ndiaye, 2008; Pauker et al., 2018; Portelli, 2004; Smith, 2019; Squizzero et al., 2021). Among my research sites in France, Italy, and the United States, the US context has been most productive in talking about race; however, having frank conversations about race is still difficult to do, especially in the current climate. When I interviewed people for *Senegal Abroad*, participants employed various strategies to alleviate their discomfort when discussing race, such as looking around before speaking, lowering their voice, translanguaging for problematic words (e.g., switching from French to English for the word *noir/black*), and opting not to talk about the subject. However, in the end, I was able to collect robust data and theorize in depth about the intersection of racial and linguistic identity through a focus on reflexivity and multilingualism in ethnographic inquiry, which I articulate below.

Outside of the methods books analyzed by Squizzero and colleagues, the past few years have started to see the emergence of instructive scholarship on how linguists should approach race and racialization (Alim et al., 2016; Bonfiglio, 2002; Charity Hudley et al., 2020; Flores & Rosa, 2015; Hill, 1998; Ibrahim, 1999; Kubota, 2009; Lippi-Green, 1997; Makoni et al., 2003; Motha, 2014; Norton, 2000; Rampton, 1995; Rosa & Flores, 2017). While I would have benefitted from this body of work when conducting fieldwork for my dissertation and for *Senegal Abroad*, the strategies I devised are in line with its guidance. Using my research as a case study, the rest of this section briefly explores the subfield of raciolinguistics and its connection to the sociological concept of racial formation, the importance of the fourth wave of sociolinguistic research for racial inquiry, and the value of reflexivity and positionality inherent in ethnographic research.

Michael Omi and Howard Winant (2015) describe racial formation as "the sociohistorical process by which racial identities are created, lived out, transformed, and destroyed" (p.102). They then present the related concept of a historically situated racial project—"an interpretation, representation, or explanation of racial identities and meanings, and an effort to organize and distribute resources (economic, political, cultural) along particular racial lines"—to explain how race is woven into any given society from macro-level social structures to micro-level personal experiences (p. 115). Building off this theory to emphasize the relationship between linguistic and racial formations, Jonathan Rosa and Nelson Flores (2017) champion a raciolinguistic perspective to explain "the interplay of language and race within the historical production of nation-state/colonial governmentality, and the ways that colonial distinctions within and between nation-state borders continue to shape contemporary linguistic and racial formations" (p. 623). Like Rosa and Flores, my own work also shows how linguistic resources are just as productive as economic, political, and cultural resources in understanding race.

My work uses multisited research to further highlight the link between racial and linguistic identity formation. While many researchers of language and race are primarily interested in the US context or a single national context (Alim et al., 2016), in my research, racial and linguistic formations differ vastly for Senegalese people depending on the specific context of the receiving country. By focusing on national discourses on race and colorblindness and societal attitudes about language acquisition and access to citizenship/belonging in each site, my comparative analysis of Senegalese migrants' lived experiences articulates racial and linguistic formations in a new light. Importantly, this multisited approach can be applied to other diasporas, national contexts, and languages, expanding our understanding of how both racial and linguistic ideologies travel and evolve.

My work exemplifies the fourth wave of sociolinguistic research, which Charity Hudley (2016) defines as a move "beyond a taxonomy view of race by working to engage members of racial and social groups in the intellectual and practical co-construction of knowledge and resources about language, culture, race, and community" (p. 388). She adds that in this model, "both linguistic and racial ideology are co-constructed and co-negotiated between researcher, individual, and community. As such, the emphasis is on what the individual, group, race, and/or culture value and see as crucial to the investigation of language, as well as linguistic social justice" (p. 388). I find this focus on co-construction and co-negotiation particularly relevant for my research, both in how I reflect on my positionality as a researcher and how my participants make sense of the world through language.

For instance, I am conscious of how I address power dynamics inherent in interviewer/interviewee interactions. For *Senegal Abroad*, I gave participants insight into relevant aspects of my background (e.g., where I was from and received my education, how I identified racially, why I was interested in language ideologies). I walked a fine line of providing them with enough information to feel at ease while also not saying so much that it would influence their responses. In addition, at the beginning of each interview, I told them I would leave time at the end for them to ask me any questions they would like about myself, an opportunity that many participants took. Even in national settings that are hostile to discussions about race, my participants engaged in thoughtful reflections on their racialized identities. I believe that my frankness helped alleviate their doubts about discussing race and gave them a space to enunciate something that needed to be said.

Furthermore, some of my participants used my racial identity to co-construct their own identity formation, such as when two interviewees, Ndiaga and Professore, cited the film *The Color Purple* to convey a racialized existence in Rome that differed from their experiences back in Senegal:

> As both Ndiaga and Professore began to share their difficulties as Black men in Rome, Professore remarked that because I, too, was Black, I could understand what they were saying. Cultural production from the United States was allowing him not only to make sense of his current environment but also to forge a connection with me. Professore was relying on my identity as an African American to co-construct a narrative of Black exclusion in white spaces. (Smith, 2019, p. 4)

This example reveals how "our own ethnic and racial identities can influence our participants' responses to questions about their own identities during face-to-face interviews" (Squizzero et al., 2021, p. 19). In other words, researcher positionality, which is sometimes maligned as lacking academic rigor or hindering objectivity, adds richness and complexity to discussions on language and race (Clemons, this volume). More importantly, when we freely give part of ourselves to our participants just as we expect them to give part of themselves through the stories they tell us, we are more likely to do research that benefits our participants (Paris & Winn, 2014).

I also addressed power dynamics by being intentional about the languages of interaction. I welcomed participants to speak in the languages in which they were most comfortable by indicating my fluency in English, French, Spanish, Italian, and Portuguese and assuring them that even though I had limited conversational knowledge of Wolof, I would be working with

Wolof-language users when transcribing and translating my data. I also encouraged interviewees to use languages I did not know such as Sereer, Pulaar, and Jola, explaining that the onus was on me to accommodate their expansive linguistic repertoires. Furthermore, I normalized switching between languages in our interviews. At the beginning of each interview, I asked participants about which language they would like us to begin and that assured them that they could change languages throughout the course of our conversation. While my own multilingual limitations precluded me from completely alleviating the linguistic power dynamic between researcher and participant, acknowledging our multilingual realities laid the groundwork for reflections on language and power (see also Thomas, 2022).

Through the course of my research, I have witnessed how people use language to negotiate racial and national belonging. For instance, in the aforementioned interview, research participants Ndiaga and Professore did not simply rely on cultural production to articulate their lack of belonging. They also illustrated this alienation through translanguaging, in which language users access a variety of linguistic features "in order to maximize communicative potential" and "to make sense of their multilingual worlds" (García, 2009, p. 140). In quoting the character Celie's line in *The Color Purple*, "I'm poor, black, I might even be ugly, but dear God, I'm here! I'm here!," Ndiaga mused, "Je suis *nero*, je suis *brutto*, ma, je suis *vivo*!" (I am *Black*, I am *ugly*, but, I am *alive*). As I argue in *Senegal Abroad*:

> By switching to Italian for the operative words *nero*, *brutto*, and *vivo*, Ndiaga foregrounded his exclusion. There was a linguistic divide between his French-speaking identity "I am" and his Italian adjectives to which society had reduced him. . . . The quoted words evoked struggle as well as defiance in the face of this struggle, and the creative multilingual usage that Ndiaga employed further reinforced his racialized position as a Black man in an Italian society that conceived itself as white. Paradoxically, he also signaled his stake in *italianità*: living in Italy and learning Italian opened the door to an Italian identity that he partially embodied by using Italian for the operative words. (pp. 79–80)

A translanguaging perspective demonstrates the role of language in social construction, but this creative use of language may not be visible in monolingual methods of data collection. The valuing of multilingualism at the beginning of each interview and the reiteration of its value throughout our conversations set the foundation for the intricate and beautiful translanguaging practices that many of my participants shared with me.

Continual Evolution

The research I do is often rooted in ethnography because this methodology can be particularly productive in foregrounding the nuances and dynamism of language and race. As Charity Hudley (2016) notes, "Ethnographic approaches allow for closer examination of linguistic discourse, interactions, and intentionality and present insights into race that reflect its true, dynamic nature" (p. 393). In other words, ethnographic inquiry, when conducted in a way that thoughtfully privileges the voices of the community studied, creates environments in which participants have the time, space, and impetus to reflect on and illustrate their experiences as linguistic beings. However, it is important to discuss the limitations of traditional ethnographic research, missteps and challenges I have navigated in the research process, and ideas for where to go from here.

First, even though ethnographic methods have evolved since the days of white anthropologists seeking out the "exotic" other in faraway lands (Bruchac, 2018; Said, 1979; Trouillot, 2003), it remains primarily a tradition where the researcher is in control. More specifically, as much as I sought to dismantle the power dynamics between my participants and myself when working on *Senegal Abroad*, I still held the power in setting my research agenda. I went into each site with research questions I wanted to explore, with a semistructured interview guide that was the blueprint for all my conversations, and with a research subjectivity that restricted the ways in which my participants felt comfortable interacting with me regardless of my intentions to minimize power differentials. Furthermore, the fact that I was only fluent in colonial languages and not in any of the Indigenous languages of Senegal highlighted the limits on my multilinguistic decolonizing efforts. At the same time, I also found myself lacking institutional power and resources both as a Black graduate student trying to earn my doctorate and as a junior scholar needing to publish for tenure. I felt that there was only so much I could do at the time to push against the conservatism of both French studies and linguistics.

In reflecting on my scholarship, while I think I accomplished a lot of good, there is always more I can do. As someone who is learning from the excellent and transformative work happening in various fields, I continually evolve in how I approach research. For instance, instead of limiting myself to ethnographic research methods, I hope to begin employing a more collaborative agenda, which identifies community-defined goals and more readily empowers participants (Bucholtz, 2021; Chetty et al., this volume; Plumb et al., this volume). While there are risks in doing collaborative work because of a lack of recognition of these types of approaches in many academic disciplines, I feel compelled to use my new-found institutional power as a tenured professor to validate and normalize theses modes of inquiry.

In rethinking my role in academia, I am also expanding who my audiences are. As a linguist who teaches in a modern languages department and whose subjectivity is heavily influenced by language learning, I know the value of incorporating my research and lived experiences into my pedagogy. When I present my work as an invited speaker, a conference participant, a workshop leader, or an instructor, I have noticed that it is primarily students who gravitate toward this approach to language. Faculty are often intrigued, but implementing what I suggest sometimes requires unlearning what they have been taught about language and pedagogy. It is thus important to show instructors what their classrooms gain when centering multilingualism. It is equally imperative that students know it is OK to demand more inclusive pedagogy. For instance, in my own language and culture courses, I have seen my Spanish-speaking students, my international students, particularly those from China, and all my racialized students, but especially those who identify as Black, become less marginalized in the classroom when they are able to make connections between their lived linguistic experiences and the course texts (Benaglia & Smith, 2022; Smith, 2022a; Smith, 2022b). Showing students how multilingual subjects (Kramsch, 2009) in the Francophone world engage with the entirety of their linguistic repertoire provides a liberating and inspiring model of language learning. It also situates my interviewees as knowledge producers and experts.

I also want empowerment to happen beyond the confines of higher education. For that reason, I have committed myself to public scholarship and to sharing my research on language, race, and belonging in as many venues as possible. For instance, I write op-eds on a range of topics such as the difficulties of claiming my voice (Smith, 2021a), my family history with African American sea chanteys (Smith, 2021b), and my anxieties around becoming a Black mother in an anti-Black world (Smith, 2020). I have participated in radio interviews on Blackness in film (Gyimah-Brempong & Sillman, 2018). I have developed digital humanities projects such as an ArcGIS story map about the life of Alvenia Bridges, a Black woman making a name for herself behind the scenes in Rock and Roll (Smith, 2021c). Translation is another way of attracting diverse publics such as the French translation of *Senegal Abroad* by a nonacademic press, which I hope will reach a vast Francophone African audience (Smith, 2022c). I am also working on several children's book manuscripts because I believe that one is never too young to learn about how language and race operate in our lives. Just as my interviewees offer academia important perspectives concerning language and race, articulating related

Concluding Call to Action

My scholarship argues that researchers' and participants' reflections on real-world language acquisition are crucial for countering the ongoing impacts of colonial linguistic hegemony and for dismantling white supremacy, which relies on the hegemony of standard language ideologies to commodify, erase, and invalidate the linguistic experiences of Black, Brown, Indigenous, and Melanated People (BBIMP)—a phrase coined by Louisa "Weeze" Doran to de-center whiteness. My experiences in fieldwork have shown me that expanding knowledge production, engaging in reflexivity, centering the voices that are least heard, and championing multilingual practices are key ingredients for decolonizing linguistics and language study. I include further explanation of these practices and key resources to consult below.

1) **Expanding and linking knowledge production:** My interdisciplinary approach allows me to engage with many different fields (e.g., literary and cultural studies, linguistics, Second Language Acquisition, music studies) to provide a more holistic perspective on how and why people use language. As seen with the *Color Purple* example, my research participants relied heavily on literature, film, and music to make sense of their lived experiences, and they constantly amazed me with their thought-provoking insight. I used their technique as a model for my book, making explicit connections between what was happening in cultural production, what was expressed in my interviews, and what these insights meant for multilingual identity formation. This made my linguistics research more legible to other fields and to nonscholars. Resources to consult include Burkette and Warhol (2021); Smith (2019); and Rampton et. al. (2018).

2) **Creating a space of reflexivity and encouraging positionality:** When scholars reflect on our own positionality and subjectivity with participants, we validate their lived experiences and increase the possibility of receiving better, more useful data, that helps us understand participants' lives and represent them accurately and sensitively. By talking openly and honestly with participants, scholars can demystify topics such as race that are sometimes seen as taboo. Co-construction and co-negotiation can also create environments that allow members of

a community to articulate the phenomena that they experience in their lives but that they may not have had the time or space to analyze before. Resources to consult include Benaglia and Smith (2022); Anya (2017); Haller (2014); Kramsch (2009); Lyons (2019); Ramsdell (2004).

3) **Centering the voices of everyday people:** The first two practices lay the groundwork for bringing marginalized voices to the center. Linguists do not have a monopoly on explaining language. Scholars must use the wisdom of everyday people such as my participants to raise awareness of how humans theorize language, race, and inclusion in their own words. This focus moves us away from top-down approaches that often overlook valuable perspectives. Resources to consult include Plumb et al. (this volume); Chetty et al. (this volume); Thomas (2024); García-Sánchez and Orellana (2019); Rampton et al. (2018); Paris and Winn (2014).

4) **Championing multilingualism and translanguaging:** The prevailing focus on monolingualism in linguistic research and modern language studies emerges from standard language discourses, linguistic hegemony, and white supremacy. It is the norm both in academia and in Western societal discourses against which multilingual practices are measured, even though the majority of the world, particularly those from BBIMP communities, use multiple languages and varieties in their everyday lives. It is imperative that we champion multilingualism and translanguaging practices in our scholarship and teaching. Resources to consult include Chung and dela Cruz (2024); Clemons (this volume); Thomas (2022); García (2019, 2009); Macedo (2019); Anya (2017); Blackledge and Creese (2014).

The days of feeling completely out of place in my academic work are behind me, but I recognize that demanding to be heard is a constant process. As I show up alongside the incredible contributors in *Decolonizing Linguistics* and *Inclusion in Linguistics* and continue to engage in interdisciplinary scholarship, I am comforted in knowing that we are taking up space, reshaping the narrative, and offering our various disciplines the possibility of true transformation. It is now on them to listen.

Note

1. The qualitative research mentioned in this chapter received IRB approval through UC Berkeley's Office for the Protection of Human Subjects and University of Washington's Human Subjects Division.

152 Decolonizing Linguistics

References

Alim, H. Samy, & Smitherman, Geneva. (2012). *Articulate while Black: Barack Obama, language, and race in the US*. Oxford University Press.

Alim, H. Samy, Rickford, John, & Ball, Arnetha (Eds.). (2016). *Raciolinguistics: How language shapes our ideas about race*. Oxford University Press.

American Council of Education. (2019). *Race and ethnicity in higher education: A status report*. https://www.equityinhighered.org/resources/report-downloads/

Anya, Uju. (2017). *Racialized identities in second language learning: Speaking Blackness in Brazil*. Routledge.

Aronson, Joshua, Fried, Carrie B., & Good, Catherine. (2002). Reducing the effects of stereotype threat on African American college students by shaping theories of intelligence. *Journal of Experimental Social Psychology, 38*(2), 113–125.

Beaman, Jean. (2017). *Citizen outsider: Children of North African immigrants in France*. University of California Press.

Ben-Ghiat, Ruth, & Fuller, Mia. (2005). *Italian colonialism*. Palgrave Macmillan.

Benaglia, Cecilia, & Smith, Maya Angela. (2022). Multilingual texts and contexts: Inclusive pedagogies in the French foreign language classroom. In Siham Bouamer & Loïc Bourdeau (Eds.), *Diversity and decolonization of the French curriculum: New approaches to teaching* (pp. 17–32). Palgrave Macmillan.

Blackledge, Adrian, & Creese, Angela (Eds.) 2014. *Heteroglossia as practice and pedagogy*. New York: Springer.

Bonfiglio, Thomas. (2002). *Race and the rise of Standard American*. Mouton de Gruyter.

Bruchac, Margaret M. (2018). *Savage kin: Indigenous informants and American anthropologists*. University of Arizona Press.

Bucholtz, Mary. (2021). Community-centered collaboration in applied linguistics. *Applied Linguistics, 42*(6), 1153–1161. https://doi.org/10.1093/applin/amab064

Burkette, Allison, & Warhol, Tamara. (2021). *Crossing borders, making connections: Interdisciplinarity in linguistics*. De Gruyter Mouton.

Campbell-Stephens, Rosemary M. (2021). *Educational leadership and the global majority: Decolonising narratives*. Springer International Publishing.

Charity Hudley, Anne H. (2016). Language and racialization. In Ofelia García, Nelson Flores, and Massimiliano Spotti (Eds.), *The Oxford handbook of language and society* (pp. 381-402). Oxford University Press.

Charity Hudley, Anne H., Mallinson, Christine, & Bucholtz, Mary. (2020). Toward racial justice in linguistics: Interdisciplinary insights into theorizing race in the discipline and diversifying the profession. *Language, 96*(4), e200–e235. doi:10.1353/lan.2020.0074

Chung, Rhonda, & dela Cruz, John Wayne N. (2024). Pedagogies of inclusion must start from within: Landguaging teacher reflection and plurilingualism in the L2 classroom. In Anne H. Charity Hudley, Christine Mallinson, & Mary Bucholtz (Eds.), *Inclusion in linguistics*. Oxford University Press.

Coppel, Anne. (2007). Les Français et la norme linguistique: Une passion singulière. *Cosmopolitiques, 16*, 157–168.

Cukor-Avila, Patricia, & Bailey, Guy. (2001). The effects of the race of the interviewer on sociolinguistic fieldwork. *Journal of Sociolinguistics, 5*(2), 252–270.

Doran, Louiza "Weeze." (2020). BBIMP. https://www.instagram.com/p/CG5SRpBHQz2/?hl=en.

Drewelow, Isabelle, & Theobald, Anne. (2007). A comparison of the attitudes of learners, instructors, and native French speakers about the pronunciation of French: An exploratory study. *Foreign Language Annals, 40*(3), 491–520. https://doi.org/10.1111/j.1944-9720.2007.tb02872.x

Ellis, Rod. (2008). *The study of second language acquisition*, 2nd ed. Oxford University Press.

Fairclough, Norman (Ed.). (1992). *Critical language awareness*. Longman.

Fanon, Frantz. 1967 [1952]. *Black skin, white masks* (Charles Lam Markmann, Trans.). Grove Press.

Flores, Nelson, & Jonathan Rosa. (2015). Undoing appropriateness: Raciolinguistic ideologies and language diversity in education. *Harvard Educational Review, 85*(2), 149–171. https://doi.org/10.17763/0017-8055.85.2.149

French Ministry of Foreign and European Affairs (2022). Les enjeux de la diplomatie française en Afrique. *France Diplomatie.* https://www.diplomatie.gouv.fr/fr/dossiers-pays/afrique/les-enjeux-de-la-diplomatie-francaise-en-afrique/

Frodeman, Robert, Klein, Julie Thompson, & Pacheco, Roberto C. S. (2017). *The Oxford handbook of interdisciplinarity*, 2nd ed. Oxford University Press.

García-Sánchez, Inmaculada M., & Orellana, Marjorie Faulstich. (2019). Introduction. In Inmaculada García-Sánchez and Marjorie Faulstich Orellana (Eds.), *Language and cultural practices in communities and schools* (pp. 1–23). Routledge.

García, Ofelia. (2009). Education, multilingualism and translanguaging in the 21st century. In Tove Skutnabb-Kangas, Robert Phillipson, Ajit K. Mohanty, & Minati Panda (Eds.), *Social Justice through Education* (pp. 140–158). Orient Blackswan.

García, Ofelia. (2019). Decolonizing foreign, second, heritage, and first languages: Implications for education. In Donaldo Macedo (Ed.), *Decolonizing foreign language education. The misteaching of English and other colonial language* (pp. 152–168). Routledge.

Gardner, Robert C., & Lambert, Wallace E. (1972). *Attitudes and motivation in second-language learning*. Newbury House.

Goldstein, Lynn M. (1987). Standard English: The only target for nonnative speakers of English? *TESOL Quarterly, 21*(3) (September), 417–436.

Gunaratnam, Yasmin. (2003). *Researching race and ethnicity: Methods, knowledge, and power*. SAGE Publishing.

Gyimah-Brempong, Adwoa, & Sillman, Marcie. (2018). Black pain, meet Black joy: Coming home to Wakanda. *KUOW.* https://kuow.org/stories/black-pain-meet-black-joy-coming-home-wakanda/

Haller, Hermann W. (2014). Evolving linguistic identities among the Italian-American youth: Perceptions from linguistic autobiographies. *Forum Italicum, 48*(2), 238–252. https://doi.org/10.1177/0014585814529230

Harris, Roxy, & Rampton, Ben (Eds.). (2003). *The language, ethnicity and race reader*. Routledge.

Heller, Monica, Pietikänen, Sari, & Pujolar, Joan. (2018). *Critical sociolinguistic research methods: Studying language issues that matter*. Routledge.

Hicks, Christina C., Fitzsimmons, Clare, & Polunin, Nicholas. (2010). Interdisciplinarity in the environmental sciences: Barriers and frontiers. *Environmental Conservation, 37*(4), 464–477. https://doi.org/10.1017/S0376892910000822

Hill, Jane. (1998). Language, race, and white public space. *American Anthropologist, 100*(3), 680–689. https://doi.org/10.1525/aa.1998.100.3.680

Holliday, Nicole R., & Squires, Lauren. (2021). Sociolinguistic labor, linguistic climate, and race(ism) on campus: Black college students' experiences with language at predominantly white institutions. *Journal of Sociolinguistics, 25*(3), 418–437. https://doi.org/10.1111/josl.12438

Ibrahim, Awad El Karim M. (1999). Becoming Black: Rap and hip-hop, race, gender, identity, and the politics of ESL learning. *TESOL Quarterly, 33*(3), 349–369. https://doi.org/10.2307/3587669

Keaton, Trica Danielle, Sharpley-Whiting, T. Denean, & Stovall, Tyler Edward (Eds.). (2012). *Black France / France noire: The history and politics of Blackness*. Duke University Press.

Kramsch, Claire. (1997). The privilege of the non-native speaker. *PMLA, 112*(3), 359–369.

Kramsch, Claire. (2009). *The multilingual subject: What foreign language learners say about their experience and why it matters*. Oxford University Press.

Kubota, Ryuko. (2009). Rethinking the superiority of the native speaker: Toward a relational understanding of power. In Neriko Musha Doerr (Ed.), *The native speaker concept: Ethnographic investigations of native speaker effects* (pp. 233–247). Mouton de Gruyter.

Linguistic Society of America. (2019). LSA statement on race. https://www.linguisticsociety.org/content/lsa-statement-race

Lippi-Green, Rosina. (1997). *English with an accent: Language, ideology, and discrimination in the United States*. Routledge.

Lozès, Patrick. (2012). "Black France" and the national identity debate: How best to be Black and French? In Trica Danielle Keaton, T. Denean Sharpley-Whiting, & Tyler Edward Stovall (Eds.), *Black France / France noire: The history and politics of Blackness* (pp. 123–144). Duke University Press.

Lyons, Kenyse. (2019). A voice from the margins: Reflections of a sister outsider on her voyage to Italy and through Italian studies. In Siân Gibby & Anthony Julian Tamburri (Eds.), *Diversity in Italian studies* (pp. 125–148). John D. Calandra Italian American Institute.

Macedo, Donaldo P. (Ed.). (2019). *Decolonizing foreign language education: The misteaching of English and other colonial languages*. Routledge.

Makoni, Sinfree, Smitherman, Geneva, Ball, Arnetha, & Spears, Arthur (Eds.). (2003). *Black linguistics: Language, society, and politics in Africa and the Americas*. Routledge.

Milroy, Lesley, & Gordon, Matthew. (2003). *Sociolinguistics: Method and interpretation*. Blackwell.

Motha, Suhanthie. (2014). *Race, empire, and English language teaching: Creating responsible and ethical anti-racist practice*. Teachers College Press.

Ndiaye, Pap. (2008). *La condition noire: Essai sur une minorité française*. Calmann-Lévy.

Norton, Bonny. (1997). Language, identity, and the ownership of English. *TESOL Quarterly, 31* (3), 409–429. https://doi.org/10.2307/3587831

Norton, Bonny. (2000). *Identity and language learning: Gender, ethnicity and educational change*. Longman.

Omi, Michael, & Winant, Howard. (2015). *Racial formation in the United States*, 3rd ed. Routledge.

Paris, Django, & Winn, Maisha T. (Eds). (2014). *Humanizing research: Decolonizing qualitative inquiry with youth and communities*. SAGE Publishing.

Pauker Kristin, Meyers, Chanel, Sanchez, Diana T., Gaither, Sarah E., & Young, Danielle M. (2018). A review of multiracial malleability: Identity, categorization, and shifting racial attitudes. *Social and Personality Psychology Compass 12*(6), 1–15. https://doi.org/10.1111/spc3.12392

Portelli, Alessandro. (2004). The problem of the color blind: Notes on the discourse on race in Italy. In Paul Spickard (Ed.), *CrossRoutes: The meaning of race for the 21st century* (pp. 355–364). Routledge.

Rampton, Ben, Cameron, Deborah, Harvey, Penelope, Richardson, Kay, & Frazer, Elizabeth. (2018). *Researching language*. Taylor and Francis.

Rampton, Ben. (1995). *Crossing: Language and ethnicity among adolescents*. Longman.

Ramsdell, Lea. (2004). Language and identity politics: The linguistic autobiographies of Latinos in the United States. *Journal of Modern Literature, 28*(1), 166–176. https://doi.org/10.2979/JML.2004.28.1.166

Rosa, Jonathan, & Flores, Nelson. (2017). Unsettling race and language: Toward a raciolinguistic perspective. *Language in Society, 46*(5), 621–647. https://doi.org/10.1017/S0047404517000562

Said, Edward W. (1979). *Orientalism*. Vintage Books.

Shih, Shu-Mei M. (2008). Comparative racialization: An introduction. *PMLA*, *123*(5) (October 2008), 1347–1362.

Smith, Maya Angela. (2019). *Senegal abroad: Linguistic borders, racial formations, and diasporic imaginaries*. University of Wisconsin Press.

Smith, Maya Angela. (2020). As a Black mother-to-be, I am already full of heartache. *Boston Globe*. https://www.bostonglobe.com/2020/06/14/opinion/black-mother-to-be-im-already-full-heartache/

Smith, Maya Angela. (2021a). Enunciating power: Amanda Gorman and my battle to claim my voice. *Yes! Magazine*. www.yesmagazine.org/opinion/2021/02/16/amanda-gorman-claiming-my-voice/

Smith, Maya Angela. (2021b). A people's song upon the waters: A familial examination of the sea chantey lays out its African American roots. *Zócalo Public Square*. https://www.zocalopublicsquare.org/2021/04/08/african-american-tradition-sea-chantey-singers/ideas/essay/

Smith, Maya Angela. (2021c). *Reclaiming Venus: The many lives of Alvenia Bridges*. http://mayaangelasmith.ds.lib.uw.edu/ReclaimingVenus/

Smith, Maya Angela. (2022a). Creating a more diverse, equitable, and inclusive French foreign language classroom. *ADFL Bulletin*, *47*(2), pp. 12-26.

Smith, Maya Angela. (2022b). Inclusive pedagogies in Italian studies: Using sociolinguistic data to decolonize the curriculum. *Italian Studies in Southern Africa*, *35*(1), 204–225.

Smith, Maya Angela. (2022c). *Sénégalais de l'étranger: Frontières linguistiques, formations raciales et imaginaires diasporiques* (Raphaëlle Etoundi, Trans.). TBR Books.

Solórzano, Daniel, Ceja, Miguel, & Yosso, Tara. (2000). Critical Race Theory, racial microaggressions, and campus racial climate: The experiences of African American college students. *Journal of Negro Education*, *69*: 60–73.

Spielberg, Steven (dir.). (1987). *The color purple*. DVD. Warner Home Video.

Squizzero, Robert, Horst, Martin, Wassink, Alicia Beckford, Panicacci, Alex, Jensen, Monica, Moroz, Anna Kristina, Conrod, Kirby, & Bender, Emily M. (2021). Collecting and using race and ethnicity information in linguistic studies. White paper. Department of Linguistics, University of Washington.

Talburt, Susan, & Stewart, Melissa A. (1999). What's the subject of study abroad? Race, gender, and "living culture." *Modern Language Journal*, *83*(2) (June), 163–175. https://doi.org/10.1111/0026-7902.00013

Thomas, Jamie A. (2022). A fish tale about "fieldwork," or toward multilingual interviewing in applied linguistics. *Annual Review of Applied Linguistics 42*, 127–136. https://doi.org/10.1017/S026719052200006X

Thomas, Jamie A. (2024). Community college linguistics for educational justice: Content and assessment strategies that support antiracist and inclusive teaching. In Anne H. Charity Hudley, Christine Mallinson, & Mary Bucholtz (Eds.), *Inclusion in linguistics*. Oxford University Press.

Trouillot, Michel-Rolph. (2003). *Global transformations: Anthropology and the modern world*. Palgrave Macmillan.

Zippia. (n.d.). The Career Expert. French teacher demographics and statistics in the US. https://www.zippia.com/french-teacher-jobs/demographics/.

Megan Figueroa is a developmental psycholinguist and research scientist in the Department of Psychology at the University of Arizona. She is also the co-host of *The Vocal Fries,* a podcast about linguistic discrimination. She completed her PhD in linguistics at the University of Arizona in 2018, where her doctoral work focused on children's morphosyntactic development and overgeneralization of linguistic patterns. Her latest work addresses the cultural mismatch between research on children's language development and the diverse realities of children's language environments and linguistic repertoires. Her perspective is shaped by her own experience growing up in a working-class Mexican American home. She recognized her family in deficit-based descriptions of language development in the literature, and she endeavors to broaden our collective understanding of language development by disrupting these inequitable and inaccurate descriptions.

Abstract: Not everything is known about how children develop language. It is understood that parents don't teach their kids language—that's just not how it works because language development is much more natural than that. But researchers act like parents *do* teach their kids language. They say some parents are better at teaching language and some kids are better at learning it. Some researchers even claim certain parents are so bad at language that their kids will hear 30 million fewer words by the time they enter school. That's 30 million fewer words for kids to learn from, they say. This is called the language gap, and it's completely ridiculous. Worse, it's straight-up racist. Time after time, language gap research claims that racialized kids and families are the ones not doing language right, while the language of middle- and upper-class white people should be imitated. This is all just another way to protect white supremacy in a settler-colonial country.

Key Words: linguistic racism, language development, language gap rhetoric, deficit models of language

8

Decolonizing (Psycho)linguistics Means Dropping the Language Gap Rhetoric

Megan Figueroa (she/her)
University of Arizona

Introduction

The US is a settler-colonial state that, since its inception, "destroys to replace" to maintain white supremacy (Wolfe, 2006). Language has always been central to the colonial project. US President Theodore Roosevelt proclaimed, "America is a nation—not a polyglot boarding house . . . There can be but one loyalty—to the Stars and Stripes; one nationality—the American—and therefore only one language—the English language" (Maher, 2017, p. 122). Indigenous communities experienced language shift and federally attempted linguicide driven by land dispossession, forced removal, and other brutal acts of settler-colonial violence (Leonard, 2021). Indigenous children were forcibly taken from their communities to attend government-run boarding schools that forbade the use of Indigenous languages, with the goal, as stated by the US Commissioner of Indian Affairs, Jonathan Atkins, that "their barbarous dialects should be blotted out and the English language substituted" (Atkins, 1978). Decades later, my father and his classmates were met with corporal punishment for speaking Spanish, the only language they knew, while attending public school in Bisbee, Arizona in the 1950s. Decades later, I would not speak Spanish because settler-colonialism, in linguistics and beyond, destroys to replace.

As scholars have shown, linguistics has played a key role in these colonizing processes (e.g., Errington, 2008). While most discussions of this issue have focused on historical linguistics, language documentation, and sociolinguistics, the field of psycholinguistics also bears responsibility for the colonial mindset of much of contemporary linguistics. In this chapter, I examine the putative "language gap" as an example of ongoing colonial and racist rhetoric that permeates psycholinguistic research. (I refer to the notion of a " language gap" and idea of "quality" language input within quotations or mark

---

Megan Figueroa, *Decolonizing (Psycho)linguistics Means Dropping the Language Gap Rhetoric* In: *Decolonizing Linguistics.*
Edited by: Anne H. Charity Hudley, Christine Mallinson, and Mary Bucholtz, Oxford University Press.
© Anne H. Charity Hudley, Christine Mallinson, and Mary Bucholtz 2024. DOI: 10.1093/oso/9780197755259.003.0009

these terms with the phrase "so-called" to emphasize the subjective nature of these descriptions and to communicate that I do not support their underlying racist assumptions.) The "language gap" is the preposterous claim that racialized and otherwise historically marginalized children are exposed to lesser "quality" language input than middle and upper-class white children, leading to "less successful" language development. "Racialized" is to be understood as the people who, through colonization, chattel slavery, and subsequent oppression, have been situated as inferior in socially constructed racial terms. It is an active and ongoing process of oppression. Given that ongoing settler-colonialism relies on rhetorical and ideological devices to maintain settlers' occupation of territory (Leonard, 2021), I argue that "language gap" rhetoric works to colonize by maintaining white supremacy through situating whiteness and its associated linguistic behaviors as both materially and immaterially valuable, while pathologizing and Othering the linguistic behaviors of racialized populations. Remediating the alleged deficiencies of racialized populations by prescribing and imposing white linguistic norms is a paternalistic, colonial, white-supremacist practice that preserves the power relationships that were violently established earlier in the settler-colonial history of the United States. This rhetoric reflects and reproduces settler-colonial violence and anti-Blackness and has no room in a decolonized and anti-racist (psycho)linguistics. At the end of the chapter, I outline some of the steps that need to be taken to move psycholinguistics toward this goal.

Psycholinguistics and the So-Called Language Gap

The notion that science is objective and that facts are value-neutral, a fundamental assumption of psycholinguistics, renders invisible the power relations that construct all knowledge (Dupree & Kraus, 2022; Else-Quest & Hyde, 2016). The knowledge that any knower brings to a given project cannot be separated from their lived experiences. Crucially, every researcher comes to a task from a particular standpoint, which provides only a limited view and understanding of the phenomenon under study (Sprague, 2005; Wylie, 2004). In addition, researchers can end up creating the phenomenon they are studying through biased research design (see also miles-hercules, 2024). In psycholinguistics, language development, and within that area of research, linguistic input, is largely studied through a white lens with a focus on white middle- and upper-class families of Western European descent (Clancy & Davis, 2019). A recent analysis of the linguistic diversity of articles in four major academic journals of child language development from their inception to 2020 (around 45 years) found that 54% of studies focused exclusively on English, and another 30% were focused on languages from the Indo-European family (Kidd & García, 2022). Further, the authors of 87% of the articles were from either North America or Europe (mostly in Northern or Western Europe). These findings are unsurprising: members of the white middle and upper classes are disproportionally represented in academia. Thus, generalizations about language development from white families of Western European descent are taken for granted as "normal" and are essentialized as "non-ideological common sense" (Fairclough, 2001, p. 31) by overwhelmingly white researchers, authors, and readers.

This is a matter of epistemology. Currently, there is no equity across epistemologies, generally, and within the field of psycholinguistics, specifically. Many racialized scholars have been told that their work engaging race and ethnicity is "not linguistics." Anne H. Charity Hudley, Christine Mallinson, and Mary Bucholtz (2020) found that many racialized linguists are not in linguistics departments at all, preferring to work in departments (though, not necessarily psychology departments) that support their research that centers on race and racial justice. This erasure of racialized scholars and students excludes their unique experiences, standpoints, and epistemologies. What happens when this is the case is that deficit perspectives of racialized children, families, and communities are promoted with little objection. As an example, Thomas Sowell claimed that "the goals and values of Mexican Americans have never centered on education" (1981, p. 266). If this work were required reading for me, I would have no trouble calling "bullshit."

Disrupting this ideological perspective requires us to abandon the objectivist stance that white supremacy can hide behind. One way to do this is by using the tool of the counterstory: "a method of telling the stories of those people whose experiences are not often told" (Solórzano & Yosso, 2002, p. 32). I engage with the "language gap" discourse not only as a psycholinguist, but also as a Mexican American woman and a first-generation college student from the US Southwest. I grew up mostly as an English monolingual in a working-class family. My parents were both union workers who grew up in poverty. Both of my parents speak what would be labeled as a "nonstandard" variety of English. My dad was born to Mexican immigrants and speaks both Mexican Spanish and Chicano English. My mom is Anglo and speaks a variety of English that is influenced by both Southern English and Chicano English; she understands some Spanish but doesn't speak the language. From kindergarten to third grade, I went to a Title I segregated public school in Phoenix, Arizona. Title I is a federal designation in the US given to schools with a high proportion of low-income families. In practical terms,

Title I schools are extremely underresourced and with largely racialized student populations. These are the types of students often described in "language gap" work as "low-income."

Given my lived experience, I am situated outside of dominant ideologies and claims to truth and knowledge about language development. I am therefore better positioned to offer a critical perspective of the deficit models of racialized children's language that I present here (Sprague, 2005). I can present a counterstory.

Simply put, the language use of racialized children, families, and communities has historically been perceived as a deficit and overtly described in terms of deficiency because the US has a foundational problem of white supremacy. Although "race" is a social construct of domination created to maintain a power dynamic that privileges white people, and not a biological reality, it has real-world consequences precisely because of racism and racialization processes (Crenshaw et al., 1995). Institutionalized racism in academia and related "helping" professions pathologizes the language use of racialized children, families, and communities, positioning them as deficient because societal structures are designed to benefit the dominant group (i.e., white people in the US context). Marking racialized groups for linguistic remediation decreases their access to opportunities and resources. This is linguistic racism. To be sure, white children living in poverty also experience some form of linguistic prejudice. However, under white supremacy, poor white children are taught to believe they can eventually hit the target of standardized linguistic competence. By contrast, even when racialized language users engage in linguistic practices that are situated as "normative" based on standardized language ideologies (i.e., when they "sound white" or "sign white"), their language will still be perceived as "deficient" when scrutinized by a white perceiving subject (Flores & Rosa, 2015). When my dad chose to speak to me as a child in English and not Spanish, he knew that raciolinguistic ideologies conflate the language use of racialized bodies with linguistic deficiency (Flores & Rosa, 2015; Rosa & Flores, 2017). He was attempting to safeguard me against these perceived deficiencies by removing Spanish from the equation because being subjected to corporal punishment in school convinced him, consciously or not, that Spanish was a hindrance to success in a white-supremacist society.

The psycholinguistic idea of "deficient" language has been repackaged across time. The current wave of deficiency discourse began with psychologists Betty Hart and Todd Risley's 1995 monograph *Meaningful Differences in the Everyday Experience of Young American Children*, which is considered by many both inside and outside of academia as a foundational text that reifies the relationship between early home language exposure and use and later academic and economic success. Hart and Risley were interested in the linguistic environments of children across socioeconomic backgrounds: were there class-based interactional differences between caregiver and child that could account for later academic success or failure? However, the belief that any caregiver could manipulate the linguistic input their child receives in such a life-altering way that the child will be set up to "succeed" in school and beyond ignores the role of structural factors like institutionalized racism in constructing "success" and "failure" (Milner, 2012).

Hart and Risley claimed that more socioeconomically advantaged parents direct both a higher quantity of language (i.e., more words) and a higher "quality" of language (e.g., exaggerated intonation, "baby talk," conversational dyads, syntactically complex sentences, the ever-changing list goes on) to their children than their counterparts from disadvantaged socioeconomic backgrounds, resulting in children in the latter group experiencing a "gap" of 30 million words by the time they are four years old. This claim was characterized in shorthand as the so-called word gap and later as the "language gap". Thus, in order to succeed academically, the poor families must "bridge the gap." Importantly, the figure 30 million is an extrapolation from averages in Hart and Risley's observational data from 42 families—collected once a month for one hour over a two-year period—a minuscule window into children's lives. This window is likely affected by the observer's paradox: "The aim of linguistic research in the community must be to find out how people talk when they are not being systematically observed; yet we can only obtain this data by systematic observation" (Labov, 1972, p. 209). Since the researchers were white and all the lower-income families were Black, it is likely that the interpretations of the observational data were even less reflective of the families' authentic linguistic behaviors. Further, only one of the middle-class families in Hart and Risley's study was Black, so the researchers conflated socioeconomic class with race while simultaneously failing to examine the systemic patterns of historical harm under institutionalized racism. That is, classism and class-based disparities are inextricable from disparities that are due to racialization processes (Blanchett, 2006). Hence, Black, Indigenous, and other racialized communities are disproportionately represented in the lowest socioeconomic groups because socioeconomic disadvantage is a key component of institutionalized racism and racial segregation is a key component of the perpetuation of poverty (Pitts-Taylor, 2019). Hart and Risley's failure to address this fundamental fact discredits the entire study.

My introduction to the so-called language gap and Hart and Risley's monograph was during my linguistics PhD program. Although many scholars, particularly sociolinguists, have debunked the idea of a language gap (e.g., Avineri et al., 2015; Baugh, 2017; Blum, 2017; Johnson, 2015; to name very few), I was assigned the monograph in a speech, language, and hearing course on language development. I immediately saw that the study questions, design, implementation, and conclusions are racist. Why did the authors assume that there must be language problems within poor families and communities instead of interrogating the idea that traditional measures of "success" position these populations as inherently deficient? Because of such research, families like mine are told to subscribe to the "right" kind of linguistic practices by changing their behavior toward white middle- and upper-class norms. Within a deficit paradigm, individual behaviors, not structural injustice, become the target of intervention. Studies grounded in the unquestioned reality of the "language gap" rely on the racial ideological stance of color-evasiveness, which emerges from a racially stratified society that relies on a narrative of "the American Dream" and values "equal opportunity, meritocracy, and dispositionalism" (Syed et al., 2018, p. 814). I use "color-evasiveness" following Annamma and colleagues' (2017) expansion of color-blind racial ideology to (1) explicitly name the erasure of racialized people's and communities' experiences via evasion and (2) move beyond the ableism inherent in a term like "color-blind" that equates blindness with ignorance.

As a first-generation college student from a working-class Mexican American family, I already knew that the United States isn't a meritocracy. If it were, I wouldn't be the first in my family to go to college. I felt out of my element in graduate-level courses because of the gatekeeping nature of academia. As an example, a friend in my PhD program told me that others in our program were made uncomfortable when I talked about being from a working-class family. Knowing that, to be assigned to read flawed scholarship that claimed families and childhoods like mine were deficient was infuriating as well as further isolating because the study immediately rang false to me, yet my white classmates didn't question it. Some even thought I was a nuisance for talking about my childhood and my family. Further, the sterile classroom environment imposed a tone of dispassionate engagement, even with a topic that was personally urgent and painful to me. I did not yet have the language to articulate how my feelings about the so-called language gap were legitimate knowledge. I now understand that in fact my viewpoint was far more relevant than my white peers or professors (Wylie, 2004), since I had grown up in a community that was directly impacted by Hart and Risley's racist generalizations and I could offer a counterstory to the dominant discourse.

I pursued the study of linguistics because I wanted to answer a single question: Why did my dad speak Spanish and I did not? A few years ago, as the co-host of a podcast about linguistic discrimination, I had the honor of interviewing Arizona's Chicano Poet Laurate, Alberto Álvaro Ríos. He shared his lived experience of using Spanish and English in the borderlands:

> You got swatted . . . for doing something bad. So, we didn't just learn, you know, our first lesson in language, we got our first lesson in making an equation. And our parents said listen to your teacher . . . You know that you're going to get swatted for speaking Spanish, and you know that you speak Spanish, and you know you get swatted for doing something wrong. You make the equation. You're feeling this with the body. Second grade comes around and the equation widens out. Your body is a little bigger and it fits more now. Because now it's been demonstrated. You get swatted for speaking Spanish and you start to recognize by second grade: your parents speak Spanish, your family speaks Spanish, and if Spanish is bad, they, then, must be bad. Now you don't say that out loud, but you have learned it through the mechanisms of the body, not the intellect. (Gillon & Figueroa, 2017)

As a kid, I didn't have the ability to appreciate my dad and his standpoint, his lived experience. All I knew was that I didn't like the situation and I wanted answers. As I got older, my lack of Spanish felt like a flesh wound and it wasn't healing. But I was beginning to understand the type of flesh wounds that my dad carried on his body when he was six years old. I already knew that by attempting to prepare me for a white-supremacist society by withholding Spanish, my dad was performing an act of love, but reading Hart and Risley in a sterile classroom in my twenties, I learned there is no winning for us in a white-supremacist society. There I was (and others like me), in the pages of their monograph, assumed deficient based on demographic variables.

The "language gap" discourse outright ignores two axioms in the field of linguistics: first, that children learn the language variety of their environment whether spoken or signed, without direct teaching; and second, that all language varieties are systematic, rule-governed, productive, creative, and equal. How, then, could some linguistic input be "quality" and other input be deficient? Practices selectively legitimizing linguistic input as "quality" are rightly termed *linguistic racism*, as they function to reproduce institutionalized inequity that emphasizes standardization and favors white supremacy. As education scholar Christopher Scott points out, schooling is "the medium in which government maintains quality control on its people" (2021). Schools become spaces of hyper-surveillance. This is facilitated and accelerated by standardized tests (Milner, 2012).

Standardization does not exist without framing one group, the most powerful, as the norm (see also Henner, 2024). Deviation from the "norm," that is, language variation and linguistic diversity, only leads to negative outcomes

164 Decolonizing Linguistics

for racialized students when success is evaluated with measures based on linguistic racism masquerading as fact. Poor Black student's below average performance on racist assessments does not exist and persist because of their linguistic deficits (whatever that means): rather, these measures are working as designed to perpetuate the status quo and structurally maintain white linguistic hegemony, specifically, and white supremacy, more broadly (Baker-Bell, 2020; Baugh, 2017). In fact, the economy of deficit in academia has served the "normal" child well, since standardized tests "serve the purpose of recreating the racial and class stratification that students and their families experience outside of school" (Williams & Land, 2006, p. 582).

Of course, these days most psycholinguists do not explicitly state that the language use of racialized groups is deficient; many scholars have even moved away from "gap" language altogether. Instead, the earlier charges of deficiency have been repackaged in coded terms and descriptions, like "quality" linguistic input. "Quality" linguistic input has been constructed in the developmental literature in a myriad of ways, some of them contradictory. For example, longer utterances and more relative clause use have been described as "necessary" for language development, but so has child directed speech defined by shorter utterances and exaggerated intonation (Anderson et al., 2021; Schwab & Lew-Williams, 2016). Putting aside the fact that children will learn the language to which they are exposed without special efforts from caregivers, a damning problem with the notion of "quality" linguistic input is that the features claimed to be "quality" are not universal characteristics of either communication or of child rearing. For example, many researchers consider one-at-a-time conversational turn-taking between parent and child a magic bullet in the fight to bridge the so-called language gap even though this communicative style is not universal. Similarly, *wordism*—the idea that the more words the better—is a value specific to certain communities and cultures (Blum, 2015). Additionally, the concept of *mean length of utterance* rewards children who produce longer utterances, an arbitrary measure of linguistic dis/ability. This ideology of "quality" is reflected in mainstream research methodologies. William Labov (1966) points out that standardized measures of language ability are

> the natural product of educational psychology, which is concerned more with discriminating among children than finding out what a given child's actual capacity is. By subjecting each child to a "controlled" stimulus, they are able to claim scientific status for the comparisons they make between individual children . . . and in fact, these pictures of the child's capacity are so profoundly misleading that they are an open invitation to educational disaster. (pp. 5–6)

Decolonizing (Psycho)linguistics 165

Labov was right. In practical terms, maintaining white linguistic hegemony through language development research under "language gap" rhetoric means measuring "intelligence," "cognitive skills," "language skills," or "ability" with instruments that are testing vocabulary knowledge. For example, many studies use receptive or expressive vocabulary as their dependent measure of children's language development. As a review of studies of the effects of linguistic environment on children's later cognitive and language development found, "The most commonly used standardized assessment to measure language or cognitive development was the MacArthur-Bates Communicative Development Inventories (MCDI)" (Zauche et al., 2016, p. 321). The MCDI is a parent-completed instrument in which caregivers indicate which words on a predetermined list their children produce or comprehend, depending on age.

However, vocabulary knowledge is socially based and dynamic. The vocabulary included on or excluded from the MCDI is also rooted in the social world, not the mind. Measuring which words children know from a predetermined list only tells researchers which words on that list children know or reported by their parents as knowing. Treating such information as important is a matter of epistemology—and standardized tests purposefully measure only one way of knowing in order to preserve white supremacy (Milner, 2012; Yosso, 2005). Further, not every caregiver is concerned with their child having a robust vocabulary, however that might be defined—my own mother told me she wasn't (C. Figueroa, personal communication, 2021). Nevertheless, by not subscribing to the "right" kind of linguistic practices or ideologies, racialized families and communities are declared by white researchers to lack the tools to support their children. This cycle inevitably continues because there is a sense that "motherhood [and increasingly parenthood] is something to be endlessly worked on by academic research" (Allen & Spencer, 2022, p. 1183). And in order to "accelerate" language development, the modes of optimization keep shifting.

Even when racialized caregivers' interactions with their child(ren) exhibit the characteristics of so-called "quality" input, it is never enough. Hart and Risley found, for example, that "the children in the welfare [i.e., low-income] families heard a prohibition twice as often as they heard affirmative feedback" (1999, p. 169). It is not the case that these caregivers failed to produce any affirmative feedback, which the researchers considered a marker of "quality" input, they did not use as much of this kind of language the researchers subjectively decided was "quality." In such research, the socially constructed idea of "quality" is forever moving further down the line—an "imagined line" that Ofelia García and colleagues (2021) refer to as "ongoing coloniality" (p. 3). Not only is it hard to pin down what exactly constitutes "quality" linguistic input given the wide range of descriptions in the literature, but racialized caregivers are unlikely ever to hit the mark when the descriptions are embedded in coloniality and institutionalized racism.

The point that is too often missing in mainstream scientific discourse on language development is that research predicated on the so-called language gap puts racialized children and their families at risk by following a familiar recipe of deficit models: first, you identify a social problem, such as the lower rates of academic "success" among low-income children who are disproportionately racialized. Then, you conduct a study to find out how affluent and impoverished children differ in some way. Next, you identify some differences and define these as the cause of the social problem. Finally, you apply an intervention to "correct" the differences among the poor children (Valencia, 1997). While there has been a discursive shift in psycholinguistics and related fields from deficiency to what Boykin and Allen (2000) call a "proactive difference stance," this does not mean that deficit thinking has been eliminated. Highlighting difference will always result in racialized children, not middleclass and upper-class white children, being Othered or even falsely labeled disabled (Annamma et al., 2013). Difference invites comparison, and locating differences often puts groups in opposition to each other (Else-Quest & Hyde, 2016). For example, proponents of the language gap perspective argue, "It is crucial to understand the source of these *differences* to design effective, evidence-based interventions" (Golinkoff et al., 2019, p. 1; emphasis added). However, the question I have is: If you really see them as differences and not deficits, why would you need to intervene at all? And why is it never the white kids who are made to change? In this way, researchers are responsible for further marginalizing racialized communities and undermining their agency (Milner, 2012). The shifting discourse from deficient to different, from quantity to "quality," are ad hoc distinctions that function solely to uphold the status quo.

Intervening in the lives of racialized families to promote the use of "quality" linguistic input isn't just unhelpful, it's dehumanizing. As Ansgar Allen and Sarah Spencer point out, this focus on the role of parents, particularly mothers, "[commits them] to a permanent labor in which they are expected to better themselves as measured by the manifest language development of their children" (2022, p. 1183). Interventions promoted by researchers are paternalistic, colonizer prescriptions for parents to abandon their familial or individual child-rearing practices in favor of linguistic behaviors associated with white people in order to maintain white linguistic hegemony (e.g., Weber et al., 2017). Psycholinguists become agents of colonialism. Importantly, given the demographics of higher education, and especially psycholinguistics, where racialized scholars and students remain extremely underrepresented, the foundational problem of white nationalism is routinely ignored and raciolinguistic ideologies often go unchallenged even as white scholars build their careers by exploiting racialized communities.

How to Move Toward a Decolonized (Psycho)Linguistics

As I (and many other scholars) have argued, "language gap" rhetoric generates inequality by selectively legitimizing linguistic behaviors associated with middle-class and upper-class white people as "quality," while positioning language use by racialized communities as inherently deficient and in need of remediation. To be absolutely clear, there is no such thing as "quality" linguistic input. "Quality" is a value judgment, not an inherent characteristic of language. This conception only serves to reproduce inaccurate and deficit-based representations of racialized children and families. As it stands, researchers blatantly misinterpret racialized children's academic performance and language development as deficient on the grounds that the linguistic input of their environments is not of sufficient "quality"—as they themselves define it—to nurture cognitive or intellectual growth. Imposing white linguistic norms on racialized communities fails to call out the underlying racism and colonial violence that undergird beliefs about linguistic deficiency in the first place.

It is a game that cannot be won. It is destroying to replace. One of the most honest descriptions of what an intervention would need to look like for children from racialized communities under a deficit perspective is from Hart and Risley: "An intervention must address not just a lack of knowledge or skill, but an entire general approach to experience" (2003, p. 9). Destroy. Replace. The institutional forces that worked to replace my dad's Spanish with English destroyed my opportunity as a child to have a relationship with my dad in Spanish, his first language.

Individual racist beliefs or intentions aren't necessary to further a deficit perspective, or to further racism more generally and to participate in a system that destroys to replace. I can't presume to know the true intentions of each and every researcher, but even good intentions often divert attention from systemic issues. The "language gap" discourse serves to uphold the status quo and avoids politically divisive ideas and solutions—uncomfortable solutions that involve true paradigm shifts and the reallocation of power and

168 Decolonizing Linguistics

resources (Wesley, 2021). Black feminist poet Audre Lorde (1984) pointed out that Black women "become familiar with the language and manners of the oppressor, even sometimes adopting them for some illusion of protection" (p. 114). "Language gap" rhetoric works to colonize by maintaining white supremacy through situating whiteness and its associated linguistic behaviors as both materially and immaterially valuable. A paradigm shift involves interrogating the systems that force racialized people to adopt the linguistic behaviors of the white middle and upper classes for success in school and beyond. It also involves changing the way "success" is measured in the educational system. One small way to do so is to stop using vocabulary—socially dependent knowledge—as a measure of language and/or cognitive development and abilities because this only rewards the "normal" child who is the product of a white and middle- to upper-class upbringing.

A paradigm shift also involves critically examining why some scientific questions have been valued over others. Researchers must admit that science is not an objective endeavor. Robin Wall Kimmerer (2013), scientist, author, and enrolled member of the Citizen Potawatomi Nation, says of the state of science:

> Getting scientists to consider the validity of Indigenous knowledge is like swimming upstream in cold, cold water. They've been so conditioned to be skeptical of even the hardest of hard data that bending their minds toward theories that are verified without the expected graphs or equations is tough. Couple that with the unblinking assumption that science has cornered the market on truth and there's not much room for discussion. (p. 160)

Scientists must challenge deeply held beliefs about the nature of "science" and the myth of "objectivity" (Dupree & Kraus, 2022). As it stands, many lack critical consciousness of the social positions they hold. Many racialized scholars within the field of linguistics have been told that their work engaging race is "not linguistics," while the color-evasiveness of white researchers allows them to position themselves as "objective."

Psycholinguists have inherited fields of inquiry, like psychology, that owe their beginnings to proving the genetic and cultural deficiency of racialized people, particularly Black people (Boykin & Allen, 2000; Winston, 2020). Further, generalizations about language development from white families of Western European descent are taken for granted as "normal" because members of the white middle and upper classes disproportionally write, review, and read scientific articles. Shifting away from a deficit framework, or a difference framework that is covertly deficit-based, will allow us to move beyond inaccurate and limiting descriptions of language and language development. Psycholinguists must begin to work within this knowledge to broaden our theories to include historical and present-day context because without acknowledging institutionalized racism, only the most egregious and/or superficial examples of racism are eradicated, if those (Delgado & Stefancic, 2001; Trawalter et al., 2020). Finally, we must reject easily digestible and simplistic descriptions of language development that are predicated on the behavior of a very narrow subset of human diversity.

A decolonized, anti-racist field of linguistics does not have room for "language gap" rhetoric. The gap metaphor is "one of the most prevalent forms of contemporary racism in U.S. schools" (Yosso, 2005, p. 75). Teachers and educators who consume research on the "language gap" can adopt deficit perspectives of racialized students and transfer them into the classroom milieu. Adair and colleagues (2017) found that teachers citing the "word gap" had lowered expectations for Latinx/e students. Those lowered expectations translated into classroom practice, such that Latinx/e students were not given learning opportunities that were agentive and promoted self-efficacy. These characteristics are valued in the school setting and serve as indicators of "ability" and "readiness." Thus, the "language gap" discourse has become a self-fulfilling prophecy, reproducing inequities that it purports to challenge (Arnold & Faudree, 2019).

The "language gap" discourse is pervasive in psycholinguistics and adjacent fields, as well as public discourse, and bridging the gap remains of utmost importance to many researchers. It is time to stop searching for gaps and scrutinize the systems that consistently position racialized children as deficient and/or disabled. If research is grounded in the idea that "quality" is an inherent characteristic of language rather than a social construct meant to uphold white supremacy, that work is complicit in the perpetuation of a deficit view of the language use of racialized communities.

What we "know" about child language development is intrinsically linked to who conducted the research, what research methodologies and instruments were used, and the larger system under which the research is published and disseminated (Syed et al., 2018). Under the current model, the types of research questions and topics that are valued are constructing an inaccurate view of language and language development. Respecting diverse standpoints, like mine, as legitimate, would allow racially offensive ideas to be understood as such so they can then be challenged. To dismiss the experiences and epistemologies of racialized researchers as "not scientific" or "too emotional" is

170 Decolonizing Linguistics

essentially promoting epistemic racism in (psycho)linguistics (Figueroa, 2022). The idea that parents could manipulate the linguistic input their child is exposed to in a way that would set them up for "success" in academia and beyond is ridiculous when examined critically from my standpoint.

Countering linguistic and epistemic racism will take enormous effort—effort that racialized people have been undertaking since settler-colonialism first arrived in the Americas. We cannot dismiss the reality that these inequities have been accepted uncritically since this country's beginnings and that they are deeply embedded in academic institutions and disciplines. Mainstream science will never interrupt the cycle of harm perpetuated by white supremacy because to do so would require a true paradigm shift and the equitable reallocation of social power (Leonard, 2021). A true paradigm shift would mean that people like me would no longer read offensive descriptions of ourselves in so-called scientific papers. It is long past time to acknowledge the racist and colonial foundation that so many place beneath their science.

References

Adair, Jennifer Keys, Sánchez-Suzuki Colegrove, Kiyomi, & McManus, Molly E. (2017). How the word gap argument negatively impacts young children of Latinx immigrants' conceptualizations of learning. *Harvard Educational Review, 87*(3), 309–334.

Allen, Ansgar, & Spencer, Sarah. (2022). Regimes of motherhood: Social class, the word gap and the optimization of mothers' talk. *The Sociological Review, 70*(6), 1181–1198.

Anderson, Nina J., Graham, Susan A., Prime, Heather, Jenkins, Jennifer M., & Madigan, Sheri. (2021). Linking quality and quantity of parental linguistic input to child language skills: A meta-analysis. *Child Development, 92*(2), 484–501.

Annamma, Subini Ancy, Connor, David, & Ferri, Beth. (2013). Dis/ability Critical Race Studies (DisCrit): Theorizing at the intersections of race and dis/ability. *Race, Ethnicity and Education, 16*(1), 1–31.

Annamma, Subini Ancy, Jackson, Darrell D., & Morrison, Deb. (2017). Conceptualizing color-evasiveness: Using Dis/ability Critical Race Theory to expand a color-blind racial ideology in education and society. *Race, Ethnicity, and Education, 20*(2), 147–162.

Arnold, Lynnette, & Faudree, Paja. (2019). Language and social justice: Teaching about the "word gap." *American Speech, 94*(2), 283–301.

Atkins, Jonathan D. C. (1978). "The English language in Indian Schools." In Francis Paul Prucha (Ed.), *Americanizing the American Indians: Writings by the "Friends of the Indian" 1880–1900* (pp. 197–206). University of Nebraska Press.

Avineri, Netta, Johnson, Eric, Brice-Heath, Shirley, McCarty, Teresa, Ochs, Elinor, Kremer-Sadlik, Tamar, Blum, Susan, Zentella, Ana Celia, Rosa, Jonathan, Flores, Nelson, Alim, H. Samy, & Paris, Django. (2015). Invited forum: Bridging the "Language Gap." *Journal of Linguistic Anthropology, 25*(1), 66–86.

Baker-Bell, April. (2020). *Linguistic justice: Black language, literacy, identity, and pedagogy.* Routledge.

Baugh, John. (2017). Meaning-less differences: Exposing fallacies and flaws in 'The Word Gap' hypothesis that conceal a dangerous 'language trap' for low-income American families and their children." *International Multilingual Research Journal, 11*(1), 39–51.

Decolonizing (Psycho)linguistics 171

Blanchett, Wanda J. (2006). Disproportionate representation of African Americans in special education: Acknowledging the role of white privilege and racism. *Educational Researcher, 35*(6), 24–28.

Blum, Susan D. (2015). "Wordism": Is there a teacher in the house? *Journal of Linguistic Anthropology, 25*(1), 74–75.

Blum, Susan D. (2017). Unseen WEIRD assumptions: The so-called language gap discourse and ideologies of language, childhood, and learning. *International Multilingual Research Journal, 11*(1), 23–38.

Boykin, A. Wade, & Allen, Brenda A. (2000). Beyond deficits and difference: Psychological integrity in developmental research. *Advances in Education in Diverse Communities: Research, Policy, and Praxis, 1*, 15–34.

Charity Hudley, Anne H., Mallinson, Christine, & Bucholtz, Mary. (2020). Toward racial justice in linguistics: Interdisciplinary insights into theorizing race in the discipline and diversifying the profession. *Language, 96*(4), e200–e235.

Clancy, Kathryn B. H., & Davis, Jenny L. (2019). Soylent is people, and WEIRD is white: Biological anthropology, whiteness, and the limits of the WEIRD. *Annual Review of Anthropology, 48*, 169–186.

Crenshaw, Kimberlé, Gotanda, Neil T., Peller, Gary, & Thomas, Kendall. (1995). *Critical Race Theory: The key writings that formed the movement*. The New Press.

Delgado, Richard, & Stefancic, Dean. (2001). *Critical Race Theory: An introduction*. New York University Press.

Dupree, Cydney H., & Kraus, Michael W. (2022). Psychological science is not race neutral. *Association for Psychological Science, 17*(1), 270–275.

Else-Quest, Nicole M., & Shibley Hyde, Janet. (2016). Intersectionality in quantitative psychological research: I. Theoretical and epistemological issues. *Psychology of Women Quarterly, 40*(2), 155–170.

Errington, Joseph. (2008). *Linguistics in a colonial world: A story of language, meaning, and power*. Blackwell Publishing.

Fairclough, Norman. (2001). *Language and Power*, 2nd ed. Longman.

Figueroa, Megan. (2022). Podcasting past the paywall: How diverse media allows more equitable participation in linguistic science. *Annual Review of Applied Linguistics, 42*, 40–46.

Flores, Nelson, & Rosa, Jonathan. (2015). Undoing appropriateness: Raciolinguistic ideologies and language diversity in education. *Harvard Educational Review, 85*(2), 149–171.

García, Ofelia, Flores, Nelson, Seltzer, Kate, Wei, Li, Otheguy, Ricardo, & Rosa, Jonathan. (2021). Rejecting abysmal thinking in the language education of racialized bilinguals: A manifesto. *Critical Inquiry in Language Studies, 18*(3), 203–228.

Gillon, Carrie, & Figueroa, Megan. (Hosts). (2017, November 13). Borderlands/La frontera [Audio podcast episode]. In The Vocal Fries.

Golinkoff, Roberta Michnick, Hoff, Erika, Rowe, Meredith L., Tamis-LeMonda, Catherine S., & Hirsh-Pasek, Kathy. (2019). Language matters: Denying the existence of the 30-million-word gap has serious consequences. *Child Development, 90*(3), 985–992.

Hart, Betty, & Risley, Todd R. (1995). *Meaningful differences in the everyday experience of young American children*. Brookes Publishing.

Hart, Betty, & Risley, Todd R. (2003). The early catastrophe: The 30 million word gap by age 3. *American Educator, Spring*, 4–9.

Henner, Jon. (2024). How to train your abled linguist: A crip linguistics perspective on pragmatic research. In Anne H. Charity Hudley, Christine Mallinson, & Mary Bucholtz (Eds.), *Inclusion in linguistics*. Oxford University Press.

Johnson, Eric J. (2015). Debunking the "language gap." *Journal for Multicultural Education, 9*(1), 42–50.

Kidd, Evan, & Garcia, Rowena. 2022. How diverse is child language acquisition research? *First Language, 42*(6): 723–735.

172   Decolonizing Linguistics

Kimmerer, Robin Wall. (2013). *Braiding Sweetgrass*. Milkweed Editions. Kindle Edition.

Labov, William. (1972). *Language in the Inner City: Studies in the Black English Vernacular*. University of Pennsylvania Press.

Labov, William. (1966). Finding out about children's language. *Working Papers in Communication, 1*, 1–30.

Leonard, Wesley Y. (2021). Toward an anti-racist linguistic anthropology: An Indigenous response to white supremacy. *Journal of Linguistic Anthropology, 31*(2), 218–237.

Lorde, Audre. (1984). *Sister outsider: Essays and speeches*. Crossing Press.

Maher, John C. (2017). *Multilingualism: A Very Short Introduction*. Oxford University Press.

miles-hercules, deandre. (2024). (Trans)forming expertise: Transness, equity, and the ethical imperative of linguistics. In Anne H. Charity Hudley, Christine Mallinson, & Mary Bucholtz (Eds.), *Inclusion in linguistics*. Oxford University Press.

Milner, H. Richard IV. (2012). Beyond a test score: Explaining opportunity gaps in educational practice. *Journal of Black Studies, 43*(6), 693–718.

Pitts-Taylor, Victoria. (2019). Neurobiologically poor? Brain phenotypes, inequality, and biosocial determinism. *Science, Technology, & Human Values, 44*(4), 660–685.

Rosa, Jonathan & Flores, Nelson. (2017). Unsettling race and language: Toward a raciolinguistic perspective." *Language in Society, 46*(5), 621–647.

Schwab, Jessica F., & Lew-Williams, Casey. (2016). Language learning, socioeconomic status, and child-directed speech. *WIREs Cognitive Science, 7*(2), 264–275.

Scott, Christopher. (2021). Country, color, and class: Talking right, talking white in the academy. In Gaillyn Clements & Marnie Jo Petray (Eds.), *Linguistic discrimination in U.S. higher education* (pp. 139–155). Taylor & Francis.

Solórzano, Daniel G., & Yosso, Tara J. (2002). Critical race methodology: Counter-storytelling as an analytical framework for education research. *Qualitative Inquiry, 8*(1), 23–44.

Sprague, Joey. (2005). *Feminist methodologies for critical researchers: Bridging differences*. AltaMira Press.

Syed, Moin, Santos, Carlos, Yoo, Hyung Chol, & Juang, Linda P. (2018). Invisibility of racial/ethnic minorities in developmental science: Implications for research and institutional practices. *American Psychologist, 73*(6), 812–826.

Trawalter, Sophie, Bart-Plange, D-J, & Hoffman, Kelly M. (2020). A socioecological psychology of racism: making structures and history more visible. *Current Opinion in Psychology, 32*, 47–51.

Valencia, Richard R. (1997). *The evolution of deficit thinking: Educational thought and practice*. Routledge Farmer.

Weber, Ann, Fernald, Anne, & Diop, Yatma. (2017). When cultural norms discourage talking to babies: Effectiveness of a parenting program in rural Senegal. *Child Development, 88*(5), 1513–1526.

Williams, Dawn G., & Land, Roderic R. (2006). The legitimation of Black subordination: The impact of color-blind ideology on African American education. *Journal of Negro Education, 75*(4), 579–588.

Winston, Andrew S. (2020). Scientific racism and North American psychology. In Ingrid Johnsrude (Ed.), *Oxford research encyclopedia of psychology*. Oxford University Press.

Wolfe, Patrick. (2006). Settler colonialism and the elimination of the Native. *Journal of Genocide Research, 8*(4), 387–409.

Wylie, Alison. (2004). Why standpoint matters. In Sandra Harding (Ed.), *The feminist standpoint theory reader: Intellectual & political controversies* (pp. 339–352). Routledge.

Yosso, Tara J. (2005). Whose culture has capital? A Critical Race Theory discussion of community cultural wealth. *Race Ethnicity and Education, 8*(1), 69–91.

Zauche, Lauren Head, Thul, Taylor A., Mahoney, A. E. D., & Stapel-Wax, Jennifer L. (2016). Influence of language nutrition on children's language and cognitive development: An integrated review. *Early Childhood Research Quarterly, 36*(3), 318–333.

PART 2
DECOLONIZING METHODS OF TEACHING AND RESEARCH

Lynnette Arnold is assistant professor at the University of Massachusetts, Amherst, which is located on stolen Nipmuc and Pocomtuck land and was built through the theft of Native lands in the Western part of Turtle Island. She seeks to advance social justice through reflexive and critical pedagogies in her linguistic anthropology courses. Her research focuses on the power of language in the experiences of families living stretched between El Salvador and the United States. These emphases carry over into her longstanding involvement with migrant justice work, most recently with the Trans Asylum Seeker Support Network, an abolitionist mutual aid collective in Western Massachusetts. Ongoing lessons from students, migrants, and community have contributed to her journey of unlearning white supremacy and becoming an accomplice in anti-racist struggles.

Abstract: In the deeply colonial field of linguistics, teaching is a vital component of decolonization. Pedagogical efforts can destabilize the normative canon and train diverse future linguists in new ways of studying language. The power of pedagogy is particularly clear in introductory classes, and this chapter suggests that incorporating a focus on race and language is vital for creating introductory courses that center the experiences of students of color. The author analyzes her experience implementing a raciolinguistic introductory curriculum as a white instructor teaching at a predominantly white institution. She evaluates curricular impact through a comparative analysis of student responses in two demographically different sections: one section was made up of students of color, while the other section was majority white. The author openly discusses her mistakes, engaging with these shortcomings to argue that decolonial teaching must ultimately include deep internal work as well as structural efforts within our institutions and the field.

En la disciplina de lingüística, la enseñanza es un componente vital de la descolonización. Hay esfuerzos pedagógicos que pueden desestabilizar el canon normativo y formar a una diversidad de futuras lingüistas en nuevas formas de estudiar el lenguaje. El poder de la pedagogía resulta particularmente evidente en las clases de nivel introductorio, y en este capítulo se sugiere que la incorporación de un enfoque que combine raza y lengua es importante para crear cursos introductorios que se centren en las experiencias de los estudiantes de color. La autora analiza su experiencia en implementar un currículo raciolingüístico como una instructora blanca que enseña clases introductorias en una Universidad Predominantemente Blanca. Evalúa el impacto curricular por medio de un análisis comparativo de las respuestas de los estudiantes en dos secciones del curso con demografías muy distintas: una sección estuvo formada por estudiantes de color mientras que la otra fue mayoritariamente blanca. La autora comenta abiertamente sobre sus errores, argumentando con la perspectiva de que la enseñanza decolonial debe incluir un trabajo interno muy profundo en combinación con esfuerzos estructurales en nuestras instituciones y en el campo de estudio.

Key Words: pedagogy, curriculum, raciolinguistics, introductory courses, higher education

9

From Gatekeeping to Inclusion in the Introductory Linguistics Curriculum

Decolonizing Our Teaching, Our Psyches, Our Institutions, and Our Field

Lynnette Arnold (she/her)
University of Massachusetts Amherst

Introduction

Teaching is a vital element of decolonial struggles.[1] Given the saliency of decolonization in much contemporary scholarship (Introduction, this volume), it is vital to clearly state how we approach this work in our local contexts (Montoya, this volume). In suggesting that teaching be approached as decolonizing work, I follow recent scholarship within linguistics and linguistic anthropology that has emphasized the deeply colonial nature of our fields (Davis & Smalls, 2021; Leonard, 2021). Linguistic scholarship too often relies on extractive methodologies and mobilizes theories that privilege Western ways of knowing the world (Kubota, 2020). The disciplinary—and disciplining—structures of our field assume and reproduce white normativity (Leonard, 2021). These colonial epistemologies and practices are grounded in a logic of dispossession that consistently targets both Native and Black communities (Davis & Smalls, 2021).

The pervasive coloniality of our field means that our teaching, too, must be decolonized, and indeed, that doing so can contribute to the decolonization of linguistics and to the academy as a whole. Here, I draw on a legacy of critical pedagogical scholarship which demonstrates the liberatory potential of teaching (Freire, 2000; hooks, 1994; 2003; Paris, 2012). This is not to say that teaching does not reproduce the theories, methods, and structures of the field; indeed, this is often the case. However, critical pedagogies can create space for change. Readings, course materials, and lectures can disrupt the canon and envision new ways of doing linguistics; these practices can then be enacted

---

Lynnette Arnold, *From Gatekeeping to Inclusion in the Introductory Linguistics Curriculum* In: *Decolonizing Linguistics*.
Edited by: Anne H. Charity Hudley, Christine Mallinson, and Mary Bucholtz, Oxford University Press.
© Anne H. Charity Hudley, Christine Mallinson, and Mary Bucholtz 2024. DOI: 10.1093/oso/9780197755259.003.0010

through assignment design and in classroom interactions. Beyond the experience of the immediate course, teaching practices have longstanding effects as they contribute to the formation of future generations of linguists.

The power of pedagogy is particularly clear in introductory level courses, which are a crucial point of entry into the field. Although these classes have the potential to recruit diverse future generations of linguists, they all too often function as gatekeeping mechanisms. Black, Brown, Indigenous, and Melanated (BBIM) students often feel "that linguistics is a field in which their experiences are not relevant" (Calhoun et al., 2021, p. e13) due to the curricular emphasis on linguistic structure and terminology, which elides their lived experience of language as a site of profound personal and sociopolitical significance. (At the suggestion of Candice Thompson, I draw here on the work of Louiza Doran (2022), who argues that the label Black, Brown, Indigenous, and Melanated (BBIM) is more specific than alternatives like "people of color" and also works powerfully to decenter whiteness).

In recognition of this fact, several universities have now begun to offer an introductory course in sociocultural linguistics (Bucholtz & Hall, 2005) as a precursor to the traditional introduction to linguistics. These courses aim to bring students into linguistics through a curriculum that focuses on language in its social and cultural context, and often fulfill a general education requirement. While such courses are an important step, I suggest that in order to truly advance inclusion, all introductory courses—regardless of their curricular focus—must consistently foreground the ways that language is fundamentally intertwined with race. This focus is vital for creating culturally relevant linguistics pedagogies for BBIM students (see Thomas, 2024).

To advance this goal, this chapter examines the curriculum of introductory sociocultural linguistics courses. I begin by reviewing past research, focusing particularly on previous efforts to design curricula specifically for BBIM students. I then outline my own experience in incorporating race and language into introductory sociocultural linguistics courses, highlighting my positionality as a white instructor at a Predominantly White Institution (PWI). I describe my efforts to revise the curriculum to center race, examining its effectiveness by comparing students' final reflections in two sections of the course with very different demographics: a large, lecture course with primarily white students and a small seminar made up entirely of first-generation BBIM students (see Mantenuto et al., 2024, for more on first-generation students). I reflect honestly on the shortcomings and challenges of my efforts to draw out important lessons learned. Ultimately, I suggest that isolated interventions are insufficient to the project of decolonization (Leonard, 2021), which requires a complete overturning of curriculum to center BBIM students in conjunction with broader efforts to unlearn our own internalized colonial attitudes and to restructure the institutions within which we work.

Race and Language in the Introductory Linguistics Curriculum

To date, scholarship on linguistics pedagogy has conceptualized introductory courses as a form of linguistics communication (Gawne et al., 2024) that counteracts dominant language myths and disseminates "basic knowledge about language" (Spring et al., 2000, p. 110). Introductory courses can also help students appreciate linguistic diversity by advocating descriptive rather than prescriptive approaches (Milambiling, 2001). While these are important aims, this approach to introductory pedagogy assumes that students come to linguistics at best with limited knowledge. Such assumptions ignore the funds of knowledge (Moll et al., 1992; Vélez-Ibáñez and Greenberg, 1992) that many multidialectal and multilingual BBIM students bring to the classroom, knowledge that is often based on deep lived experience of the complexity of linguistic diversity and the power of language to shore up racial inequality.

Envisioning students as language neophytes leads to curricula designed for a white listening subject (Flores & Rosa, 2015). The white listening subject is a racially hegemonic mode of perception that centers white normativity; it operates not only through biographical individuals but also through institutional forces such as educational policy, standardized testing, and curricular design. For instance, introductory linguistics courses often include attention to debunking "language myths" such as "everyone has an accent except me" or "some languages are just not good enough" (Bauer & Trudgill, 1999). Assuming that students hold such beliefs positions them as white monolingual speakers who lack personal experience with and understanding of the sociopolitical power of language. By centering the perspective of a white listening subject, introductory curricula make white students—and white instructors—comfortable within linguistics, while excluding BBIM students by invalidating their funds of knowledge. Too often, then, introductory courses enact colonial disposession through curricular design.

To effectively de-center whiteness and work to decolonize linguistics, I argue that introductory curricula should incorporate a raciolinguistic perspective, which emphasizes the "co-naturalization of language and race" (Rosa & Flores, 2017, p. 622). A raciolinguistic lens examines how racial and linguistic categories are simultaneously produced and naturalized, particularly through historically grounded institutional ideologies and practices.

Although there is growing research on raciolinguistic pedagogies in primary and secondary educational settings (Daniels, 2018; Hamm-Rodríguez & Morales, 2021; Seltzer, 2019), as well as in college contexts in disciplines adjacent to linguistics (Rajendran, 2019; Chang, 2020; Milu, 2021), scholarship on raciolinguistics in college-level linguistics courses remains sparse. This gap is particularly notable given the development of critical work on race and language teaching in applied linguistics (Anya, 2021; Anya & Randolph, 2019). The lack of attention to teaching race in linguistics is part of a longstanding disregard for pedagogy in the field, although this is beginning to change with the launch of the teaching-focused section of the premier linguistics journal, Language (Hiramatsu & Martinez, 2021). The consistent focus on critical pedagogy throughout these volumes on decolonization and inclusion in linguistics is thus a timely and crucial contribution to the field.

Black linguists are leading current efforts to create liberatory educational spaces in linguistics by drawing on raciolinguistic perspectives (see also Thornton, 2024). Kendra Calhoun and colleagues (2021) describe an introductory linguistics course designed specifically for Black students that aimed to draw them into the field by centering Black language and culture throughout the course; this focus consistently celebrated the linguistic agency, creativity, and resilience of Black communities. This curricular design connected students' experiential knowledge of African American English to linguistic terminology, successfully deepening their engagement by making linguistics relevant to their lives. The course was part of the Talking College initiative, a project focused on Black language and culture, race, and education. The project produced a book (Charity Hudley et al., 2022) that supports greater inclusion by highlighting the ways that raciolinguistic ideologies structure multiple facets of higher education. The course, the book, and the broader initiative all center the lived experiences of Black students as the foundation for teaching linguistics in ways that advance inclusion.

Drawing on insights from these efforts, I suggest that raciolinguistics is vital to introductory curricula for two interconnected reasons. Firstly, because the production of racial hierarchies is fundamental to the way language operates, no introduction to linguistics can be complete without including this examination; nevertheless, such topics are generally left to more advanced linguistics courses, if they are addressed at all (Calhoun et al., 2021). Secondly, if incorporated carefully, a raciolinguistic curriculum can disrupt white hegemony and coloniality within the field. A raciolinguistic perspective foregrounds the expertise of multilingual and multidialectal BBIM students (see Chung & dela Cruz, 2024; Lederer, 2024) rather than addressing a primarily white listening subject. By centering the agency and creativity of language use within BBIM communities, a raciolinguistic curriculum also counters the white perspectives and voices that have dominated the field's canonical understanding of language (Babcock, 2021; Durrani, 2019).

Developing raciolinguistic curricula in introductory courses must therefore be understood as a fundamentally anti-racist project that actively contributes to decolonization (Clemons, this volume; Ryan et al., this volume). Such work requires continual attention to the positionalities of individual instructors and their institutional contexts. The ethnoracial identity of the instructor is of utmost importance in teaching about race. Black students often do not respond well to having their own language and culture taught by non-Black instructors, even as white students tend to treat information about race from Black instructors as less credible (Weldon, 2012). As a white instructor, I understand this pedagogical work as a critical part of my obligation to take responsibility for the impacts of settler-colonialism and white supremacy, an engagement that pushes me to continually grapple with my own complicity in racial inequality.

In terms of institutional contexts, I teach at a public institution in the Northeast that is a "land grab university" (Lee & Ahtone, 2020). Under the Morrill Act of 1862, federal and state governments gave the university 366,711 acres of stolen Native land from the western part of Turtle Island; the university in turn sold this land to generate revenues to build the campus where I now teach (https://www.landgrabu.org/universities/university-of-massac husetts). This stolen Native land has been used to advance the careers of predominantly white faculty like myself and to serve primarily white students: at the time of this research, fully 69% of undergraduate students, 66% of graduate students, 80% of staff, and 76% of faculty were white (Office of Equity and Inclusion, 2021). Given the historical and contemporary ways that my university has benefitted from colonialism and supported white hegemony, there is much decolonizing work to be done. In my curricular efforts, I take inspiration from the Native American Advisory Council at my university, which, among other efforts, has worked to foster Indigenous pedagogy and institutional spaces (https://www.umass.edu/diversity/native-american-advisory-council).

At PWIs like my institution, decolonization goes hand-in-hand with efforts to disrupt deeply entrenched white hegemony. PWIs are often "racially alienating and hostile spaces" for BBIM students (Harper, 2013, p. 183). In particular, Black students report being constantly hyperaware of their language at PWIs and exerting immense physical, emotional, and psychological effort to try to meet others' expectations (Holliday and Squires, 2021; Charity Hudley et al. 2022). Although creating a truly welcoming environment for

180 Decolonizing Linguistics

BBIM students clearly involves institutional work that extends well beyond the classroom, teaching is nevertheless a fundamental part of this work. In addition, those of us teaching at PWIs may be able to use our classrooms to reach many white students, for whom a raciolinguistic perspective is a vital tool for questioning and disrupting their own complicity in linguistic racism (Baker-Bell, 2020, p. 100). In what follows, I outline my experiences in this project, following the lead of Nicole Gonzales-Howell and colleagues (2020), who suggest that honestly sharing our process and shortcomings can open up space for growth in our collective struggle for justice.

Curricular Redesign to Center Raciolinguistics

During two semesters (Fall 2019 and Fall 2020), I taught two simultaneous sections of my Language, Culture, and Communication course. One section was a large lecture course with approximately 130 students of all levels, while the other was a small seminar of 18 first-year students. Both sections of the course followed the same syllabus, explored the same readings, and had the same assignments, although the formats of the courses differed. The large class met three times a week: twice for 50-minute lectures, and once in sections, in which a graduate TA led discussions with smaller groups of approximately 20 students. The seminar-style class met twice a week for 75 minutes, and while I did deliver some short lectures, it was much more discussion-based. In the second semester (Fall 2020), the courses were both offered remotely due to the COVID-19 pandemic. Students in both sections of the course watched the same prerecorded short lectures, completed asynchronous assignments, and met synchronously for discussion. This shift in modality of instruction, compounded by the ways the COVID-19 pandemic exacerbated racial inequality (Lopez et al., 2021), no doubt shaped student's experience in the 2020 courses. However, I am unable to discuss these issues in depth in this short chapter.

In both cases, students were primarily taking the course to fulfill general education requirements, but the two groups were otherwise quite distinct. The large lecture course reflected the demographics of the PWI where I teach, while the small seminar was entirely made up of BBIM students, most of whom were multilingual and/or multidialectal. This section of the course was offered in conjunction with the Emerging Scholars Program (ESP), in which a cohort of high-achieving first-generation students takes classes together in their first year while also living in a residential community. The program, coordinated in conjunction with the Commonwealth Honors College, aims to provide focused mentoring and develop strong cohorts to help support BBIM students to succeed academically as they navigate this PWI (Residential Academic Programs, 2021).

In 2019, my first year of teaching these parallel sections, I observed striking differences in how students responded to the curriculum. For instance, halfway through the semester, students read the first chapter of Samy Alim and Geneva Smitherman's (2012) book *Articulate While Black*, which argues that Barack Obama's ability to code-switch between African American English and "standard" English contributed to his success as a US Presidential candidate. Students in the large lecture course treated this as simply another reading, or as an opportunity to engage in partisan political critique. However, in the smaller ESP section, this same reading sparked intense engagement. As multidialectal and multilingual BBIM students, the ESP scholars had deep lived experience of code-switching, and this knowledge led to an insightful conversation about the politics and consequences of using racialized varieties versus the hegemonic white "standard," I wondered what it would be like to create an introductory course where conversations like this one would be the norm rather than the exception, one in which the white normativity of the field, of myself as an instructor, and of our PWI was destabilized so that the linguistic knowledge and perspectives of BBIM students could be always front and center.

This experience led me to revise the curriculum of both sections of the course in Fall 2020 to incorporate a more consistent focus on raciolinguistics. Given the widespread Black Lives Matter protests in summer 2020, I focused in particular on anti-Black linguistic racism. The course was organized with weekly topical foci grouped into three units, as shown in Table 9.1. Assignments were designed to help students master and apply course concepts; each week students submitted a data example from news or social media and used one key concept from that week to analyze their example in greater depth. Students also completed a linguistic autobiography, discussing an experience in which they were socialized to particular ways of using language and examining how this experience revealed the entanglement of language and power.

Each week, students generally read a chapter from the course textbook—*Living Language* (Ahearn, 2017)—as well as another academic piece and sometimes news articles focused on the same theme. In 2020, I included more work by African American scholars of language and culture, but nevertheless, 50% of authors were white, 31% Black, and 19% non-Black people of color. In reporting these demographics, I exclude the news articles, as it is often difficult to find detailed information about the authors online. For co-authored

182 Decolonizing Linguistics

Table 9.1 Outline of Revised 2020 Curriculum

Week	Fall 2020	
1	Introduction: Language as Personal and Political	Unit 1: Language
2	What is language?	
3	Indexicality and Multimodality	
4	Power and Agency	
5	Language Socialization	Unit 2: Community
6	Language and Community: Identity and Performativity	
7	Gender and Sexuality	
8	Race and Ethnicity	
9	Language and Racism	Unit 3: Current Issues
10	Language and Migration	
11	Language Endangerment and Reclamation	
12	Language and Health	
13	Where do we go from here?	

readings, each author was counted individually. The textbook author was only counted once, but if she were counted once for each chapter assigned, that would bring the total representation of white authors in course readings to 67%. This dominance of white voices is a clear reflection of the longstanding exclusionary nature of linguistics, as well as of my formation in the field and ongoing struggle to move beyond my own white normativity.

To address this imbalance, I incorporated more diverse voices through multimodal materials. I wanted to bring in the perspectives of BBIM individuals in nonexploitative ways, particularly as these materials were also being used to expand the awareness of predominantly white students. For this reason, I focused on multimodal resources that foregrounded the creativity, agency, and resilience of language practices used in BBIM communities. I included short videos such as Jamila Lysicott's *Three Ways to* Speak English (2014), and also assigned documentary films in place of a second weekly reading on two occasions: *Talking Black in America* (Language and Life Project, 2020) and *We Still Live Here—Âs Nutayuneân* (Makepeace Productions, 2010). Each of these pieces highlights the perspectives of BBIM activists, educators, scholars, and artists, who theorize language in ways that emerge directly from the experiences of their communities.

A central aim in my curricular redesign was to foreground how language acts both politically and personally in the world, often reproducing but also contesting racialization and its material consequences for people's lives. For instance, during the first week of the semester, students read "How to Tame a Wild Tongue" (1987), by queer Chicana writer Gloria Anzaldúa, and Black feminist scholar bell hooks's "Language: Teaching New Words/New Worlds" (1994). In both essays, the authors use their own linguistic experiences to elucidate the deeply personal and inescapably political nature of language as both racialized violence and as a means of resistance. Following this thread through to the end of the course, the final unit foregrounded the entanglement of language in racialized inequalities by focusing on contemporary issues including racism, migration, language endangerment and reclamation, and health. As a result of this redesign, raciolinguistic perspectives were introduced from the beginning of the course and woven more consistently throughout the curriculum. There was also more course time dedicated to focused discussions of language and racial inequalities: six weeks in 2020 (46% of the course), as compared to four weeks in 2019 (31% of the course). In what follows, I trace the impact of this curricular redesign by examining students' final reflection responses to the course.

Student Responses: Tracing Impacts and Limitations

At the end of the class, I asked students as part of their course participation grade to record a two-minute video discussing what they were taking away from the course. The videos were recorded and hosted using Flipgrid (https:// info.flipgrid.com/), a platform that facilitates free video conversations for educational purposes. In the large lecture class, 87 students (67% of those enrolled) recorded a video response and in the small ESP seminar, 16 students (84%) made a recording. These differential response rates were characteristic of different levels of overall engagement in the two sections. Students in the small ESP seminar all needed to maintain high grades in order to remain in the Honors College, whereas the larger lecture section included some students who simply needed to pass the course to fulfill a general education requirement. For this study, I downloaded transcripts of these videos, and with the assistance of a research assistant, anonymized them and coded them qualitatively using the software NVivo. The Institutional Review Board only permitted this posthoc analysis on fully de-identified student work, so I was unable to utilize the demographic data of individual students in the analysis. Given the demographics of the large lecture section, identifying students by race might reveal the identity of individual respondents. Instead, I compare responses from students in the large lecture section to those from students in the small ESP seminar. Since the latter was made up entirely of BBIM students, while the former reflected the demographics of the PWI where I teach, this comparative analysis helps to reveal how a raciolinguistic curriculum is received by differently positioned students.

Across both sections of the course, students responded positively to multimodal materials such as short video clips and documentaries. In particular, *Talking Black in America* made a strong impression: it was the single most mentioned resource. Students stated that the film helped them understand how Black language has been continually shaped by structural racism even as it serves as a vital cultural resource for resistance and Black joy. Resonating with previous work (cf. Dozier, 2017), this finding suggests that incorporating multimodal recordings can be a crucial strategy for teaching about race at PWIs. To maximize their impact these resources should not simply be left for students to watch on their own time, but rather should be screened and discussed in class; this practice can actively work to decenter the voice and authority of the white instructor, contributing to the disruption of white normativity.

There was also a great deal of similarity across sections in how students described the primary impacts of the course. For both sections, the three most frequently mentioned takeaways from the course were: (1) a new, albeit depoliticized, awareness of language in their lives; (2) greater insights into the political nature of their personal experiences with language; and (3) an understanding of the political nature of language in society at large. Many students mentioned more than one of these themes in their comments. Table 9.2 shows the rate of mention for each of these themes in both sections, which was calculated as the number of mentions divided by the total number of responses for that section, in order to facilitate comparison across the two. However, looking more closely at student responses reveals that the course had very different effects for students in the two sections.

Students in the large lecture class were more likely to state that the course had sparked a new awareness about the role of language in their lives, but they did not draw connections between language and systemic racism. For instance, 20% of students in the lecture mentioned the linguistic autobiography assignment as an impactful aspect of the course. Students reported that

Table 9.2 Rates of Mention for Most Frequent Themes

Themes	Large Lecture	ESP Seminar
De-politicized new awareness of language in their life	1.87 (n=163)	1.56 (n=25)
Insights into the politics of personal experiences of language	1.52 (n=132)	2.06 (n=33)
Political nature of language in society	1.16 (n=101)	1.19 (n=19)

the assignment helped them gain deeper insight into how their language use had shaped personal experiences such as moving to another region, starting college, or joining the hockey team. Ultimately, students in the large section seemed to take away a fairly depoliticized understanding of the role of language, one in which raciolinguistic perspectives were not foregrounded.

On the other hand, students in the ESP seminar were more likely to discuss new insights they had gained into the political role of language in their lives, for instance with experiences of bilingualism or language policing. The ESP students were much more likely to mention linguistic racism than their peers in the large lecture class (ESP rate of 1.19 (n = 19) compared to lecture rate of 0.71 (n = 62)). These statements often connected their personal experiences to larger-scale raciolinguistic ideologies and structures. For instance, one student described the many societal forces that pushed them to stop speaking their home language and shared that through the course "I came to a monumental realization that previously had been the cause of inner torment and loathing: that my language loss was not my fault." For this student, the raciolinguistic perspectives introduced in the course helped to interrupt colonial discourses that blame language shift on BBIM communities.

These responses indicate that my curricular redesign had very different impacts for students in the two sections. Of course, these outcomes were likely shaped by the different format of the two classes, as students in the ESP seminar had greater opportunities for peer-to-peer dialogue than those in the large lecture section. In addition, through the ESP program, these students spent time together in their shared dormitory, so that conversations begun in class never ended there. Clearly, having space for ongoing and sustained dialogues about race and language is vital to students' ability to think through and fully take on raciolinguistic understandings.

In addition, I suggest that the different ethnoracial identities of students in the classes also profoundly shaped their engagement with the course material. For the predominantly white students in the large lecture course, the course may have been their first encounter with the entanglement of language and racial inequality, whereas for the ESP students, it provided a broader framework for naming and understanding their own experiences with language. Implementing the raciolinguistic curriculum in the context of the ESP created a learning environment in which the concerns and experiences of BBIM students were centered. As a result of their existing funds of knowledge about language and race, students from the ESP seminar were more likely to leave the course with a deeply raciolinguistic understanding of language. However, the majority white students in the lecture class generally did not fully take on these perspectives, reflecting a serious limitation of the curricular redesign, which ultimately failed to interrupt the white privilege of willful ignorance about structural racism.

One potential exception to this pattern emerged in discussions of whiteness, which, although it was mentioned less frequently than the three most prominent themes, appeared at approximately the same rate in the responses from both sections (lecture rate of 0.15 and ESP rate of 0.18). Across sections, these mentions revealed a general understanding that "standard English" emerges from and shores up white hegemony. In addition, in the lecture section, several white students reported that the course led them to grapple with their own linguistic privilege and resulting obliviousness to the racial politics of language. They stated that their newfound awareness was a basis for action. For instance, one student shared, "I now understand that language is a focal point for social change, and I've learned that as a white male, I have privilege and I can use this privilege to help spearhead progressive change towards more inclusive and equitable political policies and social standards." While this student envisioned taking political action, in an account that admittedly resonates with tropes of the "white savior," most responses suggested a more personal approach, with students saying they planned to continue educating themselves and others about harmful linguistic stereotypes, to change their own language practices to be more inclusive, or to intervene in individual situations of linguistic injustice. These findings suggest the importance of incorporating a more focused de-naturalization of whiteness and language in future iterations of the course by drawing on work such as Mary Bucholtz's (2011) book *White Kids*.

However, even this increased awareness and commitment to personal action on the part of some white students still revealed a persistent lack of understanding of the deeply historical and systemic entanglement of language and racism. Ultimately, the curricular redesign I implemented had contradictory outcomes, failing to help many white students truly confront the white supremacy of language politics, even as it created space in which BBIM students could come to more deeply understand how their experiences with language have been shaped by structural racism. In what follows, I discuss the implications of these findings for efforts to bring raciolinguistic perspectives into the introductory linguistics curriculum.

Discussion and Conclusion

Implementing a raciolinguistics curriculum in introductory courses is challenging, particularly at a PWI. Of course, it is no surprise that teaching white students about race is a difficult undertaking. Such efforts must confront deeply entrenched white ignorance (Martín, 2021; Mills, 1999; 2012), the ways in which white people's willful obliviousness to racism is both produced by and actively sustains white supremacy. Moreover, anti-racist education efforts often run up against white guilt and white fragility, the emotional and behavioral responses that recenter whiteness and subvert meaningful dialogue about racism (DiAngelo, 2018). In PWIs, it is all too easy for such responses by white students to set the tone, dominating class discussions about raciolinguistics and thereby shaping course outcomes for all students. When this occurs, anti-racist teaching efforts can counterproductively shore up the "walls of whiteness" (Brunsma, Brown, & Placier, 2013), or the multi-layered structural shields that protect white students at PWIs from having to critically grapple with white supremacy.

Through these experiences, I have come to see that teaching for inclusion is not enough. The pervasive coloniality of our field and the institutions at which we work call for a much braver approach, one that understands this pedagogical work as part of decolonial efforts. One consequence of this framing for myself as a white professor was to take seriously the important work of decolonizing my own psyche and undoing the ways that my approach to teaching linguistics has been shaped by white normativity. This is an ongoing journey of unlearning that unfolds in dialogue with my students. I am deeply grateful for the opportunity to teach the ESP seminar and will remain forever indebted to the students in the 2019 and 2020 cohorts for everything they taught me. Passing along the lessons I have learned, with the goal of contributing to more liberatory linguistics pedagogies, is one way that I wish to repay their trust and openness to learning alongside me.

Specifically, teaching these courses brought me face-to-face with my own white fragility, reflected in the piecemeal nature of the curricular revisions I undertook. I was concerned about how a more thoroughly raciolinguistic curriculum might negatively impact teaching evaluations from white students. While this is not an insignificant matter for pretenure faculty such as myself, my consideration of this issue recentered whiteness in my curricular redesign. As a result, white students were able to walk away from the course without engaging race specifically, or simply with comforting narratives about their own increased awareness and personal action. Of course, I am not suggesting that one course should be able to single-handedly disrupt deeply entrenched hegemonic whiteness. Rather, I highlight these limitations because doing so is vital to the perpetual "but" of anti-racist work: the ways that every effort brings us face-to-face with further contradictions and challenges (Gonzales Howell et al., 2020). Particularly as a white instructor working at a PWI, I seek to reflect on my own areas of weakness and learn from my mistakes in anti-racist pedagogy (Arnold, 2019). Moving forward, I aim to take up Montoya's (this volume) challenge to engage in a practice of refusal, refusing the privileges that my whiteness grants me in the eyes of the colonial institution, and taking greater risks.

Because the forces of whiteness are so strong—having shaped our field, our individual training, and the institutions at which we teach—I suggest that we must actively and consciously develop curricula that resist the centering of whiteness. Curricular design and pedagogical strategies must consistently center BBIM students, even when—or perhaps especially when—they are numerically in the minority. Such practices can help to destabilize white comfort, pushing back against narratives of racial difference and racism that feel satisfyingly familiar to white people (Delfino, 2021; Roth-Gordon et al., 2020). In arguing for BBIM-centered curricula, I take inspiration from recent work on how Black youth consistently use linguistic practices on social media to enact emphatic Blackness (Smalls, 2019; 2020). These language practices enact small-scale but nevertheless powerful celebrations of Black joy and resilience that disrupt white comfort, even as they center the creative agency of BBIM communities.

The challenge then becomes creating an introductory raciolinguistics curriculum that does not focus solely on linguistic racism but that foregrounds the resilience and resistance of language practices within BBIM communities. Revising the linguistics curriculum in this way will require going beyond scholarship in our field. Teaching about race has drawn a great deal of interdisciplinary attention, as can be seen for instance in the journal *Teaching Sociology* (https://journals.sagepub.com/loi/tsoa), where a quick search revealed 755 articles about teaching race, 70 of which explicitly discuss this work at PWIs. Beyond pedagogical scholarship, we can follow Kendra Calhoun's lead (2021), incorporating literature, music, and spoken word produced by BBIM communities into our curriculum, materials which enact and often simultaneously theorize linguistic resilience.

However, a decolonial approach to teaching must go beyond simple curricular revisions (Montoya, this volume), which will never be sufficient to disrupt deeply entrenched settler-colonialism and white supremacy. Rather, pedagogical work must be approached as one facet of broader structural efforts. My experience teaching the ESP seminar has made clear the vital importance of creating spaces within PWIs that are dedicated to BBIM students. Indeed, current research suggests that such campus counterspaces are vital to the well-being and academic success of BBIM students at PWIs (Brooms et al., 2021; Grier-Reed, 2010; Keels, 2019; Tichavakunda, 2021; Volpe & Jones, 2021).

Within the classroom, I suggest that instructors may productively adopt the idea of the "affinity group" from social movements, in which individuals who share some identity come together to learn from one another (RANT

From Gatekeeping to Inclusion **189**

Collective, 2006). In introductory classrooms, this may look like creating groups in which BBIM and white students can talk separately about course material, perhaps during some course discussion sections. Such affinity group discussions can serve a dual purpose. Most importantly, they provide BBIM students with space to discuss raciolinguistic concerns in an environment free from white fragility. At the same time, white students may have space in which to engage in racial identity development, moving from ignorance about racism toward positive anti-racist white identities (Helms, 1992; Lawrence & Bunche, 1996; Tatum, 1994; Scott, 2001). Moreover, the insights that emerge from these affinity group discussions can then be shared out with the class as a whole, bringing in different perspectives that shed light on—and potentially disrupt—white normativity in the PWI classroom.

Moreover, at PWIs, dismantling the walls of whiteness requires efforts to create BBIM educational spaces on campus that extend beyond the individual classroom to the development of dedicated new programming such as the course designed and taught by Calhoun et al. (2021) or the ESP seminar and program. Linguists must be active in supporting such university-level efforts, as conversations about language, race, and power—among students, but also among faculty and administrators—are vital to the well-being and educational success of BBIM students (Charity Hudley et al., 2022).

It is clear that curricular revisions such as the one I undertook will never be sufficient to the goals of inclusion and decolonization. Ultimately, a decolonized field is not simply one that incorporates more diverse generations of future linguists while maintaining the theoretical and disciplinary status quo. Rather, a truly inclusive linguistics is one in which the canon has been upset and the racial politics of language have taken center stage, because, as Ana Celia Zentella has consistently reminded us, "there is no language without politics" (2018, p. 191). For far too long, introductory courses have functioned as disciplinary gatekeepers, working as one cog in the institutional machinery that has kept linguistics functioning in the service of white hegemony. It is time to turn our curriculum to a liberatory purpose as part of a broader project of decolonial justice.

Note

1. I am deeply grateful to the editors, as well as to colleagues and fellow authors across this volume and its companion volume Aris Clemons, Iara Mantenuto, Candice Thornton, Jamie Thomas, and Jennifer Sclafani for their insightful comments, which pushed my thinking in productive directions and resulted in a much stronger chapter. Any remaining shortcomings or oversights are my own.

References

Ahearn, Laura M. (2017). *Living language: An introduction to linguistic anthropology*, 2nd ed. Wiley-Blackwell.

Alim, H. Samy, & Smitherman, Geneva. (2012). *Articulate while Black: Barack Obama, language, and race in the U.S.* Oxford University Press.

Anya, Uju. (2021). Critical race pedagogy for more effective and inclusive world language teaching. *Applied Linguistics, 42*(6), 1055–1069. https://doi.org/10.1093/applin/amab068.

Anya, Uju, and L J Randolph. (2019). Diversifying language educators and learners, *The Language Educator*, November.

Anzaldua, Gloria. (1987). How to tame a wild tongue. In *Borderlands/La frontera: The new mestiza*, 53–64. Aunt Lute Books.

Arnold, Lynnette. (2019). Accompanying as accomplices: Pedagogies for community engaged learning in sociocultural linguistics, *Language and Linguistics Compass, 13*(6), 1–20. doi:10.1111/lnc3.12329

Babcock, Joshua. (2021). Whiteness and pedagogies of language. *Anthropology News*, 8 (November). https://www.anthropology-news.org/articles/whiteness-and-pedagogies-of-language/.

Baker-Bell, April. (2020). *Linguistic justice: Black language, literacy, identity, and pedagogy*. Routledge.

Bauer, Laurie, & Trudgill, Peter. (Eds.). (1999). *Language myths*. Penguin Books.

Brooms, Derrick R., Jelisa S. Clark, and Jarrod E. Druery. (2021). 'We can redefine ourselves': Enhancing Black college men's persistence through counterspaces. *Journal of Black Studies, 52*(3), 277–295. https://doi.org/10.1177/0021934720976410.

Brunsma, David L., Brown, Eric S., & Placier, Peggy. (2013). Teaching race at historically white colleges and universities: Identifying and dismantling the walls of whiteness. *Critical Sociology, 39*(5), 717–738. doi:10.1177/0896920512446759

Bucholtz, Mary. (2011). *White kids: Language, race and styles of youth identity*. Cambridge: Cambridge University Press.

Bucholtz, Mary, & Hall, Kira. (2005). Identity and interaction: A sociocultural linguistic approach. *Discourse Studies, 7*, 585–614.

Calhoun, Kendra, Charity Hudley, Anne H., Bucholtz, Mary, Exford, Jazmine, & Johnson, Brittney. (2021). Attracting Black students to linguistics through a Black-centered introduction to linguistics course. *Language, 97*(1), e12–e38. Doi:10.1353/lan.2021.0007.

Chang, Sharon. (2020). Raciolinguistic ideology in first-year university (non)heritage Chinese classes. *Language Learning in Higher Education, 10*(2), 491–509. doi:10.1515/cercles-2020-2031

Charity Hudley, Anne, Mallinson, Christine, & Bucholtz, Mary. (2022). *Talking college: Making space for Black language practices in higher education*. Teachers College Press.

Chung, Rhonda, & dela Cruz, John Wayne N. (2024). Pedagogies of inclusion must start from within: Landguaging teacher reflection and plurilingualism in the L2 classroom. In Anne H. Charity Hudley, Christine Mallinson, & Mary Bucholtz (Eds.), *Inclusion in linguistics*. Oxford University Press.

Daniels, Julia R. (2018). "There's no way this isn't racist": White women teachers and the raciolinguistic ideologies of teaching code-switching. *Journal of Linguistic Anthropology, 28*(2), 156–174. doi:10.1111/jola.12186

Delfino, Jennifer B. (2021). White allies and the semiotics of wokeness: Raciolinguistic chronotopes of white virtue on Facebook. *Journal of Linguistic Anthropology, 31*(2), 238–257. doi:10.1111/jola.12310

DiAngelo, Robin. (2018). *White fragility: Why it's so hard for white people to talk about racism.* Beacon Press.

Doran, Louiza. (2022). *According to Weeze.* https://www.accordingtoweeze.com.

Dozier, Crystal A. (2017). Teaching anthropological concepts of race in higher education. *Teaching Anthropology, 7*(1), 15–33. doi:10.22582/ta.v7i1.458

Durrani, Mariam. (2019). Upsetting the canon. *Anthropology News,* 8 (April). https://www.anthropology-news.org/articles/upsetting-the-canon/.

Freire, Paulo. (2000). *Pedagogy of the Oppressed.* 30th anniversary ed. New York: Continuum.

Flores, Nelson, & Rosa, Jonathan. (2015). Undoing appropriateness: Raciolinguistic ideologies and language diversity in education. *Harvard Educational Review, 85*(2),149–171. doi:10.17763/0017-8055.85.2.149

Gawne, Lauren, McCulloch, Gretchen, Sweeney, Nicole, Alatalo, Rachel, Bodenhausen, Hannah, Riley, Ceri, & Grieser, Jessi. (2024). Creating inclusive linguistics communication: Crash course linguistics. In Anne H. Charity Hudley, Christine Mallinson, & Mary Bucholtz (Eds.), *Inclusion in linguistics.* Oxford University Press.

Gonzales Howell, Nicole, Navickas, Kate, Shapiro, Rachael, Shapiro, Shawna, & Watson, Missy. (2020). Embracing the perpetual "but" in raciolinguistic justice work: When idealism meets practice. *Composition Forum,* 44 (Summer). http://compositionforum.com/issue/44/embracing.php

Grier-Reed, Tabitha L. (2010). The African American student network: Creating sanctuaries and counterspaces for coping with racial microaggressions in higher education settings. *The Journal of Humanistic Counseling, Education and Development,* 49(2), 181–188. https://doi.org/10.1002/j.2161-1939.2010.tb00096.x.

Hamm-Rodríguez, Molly, & Morales, Astrid S. (2021). (Re)producing insecurity for Puerto Rican students in Florida schools: A raciolinguistic perspective on English-only policies. *Centro Journal, 33*(1), 112–131.

Harper, Shaun R. (2013). Am I my brother's Teacher? Black undergraduates, racial socialization, and peer pedagogies in predominantly white postsecondary contexts. *Review of Research in Education, 37,* 183–211.

Hiramatsu, Kazuko, and Michal Temkin Martinez. (2021). Publishing in the Teaching Linguistics Section of Language. *Language,* 97(2), 406–408. https://doi.org/10.1353/lan.2021.0023.

Helms, Janet E. (1992). *A race is a nice thing to have: A guide to being a white person or understanding the white persons in your life.* Content Communications.

Holliday, Nicole R., & Squires, Lauren. (2021). Sociolinguistic labor, linguistic climate, and race(ism) on campus: Black college students' experiences with language at predominantly white institutions. *Journal of Sociolinguistics, 25*(3), 418–437. doi:10.1111/josl.12438

hooks, bell. (1994). Language: Teaching new words/new worlds. In *Teaching to transgress* (pp. 222–227). Routledge.

hooks, bell. (2003). *Teaching community: A pedagogy of hope.* New York: Routledge.

Keels, Micere. (2019). *Campus counterspaces: Black and Latinx students' search for community at historically white universities.* Ithaca: Cornell University Press.

Kubota, Ryuko. (2020). Confronting epistemological racism, decolonizing scholarly knowledge: Race and gender in applied linguistics. *Applied Linguistics,* 41(5), 712–32. https://doi.org/10.1093/applin/amz033.

Language and Life Project. (2020). *Talking Black in America.* https://www.talkingblackinamerica.org/talking-black-in-america-the-film/.

Lawrence, Sandra M., & Bunche, Takiema. (1996). Feeling and dealing: Teaching white students about racial privilege. *Teaching and Teacher Education, 12*(5), 531–542. doi:10.1016/0742-051X(95)00054-N

Lederer, Jenny. (2024). Texts, tweets, twitch, Tiktok: Computer-mediated communication as an inclusive gateway to linguistics. In Anne H. Charity Hudley, Christine Mallinson, & Mary Bucholtz (Eds.), *Inclusion in linguistics*. Oxford University Press.

Lee, Robert, and Tristan Ahtone. (2020). Land-grab universities. March 30, 2020. https://www.hcn.org/issues/52.4/indigenous-affairs-education-land-grab-universities.

Leonard, Wesley Y. (2021). "Toward an anti-racist linguistic anthropology: An Indigenous response to white supremacy." *Journal of Linguistic Anthropology*, 31 (2), 218–237. https://doi.org/10.1111/jola.12319.

Lopez, Leo, III, Hart, Louis H., III, & Katz, Mitchell H. (2021). Racial and ethnic health disparities related to COVID-19. *JAMA*, *325*(8), 719–720. doi:10.1001/jama.2020.26443

Lyiscott, Jamila. (2014). *3 ways to speak English*. https://www.ted.com/talks/jamila_lyiscott_3_ways_to_speak_english.

Makepeace Productions (2010). We Still Live Here Film Information. https://www.makepeaceproductions.com/wampfilm.html.

Mantenuto, Iara, Levy, Tamaya, Reyes, Stephanie, & Zhang, Zhongyin. (2024). Increasing access and equity for first-generation scholars in linguistics. In Anne H. Charity Hudley, Christine Mallinson, & Mary Bucholtz (Eds.), *Inclusion in linguistics*. Oxford University Press.

Martín, Annette. (2021). What is white ignorance? *The Philosophical Quarterly*, *71*(4), 864–885. doi:10.1093/pq/pqaa073

Milambiling, Joyce. (2001). Opening minds or changing them? Some observations on teaching introductory linguistics. *Theory Into Practice*, *40*(4), 249–254. doi:10.1207/s15430421tip4004_6

Mills, Charles W. (1999). *The racial contract*. Cornell University Press.

Mills, Charles W. (2012). White ignorance. In Shannon Sullivan & Nancy Tuana (Eds.), *Race and epistemologies of ignorance* (pp. 11–38). SUNY Press.

Milu, Esther. (2021). Diversity of raciolinguistic experiences in the writing classroom: An argument for a transnational Black language pedagogy. *College English*, *83*(6), 415–441.

Moll, Luis C., Amanti, Cathy, Neff, Deborah, & González, Norma. (1992). Funds of knowledge for teaching: Using a qualitative approach to connect homes and classrooms. *Theory into Practice*, *31*(2),132–141.

Office of Equity and Inclusion, UMass Amherst. (2021). *Campus data*. https://www.umass.edu/diversity/data-policies.

Paris, Django. (2012). Culturally sustaining pedagogy: A needed change in stance, terminology, and practice. *Educational Researcher*, 41(3), 93–97. https://doi.org/10.3102/0013189X12441244.

Rajendran, Shyama. (2019). Undoing "the vernacular": Dismantling structures of raciolinguistic supremacy. *Literature Compass*, *16*(9–10), e12544. doi:10.1111/lic3.12544

RANT Collective. (2006). *History of affinity groups*. https://web.archive.org/web/20060519032829/http://www.rantcollective.net/article.php?id=33.

Residential Academic Programs, UMass Amherst. (2021). *Emerging scholars RAP*. https://www.umass.edu/rap/emerging-scholars-rap.

Rosa, Jonathan, & Flores, Nelson. (2017). Unsettling race and language: Toward a raciolinguistic perspective. *Language in Society*, *46*(5), 621–647. doi:10.1017/S0047404517000562.

Roth-Gordon, Jennifer, Harris, Jessica, & Zamora, Stephanie. (2020). Producing white comfort through "corporate cool": Linguistic appropriation, social media, and @BrandsSayingBae. *International Journal of the Sociology of Language*, *2020*(265),107–128. doi:10.1515/ijsl-2020-2105

Scott, Ellen K. (2001). From race cognizance to racism cognizance: Dilemmas in antiracist activism in California. In Kathleen M. Blue (Ed.), *Feminism and antiracism: International struggles for justice* (pp. 125–149). New York University Press.

Seltzer, Kate. (2019). Performing ideologies: Fostering raciolinguistic literacies through role-play in a high school English classroom. *Journal of Adolescent & Adult Literacy, 63*(2), 147–155. doi:10.1002/jaal.966

Smalls, Krystal A. (2019). Languages of liberation: Digital discourses of emphatic Blackness. In Netta Avineri, Laura R. Graham, Eric J. Johnson, Robin Conley Riner, & Jonathan Rosa (Eds.), *Language and social justice in practice* (pp. 52–60). Routledge.

Smalls, Krystal A. (2020). Race, signs, and the body: Towards a theory of racial semiotics. In H. Samy Alim, Angela Reyes, & Paul V. Kroskrity (Eds.), *The Oxford handbook of language and race* (pp. 231–260). Oxford University Press.

Spring, Cari L., Moses, Rae, Flynn, Michael, Steele, Susan, Joseph, Brian D., & Webb, Charlotte. (2000). The successful introductory course: Bridging the gap for the nonmajor. *Language, 76*(1), 110–122. doi:10.1353/lan.2000.0124

Tatum, Beverly D. (1994). Teaching white students about racism: The search for white allies and the restoration of hope. *Teachers College Record, 95*(4), 462–476.

Tichavakunda, Antar A. (2021). Black joy on white campuses: Exploring Black students' recreation and celebration at a historically white institution. *The Review of Higher Education, 44*(3), 297–324. https://doi.org/10.1353/rhe.2021.0003.

Thomas, Jamie A. (2024). Community college linguistics for educational justice: Content and assessment strategies that support antiracist and inclusive teaching. In Anne H. Charity Hudley, Christine Mallinson, & Mary Bucholtz (Eds.), *Inclusion in linguistics*. Oxford University Press.

Thornton, Candice Y. (2024). For the culture: Pathways in linguistics for Black and HBCU scholars. In Anne H. Charity Hudley, Christine Mallinson, & Mary Bucholtz (Eds.), *Inclusion in linguistics*. Oxford University Press.

Vélez-Ibáñez, Carlos, & Greenberg, Joseph T. (1992). Formation and transformation of funds of knowledge among US-Mexican households. *Anthropology & Education Quarterly, 23*(4), 313–335.

Volpe, Vanessa V., and Bryanna M. Jones. (2021). 'Enriching the Africana soul': Black college students' lived experiences with affinity housing at a predominately white institution. *Journal of Diversity in Higher Education*, 16(2), 157-169. https://doi.org/10.1037/dhe0000332.

Weldon, Tracey L. (2012). Teaching African American English to college students: Ideological and pedagogical challenges and solutions. *American Speech, 87*(2), 232–247. doi:10.1215/00031283-1668244

Żentella, Ana Celia. (2018). LatinUs and linguistics: Complaints, conflicts, and contradictions - The anthro-political linguistics solution. In Naomi L. Shin & Daniel Erker (Eds.), *Questioning theoretical primitives in linguistic inquiry: Papers in honor of Ricardo Otheguy* (pp. 189–207). John Benjamins.

Claire Bowern is professor of linguistics at Yale University. She is a Fellow of the Linguistic Society of America and the second woman to have the rank of full professor in her department. Her research is in language change and language documentation, focusing on work with Australian Indigenous communities. She has ongoing collaborations with the Bardi and Kullilli communities. At Yale she teaches classes in historical linguistics, language documentation and fieldwork, introductory linguistics, and linguistics for nonmajors.

Rikker Dockum is visiting assistant professor of linguistics at Swarthmore College. His research focuses on sound change in tonal languages and language documentation, with a special focus on Tai languages of Mainland Southeast Asia, working with the Tai Khamti community in Khamti Township, Sagaing, Myanmar, to document their language. He teaches courses including historical linguistics, linguistic field methods, phonetics and phonology, introductory linguistics, and advanced research methods.

Abstract: The study of language variation and change is both one of the oldest areas of the scientific study of language, and one of the most global. Its origins (in European traditions) are steeped in Empire and colonialism. Yet it is also an important way to study relationships and dynamics between language and society. The field also contributes crucial insights from linguistics toward an understanding of how racist attitudes have been developed and justified by language.

In this chapter, the authors discuss their experiences in decolonizing our classes in historical and introductory linguistics, as white instructors at two Predominantly White Institutions (PWIs) on the East Coast of the United States, and we give examples of some activities that we used. We use these examples both to discuss how (and why) to improve the teaching of linguistic subfields which have been said to be "too hard" to decolonize, and as a chance to think through issues and approaches.

Key Words: language change, maps, antiracist pedagogy, historical linguistics, Indigenous language

10
Decolonizing Historical Linguistics in the Classroom and Beyond

Claire Bowern (she/they)
Yale University

Rikker Dockum (he/him)
Swarthmore College

The study of language variation and change is both one of the oldest areas of the scientific study of language, and one of the most global.[1] Its origins (in European traditions) are steeped in empire and colonialism (cf. Errington, 2001). Yet it is also an important way to study relationships and dynamics between language and society. The prominence of the European linguistic past within historical linguistics across much of the world has too often obscured the fact that historical linguistics allows us to recover aspects of history for those whose pasts have been excluded from the written record, and it provides an opportunity for linguistics to contribute—along with other disciplines—to an understanding of global human cultures. It also contributes crucial insights from linguistics toward an understanding of how racist attitudes have been developed and justified by language (cf. Saini, 2019 for a discussion of similar points in genetics).

In this chapter, we discuss our experiences in decolonizing our historical and introductory linguistics classes, as white instructors at two Predominantly White Institutions (PWIs) on the East Coast of the United States. We use this as a case of how (and why) to improve the teaching of disciplines which have been thought to be "too hard" to decolonize, and as a chance to think through issues and approaches. These actions are happening at a time of broader attention to questions of belonging, diversity, equity, and inclusion in higher education. Therefore, this is a good moment to examine curricular materials along with (not as a substitute for) other aspects of racial justice in academia. These actions are not taken in a vacuum;

Claire Bowern, Rikker Dockum, *Decolonizing Historical Linguistics in the Classroom and Beyond* In: *Decolonizing Linguistics*.
Edited by: Anne H. Charity Hudley, Christine Mallinson, and Mary Bucholtz, Oxford University Press.
© Anne H. Charity Hudley, Christine Mallinson, and Mary Bucholtz 2024. DOI: 10.1093/oso/9780197755259.003.0011

for example, at Yale the department has had several initiatives around "belonging," such as a pop-up antiracist reading group and discussions of DEI topics at faculty meetings. At Swarthmore, the linguistics department held a town hall, led by students, and finalized a new course requirement in sociolinguistics. At both institutions, however, curricular content has been left to individual faculty members. For one view of the importance of curricular reform, see Arnold (2019).

Notions of Race and Historical Linguistics

Implicitly or explicitly, race has always been part of historical linguistics. At the earliest stages of the field, the tree of humanity and the tree of languages were often treated as one and the same (see, among others, Bonfiglio, 2007, 2010 for the historical conflation of language and ethnicity and Hutton 1998, 2010 for additional historical perspective). The very term "Caucasian" as a racial category, now rejected by the scientific community (Templeton, 2016), is connected to the concept of the Indo-European family and its origins, more than 6,000 years ago, in or north of the Caucasus mountains (Blumenbach, 1795; Meiners, 1785; for further context see Baum, 2006; Michael, 2021; Valone, 1996). Jacob Grimm, one of the early Indo-Europeanists and historical linguists using methods recognizable to contemporary practitioners, was clear about a direct link between race and language change (cf. Grimm, 1851/ 1984). The early work on typology was done as part of surveys in expansions of empires; compare, for example, Johann Adelung's (1806) work as part of the expeditions of Catherine the Great (see also Lass, 2014, among many others), or George Grierson's *Linguistic Survey of India* (1903–1928; cf. Majeed, 2018). And the notion of Proto-Indo-European—a family of languages including Sanskrit, Greek, and Latin "sprung from some common source, which, perhaps, no longer exists"—is from William Jones (1786), who learned Sanskrit when stationed in India as a judge appointed by the British colonial government.

Historical linguistics also, however, provides tools for undoing some of this damage. For example, historical linguists have knowledge and skills that assist language revitalization. Such tools need to be more prominently centered within linguistics. Historical linguists can help make sense of how past linguists have encoded Indigenous language practice and how to decode those records and make them more accessible, as Haley Shea et al. (2019) and Megan Lukaniec (2017) have discussed. And through linguistic reconstruction, historical linguistics can work with communities who seek to create vocabulary beyond what was recorded, or who wish to pursue ecologically valid methods of vocabulary creation (cf. Amery & Buckskin, 2012; Bodt & List, 2022).

All the more reason to grapple with the ways in which race plays a role, explicitly or implicitly, in historical linguistics. However, historical linguists, like scholars in many other subfields of linguistics, have tended to avoid discussion of race and ethnicity entirely—by defining their work in terms of "languages" rather than "cultures" and abstracting away from the concept of an ethnolinguistic group; by focusing exclusively on standardized, ancient, written linguistic varieties; or by arguing that the comparative method applies only to abstract forms rather than actual linguistic utterances associated with particular cultures. Michel DeGraff (2005a, 2005b) provides further discussion of and arguments against these points, and Mark Hale (2014) also gives context. An example of the primacy of particular varieties is Blust's (1990, p. 90) comment on reconstruction in Austronesian: "This is very different from Indo-European, where one can ignore, e.g., Hindi or Italian in higher-level reconstruction, since everything of comparative interest in these languages is found more clearly preserved in Sanskrit or Latin." However, we recognize a possible contradiction here, since historical linguistic reconstruction is also used as a means to investigate past culture, through tangible cultural reconstruction methods known as *Wörter und Sachen* (cf. Crowley & Bowern, 2010). Arguments around the abstraction of linguistic reconstructions are often tied to the necessarily incomplete and partial nature of reconstructions. It should also be acknowledged that views among practitioners vary substantially on these points.

Decolonizing?

Some discussion of decolonization is warranted. The term has both literal and metaphorical uses. Literal decolonization is the removal of Indigenous materials from colonialist structures, for example (see among others Tuck & Yang, 2012). The term is also used metaphorically, in the broader sense of inclusion of Indigenous material in the university curriculum and the creation of a more flexible, respectful, and open intellectual environment that recognizes Indigenous authorities and validates decolonialist ideas and epistemologies. We concentrate here on metaphorical decolonizations in and of our classrooms. We believe that not undertaking a review of the curriculum is to perpetuate a particular view of historical linguistics that we do not subscribe to, whether or not we explicitly link it to anticolonial, decolonial, or other critical intellectual movements. Suhanthie Motha (2020, p. 128) makes

198 Decolonizing Linguistics

an analogous point for applied linguistics, another subfield "rooted in an ontology of race and empire." As Motha discusses, this ontology is produced through disciplinary statements about "objectivity" and the divorcing of human experience from linguistics (see also Clemons, this volume). We agree with Eve Tuck and K. Wayne Yang (2012, p. 1) that "approaches that decenter settler perspectives have objectives that may be incommensurable with decolonization"; our point here is less about what to call what we do and more about what concrete steps are taken to further social justice in our classrooms.

We also wish to counter some views of the discipline of historical linguistics within academia. At the LSA's Annual Meeting in 2022, where we gave a talk based on this material (Bowern & Dockum, 2022), some colleagues asked about perceptions that historical linguistics is a discipline which looks solely into the past, without reflecting on how the past shapes the present, and is therefore irrelevant to contemporary concerns. We have four responses to this point. First is that linguistics is one of the disciplines, along with archaeology, genetics, and anthropology, that allows a detailed view into the story of human history. Knowing about human history is valuable in itself.

Secondly, by explicitly including topics of social relevance in historical classes, we shift the focus from static historicism to language dynamics: that is, to the dynamics of change and how it works. Thirdly, a socially and dynamically oriented approach allows us a better understanding of the present, for example by directly countering narratives that the languages of Native North America are only to do with the past. Studying dynamics also allows a better focus on diversity and variation, building on Shelome Gooden's (2020) call for more realistic models of language. Finally, by studying language history and how languages got the way they are, we better contextualize the present. It is possible to acknowledge past insights while creating something new, and as deandre miles-hercules (2020) puts it, while we are all molded by our academic experience, molds are, in the end, meant to be broken.

Our Positionalities

As white instructors trained in linguistics, we don't come to this topic with a lot of background in decolonizing pedagogies or broader social justice, at least in terms of explicit instruction in our graduate programs or lived experience. We have approached this as we approach any other aspect of scholarship: get educated, use our experience and knowledge of pedagogy to work out what will work for our classrooms, try things out, be willing to take risks, welcome feedback from students and colleagues at every stage, and adapt as needed.

Claire

I am white and teach at an Ivy League PWI, but one whose student body is now much more diverse (with respect to race and ethnicity) compared to what it was even ten years ago. The Yale College Class of 2024 is the first class ever to be under 50% white, for example. That said, the university's students are economically from a much less diverse group, with the vast majority coming from the top 25% of US income brackets. The linguistics department has a long-standing commitment to mentalist approaches to grammar and has had only a few sociolinguistics offerings in the last ten years, all of which have been taught by visiting faculty. The department has a very long tradition of historical linguistics, particularly in Indo-European studies, but also in linguistic fieldwork, dating back to the founding of both disciplines in the US.

The historical linguistics curricular materials presented here were developed as part of reforms toward antiracist pedagogy with the goal of introducing nonminoritized students to these topics while "staying in my lane." It followed from my and others' earlier work around broadening curriculum in other ways, such as in representation of scholars' work in advanced classes and being inclusive in both content and context. For example, as Adrienne Tsikewa (2021) has pointed out, it is possible to teach a class on language endangerment that represents a broad range of languages while decentering those languages and the experiences of language communities: that is not an antiracist curriculum.

I have long been dissatisfied with claims that some subjects are just "too hard to introduce social justice issues to." This clearly isn't true for historical linguistics, when the very foundation of the discipline is comparative ideas, built around particular models of language transmission, and deeply mired in race science. Indeed, it's a perfect opportunity to do better linguistics by engaging specifically with these questions, as well as being clear about what types of antiracist activities are most productive at PWIs at this point in time.

Rikker

I am white and was raised in conservative rural communities in the Pacific Northwest of the US. While I am the first in my family to earn a PhD, both of my parents attended college or higher. I teach at a selective liberal arts college, a PWI that has drawn a more racially and socioeconomically diverse student body in recent years, such that the student body today is roughly 33% white, but the faculty remains overwhelmingly white, at above 70% (College Factual, 2023; NCES, 2022). The linguistics department is a joint department shared across three campuses (Swarthmore, Haverford, and Bryn Mawr, all PWI liberal arts colleges) and has long focused on working with Indigenous groups, endangered languages, and language documentation (see also Riestenberg et al., this volume). It is home to such projects as Talking Dictionaries (talkingdictionary.swarthmore.edu) and Ticha (ticha.haverford.edu; Broadwell et al., 2020).

One source of my motivation to work on antiracist pedagogy is that my department has constant student interest in the intersection of language and society, despite having no sociolinguistics tenure line. Sociolinguistics also makes up a disproportionate number of senior thesis topics—by my count and categorization, roughly 25% of 127 theses on file in the five-year period 2016–2021. Beginning in fall semester 2021, a course in sociolinguistics was made a requirement for all new linguistics majors. This development has inspired me to examine all of my courses and find ways to make connections to social issues that my students and I care about. I draw additional motivation for this work from the example set by my students, both from their scholarship (e.g., Keicho, 2021), and from their activism, such as student strikes at all three campuses in fall 2020 over justice and equity issues, especially those related to Black student experiences, and the resulting commitment at Bryn Mawr and Haverford of substantial new resource commitments from the administrations (see Thompson, 2020; Velonis, 2020).

Decolonizing Historical Linguistics Pedagogy

In this section we describe some of our experiences in adapting our historical linguistics curriculum to engage more explicitly and concretely with colonialism, social justice issues, and bridges between disciplines. We hope this overview will serve as an example for others working on these issues, particularly in disciplines of linguistics which consider themselves "difficult to decolonize" because of the natures of their traditional curricula. We draw from our experiences teaching introductory linguistics, introductory historical linguistics, and an advanced historical linguistics class.

The overall objectives in all three courses were to teach students how languages change, how language is used to study the past, how to learn about the linguistic past, and how diachronic techniques are relevant to contemporary issues—and to do these things in a way that is both inclusive of languages and cultural and linguistic traditions and reflective of student experiences. This latter goal involves explicitly acknowledging and critically engaging with the discipline's past. For advanced linguistics classes, doing so prepares students for further work within historical linguistics, as well as for work elsewhere in the field that draws on diachronic frameworks. Further, it challenges students to deal with the history of linguistics itself and problematizes the ways linguists have thought about language and treated language communities in the past, in ways that are less likely to be covered in other linguistics courses.

Over the last four years, we have made incremental changes to the curricula on language change in introductory linguistics and historical linguistics classes, first as co-teachers and later at our respective current institutions. The changes entailed expanded units on sociolinguistics and integration of work on language variation and language change, along with discussion of aspects of language change that take examples from a wide variety of languages around the world, including signed languages (mostly American Sign Language, given expertise on our campuses). In the advanced historical class, we focused on applications of historical linguistics in legal settings and in language reclamation. With regard to legal settings, we studied LADO (linguistic analysis for determination of origin; see Dennis Preston, 2019, and the other articles in that volume) and the role of language and linguistic relationships in Indigenous land claims. For language reclamation, we discussed the roles that linguists have played in the creation of new vocabulary in Indigenous languages.

The following case studies are two examples of the type of innovations we made. The first is an exercise on language maps, which we use in introductory classes in linguistics and historical linguistics (see online supplementary materials). It is an exercise which can be done with a class of any size. The introductory historical linguistics class is approximately 20–30 students, while the introductory linguistics class is over 80. The second details the topics discussed in an advanced class on language change that focus on language activism. The advanced historical class is a smaller seminar, usually fewer than ten students. While the activities and discussions could be conducted with a larger group, they were designed with a small number of students in mind.

Using Language Maps to Introduce Linguistic Diversity

Students who are new to linguistics typically come to the discipline with very different amounts of background knowledge of linguistic diversity, both in the United States and globally. Few have had any explicit instruction about the number of languages in the world or US linguistic diversity. One exercise that we do early in several courses (in the first or second class, usually) is to explore students' knowledge of linguistic diversity through a discussion of language maps of different types, regions, and from different time periods. We project each map on the screen and give students some time to comment on anything they notice. They do this through sharing with a partner, calling out observations, contributing to a shared google document, or using an anonymous feedback option such as PollEverywhere. We give some samples here. A list of sources of these and other maps, including color reproductions of the figures here, is included in the supplementary website associated with these volumes.

Consider the map in Figure 10.1. Students often mention the relative numbers of languages on the west coast of the continent compared to inland; the

Figure 10.1 Language map of North America.

Source: Wikimedia Commons contributors 2022, based on a Smithsonian map of Native languages of North America, Goddard 1996.

Alt text: map of Canada, the United States, and parts of Greenland and Mexico, with the main Indigenous language families in different colors. The interior of Greenland, the southeast of the United States, and inland Mexico is blank. 30 language families and 28 isolates are defined.

highly variable sizes of the language areas; the differences between country borders and the language boundaries (e.g., between the United States and Mexico, Alaska and Canada, or between US states). These observations can lead to discussion on what this representation suggests about the sociopolitical history or influence of each of the communities that speak the languages on the map, as well as the politics of who made the map and why. Noting the blank spaces on the map brings us to discussion of many different topics: colonial history; what it means to locate a *language* on a map (rather than a community of language users); how the blank spaces in Greenland are different from the blank spaces in the southeast of the United States, for example. We also talk about maps and time periods. The map in Figure 10.1 is not a contemporary map, but neither is it a historical map depicting a single point in time. It also lets us talk about language families and isolates and name different families of Indigenous languages in North America. Students are often especially interested in the languages or families in their home regions. Finally, students sometimes ask about the location of signed languages on such maps.

For contrast, the map in Figure 10.2, drawn by @JakubMarian from https://jakubmarian.com/map-of-languages-and-language-families-of-europe/. This map, in contrast, uses country boundaries, but also represents bilingual areas (but not all bilingual areas – another topic that comes up in discussion). It also colors languages by subgroup, which allows an entry into a discussion of linguistic relatedness. Discussion of bilingualism also allows us to discuss which languages are represented. For example, Welsh and English are both shown in Wales but there is no multilingual area for London, where 22% of the population speaks a language other than English). English is not shown outside of England, even though English is widespread in many European countries. The lack of immigrant or second languages on such maps can also bring up how signed languages are represented.

Finally, Figure 10.3 shows language families of Eurasia. It separates subgroups of Indo-European but groups together many Papuan language families, leading to the impression that all parts of Eurasia are roughly equally linguistically diverse. It also lets us discuss the label *Chinese* and notions of what a language is. In our classes, we contrast Figure 10.3 with a map such as the one in Figure 10.4, which marks languages as single dot points, coded by language family (as given in Glottolog.org). Figure 10.4 allows us to discuss the relative density of languages and the different number of languages in different geopolitical units.

In discussing these points, we are able to cover numerous ideas that are new to students, that are then taken up and explored in more detail in the rest of

Figure 10.2 Map of languages of Europe.

Source: @JakubMarian from https://jakubmarian.com/map-of-languages-and-language-families-of-europe/.

Alt text: Map of languages of Europe, from the UK and Iceland to western Russia and Turkey. Most of the map is colored by country, with a few major minority languages. See main text for further discussion.

the semester. It foregrounds linguistic diversity while also highlighting historical linguistics as a discipline in which we talk about processes: to uncover the past—like archaeology but with language, as we put it—and to understand the present.

The beauty of this exercise is that it can be accomplished with virtually any language maps. The maps can be shown in any order, changed from year to year, or tailored to regions or topics of interest. We made a point of using maps from a variety of sources, including those created by amateurs and from popular websites, because these are the kinds of language maps that students

Figure 10.3 Language families of "Asia" (actually Eurasia and part of Oceania).
Source: Wikimedia Commons contributors 2013.
Alt text: Unlabeled map of Europe and Asia, colored by language family. The map is entitled Language families of Asia.

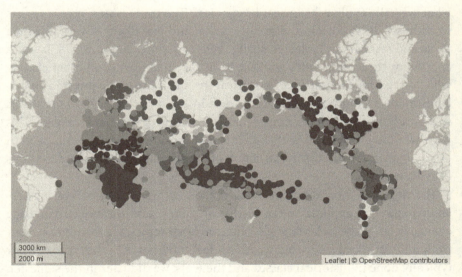

Figure 10.4 Languages of the world, from Glottolog.org.
Source: Map produced by Robert Forkel.
Alt text: world map with centroid of each language in the glottolog catalog, colored by language family.

frequently encounter outside the classroom. And in fact, "bad" maps are excellent fodder for discussion, as students very quickly learn to spot the issues and enjoy critiquing and deconstructing something that they might previously have taken at face value as accurate and reliable.

Another related exercise we have used to good effect in historical linguistics classes is a "name a language" exercise, which works well as an icebreaker at the first class. We ask students to name a language that they have learned at school or college, have heritage connections to, or have otherwise heard of, which can serve as an entry into discussion of similar topics as the maps exercise. Such an exercise also allows students to talk about speakers or signers of the language, setting an expectation that language is not divorced from usage context, even when primarily focusing on language structure later in the course. It also lays the background for a student's linguistic autobiography, a useful written assignment for early in the semester.

Applied Historical Linguistics

Our second example of decolonizing historical linguistics focuses on the setup of a syllabus for an advanced historical linguistics class, focusing on what we call "applied historical linguistics." The overarching objective was to address—theoretically, methodologically, and practically—ways in which ideas and facts about language change relate to topics in the world. It was a chance for students to work with the ideas they had learned in other classes, while discussing the impact of historical work in a broader context. This syllabus follows from our earlier joint work in the introductory class that was specifically aimed at broadening the representation of ideas and scholars. This class was taught in 2019 in this format and aspects of it have been used in other courses. We discuss the structure of the syllabus as well as our methods of assessment.

The class had three different units: evaluating hypotheses of language relationship; legal applications of historical claims; and the use of language change in language reclamation. Unlike the other topics, the first did not centrally address social justice but was a "bridge" topic between the types of work typically done in historical classes and the work we did later in the semester. In this unit, we examined Juliette Blevins' (2018) hypothesis that Basque and Indo-European are related. We studied the evidence given in her book and examined what assumptions were made about language, geography, and history. In the final part of this unit, students formed and investigated hypotheses about phenomena that should also be true (or that should be false) if the Euskaran hypothesis is true. It was therefore an exercise in reasoning through consequences. It also allowed us to have discussions of how views of the past are relevant to contemporary ideas of statehood, nationhood, and group identity.

The second unit, on the legal implications of historical linguistics, focused on two areas. The first was language and land rights, with a case study of Australia's Native Title legislation, from a linguistic (rather than a legal) standpoint. Native Title, as discussed by Sutton (2004), is the legal framework through which Australia's Indigenous peoples can seek legal recognition of their land rights. Works discussed in the class included Henderson (2002), Rumsey (1993), Berson (2012), and Walsh (1997). (More information is given in the online supplement to this chapter.) These scholars focused on the nature of linguistic evidence for the past and how that is interpreted in a legal context. Berson (2012), for example, discusses linguistic trees and how they represent a particular view of language: irrevocable bifurcations that linguists seldom believe in practice but which represent a modeling convenience. That convenience, however, can lead to an interpretation where language and ethnicity are co-defined and co-exclusive, weakening the cases of Indigenous claimants who, naturally in a multilingual region, have ties to multiple languages.

The second topic in the unit on legal issues was Linguistic Analysis for Determination of Origin (LADO), the use of language and dialect in asylum cases (Muysken, 2019 and Preston, 2019). LADO makes use of the concept of a Shibboleth to identify the origin of asylum seekers. That is, the starting assumption of a LADO analysis is that it is possible to tell where a person is from based on how they speak. Typically determinations are made through interviews between asylum seekers and interviewers, who may themselves be displaced persons. Many issues arise, from accent and dialect perception to language variation, to the impacts of testing someone in an official context in a language they usually only use in the home.

From these topics, several themes emerged: folk and linguistic theories of change and how they differ; language and geography, dialectology (variation and change), language and identity, and models of mono- and multilingualism. The Native Title readings also engage particularly with historical linguistics, trees, and such models, which are relevant for concepts of what languages are. Both topics also let us talk about "experts," conceptions of "expert testimony" and who is given expert status. For example, the testers accorded expert status in LADO determinations are the same "native speakers" who are not accorded expert status in Native Title, and whose expertise must be "translated" through anthropologists to gain credibility.

The final unit was about language endangerment and reclamation/revitalization. A key component of language reclamation for many communities is the creation of new vocabulary, especially when the language sources do not contain means of expression for concepts that contemporary language users want to use. We read work on community involvement and acquisition

(Meek, 2007; 2019), and then classic work in Australia (e.g., Amery 2000; 2009; Amery & Buckskin, 2012) on word formation processes and vocabulary development. This brings up "memory documentation"—that is, the portrayal of language documentation as "salvage" work. While this is not at all the only task of language reclamation/revitalization (cf. Leonard & Haynes, 2010), it is one that relates concretely to the rest of the class as well as to language change and historical linguistics. For example, one method of creating vocabulary is so-called cognate prediction—using the reflexes of words in related languages to create what the word would have been in the revitalized language (had it been recorded).

One clear and legitimate criticism of language revitalization is that it treats language as independent from other social, cultural, and spiritual aspects of life. A genuinely integrative approach to reclamation, as discussed by scholars such as Wesley Leonard (2017) and Theresa McCarty et al. (2018), places language as one pillar of community healing, along with others such as land and health. Discussing these points also brings in different views of what role linguists might have in language programs.

Finally, Brook Lillehaugen (cf. Broadwell et al., 2020; Lillehaugen et al., 2016) gave guest lectures in both the Yale advanced historical linguistics class and Swarthmore's historical class. Some students in the advanced class worked with Lillehaugen's Ticha project on Colonial Zapotec (ticha.haverford.edu) for their final assessment. This was a chance for students to learn about an active project which combines the study of history and historical linguistics and contemporary language work.

Each portion of the class assessed students based on class participation (engaging with the materials and leading a discussion) and reading responses. In the final part of the semester, students worked on a final project, which involved either partnering with Wôpanâak language teachers (wlrp.org) or volunteering with the Ticha project. The Wôpanâak partnership built on existing connections between Claire and jessie little doe baird. Claire and jessie had been chatting informally for some time about ways that linguistics at Yale might help advance the goals of the Wôpanâak language reclamation program. Two big structural issues have, so far, stood in the way of a partnership. First, the Yale linguistics students and faculty who would be involved do not know Wôpanâak, and it would not be a good idea for Wôpanâak teachers to spend a lot of time away from Wôpanâak community-oriented projects to teach Yale community members, since most Yale students spend a few years at most in the linguistics department. Therefore any contributions from the Yale side need to be able to be enacted without a detailed knowledge of the language. Secondly, the Wôpanâak program is already fully stretched and at full capacity, so any useful projects cannot require substantial additional participation. jessie identified the areas of greatest need for the Wôpanâak language reclamation projects, and she and Claire discussed ways that student work might be beneficial to the program. That conversation identified projects that would be useful for the language teachers, that students could do with supervision by Claire that would not take teachers' time away from existing projects for Wôpanâak speakers. The upshot is that student work couldn't directly involve projects about the Wôpanâak language or require an investment of teachers' time. Several projects were identified and completed. First was a summary of recent educational research in effective language teaching, since teachers were busy with lesson planning and felt they couldn't keep up with research findings. Students extracted some key generalizations and summarized recent relevant research. A second project supported intermediate and advanced language classes through explaining syntax research on Algonquian languages. Project members saw a big disconnection between the technical side of syntax and what language teachers need for intermediate and advanced learners. Students read a series of recently published papers in Algonquian languages of the region and summarized their key findings in clear, nontechnical ways that would help with language teaching and the interpretation of old Wampanoag sources. For example, Fernando Zúñiga (2016) discusses semitransitive constructions across several Algonquian languages, including how animacy interacts with valency in passive and antipassive constructions. Students annotated the papers with explanations designed to make the research findings more usable for teachers.

Work with the Ticha project was of a different type. The main tasks needed by project staff were transcription and analysis of Colonial Zapotec materials. Since we were joining an established project, students participated in tasks that were part of a much larger annotation and translation project. They learned about group work and workflows in digital humanities, as well as how to work with old materials.

Students had a range of reactions to the class. In general, they found it valuable and appreciated being able to link what they had studied theoretically to real-world applications. Several appreciated that the broadened their view of language change and brought up aspects of language that they had never considered. However, some said that they felt the topics were too different from one another; that is, they felt that the legal and social aspects of the class were not well conntect, which made the semester feel like several distinct classes with little to link them together. For a future iteration of this class we would pay more attention to exploring connections between the units, rather than treating them as independent case studies. One student wished that we had

210 Decolonizing Linguistics

been able to go into more detail for each topic. They noted that by covering several very different topics, we ended up only scratching the surface. Others, however, appreciated the breadth of material and the many ways in which historical linguistics connects to contemporary language issues.

Next Steps

The above examples of pedagogical interventions are a step in making a more inclusive historical linguistics curriculum. At the same time, our efforts have also led to further issues, including questions that instructors looking to enact these methods in their classrooms may have. While there is not space to fully discuss these issues here, we flag them as needing further attention and work.

One problem that came up was how to create meaningful assessment tasks that evaluate a broad range of student knowledge. When an assessment is structured solely according to linguistic content, it is fairly straightforward to construct assessments that test that knowledge (for example, research papers on particular topics, problem sets that check a student's recognition and understanding of key concepts and their analytical expertise). When the assessment also needs to include community impact and relevance, as well as being feasible to execute within the time frame of a four-week unit or a 13-week semester, it becomes more difficult. The flexibility afforded to faculty to design appropriate assessments was crucial here, and universities with more rigid instructional requirements may have more difficulty in implementing this type of project.

A related issue was how to be effective in joining existing projects. It would not satisfy the broader aims of the class if the students were the only beneficiaries of the practicum. Some types of classes require students to acquire particular skills and knowledge, and original research experiences are not appropriate for their stage of knowledge. To return to a point raised above, it would be inappropriate and disrespectful to pretend "for pedagogical purposes" that there is not already substantial work on Wôpanâak, particularly when the point of the class is to explicitly and appropriately address how linguistic work on language change has practical relevance in a variety of contexts. To do so is to place students' training above community needs, which is inappropriate. Ultimately, we solved this problem by considering the overall aims and goals of the class, as well as the broad skills and knowledge that the students obtained. That is, it was more important for students to produce a piece of work that demonstrated their ability to synthesize the literature, to translate it for others, and to have a positive impact with their work,

Decolonizing in the Classroom and Beyond **211**

than it was for every single piece of work to be exclusively diachronic and to test every topic covered in the course.

Crucially, the practical aspects of organization were only possible because of existing connections between Claire and jessie little doe baird, as well as the institutional outreach already undertaken by members of the Ticha project. It would be difficult in many places to start outreach projects specifically for the class, and we caution against doing so if the aim is simply to create an experience for the students. After all, one of the features of an antiracist pedagogy is an explicit examination of whose experiences are centered in the curriculum. The broader aims of such a class are not satisfied if the students are the only beneficiaries of the way it is structured. One of the take-home points here is that when personal connections are already in place, a great deal can be done through institutions.

We have yet to resolve how to introduce Indigenous course content without appropriation, since there are very different views in Indigenous Studies about the advisability of doing so, and how to do it appropriately. One view, which we have encountered at conferences and on social media but not in print, is that only Indigenous scholars should teach Indigenous course content. There are two main reasons for this position. One is that non-Indigenous instructors tend to, in short, screw up. The other is that teaching about Indigenous content is an inherently spiritual act, and so for non-Indigenous people to teach Indigenous content is inevitably appropriative, even when not intended to be. Another view is that it is important for Indigenous course content to have a place in the curriculum, and therefore as long as the work of Indigenous scholars is recognized and presented accurately, the instructor does not have to be Indigenous. That is, this view states that it is important for non-Indigenous instructors to incorporate (but not appropriate) Indigenous perspectives into the classroom, and to do so in a way that is respectful and accurate. A third view is succinctly summarized by Chelsea Bond (2014). Teaching Indigenous material to non-Indigenous students often involves intensive emotional labor and risk for Indigenous educators, because they are constantly forced to defend their legitimacy as instructors and scholars in a context where Indigenous peoples are overwhelmingly researched by non-Indigenous agents. They must constantly confront materials that reinforce stereotypical views of Indigenous cultures, and they must do so in a way that manages the discomfort of non-Indigenous students, who are usually the vast majority of class participants. It is therefore appropriate for non-Indigenous instructors to share some of this labor. These points of view place different weights on the roles of identity and lived experience in shaping the curriculum. We respect that there is no single Indigenous viewpoint here. Thus far we have addressed this issue by focusing on published content by Indigenous scholars whose work is aimed at general audiences or the field of linguistics (cf. Gaby & Woods, 2020; Meek, 2010; Leonard, 2017). We discuss Indigenous intellectual property rights explicitly in our classes and do not, for example, draw examples from language communities where we know there to be cultural prohibitions on who can discuss the language (e.g., Miriwoong, Acoma, and Zuni).

A final dilemma is how to draw on broad intellectual frameworks around antiracism. That is, the end goal of these curricular discussions are *not* the replication of white power structures with different content. We are trying to avoid the situation where white-centered academics put a thin layer of nominally anti-racist content onto an existing syllabus and call it decolonization. Nor is the aim to position ourselves as experts on decolonization. Rather, it's thinking about what we can do (cf. Bender, 2022), how to use opportunities for bringing up talking points and ideas, and recognizing that this work needs all of our continued involvement. This aligns with the goal of building an inclusive big tent linguistics (see Dockum & Green, 2024), and we amplify the call for all linguists to assess their own sphere of influence and make concrete changes accordingly, in order to combat harmful norms of the past and present, and to create new norms for our field.

Note

1. We are very grateful to the volume editors and fellow authors (particularly Margaret Thomas), to the students in all of our classes discussed above, as well as members of the Yale language contact and field linguistics group, and in particular Jisu Sheen. Thank you to Brook Lillehaugen and Ticha project members, and jessie little doe baird and Mashpee Wôpanâak teachers for their collaboration. We are also grateful for the audience at the LSA 2022 Annual meeting for useful comments and feedback.

References

Adelung, Johann Christoph. (1806). *Mithridates, oder allgemeine Sprachenkunde*. Vosische buchhandlung.

Amery, Rob. (2000). *Warrabarna Kaurna!: Reclaiming an Australian language*. Taylor & Francis.

Amery, Rob. (2009). Phoenix or relic? Documentation of languages with revitalisation in mind. Scholar Space. https://scholarspace.manoa.hawaii.edu/handle/10125/5025.

Amery, Rob, & Buckskin, Vincent Kanya. (2012). A comparison of traditional Kaurna kinship patterns with those used in contemporary Nunga English. *Australian Aboriginal Studies (Canberra), 1*, 49–62. doi: 10.3316/informit.407120031225422.

Arnold, Lynnette. (2019). Accompanying as accomplices: Pedagogies for community engaged learning in sociocultural linguistics. *Language and Linguistics Compass, 13*(6), e12329. doi: 10.1111/lnc3.12329.

Baker, Philip, & Eversley, John. (2000). *Multilingual capital: The languages of London's schoolchildren and their relevance to economic, social and educational policies.* Battlebridge Publications.

Baum, Bruce. (2006). *The rise and fall of the Caucasian race: A political history of racial identity.* New York University Press.

Bender, Emily. (2022). When the media comes calling: On handling sudden media interest in research and its production. In Jeff Good & Kristen Syrett (organizers), *Towards best practices in public outreach by linguists: Responsibilities, strategies, ethics, and impact.* Panel at the 96th Annual Meeting of the Linguistic Society of America, Washington, DC, Jan. 6–9.

Berson, Josh. (2012). Ideologies of descent in linguistics and law. *Language & Communication, 32*(2), 137–146. doi: 10.1016/j.langcom.2011.05.002.

Blevins, Juliette. (2018). *Advances in proto-Basque reconstruction with evidence for the proto-Indo-European-Euskarian hypothesis.* Routledge.

Blumenbach, Johann Friedrich. (1795). *De Generis Humani Varietate Nativa.* Vandenhoek et Ruprecht.

Blust, Robert. (1990). Summary report: Linguistic change and reconstruction methodology in the Austronesian language family. In Philip Baldi (Ed.), *Linguistic Change and Reconstruction Methodology* (pp. 133–154). De Gruyter Mouton.

Bodt, Timotheus A., & List, Johann-Mattis. (2022). Reflex prediction: A case study of Western Kho-Bwa. *Diachronica, 39*(1), 1–38. doi: 10.1075/dia.20009.bod.

Bond, Chelsea. (2014, Nov. 14). When the object teaches: Indigenous academics in Australian universities. *Right Now: Human Rights in Australia.* https://rightnow.org.au/opinion/when-the-object-teaches-indigenous-academics-in-australian-universities/.

Bonfiglio, Thomas Paul. (2007). "Language, Racism, and Ethnicity." In Marlis Hellinger & Anne Pauwels (Eds.) *Handbook of Language and Communication: Diversity and Change,* 619–50. De Gruyter Mouton.

Bonfiglio, Thomas Paul. (2010). *Mother tongues and nations: The invention of the native speaker.* De Gruyter Mouton.

Bowern, Claire, & Dockum, Rikker. (2022). Decolonizing historical linguistics in the classroom and beyond. *Presentation at the 96th Annual Meeting of the Linguistic Society of America, Washington, DC, Jan. 6–9.*

Broadwell, George Aaron, García Guzmán, Moisés, Lillehaugen, Brook Danielle, Lopez, Felipe H., Plumb, May Helena, & Zarafonetis, Mike. (2020). Ticha: Collaboration with Indigenous communities to build digital resources on Zapotec language and history. *DHQ: Digital Humanities Quarterly, 14*(4).

College Factual. (2023). Race/Ethnicity of Swarthmore College Faculty. Retrieved on October 24, 2023. https://www.collegefactual.com/colleges/swarthmore-college/student-life/diversity/chart-faculty-ethnic-diversity.html

Crowley, Terry, and Claire Bowern. (2010). *Introduction to Historical Linguistics.* Oxford: Oxford University Press.

DeGraff, Michel. (2005). Do Creole languages constitute an exceptional typological class? *Revue Francaise de Linguistique Appliquee, 1*, 11–24.

DeGraff, Michel. (2005). Linguists' most dangerous myth: The fallacy of Creole exceptionalism. *Language in Society, 34*(4), 533–591. doi: 10.1017/S0047404505050207

Dockum, Rikker, & Green, Caitlin M. (2024). Toward a big tent linguistics: Inclusion and the myth of the lone genius. In Anne H. Charity Hudley, Christine Mallinson, & Mary Bucholtz (Eds.), *Inclusion in linguistics*. Oxford University Press.

Errington, Joseph. (2001). Colonial linguistics. *Annual Review of Anthropology, 30*(1), 19–39. doi: 10.1146/annurev.anthro.30.1.19.

Gaby, Alice, & Woods, Lesley. (2020). Towards linguistic justice for Indigenous people: A response to Charity Hudley, Mallinson and Bucholz. *Language, 96*(4), 268–280. doi: 10.1353/lan.2020.0078.

Gooden, Shelome. (2020). Creole language prosody in the 21st century. Plenary address at the 94th Annual Meeting of the Linguistic Society of America, New Orleans, Jan. 3–7.

Grierson, George Abraham. (1903–1928). *Linguistic survey of India*. Office of the Superintendent of Government Printing, India.

Grimm, Jacob. (1851). *Über Den Ursprung der Sprache*. F. Dümmler.

Grimm, Jacob. (1984). *On the origin of language*, trans. Raymond A. Wiley. Brill.

Hale, Mark. (2014). The comparative method: Theoretical issues. In Claire Bowern & Bethwyn Evans (Eds.), *The Routledge handbook of historical linguistics* (pp. 146–160). Routledge.

Henderson, John. (2002). Language and Native Title. In John Henderson & David Nash (Eds.), *Language in native title* (pp. 1–19). Aboriginal Studies Press.

Hutton, Christopher M. (1998). *Linguistics and the Third Reich: Mother-tongue fascism, race and the science of language*. Routledge.

Hutton, Christopher M. (2010). Who owns language? Mother tongues as intellectual property and the conceptualization of human linguistic diversity. *Language Sciences, 32*(6), 638–647. doi: 10.1016/j.langsci.2010.06.001.

Jones, William. (1786). Third anniversary discourse, by the president, Asiatic Society of Bengal. February 2. http://www.eliohs.unifi.it/testi/700/jones/Jones_Discourse_3.html

Keicho, Momoka. (2021). *Raciolinguistic socialization and subversion at a Predominantly White Institution* [BA. thesis, Swarthmore College].

Lass, Roger. (2014). Lineage and the constructive imagination: The birth of historical linguistics. In Claire Bowern & Bethwyn Evans (Eds.), *The Routledge Handbook of Historical Linguistics (pp.* 43–63). Routledge.

Leonard, Wesley Y. (2017). Producing language reclamation by decolonising "language." *Language Documentation and Description, 14*, 15–36.

Leonard, Wesley Y., & Haynes, Erin. (2010). Making "collaboration" collaborative: An examination of perspectives that frame linguistic field research. *Language Documentation & Conservation, 4*, 269–293.

Lillehaugen, Brook Danielle, Broadwell, George Aaron, Oudijk, Michel R., Allen, Laurie, Plumb, May Helena, & Zarafonetis, Mike. (2016). Ticha: A digital text explorer for colonial Zapotec, first edition. https://ticha.haverford.edu/.

Lukaniec, Megan. (2017). Toward a methodology for dormant language reclamation: Deconstructing the process of using archival data for research and revitalization. Presentation at the 5th International Conference on Language Documentation and Conservation, Hawai'i, March 2017.

Majeed, Javed. (2018). *Colonialism and knowledge in Grierson's linguistic survey of India*. Routledge India.

McCarty, Teresa L., Nicholas, Sheilah E., Chew, Kari A. B., Diaz, Natalie G., Leonard, Wesley Y., & White, Louellyn. (2018). Hear Our Languages, Hear Our Voices: Storywork as Theory and Praxis in Indigenous-Language Reclamation." *Daedalus 147*(2), 160–172. doi: 10.1162/DAED_a_00499.

Meek, Barbra A., (2007). Respecting the language of elders: Ideological shift and linguistic discontinuity in a Northern Athapascan community. *Journal of Linguistic Anthropology, 17*, 23–43. doi: 10.1525/jlin.2007.17.1.23.

Meek, Barbra A. (2010). *We are our language: An ethnography of language revitalization in a Northern Athabaskan community*. University of Arizona Press.

Meek, B. A. (2019). Language endangerment in childhood. *Annual Review of Anthropology, 48*, 95–115. doi: 10.1146/annurev-anthro-102317-050041.

Meiners, Christoph. (1785). *Grundriß der Geschichte der Menschheit*. 1st edition. Meyer.

Michael, John S. (2021). The race supremacist anthropology of Christoph Meiners, its origins and reception. Unpublished Manuscript.

miles-hercules, deandre. (2020). Perspectives on African American students' linguistic experiences in the academy." In *Black Becoming for Language and Linguistics Researchers*, Panel at the 94th Annual Meeting of the Linguistic Society of America, Jan. 3 2020, New Orleans.

Motha, Suhanthie. (2020). Is an antiracist and decolonizing applied linguistics possible? *Annual Review of Applied Linguistics, 40*, 128–133. doi: 10.1017/S0267190520000100.

Muysken, Pieter. (2019). Language and origin: The perspective of multilingualism. In P. L. Patrick, M. S. Schmid, & K. Zwaan (Eds.), *Language analysis for the determination of origin: Current perspectives and new directions, language policy* (pp. 119–130). Springer International Publishing.

National Center for Education Statistics (NCES). (2022). Integrated Postsecondary Education Data System (IPEDS) Data Feedback Report 2022 for Swarthmore College. https://nces.ed.gov/ipeds/dfr/2022/ReportHTML.aspx?unitId=216287

Preston, Dennis R. (2019). Trouble in LADO-land: How the brain deceives the ear. In P. L. Patrick, M. S. Schmid, & K. Zwaan (Eds.), *Language Analysis for the Determination of Origin: Current Perspectives and New Directions, Language Policy* (pp. 131–154). Springer International Publishing.

Rumsey, Alan. (1993). Aboriginal Australia. In Michael Walsh & Colin Yallop (Eds.), *Language and Culture in Aboriginal Australia* (pp. 191–206). Canberra; Australian Institute of Aboriginal and Torres Strait Islander Studies.

Saini, Angela. (2019). *Superior: The return of race science*. Beacon Press.

Shea, Haley, Mosley-Howard, G. Susan, Baldwin, Daryl, Ironstrack, George, Rousmaniere, Kate, & Schroer, Joseph E. (2019). Cultural revitalization as a restorative process to combat racial and cultural trauma and promote living well. *Cultural Diversity and Ethnic Minority Psychology, 25*(4), 553–565. doi: 10.1037/cdp0000250.

Sutton, Peter. (2004). *Native title in Australia: An ethnographic perspective*. Cambridge University Press.

Templeton, Alan R. (2016). Evolution and notions of human race. In J. B. Losos & R. E. Lenski (Eds.), *How Evolution Shapes Our Lives, Essays on Biology and Society* (pp. 346–361). Princeton University Press.

Thompson, Elle. (2020). Bryn Mawr strike ends after 16 days. *The Bi-College News*, November 20. https://bicollegenews.com/2020/11/20/bryn-mawr-strike-ends-after-16-days/

Tsikewa, A. (2021). Reimagining the current praxis of field linguistics training: Decolonial considerations. *Language, 97*(4), e293–e319.

Tuck, Eve, & Yang, K. Wayne. (2012). Decolonization is not a metaphor. *Decolonization: Indigeneity, Education & Society, 1*(1), 1–40.

Valone, David A. (1996). Language, race, and history: the origin of the Whitney-Müller debate and the transformation of the human sciences. *Journal of the History of the Behavioral Sciences, 32*(2), 119–134.

Velonis, Adrian. (2020). Haverford strikers declare victory after final negotiations. *The Bi-College News*, November 11. https://bicollegenews.com/2020/11/11/haverford-strikers-declare-victory-after-final-negotiations.

Walsh, Michael. (1997). How many Australian languages were there? In D. Tryon & M. Walsh (Eds.), *Boundary rider: Essays in honour of Geoffrey O'Grady* (pp. 393–412). Pacific Linguistics.

Wikimedia Commons. (2013). Language families of Asia. *Wikimedia Commons*. https://commons.wikimedia.org/w/index.php?title=File:Language_families_of_Asia.png&oldid=647422621.

Wikimedia Commons. (2022). Langs N. Amer. *Wikimedia Commons*. https://commons.wikimedia.org/w/index.php?title=File:Langs_N.Amer.png&oldid=692903885.

Zúñiga, Fernando. (2016). Selected semitransitive constructions in Algonquian. *Lingua Posnaniensis, 58*(2), 207–225.

Hannah Gibson is professor of linguistics at the University of Essex. Her research is concerned with linguistic variation, particularly why and how languages change. Much of her research examines variation in the morphosyntax of the Bantu languages of Eastern and Southern Africa. Her theoretical work is articulated from the perspective of the Dynamic Syntax framework—a parsing/production-oriented approach to natural language processing which seeks to capture the way in which meaning is established in real time. Her work also examines multilingualism, language and identity, youth language practices, and the relationship between linguistics and social justice.

Kyle Jerro is senior lecturer at the University of Essex. They're interested in semantics, syntax, and the interfaces between syntax, semantics, and pragmatics. In particular, their focus has been on the question of possible verb meanings and how the meaning of a verb derives argument realisation, especially on the semantics of valency changing morphology like applicatives and causatives in Bantu languages. They've also conducted research in the areas of aspect and temporal reference, information structure, the semantics of location and directed motion, reference and fictional worlds, and the psychosemantic reality of noun classes in Bantu languages.

Savithry Namboodiripad is assistant professor at the University of Michigan, Ann Arbor and the director of the Contact, Cognition, & Change Lab. Her research focuses on how language ideologies and use interact in multilingual contexts to shape patterns of language change, and she uses experimental methods to study contact and cross-linguistic variation in flexible constituent order. Though her syntactic training was rooted in generative approaches to syntax, her current work is more aligned with usage-based, constructionist approaches. She also studies various aspects of Malayalam, which she grew up speaking, as it is used in North America and South Asia. She researches the field of linguistics as well, studying interpersonal harassment and bias in addition to the history and use of colonialist theoretical constructs such as "native speaker."

Kristina Riedel is senior lecturer in linguistics at the University of the Witwatersrand. Her research interests are focused on the interactions of agreement and word order in the Bantu languages, the morphosyntax of the Bantu language more broadly, and the interface between phonology and syntax. Her research combines descriptive and theoretical approaches to Bantu languages. She has worked on several languages of Tanzania and South Africa. She has also examined issues relating to transformation and decolonisation of higher education with a focus on Linguistics in South Africa.

Abstract: In this chapter the authors argue that syntacticians and the field of syntax have for too long avoided engaging with the colonial legacies and the implicit racist assumptions that have shaped the discipline. They take three key areas which relate to syntax—teaching, research, and citation practices—and explore the ways in which these have been intricately tied up with, or curtailed as a result of, dominant narratives about language, global hierarchies, the idealised "native-speaker," and language as a disembodied object. The authors present a case study of citation practices in Bantu linguistics, where there is an underrepresentation of African scholars in the literature. Beyond the critiques that can be directed at the discipline, as scholars who work in this field, the authors argue that there can and must be a decolonial syntax. They provide practical steps for action in the form of provocations which they urge scholars to engage with, reflect on, and implement within their praxis.

Key Words: syntax, citation practices, Bantu languages, native speaker ideology, teaching linguistics

11

Towards a Decolonial Syntax

Research, Teaching, Publishing

Hannah Gibson (she, her)
University of Essex

Kyle Jerro (they, he)
University of Essex

Savithry Namboodiripad (she, her)
University of Michigan, Ann Arbor

Kristina Riedel (she, her)
University of the Witwatersrand

Introduction: A Background to Decolonising Syntax

In this chapter, we argue that syntacticians should do more to work against the colonial legacies which have shaped our field. We focus on three core academic activities, teaching, research, and citation practices. We give examples of how colonialist constructs and practices have shaped conventions in these areas, grounding our discussion in our own disciplinary, geographic, and institutional contexts. In order to encourage movement from reflection to action, we present a series of provocations in each section which address conceptual and practical steps syntacticians can take. Finally, while we grapple with the issue, we conclude that there can and must be a decolonial syntax in order for the field to move forward.

Decolonisation in Our Local Contexts

Recent years have seen the growth of movements calling on educational and research institutions around the world to acknowledge their role in shaping assumptions about racial and global hierarchies. Following the

Gibson, Jerro, Namboodiripad, Riedel, *Towards a Decolonial Syntax* In: *Decolonizing Linguistics*. Edited by:
Anne H. Charity Hudley, Christine Mallinson, and Mary Bucholtz, Oxford University Press.
© Anne H. Charity Hudley, Christine Mallinson, and Mary Bucholtz 2024. DOI: 10.1093/oso/9780197755259.003.0012

#RhodesMustFall movement in South Africa, the imperative to "decolonise" has become associated with a call to reimagine, transform, and disrupt the role played by universities as sites and producers of knowledge (Bhambra et al., 2018; Jansen, 2019). This process includes acknowledging and calling into question how academic disciplines have shaped thinking about the world, as well as what constitutes legitimate topics of study and appropriate methodological approaches. Our contribution to this volume draws on our experiences of teaching syntax in the parts of the world in which we are based—the United States, the United Kingdom, and South Africa—and our experiences of doing research on languages spoken in colonised contexts. We situate this discussion within the larger discourse on "decoloniality" and "transformation" as it is playing out in North America, South Africa, and the UK, drawing on our own experiences and insights. Through these three focus areas, the chapter represents a critical engagement with the methodologies and practices involved in syntax.

In the UK, decolonising discourses at higher education institutions tend to focus on the curriculum and teaching, although there is a varied response to the topic, both within and between institutions (cf. for example, Andrews, 2018; Bhambra et al., 2018; Gebrial, 2018). In South Africa, the discourse tends to centre around the term "transformation" (cf. du Preez et al., 2016), which necessarily engages with racial inequalities and processes of erasure, but also links to broader intersecting social justice issues including, for example, misogyny and transphobia. In North America, scholars of critical race and Indigenous studies have argued that "decolonise" should not be used as a metaphor (cf. Tuck & Yang, 2012), but rather that it should only be used in relation to movements for Indigenous land rights, access, and repatriation. Though our thinking is informed by all of these traditions, we do not follow any one of these approaches here. Instead, we find it critical to situate notions of "decolonisation" and "transformation" within our local contexts, histories, and daily lived realities.

While there are parallels between the three locations we inhabit, there are also important differences with respect to the educational systems, the research context, and positionality with respect to the decolonial discourse. As scholars working in these contexts, we draw on our own perspectives as well as our experiences of the contexts in which we are operating. We are aware of the need for context-specific responses to these challenges, as well as the strength that comes from forging international allegiances and collaborations. We are also aware that in many ways, the issues we discuss here in relation to knowledge production transcend national boundaries. In this chapter, we aim to identify the ways in which syntax as a field of research has fallen short of engaging with decolonisation, and we aim to provoke discussion and ongoing discourse around how to bring decolonial dialogue into syntax research, teaching, and citation practice.

The approach developed here is influenced by the idea that decolonising efforts are united by two key political and methodological considerations. Firstly, decolonisation proceeds from a shared way of thinking about the world which takes colonialism, empire, and racism as its empirical and discursive objects of study; and seeks to resituate these phenomena as key shaping forces in the contemporary world where their role has systematically and perpetually been hidden and erased from majority discourses. Secondly, in so doing, decolonisation purports to offer alternative ways of thinking about the world and an alternative form of praxis (Bhambra et al., 2018). Crucially, a decolonial approach requires us to first recognize how dominant and "unmarked" ways of understanding and interacting with the world have been shaped by these historical forces. Then, we must reimagine and reinvent these practices, while also addressing material and epistemological harms. In the context of syntax, this paper aims to show some ways that colonialisation, colonial histories, and empire have shaped current research and teaching practices, and provides first steps to creating an alternative framework of approaching teaching, research, and attribution in syntax.

Decolonising and (Re)Contextualising Syntax

Syntax is concerned with the internal organisation of language. From the classification of words to the ordering of words within phrases and sentences, syntax examines the structure of language. The study of syntax has been positioned as a central component of present-day linguistics, driven in large part by notions of generative grammar following Noam Chomsky (1965) and work following; this prioritisation can be seen in terms of which classes are part of the "core" linguistics curricula, introductory textbooks, and publication patterns in flagship journals. At the same time, the history of syntax is intrinsically connected with broader positivist movements in linguistics which have valued moves towards scientism (see also Clemons, this volume) and away from studying language-in-context (Goldsmith & Laks, 2019; Sankoff, 1988). While these theoretical moves are most closely associated with "Mainstream Generative Grammar" (Cullicover & Jackendoff, 2006), there have been knock-on effects across linguistic subdisciplines, where many assumptions about structuralism and generative grammar are taken for granted (Bell et al., 2016; Flores & Rosa, 2022).

222 Decolonizing Linguistics

As noted by Anne Charity Hudley, Christine Mallinson, and Mary Bucholtz (2020), linguistics lags behind a number of other humanities and social science disciplines in its engagement with race and racism. We, as researchers in topics within the field of syntax, believe that syntax is yet further behind other areas of linguistics in addressing these issues, as well as matters related to (de)coloniality. For example, work in language documentation and reclamation has called for the centring of linguistics around the lived experiences of the people who use the languages under study (Leonard, 2018); parallel issues remain underexplored in syntax. In part, this is due to an assumption, sometimes stated and sometimes unstated, that a language user's syntactic knowledge is in some way "deeper" than or impermeable to social—including racial—factors. Indeed, the degree to which social factors are included as part of an explanation often shapes whether that explanation gets to be called "syntactic" or even "linguistic" (Birkeland et al., 2022).

As such, *by design*, factors such as racism have been ruled out as being viable objects of study, labelled as extra-syntactic or extra-linguistic. Not only does this flawed assumption limit the empirical scope of the field, affecting what gets studied, it also affects who is seen as or self-identifies as a syntactician (again, see analogous arguments for all of linguistics from Charity Hudley et al., 2020; Charity Hudley & Flores, 2022; et alia). That is, ignoring factors such as racism and colonialism in syntactic inquiry enables these structural forces to cause harm to (potential) syntacticians. By naming these factors and their insidious reach, we seek to undo any lingering assumptions that the field of syntax is immune from racism, as we highlight, call into question, and disrupt the colonial histories and heritage embedded in our field.

About Our Team and Our Foci in this Chapter

The previous sections briefly laid out the intellectual contexts which have informed our approach to writing about decolonisation and syntax. This section gives some further context as to who we are and how our lived experiences and commitments, individually and as a group, have directed our focus in this chapter. In so doing, we keep with the reflective ethos of a decolonial approach, which asks all scholars to interrogate and name otherwise invisibilised subjectivities which shape how we ask and answer questions about the world. By briefly discussing who we are, why we are writing this chapter, and how the former informs the latter, we seek to push against colonial and positivist norms of inquiry which favour uninterrogated objectivity over contextualised subjectivities alongside motivating what we chose to talk about.

This chapter focuses on three areas where syntacticians need to adopt decolonial forms of thought and praxis, through what we see as some of the core areas of the academic profession: teaching, research, publishing, and engagement with the wider academic community. We identify practices rooted in colonialism and present alternative approaches via three case studies covering these areas.

In the second section we examine teaching practices and pedagogical approaches. The writing and conceptualisation of this section were led by Kristina Riedel. Kristina taught general linguistics and African linguistics at the University of the Free State, South Africa from 2016 to 2023. She has been teaching general linguistics at the University of the Witwatersrand since mid-2023. South Africa has seen large scale student protests in recent years that shut down campuses across the country, starting in 2015 with #RhodesMustFall. In response to this movement, the first workshop on Transformation in Linguistics by the linguistics associations of South Africa was held at Rhodes University in 2016, for which Kristina co-hosted a follow-up workshop at University of the Free State in 2018. She has been invited to speak about and has co-authored studies on transformation and decolonisation (de Vos & Riedel, 2023; Gibson et al., 2021). Kristina is co-authoring an Open Access syntax textbook for South African students that has a decolonial focus with Hlumela Mkabile (UFS) and Mark de Vos (Rhodes). As a white, German, "foreign national" in South Africa, and one of a small number of scholars in her area of African Linguistics in South Africa, she seeks to contribute to a meaningful transformation of this field from her own classes to her engagement with the linguistics association while staying mindful of the challenges and contradictions this involves.

In the third section, we identify insidious colonial constructs which are pervasive in research methods and entwined with central theoretical assumptions. Hannah Gibson and Savithry Namboodiripad took the lead on this section; Hannah, who is also the lead author of this chapter, works on language contact and linguistic variation, with a focus on the morphosyntax of languages of Eastern and Southern Africa and the link between multilingualism and equitable access to resources. Much of her collaborative research has been carried out with colleagues and academic partners based in Eastern and Southern Africa. Her ongoing work on decolonisation of teaching and research is informed by her own experiences as a Black academic of mixed Black Caribbean and white English heritage in a UK higher education institution, where she has found herself both hypervisible and invisible. This positionality, combined with ongoing interactions and discussions with students and colleagues, continue to inform her views and work in relation to decolonising linguistics.

Savithry studies language contact and syntactic typology, and her research is informed by psycholinguistics and language evolution, disciplines which are underpinned by many un- or under-interrogated colonialist constructs. Relatedly, she has worked on collaborative projects investigating the role of "native speaker" in (psycho)linguistic methods and theory (Birkeland et al., 2022; Cheng et al., 2021, Cheng et al., 2022), and she has personal and scholarly commitments to developing and advocating for approaches which address historical (epistemological) harms in (psycho)linguistics in order to improve both the process and outcomes of language research (Namboodiripad & Henner, 2022; Namboodiripad & Sedarous, 2020). Along with her interactions with family and research participants in diasporic and decolonial contexts, her collaborative work on experiences of harassment and bias among linguists and language researchers (Namboodiripad et al., 2019) and the ensuing discussions have informed her efforts in this area.

In the fourth section, we present a case study of the citation of African researchers within the subfield of Bantu linguistics. Kyle Jerro led on this section. Kyle studies the syntax and semantics of argument realization and has explored these topics in Bantu languages, especially Kinyarwanda (Rwanda). As a white researcher based in the UK, they have been seeking to use their position to strengthen North–South collaborations and create a more collaborative environment that better promotes the research agendas set by African scholars. Having been recently criticized by a reviewer in a journal article submission for failing to cite "classic" works in African linguistics (i.e., grammars and papers by white colonial linguists), they have become interested in citation practices, and in particular, seek to disrupt traditions which position white researchers as experts by default.

Though we have crudely assigned ourselves to various sections, our thinking on each of these topics has grown through our personal interactions and scholarly collaborations. We form a team who have come together as a community of practice working on issues relating to decoloniality, race, and racism in higher education and linguistics. Our contributions here are also the result of a range of joint work and conversations amongst members of our team. Hannah, Savithry, and Kristina have worked jointly with Jacqueline Lück (Nelson Mandela University, South Africa) to conduct a survey of the views and experiences of students and instructors on the link between African languages and decolonisation. Hannah and Kyle have also co-taught a number of courses at the University of Essex and discussions around course content, presentation of ideas, and representation—both with each other and with students—have informed their views on teaching and the conceptualisation of a decolonial syntax. Kristina and Hannah also co-organised a workshop entitled "Towards a Decolonial Linguistics" at the 8th International Conference on Bantu Languages held online in 2021 hosted by the University of Essex. This was to our knowledge the first workshop in this biennial conference series dedicated to the exploration of issues of (de)coloniality in Bantu linguistics, and citation and authorship were topics that arose in the course of the workshop.

This chapter draws on our own individual and shared positionalities, experiences, and ongoing work, and our shared view that the field of syntax has for too long avoided engaging with decoloniality and the inherent colonial and racist bias in our study of language. We issue a call for action which is based on a critical examination of the foundations of the field and theories that emerged therefrom. In an effort to facilitate this discussion, we provide "provocations" at the end of each section as ways to disrupt racist and/or colonial systems, practices, and assumptions in our field.

Teaching Practices and Pedagogical Approaches: The Classroom Context

We discuss three key aspects of a decolonial pedagogy: teaching materials need (1) to be richer, more representative, and locally relevant; (2) to provide broader coverage of languages and structures; and (3) to be embedded in an explicit pedagogy of inclusion and student-empowerment. Addressing these requirements is a necessary (though not sufficient) step towards allowing the study of syntax to play an important role in helping racialised learners interrogate and overcome negative hegemonic ideologies associated with their own language styles.

We are not aware of any accessible materials focused on teaching syntax through decolonising pedagogy but a number of scholars have developed models for other subfields of linguistics which we recommend as resources (Calhoun et al., 2021; Namboodiripad, 2020; Sanders, 2020; also Bowern & Dockum, this volume; Sanders et al., 2024; amongst others). In a webinar for the Linguistic Society of America, Savithry Namboodiripad (2020) notes two key aspects to meaningful application of the principles above to course design: firstly, including minoritized content in all lectures rather than leaving these for one or more dedicated session, and secondly, changing topics and their order from the perceived "norm" to recentre peripheralized contexts of language use. This model is put into practice in a textbook by Andrew Nevins

(2022), which describes how minoritized languages have changed linguistic theory. The book draws on typologically diverse languages from different parts of the world, and includes chapters on syntax, morphology, phonology, and semantics.

While syntax as a research area has broadened its empirical coverage of the world's languages over the past decades, the same trend is not as evident in syntax textbooks published in English, especially (but not only) those focused on generative theories, which continue to rely on English structures and examples. For example, Olaf Koeneman and Hedde Zeijlstra (2017) explicitly avoid non-English examples, while Maggie Tallerman's (2020) textbook, which does not focus on syntactic theory, aims for a diverse set of languages and structures but takes English as a starting point. This focus on English is often justified as a way to first present patterns in a language for which students have intuitions, but this problematically and incorrectly assumes monolingualism as the norm. This also consequently has an impact on which kind of structures are covered and to which extent. Commercial publishing may also play a role here, as presenting a one-size-fits-all approach with a focus on English is presumably viewed as ensuring a wider potential audience and cuts down on costs associated of multiple context-specific resources.

Exclusionary or biased example sentences, such as those predominantly featuring male agents or gender-stereotyping activities, represent another problem (Cépeda et al., 2021; Kotek et al., 2021). While we have not been able to locate any studies of racist and culturally stereotyping linguistic examples in general linguistics materials, these problems have been identified in a wide range of educational and testing materials in other disciplines (e.g., Dos Santos & Windle, 2021; Spiegelman, 2022). Since research has shown that there is gender bias and stereotyping in linguistic examples (Kotek et al., 2021) it seems likely that a systematic survey of linguistic examples may also reveal racial bias and/or racial stereotyping.

The importance of contextually appropriate syntax teaching materials is especially clear in South African linguistics programmes. Most programmes use English as the language of instruction. This is despite the fact that less than 10% of South Africans speak English as their first language; just over 10% speak Afrikaans, and about 75% of the South African population speak a Bantu language as their first language (Statistics South Africa, 2012). Universities differ significantly in terms of student racial demographics, but across South African higher education, over 90% of students are South African (Department of Higher Education and Training, 2020), while around 70% of international students come from the predominately also Bantu-language speaking countries in the Southern African Development

Community (SADC) region (IEASA, 2019). In 2015, 49% of academic staff at South Africa universities identified as white, 35% as Black African (Breetzke & Hedding, 2018), and while race is not directly correlated to languages spoken or research and teaching expertise, in reality, and because access to language courses at university is determined by secondary school languages taken, this often means a lack of expertise in Bantu languages by white staff.

While some instructors or programmes avoid commercially published textbooks and use their own materials instead, this approach may be difficult for small departments. In South Africa, few departments that offer linguistics degrees have more than three permanent academic staff members, and linguistics programmes are often found in English departments or form part of broader language and translation studies units. Moreover, a significant number of academic staff at South African universities do not hold PhDs, meaning that they might not yet have received the type of training where creating their own research-based teaching tools is feasible, especially given time constraints. Another issue is that many African languages, especially from "Khoisan"[1] families, remain underdocumented and underresearched, so instructors have less access to journal articles. Even in cases where relevant research has been published, these publications may not be accessible given that many South African university library systems are underfunded and underresourced.

Nearly all public universities in South Africa use English as the sole medium of instruction for most subjects, including linguistics. There are no textbooks in English on the syntax of Bantu or Khoisan languages (although see Bock & Mheta, 2019 for a general introduction to linguistics for South African students, and Bock, 2021 for a reflection on the creation of this textbook as a decolonising effort). Grammars and textbooks that could be used to enhance the visibility and coverage of African languages in the curriculum often stem from the colonial and apartheid eras and use racist language (and/or language names). Some widely used sources include racist example sentences which encode colonial, white supremacist hierarchies, asking students to translate sentences such as "Have the bwana's shirts been ironed?" (*bwana* here could be translated as "master") or "This food was cooked by Ali the European"s cook" (Ashton, 1944, p. 224). While academics continue to use such sources in teaching and research, the racism therein is rarely if ever explicitly addressed. In addition to appropriately covering African language data, the inclusion of theoretical approaches to linguistic analysis is important in African higher education contexts because many African universities require a theoretical lens to be applied to a MA or PhD research project. Students who are not able to apply a theoretical model to syntactic data are therefore not allowed to write their MA or PhD dissertations on a syntactic topic. Context-appropriate textbooks for Southern Africa should cover all of these needs and thematic areas, and explicitly address issues such as racism or the perpetuation of racist worldviews which may appear in resources on African languages.

How well can a textbook that focuses on English language syntax work in the South African context? Bantu languages have a rich agreement system that includes subjects, objects, relative clauses and often locatives, as well as morphosyntactic properties which are not found in other language families such as augments and conjoint-disjoint alternations. While examples from Bantu languages are frequently found in textbooks of phonology (especially for tone) and morphology, very few examples from Bantu languages appear in syntax teaching materials. While Khoisan click consonants feature in phonetics materials, little if any discussion of the morphosyntactic structures, such as linkers, can be found in syntax or morphology textbooks. The problems associated with focusing on standardized forms of language that do not reflect South African students' own speech are also part of the larger challenge here. A syntax textbook featuring primarily (or exclusively) data from English and analyses based on English does not adequately prepare South African students to analyse the languages of the region, nor will it necessarily enable a student to develop appropriate insights into these languages for personal and/or professional purposes. This gap is left to instructors and departments to fill.

Mark de Vos and Kristina Riedel (2023) surveyed South African linguistics and language instructors and departments and showed that many self-reported being involved in curriculum transformation. Their study also showed, however, that the efforts to transform remain partial and shallow, as the majority of instructors appeared not to consider including Khoisan languages in their curricula, but simply added some Bantu language examples to existing (generally English-centric) materials. This finding suggested that when trying to adequately accommodate the diversity of students' linguistic repertoires, it is also crucial to reflect deeply on what is added to the curriculum, as well as when and how.

A study conducted by Hannah Gibson, Kristina Riedel, Jacqueline Luck, and Savithry Namboodiripad has shown that students feel that African language data is added in a tokenistic way in at least some of their classes (Gibson et al., 2021). This does little to shift the colonial paradigm of linguistics and can ultimately negatively impact communities by devaluing both them and their languages. In such instances, community members, rather than seeing themselves represented and reflected in class materials, find their language practices "exoticised" or presented out of context. We must ask: What is communicated and what is left out about these language communities? How can we do better to engage with this linguistic diversity in a meaningful way?

In addition to the potential impact on individual learners, (whether from the communities that are the subject of study or not), there are very real benefits of using a diversity of languages and varieties for teaching and learning purposes. Doing so allows for the broadest spectrum of linguistic structures and realities to be covered in a given teaching context and to be considered in theoretical systems and analyses.

While no single model can meet the needs of instructors and students in all contexts (cf. Namboodiripad, 2020), there are significant opportunities in on-line and Open Access publishing for better meeting the needs of students and instructors, including the possibility of multilingual publishing and the provision of accompanying online materials. However, while these options may not require funding or the same kind of market as commercially published textbooks, they require significant expertise and labour by expert instructors as authors, reviewers, editors, and copyeditors. In South Africa, and in the academic systems in many other countries, authoring textbooks is not weighted in the same manner as research-based journal articles or books in hiring, promotion, funding, and (where relevant) tenure, creating a disincentive for addressing the problem of inadequate textbooks. For a more detailed discussion of this, see Daniel Villarreal and Lauren Collister (this volume) on some of the colonial complexities of Open Access and Open Science.

In order to identify and put needed changes into practice, a helpful next step would be the development of supportive communities of practice across institutions and the wider region, where instructors and postgraduate students can pool resources and knowledge. We also encourage peer-to-peer training and exchange (for discussion of faculty working groups see de Cuba et al., this volume). In addition to taking place within departments, these activities could happen in online spaces. Thematic workshops at regional or subdiscipline-specific conferences can also provide spaces for raising and discussing these issues (see also Charity Hudley & Mallinson, 2018).

It is against this backdrop that we offer a number of reflective questions below for instructors of syntax courses who are developing or otherwise sourcing example sentences and topics.

1. Which languages, dialects, or linguistic varieties that form part of the students' (and my own) linguistic repertoires are included/excluded from my course materials and classroom examples? Which are excluded, and why?

2. What does the choice of names in my examples communicate to students?
3. What do the verbs, nouns and other semantic choices in my examples communicate as a worldview or normative behaviour to students (e.g., who is doing what kind of activity)?
4. How well do the syntactic phenomena discussed in my classes fit the range of linguistic structures found in the linguistic repertoires of those in the classroom and the broader society? Are my students acquiring the tools to analyse their own language use and that of the wider community/country/region? Is the diversity of structures represented appropriate for the specific context of my classroom and students? Are linguistic structures which are common in the languages/varieties in my local context treated as being exotic, unruly, or exceptional in my teaching materials?
5. What is a good balance of structures and related theories for my particular context? (e.g., to what extent should the course material be driven by theoretical considerations and the structure of the teaching materials, and to what extent should I make room for phenomena which are specifically relevant to the languages and varieties represented in the classroom?)
6. Does my department, programme, or university have a publicly stated vision of locally relevant and affirming syntax for our students? If not, why not, and how can I help develop one?

Research Methodologies: Conceptual and Practical Issues

Taking a simplistic "diversity and inclusion" approach to evaluating the state of syntax might lead one to think there are no problems to address: after all, there are syntactic analyses and descriptions of a wide range of languages, so one could survey major publications, note that a diverse set of languages is included, and stop there. This is where questioning and rejecting commonly held assumptions underlying the work in mainstream approaches to syntax, in line with decolonial or transformational approaches, is critical not only for a true assessment of the field, but also for finding ways forward. This section connects critiques from decolonial perspectives with research practices in syntax: firstly, in line with the decolonial call to recontextualize, denaturalize, and reject constructs with roots in colonialist hierarchies, we address problematic conceptual underpinnings of widely adopted theoretical approaches to the study of syntax. Building on this, we ask how rethinking these theoretical assumptions might have an effect on practical considerations involved in syntactic research.

In describing or analysing particular phenomena, syntacticians often default to factoring out influences from other languages (Bowern, 2010), from other levels of linguistic analysis, and from factors considered to be "extra-linguistic" (Geeraerts, 2010). By basing both our research and our formal models on the idealised "speaker-hearer," the "disembodied language" remains the central object of study in many dominant approaches to syntax. This perspective overlooks core and widespread linguistic practices such as multilingualism, which far outnumbers monolingualism globally. Either as a deliberate standpoint or as a theoretically informed view, engagements with both individual-level and community-level variation, interaction, and language use have been peripheralized or labelled as extra-syntactic, as opposed to being seen as central to the object of study (Charity Hudley & Flores, 2022; DeGraff, 2020; Ferguson & Gumperz, 1960; Stanlaw, 2020).

There have been major critiques of this decontextualized approach within linguistics, such as critiques of modularity (e.g., Croft, 2001) and calls for embodied and situated approaches to language documentation, description, and analysis (e.g., Enfield, 2013), but these have been motivated by a variety of factors which do not include connections to the colonialist underpinnings of traditional theories and methods. However, these critiques resonate with long-held critiques from adjacent fields such as linguistic anthropology and educational linguistics that call for linguists to question colonialist constructs such as bounded languages (Otheguy et al., 2015). Such work has shown that approaches which do not take the subjectivities of language users into account, impose etic or outsiders' categories onto domains where they may not be appropriate (Leonard, 2018). While isolating phenomena to some degree is important for practical purposes, these scholars scrutinize the way that this isolation is done. Whose categories are used? What type of data is collected and analysed? Who decides what belongs in a particular language, and what counts as "linguistics" to begin with? When linguists' labels do not align with those of language-users, whose labels are given precedence? By failing to critically consider these questions many syntactic theories have further embedded dominant thought in the field and excluded other, often less visible, modes of thought and knowledge production, perpetuating the epistemicide of European colonialism (De Sousa Santos, 2016).

A notable example of this process is the "native speaker," a term which is inextricable from the colonialist project and has been widely critiqued and theorised outside of syntax (e.g., Paikeday, 1985; Rajagopalan, 1997; Love

& Ansaldo, 2010). From a historical perspective, Stephanie Hackert (2012) traces how the notion of the "English native speaker" developed alongside English nationalism and overtly white supremacist movements such as Anglo-Saxonism. Despite these critiques, the native speaker remains a central yet undertheorised construct across syntactic frameworks (Birkeland et al., 2022; Cheng et al., 2021; Dewaele et al., 2021). By instead centring multilingual and otherwise underexamined contexts of language use and including more languages, varieties, practices, and communities in syntactic research, we will improve our research methods and our view of syntax itself (Costley & Reilly, 2021; Henner & Robinson, 2021; see also Henner, 2024). While the field of syntax includes some work on a wide range of languages, there is still a very high level of overrepresentation of what Yourdanis Sedarous and Savithry Namboodiripad have called "WISPy languages," that is, languages or varieties of languages which are Written, Institutionally supported, Standardised, and/or Prestigious (Sedarous & Namboodiripad, 2020). This shift in focus will require a destabilisation of disciplinary norms, moving from static to dynamic, from homogenous to heterogenous, and from categorical to emergent. But it is this very disruption that is needed to develop a decolonial syntax.

A reasonable question, one with which we ourselves are still grappling, is whether decoloniality is possible for scholars who are situated within spaces which have emerged directly from colonial traditions—such as syntax, linguistics, and academia more broadly (Jobson, 2020; Mayorga et al., 2019). Rather than reject the enterprise altogether, we believe that syntax makes a crucial contribution to our understanding of language and the world. We argue that a decolonial syntax is possible and that developing the subfield in this direction and exploring what this might look like should constitute a key theoretical concern for syntacticians. Though a questioning of disciplinary assumptions and boundaries is necessary, syntacticians need not and should not leave such critiques or investigations to other fields and subfields, but rather these questions must also be a central part of syntactic inquiry.

Such a set of moves has precedence within theoretical approaches to syntax, namely, in approaches which focus on individual differences and emergent grammar (e.g., Dąbrowska, 2013), and those which incorporate language users' subjectivities into linguistic representations (e.g., Höder, 2012). In the generative tradition, this approach can be seen in the focus on i-languages as the object of study (Chomsky, 1986). Related approaches which seek to explain syntactic phenomena from historical or contact perspectives have also developed theoretical machinery to address relevant empirical issues related to the dynamics of syntax, such as competing grammars (Kroch, 1989) or hybrid grammars (Aboh, 2015). We do not suggest that the existence of these approaches means that the problem is solved, nor do these represent decolonial approaches. We consider transformation of the field a process rather than an end goal which can be fully attained. Instead, these approaches provide examples of local solutions to certain analytic problems that could provide a way forward in addressing as yet untheoretical or untheorized conceptual and representational issues in the discipline.

We encourage readers to reflect on how colonialist constructs and the centring of colonial languages in syntax have led to the assumptions about how (all) language(s) are structured. For example, analyses of languages with flexible word order have been central to debates within and across syntactic frameworks, with languages exhibiting flexibility being exoticised, labelled as exceptional, or seen as requiring a fundamentally different set of analytic tools (Levshina, Namboodiripad et al., 2023). How has starting with a particular set of assumptions, rooted in hegemonic languages and ways of thinking, contributed to the exoticisation of flexible word order and how it is framed? Rather than providing an alternative analysis or set of instructions, we ask readers to imagine how syntactic analyses and descriptions of their specific phenomena might look different if variation were treated a priori as being relevant from a theoretical and descriptive perspective. In other words, the starting point often determines not only the analysis but the very questions that are asked.

We offer the following questions for reflection, whether by individual researchers, in research groups, or by reviewing scholarly work and research proposals (see also Chetty et al., this volume, for more on research funding).

1. Whose language use is analysed and modelled? Who is given authority to provide judgements or have their language use analysed? Who is excluded from these research processes? How do the answers to these questions map onto structures of oppression, either in the language community or, more broadly speaking, in the unequal relationship between language users and the analyst?
2. Are normative modes of language use centred or given precedence over others? Is a hegemonic mode of language learning and/or use treated as unmarked, or as a proxy for how a given language works in all cases? (See Figueroa, this volume; Henner & Robinson, 2021.)
3. How is description of the particularities of a language balanced with comparison across languages? Are locally relevant categories elided in descriptions and comparisons?
4. How are different modalities treated? Are embodied language use, gestures, and prosody treated as nuisance variables or even ignored?

What are points of (mis)alignment between researchers' perspectives and how the phenomenon under investigation is produced and understood by language users?

5. How is language contact treated? Is the full linguistic repertoire of language users given serious attention? Whose conceptualization of languages boundaries are considered relevant, and why?

6. How does this work connect with the needs and goals of the language communities and relevant stakeholders, and if it does not why is that the case?

7. How is funding conceived of and disbursed? For example, do funding schemes require or preclude applicants from certain parts of the world? Do the ways in which the schemes are set up perpetuate colonial and inequitable relations (cf. Chetty et al., this volume)? Do grant applications include substantive funding to support language communities?

8. How are the positionality and commitments of the researcher(s) addressed? Are there subjectivities which have gone unnamed and therefore been mischaracterised as objectivities? What additional opportunities might there be for integrating reflection into the research process?

Visibility and Inclusion In Citation Practices and Publishing

For citation practices we take the subfield of Bantu linguistics, a research interest of three of the authors, as a case study of the power dynamics of race. We show that there is a striking overrepresentation of non-African researchers publishing about African languages, and an underrecognition of work by African linguists. These factors are intricately related to who is conceived of as an "expert" (see also Dockum & Green, 2024), and we note the many intersecting hierarchies that factor into this, such as being based at an institution in the Minority World versus Majority World, enduring colonialist frames, anti-Blackness, and community membership. We use the phrase "Minority World" here to denote those countries which despite their small proportion of the global population have disproportionate wealth and influence over global affairs, including European and North American countries; this contrasts with the term "Majority World" (a term attributed to Bangladeshi photographer Shahidul Alam) which denotes the global majority, who come from countries in Africa, South America, and Latin America.

To briefly illustrate the issue, we used the search term "African Languages" in Google Scholar which lists works in order of the number of citations. On 5 October 2022, the top search returns (looking at the first three pages returned by Google Scholar) are almost exclusively white scholars from Minority World institutions, with only one African author showing in the top ten searches, Professor Emeritus Ayọ̀ Bámgbóṣé of the University of Ibadan in Nigeria, who appears third. In a search for "Bantu languages," the top three pages of results returned only two African scholars: Professor Emeritus Eyamba Bokamba of the University of Illinois at Urbana-Champaign, who appears eleventh (Bokamba, 1988) and thirteenth (Bokamba, 1976) and Professor Sam Mchombo at the University of Berkeley, who is twenty-fifth (Mchombo, 2017). Of note is that none of the African authors are women.

It is cause for concern that in this field, African scholars are not the most-cited experts. This imbalance is especially concerning given the point made by Emmanuel Ngué Um (2020) that many of the white scholars who are viewed as authorities were or are agents of colonial regimes. Similar issues have been observed with the lack of representation of women across different academic disciplines (Leslie et al., 2016) as well as the preponderance of white authors conducting research on African American English (Charity Hudley et al., 2020; Rickford, 1997). A range of potential explanations have been offered, including those which are sexist and make reference to putative cognitive differences between women and men; see Leslie et al., 2016 for discussion). Possible explanations for the undercitation of African academics include racism, Western-dominated research paradigms, and the impact of colonialism (Mufwene, 2017; 2020). Furthermore, stemming from the concentration of global wealth in Minority World countries, academics outside Africa often have better resources for research, such as more expansive libraries and facilities as well as more access to research funding. This is in addition to the more fundamental infrastructural challenges that are present for many, such as reliable electricity and internet access.

It is worth noting that comparable searches for "African Languages" and "Bantu Languages" in Scopus and Web of Science pull up a range of papers from many other, unrelated fields, due to a difference in how the results are calculated from the search terms. Given that our aim here is to illustrate the overcitation of white (male) scholars from the Minority World, we restrict our discussion to the convenience survey using Google Scholar and leave a more detailed analysis of citation patterns to future work.

Resolving this issue by giving research by African scholars its appropriate recognition (here, via citation practices as a case study) is a crucial task in decolonizing syntactic research in this area. However, there is no simple fix.

236 Decolonizing Linguistics

The problems around citation practices reflect broader issues of representation and agenda-setting within the field, and citations have been shown to be an imperfect reflection of impact, relevance, and research quality (Aksnes et al., 2019). Nevertheless, identifying these issues is an important first step, as is a broad call for cultivating a research culture which requires critical thinking around citation and publication practices, particularly with regard to racial inclusion (Charity Hudley et al., 2020; Villarreal & Collister, this volume; Chetty et al., this volume). In addition, Wesley Leonard (2018) calls for research on Indigenous languages to be grounded in the experiences of users of the language; in the context of African linguistics, then centring work on African languages around the experiences and expertise of African scholars is paramount. Beyond this recentring, we suggest that authors and publishers act to ensure that African scholars who have published on a given topic are appropriately cited. A culture of decolonial research relies on scholars who are not users of the languages they research to reflect critically on their position in the field and on how their particular own research links to other research and researchers in terms of who is conceptualized as an expert in this body of scholarship. Although this reflective exercise may take place in some scholars' private discussions and reflections, it has not yet been implemented more broadly or publicly as a central practice of African linguistics or beyond. And yet reflection is simply the first step. This reflection needs to then translate into decisive action, by individuals *and* scholarly communities, to ensure that citation and attribution of knowledge is appropriately directed, and with special focus on those whose languages are being studied.

To this end, we suggest the provocations below to aid in the disruption of assumptions around expertise, to contribute to the dialogue about best practice, and to increase and improve the recognition of knowledge held by users of African languages, as well as linguists based on the continent:

1. Does my publication cite research by experts and scholars from the community? Does my paper cite people of colour and especially women of colour? (See, e.g., the Cite Black Women Collective, citeblackwomencollective.org.)
2. Do I include work that might not be otherwise be read by scholars in my home context?
3. Are there works from the community whose language is being discussed, including works in other languages that I can cite? (See Charity Hudley Rule for Liberatory Linguistics.)[2]
4. Do I acknowledge local sources of knowledge, including nonacademic sources?

5. Do I cite existing work in a variety of theoretical veins or traditions, including theories developed or centred across the Majority World?
6. Is my work accessible to all audiences, including those outside of academic spaces, for example by being published Open Access? (See Villarreal & Collister, this volume.)

Steps Forward: Can There Be a Decolonial Syntax?

The COVID-19 pandemic prompted an increase in online seminars, reading groups, workshops, lectures, and conferences, sometimes including free versions of formerly paid events. Taking seriously the need for material solutions to material inequities caused by colonialism, we think about opportunities to disrupt the status quo in favour of new norms which could prioritise decolonial values. For example, having more free online scholarly events allows for the creation of new collaborations and forums for exchange for linguists who strive to decolonise our classrooms and our research practices. There is scope for regional collaborations to meet local needs and create local content together, such as Open Access and/or online textbooks and learning materials created by larger teams, which reduces the burden on individual instructors. However, we are also cognisant of the ways in which these changes may lead to surface-level change, or worse, further entrench inequalities. For example, with the move to online conferences, it became clear that not all participants around the world have access to fast, reliable, and affordable internet access. This disparity impacts both individuals and institutions. While removing the costs associated with international conference travel, for example, can be seen as a pathway to inclusion and equality, insufficient attention is paid to other forms of unequal access. Similarly, Open Access resources are often presented as inherently equitable, providing the opportunity for a broader range of people to access resources. However, critiques suggest that Open Access publishing may create further inequality (see also, Kramer & Bosman, 2018; Villarreal & Collister, this volume; Wellmon & Piper, 2017).

These inherent tensions and contradictions are illustrative of the challenges central to the broader question we ask in this chapter: Can there be a decolonial syntax? We believe so. We argue that viewing syntax as an observable object of enquiry and critical analysis which is separable from syntax as a field of study may represent a useful path forward. As we argue here, the field of syntax has its origins in colonial approaches, inaccurate worldviews, and racist, sexist, and other biased assumptions rooted in inequitable power dynamics and social hierarchies. We have presented three areas of focus where we believe initial steps to decolonising syntax can and should be taken.

This chapter is a call to action to those working in syntax, including ourselves. The goal has been to highlight the imperative for the field of syntax to reflect a wider range of knowledge, perspectives and peoples into its basic assumptions and theoretical models, as well as to explore how it can contribute to a more equitable, inclusive, and collaborative linguistics.

Rather than providing a diagnostic of what to do or what steps to follow—a prescriptive trap that could end up as a tick-box exercise—we have presented a series of provocations designed to aid reflection and action. As linguists reckon with the colonialist past and present of our field and its ways of knowing, we must think about practical, action-based changes and identify steps for use in our classrooms, our research, and in our writing. We must explore avenues for resource development, including the co-construction of radical anti-racist syntax resources, similar to the initiatives that have been taking place in other disciplines and other subfields of linguistics.

As syntacticians, our field has been constructed as being central in linguistics. As such, we have the responsibility to also be at the centre of a move towards a decolonial syntax, with all of the work and resistance that that might bring with it. We must acknowledge that current modes of thinking, teaching, writing, and conducting research are steeped in colonial legacies from which linguistics as a discipline has arisen. We must acknowledge that neither syntacticians nor syntax are immune from racism, in our thoughts, in our actions, or in our theorisations.

Perhaps most importantly, we must engage with our decolonial imaginations (Egido & De Costa, 2022): we must believe that a decolonial syntax is possible. It is. It has to be. Because without it, we continue to only teach to, characterise the language use of, and acknowledge the contributions of the mythical monolingual, hearing individual using a WISPy language. In doing so we not only miss a central goal of syntax—explaining human language—but we also dehumanise our students, those who use the languages we study, our academic community, and ourselves.

Notes

1. The so-called Khoisan group of languages spoken in (Southern) Africa is not a genetic group (Güldemann 2014 among others) and the term itself is also contested. Alena Witzlack-Makarevich and Hirosi Nakagawa (2017) provide a short overview of the terminology that

has been employed to refer to this group of languages. We use the term here for ease of reference and due to its ongoing use in the South African context. However, we recognise that its use is not without problem.

2. Charity Hudley Rule for Liberatory Linguistics: any published research that you conduct in a community that you do not consider yourself a part of should include an explicit discussion of the meaningful inclusion of members from that community in your research process and your efforts to increase the participation of community members at your university, in your department, and in your research area.

References

Aboh, Enoch Oladé. (2015). *The emergence of hybrid grammars: Language contact and change.* Cambridge University Press.

Aksnes, Dag, Langfeldt, Liv, & Wouters, Paul. (2019). Citations, citation indicators, and research quality: An overview of basic concepts and theories. *SAGE Open,* 1–17.

Andrews, Kehinde. (2018). The challenge for Black studies in the neoliberal university. In Gurminder K. Bhambra, Kerem Nişancıoğlu, & Dalia Gebrial (Eds.), *Decolonising the university* (pp. 129–144). Pluto Press.

Asthon, E. O. 1944. *Swahili grammar (including intonation).* Longmans, Green & Co.

Bhambra, Gurminder K., Nişancıoğlu, Kerem, & Gebrial, Dalia (Eds.). 2018. *Decolonising the university.* Pluto Press.

Bell, Allan, Sharma, Devyani, & Britain, David. 2016. Labov in sociolinguistics: An introduction. *Journal of Sociolinguistics, 20*(4), 399–408.

Birkeland, Annie, Block, Adeli, Craft, Justin, Sedarous, Yourdanis, Wang, Sky, Wu, Alexis, & Namboodiripad, Savithry. (2022, January 6–9). *Problematizing the "native speaker" in linguistic research: History of the term and ways forward.* [Paper presentation]. Annual Meeting of the Linguistic Society of America.

Bock, Zannie, & Mheta, Gift. (2019). *Language, society and communication: An introduction* 2nd edition. Van Schaik.

Bock, Zannie. (2021). Decolonising linguistics: A southern African textbook project. In Zannie Bock & Christopher Stroud (Eds.), *Language and decoloniality in higher education: Reclaiming voices from the South* (pp. 181–200). Bloomsbury.

Bokamba, Eyamba Georges. (1976). *Question formation in some Bantu languages* [Doctoral dissertation, Indiana University].

Bokamba, Eyamba G. (1988). Code-mixing, language variation, and linguistic theory: Evidence from Bantu languages. *Lingua, 76*(1), 21–62.

Bosman J, & Kramer B. (2018). Open access levels: a quantitative exploration using Web of Science and oaDOI data. PeerJ Preprints 6:e3520v1 https://doi.org/10.7287/peerj.preprints.3520v1

Bowern, Claire. (2010). Fieldwork in language contact situations. In R. Hickey (Ed.), *The handbook of language contact* (pp. 340–357). Blackwell.

Breetzke, Gregory D., & Heading, David W. (2018). The changing demography of academic staff at higher education institutions. *Higher Education, 76*(1), 145–161. https://doi.org/10.1007/s10734-017-0203-4.

Calhoun, Kendra, Charity Hudley, Anne H., Bucholtz, Mary, Exford, Jazmine, & Johnson, Brittney. (2021). Attracting Black students to linguistics through a Black-centered introduction to linguistics course: Supplementary materials. *Language, 97*(1). doi: 10.1353/lan.2021.0014

240 Decolonizing Linguistics

Cépeda Paola, Hadas Kotak, Pabst, Katharina, & Syrett, Kristen. (2021). Gender bias in linguistics textbooks: Has anything changed since Macaulay & Brice 1997? *Language, 97*(4), 678–702.

Charity Hudley, Anne, & Mallinson, Christine. (2018). Dismantling "the master's tools": Moving students' rights to their own language from theory to practice. *American Speech, 93*(3–4), 513–537.

Charity Hudley, Anne, Mallinson, Christine, & Bucholtz, Mary. (2020). Toward racial justice in linguistics: Interdisciplinary insights into theorizing race in the discipline and diversifying the profession. *Language, 96*(4), e200–e235.

Charity Hudley, Anne H., & Flores, Nelson. (2022). Social justice in applied linguistics: Not a conclusion, but a way forward. *Annual Review of Applied Linguistics, 42*, 144–154.

Cheng, Lauretta S. P., Burgess, Danielle, Vernooij, Natasha, Solís-Barosso, Cecilia, McDermott, Ashley, & Namboodiripad, Savithry. (2021). Problematizing the Native Speaker in psycholinguistics: Replacing vague and harmful terminology with inclusive and accurate measures. *Frontiers in Psychology, 12*(3):186–205

Cheng, Lauretta S. P., Kramer, Mathew, Upreti, Ria, & Namboodiripad, Savithry. (2022). Moving past indirect proxies for language experience: "Native speaker" and residential history are poor predictors of language behavior. In *Proceedings of the 42nd Annual Conference of the Cognitive Science Society*. (44): 1682–1689.

Chomsky, Noam. (1965). *Aspects of the Theory of Syntax*. MIT Press.

Chomsky, Noam. (1986). *Knowledge of language: Its nature, origin, and use*. Greenwood Publishing Group.

Costley, Tracey, & Reilly, Colin. (2021). Methodological principles for researching multilingually: Reflections on linguistic ethnography. *TESOL Quarterly, 55*(3), 1035–1047.

Croft, William. (2001). *Radical construction grammar: Syntactic theory in typological perspective*. Oxford University Press.

Culicover, Peter W., & Ray Jackendoff. (2006). Turn over control to the semantics. *Syntax 9*(2), 131–152.

Dąbrowska, Ewa. (2013). Functional constraints, usage, and mental grammars: A study of speakers' intuitions about questions with long-distance dependencies. *Cognitive Linguistics, 24*(4), 633–665.

DeGraff, Michel. (2020). Toward racial justice in linguistics: The case of Creole studies. *Language: Journal of the Linguistic Society of America, 96*(4). e292–e306.

de Vos, Mark, & Kristina Riedel. (2023). Decolonising and transforming linguistic curricula in South Africa: taking stock and charting the way forward. *Transformation in Higher Education, 8*. DOI: 10.4102/the.v8i0.200

Department of Higher Education and Training. (2020). Fact sheet on foreign students in post-school education and training institutions in South Africa. Department of Higher Education and Training, Pretoria.

Dewaele, Jean-Marc, H. Bak, Thomas H., & Ortega, Lourdes. (2021). Why the mythical "native speaker" has mud on its face. In Nikolay Slavkov, Nadja Kerschhofer-Puhalo, & Sílvia Maria Melo-Pfeifer (Eds.), *Changing face of the "native speaker": Perspectives from multilingualism and globalization* (pp. 23–43). Mouton De Gruyter.

Dockum, Rikker, & Green, Caitlin M. (2024). Toward a big tent linguistics: Inclusion and the myth of the lone genius. In Anne H. Charity Hudley, Christine Mallinson, & Mary Bucholtz (Eds.), *Inclusion in linguistics*. Oxford University Press.

Dos Santos, Gabriel Nascimento, & Windle, Joel. (2021). The nexus of race and class in ELT: From interaction orders to orders of being. *Applied Linguistics, 42*(3), 473–491. https://doi.org/10.1093/applin/amaa031

Du Preez, Petro, Simmonds, Shan, & Verhoef, Anné Hendrik. (2016). Rethinking and researching transformation in higher education: A meta-study of South African trends. *Transformation in Higher Education, 1*(1). doi: 10.4102/the.v1i1.2

Egido, Alex, & De Costa, Peter. (2022). Colonial narrative of ethics in research: Telling stories and imagining decolonial futures in applied linguistics. *Research Methods in Applied Linguistics, 1*(2), 100016.

Enfield, Nick J. (2013). A 'composite utterances' approach to meaning. In *Handbook Body-Language–Communication. Volume 1*, pp. 689–706. Mouton de Gruyter.

Ferguson, Charles A., & Gumperz, John D. (1960). Linguistic diversity in South Asia. *International Journal of American Linguistics, 26*(3), 7–13.

Gebrial, Dalia. (2018). Rhodes must fall: Oxford and movements for change. In Gurminder K. Bhambra, Kerem Nişancıoğlu, & Dalia Gebrial (Eds.), *Decolonising the university* (pp. 19–36). Pluto Press.

Geeraerts, Dirk. (2010). Recontextualizing grammar: Underlying trends in thirty years of cognitive linguistics. In Elzbieta Tabakowska, Michal Choinski, & Lukasz Wiraszka (Eds.), *Cognitive linguistics in action: From theory to application and back* (pp. 71–102). De Gruyter.

Gibson, Hannah, Lück, Jacqueline, Namboodiripad, Savithry, & Riedel, Kristina. (2021). African linguistics after #RhodesMustFall. Presentation at AILA World Congress, August 2021.

Goldsmith, John, & Laks, Bernard. (2019). *Battle in the mind fields*. University of Chicago Press.

Güldemann, Tom. (2014). 'Khoisan' linguistic classification today. In Tom Güldemann & Anne-Maria Fehn (Eds.), *Current Issues in Linguistic Theory* (pp. 1–40). John Benjamins.

Flores, Nelson, & Rosa, Jonathan. (2022). Undoing competence: Coloniality, homogeneity, and the overrepresentation of whiteness in applied linguistics. *Language Learning*. https://doi.org/10.1111/lang.12528

Hackert, Stephanie. (2012). *The emergence of the English native speaker: A chapter in nineteenth-century linguistic thought*. Walter de Gruyter.

Henner, Jon. (2024). How to train your abled linguist: A crip linguistics perspective on pragmatic research. In Anne H. Charity Hudley, Christine Mallinson, & Mary Bucholtz (Eds.), *Inclusion in linguistics*. Oxford University Press.

Henner, Jon, & Robinson, Octavian. (2021). Unsettling languages, unruly bodyminds: Imaging a crip linguistics. https://doi.org/10.31234/osf.io/7bzaw

Höder, Steffen. (2012). Multilingual constructions. *A diasystematic approach to common structures*. In Kurt Braunmüller and Christoph Gabriel (eds.) Multilingual Individuals and Multilingual Societies. pp. 241–258. https://doi.org/10.1075/hsm.13.17hod

International Education Association of South Africa. (2019). *Study South Africa (Study SA)*. IEASA, Pretoria.

Jansen, Jonathan. (2019). Introduction and overview: Making sense of decolonisation in universities. In J. Jansen (Ed.), *Decolonisation in universities: The politics of knowledge* (pp. 1–12). Wits University Press.

Jobson, Ryan Cecil. (2020). The case for letting anthropology burn: Sociocultural anthropology in 2019. *American Anthropologist, 122*(2), 259–271.

Koeneman, Olaf, & Zeijlstra, Hedde. (2017). *Introducing syntax*. Cambridge University Press.

Kotek, Hadas, Dockum, Rikker, Babinski, Sarah, & Geissler, Christopher. (2021). Gender bias and stereotypes in linguistic example sentences. *Language: Journal of the Linguistic Society of America, 97*(4), 653-677.

Kroch, Anthony S. (1989). Reflexes of grammar in patterns of language change. *Language Variation and Change, 1*(3), 199–244.

Leslie SJ, Cimpian A, Meyer M, Freeland E. Expectations of brilliance underlie gender distributions across academic disciplines. Science. 2015 Jan 16;347(6219):262-5. doi: 10.1126/science.1261375. PMID: 25593183.

Leonard, Wesley Y. (2018). Reflections on (de)colonialism in language documentation. In Bradley McDonnell, Andrea L. Berez-Kroeker, & Gary Holton (Eds.), *Reflections on Language Documentation 20 Years after Himmelmann 1998* (pp. 55–65). University of Hawaii Press.

242 Decolonizing Linguistics

Levshina, Natalia, Namboodiripad, Savithry, Allassonnière-Tang, Marc, Kramer, Mathew, Talamo, Luigi, Verkerk, Annemarie, Wilmoth, Sasha, Rodriguez, Gabriela Garrido, Gupton, Timothy Michael, Kidd, Evan, Liu, Zoey, Naccarato, Chiara, Nordlinger, Rachel, Panova, Anastasia & Stoynova, Natalia. 2023. Why we need a gradient approach to word order. *Linguistics,* (61) 4, 825-883.

Love, Nigel, & Ansaldo, Umberto. (2010). The native speaker and the mother tongue. *Language Sciences, 32*(6), 589–593.

Mayorga, Edwin, Leidecker, Lekey, & de Gutierrez, Daniel Orr. (2019). Burn it down: The incommensurability of the university and decolonization." *Journal of Critical Thought and Praxis, 8*(1), 87–106.

Mchombo, Sam A. (2017). Chichewa (Bantu). In Andrew Spencer & Arnold Zwicky (Eds.), *The Handbook of morphology* (pp. 500–520). Blackwell publishing.

Mufwene, Salikoko. (2020). Decolonial linguistics as paradigm shift: A commentary. In Ana Deumert, Anne Storch, & Nick Shepherd (Eds.), *Colonial and decolonial linguistics: Knowledges and epistemes* (pp. 289–300). Oxford University Press.

Mufwene, Salikoko S. (2017). Language vitality: The weak theoretical underpinnings of what can be an exciting research area. *Language, 93*, e202–e223.

Namboodiripad, Savithry, Occhino, Corrine, Hou, Lynn, Heaton, Hayley, Herbert, Marjorie, Canning, Dominique, & Bouavichith, Dominique. (2019). Survey of linguists and language researchers. https://sites. google.com/umich.edu/ling climatesurvey/our-team.

Namboodiripad, Savithry. (2020). Presentation at LSA webinar on 14 August 2020: Centering linguistic diversity and justice in course design. https://www.linguisticsociety.org/resource/webinar-centering-linguistic-diversity-and-justice-course-design

Namboodiripad, Savithry, & Henner, Jon. (2022). Rejecting competence: Essentialist constructs reproduce ableism and white supremacy in linguistic theory. Invited peer commentary for Flores & Rosa target article "Undoing competence: Race, linguistic homogeneity, and humanism in applied linguistics. In T. Satterfield (Ed.), *Language learning* (pp. 1-4).

Nevins, Andrew. (2022). *When minoritized languages change linguistic theory.* Cambridge University Press.

Ngué Um, Emmanuel. (2020). Had Ferdinand de Saussure spoken Wolof or Basaa . . . , the discipline of linguistics would have fared differently. *Language, Culture, and Society, 2*(1), 107–115.

Otheguy, Ricardo, Garcia, Ofelia, and Reid, Wallis. (2015). Clarifying translanguaging and deconstructing named languages: A perspective from linguistics. *Applied Linguistics Review, 6*(3): 281–307.

Paikeday, Thomas M. (1985). May I kill the native speaker? *Tesol Quarterly, 19*(2), 390–395.

Piper, Andrew and Chad Wellmon. 2017. How the academic elite reproduces itself' *The chronicle of Higher education.* Last accessed 24 October 2023. https://www.chronicle.com/article/how-the-academic-elite-reproduces-itself/

Rajagopalan, Kanavillil. (1997). Linguistics and the myth of nativity: Comments on the controversy over "new/non-native Englishes." *Journal of Pragmatics, 27*(2), 225–231.

Rickford, John R. (1997). Unequal partnership: Sociolinguistics and the African American speech community. *Language in Society, 26*(2), 161–198.

Riedel, Kristina, & de Vos, Mark. (2018). Decolonising and transforming linguistics in South Africa: Taking stock and charting the way forward. Presentation at Workshop on Language and the (De)Colonisation of the African Coast, October 1–2, 2018, Nelson Mandela University.

Sanders, Nathan. (2020). Presentation at LSA Webinar on 14 August 2020: Centering linguistic diversity and justice in course design. https://www.linguisticsociety.org/resource/webinar-centering-linguistic-diversity-and-justice-course-design

Sanders, Nathan, Konnelly, Lex, & Umbal, Pocholo. (2024). An action-based roadmap for equity, diversity, and inclusion in teaching linguistics. In Anne H. Charity Hudley, Christine Mallinson, & Mary Bucholtz (Eds.), *Inclusion in linguistics*. Oxford University Press.

Sankoff, David. (1988). Sociolinguistics and syntactic variation. In F. J. Newmeyer (Ed.), *Linguistics: The Cambridge survey* (pp. 140–161). Cambridge University Press.

Santos, Boaventura de Sousa. (2016). Epistemologies of the South and the future. *From the European South: A Transdisciplinary Journal of Postcolonial Humanities, 1,* 17–29.

Sedarous, Yourdanis, & Namboodiripad, Savithry. (2020). Using audio stimuli in acceptability judgment experiments. *Language and Linguistics Compass 14*(8), e12377.

Spiegelman, Julia D. (2022). Racism, colonialism, and the limits of diversity: The racialized "other" in French foreign language textbooks. In S. Bouamer & L. Bourdeau (Eds.), *Diversity and decolonization in French studies* (pp. xx–xx). Palgrave Macmillan, 51–64.

Stanlaw, James. (2020). Chomsky, and the Chomskyan tradition vs. linguistic anthropology. In J. Stanlaw (Ed.) *The International Encyclopedia of Linguistic Anthropology* (pp. 1–14). Wiley Blackwell.

Statistics South Africa. (2012). Census 2011 statistical release—P0301.4. Statistics South Africa, Pretoria.

Tallerman, Maggie. (2020). *Understanding syntax*, 5th ed. Routledge.

Tuck, Eve, & , K. Wayne Yang. (2012). Decolonization is not a metaphor. *Tabula Rasa 38 (2021): 61-111,* 1–40.

Witzlack-Makarevich, Alena & Hirosi Nakagawa (2019) Linguistic features and typologies in languages commonly referred to as 'Khoisan'* In Ekkehard Wolff (ed). *African linguistics*. Cambridge University Press. Cambridge. 382–416. doi:10.1017/9781108283991.012

Rajendra Chetty is a South African professor in the Faculty of Education at the University of the Western Cape, and works in the field of language education with specific emphasis on the training of language teachers. The South African context with regard to language is complex given the entanglement of language with race, class, and ethnicity and the role of language in the oppression of Black bodies. Chetty's commitment to the decolonial turn foregrounds the imperative to encompass values and dispositions that unlearn, re-form, and deconstruct linguistics and language studies. Radical intellectualism in linguistics should engage with the hidden violence of language. His thesis is that we need new ways of thinking around language, and that dominant academic cultures cannot disrupt old ways of working on and thinking about knowledge.

Hannah Gibson is professor of linguistics at the University of Essex, UK. Her research is concerned with linguistic variation, particularly why and how languages change. Much of her research examines variation in the morphosyntax of the Bantu languages of Eastern and Southern Africa. She also works on multilingualism, language and identity, youth language practices, and the relationship between linguistics and social justice. She is involved in a number of international collaborative research projects and is committed to working towards more equitable research structures and partnerships.

Colin Reilly is lecturer in linguistics at the University of Stirling and affiliated researcher in the Centre for Language Studies at the University of Malawi. He was previously a senior research officer at the University of Essex. His research focuses on multilingualism, language policy, youth language, and linguistic ethnography. He is interested in understanding the ways in which language policies can influence access to services, institutions, and opportunities in multilingual settings, particularly within education and labour market contexts.

Abstract: In this chapter the authors provide a reflective account of their experiences as scholars based in the UK and South Africa, of working in international academic partnerships. They ask: What can we as individuals do to work towards decolonial international research partnerships? What can the institutions at which we are based do to facilitate more equitable and decolonial research partnerships between North and South contexts? What is the role of funding and funders in supporting these international research collaborations, particularly in light of historical and continued inequitable power relations? The authors explore issues relating to power and equity in academic collaboration by providing personal accounts of research partnerships with which we they have been associated. They focus mainly on issues surrounding funding and the challenges which can emerge from Eurocentric funding models. The chapter concludes with points for reflection on how scholars can move towards effective, decolonial partnerships.

Key Words: methodologies, partnerships, funding, Decolonisation, "North-South"

12

Decolonising Methodologies Through Collaboration

Reflections on Partnerships and Funding Flows from Working Between the South and the North

Rajendra Chetty (he/him)
University of the Western Cape

Hannah Gibson (she/her)
University of Essex

Colin Reilly (he/him)
University of Stirling

Introduction

This chapter explores how we can adopt a decolonial approach to methodologies within linguistics through critical examination of the role of partnerships within academic collaborations in the so-called "Global North" and "Global South". We recognise that the North–South dichotomy is artificial and reductionist. However, for the purposes of the current chapter we employ these terms to reflect conceptualisations in our workplaces, as seen in funding schemes which explicitly require relationships between individuals and/or institutions in the North and South. We acknowledge, however, that the terminology is problematic and fraught, and we explore some of the issues involved in further detail below.

Decolonisation is a "double operation that includes both colonized and colonizer" (Mignolo, 2007, p. 458; cf. Fanon, 1952), and consequently we "are all today in the colonial matrix of power" (Mignolo, 2018, p. 108). While we recognise that the colonised and coloniser operate from different positions, we argue that collaborative partnership is crucial for pursuing the challenge

---

Rajendra Chetty, Hannah Gibson, Colin Reilly, *Decolonising Methodologies Through Collaboration* In: *Decolonizing Linguistics*.
Edited by: Anne H. Charity Hudley, Christine Mallinson, and Mary Bucholtz, Oxford University Press.
© Anne H. Charity Hudley, Christine Mallinson, and Mary Bucholtz 2024. DOI: 10.1093/oso/9780197755259.003.0013

246 Decolonizing Linguistics

of decolonisation and must involve individuals working from different positionalities, histories, geographies, disciplines, and epistemologies. In creating decolonial partnerships, we can "make room for new ideas and the scholars who produce them" and thereby "disrupt traditional departmental and disciplinary identities" (Charity Hudley et al., 2020, p. 312). In linguistics, this will involve challenging ideas around what language practices and contexts are valued as objects of study, and considering who gets to do research or be considered an expert on particular language practices.

There is increasing awareness of the importance of collaboration in academic research and a growing acknowledgement of the necessity of South–North research collaboration to tackle real-world challenges. There is also a heightened awareness of the inequalities which are inherent in this type of work (Coetzee, 2019; Mutua & Swadener, 2004; Tilley & Kalina, 2021). When taking a decolonial approach, collaborations can give rise to challenges and opportunities because decolonisation is a process which seeks to disrupt "the long-standing patterns of power that survive colonialism" (Maldonado-Torres, 2007, p. 243) and move towards "the possibilities of an otherwise" (Walsh, 2018, p. 17).

In this chapter we discuss the challenges and opportunities for decolonial disruption which exist when working in academic partnership, with a focus on linguistics research. We develop an autoethnographic account based on our experiences of working on several international collaborative research projects. We draw on experiences of collaborative academic partnerships between researchers based in Africa and Europe, involving different individuals and institutions, as well as on our experiences of working together on a project which focused on decolonising the curriculum at the University of Essex (UK) and the University of the Western Cape (South Africa). The chapter is structured around three sections: (1) the need to decolonise linguistics; (2) reflections on decolonial partnerships as one strategy towards that goal; and (3) suggestions for best practice in such partnerships.

We ask: What can we as individuals do to work towards decolonial research partnerships? What can the institutions at which we are based do to facilitate more equitable and decolonial research partnerships between North and South contexts? What is the role of funders in supporting these international research collaborations, particularly in light of colonial histories which continue to impact on present-day power relations and inequalities?

We recognise that not all collaborations are funded. However, we focus here on both internally and externally funded research projects to highlight the way that while funding may enable collaborations and projects which would not otherwise be possible, it can also impact and characterise these partnerships and the associated research goals and agendas. We consider funding as a clear area in which there are inequities relating to opportunities for access. Funding is often influenced by institutional affiliation, geographical location, and the availability of pre-existing resources, as well as what type of research and work they support and enable. It is also an area in which there are differences in the contexts we draw on as researchers based in South Africa and the UK. There are also differences with regard to expected outputs from projects, how these are viewed and assessed, the impact that they have for individuals' career progression (see also Riestenberg et al., this volume), and the availability of broader research infrastructure and administrative support.

Within the funding landscape, funding schemes such as the UK's Global Challenges Research Fund (GCRF; see the UK Research and Innovation website for further details) explicitly require North–South partnerships, albeit with the funding primarily administered in the North. The GCRF was a £1.5 billion funding scheme established in 2015 that was directly linked with the UK's Official Development Assistance (ODA) budget. Projects funded by the scheme therefore have to work with, and in, countries deemed eligible to receive ODA and funds must be spent following ODA guidelines. Due to the UK Conservative Government's 2021 decision to neglect their commitment to spending 0.7% of Gross National Income on ODA, and to cut the ODA budget by around £4 billion, the GCRF scheme was stopped and researchers working within it have been negatively affected (Phipps, 2021). The impacts not only affected the future of the scheme, but projects which had been awarded funding but had not commenced, and projects which were already underway and had their funding cut. As Phipps (2021, p. 40) writes, in this process there "was no respect at all for the partnerships overseas or the careful way in which researchers had built up participatory models and equitable partnerships." This example illustrates how funding structures can impact partnerships and how we need to reimagine how funding operates if we are to move towards decolonial practices. Our autoethnographic reflections in this piece focus on the role which funding has in international research partnerships, within both the GCRF scheme and other funding schemes.

We come together in our collaborations acknowledging, as Walter Mignolo (1994) puts it, that we all speak from a different locus of enunciation. Acknowledging our positionalities and reflecting on how they affect our work is an integral part of working towards effective collaborations; accordingly, we begin this chapter with brief positionality statements from all three of us as authors, these show not only who we are in respect to the work we carry out but also how our lived experiences influence our perspectives on the topic of collaborative research.

248   Decolonizing Linguistics

Rajendra

I am a Black South African, and I work in the field of language education with specific emphasis on the training of language teachers. The South African context with regard to language is complex given the entanglement of language with race, class and ethnicity and the role of language in the oppression of Black bodies. My commitment to the decolonial turn foregrounds the imperative to encompass values and dispositions that unlearn, re-form, and deconstruct linguistics and language studies. Radical intellectualism in linguistics should engage with the hidden violence of language. My thesis is that we need new ways of thinking around language, and that dominant academic cultures cannot disrupt old ways of working on and thinking about knowledge.

Hannah

I am a Black woman who grew up in the UK with a mixed Jamaican and English background. The views I share here have their origins in my experiences of working with academic colleagues in Eastern and Southern Africa as part of collaborative research projects. In these contexts, I carry substantial privilege as someone from the UK who is supported by Northern institutions both personally and professionally. I am committed to partnerships and to working with and, contributing to, the local research community. However, my experiences have only strengthened my belief that research and research partnerships need to be approached through a decolonial lens and that Northern research institutes and agendas need to be challenged where they perpetuate inequalities and do not acknowledge the ways in which colonial legacies continue to shape research.

Colin

I work in applied linguistics, focusing on multilingualism and language policy. I have worked primarily in Malawi, and also in Ghana, Botswana, Tanzania, and Zambia. As a white Scottish man based in higher education institutions in the UK, I am able to choose to conduct this type of research, and my ability to be accepted as a researcher within this field is indicative of the inherent privileges that I possess. While I am precariously employed as an early career researcher, my positionality still affords me a disproportionate amount of privilege within academia, which I have a responsibility to use to challenge the inequities faced by other colleagues within linguistics.

The intellectual and material burden of decolonisation within linguistics is one that must be shared, and I have an increasing commitment to collaborative work.

The Need to Decolonise Linguistics

Colonialism is intimately linked to language: as Felix Ndhlovu and Leketi Makalela (2021, p. 8) write, "the twin processes of colonial imperialism and Christian modernity have had the most significant influence on the spread of monolingual thinking." Not surprisingly then, linguistics as a field has "been deeply implicated in the colonial project of conquest and control" (Mazrui 2009, p. 361; Errington, 2001), and the widespread dominance of both English and monoglossic bias that pervades our research agendas and methodologies is a product of coloniality (McKinney, 2020; Pennycook & Makoni, 2020). Addressing and acknowledging the colonial history of our field is an essential step in delinking from it and improving the practice of linguistics as a discipline (Mufwene, 2020; Ndhlovu, 2020). In order to do so, we must actively move away from Euro-modernist epistemologies (Mignolo, 2018; Ndhlovu & Makalela, 2021).

As Linda Tuhiwai Smith (2008) writes, "the term 'research' is inextricably linked to European imperialism and colonialism" (p. 1). Linguistics methodologies have been built on a specific Euro-modernist worldview that does not necessarily allow us to capture the lived linguistic realities of people's lives (Mufwene, 2020; Ndhlovu, 2020). To decolonise linguistics, we must both decolonise the research that informs our teaching and decolonise how we undertake that research. This process involves addressing the ways in which knowledge is produced and whose knowledge is valued and promoted. The priority for the radical intellectual is to reflect on the ways that academic practices signify, restrain, or empower decolonial turns not only in curricula or the research process but also in real-life concerns of domination, emancipation, justice, and liberation of the increasing number of oppressed people globally. When Northern and Southern scholars collaborate, there is always the question of who speaks for whom, especially in research on the lived experience of the "subaltern" (Spivak, 1988). A crucial consideration for decolonising methodologies is the observation that in many academic endeavours, it is not the voices or intellectual production of the subaltern that are foregrounded, but the interpretation and utility of their experiences from a scholar's perspective. This can occur when scholars are operating from a Northern perspective or a Southern perspective and this must be challenged if we are to engage in research that is not exploitative.

Reflections On Power and Trust in Decolonial Partnerships

Collaborations between the North and South do not automatically mean that research partnerships are engaging with decoloniality. To do so in a meaningful way, this engagement has to include the hybrid spaces of the "Norths in the South," and the "Souths in the North," given the colonial history of spatial injustice. Moving beyond the North–South dichotomy, researchers should be guided by a commitment to radical humanism and focus on how nuances of the historical process of coloniality contribute to its invisibility in many aspects of present-day research. Radical humanism as a philosophy insists on the freedom of an individual and places emphasis on the personality of the individual as a human being. Frantz Fanon's (1952, p. 230) radical humanism sustains a capacity to speak with real power to many of the ways in which the question of the human is posed, and contested, from within contemporary forms of resistance undertaken by the subaltern in zones of social exclusion and domination.

Concerns about equitable partnerships are widespread within collaborative research, particularly when these partnerships are between colleagues from the South and North (Asare et al., 2022; Costley & Reilly, 2021; Dodsworth, 2019; Grieve & Mitchell, 2020; Kontinen & Nguyahambi, 2020; Perry, 2020; Price et al., 2020). These concerns often centre around issues of power and resources within partnerships—who has access to power and resources, and how are these used? Such considerations are affected by the history of colonialism and contemporary systems of coloniality which influence how power and resources are allocated (Dodsworth, 2019). As Mia Perry (2020, p. 1) writes, "partnerships begin on the basis of histories, understandings, and layers of contexts that are not always immediately evident, not always directly connected to you, but always influencing the starting positions and the potentials of the collaboration ahead."

Similarly, Walter Mignolo (2018) reminds us that we always speak from a particular location in power structures, be it in the North or South, and that no one escapes the class, sexual, gender, spiritual, linguistic, geographical, and racial hierarchies of the modern, capitalist, and patriarchal world-system. Therefore, a key aspect of collaborative work involves understanding, and discussing, how different aspects of the research are affected by coloniality— including which knowledge and worldviews are valued or defaulted to and how collaborators are able to influence fundamental parts of the research design (Jentsch, 2004; Perry, 2020). Without discussing the epistemological foundations and assumptions that undergird or influence any research endeavour, there is a danger of perpetuating epistemic injustice (Meredith & Quitoz-Niño, 2021).

An important reflection from our own collaborative work is that there are multiple roles and processes which may be visible or invisible and explicit or implicit to varying degrees. Individuals may automatically assume certain roles and responsibilities. While it is not necessary for everyone to participate to an equal degree in all aspects of a project, it is important to make visible and explicit the roles which all collaborators have, to discuss these as our awareness emerges and changes, and to reflect on these in an iterative and ongoing basis. Practical examples of this process include discussing who is responsible for arranging meetings, around whose schedules are they arranged and who gets to set the agenda? (For reflections on collaborative research partnerships in linguistics see Costley & Reilly 2021, Reilly et al., 2023.)

Similarly, when engaging with academic outputs such as conference talks or journal articles, the division of labour—as well as its rationale—is often not made explicit from the outset. Increasing attention must be paid to the importance of author credit within collaborative linguistics work (Amfo, 2021; Costley & Reilly, 2021). This is of course true for collaborations with colleagues based in the same country or at the same institution, but international collaborative research brings additional potential challenges, especially when different academic currencies hold at different institutions and in different contexts. For example, are publications expected in order to secure academic jobs? Are publications needed in order to apply for promotions? Are externally funded research grants valued and/or expected? It can be easy to assume that these issues are viewed similarly across contexts, but this is not the case. Having explicit discussions about who will be responsible for putting together an initial draft of a paper, which conferences will be attended and by which members of the collaboration, has the potential to mitigate against some of these complications, at least those that are within our control. Often these discussions take place against the background of constraints which us as individuals are not in a position to overhaul, however we should identify the areas in which we do have individual capacity to make a difference, and to call for wider systematic restructuring for broader constraints.

Funding Flows in Collaborations

Having briefly reviewed issues which we believe are pertinent to decolonising linguistics, we now turn to how we have experienced coloniality in our own research partnerships. We focus here particularly on funding systems and

252   Decolonizing Linguistics

reflect on questions such as: How does the funding landscape and funder's agendas affect the possibility of equitable collaboration? How do institutional systems and processes impact trust between collaborators?

Colin

Within many of my collaborative projects, and in much of the funding available from schemes in the Global North, the UK-based institution acts as the "award-holder." Our partner institutions can only gain access to funding through the UK institution. Despite the fact that a requirement to get GCRF funding, as discussed above, is that a "least developed country/lower-middle income country" is involved both in the project and in development of the grant application itself, the systems and processes within UK universities are not set up to efficiently work with universities in the Global South. In the majority of cases, partnership agreements, largely written in dense legalese by institutional representatives in the UK, must be signed by all partners. This process can lead to lengthy and drawn-out negotiations. It can also potentially lead to misunderstandings and inequity in negotiations, depending on the non–UK-based collaborators' familiarity with the language of these documents, as well as local expectations and regulations in relation to the agreement.

The project which all three of us worked on together examined the link between language policy and broader issues involved in decolonising the university. As it was a short-term project, there was not sufficient time to set up the University of the Western Cape (UWC) as a formal "partner" for the University of Essex. Our remaining option—to ensure that the funding which we had allocated in our proposal for activities led by UWC could get to UWC—was for UWC to invoice the University of Essex. We had planned for the bulk of funding to go towards hiring two student research assistants from UWC to work alongside students at the University of Essex. However, invoices could only be paid retroactively, meaning that UWC would have to set up a contract, employ, and pay students to work on the project and then claim the money from Essex. However, they could not do so without having the funding available first. This double-bind meant that due to the financial systems involved, we were unable to send any funds to UWC or to employ any students from South Africa on the project, despite the fact that this aspect of our research had been specified in our successful funding application. Our student research assistants at Essex were all excellent, producing valuable work for the project and gaining research experience and skills at the same time. Yet it was to the detriment of the project that we were not also able work with research assistants based at UWC. That one of the topics we were investigating was the decolonisation of curriculums in South Africa and the UK made the whole experience more frustrating because our South African students were not able to participate in the project on an equal level as our UK students, thereby perpetuating these inequitable relations.

In any research partnership, multiple collaborators may be involved at different levels and stages, including researchers, communities, institutions, and funders. They may all have different priorities and pressures that affects the research and how the partnership can operate. As the above example demonstrates, we cannot have equitable partnerships if the funding systems and processes that we employ are not equitable and do not allow for sharing resources effectively between all partners. Even if there is a commitment amongst individuals involved in a research project to adopt a decolonial stance as we produce knowledge, many of the institutional systems we are operating within in the UK, and universities themselves, are products of coloniality and may reproduce these processes in ways that individual researchers and other partners, despite our best efforts, are unable to overcome.

Hannah

I reflect here on the initial stages of a different international collaborative linguistics-focused research project involving two institutions in the UK and two institutions based in Africa. Unlike the programme that Colin discusses above, the funding scheme that supports this project is not restricted to joint research projects nor to working with international collaborators from specific countries. However, it allows for international partners and collaborators, which is the basis on which the proposal was made. I highlight here the practical but also the interpersonal consequences of being required to enter into formal contracts and engage with systems of compliance before the collaborative elements of the research on the project had begun.

In this case, both the Africa-based partners and I had to act as intermediaries in the communication between the UK grant-holding institution and the Co-Applicants' respective institutions. Before any funds can be transferred to any of the institutions, a due diligence process must be completed. The academic project members were responsible for obtaining the information required to complete the process. Many of the questions on the 11-page form are not those that academic staff are in a position to answer due to the nature of our job roles. This included a range of questions about institutional accounts, processes and procedures. Substantial time and effort is therefore needed not only to obtain the correct information but to also ensure that the form is signed by the relevant responsible person with the correct level of seniority.

Working on the UK side, I found this to be a deeply frustrating process. It is time-consuming and, I felt, a job that the academic partners should not be expected to do—not least because these were questions that we did not know the answers to. This requirement also meant that the first months of the project were filled with communication about the due diligence and the draft collaboration agreement rather than the focus of the research. I felt fortunate that the project partners were people I already knew—which is not the case in every partnership of this kind—and that I had collaborated extensively with one of them in the past. Were this not the case, it would be a particularly difficult note on which to start the project. And of course, on a practical level, it is frustrating to have to expend so much time and energy on such details at the outset of a project when partners are eager to begin the research.

These issues also reveal the assumptions on which funding and funding flows are based. Many UK institutions have research offices and research development support. This is because research is a key aspect of the work of UK universities, and because there is funding within the UK to which researchers are able to apply. There is therefore a larger research infrastructure which supports the research environment at my own and many other institutions, including skilled colleagues who can help with the application process, can provide figures and advice about costings, and who are familiar with online submission portals, the expectations of specific schemes and funders. It is easy for both researchers and funders in the Global North to forget that such structures and infrastructures are not found everywhere.

When researchers think about the terms on which collaborative research projects are established, run, and administered, it is therefore crucial to also think about the ways in which the ongoing and potential collaborations of those involved in the project can be supported from the outset. These interactions and collaborations must proceed in equitable and sustainable ways that invest in the research capacity of institutions and individuals both in the North and the South, as well as across all institutions and countries.

Rajendra

I think researchers, regardless of the Northern or Southern context, are conditioned and influenced by dominant philosophies and ideologies that form an essential part of their "settled" knowledge, what Frantz Fanon (1952, p. 11) refes to as their situated dimension of being human. These ideologies have a major influence on research activities and funding. Hence, the priority for the radical intellectual is to reflect seriously on the ways academic practices like funding mechanisms and programmes may be stuck in traditional, colonising ways of seeing and interacting with the "other." In my research collaboration with Northern scholars for the past two decades, I have become aware of the distinct dangers of subliminal racism and patronising behaviours towards the lived experience of the subaltern in Africa. The capitalist social order of the West is reinforced in European research funding when the lion's share of the funding is channelled directly to consultants, travel agents, experts, keynote speakers, and so on from the host country. For example, an annual literacy conference in Cape Town is funded by the British Council with the strict proviso that the keynote speaker will be a scholar from the UK, chosen by the British Council. In all the conferences held thus far, however, the keynote speakers have made no contribution to local literacy debates. They may well be experts in the UK, but this does not mean that their knowledge has universal relevance, given the integral role that local context plays in literacy debates.

Collaborative projects between the North and South also often reflect and embody the ideological tension between the West's individualism and the South's collectivism or "ubuntu." The intellectual production that emerges from the collaborative project almost always foregrounds the voice of scholars from the North. It is the intellectual practice of *speaking for* the subaltern that has generally characterised leftist thought in postcolonial countries, a practice that tends to reproduce and maintain subalternisation (Walsh 2012, p. 14). More importantly, and from a decolonial perspective, I feel that research on the subaltern in Africa must include the voice of the subaltern and their intellectual production, and should disrupt the practice where the scholar speaks for the participants or the scholar interprets their lived experience from a Western perspective. I will illustrate this danger of "who speaks for whom; and can the subaltern speak" (Spivak, 1988) with a recent example from a British funded project in South Africa.

In November 2019, a multimillion rand UKRI grant was awarded to a UK university for research in informal settlements in the Cape Flats. The research team also consisted of academics from the University of the Western Cape and the University of Cape Town, including me, and two white community workers. I was the only Black team member. The community workers received the lion's share of the funding for their "intervention work" with fire and water in three sites in the Cape Flats. Conspicuously, both civic organisations that currently engage with these issues and inhabitants of the informal settlements that experience the hazard of fire were excluded. The leader of the project from the UK dismissed my questions around the methodological framing of the project which was clearly stuck in a colonial paradigm. She argued that the proposal had been peer-reviewed by the funder and the methodology found to be appropriate. In response, I drew upon my work with the shack-dwellers in informal settlements and shared with her how the subaltern views scholars' reasoning on shack fires by passing along a press statement issued by a local organisation that advocates for settlement residents, which reads in part:

> We have heard many people suddenly becoming experts on shack fires. Some are saying the reasons that shack fires exist is because we build too close to one another. Others blame the forms of lighting or heating that people use. In some cases alcohol is said to be the cause of the fires. It is typical for middle class and elite people to think in this way. They want to blame the oppressed for their suffering rather than to blame the systems that cause oppressions. (baseMjondolo, 2018)

An important point here from a linguistic perspective is that doing research on the "other," the subaltern, requires careful consideration not only of the language spoken by the people being researched but also of the notions of who speaks for whom, who has voice, and who can speak but does not. I was ultimately forced to withdraw from the project given the reactionary stance of the project leader. My withdrawal resulted in a dichotomous situation with all white researchers and all Black research subjects. It is evident in this example that the colonial process of knowing about the "native" is far from being disrupted given the financial power and developmental agenda of empire.

Suggestions for Best Practice in Research Partnerships

We draw on our experiences as well as the literature on decolonisation and collaboration to make suggestions for linguists seeking to approach collaborative work from a decolonial perspective. Western canonical traditions of knowledge production have become hegemonic. The dominance of epistemologically conservative scholars actively reinforces these traditions in the guise of values and standards. This hegemonic notion of knowledge production involves a particular process of knowing about Native and Indigenous others that is rooted in colonialism and never fully acknowledges the other as a thinking and knowledge-producing subject. The epistemic traditions of the imagined Native and Indigenous other are disregarded, which is a form of cognitive injustice (de Santos, 2007, p. 49). A prerequisite of cognitive justice is recognising the presence of different forms of understanding, knowing, and explaining the world. The commitment from all scholars who aim for cognitive justice should be towards a radical humanism that engages with the voices and scholarship of the subaltern. For Western scholars who are already operating in privileged positions within academia, the need for this is particularly acute. This step is a crucial foundation for decolonising collaborative research.

We cannot view our collaborations as separate from the various loci and wider systems in which we operate. In this chapter we have called for actively and explicitly talking about and reflecting upon the nature of South–North collaborations from the outset and for providing regular spaces for review and discussion on shared and distinct expectations and pressures. Where appropriate and helpful, we also advocate for creating spaces for autoethnographic work as part of the research collaboration itself, as we have put forward in this chapter. These spaces are crucial for the emergence of creative responses and interactions with the changing world in which the collaboration takes place.

We offer the following questions which we hope will help all researchers to pursue the goal of decolonial research partnerships. We suggest these as useful points for consideration, while also acknowledging that collaborators may respond differently to them and may be in different positions to actively redress any inequitable practices.

For Individual Researchers and Collaborators

- How can we as individuals ensure that the interpersonal relationships that necessarily form or are strengthened as the result of a collaboration are given the optimal chance to develop positively?
- Can all individual researchers collaboratively define the terms, at least initially, on which the collaboration will take place in a way that honours the responsibilities, needs and demands of all of those involved? This issue relates to what is valued in a particular context, institution, or system, as well as what is important to individuals.
- Are the outputs of the research equally valuable and accessible to all involved in the process? This includes considerations of Open Access and posting hard copies of publications, as well as acknowledgements and authorship (see Villarreal & Collister, this volume),
- How can we ensure that all project participants are able to maximally participate and benefit in the collaborative projects?

Further resources: Mia Perry (2020) and Rafael Mitchell, Arjen Wals and Ashley Jay Brockwell (2020) for resources on creating ethical partnerships;

Chad Wellmon and Andrew Piper (2017), Jeroen Bosman and Bianca Kramer (2018) for critical discussion of Open Access; Samuel Asare, Rafael Mitchell, and Pauline Rose (2022) for research of equity in outputs and discussion of project initiations; and Melanie Walker and Carmen Martinez-Vargas (2020) for suggestions on promoting epistemic equality.

For Institutions

- Are there procedures and processes that can be delayed or delegated to other people so that the academic collaborators are not also positioned as the gatekeepers, controlling the funding flowing from the North?
- Are there processes that can be sped up or started at an earlier stage so that the work can still take place and/or timelines are not unduly impacted by the complexities of international collaborations?
- Can space be made to acknowledge that different institutions and contexts have different systems and processes in place? Can we ensure that it is not the Northern institution which dictates the terms on which these collaborations take place and on which funding flows?

Further resources: See Jude Fransman et al. (2018) for suggestions on establishing equitable partnerships; Victoria Henson-Apollonio (2005) on establishing collaboration agreements; Tiina Kontinen & Ajali M Nguyahambib (2020), Romina Israti and Alex Lewis (2020), and Richard Axelby, Bethel Worku-Dix, and Emma Crewe (2022) for reflections, and best practice suggestions, for institutional partnership.

For Funders

- Do we need to establish or look for alternative funding models? What would a decolonial funding system look like?
- Can we rethink how funds are created? How grants are assessed? How funds are disbursed and shared? Does the way in which success is measured in the eyes of the funder align with the needs and interests of all parties?

See Tigist Grieve and Rafael Mitchell (2020) for a discussion of GCRF funding criteria; Gilles Carbonnier and Tiina Kontinen (2014) on a range of collaboration issues including funding; Hilary Footitt, Angela Crack, and Wine Tesseur (2018) on issues including language use in multilingual contexts, and funding.

It is crucially important to create spaces in which different individuals and institutions are able to come together to collaborate on a project. It is also important to acknowledge from the outset that there might be differing priorities and expectations, that this is not in itself a problem. If we can acknowledge the complexities inherent in South–North collaborations, we are better positioned to move towards and operate from a position of best practice, allowing truly collaborative and equitable partnerships to be formed.

However, we are also conscious of the need to guard against decolonisation becoming a matter of virtue signalling, whereby researchers engage in performative discourses and measurement rhetoric. Additionally, we need to be wary of technical compliance, symbolic activities and tokenism, actions that are not based on any intention to radically change our discipline, but a need to show very quickly that something is being done (Behari-Leak and Chetty 2021, p. 16). These approaches leave Eurocentric worldviews intact and ultimately do not support either the best partnerships or the best research. In our partnerships, we must actively, and collaboratively, interrogate the processes and power dynamics involved as a key step in ensuring equitable collaborations.

References

Abahlali baseMjondolo. (2018). Shack fires are our daily lives. Press statement, 23 October. http://abahlali.org/node/date/2018/10/

Amfo, Nana Aba Appiah. (2021). Managing authorship in (socio)linguistic collaborations. *International Journal of the Sociology of Language 2021*, (267–268), 21–26. https://doi.org/10.1515/ijsl-2020-0078

Asare, Samuel, Mitchell, Rafael, & Rose, Pauline. (2022). How equitable are south–north partnerships in education research? Evidence from sub-Saharan Africa. *Compare: A Journal of Comparative and International Education, 52*(4), 654–673. doi: 10.1080/03057925.2020.1811638

Axelby, Richard, Worku-Dix, Bethel, & Crewe, Emma. (2022). Global partnerships on paper and in practice: Critical observations from inside a Global Challenge Research Fund capacity-development project. *Journal of International Development, 34*(8), 1496-1508.

Behari-Leak, Kasturi, & Chetty, Rajendra. (2021). Drawing a line in the sand: social mapping of responses to calls to "decolonise the university." *Journal of Decolonising Disciplines, 3*(1), 1–24.

Bosman, Jereon, & Kramer, Bianca. (2018). Open access levels: A quantitative exploration using Web of Science and oaDOI data. *PeerJ Preprints, 6*, e3520v1. https://doi.org/10.7287/peerj.preprints.3520v1

260 Decolonizing Linguistics

Carbonnier, Gilles, & Kontinen, Tiina. (2014). *North–south research partnership: Academia meets development?* European Association of Development Research and Training Institutes (EADI).

Coetzee, Carli. (2019). Ethical?! Collaboration?! Keywords for our contradictory times. *Journal of African Cultural Studies, 31*(3), 257–264. doi.org/10.1080/13696815.2019.1635437.

Costley, Tracey, & Reilly, Colin. (2021). Methodological principles for researching multilingually: Reflections on linguistic ethnography. *TESOL Quarterly, 55*, 1035–1047. https://doi.org/10.1002/tesq.3037

de Santos, Boaventura Soasa. (Ed.). (2007). *Cognitive justice in a global world: Prudent knowledges for a decent life.* Lexington Books.

Dodsworth, Susan. (2019). The challenges of making research collaboration in Africa more equitable. *Oxford Research Encyclopedia of Politics.* https://oxfordre.com/politics/view/10.1093/acrefore/9780190228637.001.0001/acrefore-9780190228637-e-1389

Errington, Joseph. (2001). Colonial linguistics. *Annual Review of Anthropology, 30*(1), 19–39.

Fanon, Frantz. (1952). *Black skin, white masks.* Grove Press.

Footitt, Hilary, Crack, Angela, & Tesseur, Wine. (2018). *Respecting communities in international development: Languages and cultural understanding.* http://www.reading.ac.uk/modern-languages-and-european-studies/Research/mles-listening-zones-of-ngos.aspx

Fransman, Jude, Hall, Budd, Hayman, Rachel, Narayanan, Pradeep, Newman, Kate, & Tandon, Rajesh. (2018). *Promoting fair and equitable research partnerships to respond to global challenges.* Rethinking Research Collaborative.

Grieve, Tigist, & Mitchell, Rafael. (2020). Promoting meaningful and equitable relationships? Exploring the UK's global challenges research fund (GCRF) funding criteria from the perspectives of African partners. *European Journal of Developmental Research, 32*, 514–528. https://doi.org/10.1057/s41287-020-00274-z

Henson-Apollonio, Victoria. (2005). Collaborative agreements: A "how to" guide. ILAC Briefs 52514, Institutional Learning and Change (ILAC) Initiative.

Hudley, Anne Charity, Mallinson, Christine, & Bucholtz, Mary. (2020). From theory to action: Working collectively toward a more antiracist linguistics (response to commentators). *Language, 96* (4), e307–e319. doi:10.1353/lan.2020.0081

Istratii, Romina, & Lewis, Alex. (2020). *Promoting the SOAS GCRF strategy: A qualitative assessment of research development processes and partnerships building in collaborative international research.* SOAS University of London.

Jentsch, Birgit. (2004). Making Southern realities count: Research agendas and design in north–south collaborations. *International Journal of Social Research Methodology, 7*(3), 259–269. doi: 10.1080/1364557021000024776

Kontinen, Tiina, & Nguyahambi, Ajali M. (2020). Institutional learning in north–south partnerships: Critical self-reflection on collaboration between Finnish and Tanzanian academics. *Forum for Development Studies, 47*(2), 219–241. doi: 10.1080/08039410.2020.1768590

Maldonado-Torres, Nelson. (2007). On the coloniality of being: Contributions to the development of a concept. *Cultural Studies, 21*(2–3), 240–270. doi.org/10.1080/09502380601162548.

Mazrui, Alamin M. (2009). Linguistics in a colonial world: A story of language, meaning and power. *Journal of Multilingual and Multicultural Development 30*, 361–363.

McKinney, Carolyn. (2020). Decoloniality and language in education: Transgressing language boundaries in South Africa. In Joeal A. Windle, Dànie de Jesus, & Lesley Bartlett (Eds.), *The Dynamics of Language and Inequality in Education* (pp. 115–132). Multilingual Matters.

Meredith, Margaret, & Quiroz-Niño, Catalina. (2021). Facilitating knowledge democracy in a Global North/South academic collaboration. *Educational Action Research.* doi: 10.1080/09650792.2020.1866632

Mignolo, Walter D. (1994). Editor's introduction. *Poetics Today, 15*(4), 505–521.

Mignolo, Walter D. (2007). Delinking. *Cultural Studies, 21*(2), 449–514. doi.org/10.1080/09502380601162647.

Mignolo, Walter D. (2018). The decolonial option. In Walter D. Mignolo & Catherine. E. Walsh (Eds.), *On Decoloniality: Concepts, Analytics, Praxis* (pp. 105–244). Duke University Press.

Mitchell, Rafael, Wals, Arjen, & Brockwell, Ashley Jay (2020). *Mobilising capacities for Transforming Education for Sustainable Futures: Opening spaces for collaborative action and learning.* https://doi.org/10.5281/zenodo.4134931.

Mufwene, Salikoko. (2020). Decolonial linguistics as paradigm shift: A commentary. In Ana Deumert, Anne Storch, & Nick. Shepherd (Eds.), *Colonial and Decolonial Linguistics: Knowledges and Epistemes* (pp. 289–300). Oxford University Press.

Mutua, Kagendo, & Swadener, Beth Blue. (2004). *Decolonizing research in cross-cultural contexts: Critical personal narratives.* SUNY Press.

Ndhlovu, Finex. (2020). Decolonising sociolinguistics research: Methodological turn-around next? *International Journal of the Sociology of Language 2021*, (267–268), 193–201. https://doi.org/10.1515/ijsl-2020-0063

Ndhlovu, Finex, & Makalela, Leketi. (2021). *Decolonising multilingualism in Africa: Recentering silenced voices from the Global South.* Multilingual Matters.

Phipps, Alison. (2021). Last word: The research cost of Britain's foreign aid cuts. *Political Insight, 12*(3), 40–40. doi:10.1177/20419058211045149.

Pennycook, Alistair, & Makoni, Sinfree. (2020). *Innovations and challenges in applied linguistics from the Global South.* Routledge.

Perry, Mia. (2020). *A critical resource for ethical international partnerships.* https://doi.org/10.17605/OSF.IO/DJTN4

Price, Roz, Snijder, Mieke, & Apgar, Marina. (2020). *Defining and evaluating equitable partnerships: A rapid review.* Tomorrow's Cities. http://dx.doi.org/10.7488/era/1008

Reilly, Colin, Costley, Tracey, Gibson, Hannah, Kula, Nancy, Bagwasi, Mompoloki M., Dikosha, Dikosha, Mmolao, Phetso, Mwansa, Joseph M., Mwandia, Martha, Mapunda, Gastor, & James, Edna. (2023) Emerging principles for researching multilingually in linguistic ethnography: reflections from Botswana, Tanzania, the UK and Zambia, *Journal of Multilingual and Multicultural Development*, 44(8), 689–701, DOI: 10.1080/01434632.2023.2194864

Spivak, Gayatri Chakravorty. (1988). Can the subaltern speak? In Cary Nelson & Lawrence Grossberg (Eds.), *Marxism and the Interpretation of Culture* (pp. 271–313). University of Illinois Press.

Smith, Linda Tuhiwai. (2008). *Decolonizing methodologies: Research and Indigenous peoples.* Zed Books.

Tilley, Elizabeth, & Kalina, Marc. (2021). "My flight arrives at 5am, can you pick me up?": The gatekeeping burden of the African academic. *Journal of African Cultural Studies.* doi.org/10.1080/13696815.2021.1884972.

Walker, Melanie, & Martinez-Vargas, Carmen. (2020). Epistemic governance and the colonial epistemic structure: Towards epistemic humility and transformed South–North relations. *Critical Studies in Education.* doi: 10.1080/17508487.2020.1778052.

Walsh, Catherine. (2012). "Other" knowledges, "other" critiques: Reflections on the politics and practices of philosophy and decoloniality in the "other" America. *Transmodernity: Journal of Peripheral Cultural Production of the Luso-Hispanic World, (1)3*, 11–39.

Walsh, Catherine. (2018). Decoloniality in/as praxis. In Walter D. Mignolo & Catherine E. Walsh (Eds.), *On decoloniality: Concepts, analytics, praxis* (pp. 1–104). Duke University Press.

Wellmon, Chad, & Piper, Andrew. (2017). Publication, power, and patronage: On inequality and academic publishing. *Critical Inquiry,* July 21; updated October 2. criticalinquiry.uchicago.edu/publication_power_and_patronage_on_inequality_and_academic_publishing

Dan Villarreal is assistant professor of linguistics at the University of Pittsburgh. As a computational sociolinguist, Dan's scholarly work sits at the nexus of two research traditions: bringing together computational methods and sociolinguistic perspectives. In particular, his research seeks to expand sociolinguists' research toolkits by making computational techniques and sociolinguistic data accessible and usable; explore how speakers and listeners make sense of the tremendous phonetic variability that characterizes everyday speech; and foster a computational sociolinguistics (and a linguistics more broadly) that addresses its research questions faster, better, and more equitably. His recent work has investigated computational methods to automatically code sociophonetic variation (and how to make these methods equitable), as well as gender segregation and speech communities in New Zealand. His research has been published in *Language Variation and Change*, *Laboratory Phonology*, and the *Journal of Pragmatics*. Dan pronounces his last name [vɪləɹiˈæl].

Lauren B. Collister is an engagement coordinator at the organization Invest in Open Infrastructure. At the time of writing this chapter, she was director of the Office of Scholarly Communication for the University of Pittsburgh Library System. Her goal as a scholarly communication professional is to set the default to Open; as part of that mission, she oversaw the Pitt Open Library Publishing program for Open Access journals and coordinates services relating to repositories, copyright, and open scholarship. Lauren's background is in linguistics; her PhD research work on multimodal online communication introduced her to the complexities of linguistic data and the meta-scholarship of publishing and access to research. She previously served as chair of the Committee on Scholarly Communication in Linguistics for the Linguistic Society of America and is the co-editor of the recently published *Open Handbook of Linguistic Data Management* from MIT Press.

Abstract: Open Methods are resources that pertain to at least one stage in the linguistics research process and are available free of charge to all who can find them. This chapter describes the current state of Open Methods in linguistics, including benefits and structural barriers to further development. Then, in the spirit of the dictum that those who do not learn from history are doomed to repeat it, the authors discuss how Open Access (a longer-developed cousin to Open Methods that focuses on publishing research) fails to adequately serve research(ers) in the global context despite its agreeable basic premise. They critically assess whether Open Methods can help decolonize linguistics research—or whether it merely allows already privileged linguistics to accrue greater privilege. The chapter ultimately presents a cautiously optimistic model for anticolonial Open Methods in linguistics, with recommendations and examples of practices and policies throughout.

Key Words: Open Methods, research methods, Open Access, colonialism, computational approaches

13

Open Methods

Decolonizing (or Not) Research Methods in Linguistics

Dan Villarreal (he/him)
University of Pittsburgh

Lauren Collister (she/her)
Invest in Open Infrastructure

In academia generally and linguistics specifically, there has been a growing movement toward the open sharing of resources that can mitigate resource barriers to research.[1] These Open Methods streamline and standardize various steps of research methodology, and creators make Open Methods freely available for other researchers to use to avoid each researcher or team re-creating processes and methodologies for each project. On the surface, this trend appears positive, even potentially heralding a democratization of linguistics research. The same was true, however, of Open Access, a longer-developed cousin to Open Methods in the Open Science movement that focuses on publishing research; despite the optimistic outlook of the 2002 Budapest Open Access Initiative declaration (Guédon, 2017), 20 years of Open Access have instead seen colonial results (Meagher, 2021). Indeed, the current landscape of Open Methods in linguistics has been influenced by power structures and resource imbalances; there is a real danger of Open Methods merely becoming an instrument reproducing the hegemony of North American and European research(ers) in linguistics, like Open Access before it. There is thus no better time to critically assess whether and how Open Methods can help decolonize linguistics research. This critical assessment leads us to present a cautiously optimistic model for anticolonial Open Methods in linguistics; we preview this model throughout the chapter with recommendations and examples of practices and policies.

Before we proceed, it's important to know that both authors enjoy structural privilege with respect to Open Methods, derived from our affiliation with a

---

Dan Villarreal, Lauren Collister, *Open Methods* In: *Decolonizing Linguistics*. Edited by: Anne H. Charity Hudley, Christine Mallinson, and Mary Bucholtz, Oxford University Press. © Anne H. Charity Hudley, Christine Mallinson, and Mary Bucholtz 2024.
DOI: 10.1093/oso/9780197755259.003.0014

wealthy research-centered US university, from the specific jobs we hold at that university, and from other identities. (We expand on our positionalities in the section "Model for an Anticolonial Open Methods.") The descriptions and recommendations mentioned in this chapter thus inherit our biases and limited perspectives, so we intend this chapter to be a starting point rather than the last word, leaving space especially for scholars from different backgrounds to iterate and expand on our ideas.

What Are Open Methods in Linguistics?

What we call Open Methods in linguistics encompasses a varied range of existing practices and products by linguistics researchers. What unites these practices and products is that they are not only *open*, as they are available free of charge to all who can find them (via the internet), but also *methodological*, as they pertain to at least one stage in the linguistics research process (e.g., data collection, data processing, data analysis, visualization). For the purposes of this chapter, we limit our discussion to Open Methods developed primarily by and for linguistics researchers, although general-purpose Open Methods such as the R statistical programming language (R Core Team, 2022) have tremendously benefited linguistics research.

While both *open* and *methodological* are difficult to precisely circumscribe, we argue that linguistics is best served by an expansive view of Open Methods. To illustrate, we provide some examples of Open Methods in Table 13.1. To be clear, this is not a representative sample (a full survey of Open Methods is beyond the scope of this chapter) but rather a judgment sample selected by Dan to illustrate the range of Open Methods in linguistics. While this list is not representative in the statistical sense (we are not claiming that three of every ten Open Methods are software), in terms of methodological traditions (given Dan's research interests, it skews toward corpus sociophonetics), or in terms of who produces Open Methods (given Dan's professional networks, it skews toward high-resource countries), all of these resources are open and methodological in different ways. When Open Methods are software, they are typically open in the additional sense of open source: the underlying computer code is published and thus available for critique, contributions, and customization by users. As Santiago Barreda (personal communication) eloquently states, "customizability allows others to 'fix' things that [creators] may not even understand as broken." Furthermore, Open Methods coexist in an ecosystem; while the customizability of Praat (Boersma & Weenink, 2021) makes building extensions possible (e.g., Barreda, 2021), its software-oriented rather

Open Methods 265

Table 13.1 Illustrative examples of Open Methods in linguistics

Category	Product	Description	Available since
Linguistic data	Corpus of Regional African American Language (Kendall & Farrington 2020)	Dataset	2018
	World Atlas of Language Structures Online (Dryer & Haspelmath 2013)	Dataset	2013
Software	Praat (Boersma & Weenink 2021)	Phonetics/phonology analysis software	1995
	NORM (Thomas & Kendall 2007)	Vowel normalization and plotting tool	2007
	FAVE (Rosenfelder et al. 2011)	Forced alignment and vowel extraction software	2011
Software extensions	Rbrul (Johnson 2009)[a]	R extension for variable rule analysis	2009
	phonR (McCloy 2016)	R package for phonetic analysis/visualization	2012
	Fast Track (Barreda 2021)[a,b]	Praat extension for formant tracking	2021
Tutorials for using Open Methods	How to train your classifier (Villarreal et al. 2019)[a]	Documentation of sociolinguistic auto-coding in R with worked example	2019
	Using Praat for linguistic research (Styler 2021)	Praat user guide	2011

[a] Also published with a companion journal article.

[b] First published when at least one author was on tenure track (see Appendix A).

than task-oriented documentation necessitates a user guide (Styler, 2021). Finally, while these resources are all freely *available*, that does not guarantee they are all equally *accessible* to potential users; Dan's own Open Method (Villarreal et al., 2019), for example, contains data in an R-specific file format, includes R code that is not legible to beginning users, and is only available in English. We bring up these examples not to gatekeep "openness," but to inspire creators to make adjustments to their resources to make them as open as possible. To that end, we have developed a "Spectrum of Open Methods" rubric (Collister & Villarreal, 2022), accompanied by a case study assessing Villarreal et al.'s (2019) Open Method. In this respect, we draw inspiration from Catherine D'Ignazio and Lauren Klein's (2020, p. 4) self-assessment of "aspirational metrics to live [their] values" for their *Data Feminism* book. In other words, a method that's imperfect but published is always more open than a method that never gets published because it's not perfect yet (Barnes, 2010).

Open Methods have gained interest in large part because they can yield efficiency gains for linguistics researchers (beyond their creators); for example, recent computational methods automate (or semiautomate) time-consuming tasks such as time-aligning segmental boundaries (Rosenfelder et al., 2011), measuring formants (Barreda, 2021), and coding sociolinguistic variables (Villarreal et al., 2019). But of equal significance is the potential of Open Methods to mitigate or circumvent resource barriers that would otherwise exclude some potential researchers, such as those with precarious positions or at low-resource institutions. For example, collecting a sociolinguistic corpus is highly resource-intensive, but researchers can use the Corpus of Regional African American Language regardless of their access to recording equipment, a travel budget, or community contacts. (We'll complicate the idea that this is always a desirable outcome in "Open Methods Reappraised: Colonial or Anticolonial?" below.) Beyond individual researchers, perceived benefits to the field are transparency in research methodology (Nosek et al., 2015), a corrective measure for the "reproducibility crisis" in psychology and other fields (Gawne & Styles, 2022), expansion of benefits for translation work (Helsinki Initiative, 2019), and promoting best methodological practices. Open Methods can also benefit the practitioners who disseminate Open Methods themselves, for example by encouraging good record-keeping practices (following the philosophy that "your most important collaborator is yourself six months ago—and they don't answer emails").

These perceived benefits, however, are largely overshadowed by the costs of producing Open Methods. Some of these costs are at the institutional level, such as web-hosting services for digital tools, computational support for resource-intensive applications, or research staff to document, develop, translate, or curate materials. These institutional costs are not trivial, and that they are more likely to be borne by already-privileged institutions (Frischmann et al., 2014) is related to the colonialist corporate capture of Open Access (see "Open Access: Optimistic Intentions, Colonial Results" below). Indeed, as mentioned above, our own positionality and exposure result in all of the Open Methods in Table 13.1 coming from researchers working at universities in high-resource countries.

We argue, however, that the primary cost barrier to Open Methods in linguistics is researcher labor. Many Open Methods begin as resources that researchers create for their own projects; the steps needed to turn a resource created for a narrow use case into an Open Method may include: making the resource flexible for multiple use cases, vetting and testing source code, anonymizing data, securing rights or permissions for sharing data, creating documentation, making the method available, translating the documentation and method into multiple languages, and getting the word out. In addition, researchers who create computer code often suffer from "code-shyness," a reluctance to share their code because they are worried about its quality (Barnes, 2010). On top of these costs are a lack of benefits; because Open Methods are not "traditional research outputs" as defined by privileged research institutions in North America and Europe, they may not count toward researchers' career advancement (see also Montoya, this volume). (Notably, several examples in Table 13.1 were published with a companion journal article—a traditional output on top of the Open Method itself.) Amid extraordinary competition for scarce faculty jobs and funding for research projects (Benedicto, 2018; Bonn & Pinxten, 2021), workers in precarious conditions generally calculate that they cannot afford the risk of spending time on Open Methods. As a result, many potentially useful resources for the broad linguistics community remain unshared and unknown except by those who traditionally hold social power and capital in the discipline, thereby reproducing exclusionary and colonial dynamics.

Open Methods thus represent an area where individual actors' best interests do not align with the best interests of the field. A growing chorus of commentators and professional societies, including the Linguistic Society of America (LSA), have advocated bringing these interests into better alignment by incentivizing Open Methods and other forms of Open Scholarship (Alperin et al., 2022; Linguistic Society of America, 2018, 2021). As of the time of writing, US linguistics departments' review, promotion, and tenure (RPT) policies run the gamut in terms of whether and how they count Open Methods toward career advancement. (See Appendix B for links to policies described here.) For example, at the University of Delaware's department, "primary evidence for scholarly excellence [i.e., research]" includes refereed articles, books, and "publicly available data collections," though not other Open Methods like software. The University of Illinois Chicago's department recognizes "the development of scholarly digital material" as secondary to journal articles, placing Open Methods alongside "conference papers [and] lectures." The Ohio State University's linguistics RPT policy gives tenure-track faculty no incentive to create Open Methods, as it does not explicitly list Open Methods as evidence of research excellence. The University of Georgia's linguistics RPT policy states that "the concept of 'publication.' . . may include linguistic corpora, software, or other digital materials," but only "if these items are subject to a stringent peer-review process." Despite good intentions, this policy fails to acknowledge the fact that linguistics doesn't have models for "stringent peer-review" of outputs like software (although good models may be adopted from other fields), nor does it specify what would count as "stringent peer-review"; in other words, scholars working under this policy have no clear guidance on how to proceed or whether Open Methods will be worth their while professionally. In short, there is no consistent policy landscape with respect to Open Methods in RPT. In fact, only one Open Method in Table 13.1 was created by a researcher on the tenure track, and the author went through the extra effort of creating a companion journal article because it would otherwise be difficult to get credit for citations or to gauge user uptake (Santiago Barreda, personal communication; see also Howison & Bullard, 2016; Huang et al., 2015). All the other examples were created by PhD students, postdocs, tenured professors, or the international equivalents thereof (see Appendix A). This pattern suggests that the pressure to conform to established scholarly expectations and metrics imposed by the tenure track creates a strong disincentive against creating Open Methods; the risks may be even higher for researchers in positions of precarious employment.

Creating the conditions for a greater proliferation of Open Methods would require change in several parts of the academic-research ecosystem. Readers at research institutions in positions of power should advocate for the inclusion of Open Methods in RPT, with clear and reasonable expectations. This call entails change at both the departmental and university levels; university leadership can guide departments to better recognize Open Methods and invest resources to support researchers who wish to open their closed methods. Furthermore, we call for journals to widen the scope of what is considered publishable, to include articles that are "purely methodological" without needing to also demonstrate direct theoretical impact or novel empirical data; doing so would create needed incentives for researchers working in departments that only recognize traditional research outputs. The publication of such "purely methodological" work has historically been limited to computational linguistics, which overlaps in disciplinary norms with engineering (Charity Hudley et al., 2023). One common past practice in linguistics is to publish methods works in handbooks, few of which are Open Access (with the notable exception of Berez-Kroeker et al., 2022). Additionally, "purely methodological" work is starting to appear in more journals. Some notable examples are the recent computational sociolinguistics research topic in *Frontiers in Artificial Intelligence* (e.g., Bartelds et al., 2020; Ghyselen et al., 2020; Kendall et al., 2021), *Laboratory Phonology* (e.g., Villarreal et al., 2020), and especially *Linguistics Vanguard* (e.g., Barreda, 2021; Hall-Lew et al., 2022), which has published special issues on using smartphones to collect data for linguistic research (Hilton & Leemann, 2021) and sociolinguistic data collection in the COVID-19 era (Sneller, 2022).

Thus far, we have laid out the case for Open Methods as lowering resource barriers to carrying out linguistics research, as well as recommendations for advancing Open Methods. This case for Open Methods, however, considers only the perspective of linguistics research in high-resource countries, rather than the resource barriers that researchers face in the rest of the world. To consider the global implications of Open Methods, we turn our focus to Open Access (OA), a cousin in the Open Science movement that has a longer track record than Open Methods. Both in linguistics and beyond, OA presents a cautionary tale of an unobjectionable moral premise that has been captured by colonialist hegemony in the guise of humanitarianism and social justice (e.g., Meagher, 2021; Nkoudou, 2020a; Roh et al., 2020). To ensure Open Methods does not suffer from a similar outcome, then, we proceed to learn from OA history.

Open Access: Optimistic Intentions, Colonial Results

Open Access as a movement grew out of the Open Source movement, and they overlap considerably not only through use of tools like copyright licenses to make work accessible and reusable, but also in the shared ideology that intellectual properties are public goods (Willinsky, 2005). The original Budapest Open Access Initiative (BOAI) declaration from 2002 began with the statement "An old tradition and a new technology have converged to make possible an unprecedented public good"; in this statement, there was a ringing optimism for the potential of technology to make research and scholarship more accessible and to put "communication at the heart of the scientific enterprise" (Guédon, 2017, p. 2). The BOAI declaration celebrated the work of enterprising academics and "DIY publishers" around the world who had been creating scholar-led Open Access scholarly journals online since the 1980s (Moore, 2020).

We agree with the basic premise that making scholarly work as open as possible is beneficial for the creators and users. In fact, many researchers assert that they agree with this basic premise as an obvious "right thing to do" with considerable benefits to the public, research participants, and other beneficiaries of research (see e.g., Day et al., 2020). However, as Charlotte Roh, Harrison Inefuku, and Emily Drabinski (2020) write, despite its unobjectionable premise, OA does not "automatically reverse the biases and norms of scholarship itself" (p. 49). Indeed, in implementation and practice in the global community, OA has suffered from many colonial practices and perspectives that hamper its uptake and distort its purpose. Recent endeavors in Open Access involve capitulation to corporate interests seeking to profit from scholarly endeavors (e.g., Priego et al., 2017). Kate Meagher (2021) points out that the interests of for-profit, capitalist scholarly publishing companies have particularly damaged OA in the Global South, resulting in "political capture of the OA agenda by Northern corporate and state interests." Other colonial practices that persist include privileging the English language in its most inscrutable form, "academic language" (Figueroa, 2022), and presuming that North American and European notions of quality and prestige are shared by all (Nkoudou, 2020b; see also Khan, this volume; Montoya, this volume; Plumb et al., this volume). We explore these issues by highlighting the response to OA from scholars in two regions: the African continent, where OA was introduced relatively recently, and Latin America, where OA was embedded in scholarly practice long before its introduction in North America and Europe.

Thomas Hervé Mboa Nkoudou has written about the mismatch between the goals of the Open Access movement and the needs and contexts of scholars across the African continent. One key aspect of the resistance to OA from African scholars is that "the desire to make African knowledge visible was not truly an African initiative" (2020a, p. 28). Reggie Raju et al. (2020, p. 57) expand on this assertion:

> There have been assumptions about the Global South remaining ignorant and underdeveloped until it has access to the Global North's knowledge. In an attempt to 'eradicate' this ignorance and promote development, there has been a push for the Global North to focus on improving the flow of information to the Global South. (see also Braithwaite & Ali, this volume; Chetty et al., this volume)

This basic colonizer principle encounters resistance to OA from African scholars, because while OA seemed to hold promise after the declarations of the early 2000s, its implementation has failed to account for "African realities" that are different from the support structures available in rich countries: "Many factors suggest that OA is a matter for the rich countries of the Global North, where basic infrastructural matters, such as regular and reasonable salaries for academics, public research grants, access to the internet, electricity, well-supported libraries, and comfortable and safe workplaces have long been settled" (Nkoudou, 2020a, p. 27). For example, according to Raoul Kamadjeu, founder of the *Pan African Medical Journal*, much African research is researcher-funded, and because of their investment of personal funds, many African researchers are resistant to depositing their data or other materials that they have collected using their own personal funds without any tangible benefit to them (Kuchma et al., 2022). The proliferation of article processing charges (APCs) demanded by for-profit journals creates a new barrier to participation in publishing because many institutions in Africa do not fund APCs (Kuchma et al., 2022), and the continued reliance on impact factors privileges journals written in English (Curry & Lillis, 2018; Lillis et al., 2010); taken together, the result is that Western notions of prestige and quality of research are replacing the local systems of knowledge and knowledge sharing, which Nkoudou calls "epistemicide: destruction of local epistemologies that are replaced, in this case, by a Western paradigm" (2020a, p. 32; see also Leonard, 2020).

In Latin America, a different reality exists: OA has long been part of the system for disseminating scholarship through a network of regional information systems supported by Latin America-based disciplinary repositories and discovery indices such as SciELO and Redalyc (SciELO—Scientific Electronic Library Online n.d.; Sistema de Información Científica Redalyc n.d.) even before the Budapest Open Access Initiative. Two-thirds of the funding for research and publishing comes from public funds, and publishing for scholars and universities has generally not been outsourced to commercial, for-profit publishers to the extent that it has in North America and Europe (Babini & Machin-Mastromatteo, 2015; but for a troubling counterexample see Priego et al., 2017). Yet so-called global movements consistently ignore this reality and attempt to impose colonizer structures and systems on regional networks that arguably are already achieving the goals of the Open movement. In Latin America, for instance, the majority of journals are university-supported and scholar-led, and these journals do not charge APCs (Alperin et al., 2008; Babini & Smart, 2006). Contrary to these well-established Open practices, when the European OA funder initiative "Plan S" was introduced to Latin America, it included provisions about paying APCs to publishers (Debat & Babini, 2020; López & García, 2019). In short, the hegemonic European view of OA presupposes corporate for-profit capture to the detriment of existing structures, raising concerns not only about who can afford to pay the fees to publish but also about the relationship between what gets published and what will make money for the publisher. As Dave Ghamandi asks, "If scholarly publishing is not controlled by its authors and readers, is it worth having?" (qtd. in Gilliland et al., 2021, p. 3).

Considering the negative impact of hegemonic OA in Africa and Latin America, resistance to imposition of a hegemonic notion of Open scholarship centers on expanding participation in both the creation of scholarship and the structures that enable scholarship. Privileged, high-resource scholars thought they were doing Africans a favor by freely sharing scholarly products from high-resource countries; however, this equality of access does not mean equity or even equality in participation in knowledge creation (Faciolince & Green,

2021). The systems in place for high-resource countries fail to match those in local contexts; these systems construct barriers of exclusion by expecting conformity to colonial paradigms. True global participation in Open scholarship requires prioritizing the various ways that people in a variety of local contexts create, contribute, share, enrich, and benefit from scholarship. Open Methods have great potential to open up participation in the creation of scholarship in particular, but only if they are designed and implemented by scholars in their local contexts and with the full participation of the community that uses and benefits from the scholarship (Hall-Lew et al., 2022; Langley et al., 2018). Furthermore, in this collaborative approach, Open Methods must reflect local needs and considerations.

Linguists should consider embedding the question of ethical and collaborative openness into their methodologies, particularly when working with communities. To put it mildly, linguistics has a long track record of methodologies that ignore and devalue communities' priorities, needs, and epistemologies, especially with respect to the documentation of Indigenous languages (Langley et al., 2018; Leonard, 2017; 2020; see also Plumb et al., this volume; Riestenberg et al., this volume). As a result, when researchers conduct language documentation research, community input is needed in the process of making recordings and other materials to discern whether access to data should be restricted for ethical and cultural reasons (Langley et al., 2018; Seyfeddinipur et al., 2019). Community ownership over research decisions and involvement at the point of creation represents a way to use methodology as a means of decolonizing linguistics. Here we suggest that readers consult Gary Holton et al. (2022), especially regarding Indigenous Data Sovereignty and the CARE principles in language data practices, and seek to apply their approach to Open Methods work. If the conditions under which the data was collected were extractive or exploitative, those ethical violations can't be wiped away just by making the data open (Nature Editorial, 2020). Some communities may resist exploitation of their resources and culture by refusing Open Access to their materials and processes, opting instead for community control and ownership because true decolonization cannot occur without money and resources directed to communities to work on projects of their own selection, design, and operation (see Montoya, this volume).

Open Methods Reappraised: Colonial or Anticolonial?

In this section, we consider who stands to reap the benefits of Open Methods, and who is left out. As mentioned above, Open Methods can lower resource barriers (removing the need to collect data, to learn how to code, and/or to learn particular methods directly from an expert), so nominally Open Methods should benefit underresourced scholars. In reality, however, Open Methods as currently practiced in linguistics primarily benefits *slightly* under-resourced scholars in high-resource countries, who still enjoy numerous manifestations of privilege in consuming and producing academic research. Rather than "lowering barriers," a better metaphor for the predominant effect of Open Methods is "tilting the playing field." We find that "tilting the playing field" happens at multiple levels: who can benefit from Open Methods, who creates impactful Open Methods, and how methodology reflects and impacts epistemology.

From our perspective, the most visible examples of Open Methods have come from high-resource countries; as mentioned above, this is true of all of our Open Methods examples in Table 13.1. As a result, research can be conducted more quickly and easily as long as it fits colonizer scholars' views of legitimate methodology. Because theory and methods are inextricably intertwined (Charity Hudley et al., forthcoming), this dominance of methods by high-resource countries raises the possibility of "epistemicide." The epistemological tug of colonizer methodologies is only heightened by "tech-solutionism," where every technological tool is sold as solving problems without engagement or critical appraisal (Braybrooke & Jordan, 2017). Even when algorithmic methods are created with good intentions, like removing hate speech from social media sites, the extractive paradigm of their creation can result in harmful consequences (see Bender & Grissom, 2024).

We find the "lowering barriers" metaphor most wanting when it comes to who can benefit from Open Methods. First, scholars still require informational and/or technological resources to discover and utilize Open Methods. For example, some scholars in Kenya and South Africa face inadequate internet access (Bezuidenhout et al., 2017), a problem that Open Methods cannot compensate for. Second, Open Methods do not work equally well for all languages or varieties (e.g., Koenecke et al., 2020), so they may benefit only researchers working on majority languages. Forced-alignment algorithms (McAuliffe et al., 2017; Rosenfelder et al., 2011), for example, automatically align segmental annotations to stretches of text; these tools can save users hours of painstaking labor, facilitating wider-scale analysis of acoustic phonetic data. However, these algorithms require language models trained on large amounts of data, and pretrained models only exist for majority languages and varieties (Bender et al., 2021; Gooden, 2022; see also Bender & Grissom, 2024). Third, taking advantage of the "latest and greatest" Open Methods often requires substantial computational resources and/or expertise. For example, a method now exists for applying forced alignment to minority languages without needing the type of huge corpus on which a language model of English would typically be trained (Barth et al., 2020); taking advantage of this method, however, requires computational know-how and time commitment far greater than simply downloading a pretrained model. Another example is the use of automatic speech recognition (ASR) to facilitate sociolinguistic transcription; whereas Google's and Amazon's ASR systems are far user-friendlier than the "latest and greatest" ASR Open Method based on the Kaldi Speech Recognition Toolkit (Chodroff, 2018), these commercial systems woefully underperform a Kaldi-based system (Markl, 2022). In short, there is a real danger of Open Methods merely becoming another instrument reproducing the hegemony of North American and European research(ers) in linguistics.

The cumulative result is this: scholars who are already privileged are likely to be disproportionate beneficiaries of Open Methods. In an example that we stress should not be taken to represent challenges facing scholars in underresourced countries as a whole, Shelome Gooden (personal communication) describes how Caribbean scholars not only don't take advantage of Open Methods, but also get left further behind as these methods—and the means for discovering them—build upon one another over time. Thus, Open Methods can actually exacerbate pre-existing resource disparities between US and Caribbean linguists; indeed, much linguistics research has grown increasingly computational and quantitative, with corresponding increases in processing power, storage, and associated costs necessary for research (Charity Hudley et al., forthcoming). Gooden's own practices, which include training Caribbean colleagues on Open Methods like Praat, represent a model to counteract this process of growing inequality. As a native Jamaican who received her graduate training in the United States and now is a professor and administrator at a high-resource US-based research university, Gooden is utilizing the opportunities afforded her to share Open Methods' benefits with Caribbean scholars.

An anticolonial lens prompts us to refine our earlier recommendation to recognize Open Methods as legitimate indicia of scholarship in RPT policies (e.g., Linguistic Society of America, 2018; 2019; 2021), adding the qualifications that these policies should consider Open Methods expansively and shouldn't require "impact" or "stringent peer-review." First, these policies should take an expansive view of Open Methods, ranging from software-heavy products to methodological know-how (Table 13.1). We further encourage departments to consider recognizing meta-practices that increase the quality and anticolonialism of Open Methods. To revisit the above example of Gooden's work in the Caribbean, while she is not *creating* an Open Method via her Praat outreach, she is nevertheless lowering resource barriers to Caribbean researchers—and in so doing, contributing to linguistics scholarship more broadly. Expansive policies can both undermine the hegemony-reproducing potential that Open Methods represent and avoid the problem of tech-solutionism (see Bender & Grissom, 2024).

Second, we discourage departments from using traditional "impact" metrics to assess Open Methods. Citation counts, a frequent measure of impact for traditional research outputs, are inaccurate for Open Methods, as many authors fail to cite software (Howison & Bullard, 2016) or data (Huang et al., 2015). When citation metrics are available and appropriate, we encourage their responsible use in evaluation, necessarily coupled with other measures that demonstrate impact. For best practices, we suggest consulting the recommendations of the "Humane Metrics" initiative (Agate et al., 2022; Humane Metrics Initiative, n.d.). As part of this rethinking of metrics and impact, we also recognize the need for linguists to listen to communities to understand what "impact" means for them. For example, Kristine Stenzel (2014) discusses the sustainability of research in a community after the completion of a project, and the misunderstanding that teaching a community to do research is a desirable outcome for the community. We encourage resistance against the idea that creating an Open Method is a proxy for community engagement and community benefit.

Third, not only is "stringent peer-review" unrealistic for Open Methods in linguistics (as discussed above), but it would also have negative colonial ramifications for Open Methods. Beyond its ostensible quality-control function, peer-review also functions as a mechanism for corporate control of academic journal content (Fyfe et al., 2017), so we fear that requiring peer-review would only further tilt the creation of Open Methods to those with pre-existing privilege. Nevertheless, we do recognize that Open Methods would benefit from quality control, especially with respect to indicators of openness like user-friendliness that are difficult for single creators to self-assess (Collister & Villarreal, 2022). As such, we would like to see professional societies like the LSA help foster structures to promote quality in Open Methods without reinscribing colonial hegemony, building on their collection of resources on ethics in linguistics research (Linguistic Society of America, n.d.). We also encourage individual researchers to advocate for Open Methods within professional organizations; for example, Lauren previously chaired the LSA's Committee on Scholarly Communication in Linguistics and, at the time of writing, is a board member of LingOA.

276 Decolonizing Linguistics

Fortunately, good models for peer review for data, software, and methods already exist. We would like to particularly highlight the peer-review policies and procedures for datasets and software used by the *Journal of Open Source Software*, the generalist journal *Data*, and the publisher PLOS (Journal of Open Science Software, 2018; MDPI, n.d.; PLOS, n.d.). The *Journal of Open Humanities Data* also provides a resource for guidance on reviewing data papers and an example of a data policy for a publication (Journal of Open Humanities Data, n.d.). The nonprofit academic organization rOpenSci peer-reviews software for the R language using a peer-review process that it touts as "transparent, constructive, non adversarial and open" (rOpenSci, n.d.). Finally, to avoid further tilting the playing field toward the epistemological and methodological agendas of scholars in high-resource countries, outlets that publish Open Methods should provide clear policy documents and recommendations so a broad range of researchers globally can contribute to the conversation around Open Methods.

Model for an Anticolonial Open Methods

Throughout this chapter, we have made many recommendations for changes in policies and practices to foster a productive and anticolonial future for Open Methods in linguistics. However, our recommendations must be understood in the context of our positionalities; we both enjoy privilege with respect to Open Methods, providing us leeway and agency to resist existing institutional structures. We derive this privilege in part through our affiliation with a wealthy research-centered US university, which affords us resources (computational resources, journal subscriptions, prestige) that facilitate learning about, implementing, and disseminating Open Methods. In addition, many of our examples come from those communities most visible to us in our lived experience; to date, our knowledge and experience of research practices and challenges beyond a small circle of high-resource countries comes mostly from secondhand conversations and reading the writings of scholars in these contexts, rather than lived experience. Indeed, this very chapter—which only exists because Dan and Lauren have been recognized as having the legitimacy to write it—is a manifestation of our privilege with respect to Open Methods.

Crucially, Dan's and Lauren's job security is not at odds with engagement in Open Methods—we both have much greater agency than do most scholars vis-à-vis Open Methods. Dan's job was created with methodological innovation in mind; his department's RPT policies were recently revised to include Open Methods, with enthusiastic support from his department colleagues.

Lauren's entire job *is* scholarly communication and open scholarship, and in her prior faculty position she was reviewed and promoted on the basis of doing that work. Her work as a librarian involved RPT policies that are framed much differently than those for faculty in disciplinary departments, for example by explicitly validating a variety of modes of scholarship as equally relevant for review. Dan is currently on the tenure track; while this position is more precarious than that of a tenured professor, it represents much greater job security than graduate students, recent PhDs, and faculty with non–tenure-track positions, and it affords Dan the visibility to disseminate Open Methods. Finally, as a L1 English-speaking, hearing, cisgender hetero, white-passing male, Dan has never had to face questions about his computational bona fides. Lauren also benefits from privileges derived from being L1 English-speaking, hearing, white, cisgender, and hetero-passing, although she also has experience as a queer person in a nontraditional, precarious employment position. As a librarian without a degree in library science and a linguist working outside a linguistics department, Lauren faces insinuations about her credentials in two worlds. Without seeking to diminish important differences in our positionalities, we stress that we both write from a position of privilege with respect to Open Methods.

Thus, while we present our model for an anticolonial Open Methods (Table 13.2), a summary of this chapter's recommendations, we stress that this model inherits our biases and limited perspectives—our recommendations are likely to be most relevant to the Northern colleagues and institutions that we are most acquainted with. As a result, we intend this model to be a starting point rather than the last word—literally, version 1.0, with the assumption of later and better versions to follow. We explicitly invite iterations, expansions, and critiques of these recommendations, especially from scholars working in underresourced contexts who can better speak to how these recommendations can better reflect their situations.

Within our model for an anticolonial Open Methods lies a tension—or a contradiction, depending on your viewpoint—in that we appeal to colonizer institutions (universities, journals, etc.) to help create an anticolonial future for Open Methods. Put differently, can Open Methods ever be anticolonial if they are supported by colonizer institutions? Would a rich university support Open Methods if it didn't envision Open Methods as upholding the larger colonialist project? These sorts of challenges align with the refusal model described by Montoya (this volume): researchers should eschew research products that are "most valued in the reward structures of the institution," such as formal theoretical work that is "practically unusable for any kind of teaching or language revitalization," instead prioritizing the needs of

278   Decolonizing Linguistics

Table 13.2 Model for an anticolonial Open Methods (version 1.0), by Dan Villarreal and Lauren Collister, used under a Creative Commons—Attribution 4.0 International License. We explicitly invite iterations, expansions, and critiques of these recommendations.

Audience	Recommended policies and practices
Individual scholars	• Cite Open Methods when using them so creators get credit, and don't be afraid to give creators constructive feedback • Invite creators of Open Methods for trainings or class visits • When creating Open Methods, consult the Spectrum of Open Methods for ideas on how to minimize resource barriers (Collister & Villarreal 2022) • Include the community in methodology development in addition to creation and description of research content • Propose a special issue of a journal on Open Methods (e.g., exploring use cases and research done using a particular Open Method) • Make connections with colleagues who want to benefit from Open Methods but are limited by resource barriers, for example by publishing in outlets that are located in your partner community, or by presenting at conferences that are attended by scholars beyond your home institution or country • Don't be afraid to share imperfect methods or code (or to be honest about shortcomings) • Reverse the one-way flow of knowledge by citing underrepresented scholars
Departments	• Explicitly include Open Methods in RPT policies, with clear, reasonable, and anticolonial guidelines (i.e., no requirement of "stringent peer-review" or traditional "impact" metrics) • Train students to use and produce Open Methods • Host symposiums and special events, invite guest speakers, and record/live-stream events so attendance isn't limited to those physically present
Universities	• Assist departments in revising RPT policies to recognize Open Methods, with clear, reasonable, and anticolonial guidelines • Mandate institutional review boards to develop ethical, anticolonial guidelines and policies on Open Methods and Open Science for human subjects research. • Hire experts in open science and foster institutional open science expertise to support researchers' creation of Open Methods • Commit monetary or in-kind support to publishers and initiatives that foster Open Scholarship and Open Methods creation, e.g., by participating in institutional subsidy models such as for the Open Library of Humanities (Open Library of Humanities n.d.) • Support local publications and conferences that explore the use of Open Methods • Record/live-stream in-person events in order to broaden participation

Table 13.2 Continued

Audience	Recommended policies and practices
Journals	• Publish more "purely methodological" work so Open Methods can be recognized via "traditional research outputs" • Utilize the Spectrum of Open Methods in peer-reviewing "purely methodological" submissions to help make them more open (Collister & Villarreal 2022) • Resist corporate capture through intellectual property transfer clauses to corporations; retain copyright with the journal or the authors • Consider switching to Open Access and/or joining collaborative organizations like LingOA • Invite special issues or special sections on Open Methods
Professional societies	• Promote and support structures to promote quality in Open Methods in an anticolonial way • Incentivize Open Methods (e.g., awards for exemplary Open Methods) • Incorporate Open Methods into training, workshops, and conferences • Resist corporate capture through intellectual property transfer of conference materials or journal publishing

the community. While these are serious challenges, we believe that the decolonization of Open Methods is unlikely if it depends only on individual selfless acts of refusal from scholars working in the shadow of employment/ funding scarcity. Instead, even a modicum of institutional support can open a path forward for anticolonial researchers affiliated with colonial institutions to gain institutional status and power in order to effect change. It is not inevitable that Open Methods will reproduce the inequities that have come to light with the Open Access movement. With conscious attention to the framing around Open Methods and incorporation of anticolonial practices, we can envision a different future.

Conclusion

In closing, Open Methods cannot be a panacea for the aspects of linguistics research that are fundamentally extractive and exploitative. Making a methodology openly available will not cover for research projects that are not, at their core, ethically or methodologically sound. For decolonization to really happen, money and resources need to be given to marginalized communities to do their work, and partnerships with these communities must first benefit

280   Decolonizing Linguistics

the community members before the career track of a researcher. The older cousin of Open Methods, Open Access, represents a cautionary tale where colonialism masquerades as openness, for example when corporate capture of open resources introduces profit and prestige motives that actively harm their creators, or when Open Access is introduced as a universal good that presumes the existence of resources that may not actually be available. Our outlook is nevertheless (cautiously) optimistic. By acting on these issues now, when Open Methods in linguistics remains at an early stage, we can ensure an Open Methods that benefits all linguistics researchers, and not only those with pre-existing privilege.

Appendix A. Table 1 author status

This appendix provides data to support the claim that "only one Open Method in Table 1 was created by someone on the tenure track". By "created", we refer to first publication (we thus exclude new authors of FAVE since its original 2011 publication).

In US higher education, *tenure* is security of employment, obtained only after a probationary period during which scholars are said to be "on the tenure track". Among scholars in Table 1 were based at US institutions of higher learning at the time, all were either pre-PhD or, like tenured professors in the US, had security of employment.

All webpages accessed March 16, 2022. If pages are no longer available at these URLs, please use the Internet Archive's Wayback Machine (https://web.archive.org/) to view versions of these pages cached on March 16, 2022. The Wayback Machine does not capture LinkedIn pages, so the Supplementary Materials contains PDF versions of the LinkedIn CVs (Rosenfelder, Fruehwald, Evanini, and McCloy) saved February 28, 2022.

Product	First published	Author	Position at publication	Country	TT or equivalent?	CV
Corpus of Regional African American Language	2020	Tyler Kendall	Associate Professor	US		https://pages.uoregon.edu/tsk/pdfs/CVTK.pdf
		Charlie Farrington	Research Associate	US		https://charliefarrington.files.wordpress.com/2021/10/farrington_cv_202110.pdf
World Atlas of Language Structures Online	2013	Matthew Dryer	Professor[a]	US		http://www.acsu.buffalo.edu/~dryer/

Product	First published	Author	Position at publication	Country	TT or equivalent?	CV
		Martin Haspelmath	Senior Researcher & Honorary Professor	Germany		https://www.ae-info.org/ae/Member/Haspelmath_Martin
Praat	1995	Paul Boersma	PhD student	Netherlands		https://www.fon.hum.uva.nl/paul/
		David Weenink	Pre-PhD[b]	Netherlands		https://www.fon.hum.uva.nl/david/
NORM	2007	Erik Thomas	Associate Professor	US		https://chass.ncsu.edu/wp-content/uploads/sites/2/2020/07/VITAE_Thomas.doc
		Tyler Kendall	PhD student	US		https://pages.uoregon.edu/tsk/pdfs/CVTK.pdf
FAVE	2011	Ingrid Rosenfelder	Postdoc	US		https://www.linkedin.com/in/ingridrosenfelder/
		Josef Fruehwald	PhD student	US		https://www.linkedin.com/in/josef-fruehwald-16b73561/
		Keelan Evanini	Research Scientist	US		https://www.linkedin.com/in/keelan-evanini-4367b01/
		Jiahong Yuan	Researcher & Associate Director	US		https://www.ling.upenn.edu/~jiahong/
Rbrul	2009	Daniel Ezra Johnson	Research Assistant	US		http://www.danielezrajohnson.com/johnson_cv.pdf
phonR	2012	Dan McCloy	PhD student	US		https://www.linkedin.com/in/dan-mccloy-08933a5/
Fast Track	2021	Santiago Barreda	Assistant Professor	US	Yes	https://santiagobarreda.com/cv/
How to train your classifier	2019	Dan Villarreal	Postdoc	New Zealand		

(*continued*)

282 Decolonizing Linguistics

Product	First published	Author	Position at publication	Country	TT or equivalent?	CV
		Lynn Clark	Academic appointee with security of employment[c]	New Zealand		https://www.canterbury.ac.nz/arts/contact-us/people/lynn-clark.html
		Jennifer Hay	Academic appointee with security of employment[c]	New Zealand		https://www.canterbury.ac.nz/arts/contact-us/people/jennifer-hay.html
		Kevin Watson	Academic appointee with security of employment[c]	New Zealand		https://www.canterbury.ac.nz/arts/contact-us/people/kevin-watson.html
Using Praat for linguistic research	2011	Will Styler	PhD student	US		https://wstyler.ucsd.edu/files/willstylercv.pdf

[a] Position dates not publicly available. Dryer was at Buffalo from 1989 and was supervising PhD dissertations in the early 2000s (http://www.acsu.buffalo.edu/~dryer/dissertations.htm), so it is highly likely that by 2013 he was Full Professor or higher.

[b] Position dates not publicly available. Praat's bibliography page (https://www.fon.hum.uva.nl/paul/praat.html) credits Weenink with a 1996 technical report, and Weenink's webpage indicates his PhD thesis was from 2006.

[c] In New Zealand, academic appointees at Lecturer or above have security of employment (contrary to US tenure-track system). Webpages reflect current positions; Dan knows personally that all three were Lecturer or above in 2019.

Appendix B. Example US linguistics departments' review, promotion, and tenure (RPT) policies

This appendix provides sources used to support the claim that "US linguistics departments' review, promotion, and tenure (RPT) policies run the gamut in terms of whether and how they count Open Methods toward career advancement."

All pages accessed March 16, 2022. If pages are no longer available at these URLs, please use the Internet Archive's Wayback Machine (https://web.archive.org/) to view versions of these pages cached on March 16, 2022.

Institution	Department	Date	Link	Direct quotations
University of Delaware	Linguistics & Cognitive Science	4/25/2016	https://cpb-us-w2.wpmucdn.com/sites.udel.edu/dist/9/2591/files/2014/12/LCS-PT4.25.2016-11xwdew.pdf	"primary evidence for scholarly excellence [includes] ... publicly available data collections" (p. 2)
University of Illinois at Chicago	Linguistics and Less Commonly Taught Languages	1/17/2017	https://lcsl.uic.edu/wp-content/uploads/sites/292/2019/04/Linguistics-PT-1.17.2017.pdf	"the development of scholarly digital material" as secondary to journal articles, placing Open Methods alongside "conference papers [and] lectures" (p. 2)
The Ohio State University	Linguistics	8/29/2016	https://oaa.osu.edu/sites/default/files/uploads/governance-documents/college-of-arts-and-sciences/division-of-arts-and-humanities/linguistics/Linguistics_APT_2016-09-06.pdf	N/A; publications for promotion & tenure described on p. 22
University of Georgia	Linguistics	9/5/2017	https://provost.uga.edu/_resources/documents/linguistics2017.pdf	"the concept of 'publication' ... may include linguistic corpora, software, or other digital materials ... if these items are subject to a stringent peer-review process" (p. 2)

Note

1. We want to acknowledge the many people whose labor improved this chapter. Andrea Berez-Kroeker, Jenny L. Davis, Tyrica Terry Kapral, and Jack Martin helped shape our thinking in the early stages of this research and shared literature and resources. Santiago Barreda, Emily Bender, Shelome Gooden, Tyler Kendall, Charlotte Roh, Betsy Sneller, and the editors of this collection provided thoughtful and helpful feedback on drafts. Any errors are ours alone.

284 Decolonizing Linguistics

References

Agate, Nicky, Long, Christopher P., Russell, Bonnie, Kennison, Rebecca, Weber, Penelope, Sacchi, Simone, Rhody, Jason, et al. (2022). *Walking the talk: Toward a values-aligned academy* (White paper). https://hcommons.org/deposits/item/hc:44631/

Alperin, Juan Pablo, Fischman, Gustavo, & Willinsky, John. (2008). Open access and scholarly publishing in Latin America: Ten flavours and a few reflections | Acesso livre e publicação acadêmica na América Latina: dez sabores e algumas reflexões,' *Liinc em Revista*, 4(2). Instituto Brasileiro de Informação em Ciência e Tecnologia. doi: 10.18617/liinc.v4i2.269

Alperin, Juan Pablo, Schimanski, Lesley A., La, Michelle, Niles, Meredith T., & McKiernan, Erin C. (2022). The value of data and other non-traditional scholarly outputs in academic review, promotion, and tenure in Canada and the United States. In Andrea L. Berez-Kroeker, Bradley McDonnell, Eve Koller, & Lauren B. Collister (Eds.), *The open handbook of linguistic data management*. The MIT Press. doi:10.7551/mitpress/12200.001.0001

Babini, Dominique, & Machin-Mastromatteo, Juan D. (2015). Latin American science is meant to be open access: Initiatives and current challenges. *Information Development*, 31(5), 477–481.

Babini, Dominique, & Smart, Pippa. (2006). Using digital libraries to provide online access to social science journals in Latin America. Association of Learned and Professional Society Publishers.

Barnes, Nick. (2010). Publish your computer code: It is good enough. *Nature*, 467(7317), 753–753. doi: 10.1038/467753a

Barreda, Santiago. (2021). Fast track: Fast (nearly) automatic formant-tracking using Praat, *Linguistics Vanguard*, 7(1). doi: 10.1515/lingvan-2020-0051

Bartelds, Martijn, Richter, Caitlin, Liberman, Mark, & Wieling, Martijn. (2020). A new acoustic-based pronunciation distance measure. *Frontiers in Artificial Intelligence*, 3(39). doi: 10.3389/frai.2020.00039

Barth, Danielle, Grama, James, Gonzalez, Simon, & Travis, Catherine E. (2020). Using forced alignment for sociophonetic research on a minority language. *Penn Working Papers in Linguistics*, 25(2), 2.

Bender, Emily M., Gebru, Timnit, McMillan-Major, Angelina, & Shmitchell, Shmargaret. (2021). On the dangers of stochastic parrots: Can language models be too big? *Proceedings of the 2021 ACM Conference on Fairness, Accountability, and Transparency*, FAccT '21, 610–623. doi: 10.1145/3442188.3445922

Bender, Emily M., & Grissom, Alvin II. (2024). Power shift: Towards inclusive natural language processing. In Anne H. Charity Hudley, Christine Mallinson, & Mary Bucholtz (Eds.), *Inclusion in linguistics*. Oxford University Press.

Benedicto, Elena. (2018). When participatory action research (PAR) and (Western) academic institutional policies do not align. In Shannon Bischoff & Carmen Jany (Eds.), *Perspectives on language and linguistics: Community-based research* (pp. 38–65). De Gruyter Mouton.

Berez-Kroeker, Andrea L., McDonnell, Bradley, Koller, Eve, & Collister, Lauren B. (2022). *The open handbook of linguistic data management*. The MIT Press. doi: 10.7551/mitpress/12200.001.0001

Bezuidenhout, Louise M., Leonelli, Sabina, Kelly, Ann H., & Rappert, Brian. (2017). Beyond the digital divide: Towards a situated approach to open data. *Science and Public Policy*, 44(4), 464–475. doi: 10.1093/scipol/scw036

Boersma, Paul, & Weenink, David. (2021). Praat software. https//:praat.org

Bonn, Noémie Aubert, & Pinxten, Wim. (2021). Advancing science or advancing careers? Researchers' opinions on success indicators. *PLOS ONE*, 16(2), e0243664. doi: 10.1371/journal.pone.0243664

Braybrooke, Kat, & Jordan, Tim. (2017). Genealogy, culture and technomyth, *Digital Culture & Society*, *3*(1), 25–46. doi: 10.14361/dcs-2017-0103

Charity Hudley, Anne H., Clemons, Aris Moreno, & Villarreal, Dan. (2023). Language across the disciplines. *Annual Review of Linguistics*, *9*(13), 1–20. doi: 10.1146/annurev-linguistics-022421-070340

Charity Hudley, Anne H., Villarreal, Dan, & Clemons, Aris Moreno. (forthcoming). (Socio)linguistics—what is it good for? A case for liberatory linguistics. In Erica J. Benson & Bayley Robert (Eds.), *Needed research in North American dialects* (pp. xx–xx). Duke University Press.

Chodroff, Eleanor. (2018). Kaldi tutorial. http://eleanorchodroff.com/tutorial/kaldi/

Collister, Lauren, & Villarreal, Dan. (2022). *Spectrum of Open Methods*. Zenodo. doi: 10.5281/zenodo.6546894

Curry, Mary Jane, & Lillis, Theresa. (2018). The dangers of English as lingua franca of journals. *Inside Higher Ed*. https://www.insidehighered.com/views/2018/03/13/domination-english-language-journal-publishing-hurting-scholarship-many-countries

Day, Suzanne, Rennie, Stuart, Luo, Danyang, & Tucker, Joseph D. (2020). Open to the public: Paywalls and the public rationale for open access medical research publishing. *Research Involvement and Engagement*, *6*(1), 8. doi: 10.1186/s40900-020-0182-y

Debat, Humberto, & Babini, Dominique. (2020). Plan S in Latin America: A precautionary note. *Scholarly and Research Communication*, *11*(1), 12–12. doi: 10.22230/src.2020v11n1a347

D'Ignazio, Catherine, & Klein, Lauren. (2020). Our values and our metrics for holding ourselves accountable. *Data Feminism*. https://data-feminism.mitpress.mit.edu/pub/3hxh4l8o/release/2.

Dryer, Matthew S., & Haspelmath, Martin (Eds). (2013). *WALS online*. Max Planck Institute for Evolutionary Anthropology.

Faciolince, María, & Green, Duncan. (2021). One door opens: Another door shuts?, *Development and Change*, *52*(2), 373–382. doi: 10.1111/dech.12633

Figueroa, Megan. (2022). Podcasting past the paywall: How diverse media allows more equitable participation in linguistic science. *Annual Review of Applied Linguistics*, 1–7. doi: 10.1017/S0267190521000118

Frischmann, Brett M., Madison, Michael J., & Strandburg, Katherine J. (Eds). (2014). *Governing knowledge commons*. Oxford University Press.

Fyfe, Aileen, Coate, Kelly, Curry, Stephen, Lawson, Stuart, Moxham, Noah, & Røstvik, Camilla Mørk. (2017). *Untangling academic publishing* (Discussion paper). https://doi.org/10.5281/zenodo.546100

Gawne, Lauren, & Styles, Suzy. (2022). Situating linguistics in the social science data movement. In Andrea L. Berez-Kroeker, Bradley McDonnell, Eve Koller, & Lauren Collister (Eds.), *The open handbook of linguistic data management*. The MIT Press. doi:10.7551/mitpress/12200.001.0001

Ghyselen, Anne-Sophie, Breitbarth, Anne, Farasyn, Melissa, Van Keymeulen, Jacques, & van Hessen, Arjan. (2020). Clearing the transcription hurdle in dialect corpus building: The corpus of southern Dutch dialects as case study, *Frontiers in Artificial Intelligence*, *3*. doi: 10.3389/frai.2020.00010

Gilliland, Anne, Kati, Rebekah, Solomon, Jennifer, Ghamandi, Dave S., Cirasella, Jill, Lewis, David, & Dawson, DeDe. (2021). JLSC board editorial 2021. *Journal of Librarianship and Scholarly Communication*, *9*(1). doi: 10.7710/2162-3309.2432

Gooden, Shelome. (2022). Intonation and prosody in creole languages: An evolving ecology. *Annual Review of Linguistics*, *8*(18), 1–18. doi: 10.1146/annurev-linguistics-031120-124320

Guédon, Jean-Claude. (2017). Open access: Toward the internet of the mind. https://www.budapestopenaccessinitiative.org/boai15/open-access-toward-the-internet-of-the-mind/

286 Decolonizing Linguistics

Hall-Lew, Lauren, Cowie, Claire, Lai, Catherine, Markl, Nina, McNulty, Stephen Joseph, Liu, Shan-Jan Sarah, Llewellyn, Clare, et al. (2022). The Lothian diary project: Sociolinguistic methods during the COVID-19 lockdown. *Linguistics Vanguard*. doi: 10.1515/lingvan-2021-0053

Helsinki Initiative. (2019). Helsinki initiative on multilingualism in scholarly communication. Helsinki: Federation of Finnish Learned Societies, Committee for Public Information, Finnish Association for Scholarly Publishing, Universities Norway & European Network for Research Evaluation in the Social Sciences and the Humanities. doi: 10.6084/m9.figshare.7887059.v1

Hilton, Nanna Haug, & Leemann, Adrian. (2021). Editorial: Using smartphones to collect linguistic data. *Linguistics Vanguard, 7*(s1). doi: 10.1515/lingvan-2020-0132

Holton, Gary, Leonard, Wesley Y., & Pulsifer, Peter L. (2022). Indigenous peoples, ethics, and linguistic data. In Andrea Berez-Kroeker, Bradley McDonnell, Eve Koller, & Lauren Collister (Eds.), *The open handbook of linguistic data management*. The MIT Press. doi: 10.7551/mitpress/12200.003.0008

Howison, James, & Bullard, Julia. (2016). Software in the scientific literature: Problems with seeing, finding, and using software mentioned in the biology literature. *Journal of the Association for Information Science and Technology, 67*(9), 2137–2155. doi: 10.1002/asi.23538

Huang, Yi-Hung, Rose, Peter W., & Hsu, Chun-Nan. (2015). Citing a data repository: A case study of the protein data bank. *PLOS ONE, 10*(8), e0136631. Public Library of Science. DOI: 10.1371/journal.pone.0136631

Humane Metrics Initiative. (n.d.). Values framework. *HuMetricsHSS*. https://humetricshss.org/our-work/values/

Johnson, Daniel Ezra. (2009). Getting off the GoldVarb standard: Introducing Rbrul for mixed-effects variable rule analysis. *Language and Linguistics Compass, 3*(1), 359–383. doi: 10.1111/j.1749-818x.2008.00108.x

Journal of Open Humanities Data. (n.d.). Peer review process. http://openhumanitiesdata.metajnl.com/about/editorialpolicies/

Journal of Open Science Software. (2018). Review criteria. https://joss.readthedocs.io/en/latest/review_criteria.html

Kendall, Tyler, & Farrington, Charlie. (2020). The corpus of regional African American language. The Online Resources for African American Language Project. https://oraal.uoregon.edu/coraal

Kendall, Tyler, Vaughn, Charlotte, Farrington, Charlie, Gunter, Kaylynn, McLean, Jaidan, Tacata, Chloe, & Arnson, Shelby. (2021). Considering performance in the automated and manual coding of sociolinguistic variables: Lessons from variable (ING). *Frontiers in Artificial Intelligence, 4*(43). doi: 10.3389/frai.2021.648543

Koenecke, Allison, Nam, Andrew, Lake, Emily, Nudell, Joe, Quartey, Minnie, Mengesha, Zion, Toups, Connor, et al. (2020). Racial disparities in automated speech recognition. *Proceedings of the National Academy of Sciences, 117*(14), 7684–7689. doi: 10.1073/pnas.1915768117

Kuchma, Iryna, Persic, Ana, Anand, Roheena, Siewicz, Krzysztof, & Kamadjeu, Raoul. (2022). *Policy into action: The UNESCO Recommendation on Open Science under the spotlight - actions for publishing*. Webinar. Open Access Scholarly Publishing Association, March 15, 2022. https://oaspa.org/webinar-policy-into-action-the-unesco-recommendation-on-open-science-under-the-spotlight-actions-for-publishing/

Langley, Bertney, Langley, Linda, Martin, Jack B., & Hasselbacher, Stephanie. (2018). The Koasati language project: A collaborative, community-based language documentation and revitalization model. In Shannon Bischoff & Carmen Jany (Eds.), *Perspectives on language and linguistics: Community-based research* (pp. 132–150). De Gruyter Mouton.

Leonard, Wesley Y. (2017). Producing language reclamation by decolonising "language." *Language Documentation and Description, 14*, 15–36.

Leonard, Wesley Y. (2020). Insights from Native American studies for theorizing race and racism in linguistics (response to Charity Hudley, Mallinson, and Bucholtz). *Language*, 96(4), e281–e291. doi: 10.1353/lan.2020.0079

Lillis, Theresa, Hewings, Ann, Vladimirou, Dimitra, & Curry, Mary Jane. (2010). The geolinguistics of English as an academic lingua franca: Citation practices across English-medium national and English-medium international journals. *International Journal of Applied Linguistics*, 20(1), 111–135. doi: 10.1111/j.1473-4192.2009.00233.x

Linguistic Society of America. (2018). Statement on evaluation of language documentation for hiring, tenure, and promotion. https://www.linguisticsociety.org/resource/statement-evaluation-language-documentation-hiring-tenure-and-promotion

Linguistic Society of America. (2019). LSA revised ethics statement, final version. https://www.linguisticsociety.org/content/lsa-revised-ethics-statement-approved-july-2019

Linguistic Society of America. (2021). Statement on the scholarly merit and evaluation of open scholarship in linguistics. https://www.linguisticsociety.org/content/statement-scholarly-merit-and-evaluation-open-scholarship-linguistics

Linguistic Society of America. (n.d.). Ethics: Further resources.' https://www.linguisticsociety.org/resource/ethics-further-resources

López, Eduardo Aguado, & García, Arianna Becerril. (2019). Latin America's longstanding open access ecosystem could be undermined by proposals from the Global North. *LSE Latin America and Caribbean blog*. https://blogs.lse.ac.uk/latamcaribbean/2019/11/06/latin-americas-longstanding-open-access-ecosystem-could-be-undermined-by-proposals-from-the-global-north/

Markl, Nina. (2022). Language variation and algorithmic bias: Understanding algorithmic bias in British English automatic speech recognition. *2022 ACM Conference on Fairness, Accountability, and Transparency*, FAccT '22, 521–534. doi: 10.1145/3531146.3533117

McAuliffe, Michael, Socolof, Michaela, Mihuc, Sarah, Wagner, Michael, & Sonderegger, Morgan. (2017). Montreal forced aligner: Trainable text-speech alignment using Kaldi. Presented at the 18th Interspeech. Stockholm.

McCloy, Daniel R. (2016). phonR: Tools for phoneticians and phonologists. R package, version 1.0-7. https://cran.r-project.org/package=phonR

MDPI. (n.d.). Data—guidelines for reviewers. https://www.mdpi.com/journal/data/guidelines

Meagher, Kate. (2021). Introduction: The politics of open access — decolonizing research or corporate capture? *Development and Change*, 52(2), 340–358. doi: 10.1111/dech.12630

Moore, Samuel A. (2020). Revisiting "the 1990s debutante": Scholar-led publishing and the pre-history of the open access movement. *Journal of the Association for Information Science and Technology*, 71(7), 856–866. doi: 10.1002/asi.24306

Nature Editorial. (2020). Henrietta Lacks: Science must right a historical wrong. *Nature*, 585, 7. doi: 10.1038/d41586-020-02494-z

Nkoudou, Thomas Hervé Mboa. (2020a). Epistemic alienation in African scholarly communications: Open access as a *pharmakon*. In Eve Martin Paul & Gray Jonathan (Eds.), *Reassembling scholarly communications: Histories, infrastructures, and global politics of open access* (pp. 25–40). MIT Press.

Nkoudou, Thomas Hervé Mboa. (2020b). Epistemic alienation in African scholarly communications: Open access as a pharmakon. In Eve Martin Paul & Gray Jonathan (Eds.), *Reassembling scholarly communications: Histories, infrastructures, and global politics of open access* (pp. 25–40). The MIT Press.

Nosek, B. A., Alter, G., Banks, G. C., Borsboom, D., Bowman, S. D., Breckler, S. J., Buck, S., et al. (2015). Promoting an open research culture. *Science*, 348(6242), 1422–1425. doi: 10.1126/science.aab2374

PLOS. (n.d.). A reviewer's quick guide to assessing open datasets. *PLOS*. https://plos.org/resource/peer-reviewing-data/

Priego, Ernesto, McKiernan, Erin, Posada, Alejandro, Hartley, Ricardo, Ortega, Nuria Rodr guez, Fiormonte, Domenico, Gil, Alex, et al. (2017). Scholarly publishing, freedom of information and academic self-determination: The UNAM-Elsevier case. Authorea, Inc. doi: 10.22541/au.151160332.22737207

R Core Team. (2022). R: A language and environment for statistical computing.

Raju, Reggie, Claassen, Jill, Madini, Namhla, & Suliaman, Tamzyn. (2020). Social justice and inclusivity: Drivers for the dissemination of African scholarship. In Eve Martin Paul & Gray Jonathan (Eds.), *Reassembling scholarly communications: Histories, infrastructures, and global politics of open access* (pp. 53–64). MIT Press.

Roh, Charlotte, Inefuku, Harrison W., & Drabinski, Emily. (2020). Scholarly communications and social justice. In Eve Martin Paul & Gray Jonathan (Eds.), *Reassembling scholarly communications: Histories, infrastructures, and global politics of open access* (pp. 41–52). MIT Press.

rOpenSci. (n.d.). Software peer review. https://ropensci.org/software-review/

Rosenfelder, Ingrid, Fruehwald, Joe, Evanini, Keelan, & Yuan, Jiahong. (2011). FAVE (forced alignment and vowel extraction) program suite. https://github.com/JoFrhwld/FAVE

Scientific Electronic Library Online. (n.d.). SciELO. https://scielo.org/en/

Seyfeddinipur, Mandana, Ameka, Felix, Bolton, Lissant, Blumtritt, Jonathan, Carpenter, Brian, Cruz, Hilaria, Drude, Sebastian, et al. (2019). Public access to research data in language documentation: Challenges and possible strategies. *Language Documentation & Conservation*, 13, 545–563.

Sistema de Información Científica Redalyc. (n.d.). Sistema de InformacióSistema de Informacin Cientíón Científica Redalyc, Red de Revistas Científicas. *Redalyc.org*. https://www.redalyc.org/home.oa

Sneller, Betsy. (2022). COVID-era sociolinguistics: introduction to the special issue. *Linguistics Vanguard*. doi: 10.1515/lingvan-2021-0138

Stenzel, Kristine. (2014). The pleasures and pitfalls of a "participatory" documentation project: An experience in northwestern Amazonia. *Language Documentation*, 8, 20.

Styler, Will. (2021). Using Praat for linguistic research. https://wstyler.ucsd.edu/praat//UsingPraatforLinguisticResearchLatest.pdf

Thomas, Erik R., & Kendall, Tyler. (2007). NORM: The vowel normalization and plotting suite. http://lingtools.uoregon.edu/norm/norm1.php

Villarreal, Dan, Clark, Lynn, Hay, Jennifer, & Watson, Kevin. (2019). How to train your classifier. https://nzilbb.github.io/How-to-Train-Your-Classifier/How_to_Train_Your_Classifier.html

Villarreal, Dan, Clark, Lynn, Hay, Jennifer, & Watson, Kevin. (2020). From categories to gradience: Auto-coding sociophonetic variation with random forests. *Laboratory Phonology*, 11(6), 1–31. doi: 10.5334/labphon.216

Willinsky, John. (2005). The unacknowledged convergence of open source, open access, and open science. *First Monday*. doi: 10.5210/fm.v10i8.1265

Ariana Bancu is former assistant professor at Northeastern Illinois University in Chicago, where she taught classes with a focus on sociocultural linguistics and psycholinguistics. She specializes in language contact, endangered languages, and multilingualism, and she ran the Trilingualism Lab, where she analyzed data from trilingual language users with the help of graduate research assistants. She has dedicated the past seven years to studying and documenting Transylvanian Saxon, an endangered, nonstandardized Germanic language used in Romania and Germany. She sees the case of Transylvanian Saxon as a prime example of how in-group and out-group language attitudes and ideologies determine the fate of a language and its users, and she extends her expertise to studying Creole languages from a community-based perspective.

Marylse Baptista has deep roots in Cabo Verde (where her parents were born and raised) and in the diasporic community of Cabo Verdeans in Massachusetts. She was born in Senegal, raised in France, and has lived in the United States for three decades. She speaks English, French, and Kriolu. She has conducted fieldwork on Kriolu in Cabo Verde for 25 years. One of the new lines in her research (with Sophia Eakins) is the use of Kriolu in the diaspora. She is a strong proponent of an anti-deficit, anti-exceptionalist perspective on Creoles and advocate for foregrounding them as the complex and creative natural languages that they are (like any language) while acknowledging the colonial linguistic territoriality, hierarchies, and subordination that they have been subjected to (like many languages/varieties). She uses theoretical, experimental, and corpus methods in investigating Creoles. She studies their structure, history, the cognitive processes underlying their formation, and theories of Creole genesis.

Felicia Bisnath is a hearing woman of Indian descent who grew up in Trinidad and Tobago and who has been living in the United States since 2019. She uses Trinidadian English and Trinidadian Creole as first languages. Her linguistics training began in Trinidad and Tobago (BA) and continued in the Netherlands (MA) and the United States (ongoing PhD). Language contact, minoritised languages (specifically Creoles and sign languages), and the role of ideology in the construction of linguistic form and in the treatment of minoritised languages in linguistics are recurring foci in her work. She has conducted research on Trinidadian French Creole, Sranan Tongo, Trinidad and Tobago Sign Language, and on the cross-linguistic occurrence of a language contact phenomenon in 37 sign languages. She has also worked on creating Creole and sign language data sets for use in introductory linguistics classes.

Danielle Burgess is a white, cis-gender woman from western New York. Her first and primary language is English. She recently completed her PhD in linguistics at the University of Michigan, experimentally investigating mechanisms of interaction and transmission that may play a role in language change across various linguistic contexts, including those which give rise to pidgins and Creoles. Her research uses artificial language learning methodologies to explore how biases in language learning and communication shape typological tendencies regarding the linear ordering of standard negation, and the extent to which such biases are universal or based on previous linguistic experience. In her research and teaching, she tries to avoid deficit perspectives of multilingual language use and acquisition, and has advocated for moving away from the vague and exclusionary term "native speaker" to recruit and describe participants in psycholinguistics research.

Sophia Eakins, a PhD student in linguistics at the University of Michigan, specializes in language contact with a particular focus on Creole languages. She has conducted research with the Cabo Verdean Creole-English bilingual community in Boston and along with Marlyse Baptista's research group Cognition, Convergence and Language Emergence, she is working to advance the scholarship and promote the visibility of Creole languages at large. Her research takes a bottom-up approach to describing and discovering the language practices of the Cabo Verdean diaspora. Questions that drive her research include: How are individual language users transgressing and creating new linguistics boundaries? What conversational, sociolinguistic, or structural factors influence language mixing? She is a hearing female born and raised in the US, in an English-speaking household.

Wilkinson Daniel Wong Gonzales is a linguist specializing in language variation, change, language contact, and language documentation in multilingual contexts. After receiving a PhD in linguistics and graduate certificates in data science and cognitive science at the University of Michigan in Ann Arbor, he moved to Hong Kong to join the Department of English at the Chinese University of Hong Kong, where he is assistant professor of applied English linguistics. Wil is particularly interested in sociolinguistics in the Philippines and in wider East Asia. He employs corpus-based, experimental, ethnographic, and computational techniques on diverse datasets, including natural speech data and social media data. He works on Sino-Philippine languages (e.g., Lánnang-uè) and other East Asian linguistic varieties, such as Colloquial Singapore English or "Singlish," Philippine English(es), and Hong Kong English.

Joy P. G. Peltier is assistant professor at the University of South Carolina in the Linguistics Program and the Department of English Language and Literature. She is a Black scholar of African American and Caribbean descent, and her family members use several languages, from Kwéyòl Donmnik to varieties of African American English. Her work centers on contact-induced and minoritized languages, such as Creoles like Kwéyòl Donmnik, as well as on multifunctional and discourse-pragmatic elements, such as pragmatic markers (e.g., Kwéyòl *èben* 'well,' English *well*, French *bon* 'well'). She is also passionate about the inclusion of minoritized languages in linguistics pedagogy and research and is engaged in collaborative research centered on the linguistic and professional experiences of Black faculty in the language sciences. She views her scholarship as an opportunity to spark "ah-ha moments" about varieties and features of language that are stigmatized or overlooked, and she draws upon a mixture of methodologies, including corpus-based analyses, metalinguistic interviews and surveys, and experimental tasks.

Moira Saltzman is a white, ethnically Jewish cis-gender woman from the midwestern United States who worked and conducted research in South Korea on and off since 2007. She recently completed her PhD in linguistics at the University of Michigan and is now assistant professor of linguistics and TESL (Teaching English as a Second Language) at California State University, Northridge. She earned her MA in linguistics from Wayne State University, and previously, she taught academic writing at the University of Michigan, the University of Detroit Mercy, and the Michigan Colleges Alliance, as well as English as a second language in public schools in South Korea. She is interested in language contact and change, and the interplay of social forces such as language use and power relationships in linguistic contact environments. Her PhD research focused on the historical development of Jejueo, the Indigenous language of Jeju Island, South Korea. Her ongoing research includes the development of a talking dictionary of Jejueo, a free online multimedia database of the language.

Yourdanis Sedarous is an Egyptian American immigrant of Coptic heritage. She regularly uses English, Egyptian Arabic, and code-switched English/Egyptian Arabic in her everyday speech. Because of her linguistic background, her research program often highlights the theoretical relevance and empirical richness provided from investigating multilingual utterances. She pursues an integrated, data driven approach to the scientific study of language by applying experimental methods to investigate both qualitatively and quantitatively the language knowledge and use of various bilingual communities, and she extends these results to inform our theories, specifically our theoretical approaches to syntax. Methodologically, she has spent a significant amount of time researching, testing, and extending different methodologies that are more inclusive of underrepresented languages and populations of language users.

Alicia Stevers is white, cis-gendered, and a first-language user of English with proficiency in American Sign Language. She is a current lecturer in linguistics at San Diego State University, and a University of Michigan linguistics PhD alumna. Her research has focused on pragmatics and discourse analysis of determiner structures, cross-linguistic analysis, and experimental pragmatics. Many of her current questions relate linguistics to theology, and how theories of pragmatics relate to interpretation of biblical texts cross-linguistically. In addition to her Michigan PhD, she has a Masters in linguistics from San Diego State University. She loves teaching, playing with her two little boys, baking cookies, and enjoying her city.

Abstract: This chapter strives to move away from hegemonic paradigms and toward decolonization by revitalizing attitudes toward Creoles: to refresh, reroute, and redefine how these languages are perceived, presented, and discussed, particularly in the Global North. The authors consulted Creole users (language experts) and linguists to better understand these two groups' representations, characterizations, and ideologies of Creoles. First, they drew upon their personal and professional connections with three Creole-using communities to interview five users each of Cabo Verdean Kriolu, Kwéyòl Donmnik, and Trinidadian English Creole. Second, they surveyed 58 linguists, combining the interview questions with questions about pedagogical approaches to Creoles. Finally, they hosted a workshop bringing together language experts and linguists from several regions to discuss how best to integrate Creole languages into linguistics classrooms. The authors report the outcomes of the research, as well as our recommendations for a revitalized approach to creolistics pedagogy.

Key Words: Creole languages, language contact, language attitudes, linguistics pedagogy, language naming

14

Revitalizing Attitudes Toward Creole Languages

Ariana Bancu (she/her)
Independent Researcher

Joy P. G. Peltier (she/her)
University of South Carolina

Felicia Bisnath (she/her)
University of Michigan

Danielle Burgess (she/her)
Independent Researcher

Sophia Eakins (she/her)
University of Michigan

Wilkinson Daniel Wong Gonzales (he/him)
The Chinese University of Hong Kong

Moira Saltzman (she/her)
California State University, Northridge

Yourdanis Sedarous (she/her)
University of Michigan

Alicia Stevers (she/her)
San Diego State University

Marlyse Baptista (she/her)
University of Pennsylvania

Bancu, Peltier, Bisnath, Burgess, Eakins, Gonzales, Saltzman, Sedarous, Stevers, Baptista, *Revitalizing Attitudes Toward Creole Languages* In: *Decolonizing Linguistics*. Edited by: Anne H. Charity Hudley, Christine Mallinson, and Mary Bucholtz, Oxford University Press. © Anne H. Charity Hudley, Christine Mallinson, and Mary Bucholtz 2024.
DOI: 10.1093/oso/9780197755259.003.0015

Introduction

The objective of this chapter is to revitalize attitudes toward Creole languages: to refresh, reroute, and redefine how these languages are perceived, presented, and discussed, particularly in the Global North (cf. Braithwaite & Ali, this volume). This is a key aspect of moving away from hegemonic paradigms and toward social justice and decolonization, which we take to mean forefronting as researchers, teachers, and language users a liberated, anti-exceptionalist narrative about Creoles and their users that emphasizes their normalcy, naturalness, creativity, diversity, and resilience. We acknowledge our subjectivity in "affirming that all languages are equal, legitimate, deeply creative, and worthy of use in all domains of life" (University of Michigan, 2021),[1] though people and institutions may assign different social values to them. This chapter is intended to serve as a conversation starter and a model for dialogue between language experts, that is, users of Creole languages with metalinguistic knowledge of how those languages are used in-community; and linguists, that is, scholars with training in the language sciences (as will become clear below, several members of our team belong to both communities of Creole users and linguists). We use a community-based research approach (Léglise & Migge, 2006) to explore conceptions and assumptions about Creoles within and across both groups.

Ten researchers came together to conduct this work and author this chapter, and each of us brought our own unique positionality to the project. All team members are hearing scholars with a shared interest in language contact who either are or were associated with the University of Michigan. The following snapshots express what each researcher chose to highlight about themselves:

Ariana Bancu is a multicultural linguist researching multilingualism, language contact, and endangered languages. She has taught at one of the most diverse universities in the Midwest and is passionate about linguistic diversity, social justice, and language documentation.

Marlyse Baptista is a linguist of Cabo Verdean descent who is a strong proponent of an anti-deficit, anti-exceptionalist approach to Creole languages. She has dedicated her career to the study of Creoles and their source languages.

Felicia Bisnath is a hearing woman of Indian descent who grew up in Trinidad and Tobago and who has been living in the United States since 2019. She uses Trinidadian English and Trinidadian Creole as first languages.

Danielle Burgess is a white, cis-gender woman from western New York. Her first and primary language is English. She experimentally investigates mechanisms of interaction and transmission which may play a role in language change across various linguistic contexts, including those which give rise to pidgins and Creoles.

Sophia Eakins is a hearing female born and raised in the US in an American English-speaking household pursuing a PhD at an R1 research institution. Her research interests revolve around language contact and change primarily with regards to Creole languages.

Wilkinson Daniel Wong Gonzales is assistant professor at the Chinese University of Hong Kong (Department of English). His research interests include World Englishes, sociolinguistics, language variation and change, language contact, and language documentation.

Joy P. G. Peltier is a Black linguist of African American and Caribbean descent whose work centers on language contact, minoritized languages, and pragmatic markers. She is fascinated by how language users' histories, attitudes, and ideologies with respect to topics like race, colonization, education, and religion are intertwined with how they approach their own language varieties and language practices.

Moira Saltzman is a white, ethnically Jewish cis-gender woman from the midwestern United States who lived and worked in South Korea for many years as an adult. Her first language is English.

Yourdanis Sedarous is a hearing female Egyptian American immigrant of Coptic descent. She regularly uses English, Egyptian Arabic, and code-switches between English and Egyptian Arabic in her everyday speech. Due to her linguistic background, her research program often highlights the theoretical relevance and empirical richness provided from investigating multilingual utterances.

Alicia Stevers is a lecturer in linguistics at San Diego State University and mom of two little boys. She is white, cis-gendered, and a first language user of English with proficiency in American Sign Language.

Our team conducted two surveys, one with language experts and the other with linguists, and a follow-up workshop to further our understanding of these two populations' representations, characterizations, and ideologies about Creole languages. We selected three Creoles in consultation with four of our team members who are language users/experts in these Creoles and have access to these populations: Cabo Verdean Kriolu (used in the Cabo Verde islands), Kwéyòl Donmnik (used on the island of Dominica), and Trinidadian English Creole (used in Trinidad and Tobago). A participant overview is provided in Table 14.1.

In the second section of this chapter, we review relevant literature that uncovers the roots of representations, understandings, and labels used for Creole languages. In the third section, we describe the Creoles that were the

296 Decolonizing Linguistics

Table 14.1 Overview of research participants' places of residence, participation formats, birthplaces (language experts only), and academic ranks (linguists only)

	All Experts' Current Place of Residence	All Experts' Birthplaces	All Experts' Participation Format(s)
Kwéyòl Donmnik Language Experts (*n* = 5)	United States (3) Dominica (1) United Kingdom (1)	Dominica (4) United Kingdom (1)	Interview (5) Workshop (2)
Trinidadian English Creole Experts (*n* = 5)	Trinidad (5)	Trinidad (5)	Interview (5) Workshop (4)
Cabo Verdean Kriolu Experts (*n* = 5)	United States (5)	Cabo Verde (3) Portugal (1) United States (1)	Interview (5) Workshop (2)
	Workshop Participants' Current Place of Residence (*n* = 9)	Workshop Participants' Academic Ranks (*n* = 9)	All Linguists' Participation Format(s)
Linguists (*n* = 58)	United States (3) Caribbean (2) Europe (3) Africa (1)	Graduate Student (4) Postdoctoral Scholar (1) Faculty Member (4)	Survey (58) Workshop (9)

focus of our study. The fourth section outlines our methodology. After that we report the survey results, the workshop outcomes, and our recommendations for a more community-centered approach to Creole language pedagogy, and a final section concludes our chapter.

The objectives of this chapter are threefold and are all interrelated: (1) the first is to change the way that Creole languages are introduced in introductory linguistics courses where they typically are discussed in a separate section of the syllabus, wrongfully conveying that they are exceptional languages to be treated separately from other natural languages; (2) this chapter promotes instead the discussion and analysis of Creole languages on the same footing and on a par with the other languages that are examined in introductory linguistics courses; (3) this in turn advances an inclusive approach to the study of Creoles, countering the harmful, colonial narratives about them while integrating the analysis of their phonetics, phonology, morphosyntax, semantics, pragmatics and other domains throughout introductory linguistics courses. Members of our team are currently contributing to the development of a database of Creole problem sets that students in introductory linguistics courses will be able to engage with.

The Framing of Creoles in the Literature

The idea that languages are homogenous, easily identifiable entities reflects colonial ideologies that assume the notion of language purity and a one-to-one relationship between race/ethnicity/nationality and language (Charity Hudley, 2016), thus erasing complex multilingual practices (see Irvine & Gal, 2000) that necessarily involve language contact and language mixing. A number of scholars (Garcia & Otheguy, 2019; Otheguy et al., 2015; Flores, 2019) have shown that the study of multilingual practices poses a real challenge to the idea that languages are distinct linguistic systems with clear boundaries. Work with multilingual language users highlights how language contact blurs these artificial lines. Creoles emerge from complex interactions and dynamics between languages and their users, and many Creoles are the products of colonial contexts. It is thus not surprising that they have been subjected to territorial, historical hierarchies and subordination that typify the inequality found in colonial environments (Errington, 2001) and rely on the notion that languages are impervious to change or to influence by contact. This results in Creoles being oftentimes reduced to "fantasmatic representation[s] of authoritative [linguistic] certainty in the face of spectacular ignorance" (Greenblatt, 1991 p. 89, as cited in Errington, 2001, p. 20). On this issue, the language contact literature (Weinreich, 1953; Thomason, 2001; Lim & Ansaldo, 2016) has clearly demonstrated that contact between language users and their languages (or dialects or idiolects) can bring about a wide range of changes, resulting in degrees of admixture in the languages in contact at the lexical, phonological, and/or morpho-syntactic levels. If all languages are subject to varying degrees of contact-induced change, then all languages undergo some type of mixing, including *prestigious* colonial varieties such as British English and American English (Baptista, under review).

We show in this chapter that linguistic ideologies are not only held by the immediate members of a community, but also by "linguists and ethnographers who have mapped the boundaries of languages and peoples and provided descriptive accounts of them" (Irvine & Gal, 2000, p. 35–36). For example, in their study on Takitaki, a contact language used in French Guiana, Léglise and Migge (2006, p. 4) aimed to determine what "the local linguistic terminology and the term Takitaki in particular suggest about how . . . different social actors conceptualize the social and linguistic reality." They analyzed the perspectives of Takitaki users, linguists working in the region, and other community members. Their results demonstrate that "different local social actors do not only project different social evaluations onto the linguistic productions referred to as Takitaki but they also have different views about the internal structure of the populations who use it" (Léglise & Migge, 2006, p. 5). It is crucial that we keep this in mind when examining the language labeling practices and linguistic ideologies at play with respect to other contact language communities. Furthermore, it is important that we consider these issues as educators when we teach about Creoles to promote a decolonized view of minoritized languages and their users in the classroom (see Arnold, this volume for more details).

In the context of linguistics pedagogy, textbooks that introduce students to the field sideline Creole languages into chapters on topics such as language contact (e.g., Fromkin et al., 2013) or language acquisition supposedly taking place under unusual circumstances (e.g., Jackendoff, 1994). This framing of Creoles as falling into a class of their own, upheld by some scholars as well (e.g., Bickerton, 1984; 2013; McWhorter, 1998; Bakker et al., 2011), is particularly problematic in introductory courses to linguistics which often provide students with an initial impression of where these languages are situated within our field. As Michel DeGraff (2020) emphasizes, contrasting the class of Creole languages against so-called normal languages systematically others the study of Creoles and excludes them from mainstream theories. This othering not only creates and transmits harmful misrepresentations of Creoles as *nonregular* languages (i.e., what DeGraff terms Creole Exceptionalism) in the domain of research, but also marginalizes their inclusion at a pedagogical level.

Inspired by Léglise and Migge's (2006) community-centered approach, we addressed these issues in this study by surveying users of three Creoles as well as linguists to further our understanding of these groups' representations and labels. Then, in a follow-up workshop, we communicated our findings to both Creole users and linguists alike to facilitate meaningful conversations within and between these groups and to generate recommendations for equitably representing Creoles in linguistics teaching.

Creoles Under Study

In this section, we provide brief profiles of the three Creoles that are the focus of this chapter, as well as information about the team members who participated in this study. All language experts interviewed for this study were recruited through the personal networks of our team members and were compensated for their time. This study was conducted with approval from the University of Michigan Institutional Review Board (HUM00204845) and was funded through Marlyse Baptista's Collegiate Professorship research funds.

Cabo Verdean Creole (Kriolu)

The islands of Cabo Verde were colonized by the Portuguese in the fifteenth century. They quickly became part of the slave trade due to their strategic location in the Atlantic Ocean between Europe, Africa, and the Americas. The enslaved populations were from the region of Cacheu and Bissau in Africa and included the Jalofo, Peul, Bambara, Bolola, Manjaku, Mandinka, and Balante people, among others. Kriolu is believed to have emerged in the early 1500s (Kihm, 1994; Andrade, 1996).

The migration of Cabo Verdeans to the United States started around the 1840s with the recruitment of many Cabo Verdean men as sailors on North American ships involved in the whaling industry. Many Cabo Verdeans settled in the New England area, one of the largest communities in the diaspora. Cabo Verde became independent from Portugal in 1975, but to this day, the only official language of the country is the colonizing language Portuguese. Portuguese is also the only language of instruction in Cabo Verdean schools although Kriolu has an orthographic script—the ALUPEK—that was officially recognized by the Cabo Verdean government in 1998. Occasional bilingual Portuguese-Kriolu programs are implemented in Cabo Verde but they are typically short-lived and nonsustainable long term due to lack of political will and lack of prioritized financial resources. Hence, although Kriolu could be used as a language of instruction, strong political forces are preventing it from gaining representation and use in the classroom.

The five Cabo Verdean language experts included in this study were interviewed by Marlyse Baptista and Sophia Eakins, who is currently studying Kriolu. The experts ranged from 33 to 52 years of age. Four identified as female and one as male. Three were born in Cabo Verde, one in Portugal, and one in the United States. Two had a college degree, and three had postgraduate degrees. None of the language experts were linguists. One of the respondents was a language activist.

Kwéyòl Donmnik (Kwéyòl)

Contributors to the emergence of Kwéyòl Donmnik include Dominica's Indigenous Kalinago community, enslaved peoples of African and

300 Decolonizing Linguistics

Caribbean descent, escaped and freed people of color, and European colonizers. Though the French arrived on the island before the British and exerted extensive influence on the Creole's lexicon, Dominica was part of the British Commonwealth for over two centuries until its independence in 1978. To learn more about Dominica and its linguistic ecology, see Lennox Honychurch (1995), Douglas Taylor (1977), and Amy L. Paugh (2012). Thus, both in Dominica and in diaspora locations such as the United Kingdom and the United States, Kwéyòl users are typically bilingual in English. Moreover, Kwéyòl is undergoing a shift. "The language is losing fluent [users] and is no longer spoken as a first language by the majority of Dominican children; by most measures, then, [Kwéyòl] would be considered an endangered language" (Paugh 2012, p. 9), and most users of the language today are community elders.

Though its use is largely restricted to language activists and scholars, there is an orthography system for Kwéyòl Donmnik. Organizations like Dominica's Komité pou Étid Kwéyòl (Committee for Creole Studies) are working both to promote use of spoken Kwéyòl and to disseminate publications written in the language, and events hosted by the University of the West Indies Open Campus on Dominica have made more space for the language to be studied, used, and celebrated. However, English remains the language of the island's school system and "Dominica schools are prime sites for the transmission of institutional norms privileging English" (Paugh, 2012, p. 22). National celebrations like Jounen Kwéyòl (Creole Day) are acknowledged by schools, but these events constitute an incredibly small portion of students' school life, and little emphasis is given to use of the Kwéyòl language itself (Paugh, 2012, p. 43).

The five Kwéyòl language experts who participated in this study were interviewed by Joy Peltier, a linguist of paternal Dominican heritage whose ties to the language community are rooted in both her familial relationships and her research. The Kwéyòl experts were between 60 and 67 years of age; four of the experts were female-identifying, while one identified as male.

Though Peltier's selection process was guided by personal and professional connections as well as by COVID-19 contact restrictions, not by a deliberate decision to interview language users ages 60 and above, this age range does reflect the language's endangered status. Four language experts were from Dominica, one was born to Dominican parents in the United Kingdom, and all five spent their formative years or more on the island. Their educational backgrounds spanned from less than high school to holding a graduate degree. Two of the experts took part in pro-Kwéyòl activism (e.g., teaching Kwéyòl, spearheading language preservation efforts), and one of these two was a linguist by training whose background in the field permeated both her volunteer work and her language-centered career.

Trinidadian English Creole

Trinidadian English Creole (TEC) developed in the nineteenth century when Trinidad was under British rule (1797–1962), through the influence of English Creole-speaking immigrants. When the British arrived, a French Creole developed by Francophones settling under Spanish rule was in use. Enslaved Africans (primarily Igbo, Kongo, Ibibio, Yoruba, and Malinke) were present from the eighteenth century, and after Emancipation (1834–1838), Bhojpuri-speaking indentured laborers came from India. The Spanish language returned to the island in the nineteenth century with the immigration of Spanish-Amerindians from Venezuela (see Mühleisen, 2013, and Winer, 1993, for more information on Trinidadian English Creole, and Williams, 1962 for more information about Trinidad and Tobago).

As for its status in education, TEC has been recognized as an official language in education since 1975 under a policy of transitional bilingualism that "tolerates" its use until students have acquired sufficient productive proficiency in Trinidadian Standard English (Craig, 1980); however, teachers are not given explicit training in how to delineate the Creole from the Standard (Yousseff, 2002). TEC is said to complement use of Trinidadian Standard English in secondary school classrooms with the latter being used by teachers when presenting formal content and the former used for commentary and informal discussion with students (Deuber, 2009). There is no official orthography for TEC.

The five TEC experts were interviewed by Felicia Bisnath, an Indo-Trinidadian linguist, who was born and raised in Trinidad & Tobago, and speaks TEC. Three of the experts were male-identifying and two female-identifying. Two were Afro-Trinidadian, two were Indo-Trinidadian, and one was Chinese-Trinidadian. They ranged in age from 20 to 48 years. Two had attained a tertiary level degree, with a third currently pursuing a bachelor's degree. The remaining two had secondary-level diplomas. All but one had lived in Trinidad for their entire lives; another had spent eleven years in Florida. At the time of the interviews, all the experts were living in Trinidad. None had backgrounds in linguistics or in promoting TEC.

Methodology

Using a community-based research approach, we designed and conducted two surveys and a follow-up workshop. The first survey targeted Creole language users—language experts—and was inspired by both the Bilingual Language Profile questionnaire (Birdsong et al., 2012) and a survey by Migge and Leglise (2006) on language naming practices. The first segment collected information about each experts' language background (e.g., how many languages they knew, age of acquisition for each), and language use patterns (e.g., domains and frequency of use). The second part probed experts' language attitudes and ideologies, capturing their perceptions of and labels for the Creoles in their communities, as well as their other metalinguistic knowledge (e.g., whether they considered their Creole to be an independent language, a dialect of another language, or something else). The third portion addressed experts' perceptions of their languages to examine whether they aligned with views commonly promoted by linguists. The survey contained both quantitative (e.g., measured using Likert scales) and open-ended questions and was administered either via Zoom or by phone in an interview format by team members who identify with our target communities. Likert scale responses were analyzed quantitatively. The open-ended responses were coded manually and analyzed qualitatively using open coding practices and Virginia Braun and Victoria Clarke's (2006, p. 87) recommendations for thematic analysis of qualitative data: we noted initial codes ("interesting features of the data"), "collocat[ed] codes into potential themes," then reviewed and refined those themes and assigned each one a name.

The second survey was designed to gain a better understanding of how linguists teach about Creole languages at the university level, as well as whether their attitudes toward Creoles align with views held by the language experts. We recruited linguists through professional listservs with members in the field. The only requirement for linguists to qualify for participation was for them to have taught introductory classes in linguistics. This survey paralleled the first one as much as possible so that we could capture both the language experts' and the linguists' views on many of the same issues (e.g., how they would define *Creole*). In addition to background information (e.g., what courses participants teach, how they incorporate Creoles in their classes), the linguist survey, which was administered through Qualtrics, contained questions related to defining Creoles and explaining their origins. Likert scale responses were approached quantitatively while open-ended questions were coded in the same way as those provided by the language experts. A total of 58 linguists, from various geographic regions (North America, the Caribbean,

Europe, Asia, Africa) and at different stages in their career (from PhD students to seasoned professors) responded to our survey.

Participants in both groups were given the option to indicate their interest in a follow-up workshop based on the results of both surveys. Our goal was to communicate our findings to the language experts and linguists, promote meaningful discussions, and generate recommendations for better integrating Creole languages into linguistics classrooms.

Results and Discussion

In this section, we report some of the recurring themes we identified in the language experts' (n = 15, five per community) interview responses and in the linguists' (n = 58) survey answers.

Labeling Practices

In an additional table that we have provided on the supplementary website associated with these volumes, we show the labeling practices captured by the interviews with the language experts. There was some variation within each language expert group. Among the Kwéyòl experts, those involved in pro-Kwéyòl activism used the term *Kwéyòl Donmnik* and strongly discouraged use of the label *Patwa*. With respect to Kriolu, the experts' labels appeared to be conditioned by the communication medium, as well as the dialect used. "Cabo Verdean Creole" is reportedly used when experts use English, and *Kriol* or *Kriolu* is preferred when using Kriolu: *Kriol* when the expert is using a windward (northern) variety of the language and *Kriolu* when they are using a leeward (southern) variety.

Both Kwéyòl and TEC experts either used or reported the existence of pejorative terms, like "broken" and "slang." Furthermore, at least one expert from each community used the name of the lexifier (the language from which most of a Creole's vocabulary is derived) as part of a label for their Creole (e.g., "French dialect" for Kwéyòl, "dialect of Portuguese" for Kriolu).

Views on the Language Status of Their Creole

Language experts in the three groups varied with regard to their views on the language status of their Creoles. Kwéyòl experts stated unanimously that their

304 Decolonizing Linguistics

Creole is a language, citing its being a fully functional communication system as the reason for the classification. Similarly, Kriolu experts viewed their Creole as "its own language," due to its structure and systematicity (e.g., having prefixes, suffixes), and they commented on the existence of Creole dialects and the presence of linguistic "mixture." The term "mixture" occurred often in the interviews, but it may not have been used with the same meaning by all language experts. Broadly, it appeared to refer to a Creole having emerged from the mixture of different languages, with identifiable elements from different languages coming together to form a new language. Kriolu experts also referred to their language as a dialect of Portuguese and were aware of the fact that Kriolu is not recognized as an official language in their country.

TEC experts were split into three groups: those who did not view it as a legitimate language, those who did, and those who were unsure. The first group viewed the Creole as "an expression of postcolonial English in the Caribbean" or a "form of English," while the second group viewed it as a "young language" or an "adapted language." The last group was unsure, saying TEC could mark the beginning of a new language.

Distinctions Between Terms: Creole, Pidgin, Dialect, and Patois

As we showed in the previous section, terms such as "Creole," "dialect," and "Patwa" surface when labeling Creoles. We asked the language experts and linguists to define and discuss the terms "Creole," "pidgin," "dialect," and "patois" to establish what they mean to each group. Roughly half of the linguists defined a Creole as a language that emerges from a pidgin and becomes the first language of a community; the other half defined a Creole as a contact language that emerges in situations of colonization, slavery, and violence. The linguists defined pidgins by drawing on factors of language use, prestige, sociohistorical contact, and the existence of community members who use it as their first language. Most commonly, pidgins were defined as emerging from a language contact situation when there is no common language available. Linguists also frequently noted the restriction in domains of use and the lack of users for whom it is a first language. Some also defined pidgins based on their emergence in colonial settings with distinct power differentials that result in their low level of prestige. The linguists defined dialects in terms of their mutual comprehensibility with other varieties and their associations with geographic regions or with particular social identities.

Participants often noted dialects' lack of prestige in comparison to standardized or hegemonic varieties (e.g., a dialect is a *subvariety of a language*). The most varied responses were the definitions of "patois." Many respondents were unsure of the definition, or reported that rather than having a linguistic definition, a patois is a popular or folk term for a dialect or Creole. Several linguists commented that "patois" is a pejorative term that could imply that a language is "imperfect," "impure," or "broken." Some linguists also associated "patois" with a particular language, such as Jamaican Creole.

Turning to how the language experts defined these terms, the Kwéyòl experts distinguished the term "Creole" from "pidgin," "dialect," and "patois" based largely on associations with mixture between a colonizing language and local varieties of language and culture. One expert characterized this mixing process as a reframed kind of *brokenness* where pieces of languages are broken off and recombined to create a new language. The TEC experts also defined "Creole" as a mixture of languages, and one expert noted its origin in the Pidgin–Creole lifecycle. Another TEC expert associated Creoles with geographic regions such as the Caribbean, where Indigenous people are referred to as "Creole." Kriolu experts defined "Creole" as a *mixture* and an independent language, even if a Creole is unwritten and its domains of use restricted (e.g., excluded from education). One Kriolu expert associated "Creole" with its origins in slavery and the mixing of African and European languages, and stated that a Creole is not as developed as European source languages such as English.

The language experts who were familiar with the term "pidgin" tended to cast it in a more negative light. One Kwéyòl expert defined pidgins as full languages much like Creoles, while another expert was dismissive of pidgins, associating them with in-group communication and word games meant to obscure one's message, much like slang. The TEC experts distinguished pidgins from the other terms as being early forms of languages or incomplete languages lacking in elegance and nuance. Most of the Kriolu experts were unfamiliar with the term "pidgin"; one defined it as a dialect of a language.

Kwéyòl experts defined a dialect as an informal, nonstandard, and local variety of any language, including of a Creole. Similarly, users of TEC defined a dialect as an "offshoot," as local, and even as a "perversion" of the rules of a dominant language. Some TEC experts associated dialects with structural features, such as differences in lexicon, syntax, and phonology. Interestingly, other TEC experts defined dialects according to what they are not, sometimes contradicting associations given by other experts. For example, one TEC expert stated that dialects are not slang, not an accent, and not a Creole.

Many of the definitions for "dialect" offered by the Kriolu experts aligned with the associations reported by the other groups. They viewed dialects as being highly localized, derived from a dominant language like Portuguese or French, and belonging to a specific group of people. The Kriolu experts also highlighted dialects' linguistic differences, particularly in their lexicons and phonology.

Although three of the Kwéyòl experts used the term "patois" (or *Patwa*) as the name for their Creole, the two other experts associated the term with "brokenness" and a "lack of development" and saw a patois as a precursor to a full language. Several TEC experts described "patois" as a mixture with French, and a few associated it with being "rough" or carrying covert prestige as a secret, urbanized language. Most Kriolu experts were unfamiliar with the term "patois," but one associated it with characteristics shared by Creoles, such as origins in colonization and slavery and being a distinct language, unintelligible to outsiders.

A comparative overview of the definitions of "Creole," "pidgin," "dialect," and "patois" reported by all four groups—language experts (three groups) and linguists—is provided in Figure 14.1. The results reported in this section not only point to the significance of labels and naming practices but also demonstrate that labels carry different meanings for community members and outsiders.

It is worth noting that scholars in other fields such as anthropology (Knörr & Trajano Filho, 2018) have a much broader conception of the terms "Creole" and "creolization" and apply them to a much wider range of linguistic situations. For instance, Knörr's (2018) concepts of creolization and pidginization are applied to language, culture, and identity and the author addresses the difference between etic and emic perspectives on classifying a language as a Creole. She explains that an emic model aims at explaining the ideology or behavior of members of a culture according to Indigenous definitions. For instance, outsiders call a Creole as such because its users refer to it by that name. In contrast, an etic model is based on criteria outside a particular culture. For instance, Mariana Kriel (2018) calls Afrikaans a Creole and describes Afrikaners as belonging to a creolized society, although not all Afrikaans users would use such labels. In brief, etic models can be viewed as universal whereas emic models are culture-specific. Similarly, in the fields of American studies and cultural studies, "Creole" is conceptualized as a multifaceted term that has been associated in various spaces, places, and time periods with "particular histories, migratory patterns, and geographies or linguistic, cultural, and ethnic identities" (Daut, 2020, p. 73).

Revitalizing Attitudes Toward Creole Languages

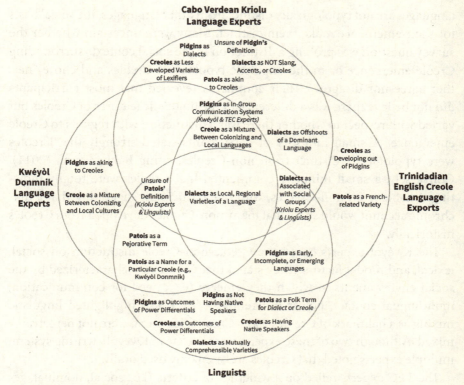

Figure 14.1 Comparative overview of definitions for "Creole," "pidgin," "dialect," and "patois" reported by Kwéyòl Donmnik, Cabo Verdean Kriolu, and Trinidadian English Creole language experts, as well as those reported by linguists.
Alternate text: Definitions for "Creole," "pidgin," "dialect," and "patois" as reported by Creole language experts and linguists.

Views on Creoles as Distinct Languages

The point of this section is to report on whether linguists and language experts consider Creoles as being distinct from non-Creoles and to examine the various perspectives on this topic within and across the two groups of participants.

We asked linguists to evaluate and discuss the following statement: "Creoles are distinct from non-Creoles." Most participants (37.93%) neither agreed nor disagreed with this statement. The other participants strongly disagreed (18.97%), disagreed (22.41%), agreed (15.52%), or strongly agreed (5.17%). Across all response categories, most commented that although Creole languages are not typologically distinct from other languages, the social basis for their emergence make them distinct. Many were uncertain whether the survey question was probing a distinction in the social contexts surrounding Creole emergence or in the linguistic typology of Creoles and chose "neither agree nor disagree." Their comments revealed that most participants did not believe there was a difference in the linguistic features of Creoles but varied with respect to whether there was a distinction with regards to Creole emergence. A small minority of participants stated strongly that Creoles were typologically distinct from non-Creoles, citing Bakker et al. (2011). Conversely, a small minority commented that Creoles were totally indistinguishable from non-Creoles, with one participant suggesting that a diachronic account would show that many non-Creoles developed from Creoles historically.

The Kwéyòl experts based the Creole-non-Creole distinction on social, lexical, and modal factors. They stated that Creoles are characterized by the social environments in which they emerge (e.g., need for communication, multilingual contact, power differentials). They also highlighted linguistic mixing as a hallmark of Creoles. Non-Creoles, for them, were not perceivably mixed. Although two of these experts were literate in Kwéyòl's writing system, multiple experts noted that Creoles are often only used orally.

The TEC experts relied on a wider set of criteria (i.e., social, nominal, geographic, temporal, lexical, and modal). One TEC expert considered a linguistic variety a Creole only if it had the label "Creole" attached to its name. These experts also drew geographic distinctions (i.e., Creoles are associated with the Caribbean, whereas non-Creoles are not) and reported that Creoles have a shorter history compared to non-Creoles. Other responses included associating Creoles with men and with informality. Aligning with the Kwéyòl experts, the TEC experts also relied on perceived language mixture as a criterion of determining Creole status.

The Kriolu experts cited lexical, developmental, social, modal, and domain-specific criteria for making the distinction between Creoles and non-Creoles. Like the other two groups, these experts emphasized that Creoles are products of language mixing, in contrast with non-Creoles. Similar to the Kwéyòl experts, they stated that Creoles are born out of particular contexts, such as slavery or colonialism, and are only spoken, whereas non-Creoles are not. Unlike the two other groups, however, one Kriolu expert also suggested that Creole structures are not as "articulated," compared to older languages like English and Portuguese. They also stated that, unlike non-Creoles, Creoles are not used in education.

Creoles in the Classroom

We asked linguists to rate and discuss the following statement: "Creole languages should be introduced to students as part of a general linguistics education." Most participants (74.14%) strongly agreed; the rest of the participants partially agreed (18.97%), neither agreed nor disagreed (3.45%), or disagreed (3.45%). Many participants believed that introducing Creole languages to students is important because it exposes them to a wide range of sociopolitical and historical interactions and processes (e.g., imperialism, colonialism, slavery). Many also commented that doing so helps students understand the nature of language: always changing, creative, and recursive/boundless. Some stated that Creoles shed new light on specific theoretical views about the nature of language (e.g., Universal Grammar) and can clarify misconceptions about languages (e.g., the notion of incomplete acquisition). Some participants noted that an introduction of Creoles serves as a good introduction to particular areas in linguistics, such as language acquisition, sociolinguistics, language contact, language variation and change, and language and power. Regarding language and power, some linguists commented that Creoles provide an example of how new language varieties can be formed through power differentials. For linguists situated in Creole-using regions, introducing the concept of Creoles served another purpose: enlightening Creole-using students about the complex processes that are involved in the creation of and discrimination against the Creoles they use. These linguists also noted that teaching about Creoles connected such students to their heritages. The few linguists who believed that Creole languages should not be in general linguistics education proposed that language variation and contemporary approaches to "informal," underdocumented varieties of all kinds should be covered rather than introducing Creoles separately (see Amado et al., 2021 for K-12 teaching materials on Creoles, developed for the Boston Public Schools.)

Follow-Up Workshop

Participants from the surveyed groups were invited to a virtual workshop over Zoom. Users of Kriolu (n = 4), Kwéyòl (n = 2), and TEC (n = 2) attended, as well as linguists from the United States (n = 4), Europe (n = 3), Africa (n = 1), and the Caribbean (n = 1). Our goals were to bring language experts and linguists together to share and discuss names for and perceptions of the

310 Decolonizing Linguistics

languages they use and research, and to generate recommendations for equitably integrating Creole languages into linguistics teaching. Language experts were compensated for participating in the workshop, while linguists volunteered their time.

The language experts discussed what they would want those inside and outside their communities to know about Creole languages in general and their language in particular, as well as what they would want to learn about Creoles more broadly and their language in particular. The linguists talked about types of courses in which they have taught about Creole languages, the kinds of information they included, and how they would like to teach about Creoles in an ideal world. We shared preliminary results from our surveys, and workshop participants shared what they learned during the workshop discussions. Throughout the workshop, priority was given to any language expert who wished to be heard.

The language experts conveyed that they want their languages to be viewed as full-fledged, independent languages that should not be confused or conflated with other Creoles or with their lexifiers. They expressed interest in the accurate description of the origins and the structural properties of their languages (this interest in Creole language history may have been triggered by a question in the language expert survey that centered on the histories of the experts' Creoles). The experts viewed Creole languages as different from each other, and they did not consider Creoles to have properties that make them more difficult than any other language to learn or understand. They pointed out that while some Creole users may view their languages as "offshoots" of another language (e.g., the lexifier) and others may not, most if not all identify strongly with their Creole. In sum, the experts viewed each of their languages as distinct, but not exceptional, and they wanted a more nuanced representation of Creole languages and their users to be integrated into pedagogical practices.

The linguists highlighted the challenges involved in making students aware of the fact that Creoles even exist, in breaking stereotypes related to Creoles (e.g., that Creoles are stigmatized or broken languages, that they are different from other languages), and in raising awareness of the importance of these languages as full-fledged, independent natural languages (Baptista, 2002; DeGraff, 2003; Baptista et al., 2010; Peltier, 2022; Peltier, forthcoming). Another challenge they reported was deciding what to teach within the brief confines of a course, taking into consideration students' levels of preparedness (e.g., how much they know about linguistic structure).

Revitalizing Attitudes Toward Creole Languages

All workshop participants—language experts and linguists alike—were in agreement that Creoles are full-fledged languages that need to be highlighted in linguistics courses rather than sidelined or treated as *an exceptional class*. Linguists pointed out that Creoles can be incorporated into a variety of courses and recommended approaches to teaching about Creoles that are more experiential and project-centered. In an ideal world, they said they would love to bring Creole language experts into their classrooms.

Recommendations

Based on the survey results and workshop outcomes, our recommendations for teaching about Creole languages in linguistics classrooms are as follows:

1. Consider integrating Creoles throughout your class rather than structurally exceptionalizing Creoles by relegating them to a single unit in a course. For example, consider comparing the history of Creoles to the history of American English or British English to bring home the idea that users of these varieties, too, speak a contact language (Baptista, under review). More advanced classes should talk about the various perspectives on Creole genesis (including exceptionalism and its harmful implications; see DeGraff, 2003) to better understand current debates around their formation. Also, use data from Creole languages for analysis wherever possible (see Calhoun et al., 2021 for a concrete model on how to integrate data from minoritized languages throughout a linguistics course). For an example exercise, please see the supplementary website associated with these volumes. Our ultimate goal is to create a repository containing problem sets that, in addition to Creoles, would also be representative of other minoritized languages like sign languages and Indigenous languages. Such problem sets would cover the phonology, syntax, semantics, and pragmatics of these languages and would come with answer keys to each problem. Several students in the Linguistics Department at the University of Michigan (Danuta Allen, Felicia Bisnath, Sophia Eakins, Demet Kayabasi, and Cecilia Solís-Barroso) are involved in developing these problem sets, a project they began in Winter 2022 in the context of a graduate seminar on Language Across Modalities that Natasha Abner and Marlyse Baptista co-taught. The repository would also contain recordings and other resources such

as YouTube videos related to the history, grammar, or users of these languages. We are in the process of developing such a repository, starting with Creole languages as our focus, and we intend to make it available online to instructors across institutions (Burgess et al., under review).

2. Reframe the narrative when you introduce Creole languages to students: forefront that they are natural, full-fledged languages (cf. DeGraff, 2005; Baptista, 2002, under review) and provide a holistic examination of the sociohistorical contexts in which they evolved.

3. The labeling and naming practices of languages is an important topic in linguistics, from both a research and community perspective. When addressing this topic in a linguistics course, consider using Creoles and pidgins as prime examples, given that users of these languages can disagree on how to name them. For instance, some may view their language as a dialect of the lexifier or a broken language whereas others may view it as an autonomous, full-fledged language (see our surveys and Gonzales, 2022). Be sure to engage students in a discussion centered on how and why these differences may emerge in a Creole or pidgin-speaking language community (e.g., (post-)colonial education practices and government policies, language activism and revitalization).

4. If possible, invite Creole language experts into your classroom, as it would directly expose students to these languages and their users and ultimately show that Creoles are used like any other natural language. If unsure where to find Creole users/experts, reach out to linguists and researchers who focus on Creole languages. Appropriate compensation to language experts visiting your classes is highly recommended.

Conclusions

In rethinking our approach to linguistics teaching with respect to Creole languages, first and foremost we sought perspectives from members of Creole-using communities to put in conversation with perspectives from within the field. That meant welcoming a diversity of experiences and viewpoints. The language experts wanted to educate others (and learn themselves) about many different topics, among them the diversity, linguistic properties, and histories of Creoles. The linguists, in turn, also wanted to teach and be educated about these topics but struggled to conceptualize where to fit them into their courses. This dilemma highlights a core issue: in the past, linguists have tried to *fit in* content about Creoles in introductory courses in linguistics. But limiting Creoles and other marginalized languages (e.g., pidgins, ethnolects, Indigenous languages, signed languages) to one topic, or one lesson, sets them apart from how students are exposed to other natural languages in linguistics. The better approach is to use Creole data for linguistic analyses and include holistic representations of Creoles throughout our linguistics classes (phonetics, phonology, morphology, syntax, pragmatics, etc.), just as we do for other languages (for an example of a textbook that integrates signed an Indigenous languages throughout the course materials, see the 11th edition of *The Language Files*, Christin Wilson and Vedrana Mihalicek, 2011; for a discussion on the more equitable inclusion of signed languages in linguistics see Hou & Ali, 2024.) This is not to suggest that we avoid lessons on the histories of Creole languages. However, limiting the narrative solely to colonialism, discrimination, and marginalization as a forefronted sidenote promotes an exceptionalist perspective, an approach to Creole languages that has harmful implications, particularly for Creole language users (for more on the negative impacts of exceptionalism, see DeGraff, 2005). As one linguist mentioned, these are topics that cannot even be fully covered in one semester, let alone one lesson. To teach our students, and others, about Creole languages in a revitalized, decolonized way, we must show rather than just tell. We must embrace in our pedagogical practices, as in other domains of our work, an anti-exceptionalist narrative about Creoles and their users that is rooted in equity, welcomes diversity, and holistically contextualizes their emergence as complete and ordinary languages.

Taking advantage of the virtual space, we were able to reach and bring together language experts and linguists from a variety of countries and timezones. This approach had both advantages and disadvantages. We conducted interviews with language experts over the phone or video chat without having to travel to their home countries, and this allowed us to complete our study in a timely and cost-effective manner. We were, however, limited in the number of people we could reach by not being on site. Similarly, while our virtual workshop made it possible for participants from all over the world to come together in the same space, we needed to accommodate several timezones and schedules, and this limited the event's duration; for this workshop, we settled on one hour. At the end of the hour, participants shared with us that they would have liked more time together and asked us to organize more events of this kind. As we have no doubt that longer, repeated workshops would lead to even deeper conversations between language experts and

314 Decolonizing Linguistics

linguists, more robust findings, and additional recommendations, we intend to facilitate such events in the future.

Note

1. For an expanded examination of our stance, we direct readers to the Standard Language Ideology Statement developed by the University of Michigan Department of Linguistics at https://lsa.umich.edu/linguistics/about-us/values-statement/standard-language-ideology-statement.html.

References

Amado, Abel Djassi, Baptista, Marlyse, Pina Garcia, Lourenço, Bolívar Humphrey, Mariano, Lima, Ambrizeth Helena, & Thomas, Dawna Marie. (2021). *Cabo Verdean heritage language and culture*. A Curriculum for the Boston Public Schools.

Andrade, Elise. (1996). *Les Îles du Cap-Vert: De la découverte à l'indépendance nationale (1460–1975)*. L'Harmattan.

Bakker, Peter, Markussen, Aymeric Daval, Parkvall, Mikael, & Plag, Ingo. (2011). Creoles are typologically distinct from non-Creoles. *Journal of Pidgin and Creole Languages, 26*(1), 5–42. https://doi.org/10.1075/jpcl.26.1.02bak.

Baptista, Marlyse. (2002). *The syntax of Cape Verdean Creole: The Sotavento varieties*. John Benjamins.

Baptista, Marlyse. (under review). In Salikoko S. Mufwene & Enoch Aboh (Eds.), *Uniformitarianism in genetic Creolistics*. Cambridge University Press.

Bickerton, Derek. (1984). The language bioprogram hypothesis. *The Behavioral and Brain Sciences, 7*(2), 173–188.

Bickerton, Derek. (2013). The evolution of language. In Daniel Reisberg (Ed.), *The Oxford handbook of cognitive psychology*. https://academic.oup.com/edited-volume/34404/chapter-abstract/291763843?redirectedFrom=fulltext.

Birdsong, David, Gertken, Libby M., & Amengual, Mark. (2012). *Bilingual language profile: An easy-to-use instrument to assess bilingualism*. COERLL, University of Texas at Austin. https://sites.la.utexas.edu/bilingual/.

Braun, Virginia, & Clarke, Victoria. (2006). Using thematic analysis in psychology. *Qualitative Research in Psychology, 3*(2), 77–101. http://dx.doi.org/10.1191/1478088706qp063oa.

Burgess, Danielle, Joy P. G. Peltier, Sophia Eakins, Wilkinson Daniel Wong Gonzales, Alicia Stevers, Ariana Bancu, Felicia Bisnath, Moira Saltzman, & Marlyse Baptista. (under review). The MULTI Project: Resources for enhancing multi-faceted Creole representation in the linguistics classroom.

Calhoun, Kendra, Hudley, Anne H. Charity, Bucholtz, Mary, Exford, Jazmine, & Johnson, Brittney. (2021). Attracting Black students to linguistics through a Black-centered Introduction to Linguistics course. *Language, 97*(1), e12–e38. http://doi.org/10.1353/lan.2021.0007.

Charity Hudley, Anne H. (2016). *Language and racialization*. Oxford University Press. https://academic.oup.com/edited-volume/27951/chapter-abstract/211528615?redirectedFrom=fulltext.

Craig, Dennis. (1980). Models for educational policy in creole-speaking communities. In A. Valdman & A. Highfield (Eds.), *Theoretical orientations in Creole studies* (pp. 245–265). Academic Press.

Daut, Marlene L. (2020). Creole. In Bruce Bergett & Glenn Hendler (Eds.), *Keywords for American Cultural Studies* (pp. 73–77). New York University Press.

DeGraff, Michel. (2003). Against Creole exceptionalism. *Language, 79*(2), 391–410. https://doi.org/10.1353/lan.2003.0114.

DeGraff, Michel. (2005). Linguists' most dangerous myth: The fallacy of Creole exceptionalism. *Language and Society, 34*(4), 533–591.

DeGraff, Michel. (2020). Toward racial justice in linguistics: The case of Creole studies (Response to Charity Hudley et al.). *Language, 96*(4), e292–e306. https://doi.org/10.1353/lan.2020.0080.

Deuber, Dagmar. (2009). Standard English in the secondary school in Trinidad. In Thomas Hoffman & Lucia Siebers (Eds.), *World Englishes—Problems, Properties and Prospects: Selected Papers from the 13th IAWE Conference* (pp. 83–106). John Benjamins.

Errington, Joseph. (2001). Colonial linguistics. *Annual Review of Anthropology, 30*, 19–39.

Flores, Nelson L. (2019). Translanguaging into raciolinguistic ideologies: A personal reflection on the legacy of Ofelia García. *Journal of Multilingual Education Research, 9*(1), Article 5.

Fromkin, Victoria, Rodman, Robert, & Hyams, Nina. (2013). *An introduction to language.* Wadsworth Cengage Learning.

García, Ofelia, & Otheguy, Ricardo. (2019). Plurilingualism and translanguaging: commonalities and divergences. *International Journal of Bilingual Education and Bilingualism, 23*(1), 17–35. https://doi.org/10.1080/13670050.2019.1598932.

Gonzales, Wilkinson Daniel Wong. (2022). *"Truly a language of our own": A corpus-based, experimental, and variationist account of Lánnang-uè in Manila* [Doctoral dissertation, University of Michigan].

Greenblatt, Stephen. (1991). Kidnapping language. In *Marvelous possessions: The Wonder of the New World* (pp. 86–118). University of Chicago Press.

Honychurch, Lennox. (1995). *The Dominica story: A history of the Island.* MacMillan Education, Ltd.

Hou, Lynn, & Ali, Kristian. (2024). Critically examining inclusion and parity for deaf Global South researchers of color in the field of sign language linguistics. In Anne H. Charity Hudley, Christine Mallinson, & Mary Bucholtz (Eds.), *Inclusion in linguistics.* Oxford University Press.

Irvine, Judith T., & Gal, Susan. (2000). Language ideology and linguistic differentiation. In Paul V. Kroskrity (Ed.), Regimes of language: *Ideologies, polities and identities* (pp. 35–83). School of American Research Press.

Jackendoff, Ray. (1994). *Patterns in the mind.* Basic Books.

Kihm, Alain. (1994). *Kriyol Syntax: The Portuguese-based Creole language of Guinea-Bissau.* John Benjamins.

Knörr, Jacqueline, & Filho, Wilson Trajano (Eds.). (2018). *Creolization and pidginization in contexts of postcolonial diversity: Language, culture, identity.* Brill.

Kriel, Mariana. (2018). Chronicle of a Creole: The ironic history of Afrikaans. In Jacqueline Knörr & Wilson Trajano Filho (Eds.), *Creolization and pidginization in contexts of postcolonial diversity* (pp. 132–157). Brill.

Léglise, Isabelle, & Migge, Bettina. (2006). Language-naming practices, ideologies, and linguistic practices: Toward a comprehensive description of language varieties. *Language in Society, 35*(3), 313–339. https://doi.org/10.1017/S0047404506060155.

Lim, Lisa, & Ansaldo, Umberto. (2016). *Languages in contact.* Cambridge University Press.

McWhorter, John. 1998. Identifying the Creole prototype: Vindicating a typological class. *Language, 74*(4), 788–818.

Mühleisen, Susanne. (2013). Trinidadian English Creole. In Susanne Maria Michaelis, Philippe Maurer, Martin Haspelmath, & Magnus Huber, *The survey of Creole languages: Volume 1* (pp. 161–169). Oxford University Press.

Otheguy, Ricardo, García, Ofelia, & Reid, Wallis. (2015). Clarifying translanguaging and deconstructing named languages: A perspective from linguistics. *Applied Linguistics Review*, *16*(3), 281–307.

Paugh, Amy L. (2012). *Playing with language: Children and change in a Caribbean village*. Berghahn Books.

Peltier, Joy P. G. (2022). *Powerful "little words" in contact and in context: Pragmatic markers in Kwéyòl Donmnik, English, and French* [Doctoral dissertation, University of Michigan].

Peltier, Joy P. G. (forthcoming). Pragmatic Markers in Kwéyòl Donmnik, French, & English: Language Contact & Creole Emergence through the Lens of Powerful Little Words. To appear in *Études Créoles*.

Taylor, Douglas. (1977). *Languages of the West Indies*. Johns Hopkins University Press.

Thomason, Sarah G. (2001). *Language contact: An introduction*. Georgetown University Press.

University of Michigan. (2021). Standard language ideology statement. Statement about standard language ideology and equity among languages. https://lsa.umich.edu/linguistics/about-us/values-statement/standard-language-ideology-statement.html.

Weinreich, Uriel. (1953). *Languages in contact: Findings and problems*. Linguistics Circle of New York.

Wilson, Christin, & Mihalicek, Vedrana (Eds). (2011). *Language files: Materials for an introduction to language and linguistics*. Ohio State University Press.

Williams, Eric. (1962). A history of the people of trinidad and tobago. Frederick A. Praeger.

Winer, Lise S. (1993). *Trinidad and Tobago*. John Benjamins.

Youssef, Valerie. (2002). Issues of bilingual education in the Caribbean: The cases of Haiti, and Trinidad and Tobago. *International Journal of Bilingual Education and Bilingualism, 5*(3), 182–193.

PART 3
DECOLONIZING RESEARCH BY CENTERING COMMUNITY AND ACTIVISM

Anne H. Charity Hudley is associate dean of Educational Affairs in the Stanford Graduate School of Education, the Bonnie Katz Tenenbaum Professor of Education, and professor of African American Studies and Linguistics, by courtesy, at Stanford University. Her research and publications address the relationship between language variation and educational practices and policies across the educational lifespan, particularly for Black students. She has a special dedication to creating high-impact practices for underrepresented students in higher education. She is the co-author of numerous publications and four books: *The Indispensable Guide to Undergraduate Research*; *We Do Language: English Language Variation in the Secondary English Classroom*; *Understanding English Language Variation in U.S. Schools*; and *Talking College: Making Space for Black Language Practices in Higher Education*. Charity Hudley is a fellow both of the Linguistic Society of America and of the American Association for the Advancement of Science (AAAS).

Christine Mallinson is the 2023–2024 Lipitz Distinguished Professor of the Arts, Humanities, and Social Sciences, professor in the Language, Literacy, and Culture Program and affiliate professor in the Department of Gender, Women's, and Sexuality Studies at the University of Maryland, Baltimore County (UMBC), where she is also director of the Center for Social Science Scholarship and Special Assistant for Research and Creative Achievement in the Office of the Vice President for Research. The author and editor of five books and numerous other publications, Mallinson draws upon interdisciplinary frameworks from linguistics, education, gender studies, sociology, and anthropology to examine language as a socially and culturally contextualized practice. Through community-centered approaches, her research aims to dismantle deficit notions surrounding cultural and linguistic difference in ways that also inform educational policy and practice. A fellow of the Linguistic Society of America, Mallinson has held many professional leadership roles, including as chair of the Linguistic Society of America's Ethics Committee and associate editor of *American Speech*.

Kahdeidra Monét Martin is assistant professor of education at Vassar College. She uses her lived experience and qualitative, community-based methods to examine linguistic variation, discourses of deviance, and the intersectional experiences of Black youth in elite independent schools as well as Black youth who are members of African diasporic religions. As a scholar-priestess, Martin examines raciolinguistics and the co-naturalization of language, race, and spirituality in the lives of African-descendant people across the lifespan. She has received two grants funded by the Henry Luce Foundation to document religious racism and conduct oral history research on members of African Diasporic religious communities, resulting in the *Embodied Memories* podcast available on YouTube and Spotify. Her scholarship can be found in *Cahiers Internationaux de Sociolinguistique*, *English in Education*, and *Linguistics and Education*, among others. She is co-author of *Classroom Talk for Social Change: Critical Conversations in English Language Arts*, which received a 2021 Divergent Book Award for Excellence from the Initiative for 21st Century Literacies Research.

Aris Moreno Clemons is assistant professor of Hispanic linguistics in the World Languages and Cultures department at the University of Tennessee Knoxville. She completed her doctoral degree in the Spanish and Portuguese Department and the Mexican American and Latina/o Studies Department at the University of Texas at Austin. Her work spans the fields of linguistics, education, anthropology, and Black and Latinx studies in order to interrogate the intersections of language, race, and identity. Originally from (all over) the Bay Area in California, she has been steeped in the traditions of anti-racist pedagogies and has dedicated herself to developing and sustaining these practices in her own research and teaching. As such, her research agenda is rooted in social change through an examination of the ways that what appears to be common knowledge is often constructed and ideologically maintained by various social institutions. Overarchingly, Aris questions the linguistic mechanisms—repetitions, stance taking, tropicalizations, and so on—responsible for the (re)construction and maintenance of racializing and marginalizing ideologies.

L. J. Randolph Jr. is assistant professor of world language education at the University of Wisconsin-Madison. He received his EdD in curriculum and instruction from the University of North Carolina at Chapel Hill. His research and teaching focus on various critical issues in language education, including teaching Spanish to heritage and native speakers, incorporating justice-oriented/antiracist/anticolonial pedagogies, and centering Blackness and Indigenousness. He has authored or coauthored several publications and given dozens of scholarly presentations on those topics. He is a coeditor of the forthcoming book *How We Take Action: Social Justice in PreK-16 Classrooms*. An advocate for equitable, accessible, and transformative language education, he has served as president of the Foreign Language Association of North Carolina (FLANC), as president of the North Carolina chapter of the American Association of Teachers of Spanish and Portuguese (AATSP), and as a board member for the American Council on the Teaching of Foreign Languages (ACTFL).

Mary Bucholtz is professor in the Department of Linguistics at the University of California, Santa Barbara, where she is also affiliated with the departments of Anthropology, Education, Feminist Studies, and Spanish and Portuguese, and with the programs in Comparative Literature and in Latin American and Iberian Studies. A fellow of the Linguistic Society of America, she directs UCSB's Center for California Languages and Cultures and is the founding director and current associate director of the educational justice program School Kids Investigating Language in Life and Society, as well as a member of the Mexican Indigenous Languages Promotion and Advocacy collective, a partnership between UCSB and a community organization that supports the Mexican Indigenous Diaspora in California. Her research focuses on language, race, gender, identity, and youth as well as on language and institutional power. She is the author or editor of over a hundred publications on these topics.

Kendra Calhoun is assistant professor of linguistic anthropology at the University of Illinois, Urbana-Champaign. She is an interdisciplinary sociocultural linguist and earned her PhD in Linguistics at UC Santa Barbara. Her work examines the relationship of language and media to identity, culture, and power, with an emphasis on African American language and culture in US education and online contexts. She has researched "diversity, equity, and inclusion" discourses and practices and their impacts on graduate students of color at multiple minority serving institutions, as well as written on ways the discipline of linguistics can be more inclusive of Black students. She has analyzed language, race, and Black digital culture on social media platforms including Vine, Tumblr, and TikTok. Her work examines how Black social media users construct and contest ideas about race and Blackness through multimodal discourse practices and how social media platforms function as both sites and tools for these practices. Her research has appeared in *Language, American Speech, Journal of Linguistic Anthropology, Oxford Research Encyclopedia of Anthropology,* and *a tumblr book: platform and cultures.*

Shenika Hankerson is assistant professor of applied linguistics and language education in the Department of Teaching and Learning, Policy and Leadership at the University of Maryland-College Park. Her research focuses on African American Language (AAL), critical sociolinguistics, critical applied linguistics, and second language writing, and addresses topics such as the effects of anti-Black linguistic discrimination on AAL-speaking students' oral and written language ideologies and practices and how Afrocentric, antiracist, and anti-oppressive instructional practices and curriculum designs can disrupt the transmission of anti-Black linguistic discrimination in language and writing pedagogy. Her scholarship can be found in *Journal of Second Language Writing, Written Communication, Language Arts Journal of Michigan*, and *Talking Back: Senior Scholars Deliberate the Past, Present, and Future of Writing Studies.*

Joy P. G. Peltier is assistant professor at the University of South Carolina in the Linguistics Program and the Department of English Language and Literature. She is a Black scholar of African American and Caribbean descent, and her family members use several languages, from Kwéyòl Donmnik to varieties of African American English. Her work centers on contact-induced and minoritized languages, such as Creoles like Kwéyòl Donmnik, as well as on multifunctional and discourse-pragmatic elements, such as pragmatic markers (e.g., Kwéyòl *èben* 'well,' English *well*, French *bon* 'well'). She is also passionate about the inclusion of minoritized languages in linguistics pedagogy and research and is engaged in collaborative research centered on the linguistic and professional experiences of Black faculty in the language sciences. She views her scholarship as an opportunity to spark "ah-ha moments" about varieties and features of language that are stigmatized or overlooked, and she draws upon a mixture of methodologies, including corpus-based analyses, metalinguistic interviews and surveys, and experimental tasks

Jamie A. Thomas is Dean of Social Sciences at Cypress College and equity facilitator for the California Virtual Campus/Online Education Initiative (CVC/OEI) and the Online Network of Educators (@ONE). She is also adjunct lecturer in linguistics at California State University, Dominguez Hills. During 2021–2022, she was a Mellon/ACLS Community College faculty fellow and principal investigator for the project Closing Racial Equity Gaps Through Online Teaching of Introductory Linguistics. In her other research, Jamie explores discourses and semiotics of antiracism, Blackness, cityscapes, and African languages in relation to language learning, embodiment, the workplace, and popular culture. She is author of the forthcoming ethnography *Zombies Speak Swahili: Race, Horror, and Sci-fi from Mexico and Tanzania to Hollywood,* and co-editor of the multidisciplinary volume *Embodied Difference: Divergent Bodies in Public Discourse.*

Deana Lacy McQuitty is associate professor and Speech Program director in the Hairston College of Health and Human Sciences at North Carolina Agricultural and Technical State University. Her research focuses on increasing the representation of culturally and linguistically diverse students into the profession of speech-language pathology. Her specific focus relates to designing programming that facilitates student-centered best practices to support students of color pursuing undergraduate and advanced studies in communication sciences and disorders. She has provided her expertise in a multitude of clinical settings and in academia, and she has been an invited speaker to discuss culturally responsive and affirming mentorship for underrepresented populations in communication and sciences disorders. Her published or forthcoming scholarship can be found in the *Journal of Best Practices in Health Professions Diversity, The Chronicle of Mentoring & Coaching,* and *Carolinas Communication Annual.*

Kara Seidel is a PhD student in the Language, Literacy, and Culture program at the University of Maryland, Baltimore County (UMBC). She received an MS in education from Johns Hopkins University in 2020 and a BA in psychology with a minor in American Studies from UMBC in 2018, where she was valedictorian of the College of Arts, Humanities, and Social Sciences. Her research interests center on the intersection of language, race, disability, and accessibility in higher education. She has presented her work in interdisciplinary venues, including at the annual meetings of the American Association for Applied Linguistics, the American Dialect Society, and the American Sociological Association.

Abstract: This chapter takes a Black Diasporic perspective on the decolonization of linguistics. The authors interrogate longstanding false institutional and ideological divides within linguistics and related fields while strengthening and fostering scholarly solidarity and collectivity for African, African American, Black, and Diasporic scholars. They share personal and professional insights on centering Blackness as part of decolonizing linguistics from their positionalities and intellectual histories as authors, as Black Diasporic scholars, and as white allies, as well as from recent autobiographical scholarship by prominent Black Diasporic linguists. Based on their findings, they offer recommendations for solidarity and collective action toward adopting transformative changes to expand Black individuals' and communities' access to linguistics, challenge the white supremacy that undergirds the discipline's ignorance about and exclusion of the Black Diaspora, and shift ideological standards for academic and scholarly success within linguistics.

Key Words: African American English, African American Language, applied linguistics, Black Diaspora, sociolinguistics

15

Solidarity and Collectivity in Decolonizing Linguistics

A Black Diasporic Perspective

Anne H. Charity Hudley (she/her)
Stanford University

Christine Mallinson (she/her)
University of Maryland, Baltimore County

Kahdeidra Monét Martin (she/her)
Vassar College

Aris Moreno Clemons (she/her)
University of Tennessee Knoxville

L. J. Randolph Jr. (he/him, they/them)
University of Wisconsin

Mary Bucholtz (she/her, they/them)
University of California, Santa Barbara

Kendra Calhoun (she/her)
University of Illinois, Urbana-Champaign

Shenika Hankerson (she/her)
University of Maryland

Joy P. G. Peltier (she/her)
University of South Carolina

Charity Hudley, Mallinson, Martin, Clemons, Randolph Jr., Bucholtz, Calhoun, Hankerson, Peltier, Thomas, McQuitty, Seidel, *Solidarity and Collectivity in Decolonizing Linguistics* In: *Decolonizing Linguistics*. Edited by: Anne H. Charity Hudley, Christine Mallinson, and Mary Bucholtz, Oxford University Press. © Anne H. Charity Hudley, Christine Mallinson, and Mary Bucholtz 2024. DOI: 10.1093/oso/9780197755259.003.0016

324 Decolonizing Linguistics

Jamie A. Thomas (she/her, they/them)
Santa Monica College

Deana Lacy McQuitty (she/her)
North Carolina Agricultural and Technical State University

Kara Seidel (she/her)
University of Maryland, Baltimore County

Introduction

Solidarity and collectivity have always been the most immediate and useful approaches to decolonization. In this chapter, we take a Black Diasporic perspective on the decolonization of linguistics.[1] Crucially, our decolonization efforts entail dismantling the longstanding institutional and ideological divide among the many subfields of linguistics as well as between linguistics and related disciplines. Our goal is to strengthen scholarly solidarity and collectivity across such false divides while fostering further conversation and organization around liberatory linguistics for African, African American, Black, and Diasporic scholars by expanding collaboration and mutual advocacy among these scholars and non-Black allies in the academy.

This chapter developed as part of Christine Mallinson and Anne H. Charity Hudley's (2022–2024) collaborative National Science Foundation-sponsored Build and Broaden Program grant, "Linguistic Production, Perception, and Identity in the Career Mobility of Black Faculty in Linguistics and the Language Sciences." All of the coauthors of the chapter are research scholars on the Build and Broaden project, which takes an intentionally collaborative and team-based approach (cf. Ledgerwood et al., 2022) to examine how US-based Black Diasporic faculty in linguistics, inclusively defined, navigate their professional experiences, with the goal of decolonizing and broadening participation in language-related fields and in academia. As Aris Moreno Clemons (this volume) notes, the Build and Broaden project "provides a template for the ways that we should engage our own linguistic histories and ideologies when approaching linguistic scholarship," because "scholarship on and about language is deeply personal."

In this chapter, we present personal and professional insights into how to begin decolonizing the discipline and centering Blackness in a broadly construed linguistics, grounded in the intellectual histories, positionalities, and research experiences of Black Diasporic scholars and their academic allies—especially white allies, given their numeric and structural dominance in the academy. We draw these insights from multiple sources: our own positionalities and intellectual histories as authors, interviews with additional Black Diasporic scholars and white allies who are navigating their careers in the US, and recent autobiographical scholarship by three prominent Black Diasporic linguists. We bring a critical Black Diasporic lens to the question of who is recognized as practicing (ideologically unmarked) "linguistics" (also termed "theoretical linguistics" or "general linguistics") and who is seen as practicing (ideologically marked) "sociolinguistics" or "applied linguistics" or other linguistics-related subfields and fields, how they do so, and why—questions that foreground issues of disciplinary boundaries and the gatekeeping that often accompanies them. Based on our findings, we put forward a collective agenda to challenge the white supremacy undergirding such divides; in so doing, we highlight the ignorance about and exclusion of the Black Diaspora that persists in linguistics, broadly defined, which non-Black academic researchers and educators of language have all too often perpetuated.

Studying Black Language in a Disciplinarily Divided Linguistics

The study of Black Diasporic languages and language varieties is a robust area in some parts of linguistics, even as it remains marginalized in other subfields and language-related areas. Across disciplinary formations, research and teaching about Black language is largely entrenched within a colonial framework. Below, we discuss Black language and Black linguists in linguistics departments, in speech-language pathology, in applied linguistics, and in English language and literacy studies and education.

Black Language in Linguistics Departments and Programs

Black language is a topic of study in nearly every linguistics undergraduate program in the US (Calhoun et al., 2021; Weldon, 2012). Discussions of Black Diasporic language are especially common in sociolinguistics courses and in sociolinguistics units in introductory courses (even as the subfield of sociolinguistics is often distinguished and separated from unmarked "linguistics"). Creole languages used in Black communities also feature heavily in courses on language contact and change. Yet the approach taken in many of these courses, and in much of the underlying research, is inherently colonial (Thomas, 2022), with Black Diasporic languages and varieties typically analyzed and theorized in comparison to hegemonic white languages and varieties and implicitly (and sometimes explicitly) positioned in a deficit relationship to whiteness. Moreover, most of the scholars who have made their careers studying Black Diasporic languages are not themselves Black (cf. Rickford, 1997), thus perpetuating extractive, colonial relationships between non-Black linguistic researchers and the users of these languages. A related issue is that because of the field's interest in linguistic typology and comparative analysis, as well as the theoretical attention garnered by Creole and African languages, many of the Black linguists housed in US linguistics departments and programs are of African or Caribbean descent, with comparatively few of African American descent (Lanehart, 2017; Lanehart & Malik, 2018).

These disciplinary and scholarly trends, and the unequal representation and participation they create in individual programs and departments, continue to negatively impact linguistics and hinder disciplinary understandings and appreciation of the linguistic innovations of communities of language users throughout the Black Diaspora. These trends also reinforce and are reinforced by other professional inequities in the field. For instance, the number of presidents of color in the nearly century-long existence of the discipline's flagship organization, the Linguistic Society of America (LSA), can be counted on one hand (Linguistic Society of America, 2019). In other words, "the scholars who most often deal with race in their research and can contribute insights based on their lived experience are less likely to hold leadership positions that would enable them to shape understandings of race within the discipline" (Charity Hudley et al., 2020, p. e202). Yet these structural inequities have gone largely unremarked within the discipline until recently (e.g., Charity Hudley et al., 2020; but see Rickford, 1997, for an important early critical statement).

Compounding these structural problems is the absence of linguistics at most Historically Black Colleges and Universities (HBCUs), despite the rich Diasporic tradition of Black language study and use at these institutions, as Candice Y. Thornton (2024) notes. Thornton profiles a number of historical and contemporary Black linguists at HBCUs, including Lorenzo Dow Turner, Temptaous Mckoy, Daryl Lynn Dance, Margaret Lee, Juanita Williamson, Sheikh Umarr Kamarah, and Desire Balboui. The latter two scholars were instrumental in helping forge a mutual exchange through the UCSB-HBCU Scholars in Linguistics Program (2018–2023), in which undergraduate students from HBCUs and other institutions spent the summer learning at the University of California, Santa Barbara (UCSB), and Kendra Calhoun, as a then-graduate student from UCSB, spent a semester learning, teaching, and researching at one of the program's HBCU partners (Calhoun, 2021; Charity Hudley & Bucholtz, 2017; Franz et al., 2022). Engaging and amplifying the work of Black linguists, especially, but not only, at Black institutions, can help create a Black-led, decolonizing linguistics—one in which anti-Blackness is rejected and Black Diasporic languages are recognized in all "their normalcy, naturalness, creativity, diversity, and resilience" (Bancu, Peltier, et al., this volume).

Speech-Language Pathology

Similar trends are evident in other language sciences, such as the study of speech-language pathology. Organizations such as the American Speech-Language-Hearing Association (ASHA) have historically outlined strategic priorities that include the recruitment and retention of more culturally and linguistically diverse professionals and practitioners, in order to achieve greater inclusion of underrepresented populations in the profession (ASHA, 2021). This goal is especially critical given statistical projections that suggest minoritized individuals will represent approximately 50% of the US population by the year 2050 (US Census Bureau, 2000). Speech-language pathologists provide therapy services to clients from birth to the end of life and must therefore be prepared to serve individuals of diverse racial, ethnic, cultural, and linguistic backgrounds in schools, hospitals, and community practices across the United States. This is a continuing challenge for speech-language pathologists who are primarily monolingual and of European American descent.

Cultural and linguistic mismatches across professionals and the communities they serve can lead to health inequities and disparities. Within speech-language pathology, health disparities arise when particular communities do not receive needed services. With regard to African Americans, for example, "It is estimated, in 2012, that almost 10% of African American kids (3–17) were diagnosed with some form of communication disorder (ranging from speech to swallowing); however, the percentage is lower for White kids at 7.8% and Hispanic kids at 6.9%" (McQuitty & Moore, 2022, p. 595). Yet despite the fact that African American youth had a higher percentage of communication disorders, they received fewer intervention services (Black et al., 2015). Morgan et al. (2016) similarly found that Black and Latinx youth are less likely to receive needed communication disorder services.

328 Decolonizing Linguistics

As Deana McQuitty and DaKysha Moore (2022) emphasize:

> The health disparities in communication disorders of need and services espe-
> cially among African American children emphasize the important role of recruiting
> and retaining more speech-language pathologists and audiologists who identify
> as a racial ethnic minority. Trust in healthcare providers is an issue in the African
> American community. Based on decades of biases, there are African American
> patients who may not trust their providers. (p. 596)

However, trust is a critical factor in getting clients to adhere to prescribed care (Murray, 2015). Throughout the healthcare industry, there is a need for more diversity among clinicians. Research suggests that patients have a higher level of satisfaction with medical visits when their doctor is of the same race (Cooper et al., 2003). Individuals from similar racial or ethnic backgrounds may also share the same language or language variety, which may include sharing semantics and/or finding commonalities among social language patterns. Training professionals and practitioners who speak the same language as the communities they serve is an important need for speech-language pathology.

Although ASHA has launched numerous initiatives and programming to address the lack of diversity within speech-language pathology, there continues to be a paucity of culturally and linguistically minoritized professionals in the organization, resulting in very few presidents of color. Mirroring the lack of linguistics programs offered at HBCUs, there is also a critical need for more undergraduate and graduate programs in language sciences such as speech-language pathology at HBCUs. Speech-language pathology is an especially important way for linguists to engage Black students, who may be drawn to the field over conventional linguistics due to its real-world impact (see also Charity Hudley et al., 2022).

In order to recruit a more culturally and linguistically diverse range of undergraduates into speech-language pathology, McQuitty and other leaders in Communication Sciences and Disorders at HBCUs have developed strategies to recruit and retain students at the largest HBCU in the nation, North Carolina Agricultural and Technical State University. North Carolina A&T has an undergraduate program in Speech Language Pathology and Audiology (SLP&A). In recent years, SLP&A has formed a partnership with the university's Middle College, an all-male high school whose population is 90% African American. In this partnership, the SLP&A program provides allied health career awareness seminars to recruit and attract the Middle College students; through these seminars, "students gained insights into the SLP and audiology job markets. Topics covered include educational requirements, the array of careers, potential salaries, and the positive impact practitioners can have on underrepresented populations in both the public schools and medical settings. As part of the program, the Middle College students engage with professionals but also interact with undergraduate students who share a similar cultural background and experiences" (McQuitty & Moore, 2022, pp. 596–597). Since the launch of this initiative, three Black male high school students have been recruited to the university as SLP&A majors. McQuitty was acknowledged by ASHA for her efforts and successes in leading this program and was featured as an invited speaker on ASHAWire's podcast, "ASHA Voice: HBCU Leaders Share Strategies for Recruiting and Retaining Underrepresented Students in CSD" (Gray, 2022). These and similar activities provide a model for linguists seeking to support Black students' interest in language-related fields.

Applied Linguistics

As a discipline, linguistics has largely limited the study of Black Diasporic languages to the analysis of decontextualized linguistic data used to advance theoretical arguments and hence rarely serves Black communities. Within applied linguistics, however, Black scholars are doing decolonizing work that centers Southern perspectives and South–South linkages and challenges Western formulations of language and languaging (e.g., Makalela, 2017; 2022; Makoni, 2011; Makoni & Meinhof, 2003; Pennycook & Makoni, 2020; Thomas, 2020; 2021; Upor & Mihayo, 2021).

Charity Hudley and Nelson Flores (2022) document recent efforts to focus on social justice and equity and dismantle anti-Blackness in applied linguistics, including the March 2022 volume of the *Annual Review of Applied Linguistics* (*ARAL*). That volume, which focuses on social justice in applied linguistics, Charity Hudley worked with editor Alison Mackey to make the applied linguistics publication model more inclusive, centering the voices of emerging scholars from a range of different racial and ethnic backgrounds, geographic areas, research specializations, and institution types, and offering each of them the opportunity to lay out their vision for what the field's agenda should be. Given this commitment, the *ARAL* volume is closely aligned with both *Inclusion in Linguistics* and *Decolonizing Linguistics*. We summarize some of these contributions to that volume below.

Brittany L. Frieson (2022) describes the racialization of English in dual-language education in the United States. She highlights the pervasive anti-Blackness that undergirds the binary terms "English speaker" and "English learner" that inform dominant discussions of dual language education.

Frieson shows how these binary categorizations misrepresent the experiences of Black students. She adopts counterstory as her methodological approach and advocates for the adoption of literacies that center Blackness.

Rachel Elizabeth Weissler (2022) uses a social justice lens to bring attention to the role of power in shaping listener perceptions of foreignness and difference. She compels us to think about the implications of these biases for assessment and measurement in language learning and shows how bias factors into more general cognitive processes. Her work is crucial for disrupting the current norms for language assessment in educational psychology and researchers' reliance on models that often have deep roots in eugenics and white supremacy.

Both Jamie A. Thomas (2022) and Sheena Shah, Letzadzo Kometsi, and Matthias Brenzinger (2022) explore how to create intentional research space for users of languages other than English through approaches guided by collaboration and community. Thomas decenters traditional white male-oriented approaches to knowledge-making and knowledge-building through a narrativized analysis that begins with her own scholarly genealogy: "As an African American woman, I . . . gather wisdom from literary giant Toni Morrison, who in turn, draws upon the insights of linguistic anthropologist and novelist Zora Neale Hurston" (p. 129). Thomas explains how Black scholarly and community traditions guide her to re-examine "what is ethically, methodologically, and sociopolitically possible in applied linguistics." Referring to the ethnographic research she carried out in Micronesia and Tanzania, she demonstrates that a shift toward multilingual, multiperson interviewing can expand and deepen the insights of language-focused research.

Relatedly, Shah and her coauthors advocate for centering collaborative language revitalization efforts to advance linguistic justice. The three authors—a user of the siPhuthi language of South Africa and Lesotho, and two outsider linguists—describe their collaborative, community-led model of research, which aims to uplift the ebaPhuthi people and the siPhuthi language. They document their efforts to ensure the integration of siPhuthi into governmental and legal domains, healthcare, policy, education, and the media. The synergies between these papers and those in the present edited volumes offer a glimpse into a new vision for linguistics that not only invites but, by necessity, requires the inclusion of Black scholars in applied linguistics and other scholars, especially in the Global South, who are doing decolonizing work across the continuum of linguistic research.

A just and equitable applied linguistics must make room for Black scholars and for Black languages and varieties. Black applied linguists who explore Blackness in language learning include Tasha Austin (2022a; 2022b), whose work centers global Blackness to counter anti-Black racism, linguistic imperialism, and harmful raciolinguistic ideologies in world language education and teacher preparation; Awad Ibrahim (e.g., 1999; 2008), who studies African immigrants learning English in Canada; L. J. Randolph Jr. (2016; 2017), whose scholarship centers social justice for heritage users of Spanish while engaging the historical diversity of Latin America, which includes the experiences of Black users of Spanish as their primary language; and Jamie A. Thomas (2020; 2021), who explores Black Diasporic and African identities in the learning and teaching of Swahili across the US, Mexico, and Tanzania, among others.

English Language and Literacy Studies and Education

Many Black linguists, following in the tradition and intellectual lineage of transformative scholar Geneva Smitherman (e.g., 1977; 2000), have had thriving careers in English language and literacy studies that emphasize the role of language in community, lived experience, and identity (e.g., Gilyard 1991; Lanehart 2002; 2009; Richardson 2003; 2007). Black scholars of language in the field of education have similarly created a legacy of transdisciplinary, community-centered scholarship. For example, David Kirkland is a scholar of English and urban education who uses ethnographic and sociolinguistic methods to understand and support the literacy of Black boys (Kirkland, 2011; 2013). Likewise, urban education scholar Valerie Kinloch engages with Black youth literacies in urban settings through community-based and youth participatory action research (Kinloch 2010; 2011). In addition, April Baker-Bell is a teacher-researcher-activist whose research establishes a framework for anti-racist Black language pedagogy to name and dismantle anti-Black linguistic racism (Baker-Bell, 2020a; 2020b).

As this section has demonstrated, there is a strong foundation for a Black-centered, Black-led, inclusive, and decolonizing linguistics, one that is informed equally by the structural and historical concerns of "theoretical" linguistics, the social questions of "socio" linguistics, and the cultural, educational, and policy issues that drive "applied" linguistics, English language and literacy studies, and education. Many of these topics have not yet been incorporated under the scholarly umbrella of linguistics. Continuing to advance these efforts requires further dismantling of traditional disciplinary boundaries by bringing together Black linguists across a wide range of subfields, programs, departments, and institutions to identify and build on common ground.

Centering Black Scholars in Decolonizing Linguistics

The following discussion is informed by the perspectives of 15 scholars in linguistics, applied linguistics, and language departments who have navigated their careers in the US: 12 Black scholars from across the Diaspora and three white allies whose careers have been actively dedicated to learning with and working toward social justice for Black and other racially minoritized groups of faculty and students (Table 15.1). The insights presented in this chapter are

Table 15.1 List of Featured Scholars

Chapter Authors	Scholar Interviewees	
Anne H. Charity Hudley	Marlyse Baptista	
Christine Mallinson	Michel DeGraff	
Kahdeidra Martin	Shelome Gooden	
Aris Moreno Clemons	Anonymous	
L. J. Randolph Jr.		
Mary Bucholtz		
Kendra Calhoun	**Autobiographical Authors**	
Shenika Hankerson	John Baugh	
Joy P. G. Peltier	John Rickford	
Jamie A. Thomas	Geneva Smitherman	
Deana Lacy McQuitty		
Kara Seidel		
Type of Contributor		
Chapter Authors	$N = 12$	
Scholar Interviewees	$N = 4$	
Autobiographical Authors	$N = 3$	
Race/Ethnicity		
Black Diasporic Scholars	$N = 15$	
White Scholars	$N = 4$	
Gender		
Women	$N = 15$	
Men	$N = 4$	
Rank		
Professor	$N = 10$	
Associate Professor	$N = 2$	
Assistant Professor	$N = 4$	
Postdoctoral Scholars	$N = 2$	
Graduate Student	$N = 1$	

drawn from multiple data sources. First, several of the authors interviewed each other and discussed our intellectual histories and our subjectivities and positionalities, whether as Black scholars (Charity Hudley, Martin, Calhoun, Clemons, Hankerson, McQuitty, Peltier, Randolph, and Thomas) or as white allies (Mallinson, Bucholtz, and Seidel). Charity Hudley interviewed three additional Black Diasporic scholars: Marlyse Baptista, Michel DeGraff, and Shelome Gooden; Mallinson interviewed a white ally who requested anonymity. Finally, we drew upon recently published autobiographical scholarship by three prominent Black linguists—John Baugh (Baugh, 2022; Conner, 2021), John Rickford (Rickford, 2022), and Geneva Smitherman (Smitherman, 2022)—for additional perspectives and further contextualization. This blend of insights reveals that personal and intellectual histories and career development are interrelated for Black Diasporic scholars in ways that can inform strategies for solidarity and collectivity as a means of advancing inclusion and decolonization.

The interviews took place via Zoom and lasted approximately 45 to 60 minutes. Six interview questions were asked, adjusted to the background of the interviewee:

1. How did you become a linguist, and why do you stick with it?
2. How has your career been colonized, and how have you worked to dismantle that colonization? (*For white scholars:* What are the ways in which you think academic careers can be colonized? How have you worked to dismantle colonization in your own or others' careers?)
3. What should we be working on across the Diaspora to decolonize our teaching, research, service, and outreach?
4. How do you perceive the appropriateness of Black language and cultural practices within the context of higher education and in your professional work? (*For white scholars:* How do you think the appropriateness of Black language and cultural practices is perceived for Black scholars in these fields?)
5. How and when do you use Black language practices in your professional work? How has your linguistic usage in teaching, research, and service and outreach positively or negatively affected your academic participation and career mobility? (*For white scholars:* How and when have you seen Black faculty in these fields use Black language practices in higher education? How and when have you seen their linguistic usage positively or negatively affect their academic participation and career mobility?)
6. How do you feel that the dynamics of linguistic production and perception reveal aspects of linguistic subordination, linguistic insecurity,

internalized racism, and implicit or explicit bias that may affect Black scholars in linguistics and the language sciences?

We discuss here three main themes that emerged from analysis of the interviews: (1) what keeps Black Diasporic scholars in linguistics, inclusively conceived; (2) how race and Diasporic identity are visible in linguistics; and (3) how decolonization is happening in linguistic research, teaching, practice, and advocacy. Based on the insights generated by the analysis, we offer key recommendations and next steps for solidarity and collective action toward decolonizing linguistics. A draft of this chapter was also shared with all interviewees to obtain their feedback, which was incorporated into the final manuscript.

What Keeps Black Diasporic Scholars in Linguistics?

The first theme that emerged from our analysis is that while Black Diasporic scholars in linguistics, understood as a broad, interdisciplinary field of inquiry, have centered their work on a wide range of specific research interests, their careers have had a common thread of being informed by their own life histories, with the goal of seeking to understand and benefit the lives and linguistic experiences of Black people. The interviews, personal reflections, and life histories that we gathered and analyzed reveal how and why Black Diasporic scholars in language and linguistics are motivated to enter the field and to persist and succeed in academia.

In *Speaking My Soul* (2022), Rickford recounts his life history and how it influenced his career path. As an undergraduate at the University of California, Santa Cruz, Rickford was influenced by the scholarship of anthropologist Roger M. Keesing and linguist Robert Le Page. He connected their work to his own upbringing in Guyana, including his family's use of Creolese and his mother's fondness for reading to Rickford and his siblings from books that included the language. As he recalled, these readings "were enough to introduce me to the ambiguous love/hate relationship that West Indians often have with what Kamau Brathwaite described as 'nation language' vs. the 'Queen's English.' And they gave me my earliest love of language and linguistics" (Rickford, 2022, pp. 29–30). Rickford knew he was "hooked," and he designed his own major in sociolinguistics. "As far as I know," he writes, "I was the first person to graduate with a major in Sociolinguistics—a brand new field—anywhere" (Rickford, 2022, p. 75). These interests converged with coursework on race and ethnicity and other events that occurred during his time in graduate school to shape his Black consciousness and his identity (Rickford, 2022, pp. 77–79). Rickford reflected, "Learning to love Black Talk (my native Creolese and African American Vernacular English, or 'AAVE') was of a piece with learning to love my black self, the African strands of my ancestry, my *me*" (2022, p. 93). From these influences developed Rickford's decades-long career of carrying out research on Black language as well as advocating for and supporting those who use it.

A very different experience motivated Smitherman to pursue linguistics as a career, as she describes in her memoir, *My Soul Look Back in Wonder* (Smitherman, 2022). She recalls that when she entered Wayne State University as an undergraduate, she was forced to undergo speech correction therapy "because I had failed the University's speech test due to my 'Negro Dialect' as it was called in those years—like saying 'foe' for 'four,' and 'thang' for 'thing'" (Smitherman, 2022, p. 22). Teacher certification programs in many states required passing a speech test, and her experience "aroused the fighting spirit" in her and encouraged her to enter the "language wars" (Smitherman, 2022, p. 22).

Several of the Black Diasporic authors and interviewees for this chapter similarly emphasized that their lived experiences surrounding Black language, identity, and culture led them to linguistics and related fields as places where they could embrace their positionality as Black scholars in their academic pursuits. In her interview, Gooden described her upbringing as a Jamaican Creole speaker. Both Creole and English were used in her school, and Gooden recalled her first exposure to language differences in elementary school:

> [My teacher] was doing what I now know is contrastive analysis, where he would ask a question, he would receive responses from his mostly Creole-speaking students in Creole. And then he would ask us, 'How would you say this in English?' And then he would . . . show us these differences.

Gooden noted that these insights were foundational to her career, which proceeded from the inherent validity of Creole languages: "[My] pursuit became about not validating the language in a linguistic sense, per se, but looking for theories that can tell me something about my language."

Meanwhile, for Black Diasporic scholars whose language was treated as deficient rather than different, challenging deficit perspectives was a central goal. As Baptista said in her interview, "I became a linguist because, later in life, I realized that Cape Verdean Creole, the language that I speak, was actually stigmatized." Although she was raised in France and attended French-speaking schools, Baptista said that "the language that I really could connect with, for me as a marker of identity, was Creole. When I first realized, in my early twenties, that actually the language was stigmatized, it made no sense to me." She went on to explain: "That's what brought me to linguistics, because I identified the field as providing me with some scientific tools that I could use to demonstrate to myself primarily, and to others, to a community, that the language that my parents spoke is a language like any other natural language." Linguistics provided Baptista with the tools to refute linguistic racism and marginalization and to honor her own and her family's linguistic experiences.

Shenika Hankerson likewise recalls moments when her language, African American Language (AAL), was stigmatized in educational settings. Hankerson was raised in Romulus, Michigan, and remembers 1985 through 1996 as being particularly traumatic years. During this time, she was taught by several teachers who used eradicationist language pedagogies in the classroom. These pedagogies prevented Hankerson from using AAL in speech and writing, and when she attempted to do so, she was penalized with lower grades and other sanctions. She also encountered similar harmful and unjust experiences during her college years. These lived experiences led Hankerson to her career in linguistics, with her research and scholarship focusing on topics such as dismantling anti-Black linguistic discrimination in language and writing pedagogy (Hankerson, 2017; 2020).

McQuitty, who grew up in North Carolina, explained that it was through her experience as a graduate student in Communication Sciences and Disorders at Southern Connecticut State University in New Haven that her passion and desire to be a change agent in the profession emerged. She recalls that in her first semester, many professors commented that her "Southern speech" was not compatible with providing speech and language services to clients in the clinic and even recommended that she enroll in a grammar course to learn to produce her vowels without a "Southern drawl," indicating their raciolinguistic biases and ideologies. Fortunately, because of her tenacity and assertiveness she utilized this feedback as a mechanism to maintain the authenticity of her speech and was supported by the department chair. Such experiences were very inspirational for McQuitty and shaped her desire to support and mentor future scholars in the discipline.

Clemons discussed how her family ties to linguistics for Black liberatory struggles made the field and its potential for social justice meaningful to her, and why these key motivations have kept her in linguistics. Clemons recalled that when she was growing up in Oakland, California, her grandmother was very involved in Stanford [University] and politics, and she worked with Stanford. Now I've come to find out my Stanford aunties were also linguists. I remember very clearly them fighting for the rights of African American Language, in what would lead up to the Oakland Ebonics debate of the 1990s.... They helped to start a school called the Nairobi School in East Palo Alto in California, which is, and was, the Black region [next to the Stanford campus]. Everything was done in English, Swahili, and French.... [It was an] educational space for kids to learn using their own languages and using other kinds of historically Black lingua francas.

Years later, in graduate school, Clemons realized that her "Stanford aunties" were linguists Faye McNair-Knox and Mary Hoover:

I was like, wait a minute, is this Auntie Faye? Is this Auntie Mary being cited in these books?... Having familial ties to linguistics is what keeps me doing it because I do see the liberatory values of linguistics . . . that linguistics can be used in order to argue for liberatory frames and for pedagogical frames that support Black students and their development and rail against the machine that is academic and "appropriate" language.

Charity Hudley also points to the liberatory potential of linguistics in shaping her career path. Her interest in linguistics began through a love of language, as she was fortunate to be able to study Geʿez in high school from a teacher who had a PhD in Semitic philology. That experience led her to a desire, as an undergraduate student, to document the language of Black people worldwide. This goal in turn led her to discover in graduate school, working with William Labov, how structural linguistic differences lead to challenges for African American students as they learn to read. This issue informed her transdisciplinary career pathway in linguistics, Black studies, English, and education and led her to investigate, as she explained in her interview, how the dynamics of language and culture impact "not just Black scholars in linguistics and related areas across their own careers, but also their own lives."

The direct engagement of Black linguists with research on Black language and culture, for the benefit of Black people and Black communities, contrasts with the often disembodied and detached linguistic approach that a predominantly white-oriented linguistics has set as the hegemonic frame of study. In Tracy Conner's (2021) interview with Baugh, he describes this fundamental intellectual difference and the educational injustice it leads to:

And not a lot of people know this, but my initial application [to the University of Pennsylvania] was rejected. The department chair said, "I'm so sorry, but you clearly have a very narrow interest," because I basically said, "I want to come study sociolinguistics with Labov. I'm a Black person. I'm interested in Black language, and he's the man." And they said, "Nope. We want somebody that's interested in the broad perspectives of the field. You know, we have Indo-European and we got this and that and we have Dell Hymes doing Native American languages. It's not enough to just want to study Black language with Labov. . . . And then Labov called me at home. And he said, "I'm so sorry that you got this letter of rejection." He said, "I did not know that that happened. I am still interested in working with you if you're still interested in the possibility of coming." (Conner, 2021, p. 464)

Likewise, when she applied to graduate school in linguistics, Charity Hudley only applied to the University of Pennsylvania to work with Labov because her desire to study Black language and culture was greater than her interest in other linguistics programs that would have tried to narrow her scope of study. As she notes elsewhere (Charity Hudley & Flores, 2022), this perspective continues to inform her work today:

It might be tempting to abandon linguistics completely and do critical work in other areas that encourage focusing our language research agendas on issues of power and oppression. But to not contend with linguistics means shutting this line of scholarship and inquiry out of the arts and sciences areas of the academy; in the US, that means keeping this teaching and research away from a great number of undergraduates and from the structurally situated conversations that being in arts and sciences provides researchers at all stages of education. (p. 146)

As these examples illustrate, our data reveal that the personal and professional desires that drive Black linguists' career choices are intertwined and are reflected in the research values that undergird their work. Taken together, these decisions and values set a comprehensive Black Diasporic research agenda based on direct commitment to supporting Black communities and Black scholars.

How Are Race and Diasporic Identity Visible in Linguistics?

Our disciplines, our institutions, and our scholarly traditions have not historically provided places and spaces for discussions of race, diaspora, identity, and colorism. Mary Bucholtz described how, when she began graduate school at the University of California, Berkeley, there was bias against the subfield of sociolinguistics, as well as against research on social topics such as gender and race: "If you said you were interested in sociolinguistics and certainly in gender, you know—that was the wrong kind of gender, you know. And, forget race! You couldn't say that." Bucholtz here alludes to the traditional disciplinary ideology that the only appropriate concept of gender in linguistics is grammatical gender, adding that studying race was not even conceivable in the field at the time. In response to that marginalization, Bucholtz recalls, "I stayed [in my graduate program] because I was so mad. I was like, 'Okay, you guys do everything possible to push me out the door. Fuck you. I'm staying.' It was really like a point of pride at that moment that kept me there." The Women in Berkeley Linguistics website (n.d.) now chronicles a number of such experiences of Bucholtz and other women-identified linguistics scholars over the years, along with the development of the Berkeley Women and Language Group that she and other graduate students coordinated and the groundbreaking research that was produced (e.g., Hall et al., 1992; Bucholtz et al.,1994; Warner et al., 1996; Wertheim et al., 1998).

Gooden, Baptista, Michel DeGraff, and Joy P. G. Peltier all described how they likewise experienced and confronted a lack of discussion about race when researching Creole linguistics. When Gooden attended the University of the West Indies, she was introduced to prominent Creole theorists Mervyn Alleyne, Silvia Kouwenberg, and Hubert Devonish and learned about Creole formation. As she recalled, the work of these scholars resonated deeply with her experiences as a Creole speaker, from her childhood to the college classroom. Nevertheless, she also remembered experiencing the common assertion in linguistics texts that "Creole languages have no morphology to speak of"—including the racist assertion that Creole languages "are similar to baby talk." Gooden described her response: "One of the first lines [of my dissertation] counters that. It starts with something like this: 'Creole languages have a rich morphological system.' Full stop." She went on to discuss the impact of her research:

> It challenges the field to deal with people saying that there's no morphology to speak of. And here I come—a newbie, saying that there's a rich morphological system. So, right there in the data, being able to challenge that, and to put that out in the work in a way that really decolonizes this idea. . . . The theory itself was not looking at the language but was looking, in kind of a colonial perspective, at the input languages . . . Perhaps some of the people who are looking at it this way are not necessarily coming from a bad place, but come from a place where you're not a native speaker of the variety, and also coming from a place of having been schooled through a particular way of thinking.

340 Decolonizing Linguistics

Building on the innovative work she carried out for her dissertation, Gooden went on to a robust research career that also explores the prosody of Caribbean Creole varieties and other aspects of cultural and linguistic diversity (e.g., Gooden, 2022; Gooden et al., 2020).

Similar pathways are seen in the careers of DeGraff and Baptista. Like Gooden's research, DeGraff's work has directly pushed back on the notions of "extreme simplicity" and "abnormal transmission" that have often been put forward in linguistics about Creole languages; he has also challenged central assumptions of linguistic theories that fallaciously position Creole languages as "exceptional" (DeGraff, 2005). Baptista, too, discussed in her interview the significance of being able to use data from Creole languages to "contrast that whole idea of simple language, to how complex those processes are when they emerge." For Baptista, it was important "to use Creole data to really challenge the theoretical assumptions out there. Because I think the idea is, how you're using your academic theories and how you have to dismantle colonization." Much of her work over her career has reflected these aims (e.g., Bancu, Peltier, et al., this volume; Baptista, 2021; Verdu et al., 2017). For Gooden, DeGraff, and Baptista, then, linguistics provided an understanding of the value of their own linguistic experiences, but also the impetus to critique the racist theories and concepts that they encountered in the discipline.

As a member of the next generation of Black linguists, Peltier is building on these scholars' groundbreaking contributions and moving the field in new, decolonizing directions. She noted that "discovering Creole linguistics—which was a journey that started when I took Marlyse [Baptista]'s language contact course as a grad student at [the University of Michigan]—sparked a profound sense of homecoming for me." Over time, she came to appreciate that decolonization is "as much an internal and personal process as it is a scholarly one. Plus, there's the structural side of things. Transforming how our disciplines and our institutions are designed and operate is something none of us can do singlehandedly, but we can each contribute to that process in our own way. All of those facets—personal, scholarly, structural—they build on one another." She started to research and learn her father's endangered Caribbean Creole, to reclaim her mother's African American English, and to confront how (post)colonial ideologies and attitudes surrounding language and Blackness have harmed her communities and her field. Peltier's anti-exceptionalist scholarship demonstrates the complexity and creativity of Creoles at the discourse-pragmatic level (Peltier, 2022; Peltier, forthcoming) and advocates for the equitable integration of these languages and their users into our work as linguists (cf. Bancu, Peltier, et al., this volume). As a new assistant professor, Peltier is also learning and researching what it is like to build a faculty life as a Black scholar in the language sciences.

Unlike Creole languages, Blackness in relation to world languages like Spanish and Portuguese is often overlooked. L. J. Randolph Jr. described in his interview how his focus on the Spanish language was shaped both by his positionality as a Black scholar and his interest in Black Spanish-speaking peoples and cultures. When he got to college, his coursework in culture and history introduced him to Afro-Cuban literature: "That's when I began to say, wow. I knew there was slavery in Mexico, for example, and I knew there were also formerly enslaved people in the United States who escaped to Mexico, but I just never made that connection that those communities were still there, still thriving." He went on to say:

> That's when I began to see myself in the curriculum, and I began to have these "aha" moments. It's not that my teachers, my professors, explicitly made the effort to do that. I did that on my own and through my own study of the language. And so I feel like that's really where my passion developed for Spanish, and I minored in Portuguese as well.

In her dissertation research on the intersectional experiences of Black current and former students in independent schools in New York City, Kahdeidra Martin (2021) found that students' lived experiences in Black Diasporic families and communities increased their motivation and sense of efficacy in language learning. In addition, they reported that linguistic variation aided their languaging competence. On being told by Spanish-dominant speakers that they had a "good accent," one participant named True observed:

> Like I was able to understand different things, and I feel like . . . the people in my building, but also my parents and the way that they speak, I'm just used to like people speaking different ways, so I feel like it's easier for my ear to pick up on it [snaps fingers] than others. (Martin, 2021, p. 140)

True credits speaking Vincentian Creole and African American Language with allowing them to notice and adapt features of the Puerto Rican and Dominican Spanishes widely used in New York City. True's experience correlates with those of other African Americans in world language education whose motivations and efforts are driven by a desire to understand and forge community with the Black Diasporic folks who live these languages (Austin, 2022b; Randolph & Johnson, 2017).

342 Decolonizing Linguistics

Clemons, who is transparent about her sociopolitical goal of coalition building around Black Diasporic experience, notes how this goal manifests in her study of Dominican Spanish. She comments:

> I work on Dominican Spanish, which is a Black language because it has a history of being in contact with other African languages, and has developed through Blackness as a diasporic kind of entity. I get asked the question, 'How can you call Dominican Spanish a Black language when clearly Dominicans of all races speak the language, and maybe more white Dominicans speak this variety in a particular area of the Dominican Republic than Black people?' And I'm like, well, if you really think about the history of the Dominican Republic since 1502, it's been a majority-Black republic, the first majority-Black republic in the Americas. So, if we reconfigure our understanding of culture as not created by the hegemonic or those who maintain power, but rather by the actual historical tools and multitudes of people, then it's not surprising that white people speak a Black language in this space.

Since colonial constructions of language and race are pervasive across academic and institutional contexts, a focus on Black Diasporic experience can lead to theoretical innovation whereby, as Clemons asserts, "reshaping our understanding of Blackness and of African Diaspora is literally reshaping the kind of ideologies we have about language and marginalized communities." She further explains that the goal is not simply to take existing categories and boundaries and rework them from a new starting point, but rather to "smash those boundaries to smithereens"—and she dedicates all her scholarship to dismantling the naturalized boundaries around language and race (Clemons, 2020; 2021; Clemons & Lawrence, 2020).

The experience of studying with other Black linguists was powerful for those who had such opportunities. For Charity Hudley, approaching her scholarship as a linguist from a Black Diasporic frame and working and learning professionally and personally with Black Diasporic linguists has enriched her work and her life. She recalled that Baptista was one of her first college professors, in a class that also included Dax Bayard, a Haitian student. Learning with these and other scholars, Charity Hudley said, has added to her own definition and lived experience of Blackness, broadening what scholarship related to Black language and culture can and should be about. As she tells her students, "I can't think of one African American who works on language (across disciplines) who worries about discipline boundaries the way that some white colleagues do. Not one." This contrast in mission summarizes the scope of the enterprise between Black and white linguists. This difference surrounding why people get involved in higher education at all has been well documented by scholars including Orlando Taylor, a speech and hearing scientist and university administrator, who said the following as a member of the Imagining Tenure committee of Imagining America, a consortium of scholars and artists in public life:

> More often than not, it is a minority scholar or the woman who tends to have more of this social idealism that leads them to want to engage in this kind of work. . . . But those who hold power in academia more often than not . . . don't value engagement, don't value civic responsibility, and therefore you have this tension where you're getting more women and people of color on the faculty, but the gatekeepers . . . [are] from another generation. And so . . . these persons may be set up for disappointments. (Taylor, quoted in Ellison & Eatman, 2008, p. 18)

This account is confirmed by young Black scholars, including Clemons, who states clearly:

> I have a desire to be an administrator to wreck things up. Like, it is very different than somebody who has a desire to be an administrator solely to represent the current power structure. Institutions often fail people, and that is cross-cultural and cross-linguistic, and if you really care about people you have to become administration to work for them. If I, being from where I am from, can get into this space and give people the ability to do the work that I know needs to be done for as long as they allow me to do it, then I will do it, even though I probably wouldn't attempt it until I achieve full [professor status].

Thinking of the desire of Black scholars like Clemons to shape the university into a safe and productive space, Taylor issues a challenge to university leaders: "I'd like to see boards of trustees or governing boards of institutions, academic senates, chief academic officers build new systems of reward and evaluation of faculty, such that this kind of work is safe" (Ellison & Eatman, 2008, p. 18).

As demonstrated by these scholars' accounts, their academic interests and their research, informed by their own lived experiences, begins from the premise that Black scholars have particular insight into Black Diasporic languages and that centering Blackness is therefore crucial for an inclusive, anti-colonial linguistics. They have worked from that starting point to address linguistic bias and racism, challenge linguistic theory, and advance understanding of AAL, Creole, and other Black Diasporic languages. They show that the validation of Black language practices does not come from academic

344 Decolonizing Linguistics

research, but rather from the lived experiences of those who use Black language and participate in Black culture—Black Diasporic linguists *been* known that!

How Is Decolonization Happening in Linguistic Research, Teaching, Practice, and Advocacy?

The scholars that were interviewed for this chapter identified multiple pathways for decolonizing linguistics, broadly defined—epistemologically, methodologically, pedagogically, and institutionally. In her work Clemons has directly challenged the epistemological and methodological traditions of linguistics, noting that the very idea of what counts as linguistic work is tangled up with colonial ideologies. She states, "I think about the way colonization comes with creating systems and norms that privilege a particular kind of scholar, a particular kind of research, a particular kind of science." And while some subdisciplines, such as sociolinguistics, have sometimes challenged epistemological traditions in the field of linguistics, these traditions still constrain how linguists can study topics such as race. Clemons observes, for example, that traditional variationist sociolinguistic studies that quantitatively analyze an established set of features are predicated on an essentialist, binary conceptualization and treatment of race and other social identity categories in ways that do not capture the lived realities and the complexities of social experience, particularly for marginalized groups. Furthermore, she notes that ideas about how research is conducted are shaped by harmful methodological practices that are often passed on through training. In linguistics, scholars from hegemonic groups are often trained to center the "other," focusing on marginalized languages and communities. This practice, which Clemons describes as "going into communities they do not belong to, taking data from communities to write descriptive books of how this language system works and is different from the standard language," results in the production of research that has little if any commitment to language users and their communities and ultimately has limited impact on how the community is able to navigate the social marginalization that often accompanies colonial power hierarchies.

Clemons (this volume) relies on her praxis of political transparency to describe the ways that she decolonizes her research process: "One of the ways . . . is by arguing for and getting support for the treatment of community members as experts of their own language, and seeing my own work as just an extension of other people's understandings of their own language, of themselves, of their identity." Ultimately, Clemons suggests the need for a shift in the power dynamic of researcher and participant through direct engagement and financial compensation. In this way, community members who have been traditionally positioned as subjects and participants are now moved into collaborator positions, which Clemons explains changes the entire research process. She asks, "What kinds of questions do we want to ask about how these communities have been positioned in society based on their language practices? And then which methodologies can we use to analyze those things?"

Study participants also emphasized the need for decolonization through pedagogical practices, including curriculum and instruction. In an interview with Clemons, Randolph discussed how learning about Black Latin Americans and Afro-Latinx communities directly impacted his anticolonial and antiracist praxis in his Spanish teaching:

I wanted to say, "Okay, how can I be as anticolonial-slash-antiracist as possible?" And so I said, "Every resource that I use is going to be from someone from an underrepresented or minoritized identity." And so that's what the whole class was about. So it was like, there were no straight white dudes in any of the sources that we looked at, or the ways that we saw that people use languages, the themes of our conversations, and I got a lot of pushback from some students who thought that I was trying to promote a certain agenda just by being inclusive. They view that as trying to promote a certain agenda. And I'm thinking to myself, "How many classes have you gone through where all you did was look at white authors and you never thought, 'Oh, what type of agenda are you trying to push here? All the people are white men'?" you know. Like, you would never think that.

Randolph then notes the immediate impact of his teaching strategies on Black students in his class and connects his pedagogical praxis to the larger need for more diverse faculty with a more diverse range of experience within the academy:

I remember there was one Black student in that class. He was a Black man and he came up to me at the end of the class and he also put this in his evaluation, which was anonymous, but I could tell who wrote it because he was the only Black person in the class, and he said, "You know, this is the first time that I saw Blackness centered in the class when it wasn't like a special unit or something like that, like the Black History unit." And he just talked about how strange that was and just how it really changed his perception of what Spanish can be and what Spanish meant and how engaged he felt in the classroom.

Decolonizing and culturally sustaining pedagogies that integrate theory and praxis have also been at the core of Martin's work as a K-12 teacher educator and instructor of first-year composition at a range of colleges and universities. For her, multimodal instruction is central to countering hegemonic linguistic norms and creating multiple access points for neurodiverse learners. In addition, culturally sustaining pedagogy that centers the knowledges of racialized people and disrupts interlocking systems of domination is important for learners of all ages. Martin and her coauthors (2019) call for a critical translanguaging pedagogy in bilingual education programs that not only encourages flexible, dynamic language use but also expressly nurtures the critical consciousness of youth. The authors state:

> Teaching students about structural and historical inequalities is critical to countering internalized oppression and raciolinguistic ideologies. Bilingual programs and multicultural pedagogy that ignore the historical legacies of racism, linguicism, and classism are not transformative at all. Instead, they participate in narratives that blame marginalized communities for their own oppression and rescind responsibility from institutions and society. (Martin et al., 2019, p. 32)

Building on her own experiences teaching multilingual Black Diasporic students in first-year writing courses as well as the work of translanguaging scholars in bilingual and English language arts education, Martin (forthcoming) reflects on "pedagogies of listening" and proposes a raciolinguistic literacy framework that centers racialization processes through all aspects of lesson design, takes a local and global approach to authentic languaging practices, and incorporates raciolinguistic literacy methods that are critically conscious and racially literate in the content, process, and products of lesson design.

Baptista also asserted the need to push back against the ways colonialist ideologies and practices have become concretized in linguistics departments. As she described, departmental and institutional expectations and requirements perpetuate "the idea that this is not what they consider linguistic work. This is not what they consider scholarly work." Decolonizing academic research, as Baptista explained, means reconfiguring priorities and values:

> Actually working with a community, what is more important than that? And trying to convey what your findings are to the community. That's how I feel I'm using my career, to dismantle colonization from that perspective and also bring in more community members and speakers into the field, in academia, or other areas that they want to be.

In a similar vein, Randolph described the process he takes in his Spanish courses:

> One way that I try to dismantle colonization is to take an unapologetically, intentionally antiracist, anticolonial approach to my teaching. In my syllabus, I tell my students that my courses are going to be different from Spanish courses that you had in the past, because we're going to focus on voices that have traditionally been marginalized, and even oppressed. . . . I try to let my students know this is what Spanish is like. This is how different communities experience Spanish.

Gooden similarly remarked that a strategy she has used to decolonize the curriculum is "being able to advocate for and put courses on the books that people would not have necessarily thought of adding, and therefore exposing the whole generation of future scholars to new topics and new ways of thinking."

Taking a broader view of the role of linguistics beyond the academy, DeGraff emphasized the need for linguists to examine and improve the ways that national and international organizations approach language and education in the context of work on human rights and economic development. He highlighted the disconnect between his own recognition that Creoles are perfectly normal languages and the United Nations Educational, Scientific and Cultural Organization (UNESCO) view of Creoles as outside the category of "language" proper, which complicates the organization's professed dedication to cultural diversity and language preservation (DeGraff, 2005; 2020). As he commented:

> The devalorization of Creole languages at UNESCO seems a direct reflection of Creole Exceptionalism dogma in linguistics textbooks. Yes, UNESCO's questionnaire for their World Languages Atlas put Creole languages in a category other than "language," on the grounds that, since Creoles come from Pidgins (a much debated hypothesis now), they don't belong to any "family"—which, then, puts Creole languages outside of the "language" category! Such devalorization goes counter to UNESCO's stated mission toward the valorization of *all* languages and cultures. This devalorization also has an on-the-ground aspect to it, as evidenced by the fact that the UNESCO's field offices in the Global South rarely use the corresponding local languages, including Creole languages as in Haiti, in their formal proceedings there, even as the same UNESCO engages local ministries of education in the production of resources in the local languages.

DeGraff noted that he has raised similar concerns about linguistic devalorization in other arms of the United Nations as well (see, e.g., DeGraff, 2019).

348 Decolonizing Linguistics

The need for continuing advocacy by linguists for decolonized and inclusive approaches to Black languages remains critical. One way to address these issues is by increasing the numbers of Black students and educators in the study of languages and linguistics, a feat that has proven difficult due to the historic conditions of Black exclusion in educational spaces. These historical conditions have led Randolph, a board member of the American Council on the Teaching of Foreign Languages, the largest world language studies organization, to assert that diversity and inclusion are primary goals of the organization (see ACTFL, 2019).

These efforts are similar to Rickford's and Smitherman's accounts of their efforts to keep Black Studies programs alive and well at their respective institutions. Both scholars made sure that their linguistic work thrived in spaces where Black people could themselves thrive, thereby serving as academic models for new generations of Black scholars at their universities. Today, for example, Baker-Bell, following in the tradition of Smitherman, holds a joint appointment in the Department of English and the Department of African American and African Studies at Michigan State University. In their interviews, Mallinson and Kara Seidel both reflected on how Rickford's and Smitherman's program-building efforts have been instrumental in laying the groundwork for the growth of interdisciplinary departments, especially those that include language and culture as a focus. Mallinson and Seidel's home department at the University of Maryland, Baltimore County (UMBC), the Language, Literacy & Culture (LLC) Program, supports large numbers of students of color and other students from backgrounds that are traditionally marginalized and underrepresented in academia. As Mallinson commented, "Most of my students are engaged in the study and pursuit of Black linguistic and educational liberation—a pathway that follows in the tradition of, and really that was made possible by, Black scholars such as John Rickford and Geneva Smitherman."

Seidel added her own perspective on the value of learning about language from interdisciplinary frameworks that draw from Africana Studies, Education, English, Gender and Women's Studies, Modern Languages and Linguistics, Media and Communications Studies, Sociology, and other related fields and disciplines: "Interdisciplinarity is crucial to understanding the ways that anti-Blackness is rooted within and between fields. It would be both irresponsible and impossible to do any of this linguistic work without the knowledge I gain as an LLC student."

The white allies who participated in this study discussed their role as white scholars in pushing back against racist, colonizing institutional practices.

Mallinson reflected on how, when she began her tenure-track job in 2006, she advocated that her program work toward greater equity and inclusion in its graduate admissions process by eliminating the Graduate Record Exam (GRE) standardized testing requirement: "As soon as I began serving on our admissions committee, it was important to me that our department immediately do away with requiring or even considering GRE scores as a basis for graduate admission." Mallinson's advocacy on this effort led to her participation, during the #BlackLivesMatter movement and the COVID-19 pandemic, in a task force to eliminate the GRE requirement in graduate admissions at UMBC university-wide (Hunt, 2023), an effort that is ongoing.

An additional anonymous participant, a white linguistics professor at a large research university in the Midwestern US, described having worked "to have target-of-opportunity hires when I was a department head, although we weren't successful, and advocated for people [of color] for tenure and promotion." At every stage, this professor recalled, there was pushback by faculty members in the department. Throughout this process, they added, "you really do see how conservative mindsets are part of the academy because the academy is so nondiverse." These mindsets accumulate over time and are revealed in

> how we define what is best versus when we critique. And critiques are harsher for people of color, and women of color in particular. And so, I've just tried to create those spaces . . . to bring those voices with me, to bring those voices into rooms, really trying to bring diverse people into the academy.

Bucholtz reflected on similar challenges in decolonizing and antiracist efforts within academic institutions: "For me, it has been a very stark recognition . . . that there's really no place that we can stand outside of the colonial legacy of academia, [including] now the neoliberal capitalist model of the academy." As a result, she described her process of "grappling with how can I, as a white scholar, try to undo white supremacy?" One important piece of the process for Bucholtz is interrogating how diversity and inclusion efforts unfold at universities:

> [For example], there are huge, profound questions about for whose benefit am I recruiting Black students to this institution? You can't *not* do it. You just have to do it in a much more careful and mindful way, and also acknowledge that you're always going to be morally compromised when you're working within the confines of the academy.

350 Decolonizing Linguistics

In the published interview (Conner, 2021), Baugh also addresses the need for and obligation of white allyship. In response to the question, "What is the present responsibility of white linguists in the fight for linguistic justice or justice more broadly?" Baugh answered:

> I think it's huge, and I am frustrated that many now sidestep these matters for fear of being judged negatively. Far too often I have been told, "Oh, as a white person I probably should not weigh in on that." Such philosophies add another burden to Black and brown scholars. We need allies on all fronts, of every kind. If you're not part of the solution, you're part of the problem. (p. 13)

Recommendations for Solidarity and Collective Action toward Decolonizing Linguistics

As Rickford (2022) asserts:

> In the case of speakers of Black Talk, the need for positive interventions is especially great, because black people face discrimination in almost every area of life—when encountering police and courts, applying for jobs and apartments, seeking health care or education, and more. In almost every case, the discrimination is worse when those black people speak Black Talk. (p. 101)

Racial justice for Black people requires linguistic justice. This goal requires a thoroughgoing decolonization of linguistics, which requires a broadening of (unmarked) linguistics to centrally include sociolinguistics, applied linguistics, speech and hearing sciences, literacy studies, education, and other fields grounded in language users' richly contextualized experiences. This goal also requires solidarity and collective action. The scholars whose insights are featured in this chapter shared multiple recommendations for how to come together, as Black Diasporic scholars and as allies, to advance the mission of decolonizing linguistics, writ large.

The first recommendation is to expand the pathways to increase the equitable inclusion of Black Diasporic scholars in linguistics, across institutions of higher education, and throughout academia. This recommendation has been made for years by a number of scholars. Charity Hudley and colleagues (2020) discuss numerous opportunities for making linguistics a more equitable and inclusive place, including revamping undergraduate and graduate curricula; redefining excellence in admissions, hiring, and promotion decisions; expanding notions of what counts as linguistics and what counts as research, and more. There is also a need for institutions and departments to reward the types of academic service that strengthen their ability to be inclusive. These recommendations are underscored by Thomas and Bucholtz (2021) in light of two pandemics of epic proportions, COVID-19 and anti-Blackness, which disproportionately harm "academia's essential workers" (p. 290). Research, teaching, and service efforts that center educational justice and disrupt colonialist power structures and white supremacy are often devalued in the academy. Such undervalued and often invisible academic labor is disproportionately allocated to and shouldered by women and faculty of color—the essential workers that institutions rely on (Reid, 2021; Social Sciences Feminist Network Research Interest Group, 2017; Trejo, 2020). It is therefore essential that those who hold institutional power be held accountable for how to use a substantive leadership role to eradicate institutional anti-Blackness.

As our anonymous study participant emphasized in their interview, taking steps toward disruption and liberation in academia

> really hit[s] the power centers—the deans, the chairs, the provosts. The junior faculty or the grad students who these topics really speak to the most just don't have power in the system. The people who have the power are the people who hire, and the people who [make decisions about] tenure and promotion.

Accordingly, this scholar suggested, there is a need for inclusive workshops on tenure and promotion specifically for deans and department chairs, as well as workshops for faculty on how to write effective and equitable letters for tenure and promotion cases. Advocacy for greater equity and inclusion is also needed in how funding agencies and scholarly journals operate and distribute opportunity—a task that also requires educating program officers, editors and editorial board members, and reviewers, as our anonymous interviewee explained:

> If people don't even think something is intellectually valid, then they're not going to give it a high score [when reviewing a grant proposal]. They've already decided it's not intellectually valid, because it doesn't occur to them that there are various ways of doing science, and that as we diversify science, in fact, we ask different questions, questions that maybe weren't even asked or even thought of as a question in the mainstream. Also doing this for journal reviewers as well. . . . So, really thinking in terms of the power structures, but also in terms of our scholars who are moving in all these trajectories—how do I incorporate the system to beat the system?

352 Decolonizing Linguistics

The second recommendation for advancing decolonization in linguistics put forward by the scholars in this chapter is to continue to center Black Diasporic and other minoritized languages and language varieties in educational spaces. Baptista highlighted the critical need to include language in all its diversity when teaching linguistics:

> I think it's all about the classroom. It's all in the classroom. I think this is where the battlefield is. When I look at Diasporic communities, and the new language varieties and identities, cultural norms, how they change, and how the language is so much part of Diasporic communities' identity, I think it's so important to represent it in the classroom.

She further reflected, "There is nothing more satisfying when I look back at my work, actually nothing more important these days, than putting the language in the classroom." One thing we can all do, "wherever we are," she says, is to keep advancing inclusive linguistic representation in education. Such action plans reverberate in the contributions throughout this volume and its companion volume, *Inclusion in Linguistics* (Charity Hudley et al. 2024).

As Baptista's comment indicates, a key part of centering Black language in education is visible representation of Black people. Gooden recalled the significance of having experienced "other Black professionals being comfortable in their own skin, in their own spaces, and using their language in spaces where they were not supposed to be used," from elementary school classrooms to higher education spaces. She recalled the joy of hearing Creole-speaking educators, ranging from her primary school teacher, who used Creole in the classroom despite the fact that the Jamaican Minister of Education had banned it, to her undergraduate and graduate professors, such as Devonish and Don Winford, who codeswitched in classes, office hours, meetings, and public lectures. Referring to Devonish, Gooden noted, "Here was somebody who was a Black professional linguist, well-published, head of a department and was comfortable in his own language in his own space." Referring to Winford, Gooden also recalled, "He would codeswitch in office hours with me, and I was comfortable. . . . I was made comfortable in my own space." As a result, she says, "now, I will codeswitch when I'm giving [linguistic] examples. And the conferences that I tend to go to are with people who are like-minded." These educators' efforts to deliberately make space to show up as their full selves in educational spaces was inspiring for Gooden, who now pays that forward to her own students and colleagues. Clemons similarly commented on how she interrogates and defies notions of professionalism and appropriateness in languaging practices:

A Black Diasporic Perspective   **353**

> I don't think I do an academic talk without integrating some sort of Black language into it—at a certain point, very clearly saying out loud and transparently that this is what I'm doing, and I don't really care what you say. If you need help understanding me, it's not because I don't know how to do it, but because you're not capable of understanding what I'm saying. . . . I'm really thankful that though I don't necessarily have the power of tenure or being senior in my field, I do have the power of other researchers who have given me the kind of tools to be able to talk back to whatever these arguments are that push us constantly towards "appropriateness" and academic language.

The third recommendation put forward by the scholars in this chapter is to continue to decolonize research in linguistics, broadly defined, through community-centered approaches. Gooden explained that valuing community-oriented work is a major part of the process of decolonizing academia, as this type of research holds great potential for centering the voices of minoritized communities and scholars: "So, we talk about what is linguistics and what is not linguistics. Who gets to decide that? [We need to be] validating that work, validating engagement with the communities . . . valuing community-engaged scholarship." Some institutions value community-centered work already or are willing to do so, Gooden notes, but many others are not. For decolonization as well as just and equitable inclusion efforts to be fully realized, community-centered research must be part of the equation, because for many Black linguists, she says, "engagement with our communities is a big part of how we're able to sustain our scholarship."

We likewise need to encourage and reward research in the community of linguists—that is, person-centered work—that engages the histories, subjectivities, and positionalities of scholars. As David Crystal (2009) and Rickford (2022) both note, memoirs and autobiographies are rare in linguistics and related fields—which limits the visibility of the interconnectedness between who scholars are, the scholarship that they produce, how it unfolds, how it is received, and how it influences the discipline. Autobiographical works and memoirs, like the narrative accounts featured in this chapter, can provide a platform for critical engagement with these issues (cf. Thomas, 2023).

The fourth recommendation is to continue to build communities of Black Diasporic scholars and allies. As Charity Hudley commented:

> We see this [chapter] as an invitation for collaboration among Black scholars of language and decolonization across the Diaspora. How can we formally come together outside of this volume? In order to have the possibilities for future collaboration,

354 Decolonizing Linguistics

we have to know that these pathways and spaces exist—and create them where they don't yet exist.

Critical sites for convening scholars of Black Diasporic and minoritized languages to share research regarding African and Creole languages include conferences such as the Associação de Crioulos de Base Lexical Portuguesa e Espanhola/Asociación de Criollos de Base Léxica Portuguesa y Española/ Association of Portuguese- and Spanish-Lexified Creoles, Colloque International des Études Créoles (Comité International des Études Créoles), Formal Approaches to Creole Studies, the Society for Caribbean Linguistics, and the Society for Pidgin and Creole Linguistics, as well as institutes such as the African Linguistics School (n.d.) and CoLang (n.d.), workshops (e.g., Kandybowicz & Torrence, 2014–2015), and initiatives such as the Massachusetts Institute of Technology-Haiti Initiative (n.d.). The UCSB-HBCU Scholars in Linguistics program discussed earlier also offers a model of academic exchange that exposed students to different historical, theoretical, and disciplinary traditions of studying Black languages. Opportunities to share, collaborate, and review through publication venues that center Black languages and/or are based in the Global South are likewise important to support. These include the forthcoming inaugural issue of a new applied linguistics journal launched by scholars at the University of Dar es Salaam in Tanzania, *Africa Journal of Second Language Studies (AJSLS)*. Other journals that expand the inclusiveness of linguistics are under discussion or in the works.

Because of the high cost of travel and other structural obstacles, in-person gatherings often exclude minoritized scholars and students, particularly from the Global South (see also Hou & Ali, 2024). Due to the COVID-19 pandemic, virtual and hybrid meeting options have greatly increased, which improves accessibility and functionality for convening scholars from around the world; these events also often include repositories for Open Access materials. Examples include the Abralin au Vivo—Linguists Online series (Abralin, 2020) and the Second Annual Advancing African American Linguist(ic) s Symposium (Bucholtz et al., 2020). There is a need to continue to develop these spaces to further promote collaborations among Black Diaspora scholars, and, as Bucholtz commented, the opportunity for impact is great:

> Things like social media and the ability to use Zoom—that's like the only silver lining of the COVID-19 pandemic, as people have realized. There are ways we can connect, there are national and international communities we can build that can transcend the institution, and frankly, that are so much more powerful than the

institution. That kind of genuine community-grounded activism, that's the only thing that's going to change the academy.

In closing, we turn to the words of Rickford: "Love is not love if it does nothing to enhance the lives of those we love, or the community members who speak the languages we love" (Rickford, 2022, p. 103). Solidarity and collectivity must be grounded in decolonization, in enacting ways of doing linguistics that make the Black Diaspora more real and more whole. That is the stuff of Black power and Black love, and, working together, Black linguists and their allies can lead the way.

Note

1. We would like to thank our interviewees for their participation in this project, as well as John Rickford, John Baugh, and Geneva Smitherman for their substantive contributions and candid memoirs. We are immensely grateful for the support of the National Science Foundation. This material is based upon work supported by the NSF Build and Broaden Program, Awards #SMA-2126414 and 2126405, "Linguistic Production, Perception, and Identity in the Career Mobility of Black Faculty in Linguistics and the Language Sciences." We also gratefully acknowledge the support of UMBC and for Stanford University's support of Anne Charity Hudley's Black Academic Lab, https://badlab.stanford.edu/. Finally, we thank our Build and Broaden research scholars network, who continue to advance critical work in pursuit of Black linguistic liberation.

References

Abralin. (2020). Abralin ao Vivo. Linguists online series. https://www.abralin.org/site/en/evento/abralin-ao-vivo-2020/

ACTFL. (2019, May 16). *Diversity and Inclusion in World Language Teaching & Learning.* https://www.actfl.org/news/diversity-and-inclusion-in-world-language-teaching-learning

African Linguistics School. (n.d.). https://sites.google.com/site/africanlingschool/

American Speech-Language-Hearing Association (ASHA). (2021). Annual demographic & employment data: 2021 member & affiliates profiles. https://www.asha.org/siteassets/surveys/2021-member-affiliate-profile.pdf

Austin, Tasha. (2022a). Linguistic imperialism: Countering anti Black racism in world language teacher preparation. *Journal for Multicultural Education, 16*(3), 246–258. https://doi.org/10.1108/JME-12-2021-0234

Austin, Tasha. (2022b). *Race, language and ideology in an urban teacher preparation program* [Doctoral dissertation, Rutgers University].

Baker-Bell, April. (2020a). Dismantling anti-Black linguistic racism in English language arts classrooms: Toward an anti-racist Black language pedagogy. *Theory Into Practice, 59*(1), 8–21. https://doi.org/10.1080/00405841.2019.1665415

356 Decolonizing Linguistics

Baker-Bell, April. (2020b). *Linguistic justice: Black language, literacy, identity, and pedagogy.* Routledge.

Baptista, Marlyse. (2021). Dynamics of language contact: On similarities, divergences, and innovations in the emergence of Creole language. In Anna M. Babel & Mark A. Sicoli (Eds.), *Contact, structure, and change: A Festschrift in honor of Sarah G. Thomason* (pp. 65–96). Maize Books.

Baugh, John. (2022). Equality matters. *Sage Perspectives.* https://perspectivesblog.sagepub.com/blog/research/equality-smatters

Black, Lindsey I., Vahratian, Anjel, & Hoffman, Howard J. (2015). Communication disorders and use of intervention services among children aged 3–17 years: United States, 2012. *NCHS Data Brief*, (205), 1–8.

Bucholtz, Mary, Charity Hudley, Anne H., & Conner, Tracy. (2020). The Second Annual Advancing African American Linguist(ic)s Symposium, August 7-8, 2020. NSF REU site: Increasing diversity in the linguistic sciences through research on language and social mobility.

Bucholtz, Mary, Liang, A. C., Sutton Laurel A., & Hines, Caitlin. (1994). *Cultural performances: Proceedings of the third Berkeley Women and Language Conference.* Berkeley Women and Language Group.

Calhoun, Kendra N. (2021). *Competing discourses of diversity and inclusion: Institutional rhetoric and graduate student narratives at two minority serving institutions* [Doctoral dissertation, University of California, Santa Barbara].

Calhoun, Kendra, Charity Hudley, Anne H., Bucholtz, Mary, Exford, Jazmine, & Johnson, Brittney. (2021). Attracting Black students to linguistics through a Black-centered introduction to linguistics course. *Language, 97*(1), e12–e38. https://doi.org/10.1353/lan.2021.0007

Charity Hudley, Anne H., & Bucholtz, Mary. (2017). *REU Site: Increasing diversity in the linguistic sciences through research on language and social mobility.* National Science Foundation. https://www.nsf.gov/awardsearch/showAward?AWD_ID=1757654

Charity Hudley, Anne H., & Flores, Nelson. (2022). Social justice in applied linguistics: Not a conclusion, but a way forward. *Annual Review of Applied Linguistics, 42*, 144–154. https://doi.org/10.1017/S0267190522000083

Charity Hudley, Anne H., Mallinson, Christine, & Bucholtz, Mary. (2020). Toward racial justice in linguistics: Interdisciplinary insights into theorizing race in the discipline and diversifying the profession. *Language, 96*(4), e200–e235. https://doi.org/10.1353/lan.2020.0074

Charity Hudley, Anne H., Mallinson, Christine, & Bucholtz, Mary. (2022). *Talking college: Making space for Black language practices in higher education.* Teachers College Press.

Charity Hudley, Anne H., Mallinson, Christine, & Bucholtz, Mary (Eds.). (2024). *Inclusion in linguistics.* Oxford University Press.

Clemons, Aris, & Lawrence, Anna. (2020). Beyond position statements on race: Fostering an ethos of antiracist scholarship in linguistic research (response to Charity Hudley et al.). *Language, 96*(4), e254–e267. https://doi.org/10.1353/lan.2020.0077

Clemons, Aris. (2020). New Blacks: Language, DNA, and the construction of the African American/Dominican boundary of difference. *Genealogy, 5*(1), 1. https://doi.org/10.3390/genealogy5010001

Clemons, Aris. (2021). *Spanish people be like: Dominican ethno-raciolinguistic stancetaking and the construction of Black Latinidades in the United States.* [Doctoral dissertation, University of Texas at Austin].

CoLang. (n.d.) *The Institute on Collaborative Language Research.* Linguistic Society of America. https://www.linguisticsociety.org/content/colang-institute-collaborative-research

Cooper, Lisa A., Roter, Debra L., Johnson, Rachel L., Ford, Daniel E., Steinwachs, Donald M., & Powe, Neil R. (2003). Patient-centered communication, ratings of care, and concordance of patient and physician race. *Annals of Internal Medicine, 139*(11), 907–915. https://doi. org/ 10.7326/0003-4819-139-11-200312020-00009

Conner, Tracy. (2021). Interview with John Baugh. *Journal of English Linguistics, 49*(4), 459–474. https://doi.org/10.1177/00754242211047891

Crystal, David. (2009). *Just a phrase I'm going through: My life in language.* Routledge.

DeGraff, Michel. (2005). Linguists' most dangerous myth: The fallacy of Creole exceptionalism. *Language in Society, 34*(4), 533–591. https://doi.org/10.1017/s0047404505050207

DeGraff, Michel. (2019). Against apartheid in education and in linguistics: The case of Haitian Creole in neo-colonial Haiti. In Donaldo Macedo (Ed.), *Decolonizing foreign language education: The misteaching of English and other colonial languages* (pp. ix–xxxiii). Routledge.

DeGraff, Michel. (2020). Toward racial justice in linguistics: The case of Creole studies (response to Charity Hudley et al.). *Language, 96*(4), e292–e306. https://doi.org/10.1353/lan.2020.0080

Ellison, Julie, & Timothy Eatman. (2008). *Scholarship in public: Knowledge creation and tenure policy in the engaged university.* Imagining America.

Franz, Hannah, et al. 2022. "The Role of the Graduate Student in Inclusive Undergraduate Research Experiences." *Pedagogy*, vol. 22(1), p. 121–141. https://doi.org/10.1215/15314200-9385522

Frieson, Brittany L. (2022). Remixin' and flowin' in centros: Exploring the biliteracy practices of Black language speakers in an elementary two-way immersion bilingual program. *Race, Ethnicity, and Education, 25*(4), 585–605. https://doi.org/10.1080/13613324.2021.1890568

Gilyard, Keith. (1991). *Voices of the self: A study of language competence.* Wayne State University Press.

Gooden, Shelome, Soudi, Abdesalam, Park, Karen, & Kinloch, Valerie. (2020). Cultural and linguistic diversity: A multifaceted approach. In Audrey J. Murrell, Jennifer L. Petrie, & Abdesalam Soudi (Eds.), *Diversity across disciplines: Research on people, policy, process and paradigm* (pp. 131–144). Information Age Publishing.

Gooden, Shelome. (2022). Intonation and prosody in Creole languages: An evolving ecology. *Annual Review of Linguistics, 8*(1), 343–364. http://dx.doi.org/10.1146/annurev-linguistics-031120-124320

Gray, J. D. (2022, May 12). ASHA voices: HBCU leaders share strategies for recruiting and retaining underrepresented students in CSD. ASHAWire. https://leader.pubs.asha.org/do/10.1044/2022-0512-podcast-diversity-higher-ed/full/

Hall, Kira, Bucholtz, Mary, & Moonwomon, Birch. (1992). *Locating power: Proceedings of the Second Berkeley Women and Language Conference.* Berkeley Women and Language Group.

Hankerson, Shenika. (2017). Black voices matter. *Language Arts Journal of Michigan, 32*(2), 34–39. https://doi.org/10.9707/2168-149x.2160

Hankerson, Shenika. (2020). Response: "I love my African American language. And yours.": Toward a raciolinguistic vision in writing studies. In Norbert Elliot & Alice S. Horning (Eds.), *Talking back: Senior scholars deliberate the past, present, and future of writing studies* (pp. 321–325). Utah State University Press.

Hou, Lynn, & Ali, Kristian. (2024). Critically examining inclusion and parity for deaf Global South researchers of colour in the field of sign language linguistics. In Anne H. Charity Hudley, Christine Mallinson, & Mary Bucholtz (Eds.), *Inclusion in linguistics.* Oxford University Press.

Hunt, Michael A. (2023). Be a gate opener, not a gatekeeper. Inside Higher Ed. https://www.insidehighered.com/views/2023/02/21/mentors-should-be-gate-openers-not-gatekeepers-opinion

Ibrahim, Awad. (1999). Becoming Black: Rap and hip hop, race, gender, identity and the politics of ESL learning. *TESOL Quarterly, 33*(3), 349–369. https://doi.org/10.2307/3587669

Ibrahim, Awad. (2008). Operating under erasure: ~~Race~~/Language/Identity. *Comparative and International Education, 37*(2), 56–76. https://doi.org/10.5206/cie-eci.v37i2.9119

Kandybowicz, Jason, & Torrence, Harold. (2014–2015). Africa's endangered languages: Documentary and theoretical approaches (National Science Foundation Awards #1360823). https://www.nsf.gov/awardsearch/showAward?AWD_ID=1360823&HistoricalAwards=false

Kinloch, Valerie. (2010). *Harlem on our minds: Place, race, and the literacies of urban youth.* Teachers College Press.

Kinloch, Valerie (Ed.). (2011). *Urban literacies: Critical perspectives on language, learning, and community.* Teachers College Press.

Kirkland, David E. (2011). Books like clothes: Engaging young Black men with reading. *Journal of Adolescent & Adult Literacy, 55*(3), 199–208. https://doi.org/10.1002/jaal.00025

Kirkland, David E. (2013). *A search past silence: The literacy of young Black men.* Teachers College Press.

Lanehart, Sonja L. (2002). *Sista, speak! Black women kinfolk talk about language and literacy.* University of Texas Press.

Lanehart, Sonja L. (Ed.). (2009). *African American women's language: Discourse, education, and identity.* Cambridge Scholars Publishing.

Lanehart, Sonja. L. (2017). Re-viewing the origins and history of African American language. *The History of English, 5,* 80–95.

Lanehart, Sonja L., & Malik, Ayesha M. (2018). Black is, Black isn't: Perceptions of language and Blackness. In Jeffrey Reaser, Eric Willbanks, Karissa Wojcik, & Walt Wolfram (Eds.), *Language variety in the New South: Contemporary perspectives on change and variation* (pp. 203–222). University of North Carolina Press.

Ledgerwood, Alison, Pickett, Cynthia, Navarro, Danielle, Remedios, Jessica D., & Lewis Jr., Neil A. (2022). The unbearable limitations of solo science: Team science as a path for more rigorous and relevant research. *Behavioral and Brain Sciences, 45,* e81. https://doi.org/10.1017/s0140525x21000844

Linguistic Society of America. (2019). *Presidents.* https://www.linguisticsociety.org/about/who-we-are/presidents

Makalela, Leketi. (2017). Translanguaging practices in a South African institution of higher learning: A case of Ubuntu multilingual return. In Catherine M. Mazak & Kevin S. Carroll (Eds.), *Translanguaging in higher education: Beyond monolingual ideologies* (pp. 11–28). Multilingual Matters.

Makalela, Leketi. (2022). *Not eleven languages: Translanguaging and South African multilingualism in concert.* Walter de Gruyter.

Makoni, Sinfree, & Meinhof, Ulrike H. (2003). Introducing applied linguistics in Africa. *AILA Review, 16,* 1–12. https://doi.org/10.1075/aila.16.01mak

Makoni, Sinfree. (2011). Sociolinguistics, colonial and postcolonial: An integrationist perspective. *Language Sciences, 33,* 680–688. http://dx.doi.org/10.1016/j.langsci.2011.04.020

Mallinson, Christine, & Charity Hudley, Anne H. (2022–2024). Linguistic production, perception, and identity in the career mobility of Black faculty in linguistics and the language sciences (National Science Foundation Awards #2126414 and #2126405). National Science Foundation. https://www.nsf.gov/awardsearch/showAward?AWD_ID=2126414

Martin, Kahdeidra M. (2021). *Counterstories of Black students and graduates of NYC independent schools: A narrative case study* [Doctoral dissertation, The Graduate Center, City University of New York].

Martin, Kahdeidra M. (Forthcoming). Speaking the pain, dressing the wounds: Developing racial and raciolinguistic literacies in the composition classroom. *Journal of Multimodal Rhetorics.*

Martin, Kahdeidra M., Aponte, Gladys Y., & García, Ofelia. (2019). Countering raciolinguistic ideologies: The role of translanguaging in educating bilingual children. *Cahiers internationaux de sociolinguistique, 16*(2), 19–41. https://doi.org/10.3917/cisl.1902.0019

McQuitty, Deana, & Moore, DaKysha. (2022). Recruiting Black males in speech and language pathology SLP: The role of mentoring and collaborations at an HBCU. *The Chronicle of Mentoring & Coaching, 6*(15), 594–597.

MIT-Haiti Initiative. (n.d.). https://mit-ayiti.net/

Morgan, Paul L., Hammer, Carol Scheffner, Farkas, George, Hillemeier, Marianne M., Maczuga, Steve, Cook, Michael, & Morano, Stephanie. (2016). Who receives speech/language services by 5 years of age in the United States? *American Journal of Speech-Language Pathology, 25*(2), 183–199. https:// doi.org/10.1044/2015_AJSLP-14-0201

Murray Traci M. (2015). Trust in African Americans' healthcare experiences. *Nursing Forum, 50*(4), 285–292. https://doi.org/10.1111/nuf.12120

Peltier, Joy P. G. (2022). *"Powerful little words" in contact and in context: Pragmatic markers in Kwéyòl Donmnik, English, and French* [Doctoral dissertation, University of Michigan].

Peltier, Joy P. G. (forthcoming). Pragmatic Markers in Kwéyòl Donmnik, French, & English: Language Contact & Creole Emergence through the Lens of Powerful Little Words. For publication in Études Créoles.

Pennycook, Alastair, & Makoni, Sinfree. (2020). *Innovations and challenges in applied linguistics from the Global South*. Routledge.

Reid, Rebecca. (2021). Retaining women faculty: The problem of invisible labor. *PS: Political Science & Politics, 54*(3), 504–506. https://doi.org/10.1017/s1049096521000056

Randolph Jr., Linwood J., & Johnson, Stacey M. (2017). Social justice in the language classroom: A call to action. *Dimension*, 99–121.

Richardson, Elaine. (2003). *African American literacies*. Routledge.

Richardson, Elaine. (2007). *Hiphop literacies*. Routledge

Rickford, John R. (1997). Unequal partnership: Sociolinguistics and the African American speech community. *Language in Society, 26*(2), 161–197. https://doi.org/10.1017/s00474 04500020893

Rickford, John R. (2022). *Speaking my soul: Race, life, and language*. Taylor & Francis.

Shah, Sheena, Kometsi, Letzadzo, & Brenzinger, Matthias. (2022). Language activists and linguists in pursuit of the SiPhuthi cause. *Annual Review of Applied Linguistics, 42*, 93–101. https://doi.org/10.1017/s0267190522000058

Smitherman, Geneva. (1977). *Talkin and testifyin: The language of Black America*. Wayne State University Press.

Smitherman, Geneva. (2000). *Talkin that talk: Language, culture and education in African America*. Routledge.

Smitherman, Geneva. (2022). *My soul look back in wonder: Memories from a life of study, struggle, and doin battle in the language wars*. Routledge.

Social Sciences Feminist Network Research Interest Group. (2017). The burden of invisible work in academia: Social inequalities and time use in five university departments. *Humboldt Journal of Social Relations, 39*, 228–245. http://www.jstor.org/stable/90007882

Thomas, Jamie A. (2020). Uncovering language-in-education policy as a challenge to Tanzanian civic engagement/descubriendo la política del lenguaje en la educación como un reto para el compromiso civil Tanzano. *Humania del Sur, 15*(28), 63–93.

Thomas, Jamie A. (2021). Ghanaian multilinguals on study abroad in Tanzania: Learning Swahili through Akan/Twi and cultures of storytelling. In Wenhao Diao & Emma Trentman (Eds.), *Language learning in study abroad: The multilingual turn* (pp. 13–42). Multilingual Matters.

Thomas, Jamie A. (2022). A fish tale about "fieldwork," or toward multilingual interviewing in applied linguistics/koasoaiepen Ropirop, de petehkpen kederpohnpeh sang pali en lokaia tohto nan "applied linguistics" de kasukuhl me pid duwen lokaia kan. *Annual Review of Applied Linguistics*, *42*, 127–136. https://doi.org/10.1017/s026719052200006x

Thomas, Jamie A. (2023). Linguistics in pursuit of justice. [Book Review]. *Journal of Sociolinguistics* 27(2): 198-203. https://doi.org/10.1111/josl.12593

Thomas, Jamie A., & Bucholtz, Mary. (2021). Personal protective equipment against anti-Blackness: Communicability and contagion in the academy. *Journal of Linguistic Anthropology*, *31*(2), 287–292. https://doi.org/10.1111/jola.12324

Thornton, Candice Y. (2024). For the culture: Pathways in linguistics for Black and HBCU scholars. In Anne H. Charity Hudley, Christine Mallinson, & Mary Bucholtz (Eds.), *Inclusion in linguistics*. Oxford University Press.

Trejo, JoAnn. (2020). The burden of service for faculty of color to achieve diversity and inclusion: The minority tax. *Molecular Biology of the Cell*, *31*(25), 2752–2754. https://doi.org/10.1091/mbc.E20-08-0567

United States Census Bureau (2000). Census 2000 statistics summary. www.census.gov/mso/www.pres-ibc/c2ss/sid008.htm.

Upor, Rose A., & Mihayo, Maziku. (2021). Dual language instruction: Teaching civics in three public primary schools in Tanzania. *Utafiti: Journal of African Perspectives*, *16*(2), 163–183. https://doi.org/10.1163/26836408-15020046

Verdu, Paul, Jewett, Ethan M., Pemberton, Trevor J., Rosenberg, Noah A., & Baptista, Marlyse. (2017). Parallel trajectories of genetic and linguistic admixture in a genetically admixed Creole population. *Current Biology, 7*(16). https://doi.org/10.1016/j.cub.2017.07.002

Warner, Natasha, Ahlers, Jocelyn, Bilmes, Leela, Oliver, Monica, Wertheim, Suzanne, & Melinda Chen. (1996). *Gender and belief systems: Proceedings of the Fourth Berkeley Women and Language Conference*. Berkeley Women and Language Group.

Weissler, Rachel E. (2022). A meeting of the minds: Broadening horizons in the study of linguistic discrimination and social justice through sociolinguistic and psycholinguistic approaches. *Annual Review of Applied Linguistics*, *42*, 1–7. https://doi.org/10.1017/S0267190521000131

Weldon, Tracey. (2012). Teaching African American English to college students: Ideological and pedagogical challenges and solutions. *American Speech*, *87*(2), 232–247. https://doi.org/10.1215/00031283-1668244

Wertheim, Suzanne, Bailey, Ashlee C., & Corston-Oliver, Monica. (1998). *Engendering communication: Proceedings from the fifth Berkeley Women and Language Conference*. Berkeley Women and Language Group.

Women in Berkeley Linguistics. (n.d.). https://lx.berkeley.edu/about/women-berkeley-linguistics

May Helena Plumb is a PhD candidate in linguistics at the University of Texas at Austin, where her research focuses on the expression of temporal-modal semantics in Diza (Tlacochahuaya Zapotec). Her broader interests extend to digital humanities and the preservation of language data, and she is committed to community-engaged research that extends beyond the academy. She is co-author of the Ticha website and co-editor of the pedagogical e-book *Caseidyneën Saën — Learning Together*. She is an NSF Graduate Research Program Fellow, and her research has been published in the *International Journal of American Linguistics* and *Digital Humanities Quarterly*.

Alejandra Dubcovsky is associate professor of History at the University of California, Riverside. She has a deep interest in how Spanish colonial sources can be reframed and rethought to prioritize Indigenous voices and perspectives. She received her BA and PhD from UC Berkeley, and a Masters in library and information science from San Jose State. Her first book, *Informed Power: Communication in the Early American South*, won the 2016 Michael V. R. Thomason Book Award from the Gulf South Historical Association. She is co-editor of *Caseidyneën Saën — Learning Together*, and her work has been featured in *Ethnohistory*, *Early America Studies*, the *Journal of Southern History*, *Native South*, and the *William and Mary Quarterly*, among others. She has served in the editorial boards of the journals of *Ethnohistory* (2015–2018), *NAISA* (2017–2020), and *Native South* (2016–2021).

Moisés García Guzmán is a teacher, language activist, and a member of the Zapotec community of San Jerónimo Tlacochahuaya, where he is the town chronicler. He received his bachelor's degree from the Technological Institute of Oaxaca (Mexico), after which he moved to California, where he received his TOEFL certification. It was during this time that he became a Zapotec language activist. He works to raise awareness of the importance of language preservation as an element of cultural identity in the state of Oaxaca. He is a member of the Ticha Project Zapotec Advisory Board, co-producer of the multilingual documentary web series *Dizhsa Nabani — Living Language*, and co-editor of *Caseidyneën Saën — Learning Together*. He has a digital language campaign on Twitter (@BnZunni).

Brook Danielle Lillehaugen is associate professor and chair of linguistics at Haverford College. She received her BA in linguistics from UC Berkeley and her PhD in linguistics from UCLA (2006). She has been collaborating with Zapotec speakers since the summer before she started graduate school and is committed to practicing a linguistics that contributes to the goals of Zapotec educators and language activists. She publishes on the grammar of Zapotec in both its modern and colonial forms, including publications in *Language Documentation and Conservation*, *International Journal of American Linguistics*, *Tlalocan*, and *Native American and Indigenous Studies*. She is co-director of the Ticha Project and co-editor of *Caseidyneën Saën — Learning Together*. Her work has been supported by the National Science Foundation, the National Endowment for the Humanities, and the American Council of Learned Societies.

Felipe H. Lopez is visiting assistant professor in the Department of Political Science at Seton Hall University and an instructor at the Universidad del Pueblo in Tlacolula, Oaxaca. He is a member of the Zapotec community of San Lucas Quiaviní and grew up speaking Dizhsa. He earned his PhD from UCLA in 2007 in urban planning, focusing on

Mexican Indigenous issues on both sides of the border. He is co-author of a Zapotec–Spanish–English dictionary and pedagogical grammar. He is a member of the Ticha Project Zapotec Advisory Board and a co-editor of *Caseidyneën Saën — Learning Together*. He also writes in Dizhsa, and his poetry can be found in the *Latin American Literary Review*, *The Acentos Review*, and *Latin American Literature Today*. He was awarded the 2017 Premios CaSa prize for the creation of Zapotec literature.

Abstract: The Ticha Project is a digital endeavor focused on knowledge repatriation and language reclamation, guided by a Zapotec agenda that centers Zapotec goals and authority. This decolonial practice forges a collaborative, reciprocal scholarship where Zapotec and non-Native experts work together in pursuit of overlapping goals, forming an interdisciplinary community which resists the individualism of academia and draws strength from an inclusive Zapotec collective. In this chapter the authors detail Ticha's working philosophy through two interrelated projects: (1) *Caseidyneën Saën*, an e-book of pedagogical materials focused on Colonial Zapotec documents, and (2) the Conversatorios, workshops led by and for Zapotec individuals that serve as important sites of Indigenous knowledge production. The authors challenge readers to find their own community-centered agenda and to grow a bigger linguistics by embracing deeply localized research.

Ticha Project na teiby zeiny guieb lo bi (ni na "digital") ni yzicy xcal nanën quën xtizhën na. Rcazën gyenën teiby ni izhiu par ra Bunyza, ra ni bsanne ra xauzanën, Bunyzado, danoën. Rcazën gyicy ni nanën ni bzuca Dizhtily loën, chiru danoën Bunyza gyieneën gualnezh quën ra buny nan ni queity na ra Bunyza gacneën saën gyenën ropta rseinyën, chiru gyeinychieën teiby guezh nan ni sutyep lo ni rseidyrëng yu rseidy sutyepneën saën rataën. Lo teiby xnez gyets xte Ticha re rniën xa na xjab xtenën, chiru ygwiën lo styop ra zeiny ni cagyienyën ni ngabne sani: (1) *Caseidyneën Saën* na teiby gyets rseidy ni na teiby xnez gyets guieb lo bi (ni na "e-book") ni rseidy nazh ra gyets Dizhzado, chiru (2) chi bdop ra Bunyza bgwe dizh nii bzub xliet xa na gal nan xte ra Bunyza. Ra ni cagyual nde rnabën load ual gacbe xii rcaz lazhad ganad tyen chile subru guecy ni racbe buny yu rseidy nezbag laty gunyberuad xai na lazhad.

Key Words: Zapotec, Indigenous knowledge, language reclamation, accessibility, digital scholarship, community-driven scholarship

16

Growing a Bigger Linguistics Through a Zapotec Agenda

The Ticha Project

May Helena Plumb (she/her)
University of Texas at Austin

Alejandra Dubcovsky (she/her)
University of California, Riverside

Moisés García Guzmán (he/him/lani)
CETis 124 Extensión San Francisco Lachigolo and
the pueblo of San Jerónimo Tlacochahuaya

Brook Danielle Lillehaugen (she/her)
Haverford College

Felipe H. Lopez (he/him/laëng)
Seton Hall University and the pueblo of San Lucas Quiaviní

Introduction

The Ticha Project is a digital endeavor focused on knowledge repatriation and language reclamation, guided by a Zapotec agenda that centers Zapotec goals and authority.[1] Ticha is thus a project in decolonial linguistics, taking this frame not as a metaphor, but as a dynamic approach and practice that centers respect of, reciprocity with, and relevance to the Zapotec community (Tuck & Yang, 2012). We strive toward a more inclusive and expansive linguistics that prioritizes the needs and work of communities exploring historical corpora in their languages (see Leonard, 2011; Hinton, 2011) and builds on community-driven digital scholarship to democratize access to these resources (see Baldwin et al., 2016; de los Monteros, 2019; Genee & Junker, 2018; Meighan, 2021; Pawlicka-Deger, 2022).

Plumb, Dubcovsky, García Guzmán, Lillehaugen, Lopez, *Growing a Bigger Linguistics Through a Zapotec Agenda*
In: *Decolonizing Linguistics*. Edited by: Anne H. Charity Hudley, Christine Mallinson, and Mary Bucholtz, Oxford University Press.
© Anne H. Charity Hudley, Christine Mallinson, and Mary Bucholtz 2024. DOI: 10.1093/oso/9780197755259.003.0017

364 Decolonizing Linguistics

In this chapter we detail Ticha's working philosophy through two interrelated projects: (1) *Caseidyneën Saën*, an e-book of pedagogical materials focused on Colonial Zapotec documents (Flores-Marcial et al., 2021a; 2021b), and (2) the Conversatorios, workshops led by and for Zapotec individuals, initially organized as a mechanism for providing feedback on drafts of *Caseidyneën Saën* and since expanded as important sites of Indigenous knowledge production. We discuss the processes of (re)defining research practices, respecting and rewarding community labor, building intellectual community, and expanding definitions of accessibility, as driven by our Zapotec agenda.

Anne Charity Hudley and her colleagues urge us to ask, "Why is your linguistics so small?" (2020, e312). We find that pursuing a Zapotec agenda helps us expand our scholarship by actively resisting colonial hegemonies. We challenge readers to find their own "Zapotec agenda" and to grow a bigger linguistics by embracing deeply localized research practices.

Zapotec Languages and the Ticha Project

Zapotec is a family of languages spoken in what is now the state of Oaxaca, Mexico, and in diaspora communities throughout Mexico and the United States. The transnational diasporic Zapotec community in California is part of what is referred to as "Oaxacalifornia" (Kearney, 1995); the greater Los Angeles area, in particular, is home to the majority of Zapotecs in California (see, e.g., Cruz-Manjarrez, 2013; Lopez & Runsten, 2004). The Zapotec language family is rich and diverse, and there is a high level of linguistic differentiation between individual pueblos in Oaxaca (see Beam de Azcona, 2016, for a linguistic profile of Zapotecan languages). García Guzmán and Lopez both speak varieties of what linguists have termed *Western Tlacolula Valley Zapotec* (Diza/San Jerónimo Tlacochahuaya Zapotec and Dizhsa/San Lucas Quiaviní Zapotec, respectively; glottocode: sanj1284). There is significant dialect diversity within Western Tlacolula Valley Zapotec; for example, Lopez (a speaker of Dizhsa), cannot fully understand Dixza (Teotitlán del Valle Zapotec), though these language varieties are both classified as Western Tlacolula Valley Zapotec. While there are endonyms for each local Zapotec variety, there is no endonym that corresponds to Western Tlacolula Valley Zapotec, nor for any other larger branch of Zapotec, nor for the Zapotec language family as a whole.

Zapotec languages have one of the longest written histories in the Americas, dating back over 2,500 years (Romero Frizzi, 2003) and including a large corpus of alphabetic texts beginning in the mid-1500s (Oudijk, 2008).

Nonetheless, the history and technological contributions of Zapotec people are rarely part of the curriculum taught in Mexico's public education system. Anti-Indigenous linguistic ideologies continue to frame Zapotec languages as deficient and as relics of a distant past, downplaying the robust history and dynamic present of Zapotec communities. Unsurprisingly, then, many Zapotec languages are not currently passed down to children, and Zapotec speakers face continued racism. (For narratives on Zapotec language and identity in Oaxaca and California, see García Guzmán & Lopez in Dizhsa Nabani, 2019; Pérez Ruiz in Enduring Voices & Endangered Languages, 2015a; Chávez Santiago in Enduring Voices & Endangered Languages, 2015b. See also Figueroa (this volume) and Henner (2024) on related colonial ideologies of language use as "deficient" or "disordered.")

In response to these issues, the Ticha Project combines digital scholarship and intentional community-building to increase access to Zapotec language and history. *Ticha* is a Colonial Zapotec word meaning "word," "language," and "text," and it speaks to our focus on (1) locating, transcribing, translating, and historically contextualizing archival documents written in and about Colonial Zapotec and (2) making these materials accessible in comprehensive and community-rooted ways. The core of the project is the Ticha website: a digital text explorer for this rich yet understudied corpus (Lillehaugen et al., 2016). Our resources are freely available to a diverse public and are intended as open educational resources; we especially seek to engage and support a transnational Zapotec audience through outreach events and dedicated content.

Our Partnership

This chapter is authored by two non-Native linguists (May Helena Plumb and Brook Danielle Lillehaugen), a non-Native historian (Alejandra Dubcovsky), and two Zapotec educators and activists (Felipe H. Lopez and Moisés García Guzmán, of San Lucas Quiaviní and San Jerónimo Tlacochahuaya, respectively). We represent a small subset of the Ticha team, a large intellectual collective which includes educators, activists, and scholars from different types of institutions and at various career stages, working across disciplinary and geographic boundaries.[2] The diversity of our team is crucial to the scholarship we describe in this chapter, and here we give a brief history of how we came to work together.

The story of our team begins in 1992, when Lopez first started working with linguists in Los Angeles, seeking ways to document his Zapotec language.

366 Decolonizing Linguistics

This led to a now decades-long collaboration with Pamela Munro at the University of California, Los Angeles (UCLA), with whom he published a Dizhsa–English–Spanish dictionary (Munro, Lopez, et al., 1999). Lillehaugen began working with Zapotec languages in 1999, just before beginning graduate school at UCLA. Later that same year, invited by Munro, Lillehaugen and Lopez joined a team of UCLA scholars (led by Munro and Kevin Terraciano) seeking to understand and translate Colonial Zapotec documents; this work resulted in several publications (e.g., Munro et al., 2017; 2018) and is ongoing. At this point Lillehaugen had a strong interest in learning about language documentation, but no experience in Mexico or in academic–community partnerships. The development of what are now deeply committed partnerships and collaborations with Zapotec language educators and activists began with baby steps, much as is described in Gabriela Pérez Báez's (2015) aptly named "'Slowly, slowly said the jaguar': Giving collaborations time to develop."

In addition to the experience and time required to build relationships, stable employment facilitated long-term collaboration. Upon starting a tenure-track position in 2012, Lillehaugen—inspired by a conversation with Laurie Allen, then the Digital Scholarship Coordinator at Haverford College—started projects that would develop into the Ticha website. Around this time, García Guzmán and Lillehaugen were put in touch by a mutual friend in Los Angeles. García Guzmán had become interested in language work after moving to California, as he realized that language played an important role in defining his Zapotec identity in the diaspora; he wanted to collaborate with linguists to learn more about his language. Meanwhile, Plumb was just beginning her linguistics career and was looking for ways to support language work in Indigenous communities. She began working as an undergraduate research assistant to Lillehaugen, learning from Lillehaugen's example of community-centered research.

These converging careers and interests came together to form the Ticha Project: initially a collaboration between Lillehaugen, Allen, linguist George Aaron Broadwell, and historian Michel R. Oudijk, in conversation with Zapotec researchers and educators, including Lopez, García Guzmán, and Xóchitl Flores-Marcial. We envisioned a project that would allow stakeholders to engage with Colonial Zapotec texts in a flexible, multilayered way, informed by linguistics, history, and lived Zapotec experience. From the beginning, this work involved—and in fact required—Zapotec perspectives; Flores-Marical, García Guzmán, and Lopez would form the inaugural Zapotec Advisory Board.

Over the next decade, the Ticha Project grew, guided by the expertise of the diverse team and by ongoing conversations with the larger Zapotec community. In 2020, the team began an initiative to expand Ticha's resources, funded by an American Council of Learned Societies Digital Extension grant (PI Lillehaugen). Dubcovsky also joined Ticha in 2020, introduced to the project through her previous collaboration with Broadwell. Together— along with Broadwell, Flores-Marcial, and Mike Zarafonetis—we co-edited the *Caseidyneën Saën* e-books and organized the Conversatorios program in 2020 and 2021 (the main focus of this chapter).

This work grew slowly and organically, reflecting the backgrounds and trajectories of people who were working to prioritize and value the Zapotec language. We each bring different perspectives to the project. Lopez and García Guzmán identify an urgent need for Zapotec youth to have access to their own language and history, and they have found Colonial Zapotec documents to be valuable in creating Zapotec-centered curricula. Dubcovsky has a deep interest in how Spanish colonial sources can be reframed and rethought to prioritize Indigenous voices and perspectives. Lillehaugen and Plumb are dedicated to linguistics scholarship that contributes to the goals of Zapotec educators and language activists. We are brought together by our overlapping commitment to Zapotec communities and by our goals of supporting Indigenous survivance through decolonial scholarship.[3]

A Zapotec Agenda

The driving force of the Ticha Project is the Zapotec agenda. The term, originally coined by García Guzmán, speaks to Richard Grounds's (2007) observation that linguists and language communities often have "separate agendas" (see also Smith, 2021, pp. 145–161). By naming and referencing the Zapotec agenda, we participate in a scholarship where community-defined goals (as well as the community-aimed goals of individual Zapotec team members) serve as the foundation of our research plan. This practice forges a collaborative, reciprocal scholarship where Zapotec and non-Native experts work together in pursuit of overlapping goals, diminishing the push–pull relationship between linguistic research and community-led language work described by Alice Gaby & Lesley Woods (2020; see also Riestenberg et al., this volume). Our work is motivated by Zapotec individuals' urgent need for knowledge and community, and we follow the priorities of Zapotec activists to create resources that can be put to immediate use addressing community needs.

The Zapotec agenda centers Zapotec intellectual authority and celebrates Zapotec survivance. Zapotec people are thus at the center of the research, from the first steps of project design to the final edits of finished materials, from putting words on the page to choosing presentation and publication venues. This collaboration is formalized through Ticha's Zapotec Advisory Board, whose members work to prioritize projects, write materials, forge liaisons with the larger Zapotec community, and create spaces for community members to interact with and contribute to the project in less formalized, less time-demanding ways. The Zapotec agenda is dynamic and constantly growing, shaped and reshaped by our team members' personal reflection, active discussion, and open conversation with the larger Zapotec community.

For García Guzmán, a key goal of the Zapotec agenda is increasing awareness of Zapotec history and spurring action in support of language reclamation. A major roadblock to this endeavor has been the lack of pedagogical resources, particularly for engaging Zapotec youth. The *Caseidyneën Saën* e-book, as discussed below, seeks to close that gap by creating a set of educational materials that connect the long history of Zapotec writing to the deep present of Zapotec language, community, and resistance. Ticha takes our goals of accessibility and knowledge repatriation further by facilitating community spaces for Zapotec people to gather and engage with topics of language, history, and identity. Our team has leveraged social media as one way to create this space (see Lillehaugen, 2019; Lillehaugen & Flores-Marcial, 2022), and our Conversatorio program, discussed later in the chapter, served as a more structured space for building intellectual community.

From Documents to Knowledge: *Caseidyneën Saën*

The original impetus for creating the Ticha website—a digital repository of high-resolution images, plain-text transcriptions, and historical context—was to improve community access to Colonial Zapotec documents, which are scattered across several colonial archives, inaccessible to most Zapotec community members (see Broadwell et al., 2020). But when fighting against centuries of violent assimilatory ideologies, policies, and practices which prevent Zapotec people from accessing their intellectual history, digitizing colonial sources is only one small part of knowledge repatriation. We asked: What can these documents tell us about the past and present of Zapotec survivance? How can we grow our scholarship to actively support knowledge-seekers in learning about Zapotec language and history?

Following the Zapotec agenda, our team developed teaching materials centered on Colonial Zapotec, and together we wrote *Caseidyneën Saën — Learning Together: Colonial Valley Zapotec Teaching Materials*, an e-book of pedagogical modules available in both English (Flores-Marcial et al., 2021a) and Spanish (2021b). Using the archival resources available on Ticha as a foundation, *Caseidyneën Saën* introduces learners to concepts in Zapotec linguistics, history, and culture. Zapotec agency and survivance are centered throughout, and even chapters about history encourage the reader to look with optimism toward the Zapotec future.

Ticha's Zapotec Advisory Board has identified a specific need to engage Zapotec youth in language reclamation, especially given the discrimination against Zapotec language and the erasure of Zapotec history in Oaxacan schools (see also Chávez Santiago in Enduring Voices & Endangered Languages, 2015b). We further recognize a more general need for Indigenous-centered learning materials in both Mexican and US classrooms (see, e.g., Yerdon, 2018; Banks, 2019; Reclaiming Native Truth, 2018, p. 13). Therefore, *Caseidyneën Saën* is geared toward high school- and college-level learners and includes resources for instructors hoping to incorporate these modules into their curricula. The volumes are written primarily, but not exclusively, for a transnational Zapotec audience; for example, each chapter includes *How does it work in your language?* exercises specifically directed at Zapotec learners.

Caseidyneën Saën was co-edited by eight individuals, with many more involved in the larger project. We practiced a collective form of work; every word of both volumes was read aloud in our editorial meetings. Moreover, through the Conversatorios described in the following section, comments and reports from Zapotec community members further shaped the final text. This process resisted the individualism of academia, drew strength from an inclusive Zapotec collective, and resulted in the creation of not only a book but an interdisciplinary community of practice that has continued beyond the book project itself.

These materials were put to work immediately. Lopez used drafts of *Caseidyneën Saën* chapters while teaching Dizhsa at the University of California, San Diego (Spring 2020). Additionally, since Fall 2020, he has taught *Caseidyneën Saën* at the Universidad del Pueblo in Tlacolula, Oaxaca, where at least 80% of the students identify as Zapotec. All of his students reported that they had never seen Zapotec written before taking the course, and several students have since become actively engaged in learning and teaching their own Zapotec language. García Guzmán's high school students at the Centro de Estudios Tecnológicos Industrial y de Servicios in Oaxaca have also shown increased interest in Zapotec history and language maintenance after learning from these materials (Fall 2021, Spring 2022). Since Fall 2020, Lillehaugen has used *Caseidyneën Saën* in linguistics classes at Haverford College, and Dubcovsky and Aaron Olivias used *Caseidyneën Saën* in history courses at the University of California, Riverside (Winter 2021) and Texas A&M University (Fall 2021), respectively, teaching key research skills while encouraging students to understand Indigenous knowledge and frameworks (see TAMIU, 2021). In addition, Ticha has sponsored several Zapotec individuals to lead workshops in their communities through the Conversatorio program, as discussed in the next section.

Learning Together: The Conversatorios

Ticha's resources are created through an iterative development process that includes community feedback at every step (Broadwell et al., 2020). While writing *Caseidyneën Saën*, in addition to the contributions of the Zapotec team members, we solicited feedback from the wider community through the Conversatorios, online workshops on Colonial Zapotec organized around chapters from the e-book. In Summer 2020, Lopez and Xóchitl Flores-Marcial, a Zapotec historian and Ticha Advisory Board member, each led a six-week Conversatorio, meeting over Zoom with Zapotec individuals from Oaxaca and Oaxacalifornia for three to six hours each week (see Broadwell et al., 2021; Lillehaugen et al., 2021). Lopez and Flores-Marcial conducted a second round of Conversatorios in Summer 2021, and later that same summer Ticha sponsored previous Conversatorio participants to design and run their own workshops in their communities.

The Conversatorios were intellectual spaces for reciprocal knowledge exchange. Lopez and Flores-Marcial used their knowledge of Zapotec language, history, and activism to facilitate a space where participants could recognize and share their own linguistic expertise, and where these myriads of experiences and perspectives were not simply acknowledged but celebrated. The style and scope of discussion was guided by the participants' interests; for example, in a Conversatorio organized by Flores-Marcial many participants turned to art to express and process their learning. Between weekly sessions, participants shared what they had learned with their local community, thereby becoming educators in their own right and cultivating a community practice of knowledge-sharing. The Zapotec agenda thus allowed us to honor the diversity and variety of Zapotec knowledge.

The Ticha Project   371

Language work can be a lonely endeavor, and building community-grounded intellectual networks is vital to the Zapotec agenda (see Lopez in Broadwell et al., 2021, 8:11–8:24). The Conversatorios brought together Zapotec individuals from 16 communities on both sides of the border, and thus forged spaces where participants could connect with others committed to Zapotec language work who they otherwise may not have met. Members of this new pan-Zapotec activist network shared technical skills and social influence, while also providing emotional support as they worked through complicated, at times traumatic knowledge and, occasionally, retraumatizing teaching experiences. (Testimonials from Conversatorio facilitators and participants offer a deeper look into these communities: see, e.g., Lopez, 2020; Velasco Vasquez in Ticha Project, 2021.)

Several Conversatorio participants expressed a desire to run similar workshops in their pueblos. In the summer and fall of 2021, we sponsored a total of eight of these spin-off Conversatorios, which took diverse forms. In one example, Janet Chávez Santiago taught an eight-week course to high school students, in collaboration with the Bachillerato Integral Comunitario in Teotitlán del Valle (BIC29). In another, Luis Gustavo Cruz led members of a community art collective to engage with Colonial Zapotec documents and create woodcuts inspired by their experiences. Empowered to make their own projects, Conversatorio participants not only experienced validation of their knowledge, but also strengthened their connection to their language, showing the power and impact of dynamic, community-based and community-led programs that valorize Zapotec knowledge and teaching.

Zapotec knowledge is regularly devalued and even outright dismissed, and a crucial struggle of language work is providing appropriate financial compensation for the intellectual and pedagogical labor of experts and apprentices alike. In the initial Conversatorios run by Lopez and Flores-Marcial, each participant was compensated for both their time and the feedback they gave to improve *Caseidyneën Saën*. Those who later ran their own Conversatorios were further compensated for their pedagogical work. In the case of Chávez Santiago's Conversatorio at BIC29, the BIC was open to collaborating with Chávez Santiago by allowing her to teach a class, but could not pay her. After the initial collaboration in Fall 2021, Chávez Santiago went on to use *Caseidyneën Saën* for three additional courses at BIC29 in the spring and fall of 2022, funded through the Ticha Conversatorio program. Ticha's access to grants, then, was an important piece in the complex landscape of relationships, knowledge, and funding required to gain space for Indigenous knowledge in the Mexican education system.[4]

A Bigger Linguistics

We hope the Ticha Project will be a useful example to other communities working with historical language corpora—our methods, materials, and code are available to any team who wants to adapt them. However, as Ticha's work is firmly grounded in a Zapotec agenda, adaptation will be necessary for use in other contexts. A replication of Ticha's materials inserted into a new community would not have the same strengths. Rather than pursuing the development of a platform that might work across contexts, we strive to work well in a single context and to build community for others seeking to do the same.

What will your specific, community-rooted research agenda be? Here we share some observations and guiding questions to help your team reflect on your research process.

1. **Ticha's research practice is centered on reciprocal knowledge exchange that values the expertise of Zapotec community members.** Where can you build infrastructure for knowledge-sharing within and between your academic and identity-based communities? What does respecting community labor look like in your context? How can you involve and train community members, including students? How can students from outside the community be involved and trained in nonextractive research methods? (Suggested reading: Cruz & Woodbury, 2014; Czaykowsa-Higgins, 2009; Driskill, 2015; Chetty et al., this volume; Riestenberg et al., this volume; Tsikewa, 2021.)

2. **Through this work, the linguists participating in Ticha are expanding their vision of what constitutes a linguist and what is included in the field of linguistics.** How can you grow as a linguist and shape how linguistics grows as a field? How are you structuring your scholarship and teams? How do community practices guide your research questions and methods? Are these practices central to your work? (Suggested reading: Clemons, this volume; England, 1992; Leonard, 2017; Mufwene, 2020; Smith, 2021; Twance, 2019.)

3. *Caseidyneën Saën* and the Conversatorios developed through long-term, frequently revisited questions around accessibility (both of Zapotec languages and of the archival and colonial materials that document Colonial Zapotec) in a transnational community that lives with the history and present of colonialism. What does accessibility look like in your context? What are the layers of accessibility beyond making materials publicly and freely available? How does your definition of accessibility specifically combat barriers constructed by colonialism and

by institutions whose policies and goals are assimilatory? (Suggested reading: Broadwell et al., 2020; de los Monteros, 2019; Figueroa, 2022; Gallagher, 2019; McCracken & Hogan, 2021; Villarreal & Collister, this volume.)

4. **To date, most of Ticha's accolades and funding have been received from entities outside of linguistics, including the interdisciplinary fields of Latin American studies and digital humanities.** Which scholarly communities are responding to your work? How can you build support networks for yourself and your community to grow? Where can you find funding and encouragement inside and outside of linguistics? How can you advocate in your institutions and with funders for more opportunities for and support of decolonial work? (Suggested reading: Charity Hudley et al., 2020; Foster, 2010; Mallinson & Kendall, 2013; O'Meara, 2010; Pfirman & Martin, 2017.)

In conclusion, we refuse to accept a linguistics that is too small. By following a Zapotec agenda we insist on a research program driven by Zapotec communities, whose questions, needs, and priorities have shaped both our knowledge and our approach. We have intentionally created spaces of and for community work that resist academic individualism and isolation, embracing a linguistics that relies on Zapotec values of reciprocity and community as research principles. We challenge you to find your own Zapotec agenda to define, grow, and strengthen your community research process.

Notes

1. The concept of *knowledge repatriation* considers Indigenous communities' access to and control of not just physical artifacts, but cultural knowledge (see, e.g., Bell et al., 2013; Wilson, 2004; also Dobrin & Holton, 2013 for application to language archives). Foundational policies in (knowledge) repatriation include the Native American Graves Protection and Repatriation Act (NAGPRA, 1990), the United Nations Educational, Scientific and Cultural Organization's Convention for the Safeguarding of the Intangible Cultural Heritage (UNESCO, 2003), and the First Archivist Circle's Protocols for Native American Archival Materials (2007).

    Following Wesley Leonard, we use the term *language reclamation* to encompass "a larger effort by a community to claim its right to speak a language and to set associated goals in response to community needs and perspectives" (2012, p. 359), which may include but go beyond the narrower goal of creating new language users, extending for example to goals of language valorization and linguistic self-determination (see also Leonard, 2007; 2011).

2. First and foremost, we are grateful to the Zapotec teachers that have shared their time and knowledge so generously with us, including Janet Chávez Santiago. Xtyozën yuad! We also

374   Decolonizing Linguistics

gratefully acknowledge the other members of the Ticha team past and present—including Laurie Allen, George Aaron Broadwell, Xóchitl Flores-Marcial, Gustavo García, Michel R. Oudijk, and Mike Zarafonetis—as well as the numerous other Zapotec community members, scholars, and students who have contributed to this project. Plumb would like to further acknowledge her mentor Nora C. England (1946–2022), whose life-long dedication to training Indigenous linguists in Latin America serves as inspiration and guidance.

This work was possible with funding from a 2019 American Council of Learned Societies Digital Extension Grant "Ticha: Advancing Community-Engaged Digital Scholarship" (PI Lillehaugen) and with previous funding from the National Endowment for the Humanities (PI Lillehaugen) and the American Philosophical Society (PI Lillehaugen). Additional funding and support was provided from the Haverford College Office of the Provost, Haverford College Libraries, and the Center for Peace and Global Citizenship at Haverford College. Plumb was supported by the National Science Foundation Graduate Research Fellowship Program under Grant No. DGE-1610403 and the Harrington Fellows Program at the University of Texas at Austin. Any opinions, findings, and conclusions or recommendations expressed in this material are those of the authors and do not necessarily reflect the views of the funders.

3. The term *survivance* frames Native survival and resilience as an active process of resistance, building toward a thriving future, in opposition to a frame of Native victimhood and tragedy (Vizenor, 1999; see also Davis, 2017 in the context of language reclamation).

4. Compensation for the Conversatorio program was possible with funding from a 2019 American Council of Learned Societies Digital Extension Grant "Ticha: Advancing community-engaged digital scholarship" (PI Lillehaugen). Any opinions, findings, and conclusions or recommendations expressed in this material are those of the authors and do not necessarily reflect the views of the funders.

References

Baldwin, Daryl, Costa, David J, & Troy, Douglas. (2016). Myaamiaataweenki eekincikoonihkiinki eeyoonki aapisaataweenki: A Miami language digital tool for language reclamation. *Language Documentation & Conservation, 10*, 394–410. http://hdl.handle.net/10125/24713

Banks, James A. (2019). Approaches to multicultural curriculum reform. In James A. Banks & Cherry A. McGee Banks (Eds.), *Multicultural education: Issues and perspectives (10th ed)*. (pp. 137–157). Wiley.

Beam de Azcona, Rosemary G. (2016). Zapotecan languages. In *Oxford research encyclopedia of linguistics*. Oxford University Press.

Bell, Joshua A., Christen, Kimberly, & Turin, Mark. (2013). Introduction: After the return. *Museum Anthropology Review, 7*(1–2), 1–21.

Broadwell, George Aaron, García Guzmán, Moisés, Lillehaugen, Brook Danielle, Lopez, Felipe H., Plumb, May Helena, & Zarafonetis, Mike. (2020). Ticha: Collaboration with Indigenous communities to build digital resources on Zapotec language and history. *Digital Humanities Quarterly, 14*(4). http://www.digitalhumanities.org/dhq/vol/14/4/000529/000529.html

Broadwell, George Aaron, Chávez Santiago, Janet, Curiel, Laura, Flores-Marcial, Xóchitl, García Guzmán, Moisés, Hernández Sernas, Rogelio, Kadlecek, Eloise, Kawan-Hemler, Collin, Lillehaugen, Brook Danielle, Lopez, Felipe H., Matías, Edith, Molina, Yaneth, Plumb,

May Helena, Santiago, Ignacio, & Velasco Vasquez, Maria. (2021, March 4–7). *Caseidyneën saën: The collaborative creation of open educational materials as a pedagogical practice and act of resistance* [Paper presentation]. *7th International Conference on Language Documentation and Conservation,* Online. https://youtu.be/4AmOX0skxXI

Charity Hudley, Anne H., Mallinson, Christine, & Bucholtz, Mary. (2020). From theory to action: Working collectively toward a more antiracist linguistics (response to commentators). *Language, 96*(4), e307–e319. http://doi.org/10.1353/lan.2020.0081

Cruz, Emiliana, & Woodbury, Anthony C. (2014). Collaboration in the context of teaching, scholarship, and language revitalization: Experience from the Chatino Language Documentation Project. *Language Documentation & Conservation, 8*, 262–286. http://hdl.handle.net/10125/24607

Cruz-Manjarrez, Adriana. (2013). *Zapotecs on the move: Cultural, social, and political processes in transnational perspective.* Rutgers University Press.

Czaykowsa-Higgins, Ewa. (2009). Research models, community engagement, and linguistic fieldwork: Reflections on working within Canadian Indigenous communities. *Language Documentation & Conservation, 3*(1), 15–50. http://hdl.handle.net/10125/4423

Davis, Jenny L. (2017). Resisting rhetorics of language endangerment: Reclamation through Indigenous language survivance. *Language Documentation and Description, 14*, 37–58. http://www.elpublishing.org/PID/151

de los Monteros, Pamela Espinosa. (2019). Decolonial information practices: Repatriating and stewarding the *Popol Vuh* online. *Preservation, Digital Technology & Culture, 48*(3–4), 107–119. https://doi.org/10.1515/pdtc-2019-0009

Dizhsa Nabani. (2019, February 7). *Dizhsa Nabani bonus episode 11: Gal rgue dich || Platicando || Talking* [Video]. YouTube. https://youtu.be/H3irk-hsiEI

Driskill, Qwo-Li. (2015). Decolonial skillshares: Indigenous rhetorics as radical practice. In Joyce Rain Anderson, Rose Gubele, & Lisa King (Eds.), *Survivance, sovereignty, and story: Teaching American Indian rhetorics* (pp. 57–78). Utah State University Press.

Dobrin, Lise M., & Holton, Gary. (2013). The documentation lives a life of its own: The temporal transformation of two Endangered Language Archive projects. *Museum Anthropology Review, 7*(1–2), 140–154.

Enduring Voices & Endangered Languages. (2015a, June 25). *Filemón Pérez Ruiz on the importance of Zapotec / Sobre la importancia de la lengua zapoteca* [Video]. YouTube. https://youtu.be/IjOqQQDpBEw

Enduring Voices & Endangered Languages. (2015b, November 16). *MEXICO—Janet Chávez Santiago, parte 1: Sobre la lengua zapoteca* [Video]. YouTube. https://youtu.be/bddESEmsZTc

England, Nora C. (1992). Doing Mayan linguistics in Guatemala. *Language, 68*(1), 29–35. https://doi.org/10.2307/416368

Figueroa, Megan. (2022). Podcasting past the paywall: How diverse media allows more equitable participation in linguistic science. *Annual Review of Applied Linguistics, 42*, 40–46. https://dx.doi.org/10.1017/S0267190521000118

Foster, Kevin Michael. (2010). Taking a stand: Community-engaged scholarship on the tenure track. *Journal of Community Engagement and Scholarship, 3*(2). https://digitalcommons.northgeorgia.edu/jces/vol3/iss2/3

First Archivist Circle. (2007). *Protocols for Native American archival materials.* https://www2.nau.edu/libnap-p/protocols.html

Flores-Marcial, Xóchitl, García Guzmán, Moisés, Lopez, Felipe H., Broadwell, George Aaron, Dubcovsky, Alejandra, Plumb, May Helena, Zarafonetis, Mike, & Lillehaugen, Brook Danielle (Eds.). (2021a). *Caseidyneën saën — Learning together: Colonial Valley Zapotec teaching materials.* PressBooks. http://ds-wordpress.haverford.edu/ticha-resources/modules/

376 Decolonizing Linguistics

Flores-Marcial, Xóchitl, García Guzmán, Moisés, Lopez, Felipe H., Broadwell, George Aaron, Dubcovsky, Alejandra, Plumb, May Helena, Zarafonetis, Mike, & Lillehaugen, Brook Danielle (Eds.). (2021b). *Caseidyneën saën — Aprendemos juntos: Recursos didácticos sobre el zapoteco colonial del Valle*. PressBooks. http://ds-wordpress.haverford.edu/ticha-resources/recursos-de-ticha/

Gaby, Alice, & Woods, Lesley. (2020). Toward linguistic justice for Indigenous people: A response to Charity Hudley, Mallinson, and Bucholtz. *Language, 96*(4), e268–e280. https://doi.org/10.1353/lan.2020.0078

Gallagher, Angela. (2019, July 15). Archives and the road to accessibility. *Perspectives on History*. https://www.historians.org/publications-and-directories/perspectives-on-history/summer-2019/archives-and-the-road-to-accessibility

Genee, Inge, & Junker, Marie-Odile. (2018). The Blackfoot language resources and digital dictionary project: Creating integrated web resources for language documentation and revitalization. *Language Documentation & Conservation, 12*, 274–314. http://hdl.handle.net/10125/24770

Grounds, Richard A. (2007). Documentation or implementation. *Cultural Survival Quarterly Magazine, 31*(2). https://www.culturalsurvival.org/publications/cultural-survival-quarterly/documentation-or-implementation

Henner, Jon. (2024). How to train your abled linguist: A crip linguistics perspective on pragmatic research. In Anne H. Charity Hudley, Christine Mallinson, & Mary Bucholtz (Eds.), *Inclusion in linguistics*. Oxford University Press.

Hinton, Leanne. (2011). Language revitalization and language pedagogy: New teaching and learning strategies. *Language and Education, 25*(4), 307–318. http://dx.doi.org/10.1080/09500782.2011.577220

Kearney, Michael. (1995). The effects of transnational culture, economy, and migration on Mixtec identity in Oaxacalifornia. In Michael Peter Smith & Joe R. Feagin (Eds.), *The bubbling cauldron: Race, ethnicity, and the urban crisis* (pp. 226–243). University of Minnesota Press.

Leonard, Wesley Y. (2007). Miami language reclamation in the home: A case study [Doctoral dissertation, University of California, Berkeley].

Leonard, Wesley Y. (2011). Challenging "extinction" through modern Miami language practices. *American Indian Culture and Research Journal, 35*(2), 135–160. https://doi.org/10.17953/aicr.35.2.f3r173r46m261844

Leonard, Wesley Y. (2012). Reframing language reclamation programmes for everybody's empowerment. *Gender and Language, 6*(2), 339–367. https://doi.org/10.1558/genl.v6i2.339

Leonard, Wesley Y. (2017). Producing language reclamation by decolonising "language." *Language Documentation and Description, 14*, 15–36. http://www.elpublishing.org/itempage/150

Lillehaugen, Brook Danielle, Broadwell, George Aaron, Oudijk, Michel R., Allen, Laurie, Plumb, May Helena, & Zarafonetis, Mike. (2016). *Ticha: A digital text explorer for Colonial Zapotec* (1st ed.). https://ticha.haverford.edu/

Lillehaugen, Brook Danielle, Flores-Marcial, Xóchitl, Plumb, May Helena, Broadwell, George Aaron, & Lopez, Felipe H. (2021). *Recovering words, re-claiming knowledge, and building community: Ticha conversatorios* [Paper presentation]. *LASA2021 virtual congress: Crisis global, desigualdades y centralidad de la vida,* Online. https://youtu.be/k5QZkyjsvHQ

Lillehaugen, Brook Danielle, & Flores-Marcial, Xóchitl. (2022). Extending pedagogy through social media: Zapotec language in and beyond classrooms. *Journal of the Native American and Indigenous Studies Association, 9*(1), 62–101.

Lillehaugen, Brook Danielle. (2019). Tweeting in Zapotec: Social media as a tool for language activists. In Jennifer Carolina Gómez Menjívar & Gloria E. Chacón (Eds.), *Indigenous interfaces: Spaces, technology, and social networks in Mexico and Central America* (pp. 202–226). University of Arizona Press.

Lopez, Felipe H., & Runsten, David. (2004). Mixtecs and Zapotecs working in California: Rural and urban experiences. In Jonathan Fox & Gaspar Riversa-Salgado (Eds.), *Indigenous Mexican migrants in the United States* (pp. 175–200). UCSD Center for U.S.–Mexican Studies and Center for Comparative Immigration Studies.

Lopez, Jasmine. (2020, November 20). Oaxacalifornia virtual life: Reproducing Zapotec culture and language. *Global SL Blog, Campus Compact*. https://compact.org/oaxacalifornia-virtual-life-reproducing-zapotec-culture-and-language/

Mallinson, Christine, & Kendall, Tyler. (2013). Interdisciplinary approaches. In Robert Bayley, Richard Cameron, & Ceil Lucas (Eds.), *The Oxford handbook of sociolinguistics* (pp. 153–71). Oxford University Press.

McCracken, Krista, & Hogan, Skylee-Storm. (2021). Community first: Indigenous community-based archival provenance. *Across the Disciplines, 18*. https://doi.org/10.37514/ATD-J.2021.18.1-2.03

Meighan, Paul J. (2021). Decolonizing the digital landscape: The role of technology in Indigenous language revitalization. *AlterNative: An International Journal of Indigenous Peoples, 17*(3), 397–405. https://doi.org/10.1177%2F11771801211037672

Mufwene, Salikoko S. (2020). Decolonial linguistics as paradigm shift: A commentary. In Ana Deumert, Anne Storch, & Nick Shepherd (Eds.), *Colonial and decolonial linguistics: Knowledges and epistemes* (pp. 289–300). Oxford University Press.

Munro, Pamela, Lopez, Felipe H., with Gracia, Rodrigo, & Mendez, Olivia. (1999). *Dìcsyonaary x:tèe'n dìi'zh sah Sann Luu'c (San Lucas Quiaviní Zapotec dictionary / Diccionario zapoteco de San Lucas Quiaviní)*. UCLA Chicano Studies Research Center.

Munro, Pamela, Terraciano, Kevin, Galant, Michael, Flores-Marcial, Xóchitl, Sonnenschein, Aaron Huey, Lillehaugen, Brook Danielle, & Schwartz, Diana. (2017). Un testamento zapoteco del Valle de Oaxaca, 1614. *Tlalocan, 22*, 15–43. http://dx.doi.org/10.19130/iifl.tlalocan.2017.468

Munro, Pamela, Terraciano, Kevin, Galant, Michael, Lillehaugen, Brook Danielle, Flores-Marcial, Xóchitl, Ornelas, Maria, Sonnenschein, Aaron Huey, & Sousa, Lisa. (2018). The Zapotec language testament of Sebastiana de Mendoza, c. 1675. *Tlalocan, 23*, 187–211. http://dx.doi.org/10.19130/iifl.tlalocan.2018.480

NAGPRA (Native American Graves Protection and Repatriation Act). (1990). 25 U.S.C. ch. 32 §3001 ff.

O'Meara, KerryAnn. (2010). Rewarding multiple forms of scholarship: Promotion and tenure. In Hiram E. Fitzgerald, Cathy Burack, & Sarena D. Seifer (Eds.), *Handbook of engaged scholarship: Contemporary landscapes, future directions*, Vol. 1 (pp. 271–294). Michigan State University Press.

Oudijk, Michel R. (2008). El texto más antiguo en zapoteco. *Tlalocan, 15*, 227–240. https://revistas-filologicas.unam.mx/tlalocan/index.php/tl/article/view/191

Pawlicka-Deger, Urszula. (2022). Infrastructuring digital humanities: On relational infrastructure and global reconfiguration of the field. *Digital Scholarship in the Humanities, 37*(2), 534–550. https://doi.org/10.1093/llc/fqab086

Pérez Báez, Gabriela. (2015). *"Slowly, slowly said the jaguar": Giving collaborations time to develop* [Paper presentation]. *International Conference on Language Documentation and Conservation, Honolulu*. http://hdl.handle.net/10125/25278

Pfirman, Stephanie, & Martin, Paula J. S. (2017). Facilitating interdisciplinary scholars. In Robert Frodeman (Ed.), *The Oxford handbook of interdisciplinarity*, 2nd ed. (pp. 586–600). Oxford University Press.

Reclaiming Native Truth. (2018). *Research findings: Compilation of all research*. Echo Hawk Consulting & First Nations Development Institute. https://www.firstnations.org/publications/compilation-of-all-research-from-the-reclaiming-native-truth-project/

378 Decolonizing Linguistics

Romero Frizzi, María de los Ángeles (Ed.). (2003). *Escritura Zapoteca: 2,500 años de historia*. Instituto Nacional de Antropología e Historia.

Smith, Linda Tuhiwai. (2021). *Decolonizing methodologies: Research and Indigenous peoples*, 3rd ed. Zed Books.

TAMIU. (2021, December 16). TAMIU Students embark on paleography project on Mexico's Indigenous people. *Campus News*. https://tamiu.edu/newsinfo/2021/12/tamiu-olivas-pale ography.shtml

Ticha Project. (2021, February 9). *Building a virtual Zapotec community: A perspective from Koreatown, Los Angeles* [Video]. YouTube. https://youtu.be/s6eaAm85h4A

Tsikewa, Adrienne. (2021). Reimagining the current praxis of field linguistics training: Decolonial considerations. *Language*, *97*(4), e293–e319. http://doi.org/10.1353/lan.2021.0072

Twance, Melissa. (2019). Learning from land and water: Exploring mazinaabikiniganan as Indigenous epistemology. *Environmental Education Research*, *25*(9), 1319–1333. https://doi.org/10.1080/13504622.2019.1630802

UNESCO. (2003). *Convention for the safeguarding of the intangible cultural heritage*. http://unes doc.unesco.org/images/0013/001325/132540e.pdf

Vizenor, Gerald. (1999). *Manifest manners: Narratives on postindian survivance*. University of Nebraska Press.

Wilson, Waziyatawin Angela. (2004). Introduction: Indigenous knowledge recovery is Indigenous empowerment. *American Indian Quarterly*, *28*(3/4), 359–372.

Yerdon, MaryBeth. (2018, March 8). Teachers, do you need better resources? You're not alone: Native knowledge 360° is here to help. *Smithsonian Magazine*. https://www.smithso nianmag.com/blogs/national-museum-american-indian/2018/03/08/teaching-native-american-history-better/

Rashana Vikara Lydner is a postdoctoral researcher in Black France: Race and the Global Francophone Diaspora at the University of Virginia's Department of French. She is an interdisciplinary scholar whose work bridges the fields of African Diaspora studies, Caribbean studies, French cultural studies, linguistic anthropology, and Creolistics. Her research mainly focuses on a transnational approach to the study of Black Popular Culture in the Caribbean (Francophone/Anglophone) at the intersections of language, identity, and power. Using qualitative and quantitative methods, she examines race, gender, sexuality, and the co-naturalization of race and Creole languages. At the core of her research is her passion for Creole languages in the Caribbean basin. She hopes that speakers of Creole languages will continue to embrace their multilingual repertoire and continue to challenge colonizing language ideologies.

Abstract: This chapter discusses popular music, dancehall, as a fruitful site for decolonizing work on Creole languages and Creole-speaking communities. Scholarship in Creolistics in the Global North has primarily been focused on the linguistic structure of creole without much attention to the social context of Creole use and the identities of their speakers. The author urges Creolists to broaden their research agenda and engage with research on the embodied experiences of Creole speakers. Dancehall music and culture is one important focus of such research, because the dancehall space is a site of struggle between high and low culture, underscores the centrality of embodiment, and welcomes the negotiation of intersecting identities. In proposing research on dancehall as a model for decolonizing Creolistics, the author illustrates the possible contributions of popular music to expanding knowledge in Creolistics on race, gender, sexuality, and Creole languages.

Key Words: dancehall, French Caribbean, French Guianese Creole, Jamaican Creole, Creolistics, Popular Culture

17

Decolonizing Creolistics Through Popular Culture

The Case of Dancehall

Rashana Vikara Lydner (she/her)
University of Virginia

Introduction

My aim in this chapter is twofold: first, to decolonize Creolists' research focus on linguistic structure and history over language users, and second, to challenge Global North Creolists' tendency to ignore important developments by their colleagues in the Caribbean (Braithwaite & Ali, this volume). I offer a model for decolonizing linguistic research, particularly in Creolistics, a subfield that focuses on theoretical, descriptive, sociolinguistic, and historical approaches to the study of Creole and pidgin languages (Roberge, 2006). I call for Creolists to take popular culture, and particularly popular music, seriously in our work on Creole languages, as it provides a site for innovative, decolonizing research on the negotiation of identity in Creole-speaking communities. Furthermore, my discussion is situated in several bodies of scholarship. First, the negotiation of cultural identity through language use has long been of concern in linguistic studies on globalization and popular music (Alim et al., 2009; Pennycook, 2003; 2007; 2010). Scholars in this area highlight how music genres become instruments for navigating and reworking global youth affiliations and local identities. Additionally, a number of scholars have focused on the intersections of popular music and Creole language, showing how speakers use Creole languages in music to express and contest national and cultural identity (Anakesa, 2010; Butler, 2002; Cidra, 2018; Cooper, 2004; Cyrille, 2002; Dawkins, 2013; Devonish, 2006; Marie-Magdeleine, 2013; 2016; Martin, 2016; Sheringham, 2016; Sieber, 2005; Zobda-Zebina, 2006; 2009; 2010).

Rashana Vikara Lydner, *Decolonizing Creolistics Through Popular Culture* In: *Decolonizing Linguistics*. Edited by: Anne H. Charity Hudley, Christine Mallinson, and Mary Bucholtz, Oxford University Press.
© Anne H. Charity Hudley, Christine Mallinson, and Mary Bucholtz 2024. DOI: 10.1093/oso/9780197755259.003.0018

382 Decolonizing Linguistics

I begin by discussing my own positionality and how it informs my research. I then point to some of the ways that Creole languages and their speakers continue to be harmed by the persistent effects of colonialism, and how Black Creolists in particular are working to decolonize the field. Next, I argue that popular culture, in the form of music, can offer Creolistics a decolonizing lens from which to conduct linguistic analysis that centers language users, their experiences, and their identities. Finally, I illustrate this argument by discussing my own research on the performance of language and identity in dancehall music in the French Overseas Collectivity, French Guiana (Lydner, 2022) as an example of decolonizing Creolistic research.

My Positionality

Scholars should share their positionality since it will help readers understands the lens through which they conduct research. Hence, I briefly share my own. I was born and raised in Jamaica and consider myself a native speaker of Jamaican Standard English and Jamaican Creole. I have always been fascinated by the cultural similarities between the anglophone and the francophone Caribbean since I started learning French in high school in Jamaica. When I moved to the US and began my undergraduate studies in French and Spanish, I became even more drawn to the French Caribbean, this time regarding the stark differences that colored our culture and Creole language use. Consequently, I did my doctoral training in French and Francophone Studies with a designated emphasis in African Diaspora Studies at the University of California, Davis. I focused primarily on a critical approach to the study of Creolistics, language and globalization, racialization, and linguistic stylization related to Black people in the French Caribbean and mainland France.

I believe music is at the core of Caribbean culture, and I grew up listening to Jamaican genres such as rocksteady, calypso, reggae, dancehall, gospel, and folk. And as an immigrant in the US, I found comfort in dancehall spaces as I tried to navigate being a Black Caribbean Woman in mostly white academic spaces, particularly in French Departments. The dancehall space has been one of the most liberating places for me, where the use of Jamaican Creole is not policed, where I can speak without wondering if I am being misunderstood and where the body becomes a vehicle of signs when speech reaches its limit. Additionally, as I am from a place where classicism, colorism, and heteropatriarchy cut deep, the dancehall becomes a place where one's Blackness, queerness, and lived experiences of being from the lower class are visible manifestations of both difference and belonging. My research interest in French Guianese dancehall music developed from this positioning. As I studied the French Caribbean, I consumed a variety of music genres such as bouyon, dennery segment, zouk, reggae, and dancehall. Popular culture and music from French Guiana have been the most intriguing, given the country's constant migratory flow, and ethnic, and linguistic diversity. Consequently, I wanted to understand how French Guianese artists and dancehall participants negotiate their own personal and local identity and intersectional identities in the face of Frenchness, heteropatriarchy, and cultural difference.

Creole Languages and the Legacies of Colonialism

The Caribbean's history of slavery and racial oppression, biased missionary and travel descriptions of the region, and the co-naturalization of Creole languages and race, including Darwinian approaches to the study of race and language (Thomas, this volume), have all worked together to produce harmful ideologies about Creoles and their speakers (Roberge, 2006; de Sousa et al. 2019). Some discourses—including scholarly discourses—maintain that Creole languages are fundamentally different from "non-Creoles" or are "failed attempts" by their speakers to acquire colonial varieties. These ideologies about Creole languages are also reflected in speaker perceptions. For example, Caribbean Creole speakers tend to refer to their language as "broken" or as an "improper" version of a colonial variety such as English or French. In Caribbean societies, the colonial variety is associated with educational opportunities and social mobility, while Creoles have been relegated to the status of folk culture, maintaining negative connotations stemming from the legacies of colonialism.

These colonial ideologies permeate linguistics as well, especially in the longstanding focus on the genesis of Creole languages: How can we group Creole languages? Did they come about through the process of pidginization? Do they represent what some linguists refer to as "normal" language change? Or are there specific characteristics or linguistic features that separate Creoles from non-Creoles? The field's preoccupation with questions related to Creole genesis has fostered the disciplinary ideology of Creole exceptionalism, which Michel DeGraff (2005) defines as a set of beliefs that suggest that Creole languages are exceptional based on structural differences and that they are in some way inferior to "normal" languages (DeGraff, 2001; 2005; see also Mufwene, 2008). Such arguments, DeGraff demonstrates, are circular, unscientific, and racist.

384 Decolonizing Linguistics

Throughout my quest to understand Creole languages in both the Francophone and the Anglophone Caribbean, I have read interdisciplinarily, drawing on the fields of Creolistics, anthropology, and literary studies and theory (Ansaldo & Meyerhoff, 2020; Baron & Cara, 2011; Bernabé et al., 1993; Brathwaite, 1971; Glissant & Dash, 1989; Édouard Glissant, 1990; Hazaël-Massieux, 2008; Kouwenberg & Singler, 2008; Palmié, 2006; Siegel, 2002; 2005; Thomas, 2004). My work is influenced by the wave of scholars who aim to critique colonizing discourses, decolonize Creolistics, and apply a decolonial framework to their analysis of Creole languages (such as Amado et al., 2024; Ansaldo et al., 2007; Bancu, Peltier, et al., this volume; DeGraff, 2001; 2005; Fuller Medina, this volume; and Mufwene, 2008). I am also influenced by research on raciolinguistics (Alim et al., 2016; Rosa and Flores, 2017; see also Smith, this volume). As the work of all of these scholars indicates, to combat colonial thinking in linguistics, any study on Caribbean Creoles must consider the intersections of race, power, and identity.

In my own research, I focus on issues related to language and identity in Caribbean Creole-speaking communities. More specifically, I use popular culture, primarily music, to examine current issues related to race, gender, and sexuality in the French Caribbean. Based on my experience, I urge those in Creolistics to conduct more research on Creole language and identity, which has often been marginalized in our field. Moreover, I implore them to consider identity work in popular music as an important avenue for unthinking the ways in which linguistic research on Creole languages and their communities have often been viewed through a colonial lens.

The Importance of Popular Music for Decolonizing Creolistics

Because popular culture is a site for the negotiation of intersecting identities and ideologies, it is a perfect space for analyzing Creole languages from a decolonizing perspective. Caribbean popular music, particularly, provides thought-provoking insights on language change and innovation as well as allowing us to take a closer look at the intersections of race, gender, sexuality, and power in Creole-speaking communities. Most importantly, in focusing on music we center speakers and their embodied experiences rather than the decontextualized linguistic analyses and often harmful theories that dominate traditional research on Creole languages. Incorporating music into research on Creole languages helps decolonize the field in several ways: by increasing the interdisciplinary engagement of Creolistics, by introducing new data and methods, and by bringing identity into focus in linguistic study.

Although Creolistics is highly interdisciplinary in some ways, there are fields that it typically does not currently engage, especially cultural studies. As a result, linguists often seem to forget that the term "Creole" has multiple meanings: racial, linguistic, cultural, and musical (Baron & Cara, 2011). All of these meanings come together in my research, which examines how individuals in the Black Caribbean musicscape use language and music to create racial and cultural solidarity. I draw on Gilroy's (1993) concept of *cross-pollination* in reference to the dissemination of knowledge production throughout the Black Atlantic. In this case, I am referring to Caribbean and Creole-specific cultural, linguistic, and musical influences which feed the evolution of old and the creation of new cultural and musical genres. By thinking about *Creole* in this broader way, I bring linguistics into dialogue with cultural studies, ethnomusicology, and other fields. More generally, using popular music as a locus of study in Creolistics allows us to view the study of Creole languages through a lens that is not only interdisciplinary but also decolonizing, cutting across the varied meanings of *Creole* to provide novel means of analyzing Creole speech, linguistic norms and innovation, ideological beliefs, and the performance of identity in ways that are meaningful to speakers themselves.

However, given the reliance on traditional linguistic methodologies in much of Creolistics, especially in the Global North, the incorporation of popular music as a site of analysis in Creolistics requires an unthinking of what is considered valuable linguistics data and methodology. In my research, dancehall stage shows, music videos, and song lyrics provide data that is preplanned and well-rehearsed and is therefore often dismissed as unacceptable by linguists who place a premium on spontaneous speech data. Yet such data deserves linguists' attention because it broadens our knowledge of the range of ways that speakers use language; in addition, it is representative of current innovations in local Creole speech. At the same time, my research shows the unique insights that can be gained from analyzing music as data, such as the importance of Creole multilingualism and transnational connections in the Black Caribbean. My analyses also introduce into Creolistics new methodologies from beyond the field, such as those from linguistic anthropology and from studies of popular music. For example, I use multimodal analysis (O'Halloran & Smith, 2012) and the analysis of linguistic stylization (Coupland, 2001) to understand embodiment and language use in the dancehall space. This more inclusive approach to linguistic methods allows me to draw conclusions about artists' repertoire choice, genre conventions of dancehall, and stylization of personas, all findings that contribute directly to linguists' understanding of Creole languages. Because these methods contextualize rather than decontextualize language, they help humanize and therefore decolonize linguistic research (Paris & Winn, 2014).

Finally, popular music also highlights the central importance of identity in language use, an issue that deserves much more attention in Creolistics. Music provides us with useful knowledge about ideologies pertaining to gender, sexuality, class, and race in the local space, which are closely connected to ideologies about language and thus allows Creolists to be part of larger conversations in linguistics and anthropology on the co-naturalization of race and language and the negotiation of Black masculinities, femininities, and sexualities through language across a range of cultural contexts (e.g., Alim et al., 2016; Alim & Smitherman, 2019; Rampton, 2010; 2017). My analysis of dancehall, for example, is a transnational study on Creole languages that examines local, regional, and transnational forms of racialization, language contact, language change, multilingualism, and intersecting identities. If Creolists take up the questions of identity that matter most to speakers, the field can both advance knowledge in a little-studied area and help move linguistics away from colonial thinking.

The Case of Dancehall

As a speaker of Jamaican Creole and an avid listener of Caribbean music, I have found dancehall music to be a fruitful site of study to undertake decolonizing work in Creolistics. Similar to its antecedent reggae, dancehall has become a Black Diasporic and transnational culture and music genre. The messages associated with dancehall and reggae are quite different even though they both focus on the lived experiences of individuals from Jamaican inner-city communities. Reggae promotes themes such as social revolution, racial pride, peace, and love while dancehall's themes mainly focus such as violence (gun violence and police brutality) poverty, and sex, among others (Hope, 2006, p. 13). As a youth genre and culture, dancehall has become a crucial site for conceptualizing Caribbean Blackness and its new global configurations amongst youth populations across the world (Cooper, 2004; Hope, 2006; 2009; 2010; Stanley Niaah, 2004; 2006; 2009; 2010; Sterling, 2010; Stolzoff, 2000).

The dancehall space is a site of identity struggle between high and low cultures and welcomes the contestation of dominant ideologies on race, class, gender, and sexuality (Cooper, 2004). Jamaican dancehall, according to Sonjah Stanley Niaah (2004), functions as a "status-granting institution" that valorizes ideologies and identities that are deemed non-normative—too vulgar or crude—by the dominant society (p. 125). Dancehall as a "status-granting institution" highlights racial, spatial, gendered, and classed lines of division while giving participants a space to express themselves without necessarily being policed by the dominant society. Dancehall artists and their listeners creatively use Creole languages to articulate their intersecting identities. In addition to Creole, they use their bodies and their sexualities to transgress monolingual ideologies, heterosexual norms, and respectability politics (Cooper, 2004; Hope, 2006; Stanley Niaah, 2010; Norman Stolzoff, 2000). Hence, they reconfigure dominant ideologies on race, gender, national identity, and sexuality through song as they navigate different spatial boundaries: local, regional, and global (see also Smalls, 2018 on emphatic Blackness).

The performers that I look at in French Guianese dancehall identify both with the radical politics of Caribbean Blackness and with creative ways of transgressing dominant society and ideologies that the dancehall space has to offer. French Guiana's relationship with dancehall is just one example of how work on popular culture can expand our knowledge of Creole language and identity in Caribbean creole-speaking communities. As French Guianese artists perform dancehall, they complicate ideas on French national identity, masculinity, and femininity. For instance, in my work on the French Guianese dancehall duo Jahyanaï and Bamby, I show how the rude bwoy and bad gyal personas are representative of Caribbean forms of masculinity and femininity that transgress respectability politics through anti-state and anti-elite linguistic and embodied performances (Lydner, 2022). More precisely, the bad gyal primarily uses embodied stylization to trouble French Caribbean gender and sexual norms as she wears provocative clothing, dances erotically, discusses sexually taboo topics, and champions sexual freedom for French Caribbean women. The rude bwoy, on the other hand, embodies his persona through a linguistic stylization that focuses heavily on the lyrical or metaphorical gun as well as anti-state ideologies.

In addition, both personas engage in Creole multilingualism and the revalorization of Caribbean Creole languages as they codeswitch between Jamaican Creole, French Guianese Creole, and taki-taki, the mutually intelligible Creole languages spoken by Maroon communities who border Suriname and French Guiana. In everyday society, both Jamaican Creole and French Guianese Creole are stigmatized and considered nonstandard or the language of folk culture, while French and Jamaican Standard English are the languages of prestige. In the dancehall musicscape, French Guianese dancehall artists are able to resist colonial knowledge production and dominant linguistic ideologies. Through code-switching in song, dancehall artists offer a

388 Decolonizing Linguistics

critique both of monolingualism and French as a dominant language. More specifically, they challenge ideologies associated with French Guianese Creole (as well as other stigmatized languages such as taki-taki) by endowing it with prestige in the French Guianese dancehall space and the French Caribbean more generally, similar to the use of Jamaican Creole in song in the Jamaican dancehall (Cooper, 2004). By code-switching and code mixing between both French Guianese Creole and Jamaican Creole, French Guianese dancehall artists strategically revalorize Creole languages, bring together the Jamaican and French Guianese cultures, and assert Black French Caribbean identity through the performance of a Black lower-class music genre.

As I show in my research, dancehall music and culture has become the newest iteration of Black resistance in French Guiana as well as an influential source of identification in trans-Caribbean discourse. Given the huge impact of music genres such as dancehall in the Caribbean, Creolists who want to study the most innovative forms of Creole languages as well as those who want to do decolonizing research can learn a great deal by examining the language of popular music.

Conclusion

Decolonizing linguistics for me means challenging old regimes of thinking as well as re-envisioning how current-day popular culture can be used to improve our field. Overall, decolonizing Creolistics means avoiding the circular arguments and racist reasoning that plague the discussion of Creole genesis. It means to contest the ideology of Creole exceptionalism as well as to ground all research in the field in a critical analysis of the co-naturalization of race and Creole language. More precisely, to decolonize Creolistics through popular culture means to take popular culture in the form of Caribbean music genres seriously as a site that can provide us not only with valuable linguistic data but also with decolonizing perspectives that center speakers and what is meaningful to them. Additionally, it means being open to new ways of collecting and analyzing linguistic data. Furthermore, it means investing in scholarship that examines identity in Creole-speaking communities. My personal call to action in Creolistics, along with the above-mentioned principles, is to produce more scholarship on creole language, gender, and sexuality across Creole-speaking communities. Work on identity in Creolistics is equally as important as work on Creole phonetics, phonology, morphology, syntax, semantics, and pragmatics. We need to produce more humanizing research on

Creole speakers and creole languages to decolonize our field and center their embodied lived experiences and creativity at the forefront of our analyses.

References

Alim, H. Samy, Ibrahim, Awad, & Pennycook, Alastair. (Eds.). (2009). *Global linguistic flows: Hip hop cultures, youth identities, and the politics of language*. Routledge.

Alim, H. Samy, Rickford, John R., & Ball, Arnetha. F. (Eds.) (2016). *Raciolinguistics: How language shapes our ideas about race*. Oxford University Press.

Alim, H. Samy, & Smitherman, Geneva. (2019). Amazing grace: An analysis of Barack Obama's raciolinguistic performances. In Àngels Massip-Bonet, Gemma Bel-Enguix, & Albert Bastardas-Boada (Eds.), *Complexity Applications in Language and Communication Sciences* (pp. 227–248). Springer.

Amado, Abel Djassi, Baptista, Marlyse, Pina Garcia, Lourenço, Lima, Ambrizeth Helena, & Thomas, Dawna Marie. (2024). Bilingual education in Cabo Verdean: Towards visibility and dignity. In Anne H. Charity Hudley, Christine Mallinson, & Mary Bucholtz (Eds.), *Inclusion in linguistics*. Oxford University Press.

Anakesa, Apollinaire. (2010). *Introduction to Guianese popular musics*. Hal Université des Antilles. http://hal.univ-antilles.fr/hal-01969584.

Ansaldo, Umberto, Lim, Lisa, & Matthews, Stephens. (2007). *Deconstructing Creole*. John Benjamins.

Ansaldo, Umberto & Meyerhoff, Miriam. (2020). Not in retrospective: The future of pidgin and creole studies. In Umberto Ansaldo & Miriam Meyerhoff (Eds.), *The Routledge Handbook of Pidgin and Creole Languages* (pp. 1–12). Routledge.

Baron, Robert & Cara, Ana C. (Eds). (2011). *Creolization as cultural creativity*. University Press of Mississippi.

Bernabé, Jean, Chamoiseau, Patrick, Confiant, Raphaël & Taleb-Khyar, Mohamed B. (1993). *Éloge de la créolité*. Gallimard.

Brathwaite, Edward. (1971). *The development of Creole society in Jamaica 1770–1820*. Clarendon Press.

Butler, Melvin L. (2002). "Nou kwe nan Sentespri" (We believe in the Holy Spirit): Music, ecstasy, and identity in Haitian Pentecostal worship. *Black Music Research Journal, 22(1)*, 85–125.

Cidra, Rui. (2018). Cabral, popular music and the debate on Cape Verdean creoleness. *Postcolonial Studies, 21*(4), 433–451.

Cooper, Carolyn. (2004). *Sound clash: Jamaican dancehall culture at large*. Palgrave Macmillan.

Coupland, Nikolas. (2001). Dialect stylization in radio talk. *Language in Society, 30*(3), 345–375.

Cyrille, Dominique. (2002). Popular music and Martinican-Creole identity. *Black Music Research Journal, 22*(1), 65–83.

Dawkins, Nickesha. (2013). She se dis, him se dat: Examining gender-based use in Jamaican dancehall. In Donna P. Hope (Ed.), *International reggae: Current and future trends in Jamaican popular music* (pp. 124–166). Pelican Books.

DeGraff, Michel. (2001). On the origin of creoles: A Cartesian critique of neo-Darwinian linguistics. *Linguistic Typology, 5*(2/3), 213–310.

DeGraff, Michel. (2005). Linguists' most dangerous myth: The fallacy of Creole Exceptionalism. *Language in Society, 34*(4), 533–591.

390 Decolonizing Linguistics

Devonish, Hubert. (2006). On the status of diphthongs in Jamaican: Mr. Vegas pronounces. In Hazel Simmons-McDonald & Ian Robertson (Eds.), *Exploring the boundaries of Caribbean Creole languages* (pp. 72–95). University of the West Indies Press.

Gilroy, Paul. (1993). *The Black Atlantic : Modernity and Double Consciousness*. Harvard University Press.

Glissant, Édouard. (1990). *Poétique de la relation*. Gallimard.

Glissant, Édouard, & Dash, J. Michael. (1989). *Caribbean discourse: Selected essays*. University of Virginia Press.

Hazaël-Massieux, Marie-Christine. (2008). *Textes anciens en créole français de la Caraïbe: Histoire et analyse*. Éditions Publibook.

Hope, Donna P. (2006). *Inna di dancehall: Popular culture and the politics of identity in Jamaica*. University of West Indies Press.

Hope, Donna P. (2009). Fashion ova style: Contemporary notions of skin bleaching in Jamaican dancehall culture. *Jenda: A Journal of Culture and African Women Studies, 14*, 101–126.

Hope, Donna P. (2010). *Man vibes: Masculinities in the Jamaican dancehall*. Ian Randle.

Kouwenberg, Silvia & Singler, John. V. (Eds.). (2008). *The handbook of Pidgin and Creole studies*. Blackwell Publishing.

Lydner, Rashana V. (2022). *Performing otherness in Guyanais dancehall: An analysis of the rude bwoy and bad gyal personas* [Doctoral dissertation, University of California, Davis].

Marie-Magdeleine, Loïc. (2016). Dancehall «lokal» et dancehall jamaïcain: entre reproduction et recherche d'authenticité. In Steve Gadet (Ed.), *Les Cultures Urbaines dans la Caraïbe* (pp. 77–100). L'Harmattan.

Marie-Magdeleine, Loïc. (2013). *Entre violence, sexualité et luttes sociales: le destin paradoxal du dancehall* [Doctoral dissertation, University of Antilles-Guyane].

Martin, Carla D. (2016). Music: An exception to Creole exceptionalism? Cape Verdean national identity and creativity post-independence. *Social Dynamics, 42*(1), 46–68.

De Sousa, Silvio Moreira, Mücke, Johannes, & Krämer, Philipp. (2019). A history of Creole studies. *Oxford research encyclopedia of linguistics*. https://doi.org/10.1093/acrefore/9780199384655.013.387.

Mufwene, Salikoko. (2008). *Language evolution: Contact, competition and change*. Bloomsbury.

O'Halloran, Kay, & Smith, Bradley A. (Eds.). (2012). *Multimodal studies: Exploring issues and domains,* Vol. 2. Routledge.

Palmié, Stephan. (2006). Creolization and its discontents. *Annual Review of Anthropology, 35*, 433–456.

Paris, Django, & Winn, Maisha (Eds.). (2014). *Humanizing research: Decolonizing qualitative inquiry with youth and communities*. SAGE Publishing.

Pennycook, Alastair. (2003). Global Englishes, Rip Slyme, and performativity. *Journal of Sociolinguistics, 7*(4), 513–533.

Pennycook, Alastair. (2007). Language, localization, and the real: Hip-hop and the global spread of authenticity. *Journal of Language, Identity, and Education, 6*(2), 101–115

Pennycook, Alastair. (2010). Popular cultures, popular languages, and global identities. In Nikolas Coupland (Ed.), *The Handbook of Language and Globalization* (pp. 592–607). Willey Blackwell.

Rampton, Ben. (2010). Crossing into class: Language, ethnicities and class sensibility in England. In Carmen Llamas & Dominic Watt (Eds.), *Language and identities* (pp. 134–143). Edinburgh University Press.

Rampton, Ben. (2017). *Crossing: Language and ethnicity among adolescents*. Routledge.

Roberge, Paul T. (2006). The development of creolistics and the study of pidgin languages: An overview. In Sylvain Auroux, Ernst F. K. Koerner, Hans-Josef Niederehe, & Kees Versteegh (Eds.), *An international handbook on the evolution of the study of language from the beginnings to the present,* Vol. 3 (pp. 2398–2413). De Gruyter Mouton.

Rosa, Jonathan, & Flores, Nelson. (2017). Unsettling race and language: Toward a raciolinguistic perspective. *Language in Society*, *46*(5), 621–647.

Sheringham, Olivia. (2016). Markers of identity in Martinique: Being French, Black, Creole. *Ethnic and Racial Studies*, *39*(2), 243–262.

Sieber, Timothy. (2005). Popular music and cultural identity in the Cape Verdean post-colonial diaspora. *Etnográfica, Revista do Centro em Rede de Investigação em Antropologia 9*(1), 123–148.

Siegel, Jeff. (2005). Creolization outside creolistics. *Journal of Pidgin and Creole Languages*, *20*(1), 141–166.

Siegel, Jeff. (2002). Applied Creolistics in the 21st century. In Glenn Gilbert (Ed.), *Pidgin and Creole linguistics in the twenty-first century* (pp. 7–48). Peter Lang Publishing.

Stanley Niaah, Sonjah. (2004). Making space: Kingston's Dancehall culture and its philosophy of "boundarylessness." *African Identities*, *2*(2), 117–132.

Stanley Niaah, Sonjah. (2006). Readings of "ritual" and community in dancehall performance. *Wadabagei*, *9*(2), 47–73.

Stanley-Niaah, Sonjah. (2009.) Negotiating a common transnational space: Mapping performance in Jamaican dancehall and South African Kwaito. *Cultural Studies*, *23*(5–6), 756–774.

Stanley-Niaah, Sonjah. (2010). *Dancehall: From slave ship to ghetto*. University of Ottawa Press.

Sterling, Marvin. (2010). *Babylon East: Performing dancehall, roots reggae, and Rastafari in Japan*. Duke University Press.

Stolzoff, Norman C. (2000). *Wake the town and tell the people: Dancehall culture in Jamaica*. Duke University Press.

Thomas, Deborah A. (2004). *Modern Blackness: Nationalism, globalization, and the politics of culture in Jamaica*. Duke University Press.

Zobda-Zebina, Mylenn. (2006). *Les musiques dancehall: Comparaison de deux sociétés Caribéennes, la Martinique et la Jamaïque* [Doctoral dissertation, Paris, École des hautes études en sciences sociales].

Zobda-Zebina, Mylenn. (2009). Dancehall in the West Indies, rap in France. *Volume!*, *6*(1), 47–59.

Zobda-Zebina, Mylenn. (2010). Musiques dancehall et utopie dans deux sociétés caribéennes, la Jamaïque et la Martinique. *Agôn (Online), 2010*(3). https://doi.org/10.4000/agon.1423.

Katherine J. (Kate) Riestenberg is an applied linguist. For nearly a decade, she worked with language teachers and activists in the US and Mexico to document, describe, teach, write, and create educational materials in Indigenous and minoritized languages. She has worked most closely with Zapotec teachers in Mexico to implement and evaluate community-based teaching methods for language revitalization. Her published work focuses on teaching methods and the nature of linguistic input and interaction available to learners in revitalization contexts. She now works as a researcher and project manager at a small technology company whose focus is addressing language barriers in healthcare and education.

Ally Freemond recently graduated from Bryn Mawr College with a bachelor's degree in linguistics. During her undergraduate career, she took part in in language documentation fieldwork in Oaxaca, Mexico. She also helped organize remote internships for fellow linguistics students that contributed to language revitalization projects. She is particularly interested in the morphosyntax of Algonquian languages.

Brook Danielle Lillehaugen is associate professor and chair of linguistics at Haverford College. She received her BA in linguistics from UC Berkeley and her PhD in linguistics from UCLA (2006). She has been collaborating with Zapotec speakers since the summer before she started graduate school and is committed to practicing a linguistics that contributes to the goals of Zapotec educators and language activists. She publishes on the grammar of Zapotec in both its modern and colonial forms, including publications in *Language Documentation and Conservation*, *International Journal of American Linguistics*, *Tlalocan*, and *Native American and Indigenous Studies*. She is co-director of Ticha and co-editor of *Caseidyneën Saën — Learning Together*. Her work has been supported by the National Science Foundation, the National Endowment for the Humanities, and the American Council of Learned Societies.

Jonathan N. Washington is associate professor of linguistics at Swarthmore College whose research interests include a range of questions in phonetics and phonology and close investigation of Turkic languages. Jonathan also develops and promotes language technology for marginalized languages, emphasizing approaches that prioritize community needs, such as decolonizing practices and free/open-source licenses.

Abstract: Published work on community-based or participatory research with Indigenous languages tends to focus on balancing community members' goals with outside researchers' academic goals. However, because inherent contradictions exist between the realities of the academy and the priorities of communities, attempts at achieving this balance rarely result in work that is truly community-based. This chapter describes two Indigenous language revitalization projects that aimed to prioritize community partners' goals rather than outcomes set by outside academic researchers. The authors offer a set of reflections based on the results of surveys conducted with the community members and students who participated in the projects. They discuss the roles of financial resources, institutional motivations, employment, and long-term connections between academic faculty and community activists in carrying out community-based work.

Key Words: Indigenous languages, community-based research, participatory research, academic research products, language revitalization, Zapotec

18

Prioritizing Community Partners' Goals in Projects to Support Indigenous Language Revitalization

Katherine J. Riestenberg
Independent Scholar

Ally Freemond
Independent scholar

Brook Danielle Lillehaugen
Haverford College

Jonathan N. Washington
Swarthmore College

Introduction

Scholarly work in linguistics related to Indigenous and minoritized languages increasingly aims to employ community-based, participatory, and decolonizing approaches (Bischoff & Jany, 2018; Czaykowska-Higgins, 2009; Leonard & Haynes, 2010).[1] However, the principles of community-engaged research are not well aligned with the realities of academia (e.g., Benedicto, 2018; Riestenberg et al., under review). Since beginning my (Kate's) work in this area with a group of Zapotec teachers in Mexico as part of a graduate school project in 2013, I have often felt stuck among a series of contradictions. Collaborative approaches require trusting relationships that are built up over time, but like a majority of academic researchers (AAUP, 2017; 2021), I faced employment instability as I worked under short-term grants or contracts. I felt immense pressure to quickly and frequently publish and disseminate academic works in particular venues, but both I and the teachers and activists

Riestenberg, Freemond, Lillehaugen, Washington, *Prioritizing Community Partners' Goals in Projects to Support Indigenous Language Revitalization* In: *Decolonizing Linguistics*. Edited by: Anne H. Charity Hudley, Christine Mallinson, and Mary Bucholtz, Oxford University Press. © Anne H. Charity Hudley, Christine Mallinson, and Mary Bucholtz 2024.
DOI: 10.1093/oso/9780197755259.003.0019

394 Decolonizing Linguistics

I worked with were much more interested in producing lesson plans, teaching materials, phrasebooks, and other practical resources. I was trained as an applied linguist but felt lonely in this space that was usually more focused on field research or documentation. I found that a rigid ideology prevented the field of linguistics from fully recognizing the value of such nontraditional research products (Benedicto, 2018). And while our field moved toward publicly accessible digital archives as the gold standard (e.g., Holton, 2012), I was working with communities that did not always want their language made publicly available.

Often in recognition of these contradictions, published work on community-based or participatory research with Indigenous or minoritized languages tends to focus on balancing community members' goals with outside researchers' academic goals. As Kristine Stenzel (2014, p. 302) writes, "Participatory projects are, by their very nature, multiple projects in which we work toward negotiating shared goals and hope to leave everybody reasonably satisfied." This notion of "negotiating shared goals" is a common theme of published work on this topic in our field, and I relied on this framing while completing much of my doctoral work. However, I later began to feel I had been working with language communities in a way that was ultimately extractive because my central focus was on research outputs that were not of interest to community members. I felt that the inherent contradictions between the realities of the academy and the priorities of the communities I was working with made it impossible to negotiate shared goals in a decolonizing and humanizing way (e.g., Leonard, 2018; Paris & Winn, 2016; Smith, 2021). I decided that my work could only truly be supportive of community members' goals if I deprioritized the kinds of outcomes that traditionally define academic success (i.e., products meant for a technical linguistics audience, such as annotated corpora and peer-reviewed journal articles).

Starting in 2018, as a postdoctoral fellow and later a visiting professor in the Tri-College Linguistics Department—which spans Bryn Mawr, Haverford, and Swarthmore Colleges—I wanted my work to prioritize the needs of the communities I worked with, even if it meant deprioritizing the kinds of output valued by academia. I found some support for working this way, especially with my chair Brook Lillehaugen, who helped me find appropriate funding and brought me into some of her work that embodied community-engaged principles. In this chapter, we describe two of these projects. Along with our student Ally Freemond and colleague Jonathan Washington, we offer a set of reflections based on the results of surveys conducted with the community members and students who participated in the projects. We discuss both the challenges and successes of working in this way, sometimes taking a critical lens to our own projects and to current approaches to community-engaged teaching and research. Overall, we want to answer the question: What happens if we deprioritize our academic goals and instead center the goals of our community partners? What conditions allow us to do so?

Project 1: Digital Resources for a Native American Language

The first project focused on creating digital resources for an endangered Native American language. As part of our collaborative agreement, we do not disclose the name of the project leader or the community in our public communications, and all of the materials produced are proprietary resources for the community not accessible to the general public. Students who work on the project agree to these terms and must delete any related files from their computers once they are no longer actively working on the project. This project has been under development in some form for over 20 years and was first envisioned by the project's lead, a linguist and language revitalization activist from the community, whom we will refer to as Hawi. The overarching goal was to create an interactive web version of a culturally significant epic narrative text. The website uses as its basis a version of the text published by a linguist from outside the community in the 1980s, which included interlinear glossing and free translations to English. Hawi added audio and video recordings of the text that he himself had gathered with individuals he considers to be, for now, the last fluent speakers of the language as well as audio that had been collected by the outside linguist.

The collaboration with our department began in 2018 when Kate was put in contact with Hawi through a mutual colleague. It began with a very simple premise: Hawi would visit the campus for one week and would attend two of Kate's Introduction to Linguistics classes. During the first class, Hawi would present to students about his community, their language, and background about the project and his work. During the second class, students would be trained to complete a crowd-sourced task that would contribute directly to advancing Hawi's website, such as proofreading or audio editing. Travel costs for these visits were covered by Bryn Mawr's Career and Civic Engagement Center. Hawi ended up returning to repeat this initiative over several semesters, and the partnership expanded to include student summer internships and independent study courses designed to further support website development. Jonathan joined the project as an additional student mentor and advisor. Kate served as the overall project manager and contributed to the pedagogical aspects of the website, while Jonathan offered technical guidance in computational linguistics. Interns were supported with paid positions through Bryn Mawr's Career and Civic Engagement Center as well as Library and Information Technology Services (LITS). LITS also financially supported the involvement of Andrew Alm, an online communications consultant with expertise in web development who had already been working with Hawi on the project. Kate and Jonathan did not receive any financial support for their work on the project, nor was there a clear way to request it from the colleges. Hawi was offered financial support through LITS but chose not to accept it. One student, Anna Thompson, continued working on the website after the summer internship and made significant progress on various aspects, including the display of the narrative text, accessible grammar explanations with examples and exercises, and a repository of audio and video recordings and other resources. A beta version of the private website was launched in spring 2021, and Hawi for the first time was able to share the website with interested members of his community which has supported new plans for teaching the language in local schools. Ongoing work led by Hawi seeks to add new features to the website that will facilitate learning and engagement with the materials.

Project 2: Tlacolula Valley Zapotec Talking Dictionaries

The second language revitalization project involved the creation or expansion of four online dictionaries corresponding to four variants of Tlacolula Valley Zapotec, a group of languages spoken in Oaxaca, Mexico and in diaspora communities in Mexico and the U.S, co-directed by Brook and activists from each community. The dictionaries are part of the larger Talking Dictionaries Project which has been based at Swarthmore College since 2005 and which originated from Gregory D.S. Anderson and K. David Harrison's work in confronting the challenges of print dictionaries in meeting community needs (Harrison et al., 2019). Dedicated work on the Zapotec dictionaries in summer 2019 was funded by a National Science Foundation Research Experiences for Undergraduates grant (Harrison, 2015–2019). This grant provided funding for a linguistics field school that trained student participants, including Ally, in collaborative documentary linguistic methods. Additional support was provided by the Haverford College Office of the Provost, Haverford College's Center for Peace and Global Citizenship, Living Tongues Institute for Endangered Languages, Swarthmore College, National Geographic Society, Endangered Language Fund, Biblioteca de Investigación Juan de Córdova, and the Tri-College Department of Linguistics. This funding supported faculty and staff travel, stipends for faculty, students, and Zapotec participants, and equipment. The three-year NSF grant and multiple sources of complementary funding allowed the team to envision a project cycle beyond the constraints of a semester (when funding is tied to a course) or academic year (the typical length of internal funding at our colleges).

The four dictionaries document the Zapotec language varieties as spoken in the pueblos of San Bartolomé Quialana (Sánchez Gómez et al., 2019), San Lucas Quiaviní (Lopez et al., 2019), Tlacochahuaya (García Guzmán et al., 2019), and Teotitlán del Valle (Chávez Santiago et al., 2019). The Zapotec project directors are each the first author of the corresponding dictionary for their community. In addition, the speakers in each sound file are credited in the dictionary entries. Multimedia such as images, videos, and tweets are embedded in dictionary entries, providing community-specific context that could not be achieved in a print dictionary (Harrison et al., 2019). During 2019, students collaborated with Zapotec dictionary leaders from these communities to expand the dictionaries, a continuous process that has involved multiple student cohorts over the past decade and still continues.

Reflective Surveys with Project Participants

In August 2020, Kate and Ally sent online surveys about the two language revitalization projects to the community project leads and students involved in the projects. They obtained IRB approval and a small stipend from Bryn Mawr College for participant incentives and summer research assistant support for Ally. Participants had the option to receive a $15 online gift card to an Indigenous or Black-owned business upon completion of the survey. The survey questions were created by Kate and Ally with the input of community partners and included a mix of closed and open-ended questions about the experience of working collaboratively on the projects (see Appendix A and Appendix B). Four out of five community partners and nine out of 16 students completed the survey. Responses to open-ended questions were coded by Ally for emergent themes using thematic analysis, roughly following the approach outlined in Graham R. Gibbs (2007), which allows for the identification of

Continuity and Relationships

One of the most consistent themes of the survey responses was the importance of project continuity and a recognition that student participation in the projects was transient while the community partners' dedication to the project was more permanent. The longevity of the established projects was a clear benefit, as evidenced in the community partner responses. Community partners stated that their projects will continue and envisioned new and expanded project outcomes each year, characterizing language preservation and revitalization as an ongoing effort. Two community partners referenced working on the project every summer as a recurring benchmark for project goals. They expressed that if they did not have students' support, the work would still continue, but that the projects clearly benefited from the resources and support that the students and the grants brought. One community partner stated that otherwise they would be making "meagre progress," as they had been doing for decades prior with little support. This response indicates that the language work could be done without the students but that the support of recurring student cohorts was a valuable resource in furthering project goals. One community partner wrote, "I wish we can keep doing this kind of work together for many more years to come." In short, the partnerships were seen as beneficial, likely because the students were supporting work that the community members already wanted to do.

Student respondents made it evident that there are unique benefits and drawbacks to joining already established projects versus joining new projects. Some noted that this work does not have a discrete end point and recognized that they were either jumping into previously existing work or just beginning the work and therefore not necessarily seeing its community impact. One student respondent stated that the lack of a clear starting point was a challenge, and that they felt better about their contributions to the project once they found a routine. Another student felt that their short period of participation in the project prevented them from seeing the "full effect" of the work. Another student wrote, "I think a challenge would be not always knowing if what you're doing is enough and that may lead to some internal challenges when working with self-directed work like this. This is something I always feel in any long-term project because there is no real 'end goal' and the work is continuous."

Academia and Institutions

Participants were asked if they thought the "academic" and "community" goals of the project aligned, leaving it to each participant to decide for themselves what these goals were. Some community leaders showed hesitancy and skepticism toward academic institutions, perhaps in reference to the colonial and extractive practices that have typically characterized Western academic engagements with Indigenous communities. One respondent wrote, "I am involved in this relationship with the Tri-College Consortium with concern for my own community. I am not necessarily concerned with fulfilling the educational needs of an American academy of higher learning." This quote shows that this community partner rightly prioritized their own community but also suggests that they felt able to participate in these projects without having to forfeit their own goals and autonomy.

At the same time, some community partner responses framed the support from academics and academic institutions as highly valued resources. One community partner participant referred to an academic faculty partner as a "trusted liaison" that handled interactions with the institution. They also recognized that language revitalization work was a component of students' education and therefore was a benefit to the institution. One community partner wrote, "I know the interaction is fulfilling some kind of need to the academy." Overall, responses indicated that student experience was not the community partners' priority, but they were aware of and proud of this aspect. In other words, community partners valued the work with students despite some skepticism toward academia and academic institutions in the US.

Among the student participants, initial feelings toward the academic goals of the project and the role of the academic institution were varied. Some student participants stated that they initially felt more aligned with academic goals or the academic lens of the work. However, multiple student participants expressed in their responses that they gained a greater understanding of the impact and longevity of the project beyond its academic scope in a way that they had not understood at the beginning of their work. One student participant stated that they initially felt that the project had an "extractive nature" before speaking to community members and realizing that "they really wanted the project." At that point, the student's perspective changed and "that was the motivation."

400 Decolonizing Linguistics

For some students, the social justice aspect of the projects was initially conceptual but became tangible throughout the work. As one student explained, "As the work progressed and I was able to see the impact our work had, I grew to appreciate that aspect much more." Another student described an experience in which they felt that the project's technical work detracted from its broader context, which suggests that they hadn't thought much about the social justice facet of the project until being asked via the survey. When asked, "What type of work do you feel like you were doing?" (see Appendix A, question 2), this was the only student who chose only "Academics" and did not choose either "Community service" or "Social justice work" as well. This student was hired to work short-term on a particular data processing task at the height of the pandemic and was not part of the regular cohort of student interns. Reflecting on this now, this was an oversight that we as project leaders on the college side could have handled better; the rest of the students surveyed were each a part of small cohorts in which the social justice aspects of the projects were discussed explicitly.

Discussion

Based on our experiences and survey findings, we now discuss the conditions that allow linguists employed in academia to facilitate projects that follow the lead of community members. For us, three overarching themes have emerged in response to this question: funding, relationships, and employment.

Funding

Financial support for this type of work is accessible in our small, liberal arts college context. Most of our funding sources focused on student learning or research experiences and did not require narrowly constrained research outcomes for faculty. This includes the National Science Foundation funding stream dedicated to Research Experiences for Undergraduates as well as college funding available to support student career training or social justice work. The requirements of internal funding tend to be flexible, and because our institutions are small, it is often possible to contact the person managing the funds directly to ask whether they would consider the project. In other words, these projects tend to have a "mish-mash" of funding from different sources, none of which are explicitly meant to create digital resources for a language community. However, we were able to manage the projects in a way that prioritized these goals. For example, Bryn Mawr's LITS, a significant funder for the Native American website project, has the primary goal of providing students with hands-on experiences that build career-focused digital competencies. This goal was compatible with the project because the community linguist was interested in working with our students to develop their skills in this way. However, such funding would work less well for a project seeking stipends that would enable young people in the language community to be involved, something we often discussed but which proved to be more challenging. Because the funding systems that we operate within are not equitable, partnerships of this sort are often not equitable, even when we attempt community-driven work (Chetty et al., this volume). It is also worth noting the role of faculty in seeking out, pulling together, overseeing, and reporting on multiple small pots of complementary funding sources to facilitate these projects. There is certainly privilege involved in having these funding sources available; the faculty labor involved is significant and potentially burdensome, especially to contingent or pretenure faculty. More opportunities for course releases and summer stipends for faculty could help to relieve some of this pressure.

Employment

Faculty were involved in these projects without clear goals toward peer-reviewed publication. For Kate, de-emphasizing publication came in concert with deprioritizing a traditional academic career altogether, and she recently accepted a position outside of academia, which has effectively ended her ability to continue being involved in these projects. Brook and Jonathan, both assistant professors when the project started, knew that the types of project outcomes described here would likely not "count" for tenure, and that they would need to submit tenure cases that did not rely significantly on this work but rather on more traditional peer-reviewed scholarship. These situations reiterate the point that this type of work has been possible by maintaining a sort of separation from traditional scholarship rather than by attempting to negotiate project goals shared by all parties. These experiences can also lead to a transformative understanding of the work of a linguist. For example, as Jonathan explained in an email exchange among the authors of this chapter, "One big struggle I had [with the Native American website project] was that . . . I have always done what I could to license computational tools I develop under Free and Open licenses and make them publicly available. The requirement of this project for resources to be proprietary [to the community]

402 Decolonizing Linguistics

goes against my long-internalized ideas of what doing something beneficial looks like, and even what science is." Now that both Jonathan and Brook have received tenure, they continue to support these projects and to involve students. Although the involvement of each student cohort is sometimes brief, the projects have a life beyond students' short participation, which is possible due to the employment stability of the faculty who maintain the project.

Relationships

Both projects we have described here are ongoing due to strong professional relationships between faculty and community leaders that were built up over years of collaboration. In the case of the Native American website project, the relationship initially relied on Kate and Hawi being introduced through a mutual colleague. The relationship continued due to the rapport that was established when Hawi saw the results of the crowdsourced work the students had completed in just a few short weeks. Although Kate is no longer actively involved with the project, she and Hawi regularly keep in touch. Jonathan and Brook have both supported students in securing summer funding to work with Hawi since Kate's departure. Brook also maintains contact with the Zapotec activists and looks forward to taking new cohorts of students to Oaxaca in future summers to continue the work on the Talking Dictionaries.

Concluding Thoughts

Decolonizing linguistics requires changing the power structures within academia. This process can begin on an individual level through specific actions, choices, and efforts that deprioritize agendas traditionally held by academic institutions. We have found that centering community goals is not necessarily at odds with creating rich learning opportunities for students, whose experiences in these projects have led to undergraduate senior theses and various career opportunities. Community goals are also not incompatible with some more traditional research objectives in linguistics; for example, the Native American website project now has a spinoff research working group investigating questions related to language structure posed by the community linguist. Importantly, however, these were not planned outcomes but rather the emergent results of collaborative projects that prioritized community goals.

Let's bring collaborative, community-led work out from these marginalized spaces in academia. Those of us who sit on tenure and promotion committees, let's be a voice for co-authored work with students and community partners and for public-facing and community-facing scholarship. When we sit on grant panels, let's mobilize our experience as academic partners in collaborative work and speak to the realities of budgets, timelines, and collaborative processes. As these volumes well attest, we are already doing this work in the spaces we find and make. Let's continue to make those spaces bigger.

Note

1. We are endlessly grateful to everyone who has made it possible for us to be involved in such meaningful and challenging work. We thank Hawi, Zapotec language activists Janet Chávez Santiago and Moisés García Guzmán, and two community activists who chose to remain anonymous. (All five declined to be included as co-authors.) Thank you as well to student participants Rosa Arasa, computer science major at Bryn Mawr College; Joe Corcoran, researcher and medical student at Temple University; Emily Drummond, linguist and PhD student at University of California, Berkeley; Graham Mauro, Haverford College class of 2020; Vinny Ong, linguistics major at Bryn Mawr College; and four students who chose to remain anonymous. We would also like to acknowledge the various funding sources mentioned throughout the paper: Biblioteca de Investigación Juan de Córdova; Bryn Mawr College Library and Information Technology Services (LITS); Bryn Mawr College Career and Civic Engagement Center; Bryn Mawr College Faculty Awards and Grants Committee; Endangered Language Fund; Haverford College Office of the Provost; Haverford College Center for Peace and Global Citizenship; Living Tongues Institute for Endangered Languages; National Geographic Society; National Science Foundation; Swarthmore College; and the Tri-College Department of Linguistics.

References

American Association of University Professors. (2017). *Trends in the academic labor force 1975–2015*. aaup.org/sites/default/files/Academic_Labor_Force_Trends_1975-2015.pdf

American Association of University Professors. (2021). *2020–21 faculty compensation survey results*. aaup.org/2020-21-faculty-compensation-survey-results

Benedicto, Elena. (2018). When participatory action research (PAR) and (Western) academic institutional policies do not align. In Shannon Bischoff & Carmen Jany (Eds.), *Insights from Practices in Community-Based Research* (pp. 38–65). De Gruyter Mouton.

Bischoff, Shannon, & Jany, Carmen. (2018). *Insights from practices in community-based research*. De Gruyter Mouton.

Czaykowska-Higgins, Ewa. (2009). Research models, community engagement, and linguistic fieldwork: Reflections on working within Canadian Indigenous communities. *Language Documentation & Conservation, 3*(1), 15–50.

Gibbs, Graham R. (2007). *Analysing qualitative data*. SAGE Publishing.

Harrision, K. David, with Fernald, Theodore, Lillehaugen, Brook, & Thomas, Jamie. (2015–2019). National Science Foundation research experiences for undergraduates

404 Decolonizing Linguistics

(REU): Building digital tools to support endangered languages and preserve environmental knowledge in Mexico, Micronesia, and Navajo Nation. #1461056.

Harrison, K. David, Lillehaugen, Brook Danielle, Fahringer, Jeremy, & Lopez, Felipe H. (2019). Zapotec language activism and talking dictionaries. In *Proceedings of Electronic Lexicography in the 21st Century Conference 2019*, 31–50.

Holton, Gary. (2012). Language archives: They're not just for linguists anymore. In Frank Seifart, Geoffrey Haig, Nikolaus P. Himmelmann, Dagmar Jung, Anna Margetts, & Paul Trilsbeek (Eds.), *Potentials of Language Documentation: Methods, Analyses, and Utilization* (pp. 111–117). University of Hawai'i Press.

Leonard, Wesley Y., and Haynes, Erin. (2010). Making "collaboration" collaborative: An examination of perspectives that frame linguistic field research. *Language Documentation & Conservation 4*, 268–293.

Chávez Santiago, Janet, Brook Danielle Lillehaugen, Allison Freemond, Neal Kelso, Jaime Metzger, Kate Riestenberg, & K. David Harrison. (2019). Teotitlán del Valle Zapotec talking dictionary, version 2.0. Living Tongues Institute for Endangered Languages. talkingdictionary.org/teotitlan

García Guzmán, Moisés, Brook Danielle Lillehaugen, Kathryn Goldberg, María Mercedes Méndez Morales, Brynn Paul, May Helena Plumb, Chantal Reyes, Cecilia G. Williamson, & K. David Harrison. (2019). Tlacochahuaya Zapotec talking dictionary, version 2.1. Living Tongues Institute for Endangered Languages. talkingdictionary.org/tlacochahuaya

Leonard, Wesley Y. (2018). Reflections on (de)colonialism in language documentation. In Bradley McDonnell, Andrea L. Berez-Kroeker & Gary Holton (Eds.), *Reflections on language documentation: 20 Years after Himmelmann 1998* (pp. 55–65). University of Hawai'I Press.

Lopez, Felipe H., Brook Danielle Lillehaugen, & Pamela Munro, with Savita M. Deo, Graham Mauro, & Saúl Ontiveros. (2019). San Lucas Quiaviní Zapotec talking dictionary, version 2.0. Living Tongues Institute for Endangered Languages. talkingdictionary.org/sanlucasquiavini

Paris, Django, & Winn, Maisha T. (Eds.). (2014). *Humanizing research*. SAGE Publishing

Riestenberg, Katherine J., Melvatha Chee, Tania Granadillo, & Shannon Bischoff. (2022.) Creating wide networks of support for Indigenous languages: The workshop on Community-based Language Research Across the Americas (CBLRAA). In Sandman, Sarah, Shannon Bischoff, & Jens Clegg (Eds.), *Voices: Perspectives from the International Year of Indigenous Languages, Language Documentation & Conservation Special Publication no. 27* (pp. 155–164). University of Hawai'i Press. https://hdl.handle.net/10125/74698

Sánchez Gómez, Aurora, Floriana Hernández Martínez, Lillehaugen, Brook Danielle, with Savita M. Deo, Graham Mauro, Saul Ontiveros, & K. David Harrison. (2019). San Bartolomé Quialana Zapotec talking dictionary, version 1.0. Living Tongues Institute for Endangered Languages. Talkingdictionary.org/quialana

Smith, Linda Tuhiwai. (2021). *Decolonizing methodologies: Research and Indigenous peoples*, 2nd ed. Zed Books.

Stenzel, Kristine. (2014). The pleasures and pitfalls of a "participatory" documentation project: An experience in Northwestern Amazonia. *Language Documentation & Conservation 8*, 287–306.

Appendix A

Student Survey Questions

1. What were your goals for the project that you participated in?

Prioritizing Community Partners' Goals   405

2. What type of work do you feel like you were doing? You may select more than one.
   Community service
   Activism
   Social justice work
   Research
   Academics
   Coursework
   Other
3. Did your feelings about what type of work you were doing change over the course of the project? After the project?
4. How relevant would you say the following skills or areas of knowledge were to the language revitalization work you took part in? If relevant, please explain or elaborate.
   Very Relevant
   Relevant
   Moderately Relevant
   Slightly Relevant
   Not Relevant
   a. Language Structure (phonetics, phonology, syntax, semantics, or morphology)
   b. Sociolinguistics (variation, linguistic discrimination, language and power, etc.)
   c. Applied Linguistics (language teaching and learning, language and education, etc.)
   d. History and Politics (colonization, international relations, geopolitics)
   e. Ethnobotany (plants and their cultural significance)
   f. Research ethics
   g. Video/audio recording and editing
   h. Digital skills (web design, social media, coding, data management, language processing, etc.)
5. What skills or knowledge did you gain while working on a language revitalization project that you later applied in your coursework? (Or could see yourself applying to coursework in the future?)
6. What skills or knowledge did you gain while working on a language revitalization project that you can see yourself using in a future career?
7. What skills or knowledge did you gain while working on a language revitalization project that you see as valuable outside of coursework and career?
8. Do you agree or disagree with the following statements? If relevant, please explain or elaborate.
   Strongly Disagree
   Disagree
   No Opinion
   Agree
   Strongly Agree
   a. The academic expectations of the project aligned with the goals of the community partners.
   b. I was involved in negotiations or dialogues about the goals of the project.
   c. The product of our linguistic work was given back to the community effectively.
   d. Questions of authorship and consent were addressed and adhered to.
9. What would you have done with your time if you weren't doing this project (e.g., homework or coursework, taken on a summer job, worked on a research project on campus)?
10. The purpose of this survey is to understand the benefits and challenges of involving students in community activist-led language revitalization work. Is there anything else relevant to this topic that you would like to add?

Appendix B

Community Partner Survey Questions

1. What have been your overall goals for the language revitalization project(s) that students worked with you on?
2. How has your understanding of the work or your goals changed over time?
3. How are you or your community now using the resource(s) that students worked with you on? Or how do you imagine using these resources in the future?
4. What skills, knowledge, or resources have you gained while working with students on a language revitalization project that you may not have gained without student participation? How are you applying or using these in your work, or how might you use them in the future?
5. What skills or knowledge do you believe students gained while working with you on a language revitalization project that they may not have gained through their typical coursework or studies?
6. Do you agree or disagree with the following statements? If relevant, please explain or elaborate.
   Strongly Disagree
   Disagree
   No Opinion
   Agree
   Strongly Agree
   a. Students' goals aligned well with my goals.
   b. I was given the lead in negotiations or dialogues about the goals of the project.
   c. I was given the lead in negotiations or dialogues about how to achieve the goals of the project.
   d. The product of the work was (or will be) effectively shared with my community.
   e. Questions of authorship and consent were addressed and adhered to.
7. What would you have done with your time if you weren't doing this project (e.g., working, studying, etc.)?
8. The purpose of this survey is to understand the benefits and challenges of involving students in language revitalization work led by community activists like yourself. Is there anything else relevant to this topic that you would like to add?

Ève Ryan is assistant professor of applied linguistics at the University of Alaska Fairbanks. Originally from Île de la Réunion in the Indian Ocean, Ève studied in Europe before moving to the United States, where she received her PhD in education from the University of California, Los Angeles. Her most recent research focuses on the bilingual development of early elementary students in a French-English dual language program in the United States.

Matt Ford is an ESL teaching assistant at the University of Alaska Fairbanks, teaching academic writing skills. He received a double BA in English and linguistics (2011) from Rowan University in New Jersey, with a specialization in Romance languages. Prior to moving to Fairbanks, Matt was the Program Director for Literacy New Jersey, a nonprofit adult literacy program specializing in ESL and High School Equivalency courses. For over 10 years, he has taught all levels of ESL, supervised instructors, led tutor training for new volunteers, and organized statewide literacy conferences. He has also led workshops in pronunciation teaching techniques, mindfulness in the classroom, goal-based curriculum development, and more. Matt is currently working on his MA in applied linguistics, focusing on the role of teacher/student emotions in the language classroom.

Giovanna Wilde is an Indigenous Yup'ik undergraduate student from Mountain Village, Alaska, attending the University of Alaska Fairbanks. Mountain Village is a small village of 800 people on the Lower Yukon in Western Alaska. The village lost its Yup'ik language due to the missionaries that came to the area. Giovanna is currently working toward a BA degree in elementary education with a Certification in Tribal Government. As an educator, Giovanna believes understanding students' language is the tool that will help improve Indigenous students' educational pursuits and ensure their success. When students' needs are met, they find their wings fly. Her goal is that one day, the students in her village will not only learn to fly, but soar. Her hopes are for more success stories among students in her village and in the Lower Yukon Schools.

Abstract: What does decolonization mean in the context of linguistics teaching in an institution of higher education in Alaska? In this chapter, the authors share some reflections based on their experience teaching and taking an undergraduate linguistics course aimed at future teachers at the University of Alaska Fairbanks (UAF). After providing a brief overview of both the Alaskan educational context and linguistics at UAF, they offer a description of the course, as well as an assessment of the course's strengths (e.g., affirming students' emotions) and limitations (e.g., missed opportunities to indigenize knowledge). The chapter concludes with a testimony from a past student of the course, illustrating and emphasizing the need for community-school-university partnerships.

Key Words: decolonization, linguistics, Alaska, teacher education, Indigenous

19

Promoting Decolonized Classrooms Through an Introductory Linguistics Course for Future Teachers in Alaska

Ève Ryan (she/her/hers)
University of Alaska Fairbanks

Matt Ford (he/him/his)
University of Alaska Fairbanks

Giovanna Wilde (she/her/hers)
University of Alaska Fairbanks

Introduction

In this chapter, we answer the call by Anne Charity Hudley, Christine Mallinson, and Mary Bucholtz (2020b) to move from theory to action and work collectively toward antiracist linguistics.[1] The propelling question at the core of our writing is whether it is "possible to sit within the academy as an applied linguist and teach, (and) prepare teachers . . . in a way that is antiracist and decolonizing" (Motha, 2020, p. 129). The advent of decolonization theory, which champions the acknowledgment of historic injustices as a precursor to the Indigenization of knowledge and ways of being (Battiste, 2013), has spurred a conversation about the need to decolonize teaching in higher education (e.g., Bhambra et al., 2018), and in linguistics in particular (e.g., Pennycook, 2021). What does decolonization mean in the context of linguistics teaching in an institution of higher education in Alaska?

Here, we share some reflections based on the experiences of Ève and Matt teaching an undergraduate linguistics course to future teachers at the University of Alaska Fairbanks (UAF). After providing a brief overview of both the Alaskan educational context and linguistics at UAF, we offer a description of the course, as well as an assessment of the course's strengths and

---

Ève Ryan, Matt Ford, Giovanna Wilde, *Promoting Decolonized Classrooms Through an Introductory Linguistics Course for Future Teachers in Alaska* In: *Decolonizing Linguistics.* Edited by: Anne H. Charity Hudley, Christine Mallinson, and Mary Bucholtz, Oxford University Press. © Anne H. Charity Hudley, Christine Mallinson, and Mary Bucholtz 2024.
DOI: 10.1093/oso/9780197755259.003.0020

Decolonizing Linguistics

limitations. We conclude the chapter with testimony from Giovanna, a previous student of the course, who has used her experiences and her position as an Alaska Native to foster an ongoing two-way collaboration between the university and her community.

Alaskan Educational Context

Alaska, which was granted statehood in 1959, displays unique characteristics that make it stand out compared to the contiguous United States (US), a settler-colonial nation-state. While the centers of economic and political power are concentrated in a few urban areas, the state is also "home to 229 federally recognized Alaska Native Villages located across a wide geographic area, whose records are as diverse as the people themselves" (National Archives Online Catalog, n.d., p. 1). Besides English, 20 Alaska Native languages are among the state's official languages (Alaska Statutes, 2014), including Yup'ik, which is the second most spoken Indigenous language in the US after Navajo. Alaska epitomizes the issues at the core of white settler-colonialism, including a history marked by the dispossession of land, languages, and ways of life (Thorne et al., 2015). From the late nineteenth century to the 1970s, Christian missionaries colluded with the federal government to forcibly remove Alaska Native children from their communities to be sent to boarding schools in an effort "to detribalize and assimilate Indigenous people into Euro-American culture" (Alaska State Archives, 2021). Schools have thus become a contested space (Thorne et al., 2015), as they promote a mostly Western curriculum featuring Standardized English as the language of instruction at the expense of Alaska Native languages and dialects, or Nonstandardized varieties of English. With respect to its educational workforce, Alaska mirrors national trends, consisting of a diverse student body that contrasts with a racially and ethnically homogeneous teaching profession. In Alaska, roughly 47% of K-12 students are white and 21% are Alaska Native (Alaska Department of Education and Early Development, 2021), whereas 90% of teachers are white, and only 5% come from American Indian or Alaska Native backgrounds (University of Alaska Fairbanks, n.d.). In addition, Alaska suffers from high teacher turnover, especially in rural areas (DeFeo et al., 2017; Kaden et al., 2016). Factors that contribute to the difficulty in recruiting and retaining teachers of color (TOCs) include: historical and current educational policies, "the often toxic environmental and operational conditions for TOCs in their preparation programs and workplaces" (Carter Andrews et al., 2019, p. 6), and the lack of exposure to topics of central relevance to people of color in K-12 classrooms. Regarding the latter, white teachers in Alaska Native Village schools often apply a curriculum that is disconnected from the local culture (Jester and Fickel, 2013).

Linguistics at UAF

As Jo-ann Archibald Q'um Q'um Xiiem and Jeremy Garcia Tuukwa (2022) explain, "the majority of teachers who teach Indigenous students are non-Indigenous; therefore, it is critical to ensure that they are better prepared to work with Indigenous students and their families and communities" (p. 42). We argue that linguistics plays an important role in this aspect of teacher preparation. Indeed, for language-minoritized students in Alaska, especially those coming from Alaska Native villages in rural areas, the disconnect between the English of the classroom and the variety of English used in the local community negatively influences their academic experience (Kwachka, 2017). Such tensions are a major area of focus in the class described in this chapter. The class, entitled "Language, Education, Linguistics," is offered annually at UAF, and is traditionally taught by a faculty member from the Linguistics Program. The Linguistics Program at UAF acknowledges the key role played by language in the health and wellbeing of Alaska Native communities, and it has a tradition of engaging in research and service that promotes "capacity building and the professionalization of Indigenous language educators" (Thorne et al., 2015, p. 143). To illustrate, the Second Language Acquisition and Teacher Education (SLATE) graduate program was created at UAF in 2006 "based on the stated goals of (1) improving Yup'ik and English education in Alaska's Yup'ik region, (2) enabling local leadership in language programming, and (3) fostering community-driven research" (Marlow & Siekmann, 2013, p. 2), and some of its graduates "serve in leadership positions beyond the university and the state" (Thorne et al., 2015, p. 152). Initiatives such as SLATE suggest that "community-school-university partnerships have helped to catalyze a sense of agency through participatory engagement" (Thorne et al., 2015, p. 155).

The Course Language, Education, Linguistics

Organization of the Course

"Language, Education, Linguistics" is taught each year at the undergraduate level. Table 19.1 describes the main features of the course as it was taught in the spring semester of 2021. Readers are encouraged to contact the first author for a copy of the latest version of the syllabus.

412 Decolonizing Linguistics

Table 19.1 Main features of the course "Language, Education, Linguistics," as taught in Spring 2021

Instructors	One faculty Instructor of Record (Ryan) One graduate Teaching Assistant (Ford)
Course length	15 weeks
Instruction format	One asynchronous lecture per week via Zoom 20 to 50 minutes Two synchronous sessions per week via Zoom 1.5 hours dedicated to a discussion of a chapter from the textbook 1.5 hours dedicated to a student-led presentation and discussion of a relevant academic or teaching article or chapter Teaching Assistant held two hours of synchronous online office hours per week Students could schedule individual appointments with the Instructor
Primary text	*Dialects at School - Educating Linguistically Diverse Students* (Reaser et al., 2017)
Course objectives	By the end of the course, students were expected to be able to: • identify some English dialect-related features in students' speech and writing • understand the ways in which English dialect differences in schools can be addressed • appreciate the complexities of teaching "Standard English" • think critically about ways to teach language awareness to students • distinguish dialect differences from language disorders
Number of students	20 undergraduate students
Students' majors and minors	Alaska Native languages Education Foreign languages Law Psychology
Students' self-reported race and ethnicity	Alaska Native / Indigenous ($n = 8$) Asian American ($n = 2$) Caucasian / white ($n = 9$) Mixed ($n = 1$)
Students' self-reported languages spoken	Inupiaq English Spanish Tagalog Yup'ik

The "Language, Education, Linguistics" class, which is cross-listed in both education and linguistics, is required for students majoring in education. All but one student in spring 2021 planned on becoming teachers, mostly within Alaska. Most importantly, students taking this course typically have very diverse language backgrounds. In spring 2021, three students identified Yup'ik as their first language. English was the first language of the majority of students, who came from both Standardized English backgrounds and Non-Standardized English backgrounds such as Alaskan Englishes (Kwachka, 2017). Some students also reported speaking Inupiaq, Spanish, and Tagalog.

Affirming Students' Emotions

Under the cover of objectivity, linguistics has historically allowed issues of racism and colonialism to go unchecked, when in fact there is no such thing as racial neutrality (Motha, 2020). In the case of Native languages, this effort to remain "objective" has in fact contributed to the reinforcement of colonial logics: objectifying Native languages (i.e., treating a language as an object or a source of data) fails to take into account the fact that a language cannot be separated from its people (Leonard, 2020). Acknowledging this context is important for Ève and Matt as linguistics instructors. In contrast, our teaching philosophy is influenced by culturally responsive pedagogy, a pedagogy "that recognizes students' differences, validates students' cultures, and asserts that cultural congruence of classroom practices increases students' success in schools" (Ragoonaden & Mueller, 2017, p. 25). This holistic approach resonates with the Alaska Native Knowledge Network (Barnhardt, 2007), "a pedagogy of place that shifts the emphasis from teaching *about* local culture to teaching *through* the culture" (p. 113, emphasis added). Teaching "Language, Education, Linguistics" in the spring of 2021, we tried to model what we hoped our students would model in their own future classrooms: that teaching linguistically diverse students means making room in the classroom for their languages, their people, their stories, and their emotions. As settler instructors, we were committed to creating an inclusive and safe classroom environment. Given that "developing trust takes time, giving of oneself, and entering into personal relationships" (Thorne et al., 2015, p. 158), we openly acknowledged aspects of our positionalities to the students in an effort to be transparent, and encouraged them to do the same. Both Ève and Matt come from privileged backgrounds, not only with respect to our race as white persons, but also in terms of our socioeconomic and educational backgrounds. Furthermore, our teaching is grounded in our experiences as speakers of dominant language varieties, including Standardized English. The fact that, as white instructors, we explicitly brought up the topic of race in some class discussions may have prompted some white students to confront language-related issues of racism that they might have resisted addressing if introduced by instructors of color (Gordon et al., 2021). Moreover, as recent newcomers to Alaska, we both have limited contextualized knowledge of the Alaskan education system, and thus strive to learn *from* our students and not simply *about* them in "ongoing conversations of learning" (Wernicke, 2021, p. 9). In that vein, we aimed to facilitate students' learning rather than to impart knowledge from a top-down approach. For example, as indicated above, pre-recorded lectures were available to students so that class time could be spent on discussions, leaving ample time to have students' voices be heard. We also took advantage of the modality (i.e., Zoom) to encourage student participation. For example, the instructors would sometimes use the muting feature for ourselves to ensure that we would not interrupt students. Also, the small group feature allowed students to interact with each other in a more intimate fashion. And finally, students were encouraged to use the chat feature to share their ideas, providing another avenue for discussion.

Fostering a nurturing classroom environment was essential as we made space for students' emotions in the classroom, which we argue is of paramount significance to a decolonizing approach. Indeed, throughout the semester, some students reported experiencing strong emotions (e.g., discomfort, sadness, anger) after completing some of the readings, discussions, and assignments as they grappled with the emotional consequences of linguistic racism and colonialism (De Costa, 2020). To illustrate, one assignment, given toward the middle of the semester and modeled after Leslie Banes and colleagues (2016), focused on self-reflexive inquiry: students were to read Amy Tan's (1999) "Mother Tongue" piece, before writing a reflection paper on their personal language history. We then devoted a whole class session to discussing students' stories, some recalling painful memories. For instance, an Alaska Native student reported listening to an Elder who recalled being punished for speaking their Alaska Native language in the classroom as a young child. We acknowledge the danger for white instructors such as ourselves of fetishizing trauma narratives, thereby retraumatizing minoritized students (Tuck & Yang, 2014). We therefore aimed to not just focus on pain narratives (Zembylas, 2014) but also to make room for stories of resilience and joy (e.g., engaging in advocacy work on campus) (Oré et al., 2016). Most importantly, this exercise served to shift the balance of power to students who came from minoritized language backgrounds. They served as authorities, using their lived experiences to illustrate and discuss academic concepts pertinent to the class. On the other hand, for settler instructors and students, such an exercise meant that the class became "a space that allows us to interrogate our ongoing participation in settler colonialism and the racialization of minoritized people, their languages, actions, desires, and knowledges; a space that lets us understand language as always political and inextricably connected to identity, culture, and knowledge" (Wernicke, 2021, p. 9). The goals of such an exercise was to promote Deep Listening, which Laura Brearley and Treahna Hamm (2013, p. 259) describe as follows:

> The Indigenous concept of Deep Listening describes a way of learning, working and being together. It is informed by the concepts of community and reciprocity. Deep Listening involves listening respectfully in ways which build community. It draws on every sense and every part of our being. Deep Listening involves taking the time to develop relationships and to listen respectfully and responsibly. It involves reframing how we learn, how we come to know and what we value as knowledge.

According to the course evaluation feedback, which we discuss further below, conducting such personal reflections in public cemented the fabric of the class, which became a trustworthy space where uncomfortable language-related discussions were embraced. Furthermore, as explained below, Deep Listening aided in evolving both Ève and Matt's teaching philosophies concerning the role of the teacher in the classroom.

Indigenizing Knowledge

In this section, we discuss some of the tensions associated with the materials selection for the course, especially regarding readings. In addition to the textbook, students were assigned a teaching or research article relevant to the unit to present to their peers before leading the follow-up discussion. Though some students commented that they were originally daunted by the difficulty of the assigned readings, they seized the opportunity to take ownership of the materials through presentations and class discussions. In fact, having students interpret theoretical concepts through the lens of their local contexts helped Indigenize knowledge by promoting "an epistemology of the colonized informed by indigenous ideas and local practices" (Shin, 2006, 148). For example, some discussions of linguistic racism naturally shifted toward the "devaluation of innovative forms of Indigenous languages," which include "varieties of colonial languages" (Gaby & Woods, 2020, e275), such as Alaska Native-influenced varieties of English. And although the class was conducted in English, we welcomed translanguaging practices: some small groups naturally switched back and forth between English and an Alaska Native language, and some students included videos in their class presentations featuring speakers from their Alaska Native communities. However, even if Alaska

416 Decolonizing Linguistics

Native students felt that the readings about other linguistically minoritized communities (e.g., speakers of African American Vernacular English, children from First Nations communities in Canada, or from American Indian communities in the contiguous United States) resonated with some of their own experiences, the same students challenged us to include local perspectives, with one student asking us at the end of the semester "What about us?" In other words, no matter how relevant the readings were to the classroom context, there were several issues. For one, the very fact that the textbook was authored by white scholars was in tension with the course's stated goal of decolonization. Furthermore, even though supplementary readings included pieces written by Black and Indigenous People of Color, by not including texts written by and about Alaskan communities, we failed to elevate Alaskan voices in the academic sphere, unintentionally reinforcing epistemological racism (Kubota, 2020). The difficulty in identifying materials pertaining to the education of linguistically diverse students in Alaska itself points to the lack of inclusiveness in linguistic research (see Charity Hudley et al., 2020a). One way that Ève plans to circumvent this issue in future iterations of the class is to expand the range of readings beyond journal articles and book chapters to include theses from alumni of the UAF graduate Linguistics Program. For example, one assignment in the latest iteration of the class in fall 2022 asks students to discuss abstracts from master's thesis projects authored by UAF alumni. Students are then asked to propose their own tentative research topic pertaining to a language-related issue that is relevant to their own community. The goals of such an assignment are to expose students to local linguistics research, to disseminate knowledge generated by Alaskan Indigenous scholars, and to potentially attract underrepresented students to linguistics by positioning them as linguists in training.

Giovanna's Testimony

The following is a testimony from Giovanna (third author), a student of the class in Spring 2021, who is currently completing her bachelor's of education as well as her Tribal Management certificate at UAF. Giovanna is an Alaska Native Yup'ik woman from Mountain Village, an Indigenous rural community in Western Alaska sitting on traditional Yup'ik land. Over 90% of the 800 residents of Mountain Village identify as Alaska Native. Due to the effects of white settler-colonialism, Mountain Village has experienced a major loss of the Yup'ik language; there are currently no fluent native speakers in residence. Throughout the 2021 semester in "Language,

Education, Linguistics," Giovanna discussed how the dispossession of Native languages and ways of life has negatively impacted the educational experiences of students in her community, and she emphasized the disconnect between the language of the classroom and the variety of English spoken in Mountain Village. Giovanna provided the following testimony in the context of our chapter collaboration, as she reflected upon her main takeaways from the course and her motivations for pursuing a graduate education in linguistics in the future.

> Every student comes into the classroom with a unique way of speaking and learning. Our Indigenous children do not think in the way that Western children do, nor do they have the same terms, labels, and identifiers for common things. This course has shown me that as a teacher, it is my responsibility to make myself aware of each student's dialect and thought process. After completing the course, I spoke with our Tribal Council about all of the things I have learned about language, education, and linguistics. I proposed a series of workshops for rural Alaskan teachers centered around the themes of this course, including dialect awareness and teacher response to nonstandard English speakers. The response has been positive; our community sees the need for our children to succeed in their education in a way that does not disregard the Indigenous experience in favor of Western culture.
>
> Language is the way our children process the world, and we must meet speakers of vernacular English where they are, and educate our teachers as to how to approach working with Native students. If we do this, our students will be able to bridge the gap between worlds, our parents in the community will feel closer and more connected to their children's learning, and we can finally begin to heal from the decades of trauma endured at the hands of the Western school system. These are all incredibly important things that will help communities like Mountain Village to thrive and succeed in a world that has often left us behind.

As Giovanna indicated in her testimony, she reached out to decision-makers in her community and made the case for dialect awareness training for teachers at the local school. The Tribal Council then reached out to the first author. With Giovanna's help, faculty members from the UAF Linguistics Program subsequently devised a teacher in-service session. At the time of the writing of this chapter, faculty members from the UAF Linguistics Program had conducted one such meeting with the local teachers and were planning another get-together. Our hope is to foster an ongoing collaboration between the university and the Mountain Village community, with knowledge flowing both ways.

Conclusion

The settler-colonial history that has marked education in Alaska, coupled with the state's linguistically diverse student population, highlight the relevance and necessity of pedagogical decolonization. As this volume attests, the field of linguistics is especially apropos for such endeavors (see Arnold, this volume; Montoya, this volume; Plumb et al., this volume; Thomas, 2024). In this chapter, we discussed decolonization in the context of linguistics teaching in an institution of higher education in Alaska by focusing on an undergraduate linguistics course targeting future teachers.

Overall, students have responded favorably to the class, as can be seen in the final course evaluations filled out anonymously by students in the spring of 2021. When asked about aspects of the course that contributed most to their learning, the majority of students pointed to class discussions, reinforcing the need for student voices to be heard. Both whole class and small group discussions allowed students to make sense of their own experiences (e.g., one student wrote: "I felt I should of been made aware of the information in this course a long time ago because it have information regarding the experiences I went through being an ELL student"), as well as to be confronted to different perspectives (e.g., one student wrote about what they felt was most valuable from the course: "hearing from my peers who together created an extremely diverse community"). Students also commented on the safe classroom climate (e.g., one student wrote: "Thank you for making me feel important and open to hearing my point of view and stories"). Some students reported undergoing attitudinal changes spurred by the course (e.g., one student wrote: "I can confidently say that as a direct result of this course I am far less likely to participate in discriminatory behavior surrounding language"). Finally, some students reflected on how the course would positively impact their future career as educators (e.g., one student wrote that the course helped them appreciate "the importance of learning about the language and cultural background of the community your students were raised [in]"). Together, these comments reinforce the ideas highlighted earlier, that is, that a decolonizing pedagogy requires "questioning common sense assumptions, privileging the situatedness of the local knowledge (and pedagogy), and understanding that one-size does not fit all" (Shin, 2006, p. 162).

For Ève and Matt, decolonization means examining not only our relationship to the Alaska Native nations upon whose traditional unceded lands we reside, but also our responsibility in perpetuating an unjust educational system that has oppressed, and continues to oppress, Indigenous communities. As the first two authors reflect on our experience teaching an undergraduate linguistics course to future teachers at UAF, we are struck by the fact that, by their own admission, most of the students' learning came from listening to their peers, emphasizing the importance of Deep Listening (Brearley & Hamm, 2013). Such an observation has forced us to reevaluate how we define the instructor's role in the classroom. Furthermore, we see the potential for practices of inclusion, including venues for possible community-school-university partnerships. We also recognize the need to constantly reevaluate our pedagogical practices as part of our commitment to identify and resolve unforeseen limitations. Part of such pedagogical inquiry will require us to evaluate the impact of the course once students become teachers in local schools, a process which may yield further opportunities for community and university collaborations and partnerships.

For Giovanna, linguistics provides an insightful lens through which to study the injustices and inequalities that have been inflicted upon my people. Language has often served as a gatekeeper, restricting minoritized students' access to the educational realm. But it can also be a tool to ease the existing barriers between home and school and to strengthen the bonds within my community. To me, decolonization means empowering my community and fostering a sense of agency, especially among the younger generation. This is the direction I envision for the field of linguistics and I am eager to take part in that movement.

Note

1. We acknowledge the Alaska Native nations upon whose traditional lands our campuses reside. In Fairbanks, the Troth Yeddha' Campus is located on the traditional lands of the Dena people of the lower Tanana River.

References

Alaska Department of Education and Early Development. (2021). 2020–2021 statewide enrollment by grade by ethnicity. https://education.alaska.gov/data-center

Alaska State Archives. (2021). Boarding schools in Alaska. https://archives.alaska.gov/education/boarding.html

Alaska Statutes. (2014). § 44.12.310. https://law.justia.com/codes/alaska/2014/title-44/chapter-44.12/article-04/section-44.12.3

Archibald Q'um Q'um Xiiem, Jo-ann, & Garcia Tuukwa, Jeremy. (2022). The struggles and triumphs of Indigenous teacher education in Canada and the United States. In Conra D. Gist & Travis J. Bristol (Eds.) , *Handbook of research on teachers of color and Indigenous teachers* (pp. 37–45). American Educational Research Association.

420 Decolonizing Linguistics

Banes, Leslie, Martínez, Danny, Athanases, Steven, & Wong, Joanna. (2016). Self-reflexive inquiry into language use and beliefs: toward more expansive language ideologies *.International Multilingual Research Journal, 10*(3), 168–187.

Barnhardt, Ray. (2007). Creating a place for Indigenous knowledge in education: The Alaska Native Knowledge Network. In David A. Gruenewald & Gregory A. Smith (Eds.), *Place-based education in the global age* (pp. 113–133). Routledge.

Battiste, Marie. (2013). *Decolonizing education: Nourishing the learning spirit.* Purich Publishing.

Bhambra, Gurminder, Gebrial, Dalia, & Nişancıoğlu, Kerem. (2018). *Decolonising the university.* Pluto Press.

Brearley, Laura, & Hamm, Treahna. (2013). Spaces between Indigenous and non-Indigenous knowledge systems: Deep listening to research in a creative form. In A.-Chr. Engles-Schwarzpaul & Michael A. Peters (Eds.), *Of other thoughts: Non-traditional ways to the doctorate* (pp. 259–278). Brill.

Carter Andrews, Dorinda, Castro, Eliana, Cho, Christine, Petchauer, Emery, Richmond, Gail, & Floden, Robert. (2019). Changing the narrative on diversifying the teaching workforce: A look at historical and contemporary factors that inform recruitment and retention of teachers of color. *Journal of Teacher Education, 70*(1), 6–12.

Charity Hudley, Anne, Mallinson, Christine, & Bucholtz, Mallinson. (2020a). Toward racial justice in linguistics: Interdisciplinary insights into theorizing race in the discipline and diversifying the profession. *Language, 96*(4), e200–e235.

Charity Hudley, Anne, Mallinson, Christine, & Bucholtz, Mallinso. (2020b). From theory to action: Working collectively toward a more antiracist linguistics (response to commentators). *Language 96*(4), e307–e319.

De Costa, Peter. (2020). Linguistic racism: Its negative effects and why we need to contest it. *International Journal of Bilingual Education and Bilingualism , 23*(7), 833–837.

DeFeo, Dayna., Tran, Trang, Hirshberg, Diane, Cope, Dale, & Cravez, Pamela (2017). The cost of teacher turnover in Alaska. https://scholarworks.alaska.edu/bitstream/handle/11122/7815/2017_3-TeacherTurnover.pdf?sequence=2&isAllowed=y

Gaby, Alice, & Woods, Lesley. (2020). Toward linguistic justice for Indigenous people: A response to Charity Hudley, Mallinson, and Bucholtz. *Language, 96*(4), e268–e280.

Gordon, Rebekah., Reichmuth, Heather, Her, Lee, & De Costa, Peter, 2021. Thinking beyond "languaging" in translanguaging pedagogies: Exploring ways to combat white fragility in an undergraduate language methodology course. In Ursula Lanvers, AmyS. Thompson & Martin East (Eds.), *Language learning in Anglophone countries* (pp. 445–462). Palgrave Macmillan.

Jester, Timothy, & Fickel, Letitia. (2013). Cross-cultural field experiences in Alaska Native villages: Implications for culturally responsive teacher education. *The Teacher Educator, 48*(3), 185–200.

Kaden, Ute, Patterson, Philip., Healy, Joanne, & Adams, Barbara. (2016). Stemming the revolving door: Teacher retention and attrition in arctic Alaska schools. *Global Education Review 3*(1): 129–147.

Kubota, Ryuko. (2020). Confronting epistemological racism, decolonizing scholarly knowledge: Race and gender in applied linguistics. *Applied Linguistics, 41*(5), 712–732.

Kwachka, Patricia. (2017). Alaskan Englishes. In Tometro Hopkins & John McKenny (Eds.), *World Englishes: North America* (pp. 187–204). Bloomsbury Academic.

Leonard, Wesley. (2020). Insights from Native American studies for theorizing race and racism in linguistics (response to Charity Hudley, Mallinson, and Bucholtz). *Language, 96*(4), e281–e291.

Marlow, Patrick, & Siekmann, Sabine. (2013). *Communities of practice: An Alaskan Native model for language teaching and learning.* University of Arizona Press.

Motha, Suhanthie. (2020). Is an antiracist and decolonizing applied linguistics possible? *Annual Review of Applied Linguistics, 40,* 128–133.

National Archives Online Catalog. (n.d.). Alaska Native communities research guide. https://www.archives.gov/files/education/native-communities/alaska-nativecommunities-guide.pdf

Oré, Christina, Teufel-Shone, Nicolette, & Chico-Jarillo, Tara. (2016). American Indian and Alaska Native resilience along the life course and across generations: A literature review. *American Indian and Alaska Native Mental Health Research, 23* (3), 134.

Pennycook, Alastair. (2021). Reassembling linguistics: Semiotic and epistemic assemblages. In Allison Burkette & Tamara Warhol (Eds.), *Crossing borders, making connections* (pp. 111–128). De Gruyter Mouton.

Ragoonaden, Karen, & Mueller, Lyle. (2017). Culturally responsive pedagogy: Indigenizing curriculum. *Canadian Journal of Higher Education 47*(2), 22–46.

Shin, Hyunjung (2006). Rethinking TESOL from a SOL's Perspective: Indigenous Epistemology and Decolonizing Praxis in TESOL. *Critical Inquiry in Language Studies, 3*(2–3), 147–167.

Tan, Amy. (1999). Mother Tongue. In S. Gillespie & R. Singleton (Eds.), *Across cultures* (pp. 26–31). Allyn and Bacon.

Thomas, Jamie A. (2024). Community college linguistics for educational justice: Content and assessment strategies that support antiracist and inclusive teaching. In Anne H. Charity Hudley, Christine Mallinson, & Mary Bucholtz (Eds.), *Inclusion in linguistics.* Oxford University Press.

Thorne, Steven, Siekmann, Sabine, & Charles, Walkie. (2015). Ethical issues in Indigenous language research and interventions. In Peter I. De Costa (Ed.), *Ethics in applied linguistics research* (pp. 142–160). Routledge.

Tuck, Eve, & Yang, K. Wayne. (2014). Unbecoming claims: Pedagogies of refusal in qualitative research. *Qualitative Inquiry, 20*(6), 811–818.

University of Alaska Fairbanks. (n.d.). Alaska teacher placement. https://www.alaskateacher.org/supply_and_demand.php

Wernicke, Meike. (2021). Four "moments" of intercultural encountering. *Teaching in Higher Education, 26* (7–8), 1130–1140.

Zembylas, Michalonos. (2014). Theorizing "difficult knowledge" in the aftermath of the "affective tur"': Implications for curriculum and pedagogy in handling traumatic representations. *Curriculum Inquiry, 44*(3), 390–412.

Carlos de Cuba has a PhD in linguistics and an MA in TESOL, both from Stony Brook University. He has taught at Stony Brook University, Pomona College, the University of Calgary, and CUNY Queens College. He is currently associate professor in speech communication in the Department of Communications & Performing Arts at Kingsborough Community College, teaching linguistics and speech communication courses. His research interests lie in the areas of theoretical and applied linguistics. Carlos is committed to the goal of equity in the classroom, and his work in this area focuses on issues of language ideology and language policy in the classroom.

Poppy Slocum is associate professor of communication studies at LaGuardia Community College, where she is committed to applying sociolinguistic theory to her teaching. She is working to help others do the same by showing how the basic linguistic principle that all languages and dialects are equally communicatively valid has consequences for a wide range of teaching, from English to biology courses.

Laura Spinu obtained her PhD in linguistics from the University of Delaware in 2010 and joined the Department of Communications & Performing Arts at CUNY Kingsborough Community College in 2017. A linguist by training, her research focuses on the relation between bilingualism and cognitive function, as well as on developing reliable acoustic classification methods for various categories of speech sounds. Spinu has a long track record of engaging undergraduate students in research, culminating in a highly successful undergraduate training program, the Kingsborough Collaborative Research & Conference Bootcamp (K-CORE). Drawing on her own research and the multitude of possibilities offered by the study of psycholinguistics, the students involved in K-CORE develop their own joint research projects and present them at conferences. As a result of engaging in scientific inquiry involving their own home dialects, students' perception shifts toward increased pride about their diverse linguistic heritages.

Abstract: This chapter describes the work of three linguists working in communication departments at two community colleges in the City University of New York system (CUNY) to counter deficit approaches toward dialectal variation in the field of communication studies (and beyond). The authors' approach includes professional presentations, curricular redesign, identifying linguistic discrimination in textbooks, and conducting professional development workshops and seminars. They believe that the things they are doing are easily reproducible, so they are shared in this chapter in the hopes that more people will get actively involved in reducing/eliminating such harmful classroom pedagogies that involve deficit views of dialectal and accent variation in educational settings.

Key Words: linguistic justice, linguistic discrimination, textbooks, undergraduate research, curriculum development

20

An Interdisciplinary Approach to Language Activism from Community Colleges

Linguistics Meets Communication Studies

Carlos de Cuba (he/him/his)
Kingsborough Community College–CUNY

Poppy Slocum (she/her/hers)
LaGuardia Community College–CUNY

Laura Spinu (she/her/hers)
Kingsborough Community College–CUNY

Introduction

As linguists working in communication departments at two community colleges in the City University of New York system (CUNY), we quickly discovered widespread deficit thinking toward dialectal variation in the field of communication.[1] Our work started with small observations of discriminatory language toward dialectal variation in public speaking textbooks (see de Cuba & Slocum, 2020b) and in a course description from a class Laura was assigned to teach. As linguists, we feel a responsibility to address these issues through reexamining course materials and doing outreach to communication studies and scholars in other disciplines as well. Decolonizing linguistics must also involve decolonizing the fields that linguistics bears on; it is not enough to stay within the confines of linguistics departments. In this chapter we share some of the activities we undertake toward decolonizing educational spaces that for far too long have treated so-called nonstandard dialect variation with disdain and hostility, as discussed by numerous researchers (Baker-Bell, 2020; Blake & Cutler, 2003; Bloome, Katz, & Champion, 2003; Cross, DeVaney, &

Carlos de Cuba, Poppy Slocum, Laura Spinu, *An Interdisciplinary Approach to Language Activism from Community Colleges*
In: *Decolonizing Linguistics*. Edited by: Anne H. Charity Hudley, Christine Mallinson, and Mary Bucholtz, Oxford University Press.
© Anne H. Charity Hudley, Christine Mallinson, and Mary Bucholtz 2024. DOI: 10.1093/oso/9780197755259.003.0021

424 Decolonizing Linguistics

Jones, 2001; Dunstan & Jaeger, 2015; Dyson & Smitherman, 2009; Godley et al., 2007; Lippi-Green, 2012; Young et al., 2018; among others).

We should note from the outset that we are not pioneers in this outreach work. Our activist work follows in the spirit of Anne Charity (Hudley), who urges linguists to become agents for social change (e.g., Charity, 2008). Much work has been and continues to be done, both in sociolinguistics and in other areas, like composition, and language and literacy (see Baker-Bell, 2020; Canagarajah, 2011; Charity Hudley & Mallinson, 2010; 2014; Conference on College Composition and Communication, 1974; 2020; Godley & Reaser, 2018; Lippi-Green, 2012; Reaser et al., 2017; Paris & Alim, 2017; Smitherman, 1995; Young et al., 2018; and countless others working for change). Geneva Smitherman (1974, p. 731) sums up the situation succinctly: "Tellin kids they lingo is cool but it ain cool enough for where it really counts (i.e., in the economic world) is just like tellin them it ain cool at all. If the problem is not the kid's dialect but attitudes toward that dialect, then why not work to change those attitudes?"

In this chapter, we detail our language activism within the field of communication studies, and our efforts to engage more linguists in this work. First, we give background about deficit language ideologies in communication studies, followed by an overview of our theoretical grounding and institutional context. Next, we present a model of outreach efforts, which include professional presentations, curricular redesign, identifying linguistic discrimination in textbooks, and conducting professional development workshops and seminars. These efforts are on the one hand specific to our situations—our work focuses on linguistic justice in communication studies and is inspired and enabled by our positions at community colleges with linguistically diverse student populations. On the other hand, these efforts are also highly replicable, and with the right institutional support can and should be conducted widely within academia.

Positionality

The three of us are linguistics PhDs who graduated in an era when full-time positions in linguistics were few and far between. Laura and Carlos spent many years working in temporary linguistics positions at various institutions in the US and Canada without finding a permanent position before both being hired for tenure-track positions in speech communication in the same job search at Kingsborough Community College. As fortune would have it, Laura and Carlos had overlapped in their graduate studies at Stony Brook so knew each other before being hired. Carlos also overlapped with Poppy at Stony Brook (Yeah, I was there for a long time:-)). Poppy skipped a lengthy and likely fruitless nomadic period chasing a linguistics position and took a position in the Humanities Department at LaGuardia Community while ABD, and has been there ever since. We were all grateful to be embraced by our colleagues in our new field and set about working in our new environments.

We all soon started running into clear cases of linguistic discrimination in our everyday practice that was being accepted unopposed. Since we all knew each other and were equally dismayed (i.e., pissed off) at what we were seeing, we quickly banded together and started strategizing about what we needed to do.

A reviewer asked us to explain our motivations for doing this work, and we were reminded of a recent talk we attended when we presented a paper at the 2022 meeting of the International Linguistic Association. In a plenary talk about his work on language revival and social justice, Ghil'ad Zuckermann (2022) explained why language revival work is (1) deontologically right, (2) aesthetically beautiful, and (3) utilitarianistically beneficial to society. We think the same can be said for valuing and protecting linguistic variation. First, we should do it because it is simply the right thing to do. Decades of sociolinguistic research tells us this. Second, we should do it because the linguistic variation we are valuing and protecting is aesthetically beautiful and has added immeasurably to our language and culture. Finally, we should do it because it is useful. In a narrow sense as instructors, if we value all students' languages we can improve their self-value and ability to be engaged and successful in the classroom. In a broader sense we can spread linguistic pride to the wider community, improving self-esteem and connecting people with their linguistic and cultural histories. We feel privileged to be in a position where we are able to make a small contribution to this cause.

Linguistic Discrimination in Communication Studies

The effort to use the insights of linguistics to decolonize Communication Studies goes back at least as far as 1970, when Walt Wolfram (1970) published a paper in the National Communication Association's journal *The Speech Teacher*. Wolfram implored speech instructors to move away from a *deficit* view of "nonstandard" dialects, in which dialectal variation is seen as a deviation from a prescribed norm, to a *difference* view in which this variation is seen as a sociocultural difference, with all varieties of language being equal in value. In the contemporary era, a movement to decolonize communication studies

426 Decolonizing Linguistics

already exists within the field. In an article called "#Communicationsowhite," Paula Chakravartty and colleagues (2018) called out the field for the marginalization of scholars of color. This article has generated considerable discussion about representation within the field (e.g., Milan & Treré 2019; Waisbord 2019). However, as of yet issues relating to language variation have not been highlighted.

Historically there has not been a great deal of interaction between the fields of communication and linguistics. We can speculate that one reason is the general siloing of disciplines in academia. On the linguistics side, Anne Charity Hudley and coauthors (2020, e209) note that linguistics has historically devalued work from departments of communication, English, modern languages, and education. On the communication side, Bryan McCann and colleagues (2020) paint a picture of communication studies as a field historically anxious about disciplinary legitimacy in the academy. Part of claiming this legitimacy involves the field trying to establish the unique value of communication studies. This inward focus matches the inward focus of linguistics. In addition, and related to the standard language ideology in the field of communication, Bryan McCann and coauthors (2020) argue that in the attempt to be seen as a legitimate discipline, communication adopted the whiteness and anti-Blackness of other disciplines that were seen as legitimate. In this context, the hostility toward dialectal variation in the field makes sense.

Critical Pedagogical Approaches to Language

Theoretically, we align ourselves with critical language awareness (Fairclough, 1992), critical language pedagogy (Godley & Minnici, 2008; Godley & Reaser, 2018), and culturally sustaining pedagogies (Paris & Alim, 2017), which all share the insight that it is not enough for sociolinguists to just recognize and document instances of language stigmatization. Nelson Fairclough (1989, pp. 7–8) argues that further action is needed:

> How—in terms of the development of social relationships to power—was the existing sociolinguistic order brought into being? How is it sustained? And how might it be changed to the advantage of those who are dominated by it?

Critical language pedagogy follows the work of Fairclough but "focuses specifically on sociolinguistic understanding of nonmainstream dialects (rather than all texts) and related ideologies, and incorporates praxis—the use of critical understandings of dialects and language ideologies to not only question but also change the ways that language attitudes uphold racism and other forms of discrimination" (Godley & Reaser, 2018, p. 21). Samy Alim and Django Paris (2017, p. 2) see the need for culturally sustaining pedagogies (CSP) as follows:

> In essence, by proposing schooling as a site for sustaining the cultural ways of being of communities of color rather than eradicating them, CSP is responding to the many ways that schools continue to function as part of the colonial project. We seek to disrupt the pervasive anti-Indigeneity, anti-Blackness, and related anti-Brownness (from anti-Latinidad to Islamophobia) and model minority myths so foundational to schooling in the United States and many other nation-states.

The history of colonialism has had a deep and damaging influence on ideologies about language. In a chapter on decolonizing teacher education with the goal of training teachers to practice culturally sustaining and revitalizing pedagogies, Michael Domínguez (2017, p. 227, citing Maldonado-Torres 2010) provides a definition of coloniality as referring to "long-standing patterns of power that emerged as a result of colonialism, but that define culture, labor, intersubjective relations, and knowledge production well beyond the strict limits of colonial administrations . . . It is maintained alive in books, in the criteria for academic performance, in cultural patterns, in common sense, in the self-image of peoples, in aspirations of self, and so many other aspects of our modern experience" (Maldonado-Torres 2010, p. 97). These colonial patterns of power extend of course to language use and the idea of a standard language. In a 2021 TED-Ed video on the history of language standardization, linguist Martin Hilpert explains:

> The basis for what is officially deemed a language was shaped by the emergence of European nation-states beginning around the 1500s. In order to establish and maintain centralized governments, clear territorial boundaries and state-sponsored education systems, many nation-states promoted a standardized language. Which form of speech was chosen to be the standard language was usually based on what people spoke in the capital. And while other forms of speech persisted, they were often treated as inferior. This tradition extended across the globe with European colonization.

This centuries-long colonial tradition continues to the present day in the form of standard language ideology, raciolinguistic ideologies and damaging deficit pedagogies in schools (see Rosa & Flores, 2017). For more on how standardization emerged in the US see Gaillynn Clements (2021).

Institutional Context

While countering standard language ideology is important for all educators, we feel a certain urgency as community college instructors in New York City given our student population, the vast majority of whom do not come from positions of hegemonic power, and few of whom come to our classrooms with so-called standard varieties of English. CUNY is deservedly proud of its record of raising families out of poverty. According to Barbara Bowen, former president of the Professional Staff Congress, the union representing CUNY faculty and staff, nearly half of CUNY undergraduates come from families whose annual income is less than $20,000, more than 60% come from families with annual incomes under $30,000, and three-quarters are Black, Latinx, or Asian (Bowen, 2019). CUNY leads the nation in fostering both individual and intergenerational economic mobility (Bowen, 2019). But as Bowen also notes, "CUNY has always been about more than expanding the economy or even changing individual lives. It is about equipping students to think critically about the causes of inequality even as they tackle its effects in their own lives." Thinking critically about language inequalities and language rights is an important part of education, not just for students but for instructors and administrators as well. As Mike Metz and Heather Knight conclude in their recent paper on English teachers' language ideologies, "By providing students accurate, precise, and contemporary linguistic knowledge and a critical narrative describing how language works in the world, teachers and students can transform social understandings of language instead of perpetuating hegemonic inequities" (2021, e254). The goal of our multipronged outreach work is to counter the impacts of deficit narratives on speakers of subordinated varieties and change the negative attitudes toward dialectal variation in communication departments and beyond.

Our Outreach Work from our Positions at Two CUNY Community Colleges

In order to counter the existing standard language ideology, we have been engaging in a number of activities that counter linguistic discrimination in the classroom and beyond at the two community colleges where we work: Kingsborough Community College and LaGuardia Community College. Additionally, Poppy regularly teaches an MA Introduction to Linguistics course in the English Department at Brooklyn College, also within

CUNY. In our various activities we target the language attitudes of students, preservice teachers, and in-service teachers. Our efforts and initiatives are fairly easily reproducible, and we share them in the hopes that more instructors will get actively involved in eliminating classroom pedagogies that involve harmful deficit views of dialectal and accent variation in educational settings. As linguists we are well placed to present arguments countering standard language ideology (Lippi-Green, 2012) to students and faculty members, and as faculty working in communication departments we are well positioned to bring discussions of language diversity to a field that, through our interactions, we have found is often not familiar with findings from linguistics, composition, and literacy and education that show the damage that deficit views can cause to students.

So how are we, as linguists, working to decolonize communication studies? Our approach depends largely on "educating the educated" (Dunstan et al., 2015). We have seen first-hand that when educators learn the basic facts of linguistic variation, the result is a broad change in their attitudes and teaching practices. In this section we outline some of the steps we are taking and that others can take as well to help eliminate linguistic discrimination from pedagogies across disciplines.

Though at an earlier stage at present, our work relates closely to the "campus-infusion model" at North Carolina (NC) State (Wolfram & Dunstan, 2021), which seeks to raise awareness of language diversity on college campuses and educate a full range of members of the campus community about language variation and diversity (2021, p. 163). (See also the outreach work of Da Pidgin Coup as described by Christina Higgins, 2021.) We share with the NC State Linguistic Diversity Program the common goals of defining what a dialect is, dispelling common myths about dialects, addressing linguistic discrimination, addressing issues of how ideologies that devalue language variation can impact students and faculty in any given discipline, work environment, and interactions with others, as well as the implications of those impacts when trying to create inclusive and respectful linguistic environments (Wolfram & Dunstan, 2021, pp. 166–167).

In the next sections we provide details of the activities we involve ourselves in toward these goals, including additional work we have done beyond our campuses to spread awareness about linguistic variation through conference presentations in outside venues, as well as work on textbooks, curricula, undergraduate research, and professional development. We discuss our outreach work linearly in the next sections, documenting how our earliest efforts led to the development of several initiatives that have impacted the field of communication studies as well as scholars in other disciplines.

Professional Presentations

We have made an effort to spread awareness through presentations at various scholarly meetings, both in the field of linguistics and beyond. Outside of linguistics, we have presented at the Eastern Communication Association (de Cuba & Slocum, 2019a), the CUNY Faculty Diversity and Inclusion Conference (de Cuba & Slocum 2019c, de Cuba et al., 2021), and the National Communication Association (NCA) Annual Convention (de Cuba & Slocum, 2019b). These presentations offer a chance to reach academics in neighboring disciplines who might not otherwise have the opportunity to hear about linguistic diversity. Indeed, we learned that for some audience members at the NCA, the idea that all language varieties are systematic and rule-governed was completely novel and caused them to immediately rethink many of their teaching practices. One audience member shared that he regularly performs a Southern accent to represent someone with an uneducated or incorrect point of view, and said he understood now why that practice was harmful, but that he'd never thought of it before. Another shared later that the talk had made him reconsider how he talks to his students about code-switching, and that he would consider opening up space for other dialects in the classroom.

To target one specific aspect of teaching, we ran a preconference workshop on linguistic discrimination at the 2021 Drexel Annual Conference on Teaching and Learning Assessment highlighting the need for linguistically sensitive assessment rubrics (de Cuba & Slocum 2021a). We believe focusing on assessment is an important path forward for linguistic justice in education. Carlos and Poppy are both involved in general education assessment at their respective institutions where they can advocate for implementing unbiased assessment tools.

We have received a lot of positive feedback on our presentations, including an opportunity to edit a public speaking textbook (discussed below), but we have also encountered a good deal of resistance, frequently hearing that the imposition of standardized language is necessary for students' success in a racist and biased society. In these situations, we highlight that deficit approaches are ineffective even if we agreed with the goal of teaching standard language (Reaser et al., 2017). We don't always convince everyone that inclusive approaches are necessary, but persuasion is often a long-term process and we know that starting the conversation is as important as finishing it.

We have also presented at linguistics conferences, including the Linguistic Society of America 2020 (de Cuba & Slocum, 2020a) and 2022 (de Cuba et al., 2022c), the CUNY Language Society and Culture Conference (de Cuba et al., 2021), the Southeast Conference on Linguistics (de Cuba et al., 2022a), the

Linguistic Association of Canada and the US (de Cuba & Slocum 2021b) and the International Linguistic Association (de Cuba et al., 2022b) to encourage other linguists to engage with faculty outside of their departments. Our work has been received warmly. For example, at the LSA in 2022 we were included in a session called "Critical Issues in Linguistics," and our talk was recognized in a meeting newsletter highlight. We have been told numerous times about the importance of our work and that people are happy that it is being done. The hope is that this recognition will turn into concrete action, with all linguists seeing anti-racist and linguistic justice work as being an important part of being a linguist.

Textbook Review and Textbook Editing

Carlos and Poppy's work on linguistic discrimination in communication departments began with noticing negative statements toward language variation in public speaking textbooks, such as "Bad grammar is much like having a bit of spinach in your front teeth," "Some business and professional people find 'improper' English as offensive as body odor or food stains on the front of a shirt," and "If you tend toward lazy speech, put more effort into your articulation." In 2020 they published a study of 17 of the most popular public speaking textbooks (de Cuba & Slocum, 2020b). A vast majority of the textbooks sampled described dialectal variants as "errors" or "mispronunciations," showing a lack of exposure to basic tenets of linguistics. A total of 70% used deficit language to discuss language variation, and 24% failed to discuss it at all.

After they presented this work at the National Communication Association in 2019, Carlos and Poppy were invited by MacMillan Learning to serve as diversity, inclusion, and culturally responsive pedagogy reviewers on the development of the new edition of a popular public speaking textbook, *A Speaker's Guidebook* (O'Hair et al., 2022). This opportunity allowed us to make a direct and broad impact by targeting textbook misinformation at the source. We plan to continue pressing publishers for change regarding language attitudes expressed in textbooks.

Curricular Redesign

Within our own departments we have worked to eliminate linguistic discrimination from our shared teaching materials, syllabi, and curricula. Specifically, Laura rewrote a course called Voice and Articulation, a commonly taught course in communication departments. The institution's catalog description presented this course as an accent reduction course, aimed at providing assistance "to overcome minor speech and voice problems most commonly found in the New York City area." After revision, the course now focuses on phonetic analysis. In the redesigned course, first taught in 2018, Laura and her students created an extensive language map of Kingsborough Community College with the support of a CUNY Research in the Classroom grant. The overarching goal of this grant was to promote the rich language diversity at the college. The students enrolled in Voice and Articulation recorded 150 of their peers reading a paragraph in their various accents of English, and subsequently used the data collected to explore aspects of language variation and change, for example to determine whether the existence of a specific Brooklyn accent (Brooklynese) that is distinct from other New York City varieties is warranted by measurable phonetic data. As a result of engaging in scientific inquiry involving their own home dialects, the students' perception shifted from initial negative attitudes toward dialectal variation to increased pride about their diverse linguistic heritages and respect for multiple Englishes, as demonstrated by the thoughts they conveyed in anonymous course evaluations:

> Before taking this class I did have somewhat of a bias against people with accents but now I've learned that accents are a part of society and there is no reason to look down upon someone because of the way they speak.
>
> I would say I have become extremely unbiased towards accents due to the experience in the research project we conducted. My group worked on stigmatized accents specifically, which opened my eyes as to the amount of people who are stigmatized.

This initiative is significant on at least one other level—by training students to do research on their home dialects and create new knowledge within this discipline, we can both legitimize marginalized languages and varieties (for instance Creoles, which are often perceived as "broken English," "broken French," by their own users; see Bancu, Peltier, et al., this volume) and cultivate a new generation of linguists with the ability to open the door to new theoretical perspectives. Students learn that their home varieties are rule based and worthy of scientific study, and in no way inferior to other languages. In addition, they refer to their languages with pride and with increased awareness of the importance of their linguistic heritage. Crucially, these students are now in a position where they can add to the body of research on their own languages. Prior to the existence of this course at Kingsborough we were missing out on a tremendous opportunity to use language varieties spoken by the diverse student body of community colleges like Kingsborough as an asset. Employing high-impact practices such as the one described above can help show people why language variation should be viewed as an asset in the classroom.

Curricular redesign is particularly important and impactful when the students targeted are future teachers. At Brooklyn College, Poppy has redesigned a linguistics course for students in the MA program for English teachers to encourage them to adopt linguistically sensitive pedagogies. For example, students read work challenging the standard language ideology, and Poppy selects linguistic problems and data sets from marginalized dialects to illustrate their systematicity. Her students reflected at the end of the 2020 semester on how the course would change their teaching practices:

> Language is such a big part of identity and I was inflicting the same identity crushing abuse on my students that had been done to me. This idea of *SAE [Standard American English, per Lippi-Green, 2012] as being the golden standard in language is just wrong and I don't have to keep perpetuating the language corrections and the linguistic and social/emotional damage to children so prevalent in the school system . . . I can make them aware of the politics of language while honoring their linguistic variations.
>
> I no longer view language diversity as linked to intellectual capacity. I know the standards I was taught were largely subjective in nature.
>
> There are so many cool nuances to how people speak and how it varies depending on where we come from. Furthermore, there is no right way to speak English which will definitely impact my teaching and understanding of how and why my students speak the way they do as well as what my students have to say.

Like Poppy, Carlos designed a new Introduction to Linguistics course at Kingsborough specifically to highlight issues of language diversity. He followed the recommendations of Kendra Calhoun and coauthors (2021) by moving discussion of sociolinguistics to earlier in the semester and focusing more on English examples early in the course (see also Plackowski, 2024). He also added a linguistic autobiography writing assignment (Charity Hudley & Mallinson, 2014; Charity Hudley et al., 2022), which the students really enjoyed. In addition, he included a number of "Crash Course Linguistics" videos (see Gawne et al., 2024) to supplement the readings and lectures. The focus on sign languages in these videos was especially welcome as Carlos felt his course needed strengthening in this area. Finally, he included detailed modules on sociolinguistic topics including language variation and language attitudes, with deep dives into Hawai'ian Creole English (HCE) and African

434 Decolonizing Linguistics

American English (for more on teaching Introduction to Linguistics in a community college context, see Thomas, 2024).

In a reflection assignment toward the end of the course, one student commented on discussion board assignments in the course, and how she would take the knowledge she gained forward.

> The discussion assignments were the most thought-provoking for me. I liked learning about how linguistics relates to the culture and perceptions of a group. Specifically, I have continued reflecting on the points discussed in the "Talking Black in America" video. Learning about AAE has helped broaden my view of language and understand how discrimination is hidden under prescriptive grammar rules. The AAE and dialect lesson also connects to my personal life, as understanding dialects is essential for my work as a tutor. I was very glad to have learned how I can help my students with reading while respecting their dialectical differences. I think discussing contrasts between speakers of different backgrounds is important in stopping the spread of ignorance and bigotry.

Another student commented on connections she made between the social conditions regarding AAE and HCE.

> The part that impacted me the most in the video was that there is a form of resilience in language. Even through slavery, people were able to find a unique way to communicate and develop their own culture; this was also something that stood out to me in the video we watched about HCE.

A third student reflected on her favorite part of the course.

> I enjoyed learning about just how complex language is. We don't give it a second thought when speaking, but there are so many variables that go into speech. The words we utter present us with so much information about who we are and where we are from. I liked learning about pidgins and creoles. There are also things like the cot/caught merger, or isoglosses- that will stick with me. I think I really enjoyed learning about how people USE the language. Now I know that everyone speaks with an accent.

Finally, Laura and Carlos have worked closely with their colleagues on the speech communication curriculum committee at Kingsborough to change the program learning outcomes, eliminating deficit language like "recognize and use standard American speech," and adding instead, "Analyze linguistic patterns and processes, communication differences vs. disorders, the development, structure, and nature of human language, and its representation in speakers' minds," and "Explain how an individual's culture, speaking patterns, and/or linguistic choices inform our understanding of the systems of language, communication, and/or matters of social justice." These changes remove noninclusive goals from the program's learning outcomes as well as the institution's catalog and website.

Undergraduate Research

Other related initiatives we have had in recent years share the goal of challenging deficit language ideologies in Communication. Kingsborough Collaborative Research and Conference Bootcamp (K-CORE) is a highly successful undergraduate collaborative research bootcamp Laura founded at her institution in 2019. K-CORE's overarching goal is to train students to conduct collaborative experimental research projects in linguistics and present them at conferences, providing hands-on experiential STEM training. Students from any major are welcome to participate. From its inception, the K-CORE program has followed a reciprocal empowerment model (Chun & Evans, 2009; McCombs, 1991), by encouraging students to take control over their own projects, thus building a sense of ownership and professional confidence from the very onset of college life. During the first cycle of the program (2019–2021), Laura mentored 15 students who delivered 22 presentations at professional conferences, such as the International Symposium on Monolingual and Bilingual Speech, the Northwest Linguistics Conference, three meetings of the Acoustical Society of America, the Web Summer School in Logic, Language, and Information, the International Seminar on Speech Production, the 2020 meeting of the Canadian Linguistic Association, and the CUNY-wide Language, Society and Culture conference. The students also had manuscripts of their work accepted for publication in conference proceedings and a forthcoming volume, *The Phonetics and Phonology of Heritage Languages*. In addition to exploring heritage language phenomena, the groups also investigated the perception of foreign-accented speech, supporting earlier research findings published in the literature and raising awareness of the stigma associated with it.

Undergraduate research serves as an excellent entryway for minoritized students to the field of linguistics, which currently suffers from severe underrepresentation of people of color. Nearly half of all community college

436 Decolonizing Linguistics

students come from underserved groups (Schinske et al., 2017; Hrabowski, 2012, but the number exceeded 70% in 2020 at Kingsborough Community College.

Professional Development

Bringing discussions of linguistic diversity into classrooms is extremely important, but in order to make a broader impact, we need to target the attitudes of faculty. In 2020, Carlos began facilitating a Faculty Interest Group (FIG) (supported by the Kingsborough Center for Teaching and Learning) focusing on language diversity in the classroom (de Cuba, n.d.). The FIG meets four times a semester. During the first year the group read *Other People's English* (Young et al., 2018) followed by *Linguistic Justice* the second year (Baker-Bell, 2020) and *Talking College* currently (Charity Hudley, Mallinson, & Bucholtz, 2022). These books are excellent entryways to discussions of language and race, and both helped facilitate important and sometimes difficult discussions.

In the FIG's first two years, faculty and staff participants came from a number of different disciplines and areas, including academic affairs, art, English, biological sciences, communication, counseling, education, health, legal studies, and psychology. Linguists often speak of the joy they feel when students have an "aha" moment when uncovering some aspect of the structural organization of language in an introductory class. In this case, the "aha" moment was with faculty colleagues, and was often much more painful, because the majority of participants came in with very limited knowledge about linguistic discrimination and many were shocked when they learned that their teaching practices were doing harm to the students they were trying to help. However, this experience was also very motivating. For example, some participants discussed pedagogical changes they were making as a result of their participation in the FIG. One of them worked to make the rubrics in the behavioral sciences department more linguistically inclusive. In addition, three FIG participants from behavioral sciences joined us in facilitating a workshop on linguistic discrimination in the classroom at the 2021 CUNY Faculty Diversity and Inclusion Conference. The following quotes are from a postsemester survey of FIG participants:

> I didn't know exactly what to expect attending the CRT [Culturally Responsive Teaching] FIG, however because we serve such a diverse body of students who speak multiple languages, I felt it would be beneficial for me to attend. . . . The

group discussions expanded my perspective on who develops and controls language, language as power, as well as how other groups learn to gain identity and power through their own evolution of a language. In my own practice, with so many students having diverse languages I learned to honor students native tongue and how they communicate in their assignments. It felt good to learn that some colleagues do things in their courses with students. I also gained some classroom ideas that I plan to implement in future semesters.

It helped broaden my own disciplinary perspectives and expanded my thinking of linguistic justice as it related to writing pedagogy in my classrooms . . . I have been thinking/reading/learning about anti-racist practices in writing/comp, so reading Baker-Bell's ethnographic framework for applying Anti-Racist Language Pedagogy, helped me see more clearly how I might conceptualize and praxis Anti-Racist Language Pedagogy in my own classes and inform my contributions to our department's collaborative curricular revision.

I have included a critical language and power focus in my legal studies classes. I have revised my grading rubrics to reflect language diversity. I am also looking for additional sources for students to engage with that reflect language diversity. I am also hoping to try out some of the approaches Baker-Bell includes in the book.

Facilitating the FIG has led to Carlos being invited to participate in a number of panel discussions on diversity equity and inclusion at Kingsborough, where the profile of issues of language discrimination can be raised to an even wider campus audience. Pre-FIG he participated as a panelist in the KCC Achieving the Dream "EquiTea" series discussing Ibram X. Kendi's *How to be an Antiracist* (2019) and Robin DiAngelo's *White Fragility* (2018). After the FIG started Carlos was a panelist for "Assessment during a Pandemic" and for another EquiTea panel, this time featuring April Baker-Bell's "Linguistic Justice"(2020) and Amber Cabral's "Allies and Advocates" (2021). The hope is that this awareness raising and the networking opportunities it brings will lead to more concrete actions toward language justice at Kingsborough.

While not all campuses may have the equivalent of a FIG, it should still be possible to find or create venues to spread the word, given that in our current climate there is interest in diversity, equity, and inclusion in academia. At Kingsborough for example The Historically Underrepresented Faculty and Staff Resource Center has been very supportive of efforts to raise awareness about linguistic diversity. Scholars interested in doing this type of work on their campuses might try to start a conversation with similar on-campus organizations, such as the office of diversity.

Conclusion

In this chapter, we've outlined a number of strategies to help counter the standard language ideology that is pervasive within and outside of academia. We've taken a varied approach, including reaching out to our colleagues via professional presentations and professional development seminars, reaching out to our students via curricular redesign and undergraduate research, and reaching out to textbook editors. Our experience has shown us that this work is successful when pursued in collaboration among faculty; such work must also apply sustained pressure both from within and from outside of different academic disciplines, as deficit pedagogy related to language is still pervasive across academia. We hope that this chapter can serve as a guide for how others can take on some of this important work.

It is no coincidence that the three of us are able to take up this work from our positions in communication departments, which often put more value on work dealing with race than linguistics departments do (Charity Hudley et al., 2020). Our goal was to find positions in linguistics departments, but as it turns out we have been able to have more impact as linguists working in another field, where there's more room to put our skills to use for social justice issues.

While we urge others to take on this type of work, we need to recognize that it is much harder without strong support from the discipline, departments, and institutions. Linguists working in linguistics departments are vulnerable in their careers if they choose to do the work without institutional support, as social justice is not treated as a part of "core linguistics" research. The lack of value placed on issues of linguistic equity can discourage potential linguists from entering our field, further exacerbating the problem of an extreme lack of diversity in linguistics (Charity Hudley et al., 2020).

In these times when calls for social justice are at the forefront of the news, we as linguists have a unique chance to help forward the conversation on linguistic and racial justice and provide a counternarrative to colonial language thinking within linguistics departments and across other fields, like communication studies. Given the suspect past of linguistics as a field when it comes to the collection of data from language informants (see Charity Hudley et al., 2020; Dockum and Green, 2024; Henner, 2024), and when it comes to race (Charity Hudley et al., 2020), we have an ethical duty as a discipline to start paying back communities which we have happily mined data from for generations. As Charity Hudley et al. 2022 remind us:

Interdisciplinary Approach to Language Activism   439

White supremacy preserves old values within the academy, including in the discipline of linguistics. These values privilege the research interests of the *over*represented, *over*served majority of powerful white scholars, which are then framed as the most pressing theoretical questions. Everyone else, particularly *mis*represented Black scholars and *dis*served Black students—whose home, community, and heritage languages and varieties are often the focus of colonizing research—are then expected to orient to these questions, rather than setting their own research agendas. (2022, p. 127).

We have a chance to change this now, if we as a field choose to take it.

Note

1. Laura gratefully acknowledges the support of the 2018 CUNY Research in the Classroom Idea Grant (#336). In addition, we humbly thank our students and colleagues for granting written permission to publish their statements; we are truly grateful for their support.

References

Alim, H. Samy, & Paris, Django. (2017). What is culturally sustaining pedagogy and why does it matter? In Django Paris & H. Samy Alim (Eds.), *Culturally sustaining pedagogies: Teaching and learning for justice in a changing world* (p. 1–24). Teachers College Press.

Baker-Bell, April. (2020). *Linguistic justice: Black language, literacy, identity, and pedagogy.* Taylor & Francis Group.

Blake, Renée, & Cutler, Cecilia. (2003). AAE and variation in teachers' attitudes: A question of school philosophy? *Linguistics and Education, 14*(2), 163. doi.org/10.1016/S0898-5898(03)00034-2

Bloome, David, Katz, Laurie, & Champion, Tempii. (2003). Young children's narratives and ideologies of language in classrooms. *Reading & Writing Quarterly, 13*(3), 205. doi.org/10.1080/10573560308216

Bowen, Barbara. (2019). Hidden in plain sight. *Clarion: Newspaper of the Professional Staff Congress/City University of New York.* October. https://psc-cuny.org/clarion/april-2019/hidden-plain-sight

Calhoun, Kendra, Charity Hudley, Anne H., Bucholtz, Mary, Exford, Jazmine, & Johnson, Brittney. (2021). Attracting Black students to linguistics through a Black-centered Introduction to Linguistics course. *Language 97*(1), e12–e38. doi:10.1353/lan.2021.0007

Canagarajah, Suresh. (2011). Codemeshing in academic writing: Identifying teachable strategies of translanguaging. *The Modern Language Journal, 95*(3), 401. doi.org/10.1111/j.1540-4781.2011.01207.x

Chakravartty, Paula, Kuo, Rachel, Grubbs, Victoria, & McIlwain, Charlton. (2018). .#CommunicationSoWhite. *Journal of Communication, 68*(2), 254. doi.org/10.1093/joc/jqy003

Charity, Anne, H. (2008). Linguists as agents for social change. *Language and Linguistics Compass, 2*(5), 923. doi.org/10.1111/j.1749-818X.2008.00081.x.

Charity Hudley, Anne H., & Mallinson, Christine. (2010). *Understanding English language variation in U.S. schools.* Teachers College Press.

Charity Hudley, Anne H, & Mallinson, Christine. (2014). *We do language: English language variation in the secondary English classroom.* Teachers College Press.

Charity Hudley, Anne H., Mallinson, Christine, & Bucholtz, Mary. (2020). Toward racial justice in linguistics: Interdisciplinary insights into theorizing race in the discipline and diversifying the profession. *Language, 96*(4), 200. doi:10.1353/lan.2020.0074

Charity Hudley, Anne H., Mallinson, Christine, & Bucholtz, Mary. (2022). *Talking college: Making space for Black language practices in higher education.* Teachers College Press.

Chun, Edna, & Evans, Alvin. (2009). Bridging the diversity divide: Globalization and reciprocal empowerment in higher education. *ASHE Higher Education Report, 35*(1), 1–144.

Clements, Gaillynn. (2021). Lifting the "diversity" wool from our eyes. In Gaillyn Clements & Marnie Jo Petray (Eds.), *Linguistic discrimination in U.S. higher education: Power, prejudice, impacts, and remedies* (pp. 1–19. Routledge.

Conference on College Composition and Communication. (1974). Student's right to their own language. *College Composition and Communication, XXV* (Fall). https://files.eric.ed.gov/fulltext/ED095540.pdf

Conference on College Composition and Communication. (2020). This ain't another statement! This is a DEMAND for Black linguistic justice! Special committee on composing a CCCC statement on anti-Black racism and Black linguistic justice, or, why we can't breathe! https://cccc.ncte.org/cccc/demand-for-black-linguistic-justice

Cross, John B., DeVaney, Thomas, & Jones, Gerald. (2001). Pre-service teacher attitudes toward differing dialects. *Linguistics and Education, 12*(2), 211.

de Cuba, Carlos. (n.d.) Culturally responsive teaching. *CUNY Academic Commons.* https://kctlcrt.commons.gc.cuny.edu/.

de Cuba, Carlos, & Slocum, Poppy. (2019a). Attitudes towards "non-standard language" in public speaking textbooks: creating a less biased future classroom. 110th Annual Eastern Communication Association Convention, Providence, Rhode Island, April 10–14.

de Cuba, Carlos, & Slocum, Poppy. (2019b). Deficit vs. difference approaches to dialects in the classroom. National Communication Association's 105th Annual Convention: Communication for Survival, Baltimore, Maryland, November 14–17.

de Cuba, Carlos, & Slocum, Poppy. (2019c). Linguistic diversity in public speaking textbooks. Minding the gap: retaining & sustaining the academic community. The 4th Biennial CUNY Faculty Diversity and Inclusion Conference, CUNY Graduate Center, March 29.

de Cuba, Carlos, & Slocum, Poppy. (2020a). Standard language ideology is alive and well in public speaking textbooks. 94th Linguistic Society of America Meeting, New Orleans, Louisiana, January 2–5.

de Cuba, Carlos, & Slocum, Poppy. (2020b). Standard language ideology is alive and well in public speaking textbooks. *Proceedings of the Linguistic Society of America, 5*(1), 369. https://doi.org/10.3765/plsa.v5i1.4715

de Cuba, Carlos, & Slocum, Poppy. (2021a). Linguistic discrimination and the oral ability: Is your rubric producing inequity? 8th Annual Drexel University Assessment Conference, "Manageability and Sustainability: The Cornerstone of Institutional Assessment." Drexel University, September 9. (Preconference workshop presentation)

de Cuba, Carlos, & Slocum, Poppy. (2021b). What is a language error and who decides? Linguistic Association Canada and the US (LACUS 2021), July 19–22, University of Toledo, Ohio.

de Cuba, Carlos, Slocum, Poppy, & Spinu, Laura. (2021). Identifying and eliminating discrimination based on accent or dialect from the classroom. Special session panel discussion at

The 5th Biennial CUNY Language, Society, and Culture Conference (LSC-5), Kingsborough Community College (CUNY), May 14.

de Cuba, Carlos, Slocum, Poppy, & Spinu, Laura. (2022a). Addressing linguistic discrimination on our campuses: Some strategies that work. *SECOL 89*. Louisiana State University, March 31.

de Cuba, Carlos, Slocum, Poppy, & Spinu, Laura. (2022b). Addressing linguistic discrimination on our campuses: Some strategies that work. The 66th Annual Conference of the International Linguistic Association, Rutgers University, April 2.

de Cuba, Carlos, Slocum, Poppy, & Spinu, Laura. (2022c). Taking action for positive change in faculty and student attitudes toward language variation. The Linguistic Society of America Annual Meeting. January 8.

de Cuba, Carlos, Slocum, Poppy, Spinu, Laura, Conte, Eric, Espinet, Ivana, Leggett, Jason, La Franceschina, Anna Maria, & Mancini, Alexandria. (2021). Identifying and eliminating discrimination based on accent or dialect from the classroom. CUNY Faculty Diversity and Inclusion Conference, April 14–15.

DiAngelo, Robin. (2018) *White Fragility: Why it's so hard for white people to talk about racism*. Beacon Press.

Dockum, Rikker, & Green, Caitlin M. (2024). Toward a big tent linguistics: Inclusion and the myth of the lone genius. In Anne H. Charity Hudley, Christine Mallinson, & Mary Bucholtz (Eds.), *Inclusion in linguistics*. Oxford University Press.

Domínguez, Michael. (2017). "Se hace puentes al andar": Decolonial teacher education as a needed bridge to culturally sustaining and revitalizing pedagogies. In Django Paris & H. Samy Alim (Eds.), *Culturally sustaining pedagogies: Teaching and learning for justice in a changing world* (pp. 225–246) Teachers College Press.

Dunstan, Stephany B., Eads, Amanda, Jaeger, Audrey J., & Crandall, Rebecca E. (2015). Educating the educated: Language diversity in the university backyard. *American Speech, 90*, 266. doi:10.1215/00031283-3130368

Dunstan, Stephany B., & Jaeger, Audrey J. (2015). Dialect and influences on the academic experiences of college students. *Journal of Higher Education, 86*(5), 777. doi:10.1353/jhe.2015.0026

Dyson, Anne Haas, & Smitherman, Geneva. (2009). The right (write) start: African American language and the discourse of sounding right. *The Teachers College Record, 11*(4), 973.

Fairclough, Nelson. (1989). *Language and power*. Longman Group.

Fairclough, Nelson. (1992). *Critical language awareness*. Routledge.

Gawne, Lauren, McCulloch, Gretchen, Sweeney, Nicole, Alatalo, Rachel, Bodenhausen, Hannah, Riley, Ceri, & Grieser, Jessi. (2024). Creating inclusive linguistics communication: Crash course linguistics. In Anne H. Charity Hudley, Christine Mallinson, & Mary Bucholtz (Eds.), *Inclusion in linguistics*. Oxford University Press.

Godley, Amanda. J., Carpenter, Brian D., & Werner, Cynthia A. (2007). I'll speak in proper slang: Language ideologies in a daily editing activity. *Reading Research Quarterly, 42*(1), 100. doi:10.1598/RRQ.42.1.4

Godley, Amanda J., & Minnici, Angela. (2008). Critical language pedagogy in an urban high school English class. *Urban Education, 43*(3) doi.org/10.1177/0042085907311801

Godley, Amanda. J., & Reaser, Jeffrey. (2018). *Critical language pedagogy: Interrogating language, dialects and power in teacher education*. Peter Lang Publishing.

Henner, Jon. (2024). How to train your abled linguist: A crip linguistics perspective on pragmatic research. In Anne H. Charity Hudley, Christine Mallinson, & Mary Bucholtz (Eds.), *Inclusion in linguistics*. Oxford University Press.

Higgins, Christina. (2021). Promoting pidgin at the University of Hawai'i at Mānoa. In Gaillyn Clements & Marnie Jo Petray (Eds.), *Linguistic discrimination in U.S. higher education: Power, prejudice, impacts, and remedies* (pp. 174–188. Routledge.

442 Decolonizing Linguistics

Hilpert, Martin. (2021). What makes a language . . . a language? Martin Hilpert. *TED-Ed* video. September 9. https://www.youtube.com/watch?v=_Z_FOtfKyfo

Hrabowski III, Freeman A. (2012). Broadening participation in the American STEM workforce. *BioScience, 62*(4), 325–326.

Kendi, Ibrahm X. (2019). *How to be an antiracist*. One World, New York.

Lippi-Green, Rosina. (2012). *English with an Accent: Language, ideology and discrimination in the United States*. Routledge.

Maldonado-Torres, Nelson. (2010). Post-continental philosophy: It's definition, contours, and fundamental sources. *Review of Contemporary Philosophy, 47*(9), 40.

McCann, Bryan J., Noel Mack, Ashley, & Self, Rico. (2020). Communication's quest for whiteness: the racial politics of disciplinary legitimacy. *Communication & Critical/Cultural Studies, 17*(2), 243. doi:10.1080/14791420.2020.1770822.

McCombs, Barbara. L. (1991). Motivation and lifelong learning. *Educational Psychologist, 26*(2), 117–127. doi: 10.1207/s15326985ep2602_4

Metz, Mike, & Knight, Heather. (2021). The dominant school language narrative: Unpacking English teachers' language ideologies. *Language, 97*(3), 238. doi:10.1353/lan.2021.0041

Milan, Stefania, & Emiliano, Treré. (2019). Big data from the South(s): Beyond data universalism. *Television & New Media*, I(4), 319–335. doi:10.1177/1527476419837739

O'Hair, Dan, Stewart, Rob, & Rubenstein, Hannah. (2022). *A speaker's guidebook*, 8th ed. MacMillan Learning.

Paris, Django, & Alim, H. Samy (Eds.). (2017). *Culturally sustaining pedagogies: Teaching and learning for justice in a changing world*. Teachers College Press.

Plackowski, Amy L. (2024). Disrupting English class: Linguistics and social justice for *all* high school students. In Anne H. Charity Hudley, Christine Mallinson, & Mary Bucholtz (Eds.), *Inclusion in linguistics*. Oxford University Press.

Reaser, Jeffrey, Adger, Carolyn Temple, Wolfram, Walt, & Christian, Donna. (2017). *Dialects at school: Educating linguistically diverse students*. Routledge.

Rosa, Jonathan, & Flores, Nelson. (2017). Do you hear what I hear? Raciolinguistic ideologies and culturally sustaining pedagogies. In Django Paris & H. Samy Alim (Eds.), *Culturally sustaining pedagogies: Teaching and learning for justice in a changing world* (pp. 175–190) Teachers College Press.

Schinske, Jeffrey N., Balke, Virginia L., Bangera, M. Gita, et al. (2017). Broadening participation in biology education research: Engaging community college students and faculty. *CBE Life Sciences Education, 16* (2), 1–11.

Smitherman, Geneva. (1995). "Students' right to their own language": A retrospective. *The English Journal, 84*(1), 21. Doi.org/10.2307/820470

Smitherman, Geneva. (1974). Response to Hunt, Meyers, et al. *College English, 35*(6), 729. doi. org/10.2307/375269

Thomas, Jamie A. (2024). Community college linguistics for educational justice: Content and assessment strategies that support antiracist and inclusive teaching. In Anne H. Charity Hudley, Christine Mallinson, & Mary Bucholtz (Eds.), *Inclusion in linguistics*. Oxford University Press.

Waisbord, Silvio. (2019). *Communication: A post-discipline*. John Wiley.

Wolfram, Walt. (1970). Sociolinguistic premises and the nature of nonstandard dialects. *Communication Education, 19*(3), 177–184. doi:10.1080/03634527009377818

Wolfram, Walt, & Dunstan, Stephany. (2021). Linguistic inequality and sociolinguistic justice in campus life: The need for programmatic intervention. In Gailynn Clements & Marnie Jo Petray (Eds.), *Linguistic discrimination in U.S. higher education: Power, prejudice, impacts, and remedies* (pp.156–173). Routledge.

Young, Vershawn Ashanti, Barrett, Rusty, Young-Rivera, Y'Shonda, & Lovejoy, Kim Brian. (2018). *Other people's English: Code-meshing, code-switching, and African American literacy*. Teachers College Press.

Zuckermann, Ghil'ad. (2022). Righting the wrong of the past and empowering Indigenous/minority wellbeing: Linguicide, language revival and social justice. The 66th Annual Conference of the International Linguistic Association, Rutgers University, April 1.

Abstract: This conclusion to *Decolonizing Linguistics* reflects on how to translate the guiding principles of decolonization into concrete action, with a focus on what can be done by the scholarly community, colleges and universities, departments, and individuals. Returning to the chapters in this volume, the conclusion explores the action plans that the authors lay out. This practical discussion begins with the fundamental recognition that decolonization is both ongoing and imperative and then considers in turn teaching and learning as a decolonizing process; decolonizing research practices; engaging in decolonization as an ongoing process; and refusing to engage in colonial ways of thinking and acting. The chapter, and the volume, concludes by calling for transparency and open, critical dialogue as linguists continue to grapple with the discipline's colonial legacy and ongoing colonial ideologies and practices and work toward a decolonized future.

Key Words: Community building, decolonization, interdisciplinarity, liberatory linguistics, public engagement, structural change

Conclusion

Decolonizing Linguistics

Anne H. Charity Hudley (she/her)
Stanford University

Ignacio L. Montoya (he/his)
University of Nevada, Reno

Christine Mallinson (she/her)
University of Maryland, Baltimore County

Mary Bucholtz (she/her, they/them)
University of California, Santa Barbara

Introduction

In this conclusion to *Decolonizing Linguistics*, we review the major themes that arise throughout the volume, interspersed with summaries of the themes that reflect how the authors conceptualize decolonization and how they are working to decolonize linguistics. We discuss the implications of these ideas and actions for the discipline and the profession, including the need to acknowledge historic and ongoing harm and move toward collective healing by bringing our whole selves into our work as linguists (Alvarez & Farinde-Wi, 2022; McKenzie, 2022). We then discuss guidance for decolonizing linguistics, categorizing opportunities for decolonizing actions that our scholarly community, our institutions, our departments, and linguists as individuals can take. Next, we discuss direct actions and recommendations for steps that linguists should take going forward, building on the themes raised by the contributors. Parallel recommendations and roadmaps are also presented in the conclusion of our companion volume, *Inclusion in Linguistics* (Charity Hudley, Mallinson, & Bucholtz 2024).

Charity Hudley, Montoya, Mallinson, Bucholtz, *Conclusion* In: *Decolonizing Linguistics*. Edited by: Anne H. Charity Hudley, Christine Mallinson and Mary Bucholtz, Oxford University Press. © Anne H. Charity Hudley, Christine Mallinson, and Mary Bucholtz 2024. DOI: 10.1093/oso/9780197755259.003.0022

446 Decolonizing Linguistics

In addition, we discuss our scholarly privilege as authors and editors in having the time and resources to undertake this conversation, write this and the other chapters, and compile both volumes. In this volume, some authors are members of historically colonizing groups, and others are from groups that have been historically colonized and are still experiencing colonization. Our conversations and collaborations, such as those demonstrated in and through both volumes, aim to carry forward the processes of decolonization and inclusion in linguistics and in the world.

Guiding Principles for Decolonizing Linguistics

As an organizing principle for ongoing actions to decolonize linguistics going forward, we present the *Charity Hudley Rule for Liberatory Linguistics*:

> Any published research that you conduct in a community that you are not a part of should include an explicit discussion of the inclusion of members from that community in your research process and your efforts to increase the participation of community members at your university, in your department, and in your research area. (Charity Hudley et al., 2022, p. 136)

As the contributions to this volume exemplify, this principle extends beyond research to include how principles of liberatory linguistics inform teaching, community action, and public engagement. Throughout this conclusion, we emphasize the direct actions that need to be taken in linguistics, including those offered by chapter authors as well as by other scholars that take us deeper and in new directions. An important area of growth is an even more invigorated emphasis on the scholarship of teaching and learning that linguistics can learn from. This focus on teaching, advising, and mentoring should be individual, but it should also be collective and communal—not the outcome of altruism or engagement but rather a crucial aspect of community building centered on decolonized education, which aims to actively undo years of individual and centuries of collective colonized education. The University of Victoria's Center for Youth and Society (n.d.) offers a concise overview of the ongoing process of decolonization in educational contexts, reminding us that decolonization is part of a more extensive process of truth and reconciliation that moves us away from assimilatory educational practices and encourages us to refocus on the true purposes and functions of education.

While great strides are being made toward decolonization in the academy, including within linguistics and related fields such as anthropology, we also recognize the existence of vocal and forceful countergroups. Powerful examples at some of our most highly prestigious universities remind us that the most resourced spaces are among the most harmful (cf. Xu, 2022). As the thoughtful and brave chapters in this volume have demonstrated, decolonizing linguistics requires action. Remaining colonized/colonizing and maintaining the status quo is a passive act. In contrast, we call for work that disrupts much more than scholarship on the printed page. We anticipate that those heavily invested in exploiting resources, humans, and knowledge will not relent easily in the face of such work. Indeed, Anne, Christine, and Mary experienced first-hand an attempt to silence our work in the form of an anonymous request to the Linguistic Society of America (LSA) that the kind of justice-centered work that we do and that we call for (namely, Charity Hudley et al., 2020) not be published in the LSA's flagship journal, *Language*. The argument put forward was that our work isn't science, but politics. We assert in response that, as countless others have said before us, the personal is political, and science and politics are absolutely inseparable; to imagine otherwise is not only naïve but also dangerous. Throughout this conclusion and the chapters in this volume, the colonialist and white-supremacist underpinnings of such arguments are clear. Without taking a critical justice lens, intellectual colonization persists in theoretical arguments (cf. "Thoughts on the LSA Resolution to Adopt the Chicago Principles on Freedom of Expression," 2022), in research and scientific processes, in funding structures, and in perceptions of who can and cannot do science in the academy and industry. As Chanda Prescod-Weinstein (2015) details, all of these aspects of research rely on political decisions regarding funding and access.

We now ask: What happens after the first rounds of justice-based scholarship and education have taken place and been resisted? How do we continue to resist and work for greater change with a commitment to restorative justice and a sense of purpose? Anonymous attacks on change-oriented scholarship highlight why collaboration and inclusion are so important to the scientific community and the scientific process. These decolonizing practices lie at the intersection of personal and the professional.

To decolonize is to seek reunion and renewal of our scholarly community so that colonizing efforts and enterprises cannot go unchecked, even if we ourselves benefit from colonizing structures—a particular tension that must be recognized by those of us who have been successful in academia. As Anne writes:

> Given all of my privileges, to decolonize is to use my academic reputation to benefit others and to call out colonization directly when I see it, as we do in this volume. We

448 Decolonizing Linguistics

have decided to take the notion of refusal literally and beware of academic efforts to profit from the collective knowledge of Black and Brown communities. Real decolonization must reach across histories and diasporas as we work together. Real decolonization refuses a divide-and-conquer model of justice with respect to academic and resource allocation. I say that very seriously from the vantage point of being an endowed chair at Stanford and the privilege and responsibility that that position bears.

What Can Our Scholarly Community Do?

This volume is a call to action for our scholarly community. We offer key driving questions to push this work forward. First, how do we decolonize our own minds? The answers may be different if we come from historically or presently colonized backgrounds, but we all must examine and interrogate our own positionality and intentionality in the work that we do. How do we make sense of our own participation in land-grab universities (see Introduction, this volume) and other colonizing institutions? Anne and Ignacio, for example, have reflected on their personal histories as scholars who both graduated from Harvard University, the oldest and most revered land and resource grabber of them all (at least in the US context), noting that "our process of continuing to make sense of our own privileges and access is the true story of how we came to be in the place to even write this chapter."

As we continue to write our own stories and to examine how colonizing and decolonizing forces have shaped those stories in ways large and small, our work must reflect these tensions. What was the story that told us we had the right to take up space in these places and in the pages of scholarly publications, and what story are we trying to write for ourselves? What we know we must do is to synthesize and amplify the work that these chapters call upon us all to do.

What Can Colleges and Universities Do?

Within our college and university structures, we must organize and press for decolonization at the institutional level. How can we refuse to work in colonized spaces and demand decolonization as the condition of our presence? As part of taking action, we can prepare ourselves for institutional leadership roles so that we can be in the rooms and spaces where decisions are made. In this way, we can work to ensure that the experiences and perspectives of those who study language are included in decolonizing efforts and policies on our campuses and in our organizations. We must educate ourselves and others about reparation, abolition, and other efforts to render long-delayed justice to the colonized peoples and communities from which colleges and universities have benefited (Shange, 2022). As we work forward, those models and conversations must greatly influence linguistic methodologies and action plans.

We have seen some of this change through changes in leadership in major organizations. As of this writing, John Baugh is the 2022 LSA president, and Marlyse Baptisa will be the 2024 president. Their work on Black Diasporic language and their leadership as Black scholars provide models that can be extended to other communities. Similarly, Bernard Perley, as 2021–2023 President of the Society of Linguistic Anthropology and the first Native president of that organization, is turning our attention to Indigenous values and priorities that should be a part of all decolonizing work (see Fine et al., 2023).

What Can Departments Do?

How should departments prioritize decolonization? Many major linguistics departments are built on the foundation of language documentation—without much or any Indigenous representation among faculty and students and with little to no consultation and collaboration with Native scholars. Those departments need to actively and purposefully recruit and retain Native linguists as faculty and students—or figure out and address why Native linguists don't want to work and learn in those departments. Some common reasons are that most linguistics departments are too far removed from Native American Studies and Indigenous Studies (see, for example, the list of Indigenous Studies Programs maintained by Georgetown University, n.d.). To meaningfully welcome Native students and scholars, linguistics departments need to build relationships with Indigenous-centered departments and programs through cross-listed classes, joint appointments, and authentic intellectual collaboration and communication efforts. These efforts are the departmental-level application of the Charity Hudley Rule.

Some programs are actively doing such work. The University of Arizona is an excellent example of how Indigenous priorities, methodologies, and interests can shape institutional structures. The American Indian Language Development Institute (AILDI) offers a range of training programs for educators and policymakers working on the revitalization and reclamation of Indigenous languages. Interdisciplinary by design, the program is supported by the Department of Teaching, Learning, and Sociocultural Studies in the College of Education, the program in American Indian Studies, the Department of Linguistics, and the Graduate College. AILDI started in 1978 as a series of workshops providing Indigenous language education to teachers, community members, policymakers, and other language activists. Initially

450 Decolonizing Linguistics

hosted by a rotating set of schools and universities, AILDI became a permanent part of the University of Arizona in 1990. This integration into an established university context has given it institutional support that strengthens both the program and the university. Indigenous language educators also have the opportunity to earn a master's degree at the University of Arizona: In conjunction with AILDI, the Department of Linguistics offers a Master of Arts in Native American Languages and Linguistics. The degree is specifically geared toward serving the needs of Indigenous community members and language activists, which is reflected both in the content of what is taught and in the structure of the program.

While the degree of integration of Indigenous priorities is especially notable at the University of Arizona, other linguistics programs have also enacted structural changes to integrate Indigenous priorities. For instance, the Department of Linguistics at the University of New Mexico houses the Navajo Language Program, which offers students training for maintaining and strengthening the Diné (Navajo) language. Instruction and research in the program are guided by Diné principles and incorporate Diné cultural knowledge and values. The Navajo Language Program collaborates with a number of organizations committed to Diné language education, both within and outside of the Navajo Nation, including the recently established Diné Language Teacher Institute, which offers Diné speakers an opportunity to receive a teaching certificate in Diné language instruction.

The University of Oregon is another institution that has developed opportunities for partnerships between the academy and Indigenous communities in service of Indigenous interests. The Northwest Indian Language Institute, which was established in 1997 in response to local tribal goals of supporting Indigenous language instruction, offers a range of resources for language maintenance and revitalization for tribes in the Northwest and nationally. These include sample curricula, research publications, assessment tools, a two-week-long summer institute for language teachers and other community members, and other professional development opportunities for educators. Another program at the University of Oregon, the Linguistics Research Experience for Undergraduates, is a National Science Foundation-funded eight-week summer program for American Indian and Alaska Native students organized by the Department of Linguistics as a means of introducing students in a culturally responsive way to higher education and to hands-on research in linguistics. These and other initiatives are models that all linguistics departments should learn from and emulate, with a focus on directly benefiting the communities that have been most affected by that department's and university's history of colonizing practices.

What Can Individuals Do?

Senior scholars and those with administrative positions both on campus and in academic organizations should advocate for specific decolonizing strategies in their long-term and strategic plans. Faculty of all ranks and work arrangements should focus on decolonization in teaching and research, as many chapters in this volume demonstrate. We urge readers to incorporate these and other decolonizing models into their teaching, mentoring, and advising and to embrace the scholarship of teaching and learning as a central part of the decolonization process.

Undergraduate and graduate students, whether from colonized or colonizing communities, must work to educate themselves about the active process of remembering, so they can actively refuse to build their careers upon the easy exploitation that colonizing academic practices and spaces offer. Refusal by all students is critically important: colonization is built on the passive complicitness of those with less power in a society, and the places and spaces where students devote their time and attention can either give power to those who colonize or pull power from them.

Action Plans for Decolonizing Linguistics

Both Decolonizing *Linguistics* and *Inclusion in Linguistics* are a useful part of these processes, but they are not sufficient on their own. We need greater organizing across communities and groups so that we can put structural pressure on those who preserve and defend colonizing practices, particularly in scholarly communication and publication. We also need greater attention to all forms of funding for linguistics and how those decisions are made. These and similar actions should be directly built on the collective experiences and suggestions of the scholars in this volume and of those who read their work and join the conversation. We focus here on the action items and plans that the authors in this volume offer us for additional steps to take. We encourage you to read the parallel suggestions in our companion volume, *Inclusion in Linguistics*, because engagement with a wide range of ideas and recommendations is needed.

Decolonization as Ongoing and Imperative

In Chapter 1, "Manifestations of Colonialism in Linguistics and Opportunities for Decolonization Through Refusal," Ignacio Montoya sets our frame for

452 Decolonizing Linguistics

action. He asserts that to use the term "decolonization" without articulating the basis of one's use of the term (e.g., whether in the sense of Tuck and Yang [2012] involving the return of land, resources, and privileges or in various other senses articulated by authors in this volume) runs the risk of erasing the Indigenous experience by ignoring the unique features of the oppression of Indigenous people in settler-colonial societies such as the United States. This erasure undermines the goals of both antiracism and decolonization, and it replicates colonial structures that seek to eliminate Indigeneity. As discussed in the introduction to this volume, there are a variety of legitimate ways of understanding and enacting decolonization. To ensure that the construct of decolonization indeed serves to disrupt and reverse the effects of colonization, we must be mindful that our use of the term is rooted in an awareness of the varied and complex structures that drive colonialism and that devalue and erase the experiences of colonized people.

In Chapter 4, "We Like the Idea of You But Not the Reality of You: The Whole Scholar as Disruptor of Default Colonial Practices in Linguistics," Nicté Fuller Medina similarly reminds us that we need not, and cannot, wait for large grants, tenure-track positions, or tenure before we act. Small movements can be impactful and can be precursors to larger-scale action, while shifts in thinking can begin immediately. Many of the authors in this volume highlight the need to first do research in order to understand the specific colonizing history and context you find yourself in. To remember is to refuse to ignore.

In Chapter 3, "The Colonial Geography of Linguistics: A View from the Caribbean," Ben Braithwaite and Kristian Ali discuss the Caribbean linguistic tradition, both past and present. They show how Caribbean linguists' rootedness in place and explicit commitment to linguistic liberation provide a powerful model for linguists elsewhere who are similarly committed to advancing Liberatory Linguistics through decolonization. The authors note how important it is for linguists in the Global North to confront the ways that geography directly maps onto power, access, and exploitation, and how these colonial processes influence the form that linguistics as a discipline now takes.

In Chapter 6, "Unpacking Experiences of Racism in European Applied Linguistics," Kamran Khan engages in the decolonizing act of remembering by highlighting the historical investment in colonialism and racism that permeates European applied linguistics and shapes his everyday life as an applied linguist. As Khan illustrates, for many racially minoritized and colonized individuals and communities, white supremacy pervades almost every space, including in academia, and inevitably shapes the extent to which one can and cannot belong.

In Chapter 2, "Racialization, Language Science, and Nineteenth Century Anthropometrics," Margaret Thomas gives us further historical context for the European and global context of colonization by examining the racist views of Paul Broca, who is often venerated as a forefather of modern psycholinguistics. She calls for linguists to interrogate how the racist ideologies of the past continue to have influence on the discipline in the present, often in ways that contemporary scholars are unaware of.

Teaching and Learning as a Decolonizing Process

One major theme and set of recommendations in the volume centers on teaching and learning as a decolonizing process. Many of the chapters engage in this work, following the memory of bell hooks, who wrote passionately about the liberatory potential of education:

> The academy is not paradise. But learning is a place where paradise can be created. The classroom, with all its limitations, remains a location of possibility. In that field of possibility we have the opportunity to labor for freedom, to demand of ourselves and our comrades, an openness of mind and heart that allows us to face reality even as we collectively imagine ways to move beyond boundaries, to transgress. This is education as the practice of freedom. (hooks, 1994, p. 207)

The paradise we envision centers on the decolonizing and Indigenizing of knowledge.

In Chapter 10, "Decolonizing Historical Linguistics in the Classroom and Beyond," Claire Bowern and Rikker Dockum discuss how and why to unlock the liberatory potential of teaching in subfields, such as historical linguistics, that are often thought to be "too hard" to decolonize. They assert that these subfields offer linguists the opportunity to think through issues and approaches to decolonization at a time when academia is paying broader attention to questions of belonging, diversity, equity, inclusion, and justice in higher education. They urge us to seize the current moment to examine and reinvent curricular materials along with—and, crucially, not as a substitute for—other aspects of racial justice in academia.

In Chapter 9, "From Gatekeeping to Inclusion in the Introductory Linguistics Curriculum: Decolonizing Our Teaching, Our Psyches, Our Institutions, and Our Field," Lynnette Arnold compares her experiences of teaching an introductory course with an emphasis on language and race to white students and to students of color at a Predominantly White Institution

(PWI). Arnold notes the challenges of teaching about race and language in this context from a decolonizing and antiracist perspective, particularly for white instructors. To address these issues, Arnold describes how she sought to rework the class to center the experiences of students of color and to de-center her own authority—for example, by sharing video resources that focus on Black language and experience and by creating opportunities for students to reflect on language in their own lives.

In Chapter 19, "Promoting Decolonized Classrooms Through an Introductory Linguistics Course for Future Teachers in Alaska," Ève Ryan, Matt Ford, and Giovanna Wilde encourage us to be creative in fostering opportunities to Indigenize knowledge, a decolonizing process that starts by acknowledging our own positionalities as instructors and honoring students' emotions as central to their learning experience. Ryan and her coauthors follow in the tradition of scholarship such as Megan Bang (in press), Douglas L. Medin and Bang (2014), Leigh Patel (2016), and Smith (2021), which give us a myriad of ways to decolonize our teaching practices.

Decolonized learning will not be fully manifested without a degree of full sovereignty and community-led education. This chapter and much other scholarship shows that we can do that educational work on the institutional level through partnerships with Tribal Colleges and Universities (TCUs) and other institutions that comprehensively support historically colonized populations. For anyone seeking to forge such partnerships, the LSA maintains a webpage entitled TCU Project Participants, which can assist in making connections with TCU students and faculty and LSA members who support partnerships with TCUs (LSA, n.d.); similarly, international partnerships are a core element of the African Linguistics School (n.d.). In California and Oregon, among other places, public universities are attempting reparations for Native students through free tuition (see, e.g., University of California Admissions, n.d.). But what supports will also be needed to fully welcome and support greater numbers of Indigenous students so they will want to come and learn in a Historically White Institution with a deeply colonial history? Who will ensure that instructors are ready to teach such students and will give them a high-quality experience?

Decolonizing Research Practices

The volume's next major theme and set of recommendations center on decolonizing research and research methodologies, which too often have been grounded in colonialist, white-supremacist research models. In

Chapter 8, "Decolonizing (Psycho)linguistics Means Dropping the Language Gap Rhetoric," Megan Figueroa interrogates the concept of the "language gap" in psychology and psycholinguistics and demonstrates how the false claim that low-income racialized children have a language deficit is a form of colonial thinking that is incompatible with an antiracist linguistics. Calling out the racism and colonial violence that undergird beliefs about linguistic deficiency in the first place, Figueroa argues that the concept must be dropped completely. In true settler-colonial fashion, deficit-oriented linguistic research "destroys to replace" (Wolfe, 2006, p. 388) by aiming to eradicate colonized people's linguistic practices in favor of a hegemonic norm.

To counter colonizing deficit models, linguists must create partnerships in which communities lead the research. In Chapter 7, "Centering Race and Multilingualism in French Linguistics," Maya Angela Smith provides an example of how linguists can center Blackness in championing multilingualism and translanguaging. She notes that the prevailing focus on monolingualism both in linguistic research and modern language studies emerges from standard language discourses, linguistic hegemony, and white supremacy. Monolingualism is the norm in academia and Western societal discourses more generally against which multilingual practices are measured, even though the majority of the world uses multiple languages and varieties in everyday life, particularly Black, Brown, Indigenous, and Melanated People (BBIMP, a term Smith borrows from Louiza "Weeze" Doran; @ accordingtoweeze). It is imperative to decolonizing efforts that we advocate for multilingualism and translanguaging practices in our scholarship and teaching. Further resources that readers can consult on these topics include Rhonda Chung and Wayne dela Cruz (2024); Aris Moreno Clemons (this volume); Jamie A. Thomas (2020); Ofelia García (2009, 2019); Donaldo Macedo (2019); and Adrian Blackledge and Angela Creese (2014).

Chapter 4, by Fuller Medina, offers additional insights on challenging colonizing norms. Writing as a person of the Global South, she cautions that scholars from the Global North should be aware of colonial tropes that position the South as an exotic and undiscovered research site that is ripe for the extraction of linguistic data. She discusses the basic legal and ethical requirements for Global North linguists conducting research in the Global South as well as the higher ethical standards to which scholars should adhere in order to decolonize academia and knowledge production. For example, she advises budgeting for honoraria for consultations with local scholars, and she calls for scholars who have legacy data to collaborate with Global South scholars who work in decolonial ways to repatriate data to communities of origin.

456 Decolonizing Linguistics

Similarly, in Chapter 1, Montoya reminds us that to advance meaningful decolonization in linguistics requires refusing to participate in the creation of extractive products. This entails *not* going into communities with the sole purpose of gathering linguistic data for us to analyze, *not* taking a standard linguistic theory and applying it to data that was collected in this extractive way (either by us or someone else), and *not* creating conventional products that are based on extraction. Instead, we must envision and enact new possibilities for what linguistics and linguistic research can be. In Chapter 5, "Apolitical Linguistics Doesn't Exist, and It Shouldn't: Developing A Black Feminist Praxis Toward Political Transparency," Aris Moreno Clemons offers one such vision and example of a decolonial linguistics. Acknowledging that all research, regardless of assertions of "objectivity," is inherently political, Clemons describes her own commitment to transparency in all aspects of the research relationship. She shows in detail how her work on Dominican language advances a Black feminist political praxis that rejects ideological hierarchies of white supremacy and colonial formations of power.

In Chapter 13, "Open Methods: Decolonizing (or Not) Research Methods in Linguistics," Dan Villarreal and Lauren Collister put forth the Open Methods movement as a potential site of decolonizing research practice. While cautioning that Open Methods, like its precursor Open Access for publications, can end up perpetuating rather than challenging colonialism, they offer a detailed preliminary model for an anticolonial Open Methods, which they envision not simply as a guide for researchers at colonizing institutions but also as a way of initiating a conversation with other linguists, especially those in the Global South. Throughout, they encourage scholars to share "imperfect" outputs and acknowledge shortcomings or limitations of our research as an important part of creating a more decolonized field.

Decolonizing Linguistics Is an Ongoing Process

A final, overarching set of recommendations from the chapters in this volume supports the idea that decolonization is an ongoing process—and, as chapter authors demonstrate, this process must not be relegated to only one sphere of action but rather embedded throughout one's work as a linguist.

In Chapter 14, "Revitalizing Attitudes Toward Creole Languages," Ariana Bancu, Joy P. G. Peltier, Felicia Bisnath, Danielle Burgess, Sophia Eakins, Wilkinson Daniel Wong Gonzales, Moira Saltzman, Yourdanis Sedarous, Alicia Stevers, and Marlyse Baptista reject the exceptionalist ideology that pervades Creole studies (DeGraff 2005) and instead call for a decolonizing approach that draws on the insights of Creole language users alongside linguists to "revitalize" the way that we think about, analyze, and theorize Creole languages and to center them and their users in introductory linguistics classes.

In Chapter 18, "Prioritizing Community Partners' Goals in Projects to Support Indigenous Language Revitalization," Katherine J. Riestenberg, Ally Freemond, Brook Danielle Lillehaugen, and Jonathan N. Washington point to the inherent and unresolvable tension between the goals of colonizing academic institutions and the goals of Indigenous linguistic activists who partner with linguists to support their community's language goals. The authors reject the widespread rhetoric of "balance" in navigating this tension, noting that such an approach leads to colonizing outcomes. Instead, they urge linguists to prioritize community goals over scholarly goals in order to carry out work that is truly decolonizing in its impact.

These themes are vitally important as we sit on tenure and promotion committees, in order to help support co-authored work and public- and community-facing scholarship. When we serve on grant panels, it is also important to mobilize our experience as academic partners in decolonizing collaborative work and speak to the realities of budgets, timelines, and collaborative processes. As both volumes attest, linguists are already doing this work in spaces we find and make. Inclusive and decolonial scholarly practices continue to make academic spaces bigger, moving us away from top-down approaches that often overlook or devalue community-centered perspectives. Further resources that readers can consult on these topics include Chapter 12, "Decolonising Methodologies Through Collaboration: Reflections on Partnerships and Funding Flows from Working Between the South and the North" by Rajendra Chetty, Hannah Gibson, and Colin Reilly (this volume); Chapter 16, "Growing a Bigger Linguistics Through a Zapotec Agenda: The Ticha Project" by May Helena Plumb, Alejandra Dubcovsky, Moisés García Guzmán, Brooke Danielle Lillehaugen, and Felipe H. Lopez (this volume); Inmaculada M. García-Sánchez and Marjorie Faulstich Orellana (2019); Ben Rampton, Constadina Charalambous, and Panayiota Charalmabous (2019); and Django Paris and Maisha T. Winn (2014).

Finally, it is important that no aspect of the study of language be exempt from conversations around decolonizing linguistics. In Chapter 11, "Towards a Decolonial Syntax: Research, Teaching, Publishing," Hannah Gibson, Kyle Jerro, Savithry Namboodiripad, and Kristina Riedel point to the colonial history of linguistics departments and argue that viewing syntax as an object of critical study in its own right rather than as an unquestioned field of scholarly knowledge is important in shedding these colonial trappings. This step

458 Decolonizing Linguistics

is crucial so that the study of syntax and other technical (and now industry-facing) areas of linguistics do not invoke a science narrative as a proxy for colonialism and white supremacy.

Doing Refusal Bravely and Collectively

Refusal is difficult and often goes against our individual interests. We need guidance on how to do refusal bravely and collectively. How can we act? We can refuse to engage in business as usual in academia. In creating course syllabi and citing scholarly sources, it is important to represent and include scholars from currently and formerly colonized countries and territories. Scholars who are already taking these actions demonstrate how outright refusal can challenge the exclusionary practices inherent to colonialism.

We also can refuse to participate in institutions and organizations that have not undertaken direct efforts to decolonize their research practices. This means we need to be more actively and publicly vocal in refusing to participate in conferences and organizations that sponsor and privilege colonized forms of research and scholarly communication. It means we need to look at the mastheads of the journals we submit to ensure that they have representation from BBIM scholars and others from formerly colonized groups. As we consider which departments and programs to work in, it means we need to ensure representation by those who use the languages and varieties under study.

In addition, we can refuse to participate in an exclusionary linguistics. In Chapter 16, Plumb et al. state it plainly: "following the set of papers that spurred this volume (Charity Hudley et al., 2020), we refuse to accept a linguistics that is too small." Creating a bigger linguistics requires us to turn our attention to scholars not only in linguistics but also in other fields who have written about how to decolonize the academy. To decolonize the study of language requires us to be in active scholarly communication with other research communities that have engaged in this work more comprehensively for a longer period of time. We cannot continue to use pragmatic arguments about waiting to get through one's own tenure and promotion pathways before shaking things up, thereby deferring the necessary work of decolonizing the academy.

A bigger linguistics is necessarily an inclusive, interdisciplinary linguistics rather than a narrow, inward-looking discipline that jealously guards and patrols its borders. Smith, in Chapter 7, provides a model for expanding and linking knowledge production by drawing on fields from applied linguistics to literary studies to musicology. Crucially, Smith's interdisciplinary perspective, which enables her to reach a wider scholarly readership, is not motivated by this goal but rather is inspired by her research participants' own meaning-making strategies and honors their multilingual lived experiences. In Chapter 17, "Decolonizing Creolistics Through Popular Culture: The Case of Dancehall," Rashana Vikara Lydner provides another such interdisciplinary model. Noting that Creole studies, especially in the Global North, largely focuses on linguistic structure and neglects both social context and language users themselves, Lydner calls for a decolonized Creolistics that attends to language use as an embodied experience. She focuses in particular on popular music, and specifically dancehall culture, as a key site for decolonial Creole research that incorporates race, gender, and sexuality as central to the ways that language is used.

Using interdisciplinarity to advance decolonial goals is not limited to research. In Chapter 20, "An Interdisciplinary Approach to Language Activism from Community Colleges: Linguistics Meets Communication Studies," Carlos de Cuba, Poppy Slocum, and Laura Spinu offer numerous ways that linguists can have a decolonizing and antiracist impact beyond linguistics by challenging harmful language ideologies that circulate in adjacent fields like communication. These efforts include not just educating students (who are often themselves future educators) but also sharing disciplinary knowledge with faculty in other fields and with textbook editors, who have enormous structural power to circulate either dangerous or liberatory language ideologies. Further, in Chapter 9, Arnold notes that linguists must be active in supporting university-level efforts to create new programming and spaces specifically for BBIM students, as conversations about language, race, and power—among students, but also among faculty and administrators—are vital to well-being and educational success (Charity Hudley et al., 2022).

Scaling up from individual departments or institutions is another crucial step in decolonial work. Chapter 15, "Solidarity and Collectivity in Decolonizing Linguistics: A Black Disaporic Perspective," by Anne H. Charity Hudley, Christine Mallinson, Kahdeidra Monét Martin, Aris Moreno Clemons, L. J. Randolph Jr., Mary Bucholtz, Kendra Calhoun, Shenika Hankerson, Joy P. G. Peltier, Jamie Thomas, Deana Lacy McQuitty, and Kara Seidel describes the model for Black faculty empowerment developed in a Build and Broaden award funded by the National Science Foundation. In this collaboration involving scholars across multiple universities, the authors offer recommendations for solidarity and collective action to adopt transformative changes that expand access for marginalized scholars and shift ideological standards for academic and scholarly success in linguistics, broadly defined. In so doing, the authors also challenge the colonialism and white supremacy that undergirds the discipline's persistent ignorance about and exclusion of the breadth and complexity of the Black Diaspora. A similar project is the

460 Decolonizing Linguistics

LSA- and NSF-sponsored Natives4Linguistics (n.d.), led by Wesley Leonard, which provides a model of building scholarly community and collaboration for Native linguists across intellectual contexts and institution types. The project's aims are to make room for Native linguists in the discipline and to incorporate Native epistemologies, methodologies, and community goals into linguistic research.

Finally, understanding the global context of the discipline and of academia is critical to the entire process of decolonizing linguistics. In Chapter 12, Chetty et al. show how collaborative partnerships provide valuable opportunities for decolonial work. They note, however, that current funding systems within the Global North are not set up to enable equitable partnerships and that change has to happen at the individual, institutional, and funder levels in order for true decolonial partnerships to be possible.

Conclusion

As the preceding discussion suggests, decolonizing linguistics depends on transparency and open, critical discussion. In Anne's Black Academic Development Lab at Stanford University, lab members work toward decolonization by talking openly about the economics of higher education, colorism, and the ongoing debate among scholars from historically colonized contexts: When do you stay and resist in a place that doesn't welcome you, even if it is your home, and when do you move on to find another place? In a situation that is still being discussed, the refusal of MacArthur "genius grant" and Pulitzer Prize winner Nikole Hannah-Jones, a Black woman, to accept a nontenured faculty position at the University of North Carolina-Chapel Hill, where she received her master's degree, exemplifies this issue in all its complexities (Legal Defense Fund, 2021). Anne is glad she worked and learned in her ancestral community as a junior scholar at the College of William & Mary in Virginia, but opportunities were limited, as reflected in the now openly discriminatory politics and policies of the state's Republican regime. Anne will never know if leaving home was the right decision, but at Stanford she now has the freedom and resources to focus on shared, collective goals and both individual and collective action. Doing decolonization requires resources, making the financial model of how to do decolonization a complicated and real question. In doing this work, we need more conversations about the economics of academic labor and more participation in groups such as the Decolonizing Wealth Project (2022) to examine the role that we can play as linguists and scholars. We have to talk about capitalism, competition, and our larger model for work and liberation, particularly in dismantling colonialism through partnerships and collective activism.

We end with some active hope. David Labaree (2018) describes the "lust for glory" in higher education in all its forms. We must be conscious of how we replicate and how we resist competitive, colonial models and how to bring others into decolonizing processes so that we can collectively build inclusive, decolonized ways of working and thinking. To do so, we have to remember that decolonization is a process. Decolonization is truly about who we choose to engage and spend our time with and how those choices lead to outcomes that are authentic, rich, and real. Decolonization is essential to true community-based work and to true collaboration and intellectual exchange. Despite our best efforts, we have not fully achieved our decolonial goals for these volumes; further work is needed to include the full Global South, particularly Latin America and Africa (Ndhlovu, 2020). Linguistics as a discipline is just beginning to identify how to produce research without reproducing colonial structures. These volumes and the conversations they have sparked (e.g., Montoya, 2022) are our best attempt at contributing to that work—and as Villareal and Collister remind us, even an imperfect attempt moves the work forward.

One of our anonymous reviewers for this volume made the excellent suggestion that readers use *Decolonizing Linguistics* and *Inclusion in Linguistics* as texts in linguistics courses. We have provided abundant teaching- and action-related resources on the supplementary website associated with these volumes, including models for making inclusion and decolonizing roadmaps, related readings from other disciplinary lenses, and further materials from the Global South in particular in order to expand the representation of these perspectives. We hope this work initiates an open, critical dialogue in linguistics that continues for years to come.

References

African Linguistics School. (n.d.) About. https://sites.google.com/site/africanlingschool/about

Alvarez, Adam J., & Farinde-Wu, Abiola. (2022). Advancing a holistic trauma framework for collective healing from colonial abuses. *AERA Open*, 8(1), 1–15. https://doi.org/10.1177/23328584221083973.

Bang, M., Marin, A., & Medin, D. (in press). Towards learning emerging from place and community: Spatial and temporal transformations. *Journal of the Learning Sciences*.

Black Academic Development Lab. (n.d.). Home. https://badlab.stanford.edu/

Blackledge, Adrian, & Creese, Angela. (2014). Heteroglossia as practice and pedagogy. In Adrian Blackledge & Angela Creese (Eds.), *Heteroglossia as practice and pedagogy* (pp. 1–20). Springer.

462 Decolonizing Linguistics

Charity Hudley, Anne H., Mallinson, Christine, & Bucholtz, Mary. (2020). Toward racial justice in linguistics: Interdisciplinary insights into theorizing race in the discipline and diversifying the profession. *Language, 96*(4), e200–e235. https://doi.org/10.1353/lan.2020.0074

Charity Hudley, Anne H., Mallinson, Christine, & Bucholtz, Mary. (2022). *Talking college: Making space for Black language practices in higher education.* Teachers College Press.

Charity Hudley, Anne H., Mallinson, Christine, & Bucholtz, Mary (Eds.). (2024). *Inclusion in linguistics.* Oxford University Press.

Chung, Rhonda, & dela Cruz, John Wayne N. (2024). Pedagogies of inclusion must start from within: Landguaging teacher reflection and plurilingualism in the L2 classroom. In Anne H. Charity Hudley, Christine Mallinson, & Mary Bucholtz (Eds.), *Inclusion in linguistics.* Oxford University Press.

Decolonizing Wealth Project. (2022). https://decolonizingwealth.com/

DeGraff, Michel. (2005). Linguists' most dangerous myth: The fallacy of Creole Exceptionalism. *Language in Society, 34*(4), 533–591. https://doi.org/10.1017/S0047404505050207

Fine, Julia Coombs, Love-Nichols, Jessica, & Perley, Bernard C. (2023). Climate and language: An entangled crisis. *Daedalus, 152*(3): 84–98.

García, Ofelia. (2009). Emergent bilinguals and TESOL: What's in a name? *TESOL Quarterly, 43*(2), 322–326. https://doi.org/10.1002/j.1545-7249.2009.tb00172.x

García, Ofelia. (2019). Translanguaging: A coda to the code? *Classroom Discourse, 10*(3–4), 369–373. https://doi.org/10.1080/19463014.2019.1638277

García-Sanchez, Immaculada M., & Orellana, Marjorie F. (Eds.). (2019). *Language and cultural practices in communities and schools.* Routledge.

Georgetown University. (n.d.). Indigenous Studies Programs. https://indigeneity.georgetown.edu/resources/programs/

hooks, bell. (1994). *Teaching to transgress.* Routledge.

Labaree, David. (2018). Gold among the dross. *Aeon.* https://aeon.co/essays/higher-education-in-the-us-is-driven-by-a-lust-for-glory

Legal Defense Fund. (2021, July 6). Nikole Hannah-Jones issues statement on decision to decline tenure offer at University of North Carolina-Chapel Hill and to accept Knight Chair appointment at Howard University. https://www.naacpldf.org/press-release/nikole-hannah-jones-issues-statement-on-decision-to-decline-tenure-offer-at-university-of-north-carolina-chapel-hill-and-to-accept-knight-chair-appointment-at-howard-university/

Linguistic Society of America [LSA]. (n.d.). TCU project participants. https://www.linguisticsociety.org/content/tcu-project-participants

Macedo, Donaldo. (Ed.). (2019). *Decolonizing foreign language education.* Routledge.

McKenzie, James. (2022). Addressing historical trauma and healing in Indigenous language cultivation and revitalization. *Annual Review of Applied Linguistics, 42*, 71–77. https://doi.org/10.1017/S0267190521000167

Medin, Douglas L., & Bang, Megan. (2014). *Who's asking?: Native science, western science and science education.* The MIT Press.

Montoya, Ignacio. (2022, Nov. 18). *Interrogating the colonial legacy of linguistics and adopting principles of decolonization* [Lecture]. CUNY Graduate Center, New York.

Natives4Linguistics. (n.d.). Home. https://natives4linguistics.wordpress.com/

Ndlovu, Finex. (2020). Decolonising sociolinguistics research: Methodological turn-around next? *International Journal of the Sociology of Language, 2021*(267–268), 193–201. https://doi.org/10.1515/ijsl-2020-0063

Paris, Django, & Winn, Maisha T. (Eds.). (2014). *Humanizing research.* SAGE Publishing.

Patel, Leigh. (2016). *Decolonizing educational research: From ownership to answerability.* Routledge.

Prescod-Weinstein, Chanda. (2015, April 25). Decolonizing science reading list: It's the end of science as you know it. Medium. https://medium.com/@chanda/decolonising-science-reading-list-339fb773d51f

Rampton, Ben, Charalambous, Constadina, & Charalambous, Panayiota. (2019). Crossing of a different kind. *Language in Society, 48*(5), 629–655. https://doi.org/10.1017/S0047404519000460

Shange, Savannah. (2022). Abolition in the clutch: Shifting through the gears with anthropology. *Feminist Anthropology, 3*, 187–197. https://doi.org/10.1002/fea2.12101

Smith, Linda Tuhawai. (2021). *Decolonizing methodologies: Research and Indigenous peoples.* 3d edition. Bloomsbury.

Thomas, Jamie A. (2020). Uncovering language-in-education policy as a challenge to Tanzanian civic engagement. *Humania del Sure, 28*, 63–93.

Thoughts on the LSA resolution to adopt the Chicago principles on freedom of expression. (2022). https://docs.google.com/document/d/1d12Cy5wdaavAdjM5FUn67zsMuvHY0xpgxADhIn5lT24/edit

Tuck, Eve, & Yang, K. Wayne. (2012). Decolonization is not a metaphor. *Decolonization: Indigenity, Education & Society, 1*(1), 1–40.

University of California Admissions. (n.d.). Native American opportunity plan. https://admission.universityofcalifornia.edu/tuition-financial-aid/types-of-aid/native-american-opportunity-plan.html

University of Victoria Center for Youth and Society (n.d.). Decolonization in an educational context. https://www.uvic.ca/research/centres/youthsociety/assets/docs/briefs/decolonizing-education-research-brief.pdf

Wolfe, Patrick. (2006). Settler colonialism and the elimination of the native. *Journal of Genocide Research, 8*(4). 387–409.

Xu, Meimei. (2022, February 21). 15 Harvard anthropology professors call on Comaroff to resign over sexual harassment allegations. *The Harvard Crimson.* https://www.thecrimson.com/article/2022/2/21/anthropology-faculty-call-for-comaroff-resignation/